From Leni Yahil, *The Holocaust: The Fate of European Jewry* (New York: Oxford University Press, 1990), 358–59.

FINLAND

Leningrad

Stockholm

Klooga　Vaivara

ESTONIA

Kaiserwald

Riga　LATVIA

LITHUANIA

Pravieniskis

Kovno　Vilna

: Sea

Stutthof

USSR

Treblinka　Bialystok

lmno　Warsaw　POLAND

Trawniki

dz　Poniatowa　Sobibor

Plaszow　Lublin-Maidanek

Krakow　Belzec

witz-Birkenau　Janowska

Lwow

Novaky

Vyhne　TRANSNISTRIA

Peciora

Budapest　Bogdanovka

Acmececta

Mostovoi

Berezowka

NGARY

RUMANIA

Djakova

iste

Belgrad　Bucharest

OSLAVIA　Black Sea

Nis　BULGARIA

Sofia

ALBANIA

Salonika　Istanbul

GREECE　TURKEY

LEGEND

International boundaries, 1933　— · —

City　○

Death Camp　●

Concentration Camp　◉

Murder Camp　□

Ghetto–Camp　■

Transit and Assembly Camp　▣

Labor Camp　◇

HITLER'S SHADOW WAR

ALSO BY DONALD M. MCKALE

War by Revolution: Germany and Great Britain in the Middle East in the Era of World War I

Rewriting History: The Original and Revised World War II Diaries of Curt Prüfer, Nazi Diplomat

Curt Prüfer: German Diplomat from the Kaiser to Hitler

Hitler: The Survival Myth

The Swastika outside Germany

The Nazi Party Courts: Hitler's Management of Conflict in His Movement, 1921–1945

HITLER'S SHADOW WAR

THE HOLOCAUST AND WORLD WAR II

DONALD M. McKALE

Cooper Square Press

First Cooper Square Press edition 2002

This Cooper Square Press hardcover edition of *Hitler's Shadow War* is an original publication. It is published by arrangement with the author.

Published by Cooper Square Press
A Member of the Rowman & Littlefield Publishing Group
200 Park Avenue South, Suite 1109
New York, New York 10003-1503
www.coopersquarepress.com

Distributed by National Book Network

Design and composition: Reider Publishing Services

Library of Congress Cataloging-in-Publication Data

McKale, Donald M., 1943–
    Hitler's shadow war : the Holocaust and World War II / Donald M. McKale.
    —1st ed.
        p. cm.
    Includes index.
    ISBN 0-8154-1211-8 (cloth : alk. paper)
    1. Jews—Germany—History—1933–1945. 2. Jews—Persecutions—Germany.
3. Antisemitism—Germany—History—20th century. 4. Holocaust, Jewish
(1939–1945) 5. Germany—History—1933–1945. 6. Germany—Ethnic relations.
I. Title: Holocaust and World War II. II. Title.

DS135.G3315 M43 2002
943'.004924—dc21

                                                                    2002002084

Manufactured in the United States of America.

FOR JANNA

CONTENTS

PREFACE

THIS BOOK SURVEYS the history of the Holocaust in World War II. I have attempted to show how the concept of racial war had an overwhelming influence on Adolf Hitler's thinking and actions, both before and during the war, and how, in his view, the Holocaust and the war were closely connected. Hopefully this will provide readers with a greater understanding of both the Holocaust and the war, and why and how each happened. Often histories of both events treat them separately or as barely related.

The intended audience for the book is the general reader or nonspecialist, including the college and university student. Since most general readers will not find them crucial and specialists on the Holocaust will not need them, endnotes have been kept to a minimum. Normally only direct quotations from original documents or from works of other writers receive a citation.

There are numerous scholars whose studies I have used or from whom I have learned much at professional meetings and discussions over the years about the Holocaust and Nazi Germany. Some of their work is cited in the notes and reading list at the end of this study.

For much of my inspiration to write this book, I wish to thank the numerous students who have enrolled in my college and university classes during the past thirty years. Based on their interest in and my discussions with many of them about the Holocaust and World War II, I have tried in the following pages to address their most frequent questions as well as those of other nonspecialists.

I am very grateful for the financial and other support for this book from Clemson University, where I have taught since 1979, and from the Class of

1941 Memorial Endowment. The latter was made possible by a generous gift to the university from its Class of 1941, in memory of fifty-seven of its members who died in World War II. Similar to most other young men of their generation, the vast majority of the class were destined for duty in the war and served their nation with extraordinary bravery and distinction. I am most appreciative of the support for my work from class members R. Roy Pearce, P. W. McAlister, Richard B. Caughman, and the late H. Betts Wilson.

I owe the greatest appreciation and thank you to my wife Janna, a wonderful and lovely person to whom this book is dedicated and without whose assistance, patience, and encouragement it would not have been completed.

Donald M. McKale
February 2002

ABBREVIATIONS AND SPECIAL TERMS

AJC   American Jewish Congress

Aktion   Literally "action"; a euphemism used by the Nazis to describe terror operations of the Germans and their foreign collaborators that included the roundup, mass shootings, and/or deportations of Jews.

Armya Krajowa   Polish underground army

Aryanization   Nazi term for the German takeover of Jewish property

BBC   British Broadcasting Corporation

Bund   Jewish Workers' or Socialist party

deportation   Mass roundup and transport by SS and German police of primarily Jews—but also occasionally of other peoples such as Gypsies—from Germany and much of the rest of Europe to death camps or other facilities in the East where they were murdered.

DP

Displaced Person; a description of the millions of refugees or deportees at the end of World War II, who found themselves displaced as a result of the war and usually unable to return to their homes.

Einsatzgruppen

Mobile and armed formations of primarily SS and German police; used to hunt down and kill Jews and other perceived enemies in the territories conquered by Nazi Germany.

ERR

Einsatzstab Reichsleiter Rosenberg; special staff of Reich leader Alfred Rosenberg; a German agency that specialized in plundering art treasures of Jews and others in the German-occupied countries of Europe.

Euthanasia

Term used by the Nazis as a euphemism to disguise their murder of the handicapped during World War II.

Final Solution

Endlösung, from the Nazi phrase "Final Solution of the Jewish question"; a euphemism for the program developed during 1941 to exterminate the Jews of Europe.

FPO

Fareinikte Partisaner Organisatzije, "United Partisan Organization"; the principal anti-Nazi resistance organization in the Vilna ghetto.

genocide

A term first used by Raphael Lemkin, a refugee Polish-Jewish lawyer in the United States, in late 1942 or early 1943 to describe the deliberate and systematic destruction of an ethnic or national group. At the time, the word referred directly to Nazi racial policies then being carried out. The word appeared in the indictments of German officers in postwar trials of war criminals. In 1948 the United Nations adopted the "Genocide

Convention," which made genocide a crime in international law. It explicitly bans killing, causing grievous bodily or spiritual harm, preventing births, or transferring children from a targeted group to some other group with genocidal intent. According to *The Columbia Guide to the Holocaust* (see "Suggestions for Further Reading"): "Hence the meaning of the word is somewhat fluid. It is sometimes used to refer to the actual physical annihilation of all members of an ethnic or national group. At other times it is employed to mean the killing of large numbers of such group members or to 'spiritual' or 'cultural' destruction."

Gestapo

Geheime Staatspolizei, "Secret State Police"; the political police in Nazi Germany.

Hiwis

Hilfswillige, "volunteers"; auxiliary units and collaborators of the Germans, especially the SS and police, recruited from among East European and Soviet peoples.

Holocaust

Term, widely used since the 1960s, to denote the systematic mass murder of European Jewry by the Nazis during World War II. The word has generally served to separate this particular massacre from other historical instances of genocide. Sometimes the term includes other victims of the Nazis as well.

ICRC

International Committee of the Red Cross; headquartered in Switzerland.

IMT

International Military Tribunal at Nuremberg, which tried the major Nazi war criminals in 1945–1946.

JRC

Jewish Rescue Committee

Judenräte	"Jewish Councils." Throughout Nazi-dominated Europe the Germans ordered the Jewish communities to establish such councils to act as intermediaries between the Jews and officials of the Third Reich. A Jewish Council (*Judenrat*) might govern a single ghetto or cluster of ghettos, as in the case of most of Eastern Europe. Or it might be held responsible for the Jews of entire countries, as in Germany, France, Belgium, the Netherlands, and Slovakia. Whether elected by the Jewish communities or appointed by the Germans, council members usually were prominent figures in prewar Jewish political and religious affairs and hence enjoyed popular confidence, at least initially.
KdF	*Kanzlei des Führers*, Hitler's personal chancellery; a Nazi party agency that handled his personal affairs, interests, and a number of specially assigned policies. It implemented at his directive the program termed euphemistically "euthanasia," the mass murder of handicapped persons.
Kristallnacht	Literally "night of broken or shattered glass"; the name for the pogrom throughout Germany organized by the Nazis and that began on 9–10 November 1938.
Mischlinge	Part-Jews or Jews of "mixed ancestry"
NSDStB	*Nationalsozialistische Deutsche Studentenbund*, "National Socialist German Students' Association"
OKW	*Oberkommando der Wehrmacht*, "Supreme Command of the Armed Forces"
OSI	Office of Special Investigations; an agency established in 1979 in the U.S. Justice Department

to denaturalize former Nazis or East European and Soviet auxiliaries of the Nazis found in the United States.

OSS   Office of Strategic Services, United States

RKFDV   *Reichskommission für die Festigung des deutschen Volkstums*, "Reich Commission for the Strengthening of the German People"; a German agency headed by Heinrich Himmler for developing and coordinating the settlement in Eastern Europe and Soviet Russia of persons of German blood.

RKPA   *Reichskriminalpolizeiamt*, "Reich Criminal Police Office"

RSHA   *Reichssicherheitshauptamt*, "Reich Security Main Office"; a government-SS agency established in September 1939 that included the Gestapo, criminal police, and SD; although officially responsible to Heinrich Himmler, it was run by Reinhard Heydrich.

SA   *Sturmabteilung*, "storm troopers"; the first Nazi paramilitary organization.

SD   *Sicherheitsdienst*, "security service"; the intelligence arm of the SS, run by Heydrich.

SIS   Secret Intelligence Service, Great Britain

Sonderkommando   Special detachment or detail of (1) concentration camp prisoners or (2) *Einsatzgruppen*.

SS   *Schutzstaffel*, "protection squad"; an elite Nazi organization headed by Himmler.

T4

Name frequently used by the Nazis for the euthanasia program, after the address of its Berlin headquarters at Tiergarten Straße number 4.

Third Reich

Nazi term, meaning "Third Empire," to describe the Nazi regime. The First Reich was supposedly the Holy Roman Empire from Charlemagne to Frederick II; the Second Reich was Germany under the Hohenzollern emperors Wilhelm I and II, 1871–1918.

Trawniki

Member of an armed auxiliary unit of the Germans, composed of East European or Soviet peoples and trained at an SS camp at Trawniki, near Lublin in former Poland.

UNWCC

United Nations War Crimes Commission, established in October 1943 by Great Britain, the United States, and fifteen other Allied nations, to identify and deal with Nazi war criminals.

VoMi

Volksdeutsche Mittelstelle, "Ethnic German Liaison Office"; handled some relations of Nazi Germany to ethnic Germans (*Volksdeutsche*) in a number of other European countries. It had competition from other German government and Nazi party agencies and was not originally part of the SS until Himmler gained effective control of it before the start of World War II.

Waffen-SS

Heavily armed units of the SS

Wehrmacht

German armed forces

WJC

World Jewish Congress

WRB   War Refugee Board, a U.S. government agency cre-
                        ated in January 1944 by an executive order of
                        President Franklin Roosevelt to rescue and assist
                        the victims of enemy oppression in Europe.

Zegota   Council for Aid to Jews, an underground organiza-
                        tion in Poland.

ZOB   *Zydowska Organizacja Bojowa,* "Jewish Fighting
                        Organization"; the chief anti-Nazi resistance organi-
                        zation in the Warsaw ghetto mainly responsible for
                        the revolt there in 1943. The organization had small
                        branches in other ghettos.

INTRODUCTION

"THE FUEHRER ONCE MORE** expressed his determination to clean up the Jews in Europe pitilessly," Joseph Goebbels wrote in his diary on 14 February 1942. "The Fuehrer," the Nazi propaganda minister continued, "realizes the full implications of the great opportunities offered by this war."[1]

During a private meeting with Goebbels that day, held while German armies occupied much of Europe and Russia in World War II, Adolf Hitler unleashed one of his many hate-filled outbursts against the Jews. As he had done often during the war (1939–1945) in both public and private, Hitler discussed the close tie, in his mind, between the massive military struggle and his implementation of what the world would eventually call the Holocaust. The Holocaust was the systematic mass murder in World War II of European Jewry by Nazi Germany.

After the war, another of Hitler's minions, Robert Ley, the Nazi Labor Front leader, confirmed the Nazis' association of the war with the Holocaust. Before committing suicide to escape trial as a war criminal at Nuremberg, Ley wrote: "We National Socialists, starting with Hitler, considered the fight which is now behind us a war merely against the Jews—not against the French, English, Americans, or Russians. We believe that they [Frenchmen, etc.] were only instruments of the Jews, and when reading the indictment, I feel inclined to believe that it actually was like that."[2]

1

The Holocaust and the War

Despite the many aspects of the Holocaust that historians and others studying it do not know or comprehend, one thing is clear: The genocide of the
Jews cannot be understood apart from the world war, the monstrous struggle
initiated by Hitler and National Socialist Germany in September 1939. The
leading authority on the diplomacy of the Third Reich and World War II,
Gerhard Weinberg, has written on the Holocaust and the war and emphasized about them: "What is needed in our teaching of both subjects is a sense
of their connectedness."[3] The book that follows owes much to his view as
well as to his superbly documented studies.

Hitler and his Nazi associates used the war in Europe, with its massive violence, as a cover or camouflage for the real war they meant to fight. This was a
"shadow war" in which they would eliminate millions of Jews—a people whom
the Nazis hated more than anyone or anything else—in Eurasia and eventually
elsewhere in the world. Already in the war's first months, in late 1939 and
1940, while the Germans searched for a solution to what to do with the vast
numbers of Jews falling under their rule, they began killing many Jews at random, and during 1941 they initiated the mass systematic murder of their victims.

Indeed, once they implemented the Holocaust, the Germans utilized
huge resources—human, physical, and technological—to carry out the "war
against the Jews"[4] that could have been channeled to fighting the military
war against the Western Allies and the Soviet Union. Also Hitler planned
for his annihilation of Jewry to serve as a prelude to a huge German reorganization of some of Europe's other peoples and races, which would include
their enslavement, expulsion, and extermination and would be completed
after the war.

During the Holocaust, the Nazis went to great lengths to conceal the
mass killing of the Jews from both the intended victims and much of the rest
of the world, the bystanders, primarily so as not to risk the further alienation
of world opinion from Germany. The fanatical anti-Semitism of Hitler and
other Nazi leaders had convinced them that the Jews formed a well-organized
"racial" group that controlled the seats of global power. Yet during 1942 and
thereafter, substantial information about what was happening to the Jews
reached the West, especially Britain and the United States.

Nevertheless, neither the Western Allies nor most of the victims of the
Holocaust realized what Hitler did about the war: He would use it, as he had

threatened publicly before, to destroy the Jews and thereby, in his view, lay the foundation for Germany's conquest of Eurasia and eventually other portions of the world. Only the physical removal of the Jews from the earth, he had decided, would pave the way for Germany's defeat of other rival peoples and politico-economic systems. These included Russian Communism, Western liberalism, and "international capital," all of which he claimed the Jews had invented or used to help them rule the world. "How many diseases have their origin in the Jewish virus!" he declared to aides in February 1942, as the genocide of the Jews he had ordered began in earnest. "We shall regain our health only by eliminating the Jew."[5]

The German armed forces set the stage for the Holocaust with their conquests first of Poland in 1939, which had three million Jews, and then of much of the western Soviet Union in 1941–1942, where nearly five million Jews lived. One of Hitler's goals in the war, which he had discussed since his earliest days in the Nazi party in Munich in 1919 and 1920, was to conquer vast new territory or living space (*Lebensraum*) for Germany, principally from the Slavs of Eastern Europe and Soviet Russia.

As part of this objective, the Germans began during the world war (initially in Poland and then in Russia) enslaving, displacing, or murdering indigenous Slavs, whom the Germans counted as racial subhumans. Before the war would end, several million Poles and much larger numbers of Russians would die. Also during the war the Germans murdered many members of other alleged "racially inferior" groups, including the handicapped, Gypsies, and homosexuals.

If the war resulted in the German victory that the National Socialists eagerly expected and assumed would give them world domination, they intended to complete their enormous project of racial purification and reorganization. Through the use of mass sterilization techniques, which they experimented with during the war, or further outright murder, they would eventually put an end—or nearly so—to racial subhumanity as they defined it. This would include similar persecution of the world's black population in Africa and America and other non-German racial groups that fell under German rule.

The Holocaust, however, formed the initial and crucial aspect of this planned "demographic reordering" of Eurasia.[6] It did so because the Nazis attempted already *during*—not after—the world war to exterminate *all* Jews in Europe and elsewhere whom the German armed forces could reach. The Nazis termed this the "Final Solution of the Jewish question." The "question," posed by anti-Semites since at least the nineteenth century, revolved around how to deliver mankind from the alleged global domination of the Jews.

Although earlier statements by Hitler made clear that he had thought about killing Jews and using war to do so, he likely issued the directive for the Final Solution verbally to his closest associates. They decided during 1941— while Germany prepared for and began the invasion of the Soviet Union, and other conditions in the war no longer restrained their radicalism on the issue—to rid first Russia and Poland of Jews, then the rest of Europe, and, as Weinberg has shown, ultimately the world.

What made the genocide of the Jews different from the persecution by the Germans of their many other victims in the world war? The historian Gordon Craig has provided a conclusive answer:

> More Jews were killed [by the Nazis] than [nonmilitary] members of any other national group. The destruction of the Jews was longer premeditated, more systematic and continuous, and accomplished by a more fiendishly ingenious combination of technological and scientific means than was true in the case of other victims. And, above all, no other group (except perhaps the Gypsies, whose extermination the Nazis did not in the end pursue with the assiduity and obsessive thoroughness that characterized their Jewish policy) was condemned to death by definition. In their desire to destroy Poland as a nation, the Nazis set out to kill the elites that might preserve it, but not all Poles were marked for death. The Jews were condemned without regard for their status, occupation, or politics; they were killed because they were Jews.[7]

To borrow from the words of a British writer, Hitler and the Final Solution were inseparable.[8] Already in the first months of the war, during 1939 and 1940, the German leadership had begun at his orders the extensive killing of the handicapped among its own people. In a less systematic way German armed forces killed large numbers of Polish Jews and Poles. Such killings during the very earliest moments of the war illustrated the willingness of Hitler and his subordinates, especially in the SS (*Schutzstaffeln*, or "protection squads"), the Nazi party's most powerful armed formation, to use the military struggle to remove Jews and other alleged "racial" enemies of Germany by murdering them.

The overwhelming majority of the Jews Germany killed in the Holocaust, almost all from Europe including Russia, came under German control as a result of the war. Recently a German historian estimated the total number of those who died in the Holocaust at "not fewer, [and] most probably more" than six million.[9]

But even before the world war, as discussed in the first chapters below, a vital connection existed between the racial and anti-Semitic measures of the National Socialist government and its foreign policy, which its leader used to prepare the country for war. One historian has termed the National Socialists' creation of a ruthless racist dictatorship in Germany after 1933 the beginning of their "*total war* against the Jews."[10]

In discussing Germany's domestic and foreign policy matters, Hitler and his followers used the word *Aryan* repeatedly and erroneously. The term did not in fact refer to anything German, including race; instead, the word meant Indo-Europeans who spoke Sanskrit and related languages and who had invaded India in prehistoric times and dominated its native inhabitants. Thus "Aryans" were Indians and Iranians, not Germans or north Europeans. The Nazis based many of their ideas, including this one, on myths originated by Aryan-racist-occult groups that had emerged in late-nineteenth-century Austria and Germany and introduced the pseudo-religious symbol, the swastika, to denote "Aryan" racial supremacy.

The Holocaust in History[11]

In 1945, with the end of the world war and defeat of Nazi Germany and its allies, the world's leaders, governments, and public hardly placed the Nazi genocide of the Jews at the center of their attention. For much of the world, torn apart by and suffering from the greatest war yet in history, the fate of Europe's Jews seemed a very marginal consideration. At the time, the most important Nazis who directed the genocide were either dead—Hitler, Heinrich Himmler, Reinhard Heydrich—or missing, or were not viewed as sufficiently important to be tried as major war criminals.

The International Military Tribunal at Nuremberg in 1945 and 1946, and subsequent war crimes trials, conducted proceedings that included crimes against the Jews, but such crimes did not assume much prominence at the time. Moreover, following World War II, interest in European affairs among the public, especially in the West, drifted quickly from the war and its horrific crimes to the "Cold War" between the West and the Soviet Union.

However, the trial in Jerusalem in 1961 of Adolf Eichmann, a key official in the German bureaucracy who helped perpetrate the Holocaust, provided for the world the first major summary of what happened during it and helped establish a place for it in history. The trial, along with revelations of subsequent concentration camp trials in West Germany in the 1960s and 1970s, initiated in Israel, the United States, Britain, and Germany a steadily growing popular interest in and scholarly literature on the subject.

Today Holocaust "consciousness" is widespread. A steady stream of publications as well as films about the Holocaust attracts an enormous public market; hundreds of schools and universities teach classes on the topic. Memorials to the victims abound in Europe, the United States, and Israel; these include museums dedicated to educating the public about the Holocaust. Scholars around the world debate, often with bitter—yet genuine—differences, the origins, nature, and meaning of what happened at places like the Jewish ghetto in Warsaw, the ravine at Babi Yar, and the gas chambers and crematoria at Auschwitz and other killing facilities.

The principal controversies center around why the Germans perpetrated the Holocaust; the degree of German planning and improvisation of it; the role Hitler played in the genocide; the attitudes and participation of ordinary Germans in it; how Jews responded to the horrific crisis in which they found themselves; and the world's knowledge of and general failure to react to the killings.

The most burning question is why and how the Holocaust could have happened. Why and how could the Germans have perpetrated it, and the victims and bystanders allowed it to occur? Chapter 1 examines why, among all the racial, political, and other groups that Hitler despised and persecuted, he singled out the Jews for his greatest hatred. Chapters 2 through 5 survey the steadily increasing yet "twisted road" of Nazi persecution of the German Jews before 1939.[12] The heart of the book, chapters 6 through 14, focuses on the war and Holocaust. Subsequent chapters discuss and analyze the world's problematic reaction to what by 1942 already became a flood of information from Europe about the Holocaust.

Several sections in the volume, including much of chapter 18, examine the response of the Jews to the catastrophe that progressively befell them. The overwhelming majority of the victims, beginning in 1933 with the Nazi regime's persecution of the German Jews and continuing well into the world war and Holocaust, had little or no realization they were destined for mass murder. According to the Israeli scholar, Yehuda Bauer: "The Germans did not know, until sometime in 1941, what they would do with the Jews: the decision to murder them was not taken until then. If the Germans did not know, the Jews cannot be expected to have known either."[13] Yet the evidence indicates also that numerous Jews, once they learned by the fall of 1942 of what awaited them, attempted in a variety of ways to resist the killers, including engaging in armed revolts. The obstacles faced by the resistance, however, were nearly always overpowering and resulted in the crushing of it.

Today's preoccupation of Jews and many others with the Holocaust, perhaps more evident than at any other time in the past, is explained in part by the historian Omer Bartov. He has written recently about the Holocaust that "due to the scope of the destruction and the exterminationist aspirations of the Nazis," more people today realize that "every Jew is a survivor by dint of having been a potential victim, including those born after the event, who would not have seen life had Hitler had his way."[14]

As this book will emphasize, the racial and other forms of hatred, the traditions of war and violence, and the creation of modern technology and of a powerful nation-state that made the Holocaust possible were products of, and deeply rooted in, Western civilization. The coalescing of such factors helps explain how the Holocaust happened so quickly, once it began in World War II. Christopher Browning, a leading American scholar of the Holocaust, has observed: "In mid-March 1942, some 75 to 80 percent of all victims of the Holocaust were still alive, while some 20 to 25 percent had already perished. Eleven months later, in mid-February 1943, the situation was just the reverse. Some 75 to 80 percent of all Holocaust victims were already dead, and a mere 20 to 25 percent still clung to a precarious existence."[15]

What led to the German decision to murder all the Jews their armed forces could reach, beginning in 1941 and 1942? Since primarily the 1970s, scholars have debated the origins of National Socialist racial policy and motivations and role of Hitler in the decision. Two schools of thought evolved: the so-called intentionalist and the functionalist (or "structuralist"). More recently, historians have moved away from the monocausal interpretations of each school and placed greater emphasis on elements from both sides to explain why the Holocaust happened.

The intentionalist view maintains that Hitler had planned since the 1920s to kill as many Jews as possible and that he implemented his plans when the opportunity arose during the war. The most extreme form of intentionalism is that of Daniel Goldhagen. In a book published in 1996 that produced both enormous popular interest and widespread controversy over the author's thesis, research methods, and claims to originality, he asserted that the Holocaust resulted from a pervasive pattern of anti-Semitism peculiar to Germany and already established in the era of the French Revolution. "From the beginning of the nineteenth century," Goldhagen emphasized, "anti-semitism was ubiquitous in Germany. It was its 'common sense.'"[16]

But not only was the German variant of anti-Semitism uniquely virulent and comprehensive, it was also implicitly genocidal from the start, what Goldhagen called "eliminationist" or "exterminationist."[17] While he noted correctly that many of the killers in the Holocaust were "willing executioners," his assertion that the genocide resulted mainly from the "preexisting, demonological, racially based, eliminationist antisemitism of the German people, which Hitler essentially unleashed," was much too sweeping to substantiate.[18]

Richard Breitman has advanced the most convincing intentionalist argument in his biography of Himmler, the leader of the SS, the Nazi party's principal military organization after 1934. Breitman calls Himmler the "architect of genocide."[19] The author demonstrates that ideas and fantasies about ridding German lands of Jews by killing them and using war to do so had circulated among Hitler, Himmler, Heydrich, and other key Nazi leaders not only before the war, but especially during 1939 and 1940.

Although the SS developed contingency plans that included the forced emigration or resettlement of Jews, only practical considerations associated with the war limited the means of Hitler and his associates to carry out what they really wanted. During 1941, when such considerations no longer existed, Hitler decided that he need not restrain his radicalism anymore and made the decision for the so-called Final Solution.

Breitman places Hitler's decision as early as March. Hitler left to Himmler, who acted as soon as conditions allowed, the implementation of the mass murder of the Jews. The recent discovery in a Moscow archive of Himmler's appointments diary lends much credibility to the view of Breitman and other intentionalists in two respects: (1) that Hitler was the decisive factor, though by no means the only one, in perpetrating the Holocaust; and (2) that the Führer was not the weak dictator, much less involved in the Holocaust, that some functionalist historians have claimed.

Functionalists, who include the German scholar Hans Mommsen, argue that the Final Solution arose during 1941 primarily from a slow radicalization of German anti-Jewish policy that resulted when other Nazi plans for eliminating the Jews from Europe—including their evacuation and resettlement—proved untenable. Some functionalists have claimed that Hitler's previous denunciations of the Jewish "menace" had been only empty rhetoric, until he felt pressures from what to do when confronted with such vast numbers of

Jews in the East falling into German hands as well as with a bitter "war-to-the-death" there.

Other functionalists, especially the German historian Götz Aly, tie together "Nazi population policy and the murder of the European Jews."[20] Aly asserts that the Holocaust, which began in the East, served as a means for Nazi planners, especially middle-level bureaucrats, to solve certain problems developing there. These included alleged overpopulation and "useless eaters" (i.e., impoverished Jews and Poles who blocked economic modernization, resettlement by the SS of ethnic Germans in the region, and expansion of German rule). The least credible interpretation of functionalists is that the decision to kill the Jews resulted from Nazi desperation following the German defeats on the Eastern Front during the winter of 1941–1942.

Still other scholars—most notably Browning, Eric Johnson, the German historians Ulrich Herbert and Christian Gerlach, the Swiss Philippe Burrin, and Ian Kershaw, Hitler's most important recent biographer—have taken a middle position in the intentionalist-functionalist debate. They maintain that Hitler played a key role in the decision-making process, but not wholly from premeditation. Instead, according to Browning, the German dictator acted from frustration with the failure of previous solutions and decided on the Final Solution during July 1941, amid the Nazi "euphoria" over what appeared to be an impending German military victory in Russia. Burrin places the decision in the fall of 1941; Gerlach maintains that Hitler issued a special directive in December.

Kershaw concludes that Hitler agreed at a meeting with Himmler in mid-September 1941 to deport the German, Austrian, and Czech Jews to the East. Although this "was not tantamount to a decision for the 'Final Solution,'" Hitler's agreement to the deportations, Kershaw maintains, "opened the door widely to a whole range of new initiatives from numerous local and regional Nazi leaders who seized on the opportunity now to rid themselves of their own 'Jewish problem,' to start killing Jews in their own areas."[21]

Similarly, Herbert and a group of young German historians have presented examples from eastern Galicia, Lithuania, Byelorussia, the "General Government" of Poland, and France that illustrate how local German officials initiated mass executions of Jews in late 1941 and early 1942. Johnson, in his study of the "Gestapo, Jews, and ordinary Germans" in the Rhineland, concludes: "The Holocaust was at times a viciously bloody spectacle perpetrated by both trained specialists and fully ordinary human beings who often had considerable decisionmaking latitude."[22]

Both functionalists and part-functionalists emphasize that the Holocaust derived in no small measure from a "killing machine" produced by twentieth century bureaucratic or industrialized efficiency. To be sure, the Germans produced the machinery of mass murder, but Lawrence Langer has called it "a mixed tale of 'inefficient efficiency.'" The gassing facilities at the death camps repeatedly malfunctioned, and the SS had the constant problem of disposing and "redisposing" of victims' bodies. Langer, moreover, observes about viewing the Holocaust as industrial mass killing: "The very image of machinery rather than man as the primary instrument of liquidation tends to absolve individual offenders and obscure the identity *and* the catalyst of the very culprits who initiated and carried out the crime."[23]

An issue that continues to arouse fierce debate among students of the Holocaust is the role of racial and political ideology as a motivator for German atrocities and behavior of "ordinary" Germans. Hundreds of thousands of Germans involved directly in the Holocaust—including SS, police, bureaucrats, transportation officials, and many in the armed forces—acted as both "ordinary men" and "ideological soldiers."[24] As this book will emphasize, some perpetrators killed for "practical" reasons, while others did so, sometimes even independently from higher-ups, because they knew they would approve from a fanatical anti-Semitism and racism.

CHAPTER ONE

GERMANY AND THE RISE OF HITLER

A T A TIME WHEN Europe still retained global preeminence, the continent's most advanced and powerful state perpetrated the Holocaust amid a massive world war. Nazi Germany and Hitler carried to the most fateful and horrific of extremes an obsessive racial anti-Semitism and willingness to use unlimited violence that originated in the West immediately before and during World War I.

What made the Germans, and not some other Western people, the driving force behind the Holocaust? Some answers seem simplistic and off the mark. This is the case, for example, with the claim that anti-Semitism was historically more embedded, widespread, and peculiarly vicious in Germany than anywhere else. Yet, however much such views may lack credibility, the Holocaust nonetheless makes the history of Germany and German anti-Semitism different from any other Western country.

The Many Faces of Anti-Semitism

Anti-Semitism, the "longest hatred" that reached back to ancient and medieval times, had no deeper tradition in Germany than in much of the rest of Europe.[1] Nearly everywhere in predominantly Christian Europe, the vast majority of people had accepted, and often acted in accordance with, the virulent Jew-hatred that had its origins in both an irrational fear of outsiders with noticeably different ways and in the teachings of early Christianity. First the Roman Catholic Church, and then the Protestants, had raised to the level of truth numerous myths alleging the evil of the Jews.

Early Christians, despite owing a substantial portion of their theology and moral precepts to ancient or Old Testament Judaism, claimed erroneously that the Jews had killed Jesus Christ. In fact, Jesus, who was himself a Jew and who lived in the ancient Roman province of Palestine, had both Jewish followers and opponents. When his followers failed to persuade significant numbers of their fellow Jews that Jesus was the Messiah, the Son of God come to save the world from sin, they gradually formed a new religion. Based on the ideas of St. Paul, Christianity sought converts among Jews as well as among the pagan populations of the Roman Empire. Both Paul and later Christian writers sought simultaneously not to antagonize the Roman authorities and to discredit their rivals by increasingly portraying the Jews rather than the Roman authorities in Palestine as responsible for the crucifixion of Jesus.

Accusing them of being "Christ killers," the ancient and medieval Christian Church "satanized" the Jews.[2] It viewed Jews falsely as agents of the Devil who conspired to rule the world, corrupted the civilizations of their host peoples and countries, and kidnapped or killed Christian children. Christian leaders warned that unless Jews converted to Christianity, they were condemned to eternal damnation. These attitudes promoted terrible anger and hatred toward Jews, whose small numbers in most Western lands made them vulnerable to the hostility toward them.

In medieval Europe, Jews suffered discrimination from church and state laws, isolation in ghettos, expulsion from their homelands, and violence and death in pogroms and massacres. Often barred from owning land and excluded from town guilds, medieval Jews concentrated in trade and money lending, occupations that frequently earned them greater resentment from non-Jews. In 1543, the German monk and founder of Protestantism, Martin Luther, in his pamphlet titled *About the Jews and Their Lies*, denounced Jews in the most vile manner and urged they be persecuted for their refusal to convert to the new form of Christianity. Later Nazi ideology would owe much of its image of the Jew to Christian and other early forms of anti-Semitism.

The creation of the Second German Empire (*Reich*) in 1871, despite its rule by an authoritarian monarchy, the army, and elite upper classes, had brought "emancipation" to the German Jews, a process begun in Prussia earlier in the century. Emancipation had originated in large measure with the spread into Central Europe of human rights ideas from the Enlightenment and the France of the 1789 revolution and Napoleon.

After 1871, emancipation heralded for German Jews a new day with the promise of full and equal participation as well as assimilation in a united and dynamic new nation. This promise had changed little with the unsettling transformation produced in the German empire at the end of the nineteenth century by rapid industrialization and modernization, both of which anti-Semites decried and attributed to excessive Jewish influence. The new empire was an economic and military power of the first rank. Its government, supported by extreme nationalist groups, pursued the ambitious policy of extending German power in Europe and the world, a course of action that would contribute significantly to the outbreak of world war in 1914.

Many German Jews accepted the premise that education formed the cornerstone of emancipation and the successful incorporation of Jews into German Gentile society. Jews entered German universities in unprecedented numbers. While they accounted for barely 1.3 percent of the population in Germany's largest state, Prussia, they represented almost 9 percent of the Prussian university student population in 1886–1887 and 8 percent in 1900.

In the German empire, most Jews were more prosperous, more assimilated, and more visible in the economy, the professions, and cultural life than elsewhere in Europe. They were also patriotic and deeply attached to their homeland. Their emancipation and increased visibility, however, helped kindle a steadily expanding anti-Semitic movement. The movement flourished in the universities and included a number of Germany's intellectual, social, and political elite. Nowhere else in Europe would the achievements of Jews produce greater resentment than among Germans.

As early as 1879–1880, a petition signed by 265,000 persons and sent to the German Chancellor, Otto von Bismarck, complained about "the growing dominion of the Jewish part of the population."[3] The petition urged the restriction of Jewish immigration in Germany, the dismissal of Jews from government posts, and the establishment of an official census for Jews. Anti-Jewish political parties also emerged.

Meanwhile, elsewhere in Europe anti-Semitism flourished much more outwardly and noticeably than in the new German Reich. In France it produced the Dreyfus affair, a national scandal in which anti-Semitic elements wrongfully accused a Jewish army captain of selling military secrets to the

Germans and unjustly imprisoned him. The affair divided France sharply and reflected the widespread anti-Jewish sentiments in the country.

In tsarist Russia violent spontaneous and state-sponsored pogroms left some Russian Jews dead, especially in the Ukraine, traditionally a hotbed of anti-Semitism. The Rumanian government prohibited most Jews from holding office and from voting, imposed economic restrictions on them, limited their admission to schools and universities, and in 1886 financed an international congress of anti-Semites. Authorities in Russia and several other lands placed Jews on trial for allegedly slaughtering Christian children as part of a Passover ritual— the deranged accusation that originated among Christians in the Middle Ages.

The rise of Zionism, a movement that urged the founding of a national home for Jews in Palestine, represented one Jewish response to the growing anti-Semitism. Also many Russian and East European Jews fled for their lives by emigrating to Western Europe, including to Germany and to the United States. By 1914, approximately 150,000 so-called Eastern Jews (*Ostjuden*) had settled in Germany. In their new country the appearance of the immigrants, who were both wholly nonassimilated and unmodern and radically different in lifestyle even from traditional German Jews, would help foster the increasingly entrenched anti-Semitism.

By World War I in both Germany and Hitler's native Austria-Hungary, the racial nationalist (*völkisch*) movement, which identified and denounced Jews erroneously as a race rather than a religion, had spread widely among the elite and middle classes and political conservatives and in the schools and universities. Unlike the traditional, or religious, anti-Semites, who believed in the possibility of Jews' assimilation into Gentile society by their conversion to Christianity, the newer brand of Jew-haters represented potentially a much greater danger for those whom they despised.

Such anti-Semites alleged that the "racial" Jew, whom they termed a diseased and filthy creature, degenerate and corrupting of other races, left the Jew unredeemable or unchangeable and therefore condemned to permanent exclusion from the non-Jewish world. Also the racial argument was intended to "delegitimise Jewish equality" and "establish a new paradigm for anti-Jewishness which sounded more neutral" and "scientific."[4] Soon anti-Semites demanded a ban on so-called mixed marriages between Germans and Jews. Jew-hatred now acquired so much social force that it would lead eventually, in the words of an important book from 1980, "from prejudice to destruction" for its victims.[5]

Germany's defeat in World War I combined with a succession of subsequent events that traumatized Germans. The long war of 1914–1918 produced an unprecedented mass slaughter of humanity and cultivated widespread hatred on all sides. Regarding German strategy at the battle of Verdun in 1916, one writer has observed that its goal "was to exterminate as many of the enemy as possible. This was a giant step towards the death camps of World War II. For the first time in memory a European nation had attempted to alter the biological rather than the military and political balance of power with an adversary."[6] Similar motives contributed to the genocide initiated under the cover of the "total war." During 1915–1916, Germany's ally, Turkey, had killed nearly one million Armenians in the eastern provinces of Anatolia. Most German officials, both in Turkey and Berlin, did nothing to stop the massacres, and some Germans apparently encouraged them.

As discussed later in this chapter, the twin shocks of military defeat in 1918 and resulting dramatic political and social changes in Germany provided fertile soil for the spread of racial and other forms of anti-Semitism of Hitler and his Nazi party followers. But despite this factor, Hitler did not become Chancellor (head of government) of Germany in January 1933 solely on the force of his or the party's hatred of Jews. By then millions of Germans, for a variety of reasons, had voted for the Nazi leader, joined his party, or responded to him enthusiastically in other ways.

Following the world war, the party would emerge by 1925 as the strongest of numerous paramilitary and völkisch hate groups that flourished on the extreme nationalist and conservative right in Weimar Germany, and especially in Bavaria. The ideology of the party and its leader represented a patchwork of late nineteenth- and early twentieth-century xenophobic, anti-Semitic, völkisch, Social Darwinist, occultist, anticapitalist, antimodernist, and anti-Marxist ideas.

Hitler's Ideology and the Nazi Party

The British historian, Hugh Trevor-Roper, once described Hitler's mind as the product of "the intellectual detritus of centuries."[7] Scholars have long debated both when and how Hitler acquired his racist and anti-Semitic views. These hatreds inhabited and consumed his mind. Born in 1889 in Austria, he eventually feared his own ancestry in a lower-middle-class Austrian-Czech family characterized by incest and illegitimacy. He did not know who his paternal grandfather was or whether he had been "corrupted" with Jewish "blood."

In fact, there is no evidence that Hitler had a Jewish ancestor, although he went to considerable lengths, once in power in Germany, to destroy proof of his genealogy. It seems probable that he learned to hate Jews and Slavs as a child in elementary school, and then added to his prejudices during his aim-less and adolescent days in pre–World War I Vienna and while he joined in 1919 the chaotic postwar political scene in Munich. In Vienna the pan-German nationalist and racist, Georg von Schönerer, and the city's popular mayor, Karl Lueger, significantly influenced Hitler's Jew-hatred. Hitler observed how Lueger mobilized mass support by fusing several anti-Semitic elements: Catholic prejudices against the "Christ killers," Viennese hostility against the Ostjuden, and modern anticapitalist resentments of the lower middle classes against Jews.

Angry and embittered at Germany's loss in the war, Hitler entered a small political party in the Bavarian capital that in 1920 renamed itself the National Socialist German Workers' party (*Nationalsozialistische Deutsche Arbeiterpartei*, Nazi). Extreme nationalist and anti-Semitic ideas dominated the tiny group, whose members came from Munich's lower middle class and beer hall element and included railroad workers, clerks, shopkeepers, and writers.

In February, the party adopted a political program filled with extremist right-wing demands. These included the revocation of German citizenship for Jews; the expropriation of department stores (a code name of the party for Jewish property) and their distribution to "small tradesmen" and "owners of small businesses;" the prohibition of the ownership of German newspapers by "non-Germans" (i.e., Jews); and the ban of such papers "which violate the public interest." In addition, the program contained the pan-German demand for "the uniting of all Germans within one Greater Germany," which included the union (*Anschluss*) of Austria and Germany.[8]

During the early 1920s, on the strength of his skills as an orator and pro-pagandist of hate, Hitler made himself the absolute leader (Führer) and dic-tator of the party. He gathered around him, to serve as party lieutenants, a band of likeminded, lower-middle-class political and social malcontents. These included Ernst Röhm, a former German army captain, very close per-sonal friend of Hitler's, notorious homosexual, and head of the party's para-military force, the "storm troopers" (*Sturmabteilung*, SA); Dietrich Eckart, a racist and nationalist poet and author of the booklet *Bolshevism from Moses to Lenin*; and Alfred Rosenberg, a Baltic German and author of *The Myth of the Twentieth Century*, which purported to provide intellectual support for Nazi racial theories.

Others whom Hitler attracted to the small party were Rudolf Hess, a former Munich university student whom Hitler named deputy leader of the party; Hermann Göring, a rotund and boastful World War I air ace with contacts to aristocratic and conservative circles; and Julius Streicher, an elementary schoolteacher and publisher of a pornographic anti-Semitic newspaper in Nuremberg, *Der Stürmer* (*The Attacker*). In 1926 Hitler first met Heinrich Himmler, a pedantic and methodical Bavarian poultry farmer who already believed in Hitler's basic ideas: German racial superiority, the menace of the Jews to Germany, and the need for Germany's armed expansion eastward to crush the "decadent" Jewish-Bolshevik and Slavic Russia and seize its extensive lands. During 1926 Hitler appointed Joseph Goebbels, a small, physically deformed writer from the Rhineland and master publicist of Nazi hate, as chief propagandist of the party and its leader in Berlin.

Despite questions about the precise origins of Hitler's ideology, what is certain is that Germany's defeat in the war stirred in him the most violent of passions against the Jews and convinced him to become a "politician." In contrast to Karl Marx, the nineteenth-century German-Jewish political economist and founder of modern communism, whose ideas about class struggles driving history Hitler despised, the latter proclaimed that racial conflict explained the important human events of the past, present, and future.

Hitler based his thought on the racial mythology developed by secret Aryan cults in late-nineteenth-century Austria and Germany and adopted by völkisch theorists. These groups had made a pseudo-religion of the legend of a heroic and "pure" Germanic race that was descended from ancient Aryans who had swept across Europe, and that was battling for survival against "an evil conspiracy of anti-German interests."[9] The latter were identified variously as the non-Aryan races, the Jews, or even the early Church. In this perpetual and brutal struggle, in which racial groups fought for land to feed and sustain their members, the non-Aryan inferiors must be enslaved, expelled, or eliminated—but never assimilated—by the stronger or superior.

According to Hitler, those races that had remained "pure" throughout history flourished and dominated; when they intermingled sexually with others, they declined. Germany, he maintained, could only expand and secure its racially "pure" master race (*Herrenvolk*) by going to war to seize extensive new Lebensraum. The bulk of the land to be conquered in this racial war, he emphasized, was that land held by the Slavs in the East, primarily in Russia.

He saw the Jews, however, as the most immediate threat to racial "purity" inside Germany and as the main element of resistance to the nation from outside it. He bitterly condemned the French and their revolution of 1789 for having initiated the spread of human rights that helped lead to the emancipation of the Jews in Germany and elsewhere in Western Europe in the nineteenth century. Indeed, this belief contributed to Hitler's hatred of France and his determination to defeat it in war.

The Jew, Hitler asserted, was evil because of his blood. This blood allegedly made the Jew inherently wicked, filled him with dangerous racial qualities, and made him the most determined and sinister enemy of Germany and all other nations. He charged that Jews, having no nation of their own, continually mingled with and lived like parasites among other peoples and nations, seeking to poison their racial "purity" and to corrupt or destroy their institutions, economic life, and positive qualities. This link by Hitler of blood with race would give the Nazis' anti-Semitic propaganda a pseudo-scientific base.

Also, Hitler alleged, borrowing from the fraudulent anti-Semitic tract, the *Protocols of the Elders of Zion*, which first appeared in 1897 in tsarist Russia, that the cunning Jew conspired secretly to rule the world. To help him do so, he had supposedly invented such doctrines and means as liberalism, democracy, pacifism, internationalism, capitalism, Marxism, and Christianity. These ideologies, Hitler claimed, contradicted the "law of nature," which had supposedly made one race, the Germanic or "Aryan," superior to all others and deserving of domination over its rivals in a brutal and continuous battle for survival.

The Nazi leader's commitment to securing living space in Russia led him to conclude that Germany was locked in an uncompromising struggle with Bolshevism, in Hitler's mind a Jewish creation. Not only had the Jews produced Bolshevism, he claimed, but also the latter served as an expression of the corrupt and destructive Jewish spirit. The Jews had used the Communist Revolution in Russia to take over that huge country, destroy its "inherently anti-Semitic" culture, and extirpate the Russian national intelligentsia along with the Russian upper classes. From Russia, Hitler argued, "Jewish-Bolshevism" intended to spread its insidious racial, economic, political, and cultural poison to Germany and to the rest of the world.

His views, in this regard similar to the many other prejudices he held about Jews and other groups of people, rested on pure legend. Bolshevism had arisen primarily from Russian nihilism and non-Jewish founders, including Vladimir Lenin and some nobility. In the summer of 1922, the 18 commissars of the Bolshevik regime included only 2 Jews, and the 150-member Supreme Soviet had 7. By 1927 the leading Jew in the Soviet regime, Leon Trotsky, had been expelled from the Bolshevik party and exiled. The greatest supporter of Bolshevism, in fact, and a significant catalyst of the Russian Revolution of 1917, had been the Imperial German government and army. They had assisted Lenin in returning to Russia, seeking thereby to continue its revolution and remove the country from the ranks of Germany's enemies in World War I.

All this Hitler chose to ignore. Instead, he deemed Germany's situation desperate, one of decay and decline, in part, he said, because its current population had already intermingled too much with other races. The Jews' most monstrous crime, he believed, had been to defile and corrupt the "purity" of the Aryan race through intermarriage and seduction of German women. As a result, he alleged, Jews, in collaboration with German Communists, Social Democrats, and liberals, had triumphed in Germany in 1918 and 1919 by engineering a disastrous political revolution in the country.

Such revolutionaries, he claimed, had "stabbed the nation in the back" by leading it to defeat in the world war and weakening it further by establishing a new government, the democratic Weimar Republic. But in making such assertions, he disregarded two important facts. First, during the war, Germany's home front had been a solid pillar of the nation's military effort and the least alienated of any major European belligerent.

Second, the Allied armies of Britain, France, and the United States had defeated the German forces in France so soundly by September 1918 that the German high command had asked the Imperial government to conclude an armistice before enemy troops invaded Germany. Hitler, however, searched for scapegoats to blame for the defeat and accused supposed traitors at home. He denounced repeatedly Rosa Luxemburg, a Jewess and leader of the Spartacus League (*Spartakusbund*), a precursor of the German Communist party, whom extreme rightists murdered in January 1919; and Hugo Preuss, a Jewish legal expert who had drafted the Weimar constitution.

Hitler's burning hatreds would eventually translate into his obsessive idea that Providence had selected him to perform an unprecedented mission in

the history of the German people. He would rescue them, he wrote on 8
February 1921 in the party's newspaper, the *Völkische Beobachter* (*Racial
Observer*), from the Jewish "corruptors of our nation."[10] Increasingly he would
define his struggle against the Jews and others whom he despised as a war,
designed to subject them to German rule or rid them from the earth.

The Hated Republic

Along with many conservative and nationalist Germans, Hitler denounced
the Weimar regime as foreign and alien to Germany, born of revolution and
forced on its people, and the product of a Jewish-Marxist plot against the
nation. Later, some scholars studying the republic viewed it as the result of a
"failed" revolution that had permitted numerous institutions and groups from
the empire to survive and continue dominating Germany, and finally to
undermine the fledgling democracy: the bureaucracy, army, industry, and
political elite.

But in a significant way, the Weimar Republic, whose principal govern-
ing groups included the Catholic Center party, the Social Democratic party,
the Democratic party, and the German People's party (*Deutsche Volkspartei*),
represented a genuine revolution and break with Germany's past. With the
advent of the republic, the German people for the first time directed their
own government, through freely elected representatives to the parliament
(*Reichstag*) and the presidency.

Moreover, the new republic provided all German citizens, including Jews
and other minorities, with political and civil equality as well as equal status
before the law. Contemporaries of the republic who despised it, including the
National Socialists, realized quickly its revolutionary nature and how significantly it had broken with Germany's history of authoritarian and conservative rule—and they vowed to put an end to the country's democratic
experiment.

Also Hitler, much as the vast majority of Germans, accused the founders
of the new republic of shackling the nation with the chains of the Versailles
treaty, the agreement ending the war and concluded with Germany by the
Allies, primarily Britain, France, and the United States. The Nazi leader
joined many other Germans in railing against the treaty and labeling it purposely ruinous and humiliating for Germany. Certainly the treaty imposed
some burdens on the country, including disarmament, losses of territory to

France and Poland, loss of German colonies, and payment of reparations to the Allies.

But the treaty was neither especially harsh nor unreasonable. According to Gerhard Weinberg, after 1919 a widespread parochialism among Germans convinced them that they alone were suffering and that the peace was unjust. Hitler and many of his countrymen chose to ignore, or failed to see, that the treaty left Germany's key resources—industry, transportation, and population— much less weakened than those of its former enemies, France, Russia, and Britain. The treaty allowed Germany to remain essentially intact as a nation, with the second largest population, after the Soviet Union, in Europe, and with a number of smaller and weaker—rather than, as before the war, two larger—states bordering Germany to the east and south.

Most Germans, Hitler included, failed to appreciate that the bulk of the war and destruction it caused had occurred in enemy territories, thanks primarily to the invasion of such lands by German armies. Even in defeat German forces were still fighting on foreign soil in France. This, along with the shock of surprise on the German home front in 1918 at the military's admission of defeat, helped produce and sustain the popular postwar myth among Germans that would infect their political life thereafter: the "stab-in-the-back" legend.

Few in Germany or elsewhere realized that the war and treaty had in fact still left the country Europe's most powerful state. The shattering experience of defeat in the war may also partially explain the rise during the 1920s of an extensive German literature that glorified war and contrasted with the predominantly pacifist writing in other Western countries.

Hatred for the treaty, the republic, Jews, and leftists especially emerged in the south German state of Bavaria. There a revolutionary government led by Kurt Eisner, a socialist intellectual and son of a Jewish merchant, had emerged already on 8 November 1918. Following his assassination in February 1919, other revolutionaries, including several Jews, played influential roles in a short-lived Soviet or communist-style republic in Munich.

Such events did not justify, but rather gave fuel to, the anti-Semitism and nationalism of numerous extreme rightist political groups in Munich. These demanded either the secession of the state from the allegedly "shameful" Weimar republic or the latter's destruction and replacement by the monarchy or by a rightist dictatorship. Civil war erupted quickly.

So-called Free Corps (*Freikorps*) units, originally government-financed volunteer paramilitary bands comprised of German soldiers and officers returning from the war, marched into Munich and destroyed with the utmost violence the Bavarian soviet regime and its leaders. The troops, although hired by the new German government in Berlin to destroy the communists, despised the government and believed zealously in the "stab-in-the-back."

In Berlin the Free Corps had crushed a Spartacus uprising, murdering hundreds of the revolutionaries. When the Free Corps attempted in March 1920 to overthrow the Weimar government, the latter disbanded the volunteer groups. Some went underground and continued to attack the republic, assassinating its leaders and engaging in other acts of political terror. Many in the Free Corps would soon join Hitler's movement; their brutality served as a rehearsal for the atrocities the Nazis would commit later.

During the early 1920s, the radicalism intensified in part because of the onset of a hyperinflation in Germany, which destroyed the life savings of millions of essentially middle class Germans. The crisis, however, resulted significantly from the republican government's deliberate undermining of the value of the German currency, the mark, to provide the regime with an excuse not to pay reparations. During 1923, French troops occupied the Ruhr industrial region of western Germany to collect reparations by force.

On 8–9 November 1923, one of the small and extreme rightist groups in Bavaria, the Nazi party and its paramilitary SA, followed up a Munich beer hall demonstration of the previous night demanding that Germany return to the monarchy, with a planned armed march on Berlin to destroy the republic. The Munich police forcibly stopped a parade of Hitler and his followers through the city's streets, killing sixteen SA men in a hail of gunfire. The so-called beer hall putsch ended with Hitler's arrest and his trial for treason in February 1924.

A local court convicted him, but thanks to a judge who sympathized with his rabid political views, the Nazi leader served only nine months of what amounted to house arrest in the Bavarian fortress of Landsberg. The trial provided him for the first time with national publicity. He also learned from the failed putsch that he must pursue political power in the future not through an armed revolt, but principally through a semilegal policy. This meant participating in the republic's elections and expanding popular support for his party while continuing to use SA bullies to conduct a reign of terror in the nation's streets.

In blaming the Jews and others for the republic as well as for the lost war and the Versailles treaty, Hitler and other German anti-Semites ignored numerous facts. For example, it mattered little to them that the tiny Jewish minority in Germany, which according to the census of 1925 numbered 564,397 (0.90 percent of the population), had proportionally contributed to the German military effort in World War I at least equal to or greater than that of other Germans.

Hitler, in his long and tedious memoir, *Mein Kampf* (*My Struggle*), published after his abortive putsch of 1923, explained what he believed Germany should have done with its Jews during the war:

> If at the beginning of the War and during the War twelve or fifteen thousand of these Hebrew corrupters of the people had been held under poison gas, as happened to hundreds of thousands of our very best German workers in the field, the sacrifice of millions at the front would not have been in vain. On the contrary: twelve thousand scoundrels eliminated in time might have saved the lives of a million real Germans valuable for the future. But it just happened to be in the line of bourgeois 'statesmanship' to subject millions to a bloody end on the battlefield without batting an eyelash, but to regard ten or twelve thousand traitors, profiteers, usurers, and swindlers as a sacred national treasure and openly proclaim their inviolability.[11]

Hitler, therefore, envisioned using poison gas during a war against at least some Jews already long before he and his followers seized power in Germany. A tragic irony, in view of the numbers of Jews Hitler proposed should have been killed, was that twelve thousand of them, as proudly noted in 1932 by the German Jewish organization, the Association to Counter Anti-Semitism (*Verein zur Abwehr des Anti-Semitismus*), had "died a hero's death for their German fatherland."[12] In addition, tens of thousands of German and Austrian Jews had received decorations for bravery during the war.

Anti-Semites like Hitler in Weimar Germany bitterly hated all aspects of the German Jewish presence in the country. They despised the civil and political equality accorded to German Jews, their belonging predominantly to the middle class, and the increasing assimilation of Jews in German society. In 1927, 54 percent of all marriages of German Jews were to non-Jews.

Jews, moreover, had made significant contributions by the 1920s to German culture—in theater (Max Reinhardt), music (Arnold Schönberg), art (Max Liebermann), philosophy (Hermann Cohen), and physics (Albert Einstein). Germany's first thirty-eight Nobel Prize winners included nine Jews. German nationalists such as the nineteenth-century composer Richard Wagner, whom Hitler admired, had denounced the role of Jews in music and art. Also Jews rose to leading positions in the republic in democratic and Marxist political parties, but in no way did they control either the parties or the republic.

Anti-Semites especially attacked what they termed the monolithic and all-powerful influence of the German Jews. This claim, too, as so many others they made, rested purely on fiction. The numerous Jewish political, religious, and social organizations in Weimar Germany differed widely—and sometimes bitterly—in their goals, memberships, and viewpoints. Among the organizations that had developed before 1919 were the local Jewish communities (*Gemeinden*), the Central Association of German Citizens of Jewish Faith (*Central-Verein deutscher Staatsbürger jüdischen Glaubens*), the Zionist Federation of Germany (*Zionistische Vereinigung für Deutschland*), orthodox and liberal Jewish groups, and the Relief Association of German Jews (*Hilfsverein der Deutschen Juden*).

During the republic, other Jewish organizations appeared or became more prominent. These included the Reich League of Jewish War Veterans (*Reichsbund jüdischer Frontsoldaten*), leftist and rightist Zionist parties, the Jewish People's party (*Jüdische Volkspartei*), youth and sport clubs, student groups, and provincial Jewish communities.

Jewish scholarship and culture in Germany grew steadily. This resulted in part from the prewar influx into the Reich of orthodox Jewish teachers and intellectuals from Eastern Europe and in part from a revival of Jewish consciousness among the traditional and modernized German Jewish population. A multiplicity of Jewish newspapers and other publications appeared, including two significant scholarly works, the multivolume *Jüdische Lexikon* and *Encyclopaedia Judaica* (whose publication the Nazis would suspend in 1934).

Yet despite the emphasis of some German Jews on their Jewishness, many others identified themselves differently. "The question of Jewish identity, as it was raised at the time," Norman Isenberg has written, "produced a whole array of competing responses."[13] Some Jews participated in German cultural and political life, and especially in its modernism, and their Jewishness remained a secondary concern. Others avoided addressing altogether that they were Jews. A growing number rejected Jewish traditions completely, choosing instead something else that might revitalize their sense of Jewishness, such as Zionism, Socialism, Eastern Jewish culture, or mysticism.

Several factors contributed to the complexity of the German-Jewish relationship. These included the spread of political and racial anti-Semitism, the rise of Zionism, acute generational conflicts in German and Jewish families alike, and the presence in Germany since World War I of large numbers of East European Jews, who held rigidly to orthodox beliefs and to a culture and lifestyle that were unmodern.

Hitler and his followers especially denounced what they termed "Jewish domination" of Germany's economy, but in fact Jews controlled none of the country's trades, industries, financial institutions, or commercial occupations. Although Jews enjoyed a disproportionately high participation in the learned professions—law, medicine, university teaching, and journalism—and in the performing arts, they in no sense controlled these areas.

Nor did they hold a prominent place in the upper reaches of German corporate and financial life. Gradually during World War I and during the destructive hyperinflation that followed, then sharply after 1925, the number of major enterprises owned or led by Jews declined. So did the relative presence of Jews on corporate managing or supervisory boards. Between 1925 and 1932, Jewish shareholders or chief executives lost control or influence in AEG (the German General Electric corporation), Agfa, Kaufhof, Salamander, the Mosse and Sonnemann-Simon publishing houses, and the Commerz and Dresdner banks.

Ownership of department store chains formed the only exception. Stores in Berlin, Frankfurt, Hamburg, Breslau, Cologne, and other cities, where nearly two-thirds of German Jews resided, with names like Tietz, Wertheim, and Karstadt, dominated. The Nazis and other anti-Semites fulminated against such stores that had a larger volume of goods and used new marketing techniques. The critics accused the stores of forcing small shopkeepers, a pillar of the German economy from before the industrial revolution, into bankruptcy.

For the Nazis, the department stores represented Jewish agents of "modernity" and subverters of traditional German values. The American historian, Karl Schleunes, commenting on the wide gap between Nazi fantasies about Jewish influence and the reality or truth about it, reminded his readers: "The notion that a people who comprised less than 1 percent of the total population could actually dominate large areas of German life was in itself evidence that assimilation was far from complete."[14]

During the 1920s and early 1930s, Hitler made his views known to many thousands of Germans who helped finance the Nazi party by paying to hear him and other party officials speak in countless public meetings. A dynamic orator and demagogue, he emphasized propaganda that shamelessly used the "big lie," which characterized nearly every aspect of his ideology, to rally the masses. Also during 1925–1926 his memoir, *Mein Kampf*, appeared, selling some 290,000 copies within seven years. He assured both his readers and listeners repeatedly that, if given power, he would ruthlessly destroy the Weimar regime and, along with it, the "traitors" of Germany whom he accused of threatening the country's existence. These included, he said, the liberals, the Social Democrats, the Communists, and above all, the force he claimed that lurked behind them all, the Jews.

Also he promised to replace the republic with an authoritarian government that would rebuild Germany's armed forces and then lead the nation in a series of wars. These would culminate in what would amount to a racial war in the East against the Slavs, primarily the Russians and their "Jewish-Bolshevik" leadership, to seize their land for more living space. In *Mein Kampf* he envisioned first a war with an extremely anti-German France, a war that would offer "the rear cover for an enlargement of our people's living space in Europe," acquired by a second war against Russia.[15]

In 1928, in an unpublished book that discussed mainly foreign policy, he revised his sequence of wars with the objective of gaining world domination. The first war would be against Czechoslovakia, Germany's closest minor enemy, which had intimate ties to France; the second against France; the third against Russia; and thereafter a fourth, against the United States. Once in power in Germany, Hitler gave up his illusion that a war with Britain could be delayed until after the one with the Soviet Union.

In promising war, he always expressed himself in explicit terms. In May 1928, he told an audience: "I believe that I have enough energy to lead our people whither it must shed its blood, not for an adjustment of its boundaries, but to save it into the most distant future by securing so much land and space that the future will receive back many times the blood shed."[16]

In short, Hitler and his followers called for a new start, a reawakened Germany, which would produce a racial or national community (*Volksgemeinschaft*). The "new Germany" would exclude racial and other supposed "enemies" of the nation, especially Jews, Communists, Socialists, liberals, and "pacifists," who had allegedly betrayed, divided, and weakened the country previously. This philosophy of hate, prejudice, and violence appealed to many Germans psychologically disoriented and embittered since World War I by a succession of traumatic experiences—military defeat, revolution, the rise of a republican government alien to many, the

Versailles treaty, runaway inflation in 1923, and world economic depression after 1929.

The Nazis and their Führer, much more so than the other political parties in the republic, seemed to buttress the beliefs of many Germans about what had gone wrong for their country, whom they thought responsible, and how they envisioned matters could be changed for the better. Even before the onset of the Depression in the fall of 1929, the National Socialists scored their first noticeable electoral successes in municipal and state elections. The Nazis and the extreme conservative German National People's party (*Deutschnationale Volkspartei*) led a bitter campaign against Germany's acceptance of the Young Plan, which revised—ironically to Germany's advantage—reparations payments imposed on the country by the Versailles treaty.

Also widespread acceptance among Germans of racial ideas, and especially of anti-Semitism and of a cultural prejudice against the Slavic peoples, helped the Nazis to move beyond their place as a fringe movement on the right in German politics. Primarily by participating in Reichstag and other elections and using the SA to brutalize party enemies in the streets and intimidate voters, they became the country's largest political party in July 1932 and the government's dominant coalition partner six months later.

Regarding the question of the Slavs, Germans after World War I focused their hatred especially on the Poles and Poland, in large part because the Versailles treaty had ceded a portion of eastern Germany to the new Polish state. This hatred fitted well into the National Socialists' bitter denunciation of the treaty.

Also Hitler's attacks on Jews, especially in his public speeches in the 1920s, according to contemporary police and news reports of Nazi meetings, formed a popular part of his appeal to party members and other sympathizers in the audiences. Repeatedly his listeners greeted the party leader's vilification of the Jews with "wild applause" (*stürmische Beifall*).

Among his chief party associates, at least one, Heinrich Himmler, the Reich leader (*Reichsführer*) of the party's second and smaller paramilitary unit after 1929, the SS, diligently read *Mein Kampf* and underlined its author's suggestion that Germany should have used poison gas against some of its Jews in World War I. Himmler, whose troops formed a subordinate adjunct to the SA, may have taken Hitler's racial thought more seriously than even Hitler himself.

Furthermore, as early as March 1930 the Nazis proposed to the Reichstag that "betrayal of the race" (*Rassenverrat*) be made a serious crime, equal to treason. The death penalty, they argued to the parliament, should await anyone "who contributes or threatens to contribute to the racial deterioration and dissolution of the German people through interbreeding with persons of Jewish blood or the colored races."[17]

Anti-Semitic violence characterized Weimar Germany during its earliest and last years. At least one historian, for example, has termed the June 1922 assassination of Germany's first (and only) Jewish Foreign Minister, Walther Rathenau, by the violent Free Corps, "a prelude to the Holocaust."[18] Beginning in 1930, every weekend Nazi hoodlums or thugs, many of them unemployed, angered, and embittered by the economic and social effects of the Depression in Germany, threatened to incite civil war in the streets of Berlin and elsewhere.

Most belonged to the Nazi party's largest paramilitary force, the SA. The so-called storm troopers, whose members wore brown-shirt uniforms and heavy jackboots, offered pay and some meaningful structure to a disoriented life. Such groups, armed with brass knuckles, pipes, chains, and other similar weapons, and crying "death to the Jews" (*Jude verrecke*), publicly and physically assaulted—and in some instances even killed—individual Jews. Especially they terrorized those whom the attackers labeled Jewish "tools," such as Communists, Social Democrats, and other so-called opponents of National Socialism.

German Support of Hitler and His Appointment as Chancellor, 1930–1933

Beginning in 1930, the governments of the republic seemed helpless to deal effectively with Germany's political and economic crises that escalated rapidly. During 1932, the deadly curse of unemployment reached 5,603,000, approximately 30 percent of the labor force. Between March 1930 and January 1933, the successive governments of chancellors Heinrich Brüning, Franz von Papen, and Kurt von Schleicher failed to receive a majority of support in the Reichstag because of the parliament's bitterly divided political parties. The bases for a moderate, stable, and operational democracy no longer existed.

Each chancellor, therefore, in order to implement his policies, relied on a series of emergency laws proposed by the chancellor and officially issued by the President of the republic, Paul von Hindenburg, the elderly and conservative former German field marshal and world war hero. The introduction of this "presidential government," however, did not result from von Hindenburg's or the chancellors' desire to save Germany's democracy.

Quite to the contrary, other motives drove the actions of the powerful conservative establishment around the President, which included representatives from the army (*Reichswehr*), large estate owners, high-ranking civil servants, and business and cultural leaders. Most of them purposely sought to establish a right-wing regime independent of political parties and the Reichstag and to keep the moderate and extreme left, the Social Democrats and Communists, out of power. Army leaders, in particular, disliked the republic because it reminded them of the defeat and revolution in 1918; also they were dissatisfied with the pace and scope of rearmament—pursued secretly with the Russians—and with the revision of the Versailles treaty that had begun during the republic.

Furthermore, many conservatives held stereotypes of Jews that associated the latter with much of what made the conservatives unhappy: the "Marxist" republic, the treaty, and the depressed German and international economy. Among East Prussian estate owners, the National Socialists effectively used the Jew as a scapegoat for the financial difficulties besetting agricultural interests. On the national level, Hitler and his followers continued to campaign in Reichstag elections on their intention to abolish the democratic system and avenge the alleged Jewish-Bolshevik humiliation of 1918.

To be sure, many Germans opposed Hitler, and some even recognized the implications of his ideas and policies. Still others believed naively that he did not mean what he said with his extreme and violent promises, while others felt that almost any change in the government would be for the better. However, by 1932 and 1933, vastly more Germans supported him enthusiastically because they hoped that he indeed meant what he said about a variety of issues.

In the Reichstag election of July 1932, the Nazis received almost 14 million votes, over 37 percent, which sent 230 Nazi deputies to the parliament and made the party the largest in Germany. Such voters made up the most diverse constituency of any political party in German history; they came from both upper and lower middle classes and the blue-collar working class, from cities and rural areas, and from both Protestant and Catholic confessions. The party's appeal was a mile wide if in some places only an inch deep.

Among the generally conservative Christian churches, the party had the most success appealing to Protestants. In 1932 party members founded an extreme right-wing Protestant group that called itself the "German Christians" (*Deutsche Christen*). The group sought to mobilize Protestants behind National Socialism, increase the party's influence in church elections in Germany's largest state, Prussia, and eliminate the Jewish Old Testament as well as some New Testament scripture from the Bible.

Unlike the Protestant churches, Roman Catholic leaders in Germany declared their official opposition to Nazism. But while Catholic bishops meeting in Fulda in August 1932 denounced the Nazi party's philosophy and activities as incompatible with the church's teachings, the bishops mentioned nothing of the party's violent and illegal attacks on the Jews and other groups.

Most Nazi voters hoped Hitler would dismantle or replace the republic. Also they viewed him and his party, including its rapidly growing paramilitary arm, the SA, as potential "saviors" of the nation from the specter of Communist revolution. Support for the German Communist party at the polls had grown markedly since the beginning of the Depression; in the Reichstag election of November 1932, the party received almost six million votes, roughly 17 percent, and one hundred seats in the parliament.

Germans, therefore, generally hoped that Hitler, if he became head of the government, would restore political order and stability as well as economic prosperity at home. Moreover, Germans voted for the Nazis because they believed Hitler would help Germany remove the stain of defeat in the world war and recapture its status as a major world power. Pervasive Nazi propaganda portrayed him as the only person in Germany who could rescue the nation from the undeserved calamities that had befallen it since 1918.

Many of the same views motivated the small cabal of powerful conservative and nationalist leaders in Berlin who, despite the decline of votes for the National Socialists in the Reichstag election of November 1932, soon urged von Hindenburg to appoint Hitler Chancellor. With Germany mired deeply in economic chaos, and the conservative Chancellor and army general, von Schleicher, having no possibility of surviving a vote of confidence in the newly elected Reichstag, his political enemies, led by von Papen, conspired to oust him and place themselves and Hitler in power.

Inside the Weimar government, conservative elite officials, many of them sympathetic to Nazi racial, anti-Semitic, and anti-Bolshevik ideas, quietly supported the Hitler movement. Behind the scenes, the German Foreign Ministry attempted to blunt negative foreign reaction to Nazism, fearing the party's growing popularity in Germany might disrupt the latter's relations with key countries. To do so, the ministry violated not only the freedom of the press, but also other democratic principles of the republic, including restricting individual freedoms of leading Jewish officials in Germany as well as the publicity abroad regarding Nazi attacks on the Jews.

During January 1933 von Papen and his fellow conservatives negotiated secretly with Hitler to establish a right-wing coalition government with the Nazis, with Hitler as chancellor. In such a government, the conservatives believed, they could control and even harness Hitler, who had never held an official political office, to their own purposes. The conservatives viewed Hitler and the National Socialists with mixed feelings. Although they found the Nazis' nationalism, anticommunism, anti-Semitism, and antirepublicanism intoxicating, they also feared the anticapitalist and quasi-socialist attitudes of some revolutionary elements in the party, especially in the SA.

Above all, the conservatives sought to save their elite positions and use the Nazis for that purpose. They believed that if Hitler succeeded in reviving Germany, they could check the radical elements in the party; and if he failed, he would be discredited among the German masses and removed from power. Amid much backroom intrigue, von Papen pushed von Hindenburg, who disliked and distrusted the former army private, Hitler, to appoint the Nazi leader chancellor of a "national" coalition government. The new cabinet would be made up of conservatives and two Nazis besides Hitler.

On 30 January, the President reluctantly appointed Hitler chancellor. That night, tens of thousands of SA and other Nazis marched through Berlin and other German cities celebrating Hitler's appointment. For Nazi opponents, it was a frightening and sad moment.

The Role of the "Jewish Question"

With Hitler's appointment to head the German government, he and his party had placed themselves in a position to mobilize Europe's most powerful state for the Nazis' political, racial, and anti-Semitic program. But few, if any, Germans—whether conservative and nationalist power brokers in Berlin or average voters—who supported the National Socialists, according to Browning, did so "for the mass murder of Europe's Jews or the wars of conquest in which Hitler's regime ultimately culminated. . . . Most of those who either voted for Hitler before 1933 or rapidly embraced the regime once it came to power did not share the passionate depths of Hitler's anti-Semitism."[19]

Yet the issue remains: What role did the so-called Jewish question play in the Nazi rise to power? That anti-Semitic appeals attracted a substantial portion of the Nazi party's members during the 1920s seems evident, especially in view of the police and newspaper accounts of Hitler's public speeches. What part of the German population voted for or was otherwise drawn to the Nazis because of their anti-Semitism is another matter.

Scholarship that provides a precise picture of the extent and significance of anti-Jewish attitudes among "ordinary Germans" during the Weimar years is limited. Yet, sufficient evidence exists to show that such attitudes played a role in the politics of certain groups and individuals. During the republic's first years, numerous anti-Semitic organizations and parties recruited followers from the traditional rightist elements, including war veterans, and from the young and politically uncommitted.

The tumultuous events of 1918–1920 had left many Germans disillusioned, embittered, and blaming the Jews and other alleged non-Germans for what had happened. Among them numbered many veterans who formed a multitude of violent volunteer forces, civil guards units, and combat leagues, the best known being the Free Corps. These forces often took politics to the streets, using assault and even assassination. In Munich, the Mecca of rightist and anti-Semitic fanaticism, fringe groups emerged such as the Thule Society, the fledgling National Socialist party, and the German Racial Protective and Offensive Association (*Deutschvölkische Schutz- und Trutzbund*), which had more than two hundred thousand members.

During the 1920s the Nazi party and SA became a reservoir for many of these forces. Above all, after 1929 the SA contributed extensively to the acts of political terror perpetrated against individual German Jews. Also some Jew-haters in the 1920s sought to defame and slander Jews with publications such as the *Protocols of the Elders of Zion*, with ritual murder propaganda, and with the desecration of Jewish cemeteries and synagogues.

Further, a radical anti-Semitism flourished in German universities. Along with other elements of right-wing extremism, it had permeated for a long time the conservative student fraternities and a völkisch student movement that had become a controlling force in university politics, the Germanic University Circle (*Deutsche Hochschulring*). The movement spread ideas of racial anti-Semitism and used political measures to attempt excluding students of Jewish "descent" from "German" student groups. The German University Circle controlled, on average, more than two-thirds of the seats in university student parliaments; in 1926, 77 percent of the Prussian students in the circle voted to retain the ban of Jews from membership in the organization.

By 1927, the rabidly anti-Jewish National Socialist German Students' Association (*Nationalsozialistische Deutsche Studentenbund*, NSDStB) made its presence felt nationally in the German Students' Union (*Deutsche Studentenschaft*). The Nazis won numerous local student union elections and in 1931 seized control of the national union. At the time, Hitler told Baldur von Schirach, the head of the NSDStB: "You have no idea how much this means to me now that I am able to say . . . the majority of the young intelligentsia stands behind me."[20]

During the Weimar years, the universities educated much of the generation that would rise during the Nazi regime, and above all during the war years, to positions of leadership in the German government and society. In the 1920s the Nazis attracted important sections of the intellectual classes, especially teachers and students. Some lower-ranking bureaucrats, lawyers, doctors, engineers, Protestant pastors, even elements in the army and upper class, joined as well.

Also the anti-Semitic movement among the university students and teachers provided a link between the fanatical, anti-Jewish völkisch extremists, with their relatively new racial anti-Semitism, and the older, more passive and socially acceptable, anti-Semitism of broad sectors of the German population. A majority of Germans shared a broad, negative stereotype of Jews, which had a long and established tradition in Germany and which doubtless broadened the appeal of the Nazi message.

This view characterized Jews as foreigners or outsiders, greedy, corrupt, degenerate, in contact with Germany's enemies from World War I, wealthy from exploiting and manipulating others financially, domineering out of all proportion to their numbers, controlling the press, and dangerously left wing. Such attitudes not only produced an indifference and apathy toward Jews among many Germans, but also led them to ignore or passively support discrimination against Jews. Moreover, the old anti-Semitism, historian Donald Niewyk has concluded, "created a climate in which the 'new' anti-Semitism was, at the very least, acceptable to millions of Germans."[21]

Numerous traditional anti-Semites belonged to the rightist German National People's party, the German People's party of Foreign Minister Gustav Stresemann, the large veterans' groups such as the Stahlhelm, and the Protestant churches. In 1924 the Stahlhelm, whose membership exceeded four hundred thousand, implemented an "Aryan Paragraph" that excluded Jews as members—even highly decorated Jewish war veterans. Many other organizations did likewise, including the Young German Order (*Jungdeutsche Orden*, with two hundred thousand members), the German National Union of Business Trainees (*Deutschnationale Handlungsgehilfen-Verband*, with four hundred thousand members), and the Reich Agricultural Association (*Reichslandbund*, with one million members).

As for the Nazi party, not all the Germans who supported it with their votes were anti-Semites. Because the intensity of anti-Semitism varied from region to region in Germany, numerous Germans were attracted first to Nazism and then to its Jew-hatred. Evidence indicates, moreover, that after 1929 Hitler spoke much less often in public about the "Jewish question." But most party members, and doubtless numerous Nazi voters, despised Jews and willingly accepted the party's public demands that they be deprived of their rights.

Most probably, before 1933 the National Socialists' anti-Jewish attacks provided the party with an element that both vaguely tied together its many political and economic promises and helped reconcile its often contradictory appeals to the middle and lower classes, farmers and consumers, and capital and labor. Creating and emphasizing the propaganda image of the Jew as "Bolshevik," "liberal," "capitalist," "traitor," "foreigner," "modernist," and "racial defiler" helped make possible the Nazis' attraction of diverse groups in the German electorate. Put another way, the Jew served Hitler's movement effectively as a scapegoat for the resentments of numerous social and political groups.

During the Weimar years, therefore, anti-Semitism represented neither a peripheral issue for ordinary Germans nor one in which all of them sought the "elimination" of the Jews. The Jew who emerged from the widespread and traditional stereotypical image held by most Germans and from the National Socialists' considerably more vicious anti-Jewish propaganda remained far removed from reality. Yet it was these images that constituted reality for groups blinded by their fear and hatred of Germany's Jews. They also help to explain, as much or more than other factors, why little or no opposition arose inside the Reich during 1933 and after to the hundreds of anti-Jewish measures implemented by the new Hitler regime.

The regime's anti-Jewish policy would produce both during and after 1933 public concern and discussions in the United States and countries of Western Europe, but not in Germany. As the following chapters will show, a substantial majority of the German population supported the National Socialist government, and especially Hitler, considerably more than most observers outside Germany would long believe.

As for Germany's Jews by 1933, they were not a completely unsuspecting group, caught unaware or by surprise by their determined enemies. During 1926 many Jews began discussing learning how to develop their bodies and defending themselves. After 1930 much of the Jewish community recognized that the only course of action for Jews was to repudiate or reject Nazism totally. Some Jewish organizations, most notably the Central Association of German Citizens of the Jewish Faith, published rebuttals to the anti-Semitism of the Nazis.

In the spring of 1931, members of the Central Association met privately with the German Chancellor, Brüning, and expressed concern about mounting Nazi physical and verbal attacks on Jews, hoping that he would issue a public condemnation of the assaults. The Chancellor, however, did nothing beyond meeting with the Jewish leaders. During 1932, public statements by Jews regarding the situation led the German government to attempt to control the remarks, primarily to keep them from generating more foreign criticism of Nazi anti-Semitism and political violence.

The small and often divided German Jewish community, which had little access to the halls of political power in the Weimar regime, and in fact was resented by many republican leaders, could do only so much in countering the mounting anti-Semitic movement. The community and its leaders found their resources severely limited, a fact wholly lost on anti-Semites who railed against the supposed international influence of Jewry. Some Jewish leaders realized that Hitler, for practical reasons, sought to play down his and the party's anti-Semitism in their drive to power. But such leaders suspected as well that after a Nazi victory and Hitler becoming Chancellor, Jews could expect little or no mercy from the new rulers in Berlin.

CHAPTER TWO

THE NAZI REVOLUTION AND GERMAN JEWS, 1933

H ITLER HAD BARELY TAKEN the oath as German chancellor, making him head of a coalition government, when he met privately with the nation's military leaders. Because few of the generals knew much about him, he sought to secure their support and allegiance and to show them how their interests in the build up of large armed forces coincided with his. On the evening of 3 February 1933, he described at length to them his plan for Germany's future rearmament and eventual war for the "conquest of new living space in the east and its ruthless Germanization." [1]

The officers listened intently. They had disliked the pace of German rearmament during the Weimar Republic; moreover, many of them had long accepted war as a necessity, especially to seize back the territory Germany had lost in 1919 to Poland. But to ensure, Hitler continued to tell the officers, that the German people would go to war in the future, radical change was needed inside Germany: the "cancer of Democracy" had to be destroyed and replaced by the "[t]lightest authoritarian State leadership." The armed forces he envisioned building, he explained, must be ideologically pure and not "poisoned" by the allegedly Jewish-inspired "pacifism, Marxism, [and] Bolshevism." [2] While he and his party consolidated their absolute authority in Germany, he would need the generals to build up the army.

The new chancellor, therefore, emphasized that only a major political revolution at home could prepare for the new and powerful Germany he promised.

He made clear, however, that the revolution he planned did not include destroying Germany's traditional institutions and elites. As he would discover, the German "establishment," the leaders of the military, bureaucracy, industry, and churches, as well as of the medical, legal, and academic professions, largely collaborated with and provided significant support for his regime. Although many among the elite looked down on Hitler as substantially lower in social rank, they found much in his ideology that attracted them to him and the new government.

The Destruction of Democracy and Human Rights

Hitler and his followers would base most of the revolutionary change they produced inside Germany on their radically different vision of how society should be organized. Germans identified by the new government as political and "racial" outsiders, and therefore also as "enemies of the state," found themselves the targets of an enormous campaign to degrade them, isolate them (both legally and in other ways) from the rest of society, and eventually force them to leave Germany.

As the foundation of this campaign, the new government attacked and destroyed the individual rights and legal equality of *all* Germans provided by the Weimar Republic. Such an assault on democracy and human rights amounted to a major political break with what had happened in Germany in 1918–1919. The Nazis viewed themselves as reversing not only the liberal ideals of the German Revolution, but also those of the revolutions in America in 1776 and France in 1789.

A most important step in the Nazi revolution, and a crippling blow to democracy, occurred on 28 February 1933. Following a fire at the Reichstag building in Berlin the previous night, which the Nazis blamed on a communist conspiracy to overthrow the new government, Hitler persuaded von Hindenburg to issue an emergency "Decree for the Protection of *Volk* and State." The so-called Reichstag fire decree would remain in effect until 1945. It suspended the basic rights of German citizens, allowed the national government to take over full powers in the German state governments, and ordered death or imprisonment for a series of crimes. These included treason, assault on government officials, arson in public buildings, incitement to riot, and resistance to the provisions of the decree.

The decree, by suspending the legal right to personal freedom, opened the way for German police to use a device called "protective custody" (*Schutzhaft*).

This enabled police to arrest and imprison suspects deemed a "threat to the state" for any length of time without trial. The nationalist and conservative members of Hitler's cabinet, by agreeing to this extraordinary grant of authority to him, showed both their incompetence and powerlessness.

During the following week, amid a campaign for a new Reichstag election, the National Socialists employed the decree to their advantage. The SA, whose lower-middle-class, violent, and unruly members now numbered in the hundreds of thousands, acted frequently as auxiliary police (*Hilfspolizei*). They arrested and imprisoned large numbers of Communists and Social Democrats. The SA locked many of the victims in unofficial or wildcat concentration camps (*wilde Konzentrationslager*) and bunkers, institutions made possible in significant part by the Reichstag fire decree. There the SA beat and tortured the prisoners indiscriminately. Some died from the brutality. Likewise, the government initiated a campaign to first muzzle and then destroy the opposition press.

Despite the growing political terror waged by the Nazis against their political enemies, the Social Democrats polled over seven million votes and the communists nearly five million on 5 March in Germany's last "free" election prior to the end of World War II. The National Socialists received 43.9 percent of the vote, substantially less than what the party needed for a parliamentary majority. However, the majority materialized when the parties of Hitler's nationalist and conservative allies in the cabinet polled over 8 percent of the vote.

Already by mid-March the Nazis began seizing control of the various state and local governments. At the local level the SA assisted in the violent removal of democratically elected officials, and Nazi supporters stormed city halls. The officials ousted were often placed under "protective custody" and imprisoned. Anyone wearing a brown SA uniform appeared free from the customary restraints of the law.

Then on 23 March Hitler combined threats of SA and SS terror with political promises to persuade the new Reichstag to approve a new law, the so-called Enabling Act. The law allowed the government to rule without constitutional forms and limitations for the next four years. This frightful surrender of the Reichstag to Hitler made him dictator of Germany, free from any real control by the parliament, his cabinet colleagues, or for that matter, the president. The law would be renewed in 1937, until Hitler declared it perpetual in 1943.

Three days before the Reichstag approved the Enabling Act, Heinrich Himmler, the leader of the SS and newly appointed police chief of Munich, opened Germany's first "official" concentration camp at Dachau, for the internment of Nazi political opponents. Himmler also asserted that Communists, whom the National Socialists identified with Jews, planned to assassinate Hitler.

Although Himmler provided no evidence for his claim, he nonetheless warned in the Nazi party's main newspaper, the *Völkischer Beobachter*, that if such an event occurred "Germany will experience the greatest mass murders and pogroms in world history, and no state power and no police will be able to halt this murder."[3] Nowhere else had one heard such a thing from a government official—a prediction about and approval of an attempt to murder a good portion of Germany's Jews if an appropriate pretext occurred.

Initial Nazi Assaults on the Jews: The Lack of a Plan

In its destruction of human rights in Germany, the new government gave a central place to organizing society along racial lines and, as the focus of this policy, the ever harsher degradation and persecution of the German Jews. The government would also single out minorities such as Gypsies and homosexuals as enemies of the new state and objects of persecution.

Two prominent historians have called Hitler's Germany "the racial state."[4] From the beginning of the regime, a vast array of agencies and organizations institutionalized racism as state policy. These included, most notably, the Reich Interior Ministry and medical or health offices, police agencies, the National Socialist party, SA, and SS; all established special offices or departments solely for studying and developing policies on racial matters, and primarily on the so-called Jewish question.

Between 1933 and 1939, the Nazis would progressively strip the German Jews—which in 1933 numbered 503,000, only 0.76 percent of the country's population—of their rights and equality as citizens, deprive them of their principal means of assimilation into German society, and persecute them in numerous ways. Simultaneously National Socialist propaganda boasted of the ever more ruthless measures taken against the victims. During its first six years, the National Socialist regime implemented roughly four hundred pieces of anti-Jewish legislation.

Much of the Nazis' initial assault on the Jews, however, had little or no central direction from the offices of Hitler's government chancellery or party headquarters. Contrary to the party's public promises to carry out an anti-Jewish campaign once the party assumed power, it had given little thought before 1933 to concrete methods of dealing with the "Jewish question." The only plans the party had made, both in its original political program of 1920 and in a lone directive of 1932, had called for depriving Jews of their ownership of department stores and their political rights by "legal process" or "through administrative means."[5]

Although such vague writings may have agreed with Hitler's initial policy of using legal and methodical measures against Nazi enemies, so as not to alienate his conservative allies, they hardly addressed the violent anti-Jewish demands of the SA and other party radicals. These groups urged the immediate and forcible removal of Jews from all aspects of German life and eventually their expulsion from the country.

Even though Hitler had long held the idea that Germany should have murdered masses of German Jews in World War I for the country to win the war, in 1933 neither he nor the party had a coherent anti-Jewish policy. At this early stage in the Nazi regime, the issue divided the party leadership into two principal groups: the realists or opportunists, on the one hand, and radicals or hardliners, on the other.

The former group included Himmler, the Reichsführer of the SS, whose power in Germany would expand significantly after 1934; Reinhard Heydrich, Himmler's second in command in the SS and chief of its Security Service (*Sicherheitsdienst*, SD); Göring, the Nazi Interior Minister in Prussia and minister in Hitler's cabinet; and Hess, the party's deputy Führer. The radicals included SA leaders such as the commander, Röhm; Goebbels, the head of a newly established Ministry for Public Enlightenment and Propaganda in Hitler's government; and Streicher, the Nazi district leader (*Gauleiter*) in Franconia and publisher of *Der Stürmer*.

Hitler sided privately with the radicals, who demanded that he make Germany *judenrein* ("free of Jews"). However, during his first years in power, he based many of his actions regarding the Jews on political opportunism. He wished for nothing to endanger his young government, which was most vulnerable to its enemies, both inside Germany and out. Moreover, he needed powerful internal allies such as the conservatives, most of whom were themselves anti-Semites to one degree or another and insisted on political stability and order, including in issues that related to Jews.

Hitler, therefore, carefully avoided the appearance of his personal involvement in the "Jewish question," and instead responded behind the scenes to pressures from "below" party activists, especially those in the SA who demanded increasingly violent and severe anti-Jewish policies. Regarding the issue, Hitler usually withdrew from or remained above the conflicts in his party and government. Nevertheless, he encouraged his followers in their assaults on the Jews. He did so both passively, with his lack of initiative in the "Jewish question," and actively, with his continued statements degrading the Jews.

Especially in areas of Germany where the National Socialists had received nearly 75 percent of the vote in recent elections, such as Upper Hesse and neighboring portions of Prussia, the SA, often acting as auxiliary police, carried out an array of outrages against the Jews. Göring, the Minister-President of Prussia, announced during a speech in Essen that he approved of the lawlessness. He rejected, he declared, the idea that "the police are a protection squad for Jewish shops."[6]

The SA correctly believed this a signal to take matters into its own hands. Bands of SA men roamed the streets shouting obscenities at Jews and subjecting them to harassments and beatings. Also brown-shirted thugs carried out brutal searches of Jewish homes, vandalized synagogues, desecrated Jewish graveyards, smashed windows of and plundered Jewish shops, and boycotted Jewish businesses and professional people. Some SA hunted down individual Jews suspected of or known to be having sexual relations with Germans or Aryans. The Jews were dragged through the streets and vilified for their alleged defilement of Germanic "racial purity."

The wild acts of terror and hooliganism created a climate of fear that affected both Jew and non-Jew alike. A Jewish woman living in Nuremberg observed: "The most frightening fact at this moment was being deprived of the protection of the law. Anybody could accuse you of anything—and you were lost."[7] Even non-Jews feared speaking to longtime Jewish friends or acquaintances as well as buying in their shops or seeking their professional help.

In concentration camps, SA killings of prisoners became commonplace. In Bavaria, where Himmler and the SS received control over the state's political police, conflicts over authority erupted between Himmler and Röhm; but while Himmler acted as commander of the state police, in the Nazi party the SS and its chief were subordinate to the SA.

Attorneys and judges reported to Hitler, the rapidly escalating instances of SA misuse of police authority and other independent actions through the Reich Ministry of Justice whereupon he demanded a halt to the SA behavior. For him, too much open SA violence threatened to undermine his nominal policy of legality and order and hence possibly even the legitimacy of his fledgling regime.

However, his concern with the SA's activities had nothing to do with the formation during March and April of an official terror organization, the secret state or political police (*Geheime Staatspolizei*, or *Gestapo*). The Gestapo originated in Prussia from an intelligence department of the Berlin police. Göring employed it primarily to deal with so-called politically unreliable elements, namely communists, socialists, and Jews. Headquartered at Prinz-Albrecht-Strasse 8 in Berlin, the Gestapo was detached from the general police. Eventually it would acquire jurisdiction in the concentration camps in Prussia and receive such extensive powers of arrest and imprisonment that the German courts of law could almost never conduct formal reviews of or limit its activities.

But neither continued appeals from Hitler nor the creation of the Gestapo impressed the SA. Yet few, if any, SA men were punished for their attacks on Jews or other alleged Nazi enemies. This, along with Hitler's public claims that SA violence resulted from communist and Jewish "provocations," made the SA's lack of response to his requests hardly surprising.

The Boycott

On 26 March 1933, Hitler informed Goebbels that he had decided on a common anti-Jewish measure that would be centrally directed from above and intended to placate the SA and other party militants. This was a nationwide boycott against Jews in the business and professional world, scheduled to begin on 1 April and continue indefinitely, presumably until Jews had been eliminated from the German economy.

Also the Nazis intended the boycott as retaliation for criticism of recent events in Germany by what the Nazis called the "Jewish-dominated" world press and foreign opinion. In the United States Jewish groups had urged that America boycott trade with Germany. Also in the United States and Britain, the press had reported widely and unfavorably on the SA terrorism and lawlessness, suppression of civil liberties, and vehement attacks on the Jews. Further, the diplomatic representatives of both countries stationed in Germany had described to their governments the Jewish persecution.

On 25 March, Göring, especially angered by the media reports, called foreign correspondents in Germany to his office at the Prussian Interior

Ministry in Berlin. He denied the claims from abroad about the mistreatment in Germany of Jews and political enemies of the government. Then shortly after this meeting, Göring secretly summoned to his office three of Germany's Jewish leaders, all heads of Jewish organizations that urged the assimilation of Jews into German society. Only at the last moment did the leader of the Zionist Federation of Germany learn of the meeting and manage to acquire an invitation to it.

That Göring initially left the Zionists out of the meeting reflected his wholly stereotypical Nazi view of Jews. He believed that all Jews were alike, the assimilationists as well as Zionists. Much as the other Nazi leaders, his hatred of Jews left him unable to separate prejudice and fantasy about them from reality. He revealed his illusions about "international Jewry" when he denounced to the Jewish leaders what he claimed were efforts by Jews to incite the foreign press to lie about events in Germany. He warned in his typically arrogant and snarling fashion that if such foreign accusations did not stop, he could not assure the future safety of the German Jews.

The Jewish leaders stood their ground. When they forced Göring to admit that some unfortunate incidents against Jews had occurred, the Nazi official's anger rose. Again revealing his belief in the influence of "world Jewry," he threatened the leaders and demanded they travel to London to inform British and American Jews about the falsehood of reports of Nazi atrocities. A few days later, one of the Jewish leaders arrived in London, but the public announcement in Germany on 28 March that the nationwide boycott would begin on 1 April ended his mission.

Hitler, for his part, initiated the anti-Jewish boycott and then removed himself from the matter, a pattern he would follow repeatedly in future Nazi anti-Jewish policy. Hopeful not to antagonize at this early stage of his rule his conservative allies in the government, who insisted on the regime keeping political stability and order, he placed the direction of the boycott not in the state's hand, but rather in the party's.

To organize and direct the boycott, he appointed a party committee headed by Streicher. But while the committee worked feverishly to publicize the boycott, the day before it began Hitler suddenly announced that it would last only one day and then possibly resume on 5 April if "international Jewry" failed to stop its anti-German activities. In reality, the boycott would last three days.

The decision to limit the boycott resulted primarily from the displeasure over the event among key conservatives. Both von Hindenburg and the cabinet, especially the Foreign Minister, Constantin Freiherr von Neurath, who worried about the diplomatic repercussions of the boycott for Germany, urged Hitler to cancel it. Pressure from the SA and the party, however, would not have allowed cancellation. Nor did Hitler wish to stop the boycott. Instead he restricted its duration and relied on Goebbels, who spoke on national radio on the eve of the boycott, to assure both von Hindenburg and party radicals that the event would meet all their expectations.

However, once the boycott began on the morning of 1 April, little of the conservatives' hoped-for moderation materialized. Some SA units started local boycotts even before the scheduled nationwide one and, posted as guards at Jewish shops, scared away prospective customers. When some visitors entered the stores, they were photographed and appeared the following day in the showcase of *Der Stürmer* and in the local press, publicly denounced as traitors to the racial community. Members of the party's Hitler Youth (*Hitler Jugend*) abused Jewish shopkeepers with vile language. Signs humiliating to the Jews, such as the swastika, and murderous slogans, such as "Death to the Jews," "Perish Judah," and "Jews Out," were smeared on walls and shop windows.[8]

Jews responded to the boycott by keeping most of their businesses open. Also, Jewish officials sent numerous written objections and protests to government agencies, including to Hitler's Reich Chancellery. Although representing a defenseless minority, Jewish leaders talked back to their oppressors with deeds and words often remarkable for their courage. Nearly every one of the many groups in the Jewish community asserted to the government the right of Jews to be German, to reside in and to love their homeland.

Some of the Jewish protests mentioned the harm done by the boycott not only to Jews, but also to Germans. Such assertions held more truth than the Nazis realized. Once the boycott began, it became evident that their propaganda about Jewish domination of the German economy hardly corresponded to reality. For example, numerous Jewish department stores, which the Nazis had long denounced as evidence of Jewish modernism and capitalist domination and now singled out for boycotting, relied largely for their financing on German banks and foreign creditors. Such stores, moreover, employed large numbers of Aryans. Rather than boycott some Jewish stores, therefore, the Nazis had to protect them and avoid risking the stores' solvency, adding to Germany's unemployment, and endangering foreign investments. Such revelations, however, were ignored by Streicher and other radicals and in no way dampened their zeal for the boycott or other attacks on the Jews.

Furthermore, the boycott confronted the Nazis for the first time with the problem of defining who and what were Jewish. For instance, did the principal ownership of stock by Jews make a business firm Jewish? If so, as the Nazis believed, what if Aryans or non-Jews acted as directors of the firm or the latter employed mostly Aryans?

The response of others to the harassment by the SA and party youth in the boycott could not have given the Jews much comfort. One historian of the economic struggle faced by the Jews in Nazi Germany has concluded: "Some of the bystanders protested, but apparently many more applauded these actions."[9] Eyewitness accounts and other scattered sources indicate that most Germans who disapproved of the boycott did so not from sympathy for their persecuted countrymen, but because they feared it would have disastrous economic consequences at a time when Germany could hardly afford them.

Much of the foreign press as well as many foreign diplomats condemned the Jewish persecution. George Messersmith, the American consul general in Berlin, informed Göring that the United States government had no control over criticism of Germany in the American press. Numerous Americans, said Messersmith, disapproved of the Nazi attack on the Jews. The Nazis, he believed, had intensified the prejudices of Germans against the Jews so significantly that the latter would have a difficult life well into the future.

The perceptive consul general also reported to his government that many of the Germans who benefited from the elimination of Jewish competition had joined the radical anti-Semites. Also after the boycott, Sir Horace Rumbold, the British ambassador to Germany, warned his government that the situation of Jews in Germany would worsen, so much in fact that it would create for Britain and other countries a mass of desperate Jewish refugees.

The widespread negative reactions from abroad soon forced Hitler to use Hjalmar Schacht, the President of the Reichsbank, to assure Britain's bankers of Germany's future intentions to follow a traditional economic policy. At the World Economic Conference in London in June, von Neurath observed a growing diplomatic isolation of Germany because of the "Jewish question." President von Hindenburg as well continued to oppose the boycott.

Retreat to Legislation

The boycott, therefore, signified a disaster for the National Socialists. With the boycott Hitler and his followers had attempted a concerted attack on the alleged "Jewish control" of the German economy based wholly on mythical and stereotypical views of the Jews. The implications and consequences of the assault required an immediate withdrawal to measures much less disruptive to the economy and more acceptable to Hitler's political allies and to the German people.

For their part, Streicher and other party radicals opposed such a retreat and anything else that indicated, in their view, an ignoring of Nazi ideology. For long after the boycott fiasco, their frustrations would lead them to initiate a series of similar and even more radical anti-Jewish campaigns. During the first months of the Nazi regime, therefore, its policy toward the Jews lacked any coordination and reflected the disagreements and tension within the Nazi movement and government regarding the issue.

Much of the regime's retreat by the beginning of April 1933 involved the decreeing of laws that provided retroactive legality for what was already happening. This was the large dismissal of Jews and other persons despised by the Nazis in cultural, artistic, and media occupations and in the civil service, especially in university and high school teaching. Also SA terrorists continued to invade German courtrooms, often either physically removing Jewish judges and lawyers and dragging them into the streets, or preventing others from entering their courtrooms or offices. Widespread firings and forced dismissals of Jewish judges occurred in Bavaria and Prussia.

These actions prompted a written protest from von Hindenburg to Hitler. The President noted "that judges, lawyers, and officials of the Judiciary who are disabled war veterans and whose record in office is flawless, have been forcibly sent on leave, and are later to be dismissed for the sole reason that they are of Jewish descent."[10] Hitler, not wishing to alienate the President or the conservatives in his cabinet, quickly produced a law that generally pleased them.

On 7 April 1933, the government decreed the "Law for the Restoration of the Professional Civil Service." Even before Hitler's assumption of power, the Reich Ministry of Interior had considered such a law. The decree of 7 April contained a so-called Aryan Paragraph that eliminated tenure and other legal safeguards for non-Aryans in the civil service, thereby leading to their dismissal. As part of the law, the government soon provided a new and important definition of non-Aryan: a person who had a "non-Aryan parent or grandparent." In June the government extended the provision to any person married to a non-Aryan.

Also the law provided for the removal of officials who did not meet their superiors' standards of suitability or could not prove their political "reliability." Apparently reflecting von Hindenburg's protest, a provision in the law exempted from it officials, Jewish or otherwise, who had already been in office by the beginning of World War I or who had fought at the front or had lost fathers or sons in the war.

The law of 7 April, as well as subsequent anti-Jewish legislation, could not have been decreed without the collaboration of senior officials in the bureaucracy, a largely elite and conservative group that associated Jews with the hated republic and its alleged corrupt party politics. In the weeks that followed the issuing of the decree, civil servants attempted to protect their jobs by flooding the Nazi party with membership applications in greater proportions than any other professional or social group.

The law not only provided the government with a corpse-like obedience (*Kadavergehorsam*) in the civil service, but it also destroyed for German Jews the equality they had previously enjoyed before the law. Eventually, nearly every Jewish official would fall victim to the decree. Thousands of them, ranging from government bureaucrats to school teachers and university professors, lost their jobs—and with them economic livelihood, social status, and professional reputation.

Immediately the Nazis applied the Aryan Paragraph to other professions and organizations. On 11 April, the government issued a "Law Concerning Admission to the Legal Profession," which banned non-Aryans from practicing as lawyers, public prosecutors, and judges. Nearly half of Jewish judges and prosecutors were dismissed from their jobs, as were almost one-third of the three thousand Jewish lawyers, who functioned as state officials and worked publicly amid the barrage of Nazi propaganda hostile to them.

Jewish doctors fared little better. In 1933 Germany had approximately 5,500 Jewish doctors, or 11 percent of all physicians. Although Hitler excluded them from application of the Aryan Paragraph, Nazi officials at local levels ignored this and banned such physicians from the list of providers for the national insurance program. Soon the Reich Ministry of Labor, responding to the local actions, extended the ban to Jewish dentists and dental technicians.

Also highly placed functionaries of the Nazi Physicians League purged Jews from the medical profession in earnest, first dismissing them from the nation's medical associations. In local areas, including Berlin and other cities, Jewish doctors suffered physical harassment from the SA or Gestapo, including beatings, boycotts, and imprisonment. State and municipal governments either banned or severely restricted the work of Jewish doctors.

The Canadian scholar, Michael Kater, has concluded that many Germans "who stood much to gain by such harassment participated enthusiastically or else incited others." Usually these included young physicians in search of employment or of a practice who took over the Aryan clients of the Jewish doctors. Old and hardened anti-Semites also participated in the attacks. According to Kater, however, much to the anger of Nazi officials, numerous Germans, including "civil servants and even members of party organizations were reluctant to surrender their trusted Jewish doctors."[11] Beginning with the so-called Nuremberg Race Laws of 1935, the Nazi government would progressively disenfranchise the Jewish doctors, and in 1938 eliminate them completely by abrogating their licenses.

It is unclear how much similar pressure from local Nazi militants resulted in the Reich government's "Law Against the Overcrowding of German Schools," decreed on 25 April. Regarding their policy toward the schools and universities, the National Socialists exploited a long tradition in Germany of intellectual anti-Semitism. The law subjected Jewish students to a *numerus clausus*, which restricted the number of Jews admitted to high schools (*Gymnasia*), technical institutes, and universities to 1.5 percent of the total enrollment. This limitation particularly hit hard the Jewish communities in Berlin and Frankfurt, where nearly half of German Jews lived. Also loopholes in the law allowed state and local authorities to permit exceptions whereby they gave Aryan children priority in admissions.

The law had several major consequences for Jews. On the one hand, it forced the Jewish communities to set up their own elementary and high school systems. On the other hand, Jewish children still permitted to attend German schools hardly had advantages. Since the government institutionalized anti-Semitism in the schools, all students, including Jews, had to take courses in racial theory, where teachers and textbooks indoctrinated them in the "racial inferiority" of Jews.

The German universities suffered a similar degradation. Vastly fewer Jewish students and other non-Aryans could attend universities, and racial teachings permeated the schools' curricula. Between 1933 and 1938 the National Socialist regime removed the tenure from and dismissed several thousand professors, many of them Jews, for racial and, to a lesser extent, political reasons.

Twenty-seven professors who had won or would win Nobel Prizes in science left their universities in Germany and later Austria. This mass brain drain would severely damage Germany's scientific production, but would also represent, according to a recent book, "Hitler's gift" to the West, especially Britain and America, to where most of the scientists escaped.[12] Germany's losses included the leading physicists—Einstein, Leo Szilard, James Franck, Otto Frisch, Rudolf Peierls, and Francis Simon—who became later the driving force behind the United States' atomic bomb project.

Most of the Aryan academics who remained in Germany, including aspiring professors who took the jobs of the purged, served the Nazi regime loyally. The corruption of faculty members even extended to those few of scholarly note, such as the "racial biologists" Eugen Fischer and Ernst Rüdin and the jurist Carl Schmitt. Other scholars, including the philosopher Martin Heidegger, greeted the Nazi regime with enthusiasm. In their classes and publications, professors taught the phony sciences of Aryan "racial superiority" and anti-Jewish ideology. They emphasized the concepts of "selection" (*Auslese*) and "extinction" (*Ausmerze*) of unfit "races," especially of Jews and Slavs.[13] Anti-Jewish research institutes, which also employed academics, spread the same nonsense. In this way, German academe provided a pseudo-scholarly legitimacy for Nazi hate propaganda and racial and political policies.

The German public, primarily for three reasons, raised little objection to the April laws and mass firings of Jews. First, despite the extensive dismissals, at least initially the laws limited somewhat the purge of Jews in the civil service, law, or medicine, mainly because at least half of the Jews targeted by the laws, and often substantially more, fell under the exclusion provisions. The Nazis, for their part, much as they had done with the boycott, badly misjudged the nature of their Jewish problem. They were ignorant of the fact that so many Jews had served in World War I or that so many others had entered their professions before 1919.

Second, the dismissals of Jews and others provided a source of new jobs and upward mobility for unemployed Germans and young people, allowing them to advance their careers in the bureaucracy and professions at the expense of those who had lost theirs. Third, the lack of negative reactions of Germans to the laws and firings suggested that the great majority of the public approved of the removal of Jews from the civil service and professions.

The widespread enthusiastic response of the German public to the Nazi regime could not help but encourage it to continue developing measures that discriminated against Jews and to establish new racial policies. On 10 May 1933 German students, assisted by SA and SS bands and Goebbels' Propaganda Ministry, burned huge piles of books written by Jews, communists, liberals, and other persons feared and hated by the government in the streets of Berlin and other cities.

During May and June the regime forcibly destroyed German labor unions, outlawed the Social Democratic party, and ordered the "voluntary" dissolution of the remaining political parties, including the Catholic Center and conservatives. These events had sharply differing results. First, the willingness of the Center party to disband, rather than to oppose Nazism, had a major psychological effect on German Catholics. The latter, whose church and clergy are discussed later in this chapter, joined the Nazi party in the millions, many believing that they had the support of the Vatican. Second, increasing numbers of socialists joined communist officials and other party-political opponents of the Nazis in "protective custody" in the concentration camps. By the end of the summer, as many as one hundred thousand such persons had been robbed of their freedom at one time or another. The Nazis had killed between five and six hundred more. Still others fled Germany into exile.

The Laws of 14 July and Cultural Purges

On 14 July, the anniversary of the fall in 1789 of the Bastille prison in Paris to French revolutionaries, the German government declared the Nazi party the only legal party in the Reich. Also that day, which the Nazis chose purposely to demonstrate their determination to reverse the ideals of the French Revolution, the government issued several other major laws. One, a decree that provided for the compulsory sterilization of persons whom the regime defined as afflicted with hereditary ailments, illustrated the significance of racial ideology to the government.

The law, which also exemplified how racism would masquerade as science and medicine under the Nazis, foresaw the sterilization of the feeble-minded, alcoholics, schizophrenics, manic depressives, genetically blind and deaf, and people suffering from Huntington's chorea. This law carried much further a draft measure of the Prussian state government from 1932 that would have permitted the voluntary sterilization of such persons.

Since before World War I, a widespread eugenics and so-called racial hygiene movement had developed in both Germany and the United States. Every medical school in Germany either possessed, or soon would, a chair and an institute of "racial hygiene." In the United States, the extensive acceptance of eugenics had resulted by 1930 in sterilization laws in more than half of the states. Hitler had studied carefully such American laws and declared that the United States had made great achievements with its race policies.

Once in power, he and his cabinet approved the sterilization law in Germany in less than six months. Apart from the moral issues raised by the decree, the National Socialist regime in fact used exceedingly insidious criteria to define hereditary illness. Justification for sterilization often reflected more the prejudices and phony science of the regime than the regulations of the law and objective medical bases.

The government sterilized numerous persons reported as "work shy" or as former members of the Communist party. Also, alcoholics were sometimes sterilized because of Hitler's belief that alcoholism was an inevitably hereditary disease, even though such a view had been scientifically disproved. As for feeble-mindedness, Nazi authorities defined it as virtually any condition perceived as abnormal.

From January 1934, when the law went into force, to 1939, the regime sterilized between 350,000 and 400,000 men and women, nearly all against their will. This number included, during 1937, on secret orders from Hitler, the sterilization of approximately five hundred black children, the offspring of black French troops and German women, born during 1924 in the wake of the French occupation of the Ruhr industrial region in Germany. Even before 1933, Germans called these African Germans or mulattoes *Rheinlandbastarde*.

Also the government sterilized numerous Gypsies, or Sinti and Roma, persons whom the Nazis classified as nomadic, "asocial," "work shy" or unproductive, and—in part because of their dark complexion—an alien threat to German racial "purity." Gypsies in Germany numbered approximately twenty-six thousand; their ancestors had left India a thousand years before and gradually migrated through Persia, Armenia, and Turkey to Europe. They first entered Germany in the fifteenth century.

Although some Gypsies had settled into a sedentary life by the twentieth century, many were itinerants, roaming the countryside in caravans, earning their living as musicians, peddlers, and fortune-tellers. Because they had traditionally lived an indigent life, the Germans often condemned them as "asocials," namely as thieves, criminals, and spies. Regarding the use of language in describing Gypsies, the historian Sybil Milton has written:

> The traditional term *Gypsy*, in German *Zigeuner*, is usually used only by outsiders from the majority society and has pejorative connotations.

The term *Roma* connotes ethnic self-description and refers to the language, Romani, spoken by the group. In Germany, the largest population group is called Sinti . . . a term based on their linguistic origins in the Sind region of India. In Austria, Roma are the larger group, whereas in Germany, Sinti are more numerous.[14]

While the Gypsies had suffered racial and other discrimination throughout much of their existence in Europe, the Nazis gave increasing attention to what they termed the "Gypsy plague." They intensified measures of control and harassment over the Gypsies. After the Nuremberg Laws of 1935, at least semiofficially, the Nazis classified Gypsies, along with Jews and blacks, as racially distinctive minorities with "alien blood." Despite this categorization, however, the German government allowed marriages between Germans and Gypsies that had only a quarter or less of such blood.

Gradually, vilification of the Gypsies increased; by 1936, they had lost their right to vote in Reichstag elections. That same year, immediately prior to the Olympic games in Berlin, the police in the capital arrested some local Gypsies and imprisoned them in the city's Marzahn camp. The camp soon became the largest German prison for Gypsies (*Zigeunerlager*); there the prisoners suffered in conditions of marginal sanitation and semistarvation.

Other victims of sterilization in Nazi Germany included roughly 1 percent of the patients, some 3,500, mainly women, who died from an operation they certainly did not ask for. Medical doctors trained in "racial hygiene" comprised most of the hereditary health courts (*Erbgesundheitsgerichte*) that made the decisions. In addition, the law forbade the sterilized to marry fertile partners. In subsequent years amendments to the law approved or reiterated authorization for "voluntary" abortions and castration, the latter primarily for sex offenders and homosexuals.

Apparently the sterilization measure had at least tacit support from the German public. Only when Germans found members of their own families and circles of friends affected by the law did they become concerned. During 1934–1935, the law produced an enormous number of denunciations (388,400), most of them from physicians. The medical establishment supported forced sterilization almost without dissent, which reflected a widespread amorality that had dominated the popular pre-Nazi eugenics movement.

Moreover, the Christian churches in Germany, which are discussed later in this chapter, responded to the law with ambivalence. The Protestants supported nonvoluntary sterilization with some hesitation and a few limitations. Dietrich Bonhoeffer, a Lutheran theologian, was among the few clergy who steadfastly opposed the regime's eugenics measures from sterilization to the later so-called euthanasia program. Although the Catholic bishops in Germany as well as the Vatican denounced the sterilization law, they compromised their position for political reasons. They offered only verbal opposition to the law because of their wish not to endanger the Concordat, the church's agreement, discussed below in this chapter, with the Nazi government.

Political repercussions of the sterilization law extended even more widely. From 1934 to 1939, a bitter struggle would ensue between the government and Nazi party for control of the law's implementation. The law, furthermore, represented the first of the Nazi regime's actions regarding family and marriage. Subsequent measures included loans granted by the state for early marriages and awards for families that produced, according to government guidelines, "genetically healthy children of the same race."[15]

In October 1935 the government would issue a so-called marriage health law, which ordered the screening of the entire German population to prevent marriages of persons viewed as carriers of hereditary degeneracy. Such measures served as harbingers of the government's massive euthanasia program, begun at Hitler's order at the start of World War II, to kill mentally and physically handicapped Germans and other peoples.

Another measure enacted on 14 July 1933, a denaturalization law, allowed the National Socialists to strip the citizenship and property from people they considered undesirable, or who had settled in Germany after 1918, and expel them from the country. On the one hand, the Nazis intended the law to help rid Germany of its approximately 150,000 Eastern Jews (Ostjuden).

However, both the Imperial and Weimar governments had viewed the Ostjuden as "foreign Jews" and refused to grant most of them German citizenship. This situation, much to the frustration of the Nazis, made the denaturalization law virtually useless when applied to the Ostjuden. Like so many other early anti-Jewish measures in the Third Reich, this one too failed to achieve what the National Socialists had intended.

Nor was the expulsion of the Ostjuden a possibility at present for the Nazi government. Many of the Eastern Jews had come from Poland, whose anti-Semitic regime eagerly sought to prevent their return to the country. Hitler, hoping to convince the world of his and of Germany's peaceful intentions, while secretly rearming the Reich for the future wars he envisioned, did not wish to alienate the Poles and would sign a German–Polish nonaggression pact in January 1934.

On the other hand, the Nazis found the denaturalization law more applicable to the emigrés who left Germany. During the first two years of National Socialist rule, the German government used the law to revoke the citizenship of thousands of German Jews as well as of political opponents, mainly leftists, of the regime who fled the country. These included Albert Einstein, the brilliant physicist who settled in the United States; Willy Brandt, an anti-Nazi socialist worker, later chancellor of the Federal Republic of Germany (1969–1974), and winner of the Nobel Peace Prize (1971); Lion Feuchtwanger, a liberal Jewish writer and drama critic; Philip Scheidemann, the socialist chancellor of the first Weimar government; Kurt Tucholsky, a journalist and author; and Thomas Mann, the novelist.

Of all the anti-Semitic measures implemented in 1933 in Germany, two enacted in the autumn would eventually have the most severe impact yet on the Jews. On 29 September, a law established the Reich Chamber of Culture (*Kulturkammer*) within Goebbels' Propaganda Ministry, which included one chamber each to regulate and control completely German film, theater, music, fine arts, literature, broadcasting, and the press. For a person thereafter to work in any of these areas required the licensed permission of the pertinent chamber.

Amid the subsequent formation of the Kulturkammer, Goebbels declared in a public speech: "In my opinion and experience a Jewish contemporary is, in general, unfit to be entrusted with German cultural assets."[16] Because the law creating the Kulturkammer contained no Aryan Paragraph with its regulations exempting some non-Aryans from dismissal, Goebbels had nothing to prevent him from refusing admission of Jews and of other "undesirables" to any of the chambers.

Even months before the enactment of law, the Nazis purged many prominent Jewish figures in the performing arts. But only during 1935 and 1936 did the chambers begin a systematic removal of non-Aryans, barring thousands of Jewish actors, filmmakers, musicians, writers, artists, and persons in related areas from participating in German cultural life.

The delay in the mass expulsions resulted from numerous factors. First, it took the chambers time to collect information on those they wished to purge. Second, relatively relaxed control procedures existed in some occupations. Third, Schacht, President of the Reichsbank and, beginning in 1934, Minister of Economics, opposed a sudden and complete elimination of Jews from German artistic life that might receive foreign criticism and adversely affect Germany's foreign trade and economic recovery. In this instance, as in others discussed in chapter 3, Schacht based his policy not on pro-Jewish motives, but on economic ones. He agreed fully with Hitler that Germany's economic recovery and rearmament should receive absolute priority.

Since Jews had made significant contributions in the performing arts and literature, the chamber of culture law represented a devastating blow for both the Jews and for German culture. Not surprising, subsequent German films played a key role in the spread of National Socialist ideology. Although most of the early Nazi films did not concentrate on anti-Semitic themes, they repeatedly contained anti-Jewish stereotypes and attitudes.

For example, *Hans Westmar*, a popular Nazi production that had its premiere in December 1933, glorified Horst Wessel, an SA man killed in a brawl with communists in 1930 in Berlin, where he lived with a former prostitute. Nazi propaganda made a martyr of Wessel, and the party transformed the marching song he composed into the movement's most important anthem. A distinguished film historian has commented about *Hans Westmar*: "Jews are subjected to a vicious attack in the film. . . . The message is clear: international Jewry has joined with Soviet Russia to enslave Germany."[17]

A week after issuing the chamber of culture decree, on 4 October, the Nazi government enacted a major press law; similar to the measure establishing the chambers of culture, it had no Aryan Paragraph. The law paved the way for the widespread exclusion of Jews from the press as journalists and editors, another profession where Jews had achieved in Germany some visibility and success.

The Christian Churches

A most conspicuous silence among Germans regarding their government's persecution of the Jews and other social and political "outcasts" existed in the Christian churches. With the exception of a few brave clergymen, the churches did nothing to oppose the regime's destruction of human rights. Most churchmen belonged to the conservative elite and sympathized to a large degree with the government's nationalism and anti-Communism. During the Third Reich, this would help to lead the churches and the vast majority of their clergy to a widespread betrayal of the Christian commandments to love one's neighbor as well as God.[18]

Hitler, a nominal Catholic, feared most the opposition to Nazism from the German Catholic bishops and much of the Center party, one of the groups that had supported the Weimar republic. Consequently, he made a special effort to negotiate an agreement with the Catholic Church. Amid the deliberations, he declared that for him to sign such an agreement, the Center party had to vote in the Reichstag for the Enabling Act, the law of 23 March 1933 that gave him dictatorial powers. The party supported the law, mainly because the party's conservative leaders, its chairman Ludwig Kaas and Hitler's vice chancellor von Papen, took their cue from the Vatican.

Both the Vatican's secretary of state, Cardinal Eugenio Pacelli, the former papal nuncio to Germany and later pope, and Kaas believed that the Center party's vote would prepare the way for a future agreement with the new German government. The agreement, Pacelli and Kaas thought, would ensure the protection of the freedom of Catholic churches and affiliated organizations in Germany from persecution by the Berlin government.

In July 1933 the Vatican and government signed the Concordat. The treaty was negotiated and implemented on behalf of Pope Pius XI by Pacelli. The Concordat authorized the Vatican to impose on German Catholics the church policy, largely invented at the end of the nineteenth century, of autocratic papal control. Also it granted numerous privileges to Catholic schools and the clergy. In return, the church in Germany (including the bishops, who had officially opposed National Socialism in 1932), its Center party, and its many associations and newspapers, withdrew from intervening in the turbulent society and politics of the Reich.

The Concordat had devastating results. It not only ensured that Nazism could rule unopposed by Germany's twenty-three million Catholics. It also left the new German government freer to act as it wished in the "Jewish question," which Hitler himself observed at a meeting of his cabinet on 14 July 1933. Further, the government failed to abide by its agreement to permit in Germany autonomous Catholic clergy as well as schools and other church organizations. Catholic churchmen in Germany who criticized the government publicly and called for racial tolerance and human rights, such as Michael Faulhaber, Cardinal and Archbishop of Munich, and Bernhard Lichtenberg, a parish priest in Berlin, formed the rare exceptions.

Moreover, the vast majority of Protestant clergy and lay people joined with the National Socialists and tolerated or even welcomed anti-Semitic measures. In some churches on Sunday morning, a swastika rested on the altar, next to the cross. Both pastors and members of their congregations frequently wore swastika armbands as they marched or processed in church services. Seminary students attending universities heard some of the most well-known theology faculty denounce Jews in lectures as a menace to Western society.

In June 1933, the Federation of Protestant Churches in Germany circulated a memorandum overseas on the so-called Jewish question in Germany. The memo termed the violence against German Jews only "isolated acts" and defended the April boycott and subsequent anti-Jewish legislation.[19] In July most Protestant leaders accepted without opposition a German government decree that established a new name and constitution for the German Protestant churches.

A driving force behind the government's effort to establish its hold on the Protestant churches was a small minority of Protestants who numbered roughly six hundred thousand and called themselves "German Christians" (Deutsche Christen). Founded primarily by National Socialists, the German Christians sought to unite their view of a racially based Christianity with Nazi ideology. German Christians preached a völkisch and "Germanic" gospel, sang nationalist hymns that praised Hitler, and called him the "savior."

Self-styled "storm troopers of Christ," the German Christians also advertised themselves as a "people's church" (Volkskirche) that formed an association of "blood" and "race," not an assembly of the baptized. Jewishness and Germanness were racial categories, they insisted. They demanded the de-Judaizing of Christianity, by which they meant the liberation of it from converted Jews, the "Jewish" and allegedly "un-German" Old Testament, and St. Paul in the New Testament. Also they claimed that Jesus had not been a Jew, but a Germanic or Aryan hero who, similar to the Nazis, opposed the Jews. A German Christian pastor in Württemberg described the "worst enemy of the church" as the "Jewish nature that has infiltrated us."[20]

Despite their relatively small numbers, the German Christians used national church elections on 23 July 1933 to gain control of the Protestant churches. They received two-thirds of the vote to capture most positions that ranged from local parish representatives to senior administrators at the national level, bishops' seats of all but three of Germany's Protestant regional churches, and some theological faculties. Hitler himself urged the election of German Christians. He subsequently appointed Ludwig Müller, a leader of the German Christians, "Reich Bishop" of the newly constituted German Protestant Church.

The bid by the German Christians to control and revamp the Protestant church soon unleashed a so-called church struggle (*Kirchenkampf*). But contrary to much belief at the time and after World War II, the struggle was less an expression of political opposition to Nazism than a competition for control within the church. The main rival of the German Christians was the Confessing Church (*Bekennende Kirche*), a group of Protestants organized originally in opposition to the German Christians' efforts to establish an Aryan Paragraph in the Protestant churches. Such a policy would expel converts from Judaism and their children and grandchildren from the Protestant clergy. The Confessing Church never broke completely with the established Protestant church, but did assert its independence from the church in several important ways. These included holding its own national synods, remaining loyal to the confessions of faith, and training some of its own clergy in illegal seminaries.

Yet most members of the Confessing Church were self-professed apoliticals, supporters of the Nazi regime, and party members. They never questioned the political legitimacy of the Third Reich. Nor was the church a champion of Judaism or of the Jews in Germany. This helped to prevent many in the church from protesting the Nazi government's brutal assaults on the German Jews and led other members to support the attacks. Only once did the Confessing Church raise its voice in official opposition to the Nazis' campaign of hatred against the Jews, in a secret memorandum from the small radical wing of the church's leadership to Hitler in May 1936.

A few in the Confessing Church, however, resisted the racial policies of the regime and German Christians. They included one of the founders of the Confessing Church, the Berlin-Dahlem Lutheran pastor Martin Niemöller. But both Niemöller and another pastor who helped establish the Confessing Church, Otto Dibelius, were nationalists and, for religious as well as social reasons, held a traditional Protestant antipathy toward Jews. Yet Niemöller, despite his anti-Semitism, denounced the Aryan Paragraph in Protestantism because he realized that its acceptance would effectively negate the teaching of baptism.

Karl Barth, a professor of theology at the University of Bonn, led the Confessing Church's opposition to the heretical nature of the German Christians. In July 1933 Barth founded a journal that denounced the German Christians' raising of race to the level of God's revelation and its resultant non-Christian and anti-Christian beliefs and activities. Barth, however, failed to note that such racial heresy was rooted in hatred toward Judaism and Jews.

Two years later, Barth, a Swiss citizen and not a Lutheran but a Calvinist, lost his professorship when he refused to swear an oath of allegiance to Hitler.

Bonhoeffer, too, had joined the Confessing Church. At least early in his career, he had linked Jewish suffering with the alleged role of Jews in executing Christ and believed that there would be a "Jewish problem" until the Jews converted to the "True Faith." But in April 1933 he published an essay attacking the German Christians and Aryan Paragraph.

Soon Bonhoeffer moved far beyond the Confessing Church's concern for institutional integrity and autonomy. He denounced the persecution of the Jews and would eventually join the political resistance that tried during World War II to kill Hitler. He did so because during the war he would recognize that a German defeat would be better for the world than one, he wrote while in prison, dominated by a regime in which "God as a working hypothesis in morals, politics, or science, has been surmounted and abolished." That, he warned, would be "the *salto mortale* [death leap] back into the Middle Ages."[21]

Bonhoeffer based his defense of the Jews on the traditional Judeo-Christian doctrine of the sanctity of human life. In one of his books he declared: "God is the Father, the Father of our Lord Jesus Christ, who became the Brother of us all." He explained that "[i]n this context 'brother' means more than 'fellow-Christian': for the follower of Jesus there can be no limit as to who is his neighbour, except as his Lord decides." Then Bonhoeffer concluded: "He who says he loves God and hates his brother is a liar."[22] For all this, and for his role in the resistance to Hitler, the Gestapo would execute him in April 1945, only days before the war's end.

CHAPTER THREE

THE REVOLUTION ENDS? BETWEEN ANTI-JEWISH VIOLENCE AND LEGISLATION, 1933–1936

ALREADY ON 17 JULY 1933, Hitler, apparently satisfied that he had consolidated his dictatorship sufficiently, declared the Nazi revolution ended. In the ensuing months he slowed the momentum of both official and unofficial anti-Jewish measures. On the one hand, the government enacted fewer anti-Semitic laws. On the other hand, orders from Nazi party headquarters in Munich directed that party members cease spontaneous actions against Jews.

Among party faithful at the local level, who continued to press for more radical policies against the Jews, such directives caused anger and confusion. At the party's annual congress in Nuremberg in September, attended by tens of thousands of SA and party members, Goebbels addressed their frustrations. In a moment of rare public candor, he explained that both domestic and foreign pressures prevented a more radical anti-Jewish policy and urged his listeners to remain patient.

The Röhm Purge, the German Army, and Austria

Goebbels' words apparently did little to placate the party radicals. Local incidents of harassment and boycotting of Jews continued. Increasingly the radicals

found a spokesman for their discontent in the person of Röhm, the commander of the huge SA. During June 1933, Röhm, writing in a party journal,
launched a sharp attack on holders of government and other offices who called
themselves National Socialists but in fact betrayed the revolution. He warned
that he and other true revolutionaries in the SA would "continue our fight"
and deserved better economic and political treatment from the government.[1]

Primarily Röhm demanded a purge of the German army's officer corps
and the formation by the SA of a revolutionary or national militia to replace
the professional army. The latter's leadership and von Hindenburg, who
insisted that the army remain the sole bearer of arms in Germany, found the
SA leader's demands wholly unacceptable. From the spring of 1934 on, Hitler
realized the growing dissatisfaction of the army command over his failure to
discipline Röhm. But he dared not ignore such feelings, especially because he
wanted to succeed to von Hindenburg's office and its military powers once
the elderly president died.

When Hitler finally acted against Röhm, his accomplices included the
SA chief's personal rivals, Göring and the SS leader, Himmler. On 30 June
1934, in the so-called Night of the Long Knives, at Hitler's order and personal direction the SS, using trucks, weapons, and barracks provided it by the
army, murdered without trial Röhm and dozens of his SA lieutenants and
other diverse opponents of the National Socialists.

In the aftermath of the bloody purge, the army and von Hindenburg
heaped fulsome praise on Hitler for protecting the army's independence. The
military elite had now cast its lot with National Socialism. As for the SS, the
Führer rewarded its loyalty to him by making the organization autonomous
of the SA, placing it directly under his personal command and allowing its
leader, Himmler, to expand the SS by adding a division of heavily armed
forces and taking over the state political police.

The purge, according to the Canadian historian, Holger Herwig, "proved
a milestone as the first state-planned and legalized mass slaughter of the Third
Reich."[2] Few Germans, however, seemed alarmed either by the killings or by
Hitler's proclamation shortly thereafter that he was the "supreme judge" in
Germany. Nor did many Germans view the purge as a revelation of the murderous potential of National Socialism. Following the purge, reports smuggled abroad by socialist informants in the Reich observed that "Hitler
undoubtedly still had as much support among the majority of the people as
he did before."[3]

Outside Germany the destruction of the SA leadership attracted a good deal of foreign attention, most of it negative. A similar reaction greeted Hitler's blundering attempt on 25 July to open the door for Germany to annex neighboring Austria, when Austrian National Socialists murdered their government's chancellor and attempted unsuccessfully to seize power in Vienna. Such a union (Anschluss) of Germany and Austria, Hitler believed, would add to the German Reich more Germans and other resources for implementing his future plans for war.

He could only offset this embarrassing defeat in international affairs, at a time when Germany was most at risk militarily, by reassuring the world of his peaceful intentions. Consequently, he continued to profess repeatedly in public his wishes for peace. There also ensued inside Germany a lengthy period of political tranquility and quiet.

Shortly after Hitler's consolidation of his authority in Germany with the Röhm purge, most Germans, including the army chiefs, welcomed with enthusiasm his takeover of the powers of the President in the wake of von Hindenburg's death on 2 August. Hitler officially combined in his person as Führer the offices of President and Chancellor. The German armed forces, whose role as the sole and official bearer of arms in Germany Hitler had secured with the purge, swore an oath of loyalty to him as did the civil service.

For the remainder of 1934, the murders of the SA leaders seemed to dampen the anti-Semitic zeal of party radicals and end, at least temporarily, local and spontaneous incidents of harassment of Jews and small-scale boycotting of their businesses. For Hitler and the German government, this proved advantageous, and perhaps not accidental. At the moment, he needed relative quiet at home, particularly regarding two issues that, as he had learned, received much unfavorable foreign publicity. The first was his government's conflict with the Protestant churches, in which he made a tactical retreat so as to pretend the regime's neutrality toward the churches. The second was anti-Jewish violence in Germany.

A Lull in the Anti-Semitic Storm and the Jewish Response, 1934

The oft-repeated accusation that German Jews should have known what was happening to them in the 1930s and left Germany sooner is both wholly simplistic and ahistorical. As victims of the Nazi persecution, the Jews faced many difficult and complex issues. This included the incremental or gradual nature of the persecution that would leave most Jews with a situation that looked unclear, at best, to them. Not even the pogrom during *Kristallnacht* ("night of shattered glass") in 1938 would provide a distinct sign of the Holocaust to come.

Although during 1933 nearly forty thousand Jews had left Germany, most of them in the initial panic at the new government, the hope existed among those remaining that the storm of both official and unofficial discriminations against them had blown itself out. The numerous anti-Jewish laws had deprived them of civil equality and banned them from professions and largely from schools. Also a gradual social isolation of them had started. With a few exceptions, most Germans, well before Nazi laws prohibited Jewish and Aryan interactions, either avoided Jews, denounced them to the authorities, or barred them from social events.

In many towns, increasingly one found "Jews not wanted" signs at the entrances to swimming pools and beaches. Private businesses, such as restaurants, hotels, movie theaters, and tennis courts preceded Nazi laws in shutting their doors to Jews. Marta Appel, a Jewess from Dortmund, recalled after the war:

> I hated to go out, since on every corner I saw signs that the Jews were the misfortune of the people. Wherever I went, when I had to speak to people in a store I imagined how they would turn against me if they knew I was Jewish. When I was waiting for a streetcar I always thought that the driver would not stop if he knew I was Jewish. . . . I did not go into a theater or a movie for a long time before we were forbidden to, since I could not bear to be among people who hated me so much.[4]

During the first weeks and months following the Nazi seizure of power, it had seemed impossible to many Jews that the new government could destroy their civil rights and permit or encourage their removal from society. The Reich Association of Jewish War Veterans (Reichsbund jüdischer Frontsoldaten), a nationalist Jewish organization formed after World War I, declared in its newsletter the right of German Jews to live in Germany as citizens with equal rights.

In this regard, the Reich Association of Jewish War Veterans reflected the views of an overwhelming majority of German Jews. Those whose families had lived in the country for many generations felt a deep attachment to their homeland and saw themselves as much or more German as Jewish. During the fall of 1933, the association informed Hitler's Chancellery that the group's members "wish to mobilize themselves entirely for the Fatherland, if that is what the hour requires."[5]

The approximately half million German Jews, in contrast to Nazi propaganda that portrayed them as part of a monolithic "national" and "international" force, in fact formed a tiny, weak, and disparate minority. Their major political and religious divisions—into assimilationist and Zionist; Orthodox, Conservative, and Liberal (or Reform)—prevented them from speaking with one voice, and thus made them even more vulnerable to the Nazi government's attacks.

Most Jews looked for comfort and assistance to both their religion and their community. It was in this regard that one found instances of bravery and indirect resistance of individual Jews to National Socialism. Jewish leaders such as Leo Baeck, the distinguished Berlin rabbi and religious philosopher, and Martin Buber, exhorted Jews to hold fast to their faith and convictions, to preserve their self-respect, and to keep up their courage.

Another Jewish leader had a different message. Robert Weltsch, the editor of the Zionist paper, *Jüdische Rundschau*, published an editorial that argued the Jew "must bear part of the blame for the degradation of Jewry" because he "did not display his Judaism with pride."[6] Later, a deeply remorseful Weltsch would regret having written what he did; he should have, he told friends, instead of calling for Jewish pride, exhorted Jews to flee for their lives.

Most Jews turned to one another for friendship and consolation. They visited their fellow Jews' private homes, even though such gatherings left them fearful of being watched by suspicious neighbors or, worse, by the Gestapo. They found solace as well in the synagogues, which were filled to overflowing and served not only as places of prayer, but also as locales where worshipers could feel a sense of solidarity and escape the increasing social isolation.

To the rabbis fell the task of providing the people with moral strength to face the daily indignities heaped on them. The night before the boycott of 1 April 1933, a Berlin rabbi, Joachim Prinz, called his sermon an "attempt at collective therapy."[7] Even in the presence of the Gestapo and other informers, rabbis dared to preach—either openly or indirectly—against the government's persecution. They would use names beginning with the initial "H," such as Haman, the prime minister of the ancient Persian empire who plotted to destroy the Jews, to make allusions to Nazi leaders, including Hitler, Himmler, and Heydrich. The congregations knew well what the rabbis meant by Haman and other similar references.

Orthodox Jews often explained what was happening by reverting to an ancient response to persecution—believing that the people were being punished for their sins. Many other Jews told themselves that the present situation represented only another in a long line of persecutions and restrictions that Jews had survived through the centuries. Still other Jews gradually accommodated to the Nazi hostility, hoping it would go no further. To maintain their own calm or that of loved ones, they expressed gratefulness for small loopholes or exceptions in government measures and pretended to dismiss the cruelties against them. Among those who could not adjust, some committed suicide; at least five thousand self-inflicted deaths among German Jews resulted during the twelve years of Nazi rule.

Jews also responded to the Nazi attacks in a political-cultural way, which some postwar historians have termed a form of resistance against the National Socialist regime. The different Jewish political groups, galvanized into action by the government's anti-Jewish measures, forged organizational alliances to assist Jews in coping with their situation. They initially created the Central Committee of German Jews for Relief and Reconstruction (*Zentralausschuss der deutschen Juden für Hilfe und Aufbau*), headed by Baeck.

The committee engaged in numerous welfare, as well as cultural, activities. Among its most important services, the committee established a Jewish school system that cultivated Jewish self-awareness and community spirit. Also the committee provided training in new occupational skills to Jews who had been forced out of their professions, made available financial aid and health care for those left impoverished or without medical attention, and assisted Jews in preparing to emigrate.

A Cultural Association of German Jews (*Kulturbund Deutscher Juden*) formed, which offered work and an audience to Jewish musicians, actors, and other artists dismissed from their jobs. The Gestapo, however, only agreed to allow the organization to continue if it dropped the words "German Jews" from its name and called itself the Jewish Cultural Association (*Jüdische Kulturbund*). The association included an orchestra, opera company, and acting troupe. It became a haven for Jewish artists and offered as well sorely needed spiritual enrichment for the besieged German Jews. Simultaneously, however, the Nazis would use the Jewish Cultural

Association as a propaganda tool to claim to the rest of the world how well Jews were allegedly treated in the Third Reich.

The Jewish press in Germany resisted the Nazi government in several ways. Jewish newspapers, although closely monitored and restricted by the Gestapo until their ban in 1939, retained a limited freedom and often discussed humanist and liberal themes. The papers frequently printed material that their readers knew to read between the lines because it protested, in disguised fashion, the regime's anti-Semitism. Some Jewish editors and journalists risked their jobs and even lives by openly criticizing Nazi propaganda that degraded Jews as less than "subhuman." In nearly every instance, the Gestapo ordered bans on newspapers and severe punishments for their editors.

Although the idea of a strong centralized Jewish leadership increased, in which Jews believed they needed one single organization that could represent them to the government, such an organization emerged only after months of extensive negotiations. On 17 September 1933 nearly every Jewish religious, political, and social group united to form a single body, the Reich Representation of German Jews (*Reichsvertretung der Deutschen Juden*), with Baeck as its president. Although the Nazi government viewed the organization with some seriousness, the regime never officially considered it a legal entity or one with which to negotiate.

As part of his office Baeck faced terrible tribulations, but he did so with dignity and courage. While he addressed religious and political differences among Jews themselves, the Gestapo harassed, threatened, and arrested him and other Jewish leaders repeatedly. Police intrusion into the Jewish community became ever more oppressive; every Jewish organization had to conduct its business in the presence of Gestapo agents. For privacy Jewish leaders met in each other's homes, and even then their fear of being watched meant they did not record all their decisions or business.

Where possible the Reich Representation of German Jews tried to lessen the excesses of Nazi anti-Semitic propaganda and to assist Jews who had been arrested or who suffered from anti-Jewish boycotts. Unclear is how much the organization managed to help the Jewish population; many of its records were destroyed after the Kristallnacht in 1938, by its own leaders or by German police and wartime Allied bombing.

Shortly after the Nazis had seized power, Baeck prophesied that "the thousand-year-old history of German Jewry has come to an end." Yet Baeck, a non-Zionist who nevertheless sympathized with the reawakening of Jewish national consciousness, refused numerous attractive offers from abroad for work that would have enabled him to escape from Nazi Germany. Einstein once remarked about him, "What this man meant to his brethren trapped in Germany and facing certain destruction cannot be fully grasped by those whose outer circumstances permit them to live on in apparent security."[8]

To many German Jews by 1934, the signs seemed to point in a hopeful direction. Increasing numbers of them had turned to Zionism, which only a minority had done previously. One writer remarked after World War II that in 1933 "a mass movement emerged out of the elite movement of German Zionism."[9] During 1933–1934, the Haluz societies, the German branch of the worldwide Zionist worker-pioneer organization, grew from five hundred to over fifteen thousand members.

The number of Jews who left Germany in 1934 dropped to twenty-two thousand. Several factors, practical and psychological, made emigration difficult. First, at least half of German Jews had reached age forty and were rarely inclined and willing to leave their families, friends, and often businesses. At the end of August, a leading English Zionist who visited Berlin reported that Baeck had told him there was no place in Germany for the young Jews: "The only thing to do is to get them out."[10]

Second, already by 1934 the Nazis forced Jews emigrating and transferring assets abroad to leave behind a substantial amount of their currency and property. The Reich Flight Tax (*Reichsfluchtsteuer*), a property tax on émigrés (and raised by the Nazis to exorbitant heights for emigrating Jews) and blocked bank accounts threatened to impoverish Jews wishing to leave the country.

Moreover, Jews faced plunder by individual Germans. Numerous post–World War II memoirs and interviews of the Jewish victims provide ample documentation. Lola Blonder wrote about two Gestapo agents looting her home as she prepared to emigrate: "They . . . took whatever little objects they liked—from the wall . . . from the tables. . . . I was used to this by now. Whenever a group of Nazis visited, they helped themselves to . . . valuables. Robbing, robbing! Every day robbing me!"[11]

Third, many German Jews had no relatives or friends abroad who could sponsor their admission into a foreign country of refuge. Nearly every foreign nation, including the United States and other Western countries, had immigration quotas. Such countries found themselves mired in the world Depression, which had produced unemployment that ran three to five times higher than normal. They did not wish to take in foreigners who had been deprived of most of their assets by their former country and who might compete for the already few jobs in their new one.

The quotas, furthermore, resulted from widespread anti-Semitism and racist attitudes among foreigners. Many such bystanders had little concern for the attacks on the Jews in Germany, either because they disliked Jews for some reason or because the oppression of the Jews seemed merely a continuation of the types of persecution Jews had suffered elsewhere in previous centuries.

Also the British issued a general limitation on Jewish emigration to Palestine, a League of Nations mandate under Britain's rule, so as not to alienate local Arabs. For the most part, the major powers viewed the whole issue of the fate of the German Jews as peripheral to decisions that dictated their political and foreign policies. Nor did such powers envision the anti-Jewish actions in Germany as a phase or step moving toward something much worse. In this regard, neither most victims nor most bystanders understood the depth of Nazi hatred for the Jews. Few German Jews or foreign leaders comprehended what such fanaticism might eventually mean for those most despised in the modern, bureaucratic, and technological nation-state that was Germany.

In part as a result of these factors, during the first months of 1935, some ten thousand Jews who had fled Germany, reported the *Jüdische Rundschau*, had begun to return. They did so in the expectation of an improved situation for Jews in Germany and because many Jewish émigrés abroad had found only impoverishment. For Jews who moved back to the Reich and for the others that had always remained there, nearly all now lived in the larger cities.

Since 1933, even isolated German Jewish families left villages for towns, and from there they frequently continued on to Berlin, Frankfurt, or other urban centers. Much of this movement resulted from the gradual impoverishment of the Jewish communities, which produced increasing dependence of Jews on one another, and particularly the dependence of poor Jews on the Reich Representation of German Jews and other Jewish relief organizations.

The increased concentration of Jews into a few large areas represented, in the words of the Holocaust historian, Raul Hilberg, "a major step" in "the destruction process" waged by the Nazis against the German Jews.[12] It assisted the National Socialists in progressively subjecting the Jews to conditions that had many characteristics of the ghetto. These included severing social contacts between Jews and Germans, identifying Jews, restricting their housing and movement, and eventually instituting Jewish administrative control over them.

The historian Marion Kaplan has described the situation differently. "Well before the physical death of German Jews," she concluded, "the German 'racial community'—the man and woman on the street, the real 'ordinary Germans'—made Jews suffer social death every day. This social death was the prerequisite for deportation and genocide."[13]

1935: Renewed Violence and Other Pressures

As some Jews moved back to Germany from abroad in 1935, new threats of increased discrimination already loomed against all German Jews. At the end of March, reports of local anti-Jewish boycotts organized by Nazi party officials led Hess, the party's deputy Führer, to order a halt to such actions. Hitler continued hoping to avoid serious anti-Semitic disturbances that would most likely, if the past were a guide, produce a negative foreign response.

Above all, he wanted nothing that would threaten to interfere with his initial significant victories in foreign affairs, which he had just achieved, or with German rearmament. In January 1935, the plebiscite in the Saar, a region in western Germany under French rule since 1919, gave Germany an overwhelming triumph and reunited the area with the Reich. Then in March Germany repudiated the arms clauses of the Versailles treaty and, in doing so, alarmed the outside world. On 16 March Hitler announced to the world that Germany would introduce general military conscription and raise an army over five times the size allowed by the treaty. A week before he had informed foreign governments that Germany once again had an air force (*Luftwaffe*).

When the Reich's most important European rivals and authors of the treaty, Britain, France, and Italy, failed to respond to Germany's violation of international law, except to denounce it verbally, the Berlin government decreed on 21 May a new military service law. The measure made Aryan descent a nearly absolute prerequisite for entry into German military service. As early as December 1933 the army had put forth on its own a proposal to use the Aryan Paragraph when appointing officer cadets. On 2 February 1934 the military had discharged all Jewish officers and soldiers.

Although the May 1935 law directly affected only those Jews who wished to enter military service, it also formally banned Jews from the armed services. The measure represented another humiliation for most German Jews, and particularly for the Reich League of Jewish War Veterans, which prided itself on helping defend the fatherland in World War I. Nor could one escape the demoralizing implications of the military law for all Jews in Germany—judged unsuitable to serve in the armed forces clearly made them citizens of a second rank.

Also Jews found disconcerting a renewed anti-Semitic campaign, more intensive than before, which began in May 1935. It included local anti-Jewish boycotts, violence, and other attacks, carried out both by Nazi party groups, especially SA units and organizations of the Hitler Youth, and government authorities. Widespread anti-Semitic propaganda accompanied the abuses.

The initiative for the renewed attacks came from several sources. One was a bitterness and discontent that festered in the SA, resulting from continued purges of its ranks, fears among its members of being dismissed and left unemployed, and resentment in it at the strengthening of the German army. To justify its survival and continued existence and to seize back power once again, the SA carried out a new wave of terror against the Jews.

Joining the SA in the renewed attacks were fanatical anti-Semites in the government and Nazi party leadership. For one thing, such officials were exultant over Hitler's recent triumphs in foreign affairs, and they expressed their jubilation by carrying out savage new attacks on the small and vulnerable Jewish minority. Central figures in this campaign included government and party officials such as Goebbels and his fellow district party leaders Jacob Sprenger of Hesse, Josef Grohé of Cologne-Aachen, and Streicher of Franconia.

These held anti-Semitic public meetings, increased incitement of Jew-hatred in the party press, and even initiated acts of violence against Jews. With regard to the press, since before 1933 Nazi publishers such as the pornographic-minded Streicher had fixated on images of illicit sexual relations between Aryans and Jews. Repeatedly his paper in Nuremberg, *Der Stürmer*, published vile propaganda that claimed rich, fat Jews raped innocent Aryan women and that Jews engaged in "ritual murders" of Christian children.

The radicals found further encouragement for their actions in Hitler's speeches. When he addressed party gatherings, which was not often in 1935, he praised the movement's battles against its enemies. On one occasion, for example, he declared: "Fighting we once conquered the German Reich, and fighting we will maintain and preserve it. Let those who are against us not be deceived! We have never shunned the fight—not then, and not now."[14]

This kind of battle-oriented rhetoric led some radicals, frustrated at the limits placed previously on their efforts to remove the Jews from the German economy and possibly even from Germany itself, to believe that they might only achieve their goal in wartime. One party militant observed this connection between the Jewish question and war during the plebiscite in the Saar. The radical declared in a speech: "If the Saar struggle gives rise to a fight or even a war, we shall not hesitate to annihilate the whole Jewish society, root and branch."[15]

The renewed anti-Jewish drive reached its peak during the summer months of 1935. In Berlin an unprecedented wave of vandalism of Jewish property and rioting broke out on the night of 16 July. In the northern and eastern portions of the city, mobs smashed windows of Jewish shops; violent attacks on Jewish businesses occurred as well in the Kurfürstendamm and Tauentzienstrasse, the fashionable shopping areas in the west.

Anti-Semitic agitation also spread to other cities. Nazi police acted as accomplices of the attackers by arresting numerous persons for alleged "racial" offenses. Both police and SA led German women accused of having sexual relations with Jews through the streets, holding over them posters describing their alleged "crime." The police interned in concentration camps Jews whom the women had supposedly associated with, charging them with "race defilement" (*Rassenschande*). State marriage offices (*Standesämter*) and judges received pressure from the SA to oppose granting marriage licenses to Jewish and Aryan couples.

By the late summer of 1935, however, the intervention of the radicals in the Jewish question again prompted opposition from some members of the German government. They feared that the militants' actions might threaten Germany's economic recovery and rearmament by arousing publicity abroad unfavorable to the Reich; this it was feared, could damage Germany's foreign trade, a necessity for Germany's massive and illegal buildup of the armed forces.

Even before Hitler had become chancellor in January 1933, the worst effects of the Depression had started to diminish, including unemployment. Thereafter, the Nazi regime used massive government spending, including for rearmament that violated the Versailles treaty, as the principal means of putting millions of Germans to work. Jobs and steady employment had contributed significantly to the widespread and enthusiastic support for Hitler among the people. Much of the work resulted from the regime's beginning, first secretly and after March 1935 openly, of construction of new armaments factories, expansion of the size of the army, creation of a large new air force, and building of a huge new navy.

Any repercussions on rearmament from the anti-Jewish violence, there-fore, concerned Hitler. The latter received warnings about such problems mainly from Schacht, one of the many among Germany's conservative elite who had pushed for Hitler's appointment as chancellor and chosen to col-laborate with the Nazis. Hitler had appointed Schacht President of the Reichsbank in 1933, Economics Minister in 1934, and Plenipotentiary-General for the War Economy in 1935. In these roles Schacht had responsi-bility for much of the government's economic policy that made rearmament and reconstruction of the German armed forces (*Wehrmacht*) possible.

Under Schacht's supervision, the government took control of imports and exports, costs and prices, wages and working conditions, raw material supplies, investments, and the flow of foreign exchange. By developing numerous swindles and other duplicitous practices, Schacht managed to cre-ate foreign credit for Germany, which had little liquid capital and almost no financial reserves. He arranged highly profitable barter deals with dozens of foreign countries, acquiring from them foodstuffs as well as raw materials— iron ore, copper, lead, zinc, oil, and rubber—vital for the military buildup.

Schacht's skill in financing rearmament made him indispensable to Hitler. But because he was an old line conservative and the only one remain-ing in the Nazi government in 1935, apart from War Minister General Werner von Blomberg and Foreign Minister von Neurath, he never enjoyed Hitler's complete confidence. Despite Schacht's efforts in acquiring foreign exchange, Germany continued to lack sufficient imports of raw materials for rearmament. Investment for developing synthetic industries had to come from inside Germany and at the expense of German domestic industries and the consumer. Also German exports had to pay for much of the foreign exchange for imports.

Especially worrisome for Schacht was any foreign interference with the German economy that would endanger a solution of such problems. He feared that violent public displays of anti-Semitism, which included boycotts and physical attacks on German Jews, could trigger, as they had done in the spring of 1933, foreign protests against Germany and boycotts of its exports.

On 20 August 1935, at a meeting with other government ministers held at Schacht's request, he emphasized "the serious damage to the German economy produced by the exaggeration and excesses of the anti-semitic propaganda and pointed out that the drift into lawlessness among other things is putting the economic basis of rearmament at risk."[16] Moreover, while meeting with Hitler at the beginning of September, he apparently convinced the chancellor that the anti-Jewish terror of party radicals threatened foreign trade and rearmament.

Hitler quietly sided with Schacht. The party received toughly worded orders from the Führer, issued through Hess and Wilhelm Frick, the Reich Minister of the Interior, to stop the anti-Semitic actions. At least officially, the German economy continued to remain off limits to the agitation. As for Schacht, he based his policies not on pro-Jewish motives, but on economic ones.

In fact, at the meeting on 20 August, Schacht made clear that he accepted Nazi goals regarding the "Jewish question." Three months later, following the issuing of the so-called Nuremberg Race Laws, he would tell the Chamber of Commerce of Saxony that "we have to agree to the Jewish policy of the Führer and, you may be surprised to hear, that of Julius Streicher as well. The race problem will be solved by the Nuremberg Laws and by throwing the Jews out of the administration, the theaters and so on."[17]

Schacht objected neither to reducing the influence of Jews in the business world nor to expelling them from it. Indeed, he played a key role in implementing rigid government controls over the economy that would steadily encourage the channeling of resources into "Aryanization," the Nazi term for the German takeover of Jewish property. Schacht presided personally over the Aryanization of nearly all Jewish-owned private banks in the Reich. He insisted only that expulsion of the Jews from the economy should take place gradually and through the enactment and use of laws. In September 1936 his Economics Ministry and the Ministry of the Interior would conclude an agreement to focus on the issue of the complete removal of the Jews from Germany.

Hitler's halt of the party radicals' violence against the Jews and their property caused ever greater unrest and bitterness among the militants. Many of them viewed the curb on their actions as a flagrant betrayal of Nazi principles and a political compromise imposed on the party leadership by the hated conservatives, namely Schacht.

Few of the militants realized the advantages the conservatives provided. Historian Shelley Baranowski has described the benefits by noting that "the regularized 'legal' anti-Semitism issuing from the state bureaucracy did not jeopardize the goals of rearmament, the revision of Versailles, or expansionism by arousing unfavorable foreign publicity," as did the violence of the SA and others in the party.[18]

Also the radicals had intended for their anti-Jewish actions to mobilize a generally apathetic German public behind the party and government. Many of the despairing, hungry, and dispossessed Germans, who previously had thronged to National Socialism, realized by 1935 that they had received little from the Nazis' promised, and the people's hoped-for, transformation of German society.

Numerous Germans in the middle classes, one of the Nazis' main pillars of support, complained of a deteriorating economic position. Shopkeepers suffered from a decline in sales at a time when government price controls had reduced profit margins and a wage freeze had diminished the public's purchasing power. Also shopkeepers protested that the party failed to help them survive by not destroying the Jewish-owned department stores.

Yet, as discussed in the next chapter, some party and government officials themselves profited significantly from the Nazi regime's increasing confiscation of Jewish property. Among the lower middle and lower classes in the country, resentment resulted from rising profits for large industry and commercial interests. But few of the discontented refused or were unable to recognize that much of the inequality of income and capital distribution resulted from Nazi economic policies geared heavily toward rearmament and big industry.

The campaign by some party leaders to use anti-Semitism as a device to rally greater political support for the regime failed. That is, violent public attacks on Jews did not distract Germans' attention from their day-to-day problems and latent resentments or raise the morale of indifferent or disaffected sectors of the German population. In fact, reports on public opinion, compiled by district and provincial government offices, the party, the Gestapo, and the SS Security Service (Sicherheitsdienst, SD), illustrated that the violence and breaches of law had increased, rather than lessened, discontent with the Nazi regime.

Even occasional whispers in the population discussed the possibility of a military dictatorship replacing the Nazis; the generals, said some gossip, had made Hitler a prisoner and a military coup loomed. But despite a certain amount of public dissatisfaction with the Nazi regime, it was more than countered by a highly significant psychological element at work in the German economy and society.

This was the connection in the minds of most Germans between the enormous popularity of the person of Hitler, the Führer, and German rearmament, economic recovery, and the resulting reduction of unemployment. Many Germans viewed Hitler as almost single-handedly responsible for the dramatic improvement in economic conditions since the Depression.

Yet Ian Kershaw, a leading authority on public opinion in the Third Reich, has demonstrated that substantially more than economic factors contributed to the popular image of Hitler among the German people. According to Kershaw, Hitler's charismatic oratory and the worship of him by Goebbels' propaganda, combined with the preexisting beliefs, prejudices, and phobias of German political culture, created a pseudo-religious Führer cult around Hitler. For many Germans, instead of assuming responsibility themselves for the many political and other problems they faced after World War I, they found it simpler to place their faith in one man who, they believed, would take care of everything.

But the image of Hitler accepted by most Germans, Kershaw has shown, stood in stark contrast to reality. As part of the myth they accepted about him, he embodied for them the strong and ruthless enforcer of "law and order;" the unselfish and detached leader who stood apart from the often corrupt, greedy, and arrogant officials of the Nazi party; the "moderate" in the party, opposed to its radical and extreme elements, including those involved in the "Jewish question;" and the genius in foreign affairs who would use "peaceful" means to rebuild the nation's strength and global prestige and remove the shackles placed on it by the Versailles treaty.

Evidence indicates that Hitler knew of the Germans' widespread discontent with his regime in 1935 and that he acted to defuse what appeared to be a tense situation, particularly involving party radicals, and one perhaps threatening even his rule. Two issues regarding the Jewish question both fueled popular discontent and needed the government's attention: alleged "racial defilement" by Jews of Aryans, and marriages between the two; and the German citizenship of Jews.

To halt the damaging outbursts of the radicals, Hitler decided to clarify the status of the Jews. Apparently he realized that his anti-Semitic movement had advanced so far that he could only achieve some control over it by implementing further legal measures against the Jews. Moreover, considerable evidence demonstrated to him that many Germans supported such measures.

The Nuremberg Laws

Hitler announced on 15 September at the party congress in Nuremberg, which the Reichstag attended in a special session, two anti-Jewish laws and a decree that established the Nazi swastika banner as the new German flag. The first measure, the "Law for the Protection of German Blood and German Honor," banned marriages and extramarital intercourse between Jews and Germans,

the employment of German women under age forty-five in Jewish house-
holds, and the flying of the German flag by Jews. The second anti-Jewish
measure, the "Reich Citizenship Law," stated that only Germans or those of
"kindred blood" could be citizens of the Reich. The Reich flag law replaced
the black-white-red flag, which had served as the colors of Imperial Germany,
with a swastika one.

The so-called Nuremberg Race Laws resulted in part from a hasty preparation of the two measures at the party congress, ordered by Hitler, by Nazi specialists on the Jewish question. This group included Bernhard Loesener of the
Reich Interior Ministry. But also since 1933, senior bureaucrats in both the
Interior and Justice Ministries had collaborated on drafts of legislation basing
German citizenship on racial criteria, banning sexual relations and marriage
between Jews and Aryans, and dissolving so-called mixed marriages. The latter resulted from Germans married to Jews or to Jews of "mixed ancestry"
(Mischlinge); the Nazis termed Germans in such marriages Jüdischversippte.

The Nuremberg Laws not only deprived Jews of much of what remained
of their political rights; the laws also invalidated the exceptions made in
April 1933 for non-Aryan veterans of World War I and state officials holding their offices before 1914. The laws, furthermore, served as the legal basis
of all subsequent government measures that would exclude the Jews from
German life and formalize their isolation and status as social and legal pariahs. In addition, Jews found their few remaining social ties to Germans now
exposed to ever more numerous denunciations by informants and party radicals, who based their attacks on the laws of September 1935.

Yet the Nuremberg Laws provided no definition of who was a Jew.
Consequently, on 14 November the government, after extensive negotiations
between the party and officials in the Interior Ministry, attempted to clarify
matters by enacting a supplementary regulation, the "First Decree to the
Reich Citizenship Law." The decree defined a Jew as anyone with at least
three Jewish grandparents or anyone with two Jewish grandparents who was
either married to a Jew or still belonged to the Jewish religion. Reflecting the
Nazi obsession with race mixing of Jew and Aryan, the decree also identified
so-called Jews of mixed ancestry (Mischlinge). It classified as first-degree
Mischlinge persons with two or more Jewish grandparents; and second-degree
Mischlinge persons with one Jewish grandparent.

But on what basis did the supplementary decree categorize someone a
Jew? The decree of 14 November said "if he or she belonged to the Jewish

religious community."[19] In reality, therefore, the decree hardly established a racial policy, but instead provided a religious definition of race. Nazi "experts" on the racial issue in both the party and the government, including a group of doctors led by Gerhard Wagner, one of the party's most rabid Jew-haters and appointed Reich Physician Leader, had tried unsuccessfully since 1933 to identify a specifically Jewish type of blood or race. However, Wagner and his associates were incapable of drawing the appropriate conclusions from their failure. At the party congress in September 1935, Wagner announced in a speech that a law banning marriages between Jews and Aryans would be enacted soon to prevent the further bastardization of the German people.

Loesener, the Interior Ministry's "Jewish expert" who played a key role in drafting the Nuremberg Laws, would claim in his postwar memoir that the laws were prepared only suddenly, at Hitler's directive, the night before he presented the decrees to the Reichstag. While nearly all historians have used Loesener's account, they disagree about its contention that the laws had resulted so haphazardly. Schleunes has commented on this issue:

> It should occasion no surprise that the Nazis would restrict the citizenship rights of Jews or their right to marry non-Jews. The surprise is that it took them until September 1935, more than two and a half years after their seizure of power, to do so. Something resembling the Nuremberg legislation had been "up the sleeve" of virtually every anti-Semitic German (and European) since the latter part of the previous century.[20]

The vast majority of the German public approved of the Nuremberg Laws. The population barely mentioned the law revoking Jewish citizenship. Generally the people applauded the "protection" law, believing that it would restore calm to the streets and put an end to the violent behavior that had besmirched Germany's image abroad as a civilized country.

The measure, thought most Germans, would confine anti-Semitic violence to the framework of law and order. Only the flag law, among those decrees announced at Nuremberg, received popular criticism, primarily from the older generation, war veterans, and officers. Abolishing a historical symbol seemed far more worthy of disapproval than ostracizing fellow Jewish countrymen.

The radicals in the Nazi party received the Nuremberg Laws with mixed emotions. Some saw the measures as a victory for Nazism in realizing the party's 1920 platform. Goebbels, at the Reich Culture Chamber's annual festival in Berlin on 15 November, declared the chamber "free of Jews" (judenrein), although he knew the claim was untrue.[21] Still other Nazi militants, however, thought the new laws too moderate.

Hitler, during his lengthy speech closing the Nuremberg rally, seemed to give the radicals confirmation of their role in the formulation of Nazi anti-Jewish policy. He praised the party "as *weltanschaulich* ['philosophical'] shaper and political navigator of German fate." Moreover, as if to underscore the importance of what the party congress had produced and of the party's future, he even mentioned the possibility of his own death, but emphasized "that the party will live on."[22]

Initial reactions of German Jews to the Nuremberg Laws reflected their cautious hope that the measures would provide them at last with a degree of security. If the laws ended boycotts and other anti-Jewish actions and propaganda assaults, while in return the Jews agreed to accept the legal status now forced on them, such hope seemed plausible. At the end of September 1935, the Reich Representation of German Jews (Reichsvertretung der Deutschen Juden), the collective voice of Germany's Jews, issued a statement declaring its willingness to work for a satisfactory arrangement with the National Socialists.

However, in what should have impressed on the Reich Representation of German Jews the serious nature of the Nuremberg Laws for Jews, the Germans forced the organization to change its name to Reich Representation of Jews in Germany (*Reichsvertretung der Juden in Deutschland*). Because Jews were no longer allowed to call themselves Germans, all Jewish organizations had to change their names. They now spoke for "Jews in Germany" rather than "German Jews."

Still, the Reich Representation of Jews in Germany acted with a measure of courage and even resistance to the Nazi government. It sent a special prayer to the synagogues throughout the country, to be read from every pulpit and serve as an honorable protest. The Gestapo forbade the prayer and arrested leaders of the Reich Represention of Jews in Germany, including its president Leo Baeck and director Otto Hirsch.

Arnold Paucker, a German Jewish survivor and postwar authority on the Jewish response to Nazism, has cited another such example of protest. He recalled sitting in a Berlin synagogue and hearing a rabbi change a traditional prayer for Germany to one that reflected the fact that justice no longer existed in the country. "Lord of the world, Father of all men," Paucker remembered the rabbi praying, "We ask you for your protection for all those countries in which Jews may go about their work free and unmolested."[23]

While many Jews chose to interpret the new quiet in the Nazi regime's behavior toward them as an effort to arrive at a modus vivendi, the reason for the calm lay elsewhere. Hitler wished to avoid anything that might lead to the Olympic Games, scheduled for 1936 in Berlin, being boycotted or cancelled—something discussed widely in international circles and especially in the United States.

Consequently, Hitler himself directed party members and other Germans to avoid anti-Semitic actions and unfavorable publicity. The Nazis even agreed to permit two German Jews to participate in the games—Rudi Ball, an exile in France who rejoined the German ice hockey team; and Helene Mayer, a half-Jewish Olympic gold medalist in fencing, who lived in Los Angeles, where she had competed in the Olympic Games in 1932.

Further, the Nazi government muted its response to the killing in Switzerland in early 1936 by a Jewish-Yugoslavian student, David Frankfurter, of an official in the Nazi party's Foreign Organization (*Auslands-Organisation*). The SS alleged that the assassination represented confirmation of the existence of an "international Jewish conspiracy" against the Reich. Two and a half years later, the assassination by another Jewish student of a German diplomat in France would lead a much more confident and aggressive Hitler, eager to begin war, to order in Germany a massive, nationwide pogrom that would devastate what remained of the country's Jewish community.

When Berlin hosted the Olympic Games in the summer of 1936, the event resulted in a propaganda success abroad for the Nazis. Travelers to Germany returned home, according to a historian of the games, "with tales of the euphoric Germans who were giving themselves up to the pervading milieu of hard work, hard play, and enchanting festivity."[24] Germany presented itself to the outside world as a contented and prospering country, united behind its government, and free of internal problems involving any of its population. Not even the brilliant victories at the games of Jesse Owens, the black American sprinter, could raise questions among most Germans about their government's doctrine of Aryan supremacy.

CHAPTER FOUR

FOREIGN AGGRESSION AND THE "JEWISH QUESTION," 1936–1938

UNNOTICED BY MOST German Jews and other Germans during 1936 and much of 1937, two factors emerged that would soon worsen, and dramatically so, the situation of the Jews. First, Hitler made major military, diplomatic, and economic moves that suddenly transformed Germany into Europe's predominant power, replacing France. This led him nearer to his goal of unleashing the war for land and for racial and global supremacy he intended to wage against the Jews, Slavs, and other peoples whom he hated.

Second, major new powerbrokers in the Nazi regime, Himmler and Göring, emerged as central figures in anti-Jewish measures. They now joined the groups and individuals that had previously fought over and shaped such actions: government bureaucrats; Nazi party radicals; and the conservative Economics Minister Schacht. The expanding influence of Himmler and Göring reflected in significant part their sharply increased role in the regime's anti-Semitism. In giving each a new base of power, Hitler had provided them both with such authority. He had appointed the Reichsführer SS, Himmler, chief of the German police, and Göring a kind of economic tsar—and successor to Schacht—responsible for preparing the German economy for war.

As for Hitler, he appeared, at least on the surface, to withdraw for a time from matters involving the Jews. Whether, as one scholar suggests, he "had no clear idea of where he wanted to go," and the initiative in Jewish affairs "had to come from other quarters," namely Göring and Himmler, is uncertain.[1] What is more definite is that by 1938 he had decided to move closer to his ultimate goal of war. Increasingly he made decisions based on situations presented to him in foreign policy by other states or on suggestions made to him by other Nazi officials, which for German Jews would soon have the most serious consequences.

Foreign Successes and the War Economy

During the remainder of 1936 and much of 1937, the relative calm in anti-Jewish measures that had accompanied the German government's preparations for and hosting of the Olympic Games, continued. The principal reason was that foreign policy, and particularly economic, issues preoccupied Hitler and the government and most other Germans as well. Above all, the regime concerned itself with solving a serious crisis in the economy that threatened to slow the pace of rearmament. This issue, too, as will be noted subsequently, would influence the Nazi regime's treatment of the German Jews.

On 7 March 1936, Hitler achieved his greatest foreign policy success to date. German armed forces reoccupied the west bank of the Rhine River, thereby breaking the provisions of both the Versailles treaty and Locarno pact of 1925, which had called for the demilitarization of the Rhineland. Hitler carried out this daring move primarily to take advantage of Fascist Italy's rupture with France and Britain over Italy's invasion of Ethiopia.

The results of the Rhineland remilitarization and the absence of drastic foreign efforts to challenge it, namely from France, Britain, and the League of Nations, were dramatic. First, the events of March 1936 completed the collapse of the post–World War I security system; the balance of power in Europe had now shifted sharply in favor of Germany and against France.

Second, Germany's subsequent rapprochement with Italy, strengthened by the two countries' joint intervention in the Spanish civil war, soon led to Germany supplanting Italy's influence in Austria and opening the possibility of a German takeover of the country. During the fall of 1936, Berlin established much closer relations to Italy and signed the Anti-Comintern pact with Japan. The two most powerful and aggressive nations of both Europe and Asia had suddenly drawn together, with Italy associated with them.

Third, inside Germany, the Rhineland coup produced frenzied acclaim for Hitler among most Germans. Kershaw has written that the triumph sent "admiration for the statesman Hitler soaring to a new pinnacle."[2] Germans' initial anxiety and worried reactions about the likelihood of a new war breaking out turned soon to jubilation and relief, once the Rhineland episode had resulted in no bloodshed. Hitler now feared considerably less that France and Britain might act to stop his future military conquests. Germany, he believed, could only grow stronger and less vulnerable as it continued to rearm and fortify its western border.

He had also sought, by achieving a spectacular coup in the Rhineland, to divert the attention of the German public from Germany's economic difficulties. The rearmament boom, while it had achieved near full employment for Germany, had nevertheless created an economic crisis. During the winter of 1935 and 1936, further shortages had emerged of imported raw materials for rearmament and imported foodstuffs. The German economy could not afford the necessary imports of both; a new propaganda campaign, launched by Goebbels in January 1936, promoted the slogan "guns or butter."[3]

These difficulties unleashed a bitter struggle over the control and direction of the economy between Schacht and Nazi party leaders, especially Göring, a close and long time associate of Hitler and commander of Germany's air force. Schacht, to help relieve Germany's shortages of raw materials, urged Hitler to increase German exports and secure a return from the Western powers of Germany's former prewar, mineral-rich colonies in Africa.

Also Schacht made the mistake of proposing to Hitler that the latter give up his plan to expand into Eastern Europe for more living space. Such areas, the minister argued, had as much or more population as Germany and would thus be of little value to the country. Schacht realized neither the fanatical extent of Hitler's commitment to Germany's expansion in the East, nor the Nazi leader's intention to depopulate the areas there by using massive force against their Slavic inhabitants.

Nor did the Economics Minister understand the impact on Hitler of the present economic crisis. The deficiencies of both food and raw materials in Germany by 1935 and 1936 made Hitler even more determined to fight a war or series of wars to conquer more territory and other resources for Germany in the East. Such wars, he planned, would be fought one at a time and when he chose to fight them.

Not surprising, therefore, Schacht soon lost his battle with Göring. The latter, along with Hitler, favored cutting back on imports and meeting the demand for raw materials as far as possible by increasing Germany's production of synthetic or substitute materials (e.g., oil, rubber, and metals) and making the Reich self-sufficient.

Consequently, in August Hitler placed Göring in charge of the Office of the Four-Year Plan, a newly created and eventually huge economic agency. Hitler directed Göring to mobilize the German economy for war by 1940. In his new position, Göring not only replaced Schacht as Germany's chief economic official. He also enormously expanded efforts to manufacture synthetic raw materials, including oil and rubber, and to increase the production of Germany's own sources of raw materials, such as coal and iron ore.

Hitler's directive to Göring, furthermore, provided the latter with a method of exacting greater booty from the German Jews. Hitler demanded that Göring hold the Jewish community as a whole responsible for any damage done to the German economy by individual Jews. Göring's initial efforts to implement this policy, which included his seizure of the foreign exchange holdings of Jews, proved disappointing. This would eventually result by mid-1938, as explained in the next chapter, in the massive intervention by the Office of the Four-Year Plan in the confiscation of Jewish property.

"Voluntary Aryanization"

Since 1933 the economic holdings of the German Jews had generally remained off limits to official anti-Jewish measures. At the time of Hitler's appointment as chancellor, Germany had some one hundred thousand Jewish-owned economic operations (using a religious definition of Jewishness), of which relatively few were large ventures. Approximately half were retail businesses, primarily in clothing, shoes, furniture, and groceries; the remainder included factories and various workplaces, private banks, publishing houses, newspapers, and practices in medicine, law, and other professions.

The value of Jewish property in Germany in 1933 was estimated at over ten billion Reichsmarks (approximately $4 billion). From its beginning, the Nazi government, mainly from concern for Germany's economic recovery and rearmament, had generally acted to restrain spontaneous anti-Jewish boycotts and violent actions against Jewish businesses by party radicals. Following the April 1933 boycott, the government had rejected various means suggested to it of pressuring Jewish firms out of business.

Almost right from the start, however, the regime frequently evaded and subverted its own decisions and actions in this regard, mainly because it received demands from party faithfuls who urged the total elimination of Jews from the German economy. Wild and anarchical attacks by local party officials on Jewish businesses left the smaller of them most vulnerable. Also Jewish shopkeepers and merchants not engaged in businesses critical to the economy found resisting Nazi attacks on them nearly impossible.

The Great Depression had already left a number of small Jewish businessmen close to bankruptcy, some of them, according to Avraham Barkai, the victims of anti-Semitic boycotts that had begun well before Hitler became chancellor. The problems became much more acute after 1933. Local party boycotts and other harassment, such as SA intimidation of customers of Jewish shopkeepers, Aryan clients refusing to pay their debts to the shopkeepers, and newspapers refusing to print advertisements of Jewish firms, weakened the businesses even more. In some instances, SA men physically attacked Jewish owners, or the Gestapo arrested the owners for alleged crimes and sent them to concentration camps.

As a result of such actions, a process of "voluntary" or nonstate-directed "Aryanization," the Nazi term for the German takeover of Jewish property, began. Between 1933 and the end of 1937, roughly two-thirds of the smaller Jewish business owners found themselves forced to close down or sell out to Aryans at whatever monstrously depressed price the sellers could get. The forced closures or sales included five of every six Jewish retailers, where the owners may have been most visible to the public.

Small Jewish businesses, however, were not the only firms attacked. In some instances, both the Nazi party and government did not hesitate to Aryanize major Jewish-held companies that the government believed had social and political importance. These included large retail outlets, such as the Leonard and Hermann Tietz department store chains, and firms that owned newspapers, such as the Ullstein publishing house. Under pressure from the party, the management of Tietz was quickly reconstructed, and by August 1933 nearly half of the one thousand Jewish employees of the store had been removed. By June 1934, the Nazi publishing company, Franz Eher Verlag, had acquired Ullstein; involved in the transfer, in addition to Eher and its director, Max Amann, were Hitler himself, Schacht, Goebbels and the Propaganda Ministry, and the large Deutsche Bank.

This haphazard process of Aryanization, however, especially angered the party radicals and a key socioeconomic pillar of their support, small German shopkeepers. Many among the latter, who generally struggled economically, hoped to profit themselves from acquiring Jewish businesses and customers. They envied and denounced what they alleged were the continued prosperity of Jewish department stores, export houses, banks, and industrial plants. Streicher, for his part, demanded that the government identify businesses officially as Jewish or Aryan.

Also zealous Nazis demanded that German corporations remove their Jewish employees, directors, and even owners. All across Germany, radicals burst into corporate offices, boardrooms, and shareholders' meetings and threatened their companies with boycotts and other hostile measures. Some of the most vulnerable companies began purges. These included the heavily indebted firms such as department and retail chain stores and breweries, along with the state-owned enterprises and those dependent on government assistance or goodwill. Into the latter category fell construction companies, automakers, and the large banks. Under such conditions, even Carl Bosch, the head of IG Farben, Germany's largest firm, could not prevent the resignation under pressure of four of the Jewish members of his supervisory board.

Large German companies followed an inconsistent but arbitrary policy toward their Jewish employees; in this regard, the companies usually responded to the party's anti-Jewish pressures on them and on their economic interests. For example, in 1935 the Hutschenreuther porcelain factory in Bavaria, after attacks on it from the local Nazi party leader, forced nearly all of its seven Jews off the company's supervisory board. During 1936 and 1937 the AEG, Germany's equivalent to General Electric, excluded Erich and Egon Loewe from the much smaller electrical company in Berlin that bore their name and took it over.

By 1937 Jews no longer had opportunities for advancement in major German firms. A few exceptions existed, as long as the Nazi party or government did not harass or threaten companies to force the latter to remove their Jewish employees. For instance, persons defined by the Nuremberg Laws as Jews still served in early 1938 on managing and/or supervisory boards of Mannesmann, IG Farben, Rheinstahl, AEG Waldhof, Feldmühle, and the Berliner Handels-Gesellschaft. Even the large Dresdner Bank, a primarily state-owned institution whose management National Socialists had taken over, still had 100 to 150 Jewish employees in Berlin in 1936, and five Jewish directors retained their posts almost until 1940.

Regarding the Aryanization of major Jewish firms, between 1933 and the end of 1937 approximately 30 percent of such firms changed hands or failed financially. In a few cases, large Jewish firms were taken from their owners with little or no compensation; this happened in 1935 to the Simson weapons factory in Thuringia. However, when the largest German businesses took over their major Jewish competitors, the terms of sale usually came closer to what was financially fair than did most other Aryanizations at the time and later.

Takeovers of Jewish businesses by German corporations resulted frequently from Jewish owners of companies approaching the Germans about selling out to them. When that happened, in some instances the Aryan firm both paid nearer the market price of the selling business and retained the latter's Jewish managers and former owners on the payroll of the new business.

Several factors explain the smaller percentage of Aryanizations of bigger Jewish businesses. First, their disappearance would have jeopardized Germany's recovery from unemployment and depression; often foreign capital badly needed by the Reich supported larger Jewish firms. Second, the few larger Jewish-owned private banks avoided heavy government or financial pressures, in part because many of their industrial customers remained with them. Third, party and state officials badgering Jewish owners of large-scale businesses agreed frequently to settle for the owners' withdrawal from managing boards to supervisory boards or from both, while leaving the owners' property rights intact.

Fourth, in instances where Nazi party activists attacked physically and destroyed bigger Jewish businesses, hoping thereby to force their Aryanization, the attackers discovered a surprising lesson. Most such firms, including the Globus department store in Lübeck, which party hooligans demolished during the night of 6 August 1935, had a small army of Aryan employees. The workers now suddenly found themselves unemployed.

Fifth, major Jewish businesses escaped destruction for a longer time because most big German companies showed minimal interest in Aryanization; whether this resulted from purely financial reasons, from legal concerns, or from principle, is unclear. Often German corporate barons had served with Jews in the world war, dealt with them in professional circles, found them loyal and cooperative, and in some cases were related to them through marriage. For reasons of personal loyalty or professional duty, such persons rejected attacks on Jewish businessmen and employees merely because of their racial descent.

Nonetheless, certain forms of prejudice existed among the German magnates. For example, they complained about allegedly corrupt Jewish influences in German cultural life, distinguished between supposedly lower-class immigrant Jews and the local or well-educated ones, and cited Jewish friends and colleagues as exceptions to the popular degrading stereotypes.

Whenever they opposed economic discrimination against Jews, the German executives acted primarily for their own financial and selfish reasons. That is, they believed that neither the depressed German economy nor the Hitler government could afford the financial losses produced by persecution of the Jews and the possible resulting retaliation from foreign countries.

To be sure, early on in the Nazi regime, a few profiteers in German big business took advantage of Aryanization. The Dresdner Bank seemed to set the standard. In September 1934 it cooperated with the Gestapo to strip the Jew Ignaz Nacher of his Engelhardt brewery firm, the second largest of its kind in Germany. A year later the bank helped to oust Alfred Orenstein and other Jews from the management of Orenstein & Koppel machine-building company, and then resold Orenstein's shares.

By late 1936 the economic and political rewards of such activity had proven so lucrative that the bank established a special section to promote Aryanization business. Meanwhile the bank forced the Jewish owners of the Gebrüder Arnhold Bank's main branch in Dresden to sell out. The tormenting of Arnhold by Martin Mutschmann, the Nazi Gauleiter of Saxony, also contributed to the bank's sale.

By the end of 1937, the executives of many large German firms, in the words of a leading scholar on German big business and the Nazis, "had reached arrangements with Nazi antisemitism that ran from the resigned to the callous. If they would not push to dispossess Jews, neither would they stand up for them."[4] Still, up to this point most of the pressure to drive the remaining Jewish business owners and executives from German economic life did not come from large German businesses.

Instead, the "little man" in the economy, the smaller German businessman, including shopkeepers and their trade associations, which sought relief from tightening supplies of raw materials and foreign exchange, demanded much more extensive Aryanization. They eagerly looked forward to the removal of Jewish competitors and, if possible, the redistribution of smaller Jewish properties among themselves.

Nor had Hitler forgotten about the Jews. In April 1937 he threatened them publicly with clearly menacing language. He explained to a group of party leaders that the final aim of his policy toward the Jews was "crystal clear to all of us" and boasted that he would make ever clearer to the enemy, "I mean to destroy you." He continued, "Then I use my intelligence, to help me to manoeuvre him into a tight corner so that he cannot strike back, and then I deliver the fatal blow."[5]

The SS and Police Empire: Forced Jewish Emigration

The years 1936 and 1937 witnessed the emergence of the SS and its Reichsführer, Himmler, as important agents in shaping Nazi anti-Jewish policy. By June 1936, with Hitler's appointment of the ambitious and absolutely loyal Himmler as chief of the German police, the SS already controlled a vast bureaucratic and armed empire. Its authority rested on the fact that it functioned largely independent of both the Nazi party and of the government and answered for its actions only through Himmler to Hitler.

A separate branch of the SS, the security service or SD, headed by Himmler's deputy, Reinhard Heydrich, operated as an intelligence section. From its origin in 1931, the SD had acted as a watchdog over the SS and the Nazi party. It also spied on alleged enemies outside the party, including communists, Jews, liberals, and conservatives. Himmler divided the numerous German police agencies into two branches, each under a main office in Berlin. Heydrich, primarily in his role as SD chief, headed one branch, a unified Security Police (Sicherheitspolizei), which combined both the Political Police (Gestapo) and the Criminal Police (Kriminalpolizei), a detective force for nonpolitical crimes.

Since the spring of 1934, another loyal Himmler associate, Kurt Daluege, had led the second part of the police, the Order Police (Ordnungspolizei, uniformed police forces). These included city or municipal police (Schutzpolizei), rural police (similar to county troopers), and small-town or community police (Gemeindepolizei). By 1938 the Order Police numbered over sixty-two thousand men.

Although military influence had characterized much of the history of the German police, Himmler, Heydrich, and Daluege instilled even more intensely within it both military discipline and absolute obedience. Beginning in 1936 and 1937, a gradual merging of the SS and police corps began, as did an extensive indoctrination of the police in Nazi ideology.

As for the SD, it mushroomed into a national intelligence service, based on well-placed citizens and other informants in German society who provided Nazi officials with extensive accounts of public opinion. Not surprisingly, Heydrich became possibly the most cynical, ruthless, and feared of the important SS figures. In Heydrich, both Himmler and Hitler found a clever and energetic servant, one whose height and blonde features fit the physical standards of their supposed Aryan ideal, and someone with the innate sense to foresee, plan, and administer their increasingly brutal anti-Jewish policies.

With Hitler's approval, the SS expanded in size by 1939 to include significantly diversified and large military formations as well as agricultural, construction, and industrial enterprises. For labor for its complex of firms, it used the inmates from its rapidly expanding network of concentration camps throughout Germany. The Nazi regime imprisoned in the camps political offenders, "asocials," common criminals, Christian opponents, would-be emigrants, and Jews. Jewish prisoners in the camps wore a yellow patch and Star of David on their clothes; other categories of inmates wore different markings.

By August 1937 four enormous camps existed, each with numerous subcamps: Dachau, Sachsenhausen, Buchenwald, and Lichtenburg, the latter used exclusively for women prisoners. In July 1938, following the German annexation of Austria, the SS constructed a camp there at Mauthausen; and during 1938–1939 the SS opened a large women's camp at Ravensbrück, north of Berlin, and a camp at Flossenbürg, in northern Bavaria.

Himmler's ambition in this growing penal and financial enterprise was to use it to make the SS economically self-sufficient and therefore politically independent and powerful. But SS businesses had developed partly from the Reichsführer's lack of success in persuading German industry to contract the captive SS labor force. He had attempted to do so since 1935, when a group of industrialists, including representatives of the huge German company, IG Farben, had visited Dachau. Industry showed little interest, however, and Himmler had developed the alternative system of SS-owned industries that would exploit by the beginning of World War II approximately one-third of the nearly one hundred thousand prisoner-laborers in the concentration camps.

The SS not only used camp inmates as forced laborers for its commercial and industrial plants. Because it was a brutal and corrupt organization, it also squeezed, coerced, blackmailed, and stole valuables from the helpless prisoners. SS torture of the inmates, including frequently forcing them to do heavy and exhausting work, made the camp system significant precursors to later camps of the world war. There both Jewish and many non-Jewish prisoners alike would be worked as slaves, often to their deaths, and their property plundered by both the SS and German industry.

The SS provided the camps with guards, the so-called SS Death's Head formations (*SS-Totenkopfverbände*). These units received extensive ideological and military training at the Dachau camp. There the SS commandant, Theodor Eicke, a vicious and genuinely fanatic Nazi, demanded blind obedience of Death's Head members to all orders from himself and other SS superior officers. Moreover, he insisted that the guards treat each prisoner with zealous hatred, as a so-called enemy of the state. Punishments for prisoners that Eicke devised at Dachau included whippings, beatings, forced labor, long periods of confinement, and even murder.

Eicke, himself a violent anti-Semite, considered the Jews the most dangerous of all the enemies of National Socialism. He reserved some of the most devastating punishments for the Jewish inmates. The brutal "Dachau model" of mistreatment of prisoners became standard throughout the concentration camp system. During 1935 the infliction of cruelties reached such a large scale in the camps, including many deaths from beatings, other tortures, and reports of inmates allegedly "shot while trying to escape," that the Reich Ministry of Justice and the Gestapo investigated.[6] Although in response the SS restricted punishment in the camps and the number of murders declined, the general tenor of excessive brutality did not.

Because the SS viewed itself as the racial-ideological elite of the Nazi state, claiming to choose its members selectively and breeding a "racial" aristocracy, it eagerly sought to play a role in the "Jewish question." In contrast to the crude and violent anti-Jewish agitation of the SA and party radicals, the SD recruited a small group of so-called Jewish experts to study the application of Nazi ideology to the Jewish question. In addition, based on its Germanic and völkisch ideology, the SS engaged in so-called racial research in medicine, archaeology, and academe.

During 1934 and 1935 the SD proposed that the Nazi government encourage the mass emigration of Jews. On the one hand, Heydrich, in the SS journal *Das Schwarze Korps*, urged the regime to cooperate with the Zionists, who "adhere to a strict racial position and by emigrating to Palestine . . . [and] are helping to build their own Jewish state." On the other hand, he continued, Germany must persecute the assimilationists among the Jews, "who deny their race and insist on their loyalty to Germany" so as to "overthrow National Socialist principles."[7]

Heydrich maintained that forced emigration served a twofold purpose of removing Jews from Germany and weakening the foreign countries where the Jews settled. Any people allowing Jews into their country, he alleged, would suffer from subsequent racial mixing and unavoidable decline. As early as May 1934, he received a memorandum from the alleged Jewish experts in the SD, who included Adolf Eichmann and Theodor Dannecker, which argued that Germany must become a land without a future for the Jews.

As part of its favoring of Zionism and championing a Germany "free of Jews" (judenrein), the SS initially supported the Transfer (*Haavara*) agreement of 1933. The German government had established this agreement with the Jewish Agency in Palestine. The arrangement provided for German Jews who immigrated to Palestine to transfer there at least some small portion of their money by arranging for the export of additional German goods to Palestine. Between 1933 and the fall of 1937, approximately 120,000 Jews had left Germany, one-third of them settling in Palestine.

Meanwhile, the SD gathered detailed records on Jews and their organizations and property in Germany, on Jews who had emigrated from the country, and on the most important foreign Jews. In the fall of 1936 the SD created a separate section for Jewish affairs, headed by Eichmann, a young and ambitious self-proclaimed "authority" on Jewish and Zionist matters. A bureaucrat with a talent for blindly following orders, he had acquired a smattering of knowledge of the Hebrew and Yiddish languages.

In 1937 Eichmann had visited Palestine briefly to explore the possibilities of Jewish emigration there from Germany. His SD section worked closely with the Gestapo, both to eliminate Jewish influence in Germany, including in the economy, and to encourage Jewish emigration. The Gestapo operated almost wholly independently of the German courts and could—and did—very nearly decide for itself what the law was, act accordingly, and ignore objections.

By 1937, however, serious obstacles had arisen to the SS plans for a Germany without Jews. On the one hand, outside the Reich, foreign countries only reluctantly accepted impoverished Jewish refugees; ironically, the Nazi regime had introduced the Haavara agreement and other measures, including Aryanization, that deprived the Jews of most of their wealth when they left Germany. Adding to the problem, anti-Semitic regimes in Eastern Europe forced waves of German Jewish immigrants to leave their countries.

As a result, many other foreign governments, which also responded to the widespread anti-Semitism among their own populations, had established immigration quotas. The United States had already implemented laws in the 1920s limiting immigration. During 1936 the British began considering the partition of Palestine and formation of a Jewish state in the land. However, because of the violent rejection of the plan by local Arabs and Britain's fears of offending the Muslim inhabitants of the British Empire, the London government abandoned it by the fall of 1937. Shortly thereafter, the British even began limiting Jewish immigration to Palestine more than previously.

On the other hand, inside Germany at least four main obstacles developed to the SS's encouragement of Jewish emigration. First, many Germans opposed the SS policy of using money of wealthy German Jews to finance the emigration of poor Jews. Opponents of the policy argued that the Jews had "stolen" the money involved from Germans by dishonest business methods and therefore the money must be seized "back" by the Germans.

Second, by the summer of 1937 even the SS, as well as some German government agencies, including the Foreign Ministry, had reversed their encouragement of German Jews to immigrate to Palestine. The SS and government offices feared the creation of a Jewish state that would surely become, they insisted, another center of power for "international Jewry." Also at the time, great concern still existed in Berlin that Britain might proceed with its plan, the details of which were revealed in July, to partition Palestine to include a Jewish state. Third, the German government's emigration office attached to the Reich Interior Ministry, functioned extremely slowly in applying legalistic and bureaucratic rules to Jews wishing to emigrate.

Fourth, the German Jews, encouraged by the relative quiet of the Nazis toward them during 1936 and 1937, did not leave Germany in droves as they had done during 1933, when thirty-seven thousand had emigrated. In 1936, roughly twenty-four thousand left the country, while in 1937 about a thousand less did so; these figures numbered only slightly higher than the ones for the previous two years.

During 1937, the Jewish experts in the SD complained that the difficulties involved with Jewish emigration created the danger that the ultimate goal would be lost from view. Anti-Jewish propaganda, they protested, had become nonexistent since 1935. Further, they demanded more systematic measures to segregate the Jews, including decreeing a law against "racial defilement" and requiring special passports for Jews and even some visual means by which to stigmatize them.

Readying the Nation for War:
The Anschluss and Czech Crisis

Not even what was soon to come satisfied the SD and other party radicals. The Jews who left Germany by the fall of 1937 did so just in time. By then the

German government would intensify dramatically its anti-Semitic measures. Hitler himself had signaled a radicalization of anti-Jewish policy in his speech on 13 September, closing the Nuremberg party congress. There he delivered a savage public attack on the Jews and associated them with Soviet Russia.

The Jews, he maintained, had created "an uncivilized, Jewish-Bolshevist, international league of criminals" that ruled "from a base in Moscow." He warned that the conquest of Russia by "this Jewish racial core" had "exceeded the dimensions of a Russian problem and become a world problem which will be decided one way or another, because it must be decided."[8]

It seems likely that, amid this extreme rhetoric, Hitler did not merely intend, as some observers have suggested, to persuade the Western Powers— particularly Britain—to remain at peace with Germany and entrust him with the defense of Europe against Communism. Instead, in light of his immediate subsequent actions, he signaled with his threatening rhetoric his readiness to begin the armed expansion that would culminate in the racial war in the East he believed necessary for Germany to acquire more land to feed its people.

At a secret conference in Berlin on 5 November he informed German Foreign Minister von Neurath, Minister of War von Blomberg, and chiefs of the armed forces that the "aim of German policy was to make secure and to preserve the racial community (*Volksmasse*) and to enlarge it." Germany, he asserted, had "the right to a greater living space than in the case of other peoples." "Germany's problem could only be solved by means of force" and by first improving the Reich's "military" and "political" situations.[9] This, Hitler continued, meant the conquest of Austria and Czechoslovakia.

These actions, however, would initially be only small ones. No later than 1943–1945, he explained further to his listeners, the much larger expansion of German territory must follow, by which he meant the conquest of Russia. While some of those present argued at the meeting and occasionally afterward with him against the plan, they focused on its risks and the speed with which he now urged it on them, but not on its merits.

Scholars have disagreed on what prompted Hitler in the fall of 1937 to move toward war. Some have shown that he had become concerned with his health and worried that he might die before acquiring the necessary living space for Germany. Others studying the issue have emphasized that by the end of 1937 German rearmament had not reached the pace and level Hitler sought. He therefore intended the 5 November meeting to test the commitment and resolve of his top diplomatic and military leaders to advance beyond the changes he had made previously in the Versailles treaty.

Still others have concluded that he wished to divert attention in Germany away from a crisis of public morale. While most Germans retained an almost religious faith in him and his charismatic leadership, police and SD reports showed much of the population apathetic or critical toward the government and party, and dissatisfied with the consumer side of the economy. In addition, the government's recently renewed attacks on Christianity had resulted in greater opposition from the small Protestant Confessing Church, led by Niemöller, whom Hitler ordered imprisoned, and from the Catholic Church.

In March 1937 Pope Pius XI had published an encyclical titled *With Deep Anxiety* (*Mit brennender Sorge*), in which he condemned the German government's treatment of the church. The encyclical became, and has remained, for many Catholics and non-Catholics alike, a symbol of the courage of Pius XI to speak out against Nazism. However, it failed to mention National Socialism and Hitler by name. Also it contained no explicit condemnation of anti-Semitism, even in relation to Jews who had converted to Christianity. During 1937 arrests of German Catholic and Protestant clergymen increased sharply.

Finally, some have claimed that by 1937 Hitler felt strong enough both politically and militarily to move toward war and, in the process, to purge from the government and armed forces the last of the conservatives. Because he believed the time had arrived to begin the aggressive policies he had long intended to pursue, he wanted around him not merely officials who agreed with him, but wholly dependent and docile marionettes.

Consequently, the conservatives still in his government now found their days numbered. On 27 November he dismissed Schacht as Economics Minister, and three months later he replaced von Blomberg, von Neurath, and army Chief of Staff General Werner von Fritsch. The purge of von Blomberg and von Fritsch, two of the highest ranking army officers, for involvements in alleged immoral offenses, weakened even further any independence left to the German military.

Most of the military leadership had welcomed the Nazi rearmament program; the indoctrination of younger officers in the principles of National Socialist ideology had also increased military support for the regime. Hitler took over the position of Commander-in-Chief of the armed forces himself. Henceforth, he used as his staff the Supreme Command of the Armed Forces (*Oberkommando der Wehrmacht*, OKW), an organizational structure that had developed since 1935 in the War Ministry. As heads of the OKW he appointed General Wilhelm Keitel and his chief assistant General Alfred Jodl, both blindly obedient to Hitler.

When Hitler's war came, and with which countries, depended not solely on his policies, but also on those of the other major powers of Europe. In March 1938 the Anschluss, Germany's takeover of Austria, Hitler's birthplace, produced little response from Britain, France, or the League of Nations. Austria was itself German and, even though the German army had occupied the country against the wishes of the Austrian government of Kurt Schuschnigg, both Hitler and some foreign observers publicly justified the Anschluss on the basis of national self-determination.

The vast majority of Austrians, furthermore, amid an outpouring of pan-German nationalist feeling, welcomed the Nazi takeover of their country. They believed that by entering an enlarged Germany they would return to their pre–World War I Great Power status. As part of this, they hoped for a dramatic improvement in their economic conditions, expecting Hitler to bring them similar material achievements that Nazi propaganda had told them he had brought to Germany.

Also millions of Austrians greeted the Anschluss as much or more in anticipation that Hitler would somehow rid their land of undesirable minorities and social outcasts, including most especially the country's 185,026 Jews. The latter formed 2.8 percent of the total population of Austria; approximately 90 percent of the country's Jews (169,978) lived in the capital, Vienna, which constituted the largest single Jewish community in German-speaking Europe. Popular anti-Semitism had a long and powerful tradition in the predominantly conservative and Catholic Austria.

While the new Nazi regime in Vienna would not disappoint the nation's many anti-Semites, Hitler's immediate interests in the Anschluss focused on the industrial and military-strategic advantages it would provide Germany. He sought the acquisition of Austrian iron ore mines and much needed gold and foreign currency reserves, and the encirclement of neighboring Czechoslovakia on three sides. The Nazi government quickly proclaimed that the union of the two states had created a new "Greater German Reich."

Czechoslovakia represented a different situation. In the summer of 1938, Hitler intended to go to war with the Czechs and seize their country. His public threats to do so produced an international crisis. At the end of September at the Munich Conference, British Prime Minister Neville Chamberlain and French Premier Edouard Daladier succeeded, along with

Italy's Benito Mussolini, in appeasing Hitler by persuading him to take only the Sudetenland. A large German-speaking minority lived in the Sudetenland, which comprised the western portion of the Czech state.

Although the world viewed the Munich settlement as a major German triumph, the agreement angered Hitler. As Weinberg has shown, Hitler believed that he had been cheated out of war. Consequently, he became more determined than ever to complete by the following spring the armed destruction of Czechoslovakia and later to go to war against Poland and then France and Britain.

Inside Germany, the bulk of the population received news of both the Anschluss and Munich agreement with enthusiasm and jubilation. Many had viewed the growing Czech crisis with great reservations and fears of war. Since 1933 most Germans had eagerly accepted the peace propaganda of Hitler and the government, which had helped to deflect a portion of the population from recognizing the real intent behind the regime's enormous rearmament program. Only a few had opposed the massive buildup of the armed forces, while the vast majority had cheered the many new jobs and steady work it provided.

Although most Germans knew nothing of Hitler's anger at what had happened at Munich, the "peaceful" takeover of the Sudetenland secured for him almost a legendary image among the people. Moreover, his seeming triumph at Munich undermined the small number of German officers around General Ludwig Beck, the army Chief of Staff, who had opposed Hitler's war plans over Czechoslovakia and had even begun preparations for a coup against the dictator. Beck, however, soon resigned his post. After Munich the German government reoriented its propaganda to prepare its people for war.

CHAPTER FIVE

THE FINAL STEPS TO WAR AND INTENSIFICATION OF JEWISH PERSECUTION, 1938–1939

ALSO TO PREPARE GERMANY FOR WAR, Hitler acted further on his obsession that the German Jews represented the most dangerous and traitorous element in the country. He and some of his closest associates had decided that, one way or another, the time had come to get rid of such a menace. Despite the conflict in his government and party over the issue, Hitler wanted the emigration of the Jews to continue, including their option of going to Palestine. But before driving them out of Germany, the government would have to complete their economic destruction; this process had started in 1933, but now it quickened dramatically, with further devastating results for the victims.

To begin with, during Christmas of 1937 Hitler directed Streicher to initiate in Nuremberg the first officially organized boycott of Jewish business in Germany since April 1933. Next, he replaced Schacht as Minister of Economics with one of Göring's stooges, Walther Funk, which signaled Göring's increasing power. The latter headed the Office of the Four-Year Plan and war economy; between the end of 1937 and December 1938, he decreed a series of laws that replaced "voluntary Aryanization" of Jewish property with "compulsory" or "state-ordered" confiscation.

Economic Destruction of the
Jews and German Rearmament

Both Göring and Hitler viewed the takeover of Jewish property as the most obvious answer to Germany's fiscal crisis produced by rearmament. The decrees issued through Göring would provide the government with a substantial percentage of the monies from the future Aryanizations. According to the economic historian Harold James, "Germany's Jews were to be made to pay for Germany's war."[1]

The first such decree, issued by Göring on 15 December 1937, reduced the amounts of foreign exchange and raw materials that Jewish firms could hold. What enterprises this meant he defined in a decree of 4 January 1938: they were firms owned or dominated by Jews or in which one personally responsible official, or one member of the managing board, or one-quarter of the supervisory board was Jewish. A month later another law forbade the awarding of public contracts to such businesses; soon the presence of even one Jew on the supervisory board would place a company under the January ban.

Göring issued still another decree, this one on 26 April, following the German annexation of Austria. The Anschluss had resulted in the mass arrests of Austrian Jews and confiscation of local Jewish businesses by Nazi party officials. Göring intended the "Decree on the Reporting of Jewish Property" to end private looting and confiscations and establish procedures for the state's control of expropriation of Jewish property.

The wealth of Austrian Jews may have reached as high as three billion Reichsmarks (approximately $1.25 billion). Since the Anschluss on 12 March 1938, the Jews in Austria had suffered massive violent attacks on their persons and property. For weeks gangs of Nazis roamed the streets of Vienna, desecrating synagogues and pillaging department stores and apartments. SA men robbed, tortured, and killed nearly at random.

Nazi thugs, moreover, cheered on by large local crowds, dragged Jews from their homes and into the streets. There the Nazis forced their victims on knees to clean political graffiti with scrubbing brushes. The attacks prompted the SS newspaper, *Das Schwarze Korps*, to observe admiringly: "The Viennese have managed to do overnight what we have failed to achieve in the slow-moving, ponderous north up to this day. In Austria, a boycott of the Jews does not need organizing—the people themselves have initiated it."[2]

Although the Austrian Jews held a prominent place in the country's business, finance, and professions, they hardly exercised the influence that most Austrians imagined and resented. To be sure, Jews lived largely in self-segregated portions of Vienna, but they were divided into cultural and political factions often different from and hostile to one another: Western Jew and Ostjude, believer and nonbeliever, assimilationist and Zionist, and modern and traditional orthodox.

Jewish organizations in the capital numbered well over four hundred and included religious or prayer groups, welfare associations, Zionist groups, professional societies, student clubs, and affiliations of war veterans. Such divisions had contributed to the difficulty of Austrian Jews to comprehend the rise in Austria and Germany of anti-Semitism and Nazism; after 1934, when the Austrian Nazis had failed to seize power, most local Jews believed they had little to worry about.

The Anschluss and subsequent massive assaults on the Austrian Jews caught the majority of them by surprise. While many committed suicide, within two years, over half of the others would flee the country, stunned and convinced by the enormous outburst of popular anti-Semitism that they could not stay in their homeland.

Göring's decree of 26 April directed Jews in the Greater German Reich to register their property, both domestic and foreign, in excess of 5,000 Reichsmarks. Also the decree required the Jews to have the property appraised by the government and, in the future, receive permission from the government to sell or lease it. The decree, moreover, gave Göring the authority to ensure that the use of the property would be "in keeping with the interests of the German economy."[3]

The decrees issued between December 1937 and April 1938 provided the "legal" bases for the ensuing massive and forced confiscation of the remaining Jewish property in the Reich. In April 1938, the German government estimated the value of Jewish wealth in the old Reich at between five and six billion Reichsmarks ($2–2.5 billion); this meant that since 1933 over half of the wealth of German Jews had been Aryanized. On 14 June 1938, still another decree further tightened the definition of a Jewish enterprise; it now meant a business in which one or more members of the supervisory board were Jewish.

The Nazi government, however, had already signaled its desire for large-scale Aryanization in mid-November 1937. Wilhelm Keppler, Göring's adviser in implementing the Four-Year Plan, summoned the chief agent of the German industrialist Friedrich Flick to Hitler's chancellery in Berlin. Keppler directed the emissary to inform Flick that he should begin the takeover of the huge brown coal and lignite mining operations in the Reich owned by the Czechoslovakian Jewish families of Julius and Ignaz Petschek.

Subsequently, Göring assisted Flick in acquiring, at a vastly depressed price, a group of Julius Petschek's German mining companies. Then in December 1938, following the German takeover of the Sudetenland in Czechoslovakia, Göring's own industrial and steel empire, the state-owned *Reichswerke* Hermann Göring, a portion of whose assets remained in his personal possession, acquired the even larger holdings of the German mining companies of Ignaz Petschek.

The Petschek properties had special value for German rearmament. Brown coal provided fuel and raw material for producing electricity, synthetic petroleum, and other chemical products. Also Göring, in return for the favors he gave industrialists regarding Aryanization, solicited funds from them and other Germans with wealth, in a kind of systemized bribery and corruption.[4]

The rapacious director of the Four-Year Plan added such monies to government resources, which he used to finance his eight large and lavish personal residences. His social background, political position, and appetite for luxury drew him almost inexorably to the wealthy and to depravity with public funds. Moreover, as noted later in this chapter, he filled his residences with valuable, but stolen, artworks and similar treasures he acquired from Jews and other victims of Nazi plunder.

With Göring leading the charge, the Nazis unleashed in the summer of 1938 a much more widespread and ruthless assault on Jewish firms and executives than any before. Soon, nearly all Jewish board members of major German firms had lost their positions. Whatever reservations remained among German corporate leaders about Aryanization evaporated quickly. The barons of both industry and finance, persuaded by the recent flood of government decrees to do so, exploited the regime's new policy of forced Aryanization by rushing to take over Jewish firms. For most German businessmen, the government had succeeded in changing the Jews from persons whom the businessmen had once thought it in their interest to defend to persons whom it was in their interest to exploit.

Especially the huge German financial corporations, the Deutsche, Dresdner, and Commerz banks, involved themselves significantly more in Aryanization.

Each of the banks received some assistance from the Gestapo. Often from Aryanization the banks collected large brokerage commissions, loaned the necessary capital to German firms, speculated on shares of the Aryanized businesses, and made their own advantageous confiscations of Jewish property.

In April 1938, for example, the Deutsche Bank and Berliner Handels-Gesellschaft divided nearly a million marks for brokering the takeover of a large Jewish factory. By the fall, the Deutsche Bank had acted as intermediary or financier in approximately 330 Aryanizations and had assisted in 75 major takeovers. These included numerous substantial Jewish firms in the tobacco, textile, and leather industries as well as Jewish-owned banks. Between 1932 and 1939 the number of German banks decreased from 1,350 to 520, and most of those expropriated were small Jewish institutions. The Dresdner Bank probably facilitated even more such takeovers.

According to the decrees that had established compulsory Aryanization, both German government and Nazi party officials had to approve all such transactions. As explained later in this chapter, the government took a substantial percentage of the money from both sides in the deals. Officials of the Four-Year Plan nearly always mistrusted both the Jewish owners and large German businesses and prevented them from profiting too much. In most instances, the government sharply reduced the amounts on which the two parties had agreed. Nevertheless, from the summer of 1938 on Aryanizations resembled fire sales. Unlike before, large German companies obtained control of Jewish firms for a fraction of the latter's value.

Not surprising, these takeovers promoted the already established tendency in many German industries toward capital concentration and monopoly. This was especially true in iron and steel, an area vital to rearmament. Benefiting were firms that were already large, such as Otto Wolff, which acquired the Thale iron and steel works, Friedrich Flick, which took over Rawack and Grünfeld Montaneninteressen (and a portion of the Petschek holdings), and Mannesmann, which assumed control of the Wolff-Netter-Jacobi firm and the Hahnsche works.

Who profited most from the massive pillaging of the German Jews? Ironically, the banks netted less than they grossed from Aryanization because they lost large funds through the removal of the deposits of Jews. Further, the banks lost big sums in non-Aryan accounts taken by the German government as payment for the exorbitant emigration taxes and currency conversion the state demanded from Jews fleeing the country.

Thus, regarding the motivations of the large banks in Aryanization, Harold James has concluded: "Deutsche Bank and its chief rival, Dresdner Bank, tried not for higher profits but to extend the grasp of their [political] influence." The latter would be most important later, "when the political market was shaken up by the German [wartime] conquests and when new opportunities [for Aryanization] became apparent."[5] Once that happened, the chances for making much larger profits and "the scope for implementing a political philosophy based on a racist nationalism became much greater."[6]

Along with the German firms that seized the Jewish businesses, the German government gained the most financially from Aryanization. Through special Aryanization levies, it took 60 to 80 percent of the amount paid for large-scale property transfers. Consequently, during 1938–1939 the regime acquired several billion Reichsmarks that Jews had possessed—almost as much as the Nazis had taken from the Jews between 1933 and early 1938—as well as increased tax income from stock transactions. James has described the importance of the state-ordered Aryanization: "A major motive of state policy was here the extraction of economic advantages for the state: the acquisition of assets in a period in which the funding of the rearmament-driven government debt was becoming increasingly problematic, and, as German war preparations advanced, a desperate search for foreign exchange, needed to acquire otherwise unavailable raw materials."[7]

The Plundering of Art

Also the government, as well as a number of National Socialist leaders personally, profited from the German looting of Jewish-owned and other art. Seizures of such property occurred on a large scale in Austria, following the Anschluss, as well as in the old Reich. In Vienna in the wake of the Anschluss, Nazi authorities, led by SS chiefs Heydrich and Karl Wolff, arrested and imprisoned the extraordinarily wealthy Baron Louis de Rothschild.

Rothschild remained in custody for nearly nine months, until he, in effect, ransomed his property for his freedom. His estate possessed more than a thousand paintings, including Rembrandts and other masters. The Nazis wanted the collection so desperately that on 12 December 1938 Himmler, along with other high-ranking SS officers, visited the baron and concluded the deal for his release.

Elsewhere in Vienna the SD and Gestapo seized vast amounts of art from Austrian Jews. By January 1939 Himmler reported to Hitler's Reich Chancellery that between sixty and seventy million marks worth of art had been confiscated; the works included thirty-six by Pierre Paul Rubens, eighteen by Titian, and twenty by Lucas Cranach. In June Hitler himself traveled to Vienna and viewed the stolen treasure. There he established detailed plans for the confiscated artworks, much as he had done in Germany previously with the government's seizure of so-called degenerate art (*entartete Kunst*), discussed later in this chapter. He zealously insisted on determining the fate of looted art.

Bitter infighting over administering the artwork ensued among local Austrian Nazi officials, including Arthur Seyss-Inquart and Joseph Bürckel, and representatives of Hitler and the government in Berlin. Numerous Austrian and German officials raked off pieces of art and furniture for themselves, while the other artworks were sold by the government usually at bargain prices, to museums in Vienna and the rest of Austria.

In Germany, following the Kristallnacht on the night of 9–10 November 1938, the government initiated a similar massive pillaging of Jewish-owned art. During the remainder of the month, the Gestapo seized in Munich alone over 950 pieces of art from 58 Jews and an art dealership. Local museum directors not only assisted the Gestapo, particularly by providing storage space for the confiscated artworks, but they also purchased at rock-bottom prices numerous pieces from the government and increased their collections. Inasmuch as the price lists they used contained the names of the former Jewish owners of the art, the directors knew of its origins.

The role of the SS and the Gestapo in the confiscation of artwork in the Greater German Reich, and later during World War II in Nazi-occupied Europe, increased even further the power of Himmler in the Nazi regime. Nearly all leading National Socialist officials, however, including Hitler, Göring, Goebbels, and Himmler exhibited an intense interest in art and enriched themselves by amassing art collections that they pillaged from Jews and other "enemies of the state."

For the Nazis art mainly provided a means to an end. Beyond controlling art policy and collecting artworks to further their own political careers and provide them with social recognition, they used art to express the basic principles of Nazi ideology. This included the belief in the alleged Aryan race as the superior producer of culture, in the superiority of German culture over that of other races and nations, and in artistic legacy as a symbol of racial and military virility. Much of the Nazis' art policy resulted from the desire of Hitler and his associates to establish large shrines to German culture, primarily in Berlin and in Hitler's Austrian hometown, Linz.

The massive Nazi takeover in 1938–1939 of Jewish-owned art in Germany represented a climax in the gradual exclusion of German Jews from the cultural life of the country. This removal had begun with the Nuremberg Laws in 1935. It continued with Goebbels' enactment in February 1936 of a decree that forbade Jewish art dealers or other providers of culture (such as book dealers) from membership in the Reich Chamber of Culture.

Further, the regime had attacked Jewish artists, whom it accused of producing modern and nontraditional art. The assault included Goebbels' decreeing a ban on art criticism in November 1936. The Nazis aimed the decree at the press as well as art, basing the law on the mythical premise that Jews controlled both the art market and press and had used the latter to promote modern art for huge profits.

Antimodernism in the Third Reich had racial anti-Semitism as a key element, which expressed itself in the purge of artworks of all Jewish artists (e.g., Otto Freundlich, Marc Chagall, and Ludwig Meidner) from German museums. During 1937 Hitler authorized Adolf Ziegler, the President of the Reich Chamber of Visual Art and the Führer's favorite—but mediocre—painter, to strip all galleries and museums in the Reich of what the Nazis called "degenerate art." This resulted in the takeover of approximately seventeen thousand examples of expressionist, abstract, cubist, and surrealist works of art, a number of them done by Jewish artists.

In July, Ziegler organized the first portion of the seized collection into the Exhibition of Degenerate Art in Munich. However, to the great embarrassment of the Nazis, the exhibition proved to be the most popular display of painting ever staged in Germany. More than two million visitors saw it in Munich, and another three million viewed it on tour in other cities of the Reich, including Berlin and Vienna. By comparison, a second exhibition, this one of "approved" Nazi works, aroused far less interest.

Although Goebbels never considered, according to the art historian Jonathan Petropoulos, whether some of the millions who visited the "degenerate art" exhibit did so "to bid a sad farewell to modern art in Germany," the Propaganda Minister moved to ensure that Jews would not visit the exhibition again.[8] In November 1938 he issued a decree that banned Jews from entering museums and theaters or attending cultural events.

In addition to the massive campaign of Aryanization and other forms of stealing of Jewish property that the German government implemented in 1938–1939, the regime imposed still more harsh economic and social measures on the Jews. In July 1938, the government notified Jewish physicians that they must close their practices within three months. In September Jewish lawyers were given until 30 November to do the same.

Another decree provided for the liquidation of Jewish real estate, brokerage, and marriage agencies catering to non-Jews. Still another law excluded Jews from certain commercial occupations, resulting in the immediate dismissal of thirty thousand Jewish salesmen. In October Göring announced that it was necessary for the Jews to be completely "removed from the economy."[9] Also the Nazi government issued two decrees aimed at both identifying and further humiliating Jews: the first established for Jews compulsory Jewish names, principally "Israel" for men and "Sarah" for women; and the second required Jews to possess identification cards and special passports marked with a "J."

Some foreign observers not only sensed what was behind the Nazis' expanding economic persecution of the Jews, but they also peered into the future. John Wiley, the American consul general in Vienna and a veteran diplomat, informed Washington that the German policy toward the Jews might be "inspired by the possibility of war and the desire to eliminate a hostile element in the population. If there is war, Heaven alone knows what will happen to these unhappy and wretched people."[10]

Renewed Anti-Semitic Violence

Along with the German government's massive economic assault on the Jews in 1938 in both Germany and annexed Austria, the SS, German police, and Nazi party attempted to dispose of the German and Austrian Jews by literally forcing them out of the country. Consequently, the nationwide pogrom on the night of 9–10 November 1938—the Kristallnacht, named for the glass from the broken windows of Jewish shops and synagogues that littered the streets afterward—represented the peak, rather than the beginning, of extreme Nazi anti-Jewish violence during the year.

For most of 1938, as fears and expectations mounted of impending war, Himmler's SS and police concentrated on intensifying the pressure on German Jews, primarily to achieve their removal from Germany before war started. As noted in chapter 4, the SS had urged the forced emigration of the German Jews since 1935. Based on the general relationship between Himmler and Hitler, it seems clear that the former, despite his ambition for both himself and the SS, acted on Hitler's orders or wishes.

Perhaps even more correct, Himmler would not have acted against what the Führer wanted. Unclear is whether Hitler gave his loyal associate special instructions for the SS regarding a forthcoming war against the Jews and other "racial" enemies, or whether Himmler moved on his own to prepare for carrying out Hitler's public and private threats against international Jewry.

In June 1938 the police and party unleashed a widespread campaign of anti-Semitic terror in Berlin as well as other cities; police carried out house-to-house searches and arrests, raided cafés, and emptied cinemas of Jews. The authorities placed those who had criminal records, no matter how minor, in concentration camps. SS guards tortured the newly imprisoned and only released them with a warning to leave the country soon, or else.

The Nazi party, too, escalated the pressure on the Jews. As it had done previously in 1933 and 1935, the party unleashed a widespread campaign of anti-Semitic propaganda and conducted random acts of violence against Jews. Unlike the earlier terror campaigns, which the government had moderated or halted, this time the regime encouraged the party's actions. At the end of April 1938 local Nazis initiated a boycott in Frankfurt.

A month later, pogroms sponsored by the party and assisted by the police broke out in Berlin. These resulted in the vandalizing of Jewish institutions, businesses, and private homes, and in the abuse, torturing, and arbitrary arrests of Jews. Also during May a Nazi mob demolished a synagogue in Munich. In June, again in Berlin, local party officials zealously competed with the police in persecuting Jews. Party members defaced Jewish stores with signs bearing swastikas, marked clinics and lawyers' offices, and smashed and gutted Jewish businesses.

In addition to the escalating violence, the police and SS gave Jews deadlines by which they had to leave the country, often brutally pushed them across borders, and even carried out mass expulsions. The Germans implemented their first deportations in Austria. Following the Anschluss, the police planned to expel all Jews from the Burgenland, a province in eastern Austria, ostensibly for strategic reasons, and to forbid Jews from residing within fifty kilometers of the border. By 11 August 1938 the authorities had ordered some twelve hundred Jewish men, women, and children to leave the Burgenland and pushed them over the frontiers into Hungary and Czechoslovakia.

Furthermore, the SS placed Eichmann in charge in Vienna of a new office, the Central Agency for Jewish Emigration (*Zentralstelle für jüdische Auswanderung*). It served as the sole Nazi institution authorized to issue exit permits for Jews from Austria. Eichmann quickly acquired "expertise" in the forced emigration of Jews, which involved the takeover and use of their property, as well of funds solicited from foreign Jews to finance the emigration of poor Jews. Moreover, Eichmann gave the Austrian Jews a choice between forced labor and imprisonment in a concentration camp on the one hand, and leaving Austria on the other.

Within six months Eichmann claimed to have forced the emigration of forty-five thousand Jews, approximately one quarter of those who lived in Austria. By May 1939, that figure had topped one hundred thousand, over half the number of Jews in the country at the time of the Anschluss. One who left Vienna was Sigmund Freud, the world famous physician and psychoanalyst. Within the next two years, an additional twenty-five thousand Jews would leave Austria.

They fled their homeland because the colossal outburst of anti-Semitism following the Anschluss persuaded them that they dared not remain. The Nazi party, clearly empowered by the state's terror against Jews and supported by Austrian popular opinion, continued to engage in humiliating and violent physical attacks on them. Such assaults had begun the day of the Anschluss and lasted into the summer and fall of 1938.

The stepped-up pressure on the Jews to force them from the Reich led at the end of October 1938 to the first mass deportation of Jews from the country. At Himmler's order, and without warning to the victims, the German police rounded up approximately seventeen thousand Jews of Polish citizenship, shoved them into trains, and brutally herded them over the Polish border. Himmler intended to expel the Jews before a new Polish law took effect that prevented the automatic right of Polish citizens living abroad to move back to their country.

A week later, during the night of 7–8 November, SA and SS men unleashed a violent pogrom in Kassel that spread throughout much of northern Hesse. The National Socialists set synagogues on fire, demolished Jewish businesses and homes, and placed Jews under "protective custody." These pogroms, including the ones in Austria during late October, represented a carefully planned action, which some historians have viewed as the beginning of the nationwide Kristallnacht. The Nazi press reported widely on the attacks in Kassel, which two days later spread throughout the Reich.

Seen in this context, the 7 November assassination in Paris of a German diplomat by a young Polish Jew served only as an immediate pretext for what the Nazis had already decided on—the most devastating assault yet on Germany's Jews. As a result of Himmler's action against the Polish Jews in Germany, Herschel Grynszpan, a seventeen-year-old Polish Jew living in Paris, decided to retaliate against Germany. He had just learned that his parents had been among those forcibly deported by the Reich to Poland. The young Grynszpan shot and killed Ernst vom Rath, an official at the German embassy in Paris.

As news of the shooting reached Germany, Hitler and the Nazi party leadership had assembled in Munich for the party's celebration of its failed beer hall putsch of 1923. On 8 November Himmler, on his arrival in Munich, had addressed in secret a meeting of SS generals, but he said nothing about what had happened in Paris. Instead, he prophesied that within ten years the world would witness an unprecedented racial conflict to the death, a long war of annihilation that would pit Germany against international Jewry. In this gigantic struggle, the Reichsführer declared, the SS would have to obey his orders without pity, even those directives to eliminate and punish the enemy harshly, if it was to save the German *Volk*. One day, Himmler concluded, the world would have no place left for the Jews.

On the evening of 9 November, news that vom Rath had died hit the Munich party festivities like a bombshell. At a reception for party "old fighters," Hitler and Goebbels sat together, discussing privately and at length what had happened. Most historians believe that Goebbels, who had fallen from Hitler's good graces because of his many extramarital affairs, jumped at the chance to push for action against the Jews and regain Hitler's favor. But if so, the Propaganda Minister only supported what had already started—a carefully calculated, widespread, and violent Nazi campaign against the Jews.

Furthermore, portions of Goebbels' diaries discovered long after the war, during 1992 in newly opened Russian archives, would confirm Hitler's central role in making the decision for the pogrom. But that fateful night, he soon left the reception, thereby disassociating himself from what soon followed and making others the scapegoats for it with the German and foreign public.

Goebbels addressed the crowd. A notorious extremist on the Jewish question, he angrily blamed international Jewry for vom Rath's death and observed that already popular disturbances across Germany had developed against synagogues. The Führer, he claimed, wished for the party neither to prepare nor to organize anti-Jewish actions, nor should it oppose sponta-neous outbreaks.

The party and SA men present understood what Goebbels intended: Hitler should not be associated with the forthcoming "spontaneous" attacks on Jews or Jewish buildings. When the evening gathering ended, the party's Gauleiters notified their districts and SA chief Viktor Lutze his men in Munich that they should carry out a nationwide pogrom. The latter would, they directed, involve primarily assaults on synagogues and Jewish businesses.

The Kristallnacht

During the next twenty-four hours, SA and other party thugs unleashed a tidal wave of violence all across Germany, termed by contemporaries as the Kristallnacht. Armed with hammers, axes, crowbars, and torches, mobs destroyed, burned, and plundered more than one thousand synagogues and over seven thousand Jewish businesses. The attackers, many of whom were nonparty members and ordinary Germans incited to a fever pitch, also ran-sacked countless apartments, dumping their furnishings on the streets outside to be looted. In addition, they murdered approximately a hundred Jews.

In Vienna alone, the Nazis burned 40 to 50 synagogues, looted 4,038 Jewish shops, and arrested over 6,000 people, of whom they murdered 27. Hundreds of Jews committed suicide. Some of the local populace in the Austrian capital not only encouraged the frenzied violence, but also partici-pated actively in it.

As the pillaging and destruction in Germany, Austria, and the Sudetenland generally wound down—but did not end completely—on 10 November, the SS and the police, which had received orders from Hitler neither to partici-pate in nor to oppose the violence, seized thirty-five thousand Jews and locked them in concentration camps. Scattered violence continued for the next several days. The pogrom was the worst in Central Europe in several centuries. Everywhere it left not only broken glass from Jewish shop windows and smoldering remains of synagogues strewn throughout the country, but also many lives further broken and devastated by Nazi hatred.

While the mass of destruction from the pogrom pleased Goebbels and other radical anti-Semites, it appeared to be a disaster to other Nazis involved in the Jewish question, namely Himmler and Göring. They disap-proved of what had happened for several reasons. First, the Kristallnacht had done further damage to Germany's foreign relations and image abroad; foreign opinion reacted very unfavorably and resulted in a more extensive foreign boycott of German goods. While both Himmler and Göring favored punishing Jews, they preferred for it to be done quietly and with little or no notice abroad or at home.

But many Western leaders and much of the press condemned the pogrom. Hugh Carleton Greene, the Berlin correspondent of the London *Daily Telegraph*, wrote: "Mob law ruled in Berlin throughout the afternoon and evening and hordes of hooligans indulged in an orgy of destruction. I have seen several anti-Jewish outbreaks in Germany during the last five years, but never anything as nauseating as this. Racial hatred and hysteria seemed to have taken complete hold of otherwise decent people."[11]

On 14 November Hans Heinrich Dieckhoff, the German ambassador in Washington, reported to his government on "the storm at present sweeping across the United States" against the Kristallnacht.[12] That same day the United States recalled its ambassador from Germany, Hugh Wilson, as a protest against what had happened and did not return him to his post; Berlin soon ordered Dieckhoff home.

A few Western leaders, however, did not respond to the Kristallnacht. The aging Pope Pius XI, while he had come to view Nazism as a greater threat to Christianity than Communism, remained silent about what had happened. Although he planned to publish an encyclical that would provide some kind of public statement on anti-Semitism, the Pope died before he could do so. Copies of a draft of the statement prepared for the Pope by several Jesuits, discovered years later, revealed that it focused on the Church's opposition to racism and its belief in the unity of humankind. However, the lengthy document was less than a ringing denunciation of anti-Semitism. Its section on the Jews, while condemning racist views of them, fully reflected the centuries-old Church attitudes. The Jews, it said, "blinded by a vision of material domination and gain," had failed to recognize Jesus as Savior.[13] Pius's successor, Eugenio Pacelli, the former papal envoy to Germany, would say nothing publicly about the Kristallnacht or Nazi anti-Semitism in general.

Second, Göring, who headed the preparation of the German economy for war, disliked the widespread destruction of property resulting from the pogrom. Costs from the damage exceeded twenty-five million marks, much of it done to property owned by Germans and rented to Jewish shopkeepers and residents.

Third, the German population generally responded to the Kristallnacht with apathy or in a negative fashion. Crowds that night had stood by and watched the burning of the synagogues and other violence. Many Germans regretted the destruction of property and other barbaric behavior, although not because of what had happened to the victims. Instead, most worried about the disapproval of foreign opinion and its potential damage to the German economy.

Other Germans, such as Catholics in the south, viewed the wanton violence as an affront to German culture and decency. Some people, to be sure, abhorred the persecution of the Jews. The anti-Nazi Catholic priest in Berlin, Father Lichtenberg, denounced the atrocities from the pulpit, as did Julius von Jan, a Protestant pastor in Württemberg. Both men, however, paid dearly for their courage; an angry Nazi mob beat and imprisoned Jan, and Lichtenberg died in prison during World War II.

Perhaps most revealing, hardly any Germans mentioned the approximately one hundred Jews murdered during the pogrom and the German courts' acquittals, without exceptions, of the murderers. In this regard, no one in either the judiciary or the public inquired about or criticized what had happened. This could not help but signal to the Nazi leadership that the murder of Jews would not be opposed by the judiciary or meet with sanctions. As for the German population, it too responded to the murders with silence.

The Kristallnacht illustrated that as long as the government's anti-Jewish policies avoided producing a public sensation and uproar or the destruction of German property, most Germans would respond to such policies primarily with indifference. Furthermore, the Nazis noted with satisfaction the magnitude of popular support the Kristallnacht received in Vienna. Anti-Semitic violence there was much greater than in any other city in Germany. According to Evan Bukey's recently published study on the subject, "In no other municipality did crowds of ordinary people eagerly join in the savagery; in no other locality did attacks on Jews persist into December—and beyond."[14] In the aftermath of the pogrom, moreover, virtually no one in Vienna attempted to comfort Jews or to express regret.

Finally, fourth, the Kristallnacht concerned Himmler and Göring for personal reasons. Two of their primary political rivals, Goebbels and the SA, had helped to spearhead and carry out the night of violence, in large part with the hope of finding their way back to political influence in Germany. For Himmler, who had worked since 1935 to make himself and Heydrich the principal authorities in Jewish policy second to Hitler, the Kristallnacht seemed an effort by two arch opponents to infringe on the SS's sphere of influence.

In the aftermath of the disaster, Hitler accepted a proposal from Goebbels to make the Jews pay a massive fine of a billion Reichsmarks for the damages the victims had allegedly caused. Furthermore, Hitler intervened directly with Göring three times between 9 and 11 November, to inform the latter of exactly what he wanted done on the Jewish question. Hitler expressed his wishes orally in a personal meeting, then by phone, and finally by a command from Martin Bormann, the staff chief of the deputy party leader, Hess. As he had done before and would do later, Hitler never wrote down what he wanted regarding the Jewish question, but instead gave commands orally.

Initially he directed that Göring concentrate the whole Jewish question under his leadership and that it "be summed up and coordinated once and for all and solved one way or another." [15] Then Göring was ordered to complete the elimination of the Jews from the German economy. Last, Hitler commanded Göring to negotiate with the Western Powers about deporting the Jews from Germany, possibly to the French-held island of Madagascar.

Göring mentioned each of these directives at a conference in his Air Ministry office on 12 November, held with a number of officials from various agencies and Goebbels and Heydrich. The meeting discussed the economic consequences of the Kristallnacht and ways to remove Jews from the German economy. When discussion focused on identifying, fining, and restricting the Jews within Germany, Heydrich warned that such measures would fail. He put forth the SS view of the issue, arguing that in the end "there is still always the basic problem of getting the Jew out of Germany." [16]

Heydrich also urged the creation of a new Central Agency for Jewish Emigration in Berlin, patterned after the successful model that his subordinate, Eichmann, had established in Vienna. Following Heydrich's remarks, Göring came close to saying what Himmler had told SS generals three days before, but only in different words. He emphasized that in the event of war, "Germany will first of all make sure of settling accounts with the Jews." [17]

Also on 12 November, Göring, at Hitler's order, issued decrees that imposed the fine of one billion Reichsmarks on the Jews, in addition to the costs of the damages to their own property (which the state would collect by confiscating their insurance payments). These and subsequent decrees would further formalize the process of forced Aryanization of Jewish-owned property, begun by the German government a year earlier. On 20 November 1938 a law provided for the attachment of the property of "enemies of the people and state." Then on 3 December Göring enacted a decree that ordered the forced disposal (i.e., Aryanization) of Jewish property.

As a result, Aryanizations now accelerated even more, producing an even greater plunder of Jewish property than previously. By 1 April 1939, the German government had administered the takeovers by primarily large German businesses of nearly half of the 39,532 Jewish businesses in operation a year earlier. Still other decrees after the Kristallnacht forbade Jews to own stocks, bonds, jewelry, and paintings; concentrated them in separate housing; and severely curtailed their use of public facilities and transportation and their attendance at cultural events.

The Propaganda Ministry, moreover, made Jews a target of the first openly anti-Semitic films in Nazi Germany. To be sure, as noted in chapter 2, films had traditionally played a significant role in the spread of National Socialist ideology and contained anti-Jewish stereotypes. During the fall of 1938, however, the ministry ordered the German film company to produce movies with such themes as the "Jewish world conspiracy," völkisch ideology, and pseudo-anthropological and racial theories.

The National Socialists intended, with the propagation of these ideas in film and other forms of media, to prepare German public opinion to favor a "solution of the Jewish question." The first principally anti-Jewish films, *Robert and Bertram* and *Leinen aus Irland* (*Linen from Ireland*), appeared in 1939 in the form of comic caricatures of Jewish "subhumans" (*Untermenschen*). They emphasized viciously negative and mythical stereotypes, which alleged that Jews infiltrated Aryan society and that Jewish men lusted after pure, blond Aryan women.

Both films ended with the efforts of the Jews, in which the latter appeared as forever cunning, wholly frustrated. A year later, during the fall of 1940, a second wave of anti-Semitic films would appear in Germany, as expectations of Nazi officials of a quick victory in the world war prompted them to intensify developing schemes to rid Germany and German-controlled Europe of Jews. This would be done in the most complete and extreme way possible in accordance with Germany's foreign and domestic situations.

Amid the Czech and Polish Crises: Emigration or Death?

In the weeks that followed the Kristallnacht, a struggle developed among the highest level Nazi officials over Jewish policy. On the one hand, Göring, a relative moderate on the issue, worried that if the Jews left Germany, the nation's economy and rearmament would lose significant funds. He therefore suggested forcing foreign Jews to provide the capital, and negotiate an agreement, for the mass emigration of Jews from Germany.

On the other hand, an alliance of Nazi radicals on the Jewish question, some of whom had been previous enemies, opposed a negotiated settlement. These included Goebbels, Himmler, Heydrich, and Joachim von Ribbentrop, the German Foreign Minister. They approved not only of forced emigration, but also of policies even more extreme. *Das Schwarze Korps*, for example, prophesied that the poverty-stricken Jews left in the Greater German Reich would necessitate "exterminating the Jewish underworld in the same way as, under our government of law and order, we are accustomed to exterminating any other criminals—that is, by fire and sword."[18] Heydrich, in Himmler's presence, addressed senior SS officers, during which he called the Jews eternal subhumanity and criticized previous expulsions of Jews in history as failing to resolve the Jewish problem.

Hitler, as always, sided with the radicals. In remarks in Berlin on 24 November 1938 to the South African Defense Minister, Oswald Pirow, he told his pro-German guest that "world Jewry," which in this case appeared to refer primarily to American Jews, regarded its European members as "the advance troops for the Bolshevization of the world." He spoke heatedly of the Jewish "invasion" from the East and declared to Pirow that his mind was irrevocably made up: "One day the Jews would disappear from Europe."[19]

By the end of 1938, increasingly in the highest echelons of the Nazi leadership, German Jews had only two possibilities: emigration or death. Even well informed foreign diplomats in Berlin, including Raymond Geist, the American consul general, perceived the emerging dire situation. Geist administered the American embassy, following Washington's recall of its ambassador from Germany in protest against the Kristallnacht. Apparently the only member of the diplomatic corps—and indeed of the Department of State—to voice the need for the West to assist the German Jewish refugees, Geist wrote to Washington on 5 December:

> The Jews are being condemned to death and their sentence will be slowly carried out; but probably too fast for the world to save them.... After we have saved these refugees, and the Catholics and Protestants have not become new victims of the wrath here, we could break off relations and prepare to join in a war against them [the Germans]. We shall

have to do so sooner or later; as France and England will be steadily pushed to the wall and eventually to save ourselves we shall have to save them. The European situation was lost to the democracies at Munich and the final situation is slowly being prepared. The age lying before us will witness great struggles and the outcome when it comes will determine the fate of civilization for a century or more.[20]

The prospects for the emigration of Jews from Germany were nearly nonexistent. Even under the impact of the devastating persecution, fewer than half of the Jews who had lived in Germany in January 1933 had left the country. Considerably more Jews were in the process of fleeing Austria. Although large numbers of them now tried desperately to get out of Germany, most simply could not do so. Approximately three hundred thousand had applied for United States immigration visas, but the annual American quota for Germany and Austria combined barely reached twenty-seven thousand.

Nevertheless, it should be noted that President Franklin Roosevelt, after his reelection in 1936, felt secure enough politically to allow a significantly larger number of visas to be issued. At the time, most Americans opposed admitting refugees, and Roosevelt acted against strong opposition from the public, which considered the President's policy pro-Jewish. Anti-Semites such as the Catholic radio priest, Father Charles Coughlin, railed publicly against both Roosevelt and the Jews. Other notorious anti-Semites, who included Henry Ford, the automobile manufacturer; Gerald L. K. Smith, the evangelical fundamentalist preacher; and members of the racist organization, the Ku Klux Klan, also associated refugee and other Jews with the Soviet Union and warned of the alleged Jewish-Communist conspiracy to dominate the world.

Moreover, powerful patriotic or military organizations, including the American Coalition and American Legion, as well as some officers in the United States Army, thwarted all efforts to open America to refugees from Nazi Germany. In 1938 an American general, George Van Horn Moseley, caused a scandal for the Army when he suggested in public that refugees should be accepted only "with the distinct understanding that they all be sterilized before being permitted to embark. Only that way can we properly protect our future."[21]

Most other countries in the world as well still refused to accept substantial numbers of Jews. This had become apparent in July 1938, when

Roosevelt invited nearly forty nations to send representatives to an international meeting on the issue in Évian, France. The Évian Conference produced little relief for the desperate Jews, except for the creation of a body called the Inter-Governmental Committee on Refugees. The committee intended to negotiate with Nazi Germany to find countries around the world where Jews could establish new homes, and to help finance resettlement.

Between 1933 and the end of 1938, the largest single group of Jewish refugees from Germany and Austria, some 132,000, had found new homes in the United States. In comparison, approximately 55,000 Jews had immigrated to Palestine, 40,000 to England, 20,000 to Argentina and Brazil, 9,000 to Shanghai, 7,000 to Australia, and 5,000 to South Africa. Such figures, however, are deceiving unless viewed in light of the size, population, and resources of the various countries.

During December 1938 and January 1939, Göring, with Hitler's approval and initially with the assistance of Schacht, negotiated with the Inter-Governmental Committee. Despite Göring's willingness to work for a negotiated emigration, he was determined nevertheless to rid Germany of its Jews. On 6 December 1938, he discussed with other Nazi officials what he termed—cynically—the "good" side of the November pogrom, by which he meant, he said, that the German people had seen that Jews could no longer live in Germany.

Göring attempted to arrange for the emigration of approximately 150,000 of the 350,000 Jews still in the Greater German Reich. At the end of January, Helmut Wohlthat, one of Göring's economic experts, reached an agreement with George Rublee, an American lawyer and director of the Inter-Governmental Committee. Although Göring supported the agreement, Himmler and Heydrich, who favored nothing less than forced emigration, opposed it.

The two directed the SS's new Reich Central Agency for Jewish Emigration in Berlin to proceed with the policies, first worked out in Vienna by the agency's chief, Eichmann. These involved financing the emigration of poor Jews through monies extorted from wealthy and foreign Jews and the illegal confiscation of Jewish property. Göring, acting as head of the Four-Year Plan and obviously with Hitler's approval, had ordered the establishment of the Reich Central Agency on 24 January 1939, and placed it under Heydrich. In addition, Göring directed Heydrich to promote the emigration of the Jews from Germany "by all possible means."[22] The operation of the agency, in turn, fell to Eichmann.

Although Göring believed that Hitler would approve the Wohlthat-Rublee agreement, the course of events proved otherwise. Not only did Hitler not sign the agreement, but he sided, as he had done repeatedly in Jewish policy, with the party radicals. On 21 January 1939 he told the Czech Foreign Minister Frantisek Chvalkovsky privately, while the two discussed the alleged influence of Jews in Czechoslovakia: "With us the Jews would be destroyed. Not for nothing had the Jews made November 9, 1918; this day would be avenged."[23]

Hitler's remarks indicated that the approach of war intensified his deeply held fear of and hatred toward the Jews. He had associated the defeat of Germany and revolution of November 1918 with the alleged intrigues of the Jews and Marxists and was determined that this would not be repeated. The outbreak of a new war, in his view, would create the conditions in which an extreme solution to the Jewish question, namely eliminating the Jews one way or another, would be necessary. The war would also make such a solution appear more acceptable and suitable and less subject to world opinion.

On 30 January he spoke to the Reichstag in a major and carefully calculated public speech tying his foreign policy and the Jewish question together. How much his remarks represented evidence that eventually he intended to carry out the Final Solution, or Holocaust, is unclear. Yet, as noted previously, the idea of slaughtering thousands of German Jews had presented itself to him many years before, he had deliberated on it in Mein Kampf, and associated the killing with war.

Perhaps appropriate in describing Hitler's views are the words of the prosecutor in Dostoyevsky's The Brothers Karamazov. He said about Dmitri at the latter's trial for murdering his father: "I was firmly convinced that he had pictured the fatal moment beforehand, but had only pictured it, contemplating it as a possibility. He had not definitely considered when and how he might commit the crime."[24]

When and how Hitler would vent his fury on the Jews depended on the situation and opportunities presented to him. In the speech on 30 January, he assumed that the Jews controlled his opponents in the West, namely Britain and France, and that both Western Powers, because of what they had done at the Munich Conference, would attempt to block his imminent and long-planned war of expansion eastward. He still intended by the spring of 1939 to occupy militarily the remainder of Czechoslovakia and integrate the western and central portions of the country into Germany.

During the long speech he castigated the Western Powers for their refusal to accept immigrant German Jews. He then warned such powers that if they went to war to stop him, not only would they suffer severely militarily, but also the Jews would be destroyed:

> And there is yet one more topic on which I would like to speak on this day, perhaps not only memorable for us Germans: I have been a prophet very often in my lifetime, and this earned me mostly ridicule. In the time of my struggle for power, it was primarily the Jewish people who mocked my prophecy that, one day, I would assume leadership of this Germany, of this State, and of the entire Volk, and that I would press for a resolution of the Jewish question, among many other problems. The resounding laughter of the Jews in Germany then may well be stuck in their throats today, I suspect.
>
> Once again I will be a prophet: should the international Jewry of finance (*Finanzjudentum*) succeed, both within and beyond Europe, in plunging mankind into yet another world war, then the result will not be a Bolshevization of the earth and the victory of Jewry, but the annihilation (*Vernichtung*) of the Jewish race in Europe.[25]

How much of his attack on the Jews Hitler also aimed at the United States is unclear. He had long expected an eventual war against America, following his conquest of Europe, Britain, and the Soviet Union, and believed the mixed racial composition of the United States made it militarily weak and incompetent. Also his explanation of Germany's defeat in World War I, in which he accepted as true the stab-in-the-back myth, left him ignorant of America's important military role in the war's outcome.

During the mid-1930s, as German historians discussed initially and Weinberg most recently, Hitler had ordered the start of construction of a large navy of super-battleships that Germany would need to attack the United States. By 1937 the German air force had plans on drawing boards for the so-called New York Bomber. Hitler would postpone hostilities with America for as long as possible, however, until he could win the war he planned in Europe and Russia, and Germany could produce the naval power it lacked.

As a significant part of his contempt for America, Hitler despised President Roosevelt as much or more than any of his other political enemies. Roosevelt, much earlier than most other Americans, recognized the threat posed by Nazi

Germany to world peace. After 1936 the President increasingly sought to awaken the American public to the danger. The mere mention of Roosevelt's name drove Hitler into a frenzy. In the words of one historian, "Hitler believed that Roosevelt was a Jew-manipulated [Woodrow] Wilson, attempting to push other nations into a belligerent alliance against Germany."[26]

Given these circumstances, neither of the schemes discussed by the Germans for the emigration of the German Jews—the Göring-Wohlthat or SS plans—intended to remove all Jews from Germany. For one thing, Hitler wished to keep some Jews as hostages to help persuade the Western Powers not to go to war. The idea of using Jews as hostages testified to the linkage in Hitler's mind between war and the alleged Jewish world conspiracy.

Hitler received support for his thinking from the SS. *Das Schwarze Korps* commented on 27 October 1938: "The Jews living in Germany and Italy are the hostages which fate has placed in our hand so that we can defend ourselves effectively against the attacks of world Jewry."[27] For another thing, if the West declared war on Germany to stop the latter's expansion to the East, both Hitler and other Nazi leaders believed that the Jews remaining in Germany would pose a serious threat to the country's security. To develop options for dealing with the Jews remaining in Germany in the event of war, the Reich Ministry of Interior held two meetings of top-level officials whose agencies or ministries would be involved in coordinating anti-Jewish measures under Heydrich's direction.

At the second meeting on 28 February 1939, Heydrich's deputy chief of the security police and of SD, Dr. Werner Best, attended, as did Eicke, the inspector-general of concentration camps, and representatives from the High Command of the Armed Forces (OKW) and other police offices. There the participants agreed that, since no Jew could perform military service, the appropriate alternative would be forced labor.

A consensus developed at the meeting that the estimated two hundred thousand male Jews available would be subjected to special police registration; employed in heavy labor columns or gangs, closely guarded by police; kept well away from German workers; and sealed off in either special labor camps or concentration camps. In such conditions, if history provided a guide, many of the Jews would die.

In addition to Hitler's remarks on 21 and 30 January 1939, still further evidence existed that the idea of using war to kill Jews had presented itself to him and other Nazi leaders. On 10 February he met privately in Berlin with leading officers in the armed services and predicted that if war began, it would be a racial struggle and would decide the fate of the German people.

A few weeks later Goebbels mentioned eliminating Jews more humanely in peace than during war. Himmler, for his part, in 1927 had already highlighted the passage in his copy of Mein Kampf in which Hitler had proposed using poison gas to kill twelve thousand German Jews in World War I. Göring's remarks during the meeting of 12 November 1938 in the Air Ministry pointed in the same ominous direction.

Also the American consul general in Berlin, Geist, who dealt personally with Himmler and Heydrich and had sources of information inside the Gestapo, predicted to his government that the Nazi persecution of the German Jews would pass through several, increasingly severe, phases. These would include placing healthy Jews in labor camps, confiscating the wealth of the whole Jewish community, isolating and putting extreme pressure on them, and removing as many as possible by force.

Geist warned Washington in May 1939 that if the Jews could not be resettled from Germany soon, it would likely be too late for them. Based partially on this information, President Roosevelt urged, albeit unsuccessfully, American Jews and others concerned about the refugee problem, to pay for Jewish hostages and gain their exit from Germany. Negotiations over German Jewish emigration dragged on until World War II began.

Geist's information did not describe a German plan to murder all German or European Jews. Instead, it appears to have reflected two realities that existed by then regarding the German leadership and the Jewish question. First, in the spring of 1939 Berlin continued to implement the SS policy of forced emigration of Germany's Jews. With the Jews now essentially eliminated from German economic life, and with Eichmann's success in forcing them to leave Austria, such emigration appeared—especially in peacetime— the only logical solution to the "Jewish question."

During the months following, Heydrich not only established control over the emigration of Jews from the Greater German Reich, he also seized hold over the Jews themselves. He obtained the latter by taking over the main organization of Jews representing their interests, the Reich Representation of Jews in Germany (Reichsvertretung der Juden in Deutschland). He renamed the organization the Reich Association of Jews in Germany (*Reichsvereinigung der Juden in Deutschland*), replaced its elected leaders with appointees by the Security Police, and supervised its work.

Despite the increased control of the Nazis over the Reich Association of Jews in Germany, the latter circumvented their orders and distributed illegal material. In December 1938 the association secretly mimeographed and sent to numerous German Jews an article in *Das Schwarze Korps*, which predicted every stage of what eventually would lead to the Nazis' Final Solution of the Jewish question. Titled "Jews, What Next?" and placed beside a cartoon caricature of blacks in America being lynched by hanging and killed in the electric chair, the article proclaimed that "we are solving the Jewish Question piecemeal, by single measures forced on us by the Jews themselves and their friends." It proposed the impoverishment of the German Jews, their isolation and further demise in ghettos, and destruction through death, "a process of natural elimination."[28]

Even the most frantic efforts by Jews to emigrate continued to prove problematic and largely fruitless. The dramatic incident in May 1939 of the ill-fated passenger ship, the *St. Louis*, illustrated the tragic situation. Both Cuba and the United States refused to permit the ship, carrying nine hundred German Jewish refugees, to dock and unload its desperate human cargo on their shores, and forced the ship to return to Europe. Most of the passengers, as a result, had to disembark in Belgium and Holland and would die later at the hands of the Germans in World War II.

As for Britain, although it accepted more than ten thousand German Jewish children as refugees, it nevertheless placed pressure on the states of Southeastern Europe not to allow ships with Jewish immigrants to depart for Palestine. The British had decided to cut off Jewish immigration into Palestine primarily for three reasons. First, the belief continued in London that Britain must appease the Arabs in Palestine. The influx of Jews into Palestine from Europe had embittered local Arabs. During the winter of 1938–1939, as Britain turned from appeasement of to resistance to German aggression, it not only introduced the first-ever peacetime conscription of troops, but also transferred soldiers from Palestine to the British Isles.

Second, Britain's reliance in World War I on Muslim troops from India and elsewhere meant that in any new war with Germany, a vast recruitment of such troops could be expected. This, too, helped to explain Britain's appeasement of Arab demands in Palestine and curtailment of Jewish immigration into the country. Third, generally anti-Jewish and pro-Arab attitudes dominated among most of the officials in the British Foreign and Colonial Offices who helped to set policy for the Middle East.

As for France, by 1939 over 150,000 Jewish refugees had entered the country since 1919, approximately 40 percent of them coming from Germany, Austria, and Czechoslovakia, and the rest from Eastern Europe. The East European Jews settled mostly in Paris and comprised about 90,000 of the city's total Jewish population of 150,000. In contrast, the number of German Jews residing in Paris when the war began reached ten thousand. Native French Jews, therefore, made up barely one-third of the capital's Jewish population.

On 17 May 1939 the census for the Greater German Reich showed a Jewish population of 330,892. Of this number, approximately 190,000 remained essentially trapped in the old Reich and 94,601 in the former Austria. A further 44,573 foreign and stateless Jews lived in the Reich. The Czech provinces of Bohemia and Moravia, which now formed a German Protectorate, had 118,310 Jews.

On 15 March 1939, in accordance with Hitler's long-held intentions, German armed forces had completed the dismemberment of Czechoslovakia. Germany occupied Bohemia and Moravia, making the Protectorate an appended territory destined for eventual integration into the Reich, and allowed the viciously anti-Semitic Slovakia, where approximately eighty-seven thousand Jews lived, to declare its independence. In reality, however, Slovakia would serve as a puppet state of Germany that largely cooperated with the Germans both in the world war and the Holocaust.

Before Germany banned the emigration of Jews from the Reich on 23 October 1941, roughly twenty-three thousand more Jews would leave the country. Unfortunately, many went to Belgium, Denmark, France, and the Netherlands; the conquest of each country by German forces at the beginning of World War II would force the Jews again under German rule and lead to the subsequent deportations and deaths of many.

In addition to the German policy of forcing Jews to leave Germany, a second reality also existed by the spring of 1939 regarding the German leadership and the Jewish question. As previously noted, some of the highest ranking German officials, including Hitler, held the idea that once they began the war they planned in the East, the opportunity would present itself to go much further, possibly even to kill a number of Jews, German as well as other.

Hitler's dismemberment of the remainder of Czechoslovakia in March 1939 led Germany a step closer to war. Despite a renewed nervousness in the German population about the possibility of war, the fact that Hitler had successfully annexed large territories without shedding blood made him extremely popular and admired among most Germans.

Also as he expected, the Western Powers now decided which war he would choose to fight first—his long-planned struggle in the East against the Slavs or a war in the West to neutralize France and Britain. Following the destruction of Czechoslovakia, Britain and France suddenly shifted their policy from appeasement of Germany to opposing the Reich, by guaranteeing the sovereignty of Poland and the rest of Eastern Europe against a German attack. As Weinberg has demonstrated, Germany, Hitler decided, would have to go to war first with the Western Powers.

To prepare for war against France and Britain, Hitler moved to protect Germany's eastern border by subordinating Lithuania, Hungary, and Poland to Germany. So as not to be cheated out of war this time, as he believed he had been at Munich earlier, he made impossible demands on Poland. These included the Poles ceding to Germany the free city of Danzig as well as a piece of land across the Polish corridor, a tiny portion of Germany given in 1919 to Poland and that separated Germany from East Prussia. The Polish government flatly rejected the German demands, while the governments of both Lithuania and Hungary agreed to subordinate themselves to Germany.

With the Polish refusal in hand, Hitler began military preparations in April 1939 to invade Poland and conquer it quickly, before he moved against the West. If the Western Powers entered the war on Poland's side, he was willing to run the risk of a wider or general war sooner rather than later. Moreover, on 23 August he stunned the world when von Ribbentrop, the German Foreign Minister, concluded a German–Soviet nonaggression treaty in Moscow. As part of the treaty, Joseph Stalin, the Soviet dictator, agreed secretly to divide Poland between Russia and Germany.

Stalin's purge of the Red Army in the late 1930s, coupled with the widespread economic and political turmoil that had characterized the Soviet Union since the Communist revolution, had left the country severely weakened. Stalin believed naively that the best means to avert war from Russia was not only to encourage Germany to attack the Western Powers, but also to assist it in doing so. For this reason, he agreed in the treaty with Germany for Russia to provide its new ally with oil, grain, and metals, as well as with other raw materials important for war production, some of them from East Asia transported across the Soviet Union.

Hitler, for his part, explained both the foreign policy and racial-ideological reasons for concluding the Nazi–Soviet agreement to Carl Burckhardt, the League of Nations commissioner in Danzig. "Everything I undertake," he told Burckhardt, "is directed against the Russians; if the West is too stupid and blind to grasp this, then I shall be compelled to come to an agreement with the Russians, beat the West, and then after their defeat turn against the Soviet Union with all my forces. I need the Ukraine so they can't starve us out like in the last war."[29]

Hitler's Orders to the Wehrmacht for Poland

The day before Germany signed the treaty with Russia, Hitler addressed commanders of the Wehrmacht about the upcoming attack on Poland. The war against the hated Poles, he said, would be the start of the war in the East he had long envisioned against the Slavs to seize their land. The "aim of the war," he told the generals, "is not to attain certain lines, but consists in the physical destruction of the opponent."

He was sending to the East, he continued, special SS units that had "the order to kill without pity or mercy all men, women, and children of Polish race or language. Only in such a way will we win the vital space that we need. Who still talks nowadays of the extermination of the Armenians." He admonished his listeners: "Be hard. Be without mercy. Act quicker and more brutally than the others." Moreover, he emphasized, "in Russia will happen just what I have practiced with Poland."[30]

Unlike the Sudeten crisis a year earlier, when Hitler had received some resistance from his military commanders to his war plans, the officers this time voiced no such objections. Their hatred for what they viewed were the inferior Poles and an illegitimate Polish state, the latter a product of the despised peace settlement of 1919, led in part to their enthusiasm for an invasion and anticipated quick defeat of the country.

In the Wehrmacht Hitler found some of his most faithful allies. Following the introduction of compulsory military service in 1935, the armed forces had grown rapidly. Most of the generals identified largely with Hitler's rearmament and major foreign policy goals. The influx by 1939 of young recruits and reserve officers meant that the majority of the Wehrmacht's enlisted men and officers had received indoctrination in National Socialist ideology at school and in numerous party organizations.

Progressively since 1933–1934, the armed forces had removed and then banned Jewish officers and soldiers from military service and prohibited non-Jewish officers from marrying Jews. As for the German civilian population, while most did not want war, they nevertheless held the same dislike of the Poles as the German generals and soldiers, and wished for a settlement of the "Polish question," preferably through diplomacy or a short, limited war.

On the morning of 1 September 1939, German armies invaded Poland. Two days later Britain and France, the two Western Powers committed to defending Poland against an unprovoked attack, declared war on Germany. Almost simultaneously, Britain's Dominions and the British-controlled government of India joined in the war on the side of London and Paris. Contrary to what the world, including most Germans and other peoples, had hoped for, another world war had begun.

CHAPTER SIX

THE BEGINNING OF RACIAL WAR, 1939–1940

F ROM THE START OF World War II in September 1939, Hitler and the German leadership fought a radically new kind of war, a murderous racial struggle conducted under the cover of traditional military campaigns. The National Socialists would attempt to use the war to establish the global domination of Germany. To this end, they began a massive operation to reconfigure the races and land of Europe and Russia, of which first the persecution, expulsion, and random murder of Jews, and then later their systematic extermination, would form the crucial part.

Moreover, to help enrich themselves as well as numerous other Germans and pay for the series of wars Hitler would lead them in, beginning with the attack on Poland, the Nazis would plunder the Jews and their many other victims unmercifully. The massive wealth seized from European Jewry alone and Hitler's efforts to limit the wartime financial and other sacrifices of the German people were designed by Hitler and his associates to prevent disaffection of the people from the war and a potential stab in the back.

In Poland, the initial German attack on the large number of Polish Jews in German-occupied territory depended significantly, as would the Holocaust perpetrated later by the Germans, on Germany's military situation and foreign policy considerations. Once the Germans invaded Poland, and Britain and France entered the war against Germany, Nazi leaders worried about the influence they believed international Jewry held in the West. As shown in the previous chapter, Hitler envisioned using some Jews as potential hostages in dealing with the Western Powers. Nevertheless, during the fall of 1939 and 1940, the German persecution of the Polish Jews would already include the haphazard killing of the victims, in which the numbers of deaths reached substantial proportions.

In her study *War against the Jews*, Lucy Dawidowicz observed that Hitler "associated his declaration of war on September 1, 1939 with his promise to destroy the Jews. . . . The disorder of war would provide Hitler with the cover for the unchecked commission of murder. He needed an arena for his operations where the restraints of common codes of morality and accepted rules of warfare would not extend."[1]

From the moment the Germans entered Poland, their actions illustrated the validity of this view. Despite Hitler's emphasis to his military commanders on the widespread killing of the Poles, which German troops would begin implementing when they invaded Poland, the conquerors focused immediately much of their terror and killing on the Polish Jews. At least four factors appear to explain this.

First, the rapid conquest of Poland increased enormously the number of Jews under German control. Second, the masses of Polish Jews were almost wholly helpless and at the mercy of German armed forces, SS and police as well as Wehrmacht. Third, most members of such forces had been conditioned for years by Nazi propaganda and Hitler to hate Jews more than anyone else or any other thing in the world. Jews, in Nazi racial ideology, were even less than the so-called subhuman Slavs and to be treated accordingly.

Fourth, the SS and police units received from Himmler and Heydrich directives for increasingly harsher treatment of the Polish Jews. Principally in two ways the SS hierarchy, while not formally ordering the widespread murder of the Jews, nevertheless encouraged the random killing of large numbers of them. First, the types of persecution ordered by the SS—mass expulsion, expropriation, and ghettoization—would inevitably lead to the deaths of many of the victims, especially the elderly and sick. Second, the SS leadership gave its approval of the killings, which would include mass shootings of Jews, not only by doing nothing to punish the killers, but also by using codewords to describe and hide the killings and rewarding the killers with promotions and increased pay.

In this regard, the first year of German rule in Poland resembled a continuous, but vastly expanded and more deadly, Kristallnacht. During the Polish campaign and subsequent German occupation of western Poland, tens of thousands of Polish Jews would perish, from both mass killings carried out by the Germans and from their other brutal actions. Estimates of the number of deaths in the Warsaw ghetto alone from starvation and disease by July 1942, before the Germans began deporting the ghetto inhabitants to their death, run as high as one hundred thousand.

The War's Beginning and the German Jews

For the approximately 330,000 Jews living in the Greater German Reich and Protectorate of Bohemia-Moravia, the outbreak of war suddenly made it even more difficult for them to survive Nazi persecution. In Germany the authorities implemented further severe measures against the Jews. The Gestapo could search, arrest, and detain Jews and other so-called enemies of the state at will.

Beatings and imprisonment of Jews increased; many more died in concentration camps. In October 1939 the newly formed Reich Security Main Office (*Reichssicherheitshauptamt*, RSHA) issued a directive that ordinarily no person placed in "protective custody" in a camp could be released for the duration of the war. This order, along with the Reichstag fire decree of February 1933, gave the police and SS the power of life and death over camp prisoners.

For the Jews who managed to avoid imprisonment, the German government reduced further their supply of food, clothing, and other daily needs; drafted them by the thousands for hard labor in cities and on farms; and seized what little remained of their property. Jews in slave-like work details constructed ghetto barracks for Jews—so-called Jew houses—in large cities and labored in armaments factories.

The Nazis had nearly completed the social isolation of the Jews. In Bavaria, for example, approximately ten thousand Jews remained in the state, less than a third of the number living there in 1933. One found only a handful of Jews still in the Bavarian countryside or small towns. Most had moved to the slightly greater security of larger Jewish communities in the cities, such as Munich, Nuremberg, Augsburg, and Würzburg. Municipal laws separated Jews from non-Jews in housing; most Jews had lost their residences to Aryanization and were forced to live in crowded "Jew houses" and ghettos. In Munich the best of the Jewish dwellings taken over from their owners through Aryanization and other theft had gone to Nazi party functionaries, civil servants, and officers.

The Gestapo and SS, and especially the ambitious Eichmann, continued to exert relentless pressure on the Jews to increase their emigration from Germany, Austria, and the Protectorate. Himmler emphasized that emigration would serve the dual purpose of ridding the Greater German Reich of Jews while bringing in foreign currency, which the world presumably would pay in exchange for their release.

In the Protectorate, which the Germans ruled directly, they had mounted since July 1939, when they established in Prague a Central Agency for Jewish Emigration, a systematic operation to confiscate Jewish property and either force the Czech Jews to leave the country or die from impoverishment. Moreover, through Aryanization and the transfer of Czech assets into German hands, the Germans aimed both at depriving the Czechs of their nationhood and making the Protectorate immediately lucrative to its new rulers.

Poland: Persecution and Mass Killings of Jews and Poles

By the end of September and first days of October 1939, German and Soviet troops had overwhelmed Poland. The fighting there ended. Foreign troops now occupied and divided the whole country, according to the Nazi–Soviet pact and subsequent agreements between Berlin and Moscow. Germany held the western portion of Poland to the Bug River, which included Warsaw, the former Polish capital, and the Lublin district in the south and east of the conquered state.

In the former Poland, the Nazis acquired control over the fate of approximately 1.9 of the 3.1 million Jews who lived there. Of the Jewish communities in Europe in 1939, that of Poland had been the largest. By itself Warsaw had approximately 450,000 Jews, one-third of the city's population and almost as many Jews as had lived in Germany in 1933; the city was Poland's most important center of Jewish cultural and political activity.

This among other reasons, had made the city a special military target of the Germans. Amid the German invasion of Poland, Warsaw suffered the most massive destruction, as torrents of bombs turned portions of the city into ruins. On 16 September, the eve of Rosh Hashana, the Jewish New Year, German planes bombed the Jewish quarter, flying so low that there could be no mistaking the attackers' deliberate intent. The invasion and bombardments killed as many as twenty thousand Polish Jews.

Outside Warsaw, once the Germans moved into the areas of Poland they had been given in the Nazi–Soviet pact, they began uprooting and destroying ancient Jewish communities and expelling and deporting their inhabitants. In this brutal campaign, the Germans found little or no opposition from the Poles, whose predominantly Catholic nation had a long history of widespread anti-Semitism and anti-Jewish measures. In some instances, in fact, as the Germans invaded and occupied their portion of Poland, Poles would collaborate eagerly with the occupiers in persecuting the Jews.

Despite this prewar history, the Jewish communities located in hundreds of small Polish towns and villages as well as cities had managed to create their own brilliantly rich civilization, centered around achievements in religion, culture, and business. But for some time before the Nazis invaded Poland, Polish Jews had lived in an extreme economic crisis. A wave of pogroms in Poland during 1936–1937 had worsened the situation.

By 1939 nearly one-third of the Jews lived near or below the poverty level, with many close to starvation. This would limit severely their ability to offer physical and economic resistance to the Germans. Also, while in the past the clustering of Jews in communities had bettered their lives, under the Germans it would hasten their destruction. Unarmed and otherwise helpless, the Jews had no protection.

Much of their ruin was the work of mobile formations of SS and German police called *Einsatzgruppen*. These units, which the Germans had used previously in Austria, the Sudetenland, and Czechoslovakia, accompanied the German armed forces (Wehrmacht) into Poland to combat elements believed hostile to Germany behind the lines of the regular troops. Although technically subordinate to the army and dependent on it for fuel, ammunition, and provisions, the Einsatzgruppen in fact had only responsibility to the men who commanded them and assigned them their functions. At the highest level, these were Himmler and the chief of the newly established Reich Security Main Office (RSHA), Heydrich.

Also involved in the attack on the Jews in Poland were other militarized German formations. These included initially twelve Order Police (Ordnungspolizei, uniformed or general police) battalions headed by Kurt Daluege; and armed SS formations, three *Waffen*-SS Death's Head regiments, commanded by Eicke and created from concentration camp guards he had trained. All such police and SS units had received extensive instruction in Nazi ideology, military discipline, and absolute obedience to the commands of their superiors.

Himmler and Heydrich, because of their fanatical desire to implement Hitler's orders in Poland for a ruthless racial war, initially attempted to keep the Wehrmacht out of the murderous campaign unfolding behind the front lines. Although most German military leaders despised the Polish Jews and Poles and welcomed the destruction of Poland, the SS leaders and Hitler were still uncertain of the army's response to Hitler's directive for a racial war in the East.

A few officers in the German army remained sensitive about following the rules during war of international law. Based principally on the Geneva Conventions of 1906 and 1929, and Hague Conventions of 1899 and 1907, such rules set forth general protections in wartime for both combatants and civilians. For civilians the conventions prescribed that they be protected from deliberate or even indiscriminate attack and murder. For the soldiers who became prisoners of war, although they would lose their liberty, they were to retain in enemy captivity their lives, health, and dignity.

However, from the start of the fighting in September 1939, Hitler and his associates in the SS, and the Nazi party, as well as numerous troops of the Wehrmacht, wholly ignored the laws of war. At Himmler's order, the day the invasion began Eicke gave a lengthy speech to the three Death's Head regiments heading for Poland, during which he emphasized that even the harshest and most severe directive had to be carried out with absolute obedience. All SS men had to perform their duties to the maximum and devote themselves to Hitler's state and the German fatherland unto death.

Also Himmler wasted no time in letting his followers know that their obligations included destroying large numbers of both Polish Jews and Poles. Regarding the latter, while in Poland on an inspection tour of the Einsatzgruppen, he ordered the units through Heydrich and senior SS and police officials to arrest, imprison, and kill Poles who resisted German rule and others considered hostile to Germany. These included particularly members of the Polish nobility, Catholic clergy, intelligentsia, and Communist party.

Moreover, some Wehrmacht troops murdered Polish prisoners of war to the last man, plundered and raped unarmed civilians, and participated in the massacres of the Polish intelligentsia and clergy. Such killings produced little response from the rest of Europe and the world; the murder of Catholic priests, for example, brought no public condemnation from even the Vatican.

Regarding the Polish Jews, the Einsatzgruppen, following similar orders from the RSHA, expelled vast numbers of the Jews from their homes. They forced the victims to leave behind their property, which would amount to billions in Reichsmarks and which the invaders would seize for themselves, and flee with a few belongings in chaos on foot and pulling carts and wagons to the large cities. Jews suffered wild and wanton humiliations, terror, and physical abuse, usually amid much laughter and obscenity from their tormentors.

The Germans ordered pious or Orthodox Polish Jews, whose traditional Jewish dress of hat and long coat and whose beard and side-locks identified them, to desecrate and destroy sacred Jewish objects. Some were made to set fire to synagogues and some to pile Torah scrolls in the center of town, where the Germans compelled other Jews to burn the pile and dance around the fire. Still other Jews were forced to scrub floors and lavatories with their prayer shawls or had their side-locks cut or torn from their faces.

The invaders killed the helpless victims in large numbers. During the first fifty-five days of the German conquest and occupation of western and central Poland, at least five thousand Jews were murdered behind military lines. Many were summarily shot by Einsatzgruppen, others by Order Police or Death's Head regiments, usually after being forced to plead in desperation for their lives.

On 4 September German police units killed approximately 180 Jews in Czestochowa, a city in southwestern Poland. Some Wehrmacht troops as well participated in the shootings. On 8 September, in nearby Bedzin, the army and other units drove two hundred Jews into the synagogue and locked and set it afire. Five days later, at Mielec, fifty-five Jews were burned alive, some in a locked synagogue.

Furthermore, at Heydrich's order the Einsatzgruppen forced the Jews from the countryside into cities. There the Germans would soon concentrate them in ghettos. Some Order Police battalions received directives to report the number of executions they had performed, and later their superiors, employing a euphemism in official directives, cautioned them not to discuss their "special duties."

The nature of this campaign of isolation, expropriation, deportation, imprisonment, and murder of perceived Jewish enemies indicated that it would extend in Poland far beyond the duration of the German military campaign there. All these were "stages," Heydrich explained on 21 September to Einsatzgruppen commanders, RSHA office chiefs, and Eichmann, that would eventually lead to a "final goal" of Jewish policy "that must be kept strictly secret."[2]

During the meeting Heydrich informed his listeners about the plans of Hitler and Himmler for the intended future of the Jews and Poland. The old German provinces in western Poland, he said, would be incorporated into the

Reich, while further east in Poland a new dependent state would be established, with its capital in Krakow. The latter region, noted Heydrich, would become a huge dumping ground for Jews from both the new German provinces and the old Reich. The new Polish "state" would concentrate the Jews in cities and then ghettos and provide subsequent possibilities for deporting the Jews elsewhere.

Heydrich's reference to a "final goal" did not indicate that the Germans had made a clear decision on the fate of the Polish or other—German, Austrian, or Czech—Jews under their rule. Such a goal would involve cumulative radicalization (i.e., it would be realized over a period of time and require a series of steps or stages, such as establishing ghettos) to accomplish. Yet Heydrich committed the RSHA to the planning and preparation for the mass deportation of Jews to a portion of Poland controlled by the Germans. Also Heydrich's discussion of a "final goal" of Jewish policy symbolized the view regarding the subject of at least several ranking Nazi officials, including Hitler. They deemed necessary the elimination of the Jews from Germany and elsewhere, by one method or another.

In Poland, meanwhile, some units of the Wehrmacht, acting on their own initiative, continued to participate in the violent actions against the Jews. At the end of September and beginning of October 1939, Wehrmacht forces drove four thousand Jews out of the Polish city of Tarnobrzeg. Soldiers also took part in murdering Polish Jews; during September alone, the troops shot at least twelve hundred. One of the onlookers of the Wehrmacht massacre of Jews in the town of Konskie was the prominent German film director, Leni Riefenstahl. She had volunteered to visit the front as a reporter. While she witnessed killings by the army, other German troops watched mass executions of Jews, including women and children, by the Einsatzgruppen, which shot the victims in the back of the neck and buried the corpses in large earthen pits or graves.

To be sure, the commander of the German army in the East, General Johannes Blaskowitz, and at least two army unit commanders, Field Marshals Wilhelm List and August von Mackensen, vigorously opposed and even restricted the murderous activities of the Einsatzgruppen and senior SS and police officials against the Polish Jews. Also other officers, such as Admiral Wilhelm Canaris, head of German military intelligence (*Abwehr*), objected to the killings.

But their superiors acted differently. Both General Wilhelm Keitel, chief of the OKW, and army Commander-in-Chief Walther von Brauchitsch, realizing

Hitler's determination to persecute the Jews, did nothing to halt the atrocities. Brauchitsch even defended such actions that he proclaimed were "dictated by our racial politics which are essential for securing German Lebensraum and which the Führer has ordered carried out."[3] Both men, similar to most other German military commanders at the highest level, lacked both moral principles and courage. In addition, they received large bribes from Hitler to motivate them further not to oppose his orders.

Germanization, the General Government, and Jewish "Reservation"

Much like Heydrich had described previously, Hitler divided the German-occupied portion of Poland and implemented there an administrative scheme that eventually would remove as far away from Germany as possible both Polish and German Jews. First, he annexed the areas of western Poland, which included the Wartheland (or Warthegau), Polish Silesia, and areas bordering East Prussia, directly to the Greater German Reich. He ordered these lands cleared of Poles and Jews and "Germanized," or resettled with German colonists, including ethnic Germans (*Volksdeutsche*) from Eastern and Southern Europe.

Second, the expelled Poles he ordered deported to a substantial area in central Poland, a special category of exploited territory called the General Government. There the Germans would experiment with the most extreme of policies for ruling occupied territories and subject peoples. These included forcing the Poles to deliver food to the Germans, raising vast levies of forced labor, and killing masses of the Polish political, intellectual, and religious elite.

Third, also inside the General Government, Hitler ordered the deportations of Jews from the annexed territories of western Poland, which numbered approximately six hundred thousand, to the region around the city of Lublin. The latter was located in the General Government, some one hundred miles southeast of Warsaw near the line dividing Poland between Germany and the Soviet Union.

At Lublin the Germans constructed a so-called reservation, a large slave labor and concentration camp facility. While the reservation represented a new element in German Jewish policy, it nevertheless included stages consistent with the earlier SS plan for German Jews. In Lublin the Germans imposed on the Jews deported and imprisoned there forced labor as well as isolation, pauperization, and death.

Even though Hitler placed the General Government under the civilian administration of Hans Frank, a notorious Nazi lawyer, longtime associate of the Führer and Reich Minister in the German government, the SS moved quickly to seize control of the whole process of Germanizing western Poland. Germanization posed enormous practical difficulties. It involved settling ethnic Germans, or Volksdeutsche, in Poland expelling huge numbers of Slavs, Jews, and Gypsies from the areas intended for Germanization, expropriating their property; and deciding which Poles would be Germanized or used for forced labor. Also other offices, including the Wehrmacht and racial-political department (*Rassenpolitisches Amt*) of the Nazi party, developed in the fall of 1939 initial plans for the resettlement of Germans in Poland.

Himmler, in bidding to take charge of Germanization, exploited his frequent access and close relationship to Hitler. The latter, for example, approved the creation of the RSHA, a large combined government-SS organization under Heydrich that directed the Einsatzgruppen. The RSHA combined in one structure two government police agencies, the detective forces (*Kriminalpolizei*, Kripo) and Gestapo (political police), with the SD, the intelligence organization of the SS. Heydrich also assumed leadership of a rapidly growing bureaucracy of SD and police officials, led by Eichmann, charged with carrying out the deportations and evacuations of Jews and Slavs.

On 7 October Hitler signed a secret decree that made Himmler head of the Reich Commission for the Strengthening of Germandom (*Reichskommission für die Festigung des deutschen Volkstums*, RKFDV), an agency with broad powers to develop and coordinate the planned Germanization schemes in the East. Eventually, by mid-1940, the RKFDV would begin terming its Germanization project *Generalplan Ost*.

This activity also involved a multitude of other SS offices, including the Race and Settlement Main Office (*Rasse-und Siedlungshauptamt*) and Ethnic German Liaison Office (*Volksdeutsche Mittelstelle*, VoMi). At the time of Himmler's appointment to lead the RKFDV, Hitler informed Keitel that the military would be relieved of all administrative matters in Poland, which the SS and RSHA would now handle.

Meanwhile, even before Himmler and Heydrich began resettlement operations in Poland, one of their subordinates, Eichmann, organized the first deportations of Jews to the Lublin reservation. He eagerly sought to win laurels for himself and perhaps envisioned becoming the future governor—like Frank in Poland or later Heydrich in Czechoslovakia—of a "Jewish state." Eichmann variously claimed authorization for his action from the Gestapo chief Heinrich Müller, Heydrich, Himmler, and even Hitler.

Despite receiving no such authority, Eichmann deported several thousand Jews from former Czechoslovakia, Polish Silesia, and Austria to a town called Nisko, located on the line between German and Russian Poland. The Gestapo soon halted the deportations, however, because their poor coordination resulted in hundreds of deaths and the forcing of numerous other deportees across the line into Russian territory.

Despite Eichmann's blunderous operation, the RSHA sent tens of thousands of Jews from western Poland in unimaginable conditions—in sealed, overcrowded, unprovisioned, and unheated railroad freight cars—to the Lublin reservation. Chaos often reigned, with further difficulties created by the uncoordinated direction of the trains. Most deportees had to abandon nearly all their possessions and arrived at Lublin owning little more than what they wore. As a result the deported Jews suffered severely. In February 1940 the SS chief of the Krakow district, Dr. Karl Wächter, reported about the deportation of the Warthegau Jews to his area that "there were many deaths during the journeys and a large number of physical injuries and cases of frostbite."[4]

During May an Order Police unit, Reserve Police Battalion 101, arrived in the Warthegau; over the next five months the battalion evacuated approximately thirty-seven thousand Poles and Jews and carried out "pacification actions" in villages and woods. One battalion member recalled after the war that the unit's superiors "objected that we struggled under the burden of the old and sick" and directed the battalion, with typically guarded words so as to conceal the real meaning of the order, to kill such persons. "To be precise," said the reservist, "they did not initially give us the order to shoot them on the spot, rather they contented themselves with making it clear to us that nothing could be done with such people."[5]

Similar murderous activities characterized the work of other German units employed against the Jews and Poles. For a time during the first months of the occupation of Poland, the Nazis organized bands or "militia" of ethnic Germans (*Volksdeutschen Selbstschutz*) that assisted in the persecution of the Poles, primarily Jews and members of civilian elites, and their expulsion from the Warthegau.

These ethnic German bands had as many as one hundred thousand men and participated in mass executions, beatings, and tortures—which included rape, castration, and dismemberment—of their victims. The groups murdered at least ten thousand Polish Jews and Poles. German commanders of the Selbstschutz included two SS officers who would become notorious later for their killings of vast numbers of Polish Jews in the Warsaw ghetto and death camps, respectively: Jürgen Stroop and Odilo Globocnik. During the war, the Volksdeutsche of Europe, in the words of one scholar, would become "Himmler's auxiliaries."[6] Not only did some join Waffen-SS units, but also they would participate in the Nazi assault on and destruction of the Jews.

The deportations soon transformed Lublin into a massive concentration camp, overcrowded, chaotic, impoverished, and rampant with disease. Throughout the General Government, the Nazi authorities subjected the Polish Jews to a whole series of repressive measures. These included brutal forced labor, often done in camps with slave-like living and working conditions, and wearing clothing marked with the Jewish star.

Altogether, by the spring of 1940, in the German-annexed western Polish territories, which included the Lodz region and Eastern Upper Silesia, approximately 550,000 Jews—a substantial percentage of the total number— and 10 percent of the Poles were deported. Their homes, money, household goods, and jobs were expropriated and given to ethnic German settlers. Many of the latter, approximately 120,000 Volhynian and Galician Germans from a section of eastern Poland then in Soviet hands, were moved into the western territories, following an agreement concluded by Germany with the Soviet Union. Similarly, sixty thousand Baltic Germans arrived in the harbors of Danzig, Stettin, and Swinemünde, awaiting resettlement in Poland.

To make room for the ethnic Germans, the Nazis deported masses of Polish Jews and other Poles to the General Government, leaving less space there for the many other Jews the Nazis intended to deport, including those from the Greater German Reich and Protectorate. The enormous problem of dealing with so many Jews, whether dead or alive, led Himmler and Heydrich by the end of 1939 and beginning of 1940 to consider the most radical means yet among the Nazis regarding the issue.

Murderous Ideas and Gassings of the Handicapped in Poland: Earliest Phase of the Holocaust?

RSHA office chiefs who met on 19 December 1939 titled the agenda for their conference the "Final Solution of the German Jewish Problem" (*Endlösung des deutschen Judenproblems*). The meeting examined the basic question of whether a Jewish "reservation" could be established in Poland, or whether something else should be done with the Jews. More specifically, the RSHA officials discussed carrying out in the General Government a massive "disposal" of the large numbers of Jews sent there.[7]

During the next days the meaning of the "disposal" option began to unfold. Heydrich, as part of his plans, moved it forward significantly. He appointed Eichmann head of a new special section for Jewish affairs in the RSHA and authorized him to coordinate Gestapo activities for all "deportations" and "evacuations" of populations. Himmler worked out his ideas on the matter with Heydrich and Oswald Pohl, the senior administrative and economic officer of the SS. Pohl supervised the large SS commercial and industrial enterprises that helped make the organization financially independent of both the Nazi party and German government.

With both Heydrich and Pohl, the Reichsführer SS raised the possibility of the mass extermination of the Jews by killing them in concentration camps with poison gas and burning their remains in crematoria. This idea, it should be recalled, was not new to Himmler. But he now resurrected the concept among his closest associates and in secrecy. Evidently he discussed it not as a total solution of the Jewish question, but as a means of removing large numbers of both Jews and Poles to help facilitate the massive planned project of Germanization.

Both Himmler and Heydrich, moreover, had been influenced by an actual program of mass murder that Hitler himself had authorized and the Nazi party and government had begun to implement. As this chapter will discuss later, the Nazis viewed this program too as connected directly to the war. The so-called euthanasia program involved the murder of tens of thousands of handicapped Germans whom the Nazis viewed as "life unworthy of life" racially and economically, by using primarily gas chambers and crematoria at specially selected killing installations. Himmler and Heydrich, as well as senior officials in the RSHA, studied the murders carefully and even assisted them. Heydrich consulted frequently with several SS doctors involved in the selections and gassings.

But even before the euthanasia murders had started in Germany, during late 1939 and the early months of 1940, along the borders of the Reich and the newly occupied Polish territories, the RSHA had practiced euthanasia by systematically killing the handicapped, some of them Jews. In part, the RSHA carried out the killings to free hospitals and asylums for use as transit camps for the ethnic Germans from Volhynia, Lithuania, the South Tyrol, and Southeastern Europe. In East and West Prussia, areas bordering on the annexed portions of Poland, SS firing squads executed several thousand handicapped patients and buried them in mass graves.

Thus, at least a full year, and possibly even more, before the Einsatzgruppen would begin shooting Jews in a systematic fashion during the summer of 1941 in the newly occupied areas of Soviet Russia, the Holocaust had its initial beginnings. The first Jews murdered by the Germans in a methodical way were those institutionalized as handicapped.

A special SS detachment (*Sonderkommando*), led by a young former Gestapo agent and commissar of detectives, Herbert Lange, carried out executions by using poison gas. The Lange detachment killed several thousand patients, including Jews, seized at hospitals in West Prussia, Pomerania, and the Warthegau in western Poland by piping carbon-monoxide gas into specially constructed airtight compartments inside motorized trucks or vans.

The detachment loaded forty patients into its gas van on each trip, killed the victims during the journey, buried their bodies in the countryside, and returned with the empty van approximately three hours later. Himmler apparently discussed such matters with Hitler. To conceal the killings the Nazis employed what had already become a consistent pattern: the use of euphemisms to explain what was happening. They described the gassing of the mental patients in Poland as "evacuation."

At approximately the same time, on 23 November 1939, Hitler met with his military commanders, a few of whom had failed to support the brutal anti-Semitic and anti-Polish actions of the Einsatzgruppen and police in Poland. He reminded them that the war was now no longer solely a military operation, but "a racial struggle." Noting the military's preparations for the attack soon in Western Europe, he observed that "[w]e can oppose Russia only when we are free in the West."[8]

Although neither Himmler nor Heydrich acted immediately on the idea of placing gas chambers and crematoria in concentration camps, the SS nevertheless began in the early months of 1940 selecting sites for new camps in the East. In January it investigated a former Polish military barracks near the town of Oswiecim, a few miles from Krakow in Upper Silesia. This region had been under Polish rule since 1918, but in the fall of 1939 it was incorporated into Germany after its occupation of western Poland.

The site, which the Germans renamed Auschwitz, seemed well suited for a camp. It had an isolated location; rail communications to Austria,

Czechoslovakia, and the General Government; availability of resources such as coal, lime, and salt; and potential for enlargement. The SS established a camp there in April and May 1940, using hundreds of local Poles and Jews as slave labor and thirty specially selected hard core German criminals from Sachsenhausen to act as overseers in the camp.

Farther north the SS constructed a concentration camp at Soldau in East Prussia, ostensibly to assist the resettlement of Poles, but in fact to use it for murdering many of them as well as other unwanted persons. There too the Lange detachment killed many of the victims in gas vans. In one large killing operation from 21 May–8 June 1940, 1,558 German and 400 Polish mentally handicapped patients from East Prussian hospitals were assembled at the Soldau camp and killed by Lange's unit.

Later, at the end of 1941, Lange's commando would perform the same work at Chelmno (Kulmhof), the first death camp established by the Germans, near Lodz. By the fall of 1941, the SS had murdered more than thirty thousand handicapped persons in western Poland and border regions including numerous Jews, in part to make room for Himmler's planned resettlement there of ethnic Germans.

Nazi Rivalries

Meanwhile, the mass deportations by the RSHA and SS of Polish Jews and other Poles to the General Government continued. Originally, the RSHA intended to deport all Jews and nearly half of the Poles in western Poland to the General Government. This would number more than five million persons, robbed of their economic means and impoverished, unloaded into a territory that already had twelve million inhabitants and was little larger in size than Bavaria and Baden-Württemberg combined.

The deportations angered Frank, the territory's governor. Although a vicious anti-Semite and German nationalist who did everything possible in "his" domain to destroy Jews living or transported there, he resented nevertheless the administrative difficulties and infringements on his authority caused him by the deportations. He opposed the dumping of millions of poor Jews, Poles, and Gypsies in the territory, driving down its standard of living, compounding its already chaotic economic conditions, and frustrating his ambitions to sole rule.

Living in luxury in the Krakow castle, "King Frank," as some fellow Nazis called him, pretended to be a cultured leader who entertained guests by playing Chopin's piano music. Along with Göring, Frank looted extensive Jewish and other art treasures in the General Government. One of the Nazis' primary objectives was to seize "Germanic" art that had found its way to Poland over the centuries and "repatriate" it back into German hands—which meant the highest level Nazi leaders stealing Polish art collections.

Frank and Göring jealously guarded their plundering in the General Government from Himmler, whose special SD detachment and later seizure units (*Erfassungs-kommandos*) looted art in the portions of Poland incorporated into the Reich. Göring, to assist Frank in seizing art treasures in Poland, appointed Kajetan Mühlmann, an Austrian SS officer, as his "special commissioner."

Also Frank appealed to Göring to halt the deportations to the General Government, a subject on which he carefully avoided even the appearance of opposing Hitler's wishes. Frank argued that orderly conditions, without further deportations, would enable the resources of the territory to contribute to the German war economy. Göring, still the powerful head of the Four-Year Plan and Air Force and named during 1939–1940 by Hitler as his successor and as *Reichsmarschall*, agreed with Frank.

During February and March 1940 Göring issued directives that, for the next nine months, greatly reduced deportations of Jews, Poles, Gypsies, and other alleged "undesirables" to the General Government. The bureaucratic struggle for power also ended the idea of establishing a Jewish "reservation" there. The decision to scale back the deportations resulted as well from the Wehrmacht's sporadic opposition to the atrocities associated with them.

Himmler, however, continued to insist that the SS and police control the fate of the Jews and the planned racial reordering of the populations in the occupied East. Hitler, although he allowed Göring to reduce the deportations to the General Government, nevertheless sided with Himmler. The SS, consequently, continued some deportations; during 12–13 February, it sent approximately a thousand Jews from Stettin to the concentration and labor camp complex at Lublin, primarily to seize the dwellings of the Jews in Stettin for ethnic Germans from the Baltic States that had arrived there.

Himmler, as Reich Commissioner for the Strengthening of Germandom, maintained charge of settling ethnic Germans in the annexed territories of western Poland. From such lands he sought to continue expelling Polish peasants eastward, primarily into the General Government. At the end of May 1940, the Reichsführer presented Hitler with a memo, in which he urged the preservation of the racially valuable Germanic inhabitants in the East and the physical destruction of the Poles. The latter, he proposed, could be achieved by eliminating all but the simplest primary education among the Poles. Himmler's view resulted not only from his extreme racist ideas, but also from his sense of what Hitler would likely consider and accept or desire.

The SS as well won its quarrel with the commander of the German armies in the East, General Johannes Blaskowitz, who opposed the atrocities committed by the Einsatzgruppen in Poland. When Blaskowitz failed to rouse for his view the support of Brauchitsch, Commander-in-Chief of the German army, and other leading military officers, Hitler replaced Blaskowitz in May 1940. Moreover, another sign of the military's diminishing influence vis-à-vis the SS was the latter's progressive expansion of its armed formations, the *Waffen-SS*. These formations were organized and equipped as regular military units and would fight alongside the Wehrmacht on most future battlefronts, beginning with the conquest of the Netherlands in April 1940.

The Ghettos

The virtual ending of deportations of Polish Jews to the General Government, and therefore also solving the Jewish question by establishing a massive Jewish "reservation" there, accelerated the SS policy of reviving medieval ghettos in Poland. The SS used the ghettos for a variety of brutal purposes: as reservoirs of slave labor for the German war effort, as places for the further killing of Jews through starvation and neglect, and eventually as staging areas from which the masses of Polish Jews could be deported to the General Government or elsewhere. Also some officials in the RSHA viewed forcing Jews into specially confined areas, or ghettos, of Polish cities as a means of providing space for the resettlement of ethnic Germans in Poland.

Heydrich, in his first order to the Einsatzgruppen in Poland on 21 September 1939 had mentioned the necessity for ghettoization. The Germans established the first ghetto in April and May 1940 in Lodz, the second largest city in Poland; the ghetto held 160,000 persons. Soon ghettos spread to the General Government. The largest, in Warsaw, was created in October 1940 and initially had 445,000 inhabitants; only a few months before, a Polish mob had destroyed many houses in the city's Jewish quarter in a three-day pogrom-like attack. Other ghettos were formed in Krakow in March 1941, in Lublin and Radom in April, and in Lwów (Lemberg) in December. The Germans constructed several hundred more ghettos in smaller towns. Later, the German invasion of the Soviet Union in the summer of 1941 would lead to the formation of ghettos in the Baltic States and other portions of western Russia.

The Germans created ghettos by fencing or walling off portions of prewar Jewish neighborhoods; in Warsaw and other cities, the Germans forced the Jews to pay for the construction of the walls. Nazi control of the ghettos made them into frighteningly overcrowded, starving, disease-ridden, and death-filled slums. For the inhabitants who left the ghetto without permission, Nazi officials decreed the death penalty and enforced it savagely.

Control of Polish ghettos produced bitter struggles among the SS and German police and local German civilian officials; gradually the SS and police emerged victorious, but "their prize," Raul Hilberg concluded, "was a heap of corpses."[9] Order Police often guarded the ghettos, such as Reserve Police Battalion 101 did in Lodz between November 1940 and May 1941.

To administer the ghettos for them and attempt to force the Jews to participate in their own destruction, the Germans exploited the prewar traditional organization of Jewish communities, which had centered in the *kehillah*, or community councils. Generally the kehillah had dealt with charities and communal affairs. The Germans ordered each ghetto to establish a so-called *Judenrat* (Jewish council), comprised of prewar elders and rabbis in the local Jewish community.

The Jewish councils essentially performed, under the absolute and brutal subjugation to German authority, the functions of a city administration; the Judenrat chairman became, de facto, a mayor. Eventually the Judenräte developed administrative staffs or bureaucracies whose officials served as ghetto police (*Ordnungsdienst*), conscripted forced or slave labor for the Germans, and cared for issues of housing, health, welfare, registration, and finances in the ghetto. The council functionaries, Hilberg concluded, "were paid and unpaid, capable and incompetent, honest and self-serving. Patronage, favoritism, and outright corruption became inviting possibilities and soon enough were commonplace."[10]

The ghettos provided the Germans with a crucial mechanism to assist them in their various stages of initially controlling and then destroying the

Polish Jews. To begin with, the ghettos sealed off or isolated completely the Jews from the rest of society. Also they contributed to the further impoverishment of their inhabitants; the latter had been forced violently into the ghettos, nearly always stripped of their worldly possessions. Without significant capital or valuables, most were rendered helpless. Slave labor factories in numerous ghettos produced war materiel for the Germans, but offered the workers little in return, except exhaustion and death from overwork.

Moreover, the Germans delivered to the ghettos far less than the bare minimum of food, coal, and soap. In the huge Warsaw ghetto, for example, the people received an official food allowance of only 184 calories per person per day, a starvation diet that was slightly more than one-quarter received by the Poles outside the ghetto. Also most buildings in the ghetto had no heat. Persons unable to acquire food or other necessities on the flourishing black market trade with the rest of Warsaw, either because they had no resources or because they could not work, did not survive long.

Generally, the inhuman conditions in the Warsaw ghetto paralleled those of the other ghettos. The greatest tragedy for ghetto inhabitants was that thousands of them died daily, victims of the horrific conditions in which they had to exist, which produced starvation and deadly diseases such as typhus and influenza. Although some sought release from their pain and hopelessness in suicide, many fought for life with their last ounce of strength, even begging food or snatching it from others.

But usually they too died when, after sustained undernourishment, they could no longer digest food normally. The heart, kidneys, liver, and spleen shrank in size, weight dropped, and skin shriveled. A ghetto physician wrote:

> Active, busy, energetic people are changed into apathetic, sleepy beings, always in bed, hardly able to get up to eat or go to the toilet. Passage from life to death is slow and gradual, like death from physical old age. . . . People fall asleep in bed or on the street and are dead in the morning. They die during physical effort, such as searching for food, and sometimes even with a piece of bread in their hands."[11]

One commonly saw corpses lying on the sidewalk or street, covered with newspapers, pending the arrival of cemetery carts. In January 1941, 898 died in the Warsaw ghetto alone; during January 1942, the figure had exploded to 5,123. The ghettos, therefore, marked a significant stage in the Nazis' intended destruction of the Polish Jews; nearly one-fifth of the victims died from starvation and disease, most of them in the ghettos and labor camps.

The Jews responded to the horrors they faced as best they could. Many reacted passively. In some instances, the instinct to remain alive triumphed over the will to resist. Some ghetto inhabitants took the last crumbs of bread or other tiny morsels of food from families or friends, leaving the latter to starve or die. The SS purposely created in the ghettos, and later in the death camps, situations that forced many of the victims to participate in their own destruction. Unarmed and peaceful, badly deprived of food and nourishment, undefended by other peoples around them, those imprisoned in the ghettos found themselves utterly helpless.

Some historians have claimed that Jewish history, based on nearly two thousand years of survival of exile and persecution, betrayed many ghetto Jews into believing they could save at least a portion of their communities by cooperating with or appeasing and accommodating their oppressors. But extensive research since the 1970s and 1980s into Jewish sources, including ghetto diaries, publications, postwar accounts by survivors, and even German reports, has shown that the Jews did not, as some critics once claimed, solely "go to their deaths like lambs to the slaughter."

Most of those imprisoned behind the ghetto walls had little knowledge of, and no way of knowing, the final outcome of their fate. As discussed in later chapters, only during the last half of 1942 would word begin to spread among inhabitants of ghettos in Poland near the Nazi death camps that death awaited them and that the possibility of survival was gone. Small resistance organizations inside some ghettos, many of which formed during 1940–1941, planned and even attempted revolts against the Germans.

Meanwhile, many ghetto dwellers exerted vast amounts of energy, both openly and secretly, in assisting one another and in communal welfare. This included establishing soup kitchens, hospitals, and schools; distributing clothing; subsidizing housing; and organizing cultural activities of all kinds. To help themselves survive, such persons engaged in clandestine activities, particularly smuggling that usually involved Polish partners outside the ghetto and deadly risks if caught by the Nazis or Jewish police. Only a few ghetto Jews had advantages that could help protect them, at least for a time, because of their status, most likely earned before ghettoization, as members of the Jewish ghetto administration, or because they had a special skill or occupation (e.g., craftsmen and artisans).

But most ghetto inhabitants suffered severely and faced a daily struggle to survive. They usually had a long day of hard work to make ends meet and often would have to endure beatings from the Germans or Jewish police. Still other Jews were too unskilled or physically weak to be absorbed into the ghetto economy; they lived shrinking lives that eventually ended in destitution, starvation, disease, and frequently death.

Especially the Judenräte illustrated the variety of Jewish responses as well as the terrible dilemmas faced by the Jews in the ghettos. The Germans forced the Jews to establish the councils, someone had to serve on them, and the councils had to provide services for the Germans. In the Warsaw ghetto, the Gestapo took Adam Czerniakow, a chemical engineer by profession and prewar chairman of the local Jewish community, to the headquarters of the local Einsatzgruppe and ordered him to form a Judenrat. While the councils made desperate efforts to lessen the suffering and stop the mass death in the ghettos, they also followed German orders and forced the ghetto inhabitants to obey.

In this regard the Jews most widely detested the Jewish ghetto police because of their frequent role in cooperating with the Germans in delivering ghetto inhabitants for slave labor or, beginning in 1942, for deportation to the death camps. The police became in many ghettos units of traitors, collaborators of the Germans. But in at least fourteen ghettos the police would participate in the Jewish resistance.

The reasons for joining the police were obvious: hope for food and exemption from deportation and expectation of status. Yet members of the Jewish police often suffered themselves from brutal forms of extortion and blackmail by the Germans to persuade them to take part in the labor conscription and later deportations. If they did not do so, they were warned, their families would suffer the same fate. This German use of the tactic of collective responsibility—punishing an entire family, group, or community for the act of one individual—played a prominent role in how the Germans exercised control over the ghettos.

A similar dilemma confronted the heads of the Judenräte. Some historians have viewed Czerniakow, chairman of the council in the Warsaw ghetto, as merely a tool of the Germans, constantly intervening and negotiating with them, but with little success, to obtain concessions for the ghetto. Others see him as a valiant leader who, until his suicide in July 1942, when confronted with the Germans' demands to deliver deportees, struggled by using various means to maintain Jewish communal existence. He continually exploited differences among the Germans to help him buy time, as well as what he believed was protection, for the ghetto.

Another ghetto chairman, Chaim Rumkowski in Lodz, ruled as a dictator and believed he governed a Jewish state. He thought erroneously that he alone could save a portion of the people by bargaining with the Germans to save lives in exchange for supplying Jewish labor. The people called Rumkowski "King Chaim." Tall, blue eyed, silver haired, and clean shaven, he was in his sixties, had little education, and had been a marginal business-man before and after World War I.

The flamboyant Rumkowski rode about the ghetto in a horse-drawn carriage, had his portrait placed on banknotes, and often made speeches that contained phrases such as "my Jews," "my children," and "my factories." When the Germans began seizing Jews off the streets in Lodz for forced labor soon after the invasion of Poland, Rumkowski was noteworthy among the Jewish leaders who proposed for the sake of peace to deliver daily quotas of Jews to the invaders. Unclear is whether this signaled to the Germans that he could be counted on to continue delivering Jews on command or that this may have been what he intended for them to understand.

Regarding the Judenrat leaders the historian Michael Marrus has written: "Opinion on these leaders differs, even today. To some the outstanding fact about such Judenrat chiefs is their arrogant, single-minded, ruthless style of rule." But such leaders also had a different vantage point: "Attacked from every quarter at once, increasingly isolated at the top, facing impossible demands, they often felt that they were the only hope for a squabbling, bitterly divided Jewish community."[12] Occasionally Judenräte clashed with ghetto resistance organizations, but usually only if the groups' activities were learned of by the Germans and they threatened reprisals against the ghetto.

As for the Nazi leadership, many of its members ridiculed the ghettos and those inside desperately struggling to stay alive. Nazi propaganda, wholly ignoring the horrors the Germans inflicted on the ghettos and their inhabitants, used the latter to defame the Jews of Eastern Europe and buttress the prejudices of many Germans against Jews in general. The Nazi leisure organization, Strength through Joy (*Kraft durch Freude*), organized bus tours of Germans to the Warsaw ghetto. When the buses took German soldiers through the streets, the passengers acted like it was a visit to the zoo to see the animals. They laughed at the emaciated and suffering ghetto dwellers, and often lashed out at them with long whips.

At the ghetto cemetery the visitors interrupted funerals and forced the families of the dead and the rabbis to pose for photographs. One visitor, Alfred Rosenberg, head of the Nazi party's Foreign Policy Office (*Aussenpolitisches Amt*) and a longtime associate of Hitler's, reported to the German government's press office that the ghettos "cannot represent the final solution of the Jewish question . . . . If there are any people left who still somehow have sympathy with the Jews then they ought to be recommended to have a look at such a ghetto."[13]

Soviet Complicity in Nazi Policy in Poland

Once war broke out in September 1939, and Germany and the Soviet Union conquered Poland and divided it among them, the Soviet regime was drawn quickly into collaboration with the German persecution of Polish and other Jews. In addition, the Soviets would persecute and kill large numbers of Poles, including massacring and burying in earthen pits fifteen thousand captured Polish officers in the Katyn forest near Smolensk. A long history of anti-Semitism had existed in Russia, especially in the Ukraine and the Baltic States, where many of the approximately five million Jews of the country lived. Before World War I, hundreds of thousands of Russian Jews had emigrated to Central Europe or America to flee the tsarist government-sponsored pogroms.

The Soviet regime had never made anti-Semitism an official policy, but once Stalin had taken over in the Kremlin the Jewish population and its leaders faced an uncertain future. For a time during the 1920s, Soviet authorities had considered establishing a homeland in the Crimea for the Soviet Jews, and thousands of the latter had left the Ukraine and Byelorussia, the old Pale of Settlement, for the Crimean steppe. Stalin, however, changed the plan in the 1930s. He decided to resettle the Jews in the Soviet Far East, in a desolate area along the border with Japanese-held Manchuria. Although some Jews moved across Siberia to the so-called Jewish Autonomous Region, the latter proved, in the words of a British historian, "a failed experiment in Soviet apartheid."[14]

During Stalin's terror purges of the 1930s, Jews figured prominently as victims. Although the Kremlin never gave anti-Semitism as a reason for the persecution of Jews in the senior ranks of the Communist party and government, such persons and their families nevertheless suffered significantly. Most were arrested, imprisoned, and murdered, based on trumped up charges of spying for the West or having contact with "Zionist circles." The unstable international situation in May 1939 helped avert possibly the worst persecution of Jewish leaders in Russia. This was the Stalin regime's planned purge of the former Soviet Foreign Minister, the pro-Western Maxim Litvinov, and his staff in the Foreign Affairs Commissariat.

Despite such treatment of Jews in the Soviet Union, when the combined German–Soviet attack on Poland began in September, thousands of Polish and German Jews fled to the Soviet side of the new German–Soviet border. Stalin, however, whom Nikita Khrushchev would later call "a dyed-in-the-wool anti-Semite," feared Germany and believed that the best way to avert war from Russia was to collaborate with the Nazis both economically and politically.[15] The Red Army turned many of the Jewish refugees back to the German-held territory, where German mobile killing units would shoot the helpless victims.

Moreover, the Soviet government rounded up and shipped back to Germany German Jews who had fled to Russia during the 1930s. There nearly all were imprisoned and soon murdered. Stalin's regime exiled still other Jewish refugees from German occupation to Siberia or Central Asia or threw them into prison or labor camps. Only when Germany invaded the Soviet Union in June 1941 would Stalin release the Jews.

In Soviet-occupied Eastern Poland, where Jews had already suffered from discrimination by the Poles, the new rulers launched a widespread attack that quickly destroyed the communities of small-town—*shtetl*—Jews and the traditions of Jewish life. Approximately one million Jews lived in the Soviet zone. The Soviets arrested and deported Jewish leaders; closed down Jewish organizations and youth groups; and boarded up synagogues and used them for stables or warehouses.

Marxist hostility to religion and class distinctions led to special attacks on the wealthier and more cultured Jewish elements. Jewish slaughterhouses closed down. The public practices of circumcision and bar mitzvah were prohibited. Also the Russians abolished the Sabbath as an official holy day, along with Jewish holidays and festivals. The livelihood of small town Jewish artisans, their shops and market stalls, was also destroyed.

Only after Germany invaded the Soviet Union did Stalin order a reversal of official policy toward the Jews. He released numerous imprisoned Jews and attempted to rally Jewish support for the hard-pressed Soviet military. Over a million Jews responded by joining and fighting in the Red Army. But chapter 8 will show how Stalin and his regime would do little or nothing to protect the several million Soviet Jews from slaughter, or near, so by the German forces advancing into western Russia.

Frequently, local Soviet populations, primarily in Crimea, Ukraine, and the Baltic States, would assist the Germans by carrying out pogroms, in which Jews were killed and their property seized. Local peoples flooded the Einsatzgruppen, the mobile killing units that entered Russia to murder all Jews, with denunciations of Jews, Communists, or other undesirables. As a consequence, most Soviet Jews who died at the hands of the German occupiers were murdered in the orgy of killing in the first nine months of the occupation.

"Euthanasia": Precursor to the Holocaust

Himmler's idea about the use of poison gas and crematoria against German racial enemies should be seen in relation to a second principal factor discussed in this chapter, which also illustrated the special racial character of the war in the view of top German leaders. This was Hitler's secret written order of October 1939 establishing a program that the Germans called euphemistically "euthanasia," or mercy killing.

Hitler backdated the document to 1 September 1939. He did so in part to mislead the German public or others if the document ever became known, and in part because that was the way he and those who administered the program envisioned it—as connected to the beginning of what they saw as essentially a racial war. Furthermore, it is possible that Hitler decided to begin the systematic killing of certain racial groups first with the handicapped, rather than with the group he most hated, the Jews, because of the generally negative reaction of the German public to the Kristallnacht a year earlier.

Euthanasia was in fact an operation of systematic mass murder. The Nazi party and government bureaucracies, German medical personnel, and SS carried out the operation against groups among their own German people whom the murderers viewed as "life unworthy of life" (*lebensunwertes Leben*) racially and economically. Particularly singled out for killing were mentally and physically handicapped persons, whom the killers viewed as biologically degenerate animals, economically nonproductive, and "useless eaters."

From its beginnings the Nazi regime had applied a series of racialist measures to the German people. In July 1933 the government had decreed compulsory sterilization for Germans allegedly afflicted with hereditary diseases. In addition, it had encouraged early marriage and numerous children among healthy Aryans. Both before and during Nazi rule, German eugenicists (including anthropologists, geneticists, and psychiatrists), so-called racial hygienists, physicians, and völkisch theorists had urged that Germany refuse to care for its incurably ill and allegedly inferior races and ethnic groups.

In 1935 Hitler told Gerhard Wagner, the Reich physician leader, that once war began he would implement compulsory euthanasia. Even before World War II, however, Hitler had authorized his private chancellery (*Kanzlei des Führers*, KdF), a Nazi party agency in Berlin headed by longtime party activist Philipp Bouhler, and the Führer's personal physician, Karl Brandt, to institute a program of killing children suffering from physical or mental handicaps. The Nazis considered healthy children especially crucial for the future of the racial community, or Volksgemeinschaft.

They claimed, therefore, that if the alleged racial and eugenic purity of the community was to succeed, children viewed as diseased or deformed had to be eliminated. An incident in 1938 provided the immediate pretext for Hitler to start the euthanasia program that he had previously intended. A German family named Knauer that had a newly born infant with severe handicaps appealed to Hitler through the KdF to grant permission to have the child killed. He gave his consent, and the child was murdered.

Of Hitler's four chancelleries—which included the Nazi party chancellery in Munich and the government's presidential chancellery and Reich chancellery in Berlin—the KdF was relatively small and the most hidden from public view. Its bureaucrats could therefore direct the killings without involving too many people and without becoming too visible. Hitler did not wish to risk public disapproval of the euthanasia program directed at either the government or party before the program had achieved a certain level of support.

Clearly he feared that the public would not approve of such killings and that they might spark popular unrest against his regime. According to Henry Friedlander, in his carefully researched account of the program, Hitler decided to go ahead with euthanasia "because he intuitively felt that he could do it, make it stick, and get away with it. This may not be surprising, but it is startling that the entire party, government, military, and professional elite accepted such a radical, irrational decision."[16]

From the beginning, therefore, the KdF kept the planning and implementation of euthanasia secret. But this became especially difficult when, during the summer of 1939, Hitler also initiated the policy of killing mentally and physically handicapped adults. This project involved far larger numbers of victims than did the children's euthanasia.

Hitler placed the adult euthanasia also under the direction of the KdF, Bouhler, and Brandt. As planning for it unfolded, however, the KdF faced a major problem, namely, convincing the larger number of cooperating professionals, primarily physicians, that they would not be prosecuted for killing patients. Hitler had consistently resisted the promulgation, and thus publication, of a law authorizing the killings, particularly in wartime.

As a result, the KdF functionaries, to convince their collaborators, and possibly to protect themselves as well, asked the Führer for a written directive. In October he signed a document prepared by the KdF, authorizing the killing of handicapped patients, but predated it to 1 September, the day he began the war. Although almost everyone accepted Hitler's word as law, the authorization did not actually have the force of law. The document served, however, as the legal basis for the ensuing vast euthanasia killing operation and persuaded numerous German physicians and civil servants to collaborate in it.

To help hide the KdF's role in the adult-killing operation the chancellery created an umbrella organization to serve as a front. Bouhler appointed Viktor Brack, his chief of staff who had longtime connections to Himmler and the SS, to run the program. Brack eventually established a central office in Berlin, in a confiscated Jewish villa at number 4 Tiergarten Straße; because of this address, adult euthanasia soon received the name "Operation T4," or simply T4. Also the KdF created numerous other front organizations to protect the identity of the various T4 offices involved in the program. For the same reason, officials in the chancellery used code names when working on T4 matters.

An unusually small number of men managed T4; they included approximately fifteen business and office clerks, accountants, and personnel, transport, and finance officials. They were a relatively young and unexceptional group, few had professional degrees, and most had worked in business after high school. Almost all had joined the Nazi movement before Hitler's rise to power, and several belonged to the SA or SS.

A variety of factors generally determined their recruitment, including their loyalty to the party and those who signed them on as well as their willingness to collaborate in a killing enterprise. Apparently none of the T4 managers refused to join the KdF's operation; all knew fully what was happening, they visited the places where killings occurred, and they watched the procedure.

They agreed to manage mass murder for a variety of reasons. The work in the KdF advanced their careers, placed them near the center of power, gave them material benefits, and provided them with a secure job on the home front away from the dangers of fighting in the war. In addition, the T4 killers accepted the eugenic and racial ideology of the National Socialists, which viewed the handicapped as inferior and the Jews and other non-Germans similarly.

Recruitment of a medical staff for T4, except for hiring a limited number of physicians already involved in children's euthanasia, was done almost randomly. As the key psychiatrist for adult euthanasia, Bouhler hired the only suitable one he knew, Werner Heyde, an SS officer and professor and senior physician at the University of Würzburg. For evaluating and deciding the fate of the handicapped adults, whether they would live or die, T4 recruited groups of so-called senior and junior medical experts.

By far the largest group, the junior experts, numbered approximately forty physicians that included nine university professors of medicine. Most were hired through a network of personal contacts and recommendations as well as information from local Nazi party offices concerning the person's ideological reliability. All of the physicians received the option to refuse to participate in the operation, but very few did. Senior physicians had the same motivation as the managers, while the junior ones were primarily murderers with medical degrees.

Operation T4, with the assistance of the Reich Ministry of Interior, the medical profession, and SS, developed an elaborate system for identifying mental patients, epileptics, and the feebleminded, shipping them to places designed and equipped for murdering them, killing those so identified and shipped, and then disposing of the bodies. To murder the large number of handicapped adults, the T4 bureaucrats and physicians had to devise a method different from the cumbersome and slow acting medications used to kill the relatively fewer children.

Brandt, following discussions with the physicians about the use of poison gas, met with Hitler. They talked about the various killing methods, and then quickly agreed on using gas. Brandt, Bouhler, Brack, and state secretary for health in the Interior Ministry, Dr. Leonardo Conti, observed the first successful gassing of victims in a sealed chamber at an old jail building in Brandenburg/Havel near Berlin.

Beginning during the winter of 1939–1940, thousands of Germans were taken from hospitals, mental institutions, and old peoples' homes and transferred to six institutions that can only be called murder factories. These killing centers systematically killed the patients and then burned their remains; they represented an unprecedented institution of the type that would eventually symbolize Nazi Germany. The Nazis would transfer these techniques of mass killing to the later death camps that helped produce the Holocaust.

T4 located the euthanasia killing centers in the old jail at Brandenburg and in hospitals at Grafeneck (Württemberg), Hartheim (Austria), Sonnenstein (Saxony), Bernburg/Saale (Prussian province of Saxony), and Hadamar (Hessen). Each center had a chamber, camouflaged as a shower, into which SS and other engineers piped carbon monoxide gas, and a crematorium to burn the victims' bodies. To perform the killings, T4 hired a number of younger and ambitious physicians who had not yet received their medical certification as well as rank-and-file staff, who did routine or physical labor.

Many persons selected for killing were not mentally or physically handicapped, but rather the blind, the deaf and mute, the epileptic, and the feebleminded. A majority of those killed, in fact, were orderly and conscious, often suspected their fate, and had to be coerced before they entered the large gray buses, disguised as coffee delivery vehicles, used to transfer them from hospitals or other institutions to the killing centers. Although most of the victims were able to know fully and object to their fate, obviously no one asked if they wished to die; nor did anyone ask their families and legal guardians for permission to kill them.

Instead, T4 attempted to hide the murders from both the families and the public by erecting an elaborate system of deceptions in transporting the victims, in the paperwork tracking their fate, and in the killings themselves. The selection of many more persons beyond the handicapped reflected in part the desire of T4 managers and physicians to create work for themselves. They had a keen interest in retaining their jobs and benefits at the home front and thereby avoiding service in the war.

Gas chambers usually held from twenty to seventy-five patients who, according to eyewitnesses to the gassings, died painful deaths over a period of five to ten minutes. Staff members then dragged the bodies from the chambers and, before burning them, looted and mutilated the corpses for dental work containing gold. Moreover, the young physicians at the killing centers, as well as at scientific institutes in Germany, exploited the euthanasia victims for purposes of alleged medical "research," by performing autopsies and removing organs. As the final step in the destruction process, the centers sent families or guardians fraudulent death certificates, listing death from "natural" causes.

The killers, however, could not keep euthanasia secret. Quickly family members became suspicious, particularly when some received more than one death certificate containing conflicting causes for the death of their loved one. By mid-1940 rumors had spread among the German population, including children, about the mysterious events in certain mental hospitals. In at least one instance, the town near the Brandenburg killing center apparently noticed the crematorium and its smell, which possibly contributed to the closing of the center in September.

By year's end local hostility to euthanasia had led Himmler to suggest closing Grafeneck, which subsequently happened. Also the killings provoked widespread opposition among the German public. Several hospitals and other institutions refused to surrender their patients for murder; at times near riots occurred when T4 buses arrived to take patients for what many suspected was certain death.

Some in the Christian churches began to protest the killings, although not until public knowledge of them had spread widely. About six months after the killings had started, Theophil Wurm, the Protestant bishop of Württemberg, protested in writing to Wilhelm Frick, the Reich Interior Minister, and asked: "Does the Führer know, does he approve?"[17] Several other clergy, including the directors of Protestant hospitals and welfare organizations, Paul Gerhard Braune and Friedrich von Bodelschwingh, spoke to government officials to request their help in ending euthanasia.

In Berlin, the Catholic priest, Bernhard Lichtenberg, criticized the government in writing; during October 1941 he was arrested, tried, and sentenced to two years in prison. In 1943 he would die while on his way to the Dachau concentration camp. Lichtenberg's fate, however, also resulted because he protested publicly the persecution of the Jews.

The Catholic Church hierarchy objected as well to the killings, and did so with the backing of the Vatican. But similar to the Protestants, public knowledge of the killings had become widespread before the Fulda Conference of Bishops, the senior body in the German church, lodged a formal complaint with the Nazi government. Moreover, the church attempted to gain a compromise with, and special favors from, the government. In the latter regard, the church sought to have priests excluded from the euthanasia program and to gain the right to provide sacraments for the persons selected to die. Had such measures been implemented, they would have suggested that the church approved of the killings. The Vatican, however, intervened on 2 December 1940 and issued a blunt statement: "The direct killing of an innocent person because of mental or physical defects is not allowed."[18]

Individual bishops in Germany, however, denounced euthanasia, including Cardinal Faulhaber of Munich, Antonius Hilfrich of Limburg, and Wilhelm Berning of Osnabrück. The protest of the bishop of Münster, Clemens August Count von Galen, received the greatest notoriety. Although he had learned of the killings over a year before, he delivered on 3 August 1941 a public and passionate sermon denouncing euthanasia.

Emphasizing its illegality and God's commandment "Thou shalt not kill," von Galen warned parishoners: "If you establish and apply the principle that you can kill 'unproductive' fellow human beings then woe betide us all when we become old and frail!" Clearly reflecting something he feared or had heard the government might be contemplating, he raised the specter that wounded German soldiers could be killed.

On 24 August Hitler ordered a temporary halt to the gassings at the killing centers. He probably acted less from the church opposition than from the far-reaching public knowledge about the killings and growing opposition to their illegality from some in the German judiciary. Also by then even neutral countries as well as the nations fighting against Germany knew of the "secret" of euthanasia.

Further, Hitler doubtless acted because by late August 1941 the German invasion of the Soviet Union had begun and was not going as smoothly or quickly as he had expected. The Germans were suffering much larger casualties in Russia than anticipated. In issuing his directive, Hitler wished to maintain morale at the front by removing any impression that the German government would kill (i.e., euthanize) its own severely wounded soldiers rather than care for them. This was done by temporarily stopping the most noticeable aspect of the program in Germany to kill the handicapped.

Estimates of the numbers of persons killed in the euthanasia program between 1939 and the fall of 1941, some based on recently discovered hospital records and former East German secret police files, vary widely, but most certainly exceeded seventy thousand. At Hadamar, for example, the staff held a special party to celebrate the cremation of the ten thousandth body at the killing center.

Hitler's stop order, however, represented only a tactical retreat. He decided to defer a portion of the euthanasia program until after the war when, he expected, a German victory would allow persons such as the Catholic bishops and other clergymen to be included in the killings. Despite the stop order, the killing of German infants and elderly cripples in hospitals continued. In fact, more Germans were killed after Hitler's directive than before.

Furthermore, Bouhler and Himmler shifted the focus of the program to killing concentration camp prisoners in Germany and in the occupied Polish territories, including handicapped inmates and others who were sick and allegedly incapable of work. Prisoners taken from the camps and killed also included Jews who were neither mentally nor physically handicapped but who were selected solely because they were Jews. In the occupied territories, euthanasia killings would continue to the war's end.

The Germans code-named this operation 14 f 13, in which 13 referred to the "special treatment" (*Sonderbehandlung*) of sick and frail prisoners. As noted previously in this chapter, the SS had collaborated in the euthanasia program from its beginning and, after 1941, provided the victims from the camps for the 14 f 13 program. On 27 April 1943 Himmler restricted the program to mentally ill prisoners, because the SS and German war economy needed to maintain the concentration camp labor force. By 1944 the Germans practiced yet another related project, "wild euthanasia," in which they murdered mental patients in hospitals throughout Germany by deliberate starvation and lethal injections or overdoses of medicine.

Also by the fall of 1941 the German government and Operation T4 made a concerted effort to gain the approval of the German population for the regime's planned future euthanasia killings. The Propaganda Ministry and T4 produced a mass of propaganda, including the production of the successful propaganda entertainment film, *Ich klage an* (*I Accuse*). This film and other forms of propaganda favoring euthanasia—focusing on "mercy deaths" that actually had no relation to the killing program—had some influence, although they did not reverse popular opposition. A small minority of Germans, for reasons ranging from selfish or materialistic motives to beliefs in Nazi racial ideology, wanted their handicapped relatives killed and so requested it.

The euthanasia program was significant in at least three ways. First, it provoked widespread criticism and opposition from the German people. Unfortunately, the same people failed to respond similarly to their government's massive killings underway during late 1939 and 1940 of non-Germans, particularly Polish Jews and Poles. Reports of such killings had filtered into Germany from their beginning, mainly from some German troops in Poland telling their families and friends back home. Second, the difficulty caused for Hitler by opposition inside Germany to the euthanasia killings may explain why he apparently did not authorize the Final Solution of the Jewish question in a written order.

Third, through the euthanasia program the Nazi regime developed a solid core of experts, as volunteers or willing participants, in day-to-day bureaucratic mass murder. Soon such individuals would find other employment; many of them, along with the killing techniques they developed, would be transferred to the former Poland, to assist in the murder of far more Jews and Slavs in the death camps.

According to Friedlander, the euthanasia killings "were Nazi Germany's first organized mass murder, in which the killers developed their killing technique. . . . The killers who learned their trade in the euthanasia killing centers of Brandenburg, Grafeneck, Hartheim, Sonnenstein, Bernburg, and Hadamar also staffed the killing centers at Belzec, Sobibor, and Treblinka."[19]

CHAPTER SEVEN

EXPANDING THE
RACIAL WAR, 1940

T HE PROTESTANT BISHOP'S query of the Nazi government about
euthanasia, "Does the Führer know, does he approve?" illustrated the
continued popularity of Hitler among the German population during the initial German victories in the war. Although Germans had entered
the war with a somber mood and reluctance that contrasted sharply with the
enthusiasm with which they had greeted war in 1914, this soon changed.

Germany's destruction of Poland and subsequent conquest in the spring
of 1940 of Denmark, Norway, the Low Countries, and particularly France
produced even greater admiration among most Germans for Hitler. In this
regard, he stood at the zenith of his political career. Germany's brutal racial
policies in Poland added to his popularity. Before the war Nazi propaganda
had reinforced German hatred for the Poles by depicting a diabolical
Poland, allegedly committing atrocities against its approximately one million ethnic Germans.

According to SD reports on public opinion, many Germans reacted to
executions of Polish Jews and Poles, as reported by German soldiers on leave,
by saying that it was "only fair and just that murderers of ethnic Germans had
been shot just like the guerrillas."[1] Also Germans viewed stories of atrocities
committed in Poland by German soldiers as the same enemy propaganda—
whose claims had been substantially true, however—put forth in World War
I about German atrocities in Belgium. In Bavaria, during the initial months
of the war, little mention of the Jewish question occurred in the opinion
reports of Nazi authorities.

Conquests in Northern and
Western Europe and Jewish Persecution

Another example of how much Hitler and other Germans in charge of the war in late 1939 and 1940 viewed it essentially as a racial struggle—as they did with euthanasia and the conquest of Poland—involved Germany's military conquest of much of Northern and Western Europe. Hitler attacked in the West in the spring of 1940, as he had told Carl Burckhardt earlier, so as to protect Germany's flank when he sent its armed forces east. There he would wage a gigantic racial war against the alleged Jewish-Bolshevist and Slavic subhumanity of Russia.

In the newly conquered countries of Northern and Western Europe, the Germans based much of how they treated each country's relatively small Jewish population on several factors. First, the conquerors attempted, with the least expenditure of effort and resources, to administer, exploit, and loot each country to provide for Hitler's intended expansion of the war in the East. This left the countries with differing degrees of independence from German occupation or other forms of control, which almost always influenced the treatment of local Jews.

Second, the National Socialists appeared concerned for public opinion in the West regarding the Jewish question and for what they perceived was the influence of international Jewry in the West. In contrast to the widespread, chaotic, and random massacres of Polish Jews and Poles in the East, the Germans, at least initially, treated the Jews and native peoples in Northern and Western Europe differently.

There, during the first year and a half of German occupation, the Nazis attempted primarily to imitate the anti-Jewish measures they had implemented by 1939 in the Reich, but at a swifter pace. Before the invasion began in the West, the German leadership decided that its forces occupying Belgium and Holland would have to act according to the dictates of international law and refrain from violence and pillage so as to avoid creating the impression that Germany intended to annex both countries. Regarding the racial issue, the OKW directed its forces on 22 February 1940 that "no initiative should be taken. . . . One must not support special actions against an inhabitant *solely* because he is a Jew."[2] Plundering Jews in the West and implementing other harsh measures against them would proceed in relation to the victory in the war that the National Socialists expected.

A third factor also influenced the German treatment of the Jews in nearly every occupied country of Northern and Western Europe. In each the Germans found much smaller Jewish communities than those in Eastern Europe. Also the Jews in Northern and Western Europe had enjoyed equal civil and political rights for over a century, and they identified with their native states as full citizens. Moreover, in each of the occupied countries there lived German, Austrian, or other Jews who had previously fled Nazi persecution. As a result, at least in some instances the Nazis found significant numbers among the native peoples sympathetic to the Jews, which made it much less easy implementing anti-Jewish measures than in the East.

Denmark

During April and early May 1940, the Germans attacked and conquered Denmark and Norway. Denmark formed an unusual case, regarding both the German administration of the country and treatment of its approximately ten thousand Jews. Germany's use of Denmark in the war dictated the Reich's policies toward both issues. German forces overpowered Denmark so quickly that neither the Danish government nor king offered any resistance or had the opportunity to escape.

The Danish government, a parliamentary monarchy, cooperated fully with the Germans. This meant that Germany found exploiting Denmark easier by leaving most of its political administration intact and merely supervising it rather than by controlling the country directly. A temporary agreement with the Danes gave the occupiers considerable advantages, including important military bases on the Baltic and North Sea coasts and large quantities of food. In return, at least for the present, the Germans left most of the Danish Jews alone; also the Copenhagen government defended the rights of its Jewish citizens.

Even though by 1942, and most probably earlier, Berlin had decided to seize the Danish Jews and deport and murder them, this plan would not be assured of success. As long as the Danish government had principal authority over local political affairs, the Germans would experience difficulty capturing the country's Jews without expending substantial effort to do so and to overcome Danish resistance. In fact, as discussed in chapter thirteen, such resistance arose in August 1943 when the German occupation authority proclaimed a military emergency, removed the Danish government, and began preparations to deport Danish Jews to the German death camps in Poland.

Norway

By 3 May 1940 the Germans had defeated the unprepared, inadequate, and poorly armed Norwegian forces following a series of surprise sea and airborne landings at Oslo and other ports scattered over enormous distances. The Norwegian government, including the king, escaped to London, while Norwegians refused to give in and submit to the rule of Vidkun Quisling, one of their own who had traitorously assisted the Germans in their invasion. Quisling, who had served previously as War Minister, led a party of Nazi sympathizers in Norway. Soon the Germans replaced Quisling and appointed a Nazi party district leader from Germany, Josef Terboven, to govern the country.

Initially Quisling's followers unleashed a campaign of terror against the small Norwegian Jewish community of approximately eighteen hundred persons. Then in the autumn of 1940 Terboven issued a decree banning the employment of Jews in the professions. During 1941, the occupation government forced all businesses to register their employees by religion and directed that an inventory be made of Jewish-owned real estate.

Much of this would form a prelude to the confiscation of Jewish businesses in 1942, the identification and marking of Jews, and extensive roundups and imprisonment of Jews by the SS and Norwegian police. Some assistance for the Jews resulted from Norway's long border with Sweden, which provided opportunities for Jews to escape, and an effective Norwegian resistance movement, aided from England.

The Netherlands

On 10 May the Germans attacked the Netherlands, Belgium, France, and Luxembourg simultaneously. The Dutch, who suffered the terrible bombing and destruction of Rotterdam by the enemy, surrendered on 15 May. Although the Dutch queen and leaders of the government fled, and the people seemed to believe they had little to worry about from their conquerors, they soon learned otherwise.

The Germans viewed the Dutch as fellow Aryans who had abandoned their true ancestry, but could be reabsorbed or annexed into a Greater Germany. Hitler, therefore, quickly replaced the German military administration in Holland with a Reich commissioner, Arthur Seyss-Inquart, an

Austrian Nazi who had played a key role in the Anschluss in 1938. Most recently Seyss-Inquart had served in Poland assisting Hans Frank in exploiting and terrorizing the Polish Jews and Poles.

Seyss-Inquart ruled Holland with the force of the SS. In addition to stripping the country of its large food exports and preparing it for incorporation into Germany, the occupation regime implemented quickly a number of repressive measures against the approximately 140,000 Dutch Jews. These included firing Jews from their jobs as well as forcing them to take a census and register their businesses with the government. Holland had the longest record in Europe of treating Jews respectably, which seemed reflected in the public denunciation of the anti-Jewish measures by most of the Protestant and Catholic churches as well as by the faculty and students at the University of Leiden.

But the protests had little practical effect. Soon, acts of terrorism by Dutch Nazis and SS against the impoverished Jews in the Jewish quarter in Amsterdam led to the Germans' forcing the Jews to organize a Judenrat, the first Jewish council established in Western Europe. Armed clashes occurred between Jews and their oppressors, during which a Dutch Nazi died and a German police patrol was sprayed with ammonia.

The Germans retaliated with mass collective punishment, ordered personally by Himmler. They seized and tortured more than four hundred Dutch Jews and then deported them to concentration camps in Germany. Most of them arrived in May 1940 at Mauthausen, possibly the deadliest of all the existing camps; none of the victims survived.

These events, along with German efforts to send Dutch workers to Germany, provoked the first major anti-Nazi uprising in German-occupied Europe. During 25–26 February 1941, a Communist-inspired general strike broke out in Amsterdam and elsewhere in the country, but the Germans quickly suppressed it. Thereafter they separated Jewish affairs from general politics, worked further to isolate the Jewish population, and steadily implemented more anti-Jewish measures.

Also the Germans used the Judenrat and its chairmen, the diamond merchant Abraham Asscher and Professor David Cohen, to calm both the Jewish and general Dutch resistance. Both men, encouraged by the Germans in their belief, would assume erroneously that they could protect the Jews by cooperating with the Germans. During June 1941, following a visit by Himmler to Mauthausen, the Germans seized another group of Dutch Jews in Amsterdam and sent them to their deaths at the camp.

Belgium

The Belgian army surrendered to Germany on 28 May 1940, which helped to place the Anglo-French forces in Belgium and northern France in an untenable position and contributed to the evacuation of many of them from Europe at Dunkirk. Although most of the Belgian government fled to London, the king, Leopold, chose to remain and became a German prisoner. His decision deeply divided the Belgian people toward him and would result following the war in his eventual abdication.

The Germans, as they did in the Netherlands, intended to include Belgium in Germany along with a portion of northern France, although Hitler postponed a final decision on the borders of the future country. Perhaps because he expected to use Belgium as a base for the future invasion of Britain and had no immediate plans to annex the country, he allowed the creation there of a German military administration.

The military governor placed in charge of Belgium, General Alexander von Falkenhausen, established the least tyrannical of all the German occupation regimes in the war. At heart an opponent of Hitler and Nazism who would pay later for his opposition with his life, von Falkenhausen attempted to avert or limit the types of horrors imposed on other conquered peoples. Also because Belgium was not to be annexed immediately, the approximately ninety thousand Jews, most of whom were not Belgian citizens but Jews who had fled to Belgium from Germany and Eastern Europe, were singled out only gradually from the rest of the population.

Although von Falkenhausen restrained the efforts of Himmler and Göring to interfere in Belgium and would later hold down the deportations of Belgian Jews to the East and their murder, his regime nevertheless enacted numerous anti-Jewish measures. These prohibited Jews from working in public jobs, including the legal, teaching, journalism, and broadcasting professions; defined who was a Jew; and required Jews to take a census. Not only did the Belgian government-in-exile declare such orders null and void, but also inside Belgium many in the population denounced the measures. Most Belgians, in fact, viewed the Germans as savages who had returned to plunder the country for a second time since World War I.

France

The expulsion of Anglo-French troops from Europe at Dunkirk and France's surrender to Germany in June 1940 left France divided into two zones. One included northeast France and ports along the English Channel and Atlantic coasts occupied by German troops, and the other was a generally larger and unoccupied area in the south, but which collaborated with the Germans, under the Vichy regime. In the former, partly because the Germans expected it to serve as a base for the future invasion of Britain, Hitler established a military administration in control, headquartered in Paris.

In the occupied zone, the military administration moved more slowly against the Jews than did the Vichy regime. On 27 September the German command published the definition of a Jew according to the Nuremberg Laws. This led soon to the registration of Jewish-owned businesses and factories and in November to the appointment of French trustees for Jewish businesses. The latter was designed so that the French could also benefit along with the Germans from the German plan to remove the Jews from the French economy. On 12 November the military administration ordered Jewish businesses sold or expropriated for Aryanization.

The influence of the military administration in Paris extended as well to Vichy, inasmuch as the Vichy government held to the principle that a unified administration existed for all of France and applied laws and regulations issued in occupied France also to the unoccupied region. Headed by the revered World War I hero Marshal Philippe Pétain, the Vichy regime provided the Germans with significant advantages. First, allowing Vichy and its forty million people their ostensible freedom enabled the Germans to avoid the possibility of continued French resistance from France's colonies in North Africa. Second, the regime meant that the Germans did not have to form an administration for a vast area and population that provided Vichy with widespread popular support.

Although the Germans used only a small supervisory bureaucracy in Vichy that controlled the government's administration and police, Vichy and its leaders ruled for the Germans more thoroughly and industriously than the Germans themselves could likely have done during the war. Vichy policies of nationalism and an authoritarian government reflected the feelings of many of its people as well as of the French Catholic Church. Large numbers of Frenchmen had become disillusioned with republicanism and foreigners by the 1930s and hoped that during the new European war Pétain would save France from the suffering it had experienced in World War I.

The sentiment of French opinion against foreigners and so-called outsiders, combined with a long history of anti-Semitism in the country, produced considerable anti-Jewish activity on the part of Vichy. In this regard, most recently Philippe Burrin has documented the widespread "collaboration and compromise" of not only France's politicians and police with the Germans, but also of the country's public, including its economic elite, intellectuals, and the Catholic clergy.[3]

Roughly three hundred thousand Jews lived in France, of whom nearly half were foreign Jews who had fled since World War I from Eastern Europe and, more recently, from Nazi Germany. A further ominous sign for the Jews in France was the German killing during the invasion of the country of others viewed by the Germans as "racial enemies," black colonial troops fighting in the French armies.

Following the French surrender, large numbers of both native and foreign Jews fled southward to Vichy, hoping to escape persecution by the Germans. But very early the Vichy government signaled the German military administration in Paris its willingness to cooperate with the Germans by adopting a sharply anti-Jewish policy. On 22 July 1940 the government established a commission to examine and revoke the citizenship of Jews who had been naturalized only recently. At the end of August the regime removed the ban on anti-Semitic propaganda.

Then on 3 October, in proclaiming the so-called Jewish Statute (*Statut des Juifs*), the government defined Jews according to the Nuremberg Laws. It immediately imprisoned foreign Jews in special camps, removed them from the civil service and army, and began the confiscation or Aryanization of their property and the application of restrictive legislation to them. By the end of 1940, Vichy had arrested thirty thousand foreign Jews, compared with twenty thousand in the German-occupied zone.

Vichy leaders held the belief, almost wholly erroneous, that the anti-Jewish measures would likely provide Vichy with Nazi Germany's gratitude and a bargaining advantage with the Germans on other issues. Many Frenchmen, long hostile to Great Britain, thought that collaboration with Germany would make France a partner in the alleged "New Order," which German propagandists proclaimed Hitler was building in Europe.

The Germans, however, never responded by granting greater authority to France either in the Jewish question or in other areas of national interest. Instead, while the Nazi occupation authorities relieved themselves of administering much of the persecution, they consistently pressed Vichy leaders for greater anti-Jewish measures. Once both leading ministers of Vichy, first Pierre Laval as vice premier during June–December 1940 and later as premier, and then Admiral Jean-François Darlan as naval minister and vice premier during 1941–1942, established the government's anti-Semitic policy, and when the head of state, Pétain, covered it with his blessing, the weight of the regime moved rigidly against the Jews.

Although unknown at the time, the first two years of Vichy anti-Jewish measures would prove most destructive for the Jews in France by clearing the way, both legally and practically, for the deportations to the East that would begin in the spring of 1942. Although during 1940–1941 the Germans complained about the low number of Aryanizations carried out by the Vichy regime, the latter nevertheless implemented such a policy. The owners of large German industrial firms and banks showed a keen interest in such businesses and attempted to acquire them by whatever means possible.

The Nazis also showed an avid interest in the art treasures owned by French Jews, and particularly by the Rothschild family. During the fall of 1940, Alfred Rosenberg won a power struggle over a multitude of other high level Nazi figures, including von Ribbentrop and Goebbels as well as the German army, for control of Jewish-owned and so-called Germanic artworks in the occupied Western countries.

For plundering such treasures, Rosenberg headed the most effective agency the world has seen, a Nazi party organization with the title of Special Staff of Reich Leader Rosenberg (*Einsatzstab Reichsleiter Rosenberg*, ERR). Initially the ERR, which had a complex web of staffs and work details and groups throughout Western Europe, looted primarily archives and libraries of the declared enemies of National Socialism. Later, the ERR would seize massive artworks and other treasure in German-occupied Greece.

On 17 September Hitler, who was himself amassing a mammoth art collection and was determined personally to decide the fate of the confiscated art, issued an order through Keitel and the German military administration in France. The directive mandated that Rosenberg, the Führer's longtime subservient and malleable Nazi party "philosopher," had sole jurisdiction over the plunder.

Before 1941, as a result, Rosenberg seized nearly three-fourths of the ERR's wartime lootings. The agency confiscated almost four thousand pieces of art owned by the various branches of the Rothschild family alone. Other important collections stolen by the agency belonged to the Kanns, the Seligmanns, the Wildensteins, the David-Weils, the Levys, and the Cassels.

To fend off continued powerful German rivals for the looting of artwork, including Göring, as well as to acquire more funds for his operation, Rosenberg joined forces with the powerful Reichsmarschall. As part of their alliance, Göring placed trains and guard staffs of the German air force, which he commanded, at the ERR's disposal for transporting and protecting the stolen art pieces. This represented yet another example of how the Nazi racial war and attack on the Jews took supplies and personnel from the "other" war, the military one.

Furthermore, immense wealth flowed to Göring from his assistance to the ERR. Within little more than a year, he acquired approximately six hundred artworks, which included paintings by the eighteenth-century Frenchman, François Boucher, and seventeenth-century Spanish master, Diego Velásquez. On 5 November 1940 Göring issued an order that established a hierarchy of Nazi leaders who had precedence in selecting art from the booty: Hitler had first choice, followed by Göring, Rosenberg's agency, appropriate German museums, and finally, French and other art dealers.

At Göring's first visit to the ERR's storage facility in Paris, the *Jeu de Paume*, he selected fourteen works of the fifteenth and sixteenth centuries that came from the Seligmann brothers' collection, valued at an estimated one million Reichsmarks. For those artworks that did not conform to Hitler's tastes, the ERR bartered and sold them at a discount to art dealers in France and Switzerland. Altogether during the war, 29 railroad transports comprising 137 cars carrying 4,174 crates that contained 21,903 items—paintings, furniture, and various kinds of objects of art from all eras of history originating from all over the world—were shipped out of France.

In the Netherlands, the ERR proceeded in a more cautious manner, inasmuch as the Nazis viewed the country as Aryan and implemented a less harsh and lawless occupation than elsewhere. Nevertheless, a special office directed by Seyss-Inquart, the Nazi Reich commissioner in the Netherlands, confiscated at least 1,114 paintings from the art collections of Dutch Jews.

The Madagascar Plan

The German army's lightning and stunning defeat of France in June 1940 and expulsion of the British from the European continent at Dunkirk persuaded numerous German leaders in Berlin that the war would soon be over. Hitler, in a speech to the Reichstag on 19 July, called on Britain to conclude peace with Germany. As a result, postwar planning in the German capital began at a feverish pace and resulted in the development by Nazi officials of numerous schemes for the expansion of German rule in Europe and elsewhere.

Some, for example, began redrawing the map of Europe, indicating that Germany would annex at the war's end numerous countries like Norway,

Holland, Belgium, Luxembourg, Denmark, Switzerland, and Sweden. Other officials envisioned that Germany's victory in the West would enable it to seize from Britain, France, Portugal, and Belgium a huge contiguous empire in Central Africa stretching from the South Atlantic to the Indian Ocean.

Also Germany's military and diplomatic situation influenced the ideas of German planners toward the Jews. Some Nazis devised measures they believed would move them closer to their goal of producing a vast racial restructuring of Europe. Germany's recent victories in the West appeared to open up the possibility of dealing with the first priority of this project: ridding Europe of its Jews and thereby achieving, in the words of some Nazi leaders, a final goal or solution to the Jewish question.

In Berlin the day of Hitler's speech urging Britain to surrender, Goebbels discussed at a meeting of his Propaganda Ministry staff what he intended soon to do with the Jews of the city. "Immediately after the end of the war," he declared confidently, "all 62,000 Jews still living in Berlin will be deported to Poland within a period of no more than eight weeks."[4]

Others in the bureaucracy had different ideas. The so-called Lublin reservation, discussed in the previous chapter, to which the Nazis had planned to transport all Polish Jews, had produced problems. Discussions in Berlin, originating in the German Foreign Ministry and then taken up briefly by the SS, now focused on deporting the Jews to Madagascar, a French island colony off the east coast of Africa. The surrrender of France and seemingly imminent defeat of Britain, which controlled the sea, appeared to some Nazi officials to make the so-called Madagascar Plan feasible.

The idea of resettling the Jews of Europe in a foreign colony, such as Madagascar or somewhere else on another continent, had occurred previously to the Nazis. Between 1938 and 1940, Streicher, Göring, von Ribbentrop, Rosenberg, and even Hitler had discussed the idea, but no concrete plans to implement it had yet emerged. On 17–18 June 1940, both von Ribbentrop and Hitler, in their meetings in Munich with the Italian leaders, Mussolini and his son-in-law and Foreign Minister, Count Galeazzo Ciano, regarding the future of the French empire, had mentioned the plan to use Madagascar for a Jewish "reservation." Then at the beginning of August, Hitler told Otto Abetz, the German Ambassador in France, that "he intended to evacuate all Jews from Europe after the war."[5]

During the following weeks, Franz Rademacher, a functionary of the Foreign Ministry's "Jewish desk," drafted with von Ribbentrop's approval a plan that envisioned forcing the defeated France to cede Madagascar to

Germany. Quickly, officials in Heydrich's RSHA, Eichmann and Dannecker, the so-called Jewish experts of the Gestapo, countered with a similar scheme.

On the one hand, Rademacher's plan proposed that the Foreign Ministry conduct negotiations for the treaty with France as well as for special treaties with other European countries to acquire control over the Jews to be shipped to the island. Rademacher envisioned resettling 6.5 million Jews on Madagascar, which included Jews from Europe and other parts of the world, except for the United States and Russia. The plan gave the SS the tasks of rounding up the Jews in Europe, seizing their property, and supervising the security of the super-ghetto through a police governor directly subordinate to Himmler.

Transportation of the Jews to Madagascar, however, would not be a job of the SS, but of Phillip Bouhler's staff in the Führer Chancellery. The collection, control, and exploitation of Jewish property, which would be placed under a newly created intra-European bank and be used to finance the resettlement, would fall to Göring's Four-Year Plan. Rademacher wrote about his plan: "The imminent victory [over Britain] gives Germany the possibility and, according to my opinion, also the obligation to solve the Jewish question in Europe. The desirable solution is: All Jews out of Europe."[6]

On the other hand, the RSHA plan proposed by Eichmann and Dannecker claimed near exclusive control of the operation for the RSHA and SS. Heydrich, in a blunt letter to von Ribbentrop of 24 June, reminding the latter that the SS had been in charge of Jewish emigration since January 1939, sought to ensure that the Foreign Ministry did not intrude on his jurisdiction in the Jewish question. Although the ministry represented no real threat to SS or security police control regarding the issue, Heydrich opposed conceding influence to the ministry or anyone else.

Moreover, Heydrich suggested in the letter that he disapproved of any Madagascar-like project by ruling out emigration. "The *total* problem," he informed von Ribbentrop, "could no longer be solved through emigration since there were three-and-one-quarter million Jews in the areas *currently* under German control [meaning more were expected]. A territorial Final Solution would therefore be necessary." He closed by asking that the Foreign Minister notify him of "any future discussions about the Final Solution to the Jewish Question."[7]

Although the Madagascar scheme represented yet another plan of some German officials for getting rid of the Jews, it presumed wholly unrealistic and impractical conditions and circumstances. For example, although Nazi functionaries envisioned the evacuation from the island of the few French settlers there, the plans made no provisions for the roughly four million local inhabitants on the island, whom the Germans apparently intended to displace to make way for the deportees.

Much has been written and debated by scholars about the Madagascar project. The original proposal for it in the Foreign Ministry may have resulted from von Ribbentrop's efforts to gain control over Germany's anti-Jewish measures as a part of German foreign affairs. Also the evidence suggests that Heydrich took the Madagascar Plan much less seriously than did others. The plan as put forth in 1940 did not originate with him or the RSHA; and, above all, he concerned himself less with the plan than with protecting the jurisdiction of the SS over the Jewish question from potential rivals. He viewed the solution to the question as a police matter, not a foreign policy one.

What he meant in his letter to von Ribbentrop by references to "a territorial Final Solution" and "the Final Solution to the Jewish Question" is unclear, except that he had ruled out emigration because of the vast numbers of Jews then under German rule. He already realized that any European solution to the Jewish question depended on Germany's control of all the Jews of Europe.

According to Eichmann's estimates in the late fall of 1940, Germany would have to remove almost six million Jews from the lands it ruled west of the German–Soviet demarcation line to solve the Jewish question; he included in his figures the Jews of the French colonies in North Africa. Millions more Jews in Russia and Eastern Europe remained free of German control. In light of the role played by the RSHA in Poland in the wholesale destruction of its Jewish communities, the concentration of Jews in ghettos, the efforts—generally frustrated by Frank—to establish a Jewish "reserve" in the General Government, and the continued killing of numerous Polish and German Jews, it seems plausible that Heydrich meant what, in fact, the Final Solution would eventually become: extermination.

Also it appears likely that he preferred killing Jews as a much simpler solution to the problems that the RSHA and SS had produced by the fall of 1940 with their deportation and resettlement policies. The argument of some functionalist historians that such problems helped give rise to the Madagascar Plan seems less persuasive than their view that it may have contributed to the decision for the Final Solution. To be sure, if the Germans had implemented the Madagascar Plan, substantial numbers of Jews sent there would have died. The Nazis, in drawing up their plans to deport the Jews to the island, made no provision to supply them with food, clothing, and other basic necessities of life. Also the land size, climate, and economy of the island could not have sustained the millions of mostly highly urbanized Europeans.

By the winter of 1940–1941, the SS had transported nearly 250,000 ethnic Germans from Eastern and Southern Europe to western Poland for resettlement. Most of the settlers were placed in transit camps, awaiting the availability of more "living space" in the region provided by the removal of local Polish Jews and Poles. Moreover, the SS planned soon to resettle in Poland large numbers of other ethnic Germans from Lithuania as well as the Bukovina and Bessarabia in Rumania, which the Soviet Union had annexed.

Still other resettlement schemes, which the German government's Agricultural Ministry promoted, envisioned shipping to Germany's conquered Eastern territories at least one and a half million peasants from the poorer agricultural regions of Germany. Further, a treaty between Germany and Italy provided for two hundred thousand Germans from the South Tyrol to be resettled in the East.

In the view of some functionalist scholars, these problems associated with the real or planned resettlement of ethnic Germans in the East were aggravated by the continued presence in western Poland and the General Government of nearly two million Polish Jews and millions more Poles. Overpopulation and chaotic conditions in the East threatened to overwhelm Nazi plans for using the war to dominate Europe and to carry out a massive racial reorganization on the continent.

By the spring of 1941, Eichmann's section in the RSHA, responsible for arranging the "evacuations" of Polish Jews and Poles, had deported "only" 408,525 persons to the General Government—not the 5 million the RSHA had originally planned on. The RSHA had imprisoned most of the Jews in German-occupied Poland in ghettos and slave labor or concentration camps.

Although tens of thousands of the ghetto and camp inhabitants died from starvation, disease, and other causes, some lower-level officials and social planners in the RSHA and German government complained about the costs of maintaining such places. For example, the Lodz ghetto, the officials estimated, cost the Reich 2.5 million Reichsmarks per month, and the Warsaw ghetto 4.6 million. Also one of Eichmann's subordinates, the head of the SD office in Posen, Rolf Heinz Höppner, urged that some quicker and more humane means be developed for killing the Jews incapable of work.

It is doubtful, however, that such lesser functionaries articulated this vision to their superiors, Himmler and Heydrich, who combined it with their fanatical anti-Semitism and changed these economic motivations into what became the Final Solution. One has difficulty imagining, as one scholar has noted, "that the rulers in Berlin really listened to their minions in Poland."[8] Furthermore, some local German officials and economic experts in Poland did everything in their power to prevent the destruction of the ghettos. Their motives ranged from trying to use underpaid Jewish labor to produce essential goods for large profit to taking bribes from the Jews, which helped produce a good life, and the fear that with the destruction of the ghetto many such officials might be sent to serve at the front.

More likely, therefore, Höppner and other second-echelon officials took their cue from their superiors in Berlin; as noted previously in this book, ideas about killing Jews and using war to do so had occurred to Hitler, Himmler, and Heydrich before the world war had begun. Each had discussed his views with groups of senior officers in the SS, RSHA, and Wehrmacht and, moreover, either ordered or approved the widespread killings of Jews, Poles, and persons with handicaps.

In addition, with the exception of the euthanasia program inside Germany, each Nazi leader had gained the assurance that the numerous German officials involved in the killings and the German public would accept such actions. The ideas and actions of Hitler and his SS leadership show a steady progression toward, and planning for, the Final Solution, and their improvisations in planning and implementation resulted as much or more from the military situation in the war as from economic and resettlement failures in the East.

Still another factor suggests Heydrich's general disinterest in the Madagascar Plan. In his letter to Ribbentrop of June 1940 regarding the plan, he informed the Foreign Minister that Hitler had reserved the key role in Jewish policy for the SS, which meant Himmler and Heydrich. That Heydrich showed little genuine interest in the Madagascar scheme meant that Hitler also cared little for it; Heydrich would not have asserted himself against Ribbentrop if he had not believed he had Hitler's authorization in the matter.

Göring's directive of January 1939, which he could have issued only with Hitler's approval, establishing Heydrich's jurisdiction over Jewish emigration, clearly illustrated this. It is therefore likely that Hitler never considered seriously shipping the Jews to Madagascar. In October 1940, for example, he ordered Rosenberg not to publish an article which the latter had written favoring the project.

But an even more important indication of Hitler's lack of enthusiasm for the plan was that amid the sudden interest in it among some German officials, Himmler had decided that Germany would not include the Ostjuden, or Jews in Eastern Europe, in any shipment of Jews to the distant island. He recommended that Germany hold the Eastern Jews as "hostages" in the East, possibly because he viewed them as a useful weapon against Britain, but more likely because he knew of Hitler's plans already to attack the Soviet Union soon. A gigantic war in the East would provide perfect cover for killing the many millions of Jews left there.

In still another way Hitler and his SS associates revealed their lack of serious interest in other solutions to the Jewish question than murdering Jews. They rejected a proposal made by Viktor Brack, a key figure in the euthanasia program, to sterilize millions of Jews by using powerful X-rays, a procedure Brack had investigated extensively. Himmler, and most likely Hitler too, instead considered sterilization a possibility for all adult Poles.

Aside from these views of the SS and RSHA leadership and Hitler toward the Madagascar Plan, something else by the fall of 1940 made the plan unrealizable: the German failure to force Great Britain to conclude a compromise peace, followed by the inability to win the Battle of Britain, which resulted in the continuation of the war. The conditions of war, along with Britain's superior fleet, not only reduced drastically any chances of forced Jewish emigration from Europe, but they also made the distant island inaccessible to the Germans.

The principal tangible result of the plan was the deportation of approximately seventy-thousand Jews from Alsace and Lorraine, the former French provinces incorporated into Germany, and Baden and the Pfalz in southwestern Germany, to the Gurs concentration camp in Vichy France. There many of the victims died of malnutrition and disease.

But even long before the German defeat in the Battle of Britain, Hitler had made plans to shift Germany's military attack away from the West to the Soviet Union. That would open the way to a new and equally inconceivable, though unfortunately more realizable and horrific, kind of final solution of the Jewish question.

Once the British refused Hitler's offer to conclude peace and chose to continue in the war, the Jews under German control lost any value the Nazis had
placed on them as possible hostages for dealing with the West. For Hitler and his
highest-level associates in the SS, the military triumphs in the West would
encourage them to begin drawing up plans not only to invade the Soviet Union,
but also to murder in the process the approximately five million Jews there.

Earliest Preparations for War in the East

During June 1940, with the German offensive in the West moving forward
so successfully, Hitler directed the OKW to begin preparations for attacking
Russia. Britain's subsequent refusal to withdraw from the war made Hitler
even more determined to attack in the East. He believed that the British
were remaining in the war because they expected Russia and the United
States to replace France as their allies.

Furthermore, Hitler and his subordinates assumed that the Russians, with
their alleged racial and cultural inferiority and "Jewish-Bolshevik" leadership,
were incapable of any effective military defense. This view made a planned
land operation in the East appear much more inviting than continuing the
risky attack against Britain across the English Channel. At last, furthermore,
in Hitler's view the time had come for him to realize his long-held ambition
of seizing vast new living space in Russia that would include the rich agricultural lands of the Ukraine, mineral resources of the Ural and Caucasus mountains, and forests of Siberia.

At a conference with his military advisers on 31 July, Hitler decided to
launch the assault in the East in the late spring of 1941 rather than the fall of
1940. Germany began a massive transfer of troops and equipment from West
to East. On 27 September Berlin signed the Tripartite Pact with Japan and
Italy. The Germans hoped particularly to use their new "Berlin-Rome-Tokyo
Axis" alliance to persuade the Japanese to resume their armed expansion in
Asia and enter the war.

Japan's entry into the struggle, in Hitler's view, would tie up the United
States in the Pacific Ocean, while a Japanese attack on British possessions in
Southeast Asia would divert Britain's resources away from its war in Europe
against Germany. In addition, German negotiations with Rumania produced
an agreement that allowed the Wehrmacht to begin sending units there that
would participate in an attack against the Soviet Union.

After considerable planning by the military staff at his direction Hitler, on 18 December 1940, issued a general directive for the invasion of Russia, code-named "Barbarossa." Based on their prejudices against the Slavs, which the victory in the West seemed to strengthen, the Nazi leaders presumed that Germany would complete the war in Russia in roughly three months, at the latest by the end of the summer or early fall of 1941.

Consequently, the Germans made few preparations for winter fighting. They based Barbarossa on two main concepts. First, huge German army groups would strike heavy initial blows near the Russian border to cut off and destroy Red Army forces. Second, the Germans aimed at establishing a battleline running approximately from Archangel on the Arctic Ocean in the north to the northern shore of the Caspian Sea in the south. The Soviet system, the Germans presupposed, would collapse in chaos and defeat within a matter of weeks under the massive armed German blows.

But even before Hitler had issued the operational order for attack in the East, the defeats suffered by the Italian armies during the final months of 1940 in Greece and North Africa complicated matters for the Germans. Mussolini had earlier participated in the German campaign against France and even sent planes to Germany to use in the Battle of Britain. Defeat of the Italians in Greece likely would open up a Balkan front in the war, creating a major problem for the Germans' concentration of their land and air forces for attacking Russia.

A defeat of the Italians in North Africa by the British not only threatened to open the Mediterranean Sea to British shipping. Also such a defeat of Italy might open it to attack from the south, lead to the collapse of Mussolini's government, and persuade the French colonies in North and West Africa to defect from Vichy France. As a result, during the final months of 1940 Hitler moved to assist his only Western European ally. In December the Germans provided air transport assistance to the Italian forces in Albania. When the British won their first major victories against the Italian forces at the Egyptian–Libyan border, the German air force quickly dispatched an air corps from Norway to assist the Italians in attacking British shipping.

Parallel to and in connection with the military plans for war in the East, a lengthy discussion unfolded in Berlin among SS and police leaders regarding racial policy, including measures against the Jews. The massive military blows against Russia envisioned by Operation Barbarossa would allow the Germans to cut off and seize quickly the masses of Jews in western Russia. On

10 August 1940 Himmler met with eleven of the most senior and powerful SS and police officers.

All present were, or had been, involved in the planning for or conduct of anti-Jewish measures, racial policy, the resettlement of ethnic Germans in the East, the concentration camps, the euthanasia program, and the Einsatzgruppen. They included Heydrich (RSHA); the five Higher SS and Police Leaders (*Höherer SS- und Polizeiführer*) from the East; Ulrich Greifelt, Himmler's deputy head of the RKFDV; and Oswald Pohl, head of the SS Budget and Construction Office and responsible for the economic administration of the concentration camps.

No record of the meeting survived the war. One suspects, however, that the gathering of so many SS and police leaders in a major conference, which Himmler disliked inasmuch as he preferred to work secretly and behind the scenes in such matters, involved the most important issues of racial and resettlement planning. A hint of the meeting's subject probably appeared a few days later.

Greifelt wrote to Wilhelm Frick, the Reich Interior Minister, objecting to the latter's wish to extend the Nuremberg Laws to the territories annexed by Germany in the East. According to Greifelt, no need existed to introduce such laws there to prohibit Poles and Jews from breeding. "[A] final cleansing of the Jewish Question and the mixed-blood [Mischling] question," he declared, "was foreseen for after the war."[9] Such a moment, a German triumph in the war, most German officials and Hitler confidently expected soon, following Germany's quick defeat of Soviet Russia.

Three weeks later, on 11 September, Heydrich dispatched a memorandum to Hans Lammers (the head of Hitler's Reich Chancellery), Martin Bormann (a deputy leader of the Party Chancellery), and Otto Hoffmann (an official in the SS Race and Settlement Main Office [*Rasse- und Siedlungshauptamt*]). There Heydrich discussed how best to solve the problem of racial mixing and Germanization in the Protectorate of Bohemia and Moravia. He particularly focused on suggestions for cleansing Bohemia racially in order to make it entirely German.

Simultaneously the RSHA began to reach beyond the frontiers of the Reich and General Government to capture control of foreign Jews. It sent an official, Dieter Wisliceny, from Eichmann's Jewish department to Slovakia as an adviser to the Slovak government and then succeeded in blunting an effort by the German Foreign Ministry to establish a similar adviser there.

During the following months, Wisliceny pressed Slovak officials to cooperate with Germany's anti-Jewish policies.

Richard Breitman, in his biography of Himmler, has shown that plans now seemed to intensify that were directed toward the extermination of the Jews. Complaints reached Himmler about the masses of useless Jews in Poland who must be dealt with. Heydrich discussed the idea of SS doctors eliminating the Jews in the Warsaw ghetto by introducing epidemics into it. Meanwhile, Himmler and Heydrich began to win their bitter rivalry with Frank over the deportations of Jews to the General Government.

On 2 November 1940 Himmler secretly ordered Odilo Globocnik, the SS and police leader in the Lublin district, to continue with developing a Jewish "reservation" in the region. This, the Reichsführer directed, would include SS industrial, construction, military, and training installations to expand SS and police power throughout the East. Simultaneously, inside Germany, before the SS could begin deporting the remaining German Jews to the East, Heydrich focused on implementing even harsher anti-Jewish measures. These included eliminating pension payments and abolishing the remaining social benefits for German Jews with relatives who had emigrated.

During December Himmler mentioned further broadly conceived plans, consistent with the ideas discussed by Hitler and others on the subject, for the Jews of Germany. In a speech in Berlin to party leaders, he called for merciless German domination in the East, the creation of a vast pool of seasonal laborers in the General Government on whom Germany could draw, and the emigration of Jews that would leave more living space for Poles. Himmler did not mention where Jews would go, but he opposed their remaining in Poland. Later, while addressing senior SS officers, he declared that one purpose of the impending campaign against Soviet Russia was to reduce the Slavic population by some thirty million people.

When, on 18 December, Hitler signed the secret directive ordering Operation Barbarossa against the Soviet Union, that night at the Reich Chancellery Himmler met alone with the Führer for a long and private conversation. No record exists of what they discussed, but one could hazard the guess that they spoke about the meaning of what Hitler had ordered. During the ensuing weeks, planning quickly accelerated in the RSHA and SS for the massive expansion of the racial war in the East, in which the Final Solution, which meant increasingly the extermination of the millions of Jews there and in the rest of Europe, would play the key role.

But for the moment at least, some limitations still existed on the radicalism of Hitler and Himmler regarding the Jewish question. First, unclear
were the views on the possibility of killing the Jews among elements in the
German army and leading Nazi officials outside the SS. Also the invasion of
Russia, which would place enormous numbers of Jews under German rule,
had not started. Nor would the mass murder of Jews serve Germany's present
foreign policy interests.

Regarding the latter, keeping the United States from joining the side
of Britain and the Soviet Union in the war necessitated Hitler restraining
his most extreme wishes in the war and Jewish policy. Although he had
nothing but contempt for the military capability of the United States, he
still wanted to postpone hostilities with America until Germany dominated
Europe, Britain, and Russia and until it had built a navy large enough to
take the war to the Western Hemisphere. Moreover, he believed that Jews
controlled President Roosevelt, whose government had criticized sharply
since 1933 Germany's anti-Jewish policies. To keep America out of the war
for the present, he thought, Germany must avoid, while it dealt militarily
with Russia and then Britain, alienating Washington and its supposed
Jewish rulers.

Film Advertisements for the Final Solution?

Amid the various Nazi proposals for what to do with the Jews that emerged
during the last half of 1940, the Nazi government sought both to intensify
anti-Semitism among the German population and prepare the latter for a
radical solution to the Jewish question. The medium of film provided a most
important means for this purpose. It was no coincidence that the most vicious
attacks on the Jews in Nazi films, which the Propaganda Ministry carefully
controlled and produced, appeared in the late summer and fall in connection
with the burgeoning German plans for war in the East.

Two movies, The Rothschilds (Die Rothschilds) and The Jew Süss (Jud Süss),
and a so-called documentary film, The Eternal Jew (Der ewige Jude), were
released within a short period of time. The Rothschilds used the background of
the Napoleonic wars to portray the financial power and cunning of the
wealthy Jewish banking family; the movie alleged that the family had
acquired its fortune at the costs of the Germans and that the Jews dominated
a weak and corrupted British society.

The Jew Süss concentrated on the "rootlessness" of the Jews and their supposed interest in penetrating and dominating Aryan society. Arguably the greatest and most powerful hate film ever produced in Nazi Germany, it portrayed a conniving, "assimilated" Jew, Süss Oppenheimer, at the court of an early eighteenth-century Württemberg duke. Süss had enormous power as the duke's financial adviser and persuaded the ruler, himself an avaricious and dissolute man, to grant the Jews the right to live in Stuttgart.

The alleged evil Jew and his clique then conspired to suck the blood of the good people of Württemberg. Süss raped the blond Aryan daughter of a local counselor of the realm, Dorothea, who committed suicide because of the dishonor. When the duke died, the righteous wrath of the people caused the now powerless Süss to be arrested, tried before a court, and ultimately hanged in a cage. The Jews were then banned from the city and countryside. A noted German dramatist, Eberhard Wolfgang Möller, wrote the script for the film; possibly more than any other artist, Möller illustrated the connection between Nazi cultural depravity and the Holocaust.

Millions of Germans saw *The Jew Süss*. Himmler ordered the SS and police, including security personnel at the concentration camps, to view the film. The Nazis also employed the movie to indoctrinate German youth; in one instance, a group of Hitler Youth, after it had seen the film, trampled a Jewish man to death. In Poland, shortly before the Germans began the deportations of Polish and other Jews to the death camps, the Germans showed the film in small Polish cities, primarily to enflame the anti-Semitic sentiments widespread among the local population and ensure that it did not assist the Jews.

The Eternal Jew premiered in November 1940. The film contained the vicious and pornographic anti-Semitism of the kind found in Streicher's paper, *Der Stürmer*. Presented as a documentary about the role of the Jews in world history, it portrayed them as lowly parasites and money-mad, immoral, and racial corrupters of the world. Scenes of ritual animal slaughter, kosher style, proclaimed the supposed grotesque sadism of the Jewish religion.

The appearance of *The Eternal Jew* simultaneously with the other two anti-Semitic movies was no accident. An expert on Nazi film propaganda has termed the films "advertisements for the Final Solution":

"The films *The Eternal Jew* and *The Jew Süss* represented the Nazi commitment to exterminating the Jews. . . . These two motion pictures represented a Nazi synthesis, for they brought to mass audiences the murder policies formerly espoused by individuals and publications which lacked power and prestige beyond obsessed psychotic anti-Jewish circles. . . . The millions of Germans who saw these films in 1940 and 1941 must have realized what the government intended to do to the Jews and was doing to them. Only the individual possessing extraordinary powers of self-deception could leave *Jud Süss* thinking it was merely a historical tale with a moral twist, the triumph of good over evil. These films were a formula for action, not a denunciation of the Jews."[10]

CHAPTER EIGHT

THE RACIAL WAR
IN THE EAST, 1941

O N 2 JANUARY 1941, barely two weeks after Hitler had signed the directive authorizing Operation Barbarossa, Himmler made known his intention to expand the concentration camp at Auschwitz. The camp, located in former southwestern Poland, lay just inside the area annexed to the Reich. To the present camp the Nazis planned to add a second, much larger, facility. At the moment, Auschwitz held approximately ten thousand inmates, which included Polish political prisoners and slave laborers, alleged criminals, and a small number of Jews.

The proposed expansion was part of Himmler's order, issued through Heydrich, for a major new division in the concentration camp system, in which particular camps would hold prisoners of a certain category. Beyond the solely existing "Auschwitz I" camp, the Reichsführer's directive mentioned an "Auschwitz II" slated for use in imprisoning dangerous criminals. Himmler had taken a special interest in Auschwitz, but not as a place for criminals and Poles. Instead, later he would use the camp for the mass killing of mostly Jews.

That such preparations were made simultaneously with the military planning that had started for the invasion of Russia was hardly a coincidence. Germany's attack on Russia, SS leaders and Hitler realized, would increase enormously the numbers of Jews under German rule. This realization provided the moment, as Weinberg has emphasized, when "the Germans decided the time had come to shift from persecution to extermination" of the Jews.[1]

Plans for the Final Solution in Early 1941

As 1941 began, the highest-ranking SS leaders continued to direct their thinking and planning on the Jewish question toward the physical extermination of
the Jews—mass murder—as the only desirable Final Solution. Hitler now
entrusted Heydrich with preparing a preliminary plan for such a solution, and
by the end of January the RSHA chief had presented a proposal to the Führer.

Historians Breitman and Charles W. Sydnor provide three independent
sources that confirm this task given Heydrich. First, Theodor Dannecker,
whom the RSHA had recently sent to Paris to organize the control of Jewish
policy for all of France, mentioned in a 21 January 1941 memorandum both
Heydrich's authorization from Hitler for a Final Solution and Heydrich's submission of his plan to Hitler and Göring. Dannecker observed that implementation of Heydrich's plan would necessitate a huge effort and the most
careful preparation of both the deportations to and settlement in the territory, still to be determined, where the solution would be carried out.

Second, on 20 March 1941, Eichmann mentioned the same details as
Dannecker, but added a further piece of information: the territory where the
Final Solution project would be carried out would be the General
Government of Poland. Eichmann, discussing the matter in the Propaganda
Ministry and using words to satisfy Goebbels' queries about removing Jews
from Berlin, said that Hitler had commissioned Heydrich with the "final
evacuation of the Jews."[2] By 1940, as noted in the last chapter, "evacuation"
had become a euphemism of the SS for the gassing of mental patients in
Poland. Third, on 20 May 1941, another well informed source in the RSHA,
Walter Schellenberg, a Gestapo official who would soon head the RSHA's
foreign intelligence division, in issuing a directive prohibiting the emigration
of Jews from France and Belgium, mentioned "the undoubtedly imminent
final solution of the Jewish question."[3]

Still other signs indicated that during the early months of 1941 urgent
and important matters preoccupied the attention of Hitler and the principal
SS figures. On 24 January Heydrich met for two hours with Göring at the latter's Carinhall estate; later in the day the two men conferred with Himmler
in Berlin. Most of the next afternoon and evening Göring met privately with
Hitler at the Führer's Berchtesgaden villa.

Five nights later, Hitler, in a speech in the Berlin *Sportpalast* celebrating
the eighth anniversary of the Nazi seizure of power, reminded the world of his

warning on 30 January 1939 that the Jews of Europe would be exterminated in any new war:

> And I should not like to forget the indication that I had already given once, on September 1, 1939 [sic], in the German Reichstag. The indication then, to wit, that if the rest of the world would be plunged into a general war by Jewry, the whole of Jewry would have finished playing its role in Europe!
>
> They may still laugh today at that, exactly as they laughed at my prophecies. The coming months and years will prove that I also saw correctly here.[4]

In the speech Hitler misdated his threat of 30 January to 1 September 1939. He did so on purpose, to associate the killing of Jews, which he and the SS were now planning, with the war.

The intentions in early 1941 for the mass extermination of the Jews remained confined to Hitler, the highest reaches of the SS, and Göring. Little indication exists that at the moment this limited circle shared this most radical of plans with other Nazi leaders. Hitler also found himself pushed toward the solution of destroying the Jews by the growing, and often contradictory, pressures from various Nazi party and government officials regarding the Jewish question.

On the one hand, party Gauleiters who also served as Reich governors or presidents in their districts demanded that such regions in the Greater German Reich be cleared of Jews by having them deported elsewhere. In addition, the RSHA pressed for further deportations of Poles and Jews, numbering approximately 831,000 persons, from the annexed Polish lands to the General Government and for the further resettlement of ethnic Germans in the annexed territories. SS offices as well demanded more space in the annexed lands for their Germanization schemes.

On the other hand, Hitler realized the problems involved in deporting more Jews to the General Government, where the governor, Frank, already complained that the area had no more space for Jews or any other alleged undesirables. Nevertheless, Hitler's sympathies lay with the RSHA and Gauleiters, and in January 1941 he approved a new program of deportations to the General Government. These would include two thousand Jews deported each day from the annexed Polish lands, and an additional seven thousand Jews from Austria.

But because the deportations would require the use of at least two freight trains per day, the operation caused transport problems for the German military buildup in Poland, in preparation for the attack on the Soviet Union. Furthermore, concerns about a growing shortage of labor for German war industries led Göring to attempt to have Jews sent from Poland to the Reich to help alleviate the shortage. Hitler, however, rejected Göring's effort and banned the employment of Jews from the East in Germany. The Nazi leader was determined to remove the Jews from Germany as well as from Poland, and he therefore subordinated the practical considerations of the German conduct of the war to the need he perceived for killing the Jews.

Also when he met privately on 17 March with Frank, Hitler apparently said nothing about his decision to use the General Government for the Final Solution that he and the SS were planning. When Frank opposed further deportations of Jews to the General Government, Hitler agreed to limit the number of deportees according to the territory's capacity to take them. But he also told Frank that the General Government would be rewarded for its achievements by being made the first territory free of Jews.

Three days later, as noted above, Eichmann, when he conferred with Goebbels and others in the Propaganda Ministry, mentioned only the "final evacuation" of the Jews to the General Government. But having a final evacuation of Jews to German-occupied Poland and simultaneously making that area free of Jews could only happen in one way (i.e., by destroying all Polish Jews as well as those who had been sent there).

Breitman has concluded that Hitler decided on the Final Solution by March 1941. Breitman's research on Himmler and sophisticated analysis of captured SS and other German records adds substantially to the claim of intentionalist historians that the top of the Nazi hierarchy planned for the war to result in the mass murder of the Jews. He observed in his biography of Himmler: "Hitler had approved the mass murder of the Jews in Poland. The locations and methods were apparently still open; they would have been up to Himmler to figure out."[5]

By March Hitler believed that he no longer needed to restrain his radicalism regarding the Jews. He had made the decision to kill the Jews because now few or no limits remained on him to do so. Support for the killings existed among key elements in the Nazi party and government, Germany would soon invade Soviet Russia, which had vast numbers of Jews to deal with, and the United States had just approved the Lend-Lease program, providing warships and other military equipment to Britain.

The Lend-Lease bill left President Roosevelt free to decide on the kind of British repayment. The bill became law on 11 March, but Roosevelt had introduced the legislation to Congress in January. Its passage indicated that the American public believed Germany posed a significant enough threat to warrant drastic American support of Germany's enemies. Despite the continued hope of most Americans that the United States would stay out of the war, the country began expanding its rearmament. America's entering the war now seemed only a matter of time.

Hitler no longer had reason to concern himself with seeking to avoid American intervention in the war; in fact, in his view the prospect of American involvement made even more necessary the rapid conquest of Russia and destruction of the Jews. Furthermore, in the aftermath of Germany's victories in Western Europe, Hitler had resumed work on building the huge navy Germany would need for war against the United States. Once the triumph he anticipated soon in Russia occurred, he planned to emphasize the naval program anew.

Plenty of evidence exists to fuel the belief that Hitler, Himmler, and Heydrich purposely tried to conceal, at least for a time, their plans for the Final Solution from Nazi officials outside the SS. Previously Hitler and the Führer Chancellery had practiced a number of deceptions to withhold from the German public the facts about the so-called euthanasia program. In that instance, Hitler's written authorization of the program had caused trouble for him once news of the unpopular killings of the handicapped leaked out and public opposition forced him to reduce the program temporarily. This may explain in part why he apparently did not issue a written order for the mass killings of the Jews. Moreover, the history of the SS and its bitter rivalries with other Nazi offices and agencies demonstrates that the SS rarely, if ever, shared information about its racial, political, or other plans until it had to do so.

During the spring of 1941, still other actions on the part of Hitler and his highest associates in the SS indicated their murderous intentions. In March Himmler first visited the Auschwitz concentration camp, which then held 10,900 prisoners, most of them Poles and supposed criminals. While there he ordered the camp's expansion, including the construction of a massive second camp facility.

Himmler ordered the existing camp enlarged to hold thirty thousand prisoners. Also the Reichsführer focused his attention on the Upper Silesian camp because of the decision by February 1941 of IG Farben, the giant German industrial firm, to build a major factory near the camp. Peter Hayes has shown that Farben's selection of the site for its plant at Auschwitz may not have hinged on the presence of the camp's slave labor force for use by Farben. Instead, the firm made its choice because it desired a location in eastern Germany and one that had geographic advantages, including a rail line and proximity to supplies of water, lime, and coal.

For Himmler, Farben's large plant at Auschwitz offered him two advantages. First, it provided the SS with the opportunity to contract to industry on a much larger scale the concentration camp labor force; and second, the SS could acquire from Farben the managerial and technical skills it sorely lacked to make it what Himmler had always aimed for, an economically self-sufficient organization.

Soon the SS and Farben had concluded an agreement involving both in the construction of the factory, which originally intended to produce primarily synthetic rubber (*Buna*). But according to Hayes, Farben was not "a merely passive victim of Auschwitz's tragic history." The company's "decision to occupy the site, however unintended and unforeseeable the consequences," would contribute "mightily to the camp's expansion and its eventual evolution into a manufacturer of death."[6]

Immediately Himmler directed the SS commandant of Auschwitz, Rudolf Höss, to establish a massive new camp at Auschwitz, at nearby Birkenau, which would become Auschwitz II. Himmler alleged to Höss that the new facility would hold one hundred thousand Russian prisoners of war. More likely, however, Himmler foresaw another function for Birkenau, given Hitler's secret mandate to the SS to prepare the Final Solution and his and Himmler's long-held idea about the mass killing of Jews.

Also illustrating the willingness of the SS leadership to send Jews to their death, later in the month Himmler visited Dachau; while there he ordered all concentration camps to kill their Jewish prisoners who reported sick. Moreover, at the end of March 1941, Heydrich met with Göring and reported to the latter briefly about the solution of the Jewish question and gave Göring a copy of his draft plan. Apparently Göring approved of the plan. He did so after the two agreed on a minor change in the proposed German civilian administration for the future occupied Soviet lands.

This agreement, which Heydrich mentioned in a memorandum about the meeting, indicated that at least Heydrich planned for a portion of the Jews of Europe to be exterminated in Russia. Göring, furthermore, urged that the German troops invading Russia receive instructions about the danger posed by Soviet elements such as the police, political commissars, Jews, and others, to prepare the troops for confronting the enemy. For Heydrich, as for Hitler and Himmler, this meant a merciless and tireless struggle carried out by German forces in Russia, with the utmost obedience to orders, against Bolsheviks and their so-called partisans, agitators, guerrillas, saboteurs, and the alleged cause of all such troublemakers, Jews.

Final Preparations for Attacking Russia: Mobile Killing Units and the Wehrmacht

Because the invasion of Russia would increase enormously the number of Jews under German control, by approximately 4.7 million persons, Hitler directed on 13 March 1941 that enlarged mobile units of the SS and RSHA, Einsatzgruppen and police battalions, move into the Soviet Union with the Wehrmacht to perform "*special tasks* for the preparation of the *political administration*."[7] Because the directive mentioned neither Jews nor other peoples in the East, some historians have claimed that the order represented no mandate to murder Jews.

However, such phrases as "special tasks" were euphemisms used by the Nazis to conceal the killing of as many Soviet Jews as the Germans could capture, including the elderly, women, and children, and other specially identified civilians. As noted repeatedly in this book, both Hitler and Himmler had always attempted to camouflage carefully their roles in the "Jewish question." Above all, they believed fanatically that Jews formed the principal force behind every alleged German enemy in Russia, from "communists" to "partisans."

To carry out the tasks given him and the SS by Hitler, Himmler also received in the 13 March directive the authority to "act independently and on his own responsibility." The directive ordered as well the Einsatzgruppen and police to cooperate with frontline German troops and army units in the rear. In this regard Poland had provided the Germans with a means to practice for what they intended to do in Russia. In Poland the Einsatzgruppen and other killing units had begun to slaughter both Polish Jews and Poles by the tens of thousands.

Hitler now directed that the same would happen to the hated and supposedly Jewish-dominated Russians, but on a much larger and, in the case of

Russian Jews, systematic scale. It is uncertain whether, when he ordered the use of the mobile killing units in the forthcoming military campaign in Russia, Hitler had already decided that after the Jews there had been murdered, he would extend the killings to all other Jews in areas of Europe or elsewhere under German rule.

What is clear, however, is that with the 13 March directive Hitler and his associates decided to carry out a methodical and planned operation of mass murder, the killing of the millions of Jews in Soviet Russia. This went far beyond all previous anti-Jewish measures in history. Down through the centuries, these had included brutal physical attacks on Jews as well as their exclusion, expulsion, forced religious conversion, and economic destruction.

Further evidence of the plans for the mass killings of Soviet Jews and other Russians emerged from subsequent instructions issued by Hitler and the OKW for the invasion of the Soviet Union. During March Himmler and Heydrich had begun discussions with high military officials, including Keitel, Franz Halder, and von Brauchitsch, for a formal agreement between the SS and police and the Wehrmacht regarding the Russian campaign.

On 30 March Hitler informed approximately 250 generals and other senior military officers that the upcoming struggle in the East would be a war of annihilation that would result in a massive racial reordering of Eurasia. First he described the war as a "struggle between two *Weltanschauungen*." "It is a war of extermination," he declared. "The struggle will be very different from that in the west. In the east toughness now means mildness in the future. The [German] leaders must make the sacrifice of overcoming their scruples." He urged the "destruction of the Bolshevik commissars and the Communist intelligentsia," which he had always equated with the Jews.[8]

Based on Hitler's directive, a few weeks later, General Erich Hoepner, commander of the 4th Panzer Group scheduled for participation in the Russian campaign, relayed an even more explicit message to his troops regarding future warfare in the East:

> The war against Russia is an essential stage in the existential battle of the German people. It is the ancient battle of the Germanic peoples against the Slavs, the defense of European culture against Muscovite-Asiatic floods, the repulsion of Jewish-Bolshevism. This struggle must have as its goal the destruction of contemporary Russia and thus must be conducted with unheard of harshness.[9]

Reflecting this view of the necessity for a savage racial struggle in the East, and the desire of Hitler, Himmler, and Heydrich to eliminate allegedly the most dangerous enemy—the Jew—first, a series of directives from Hitler and the OKW instructed the Wehrmacht to disregard international law on the conduct of war. The Wehrmacht received orders to slaughter certain categories of Soviet prisoners of war, including political commissars and Jewish POWs; annihilate the Bolshevik political elite; and deal similarly with any real or suspected opposition from the Soviet civilian population, citing Jews specifically. Before the German soldiers participated in such atrocities against civilians, they received promises of amnesty.

Moreover, the Germans anticipated extending to the areas of newly overrun Russia the mass murder of persons in mental institutions and homes for the elderly, a continuation of the euthanasia program that had operated in Germany since the start of the war. Of the remaining Soviet population, the Germans intended that various forms of murder, including starvation, would decimate a further twenty to thirty million persons. Germany's seizure of the rich agricultural lands and food of the Ukraine would cause mass famine and death in much of Russia, but the Germans saw this as an advantage. Of the Russians left alive, Germany would use them as slaves in the service of German settlers, whom the SS would move into the huge new German living space.

Despite the claims of post–World War II German military memoirs to the contrary, most of the Wehrmacht officers, whose bond with Hitler had been sealed further with the brilliantly successful German military campaigns in Western Europe, agreed with, understood, and supported Hitler's ruthless plans for the East. According to the military historian Jürgen Förster:

> The military leaders did not merely comply with Hitler's dogmatic views; they were not mere victims of an all-absolving principle of obedience. The military leaders, too, believed that the dangers of Russia and Bolshevism should be eliminated forever. . . . Had it not been Jewry and Bolshevism that had stabbed the armed forces in the back and had caused the downfall of Imperial Germany?[10]

Amid the preparations for the war in Russia, Himmler sought to protect his bureaucratic empire and safeguard the ultimate authority awarded him by Hitler over the killing operations of Jews in the East from others even under his own command, including Heydrich and Daluege. He appointed three Higher SS and Police Leaders (*Höherer SS- und Polizeiführer*) who, with mobile killing units of their own, would also participate in the invasion.

While Heydrich and the RSHA had virtual control over the Einsatzgruppen, the Higher SS and Police Leaders would receive their orders directly from Himmler. They would provide him with information from the front and have for their use SS and police troops, including Waffen-SS units and Order Police battalions, as well as Einsatzgruppen. Given their crucial functions, Himmler installed as Higher SS and Police Leaders in the East his most loyal SS generals and key police associates: Hans-Adolf Prützmann for northern Russia, Erich von dem Bach-Zelewski for central Russia, and Friedrich Jeckeln for the Ukraine.

Also shortly before the start of the invasion of Russia, Himmler met with Hitler about a subject on both of their minds—the possible use of poison gas in the campaign. International law had banned the use of gas in war. Although Hitler decided not to use the weapon in Russia, Himmler had the subject on his mind and knew of its potential to kill and its availability. Moreover, the Wehrmacht had previously investigated a gas comprised of prussic acid or hydrogen cyanide, and contacted a German pesticide manufacturing firm, the Degesch corporation, a subsidiary of IG Farben, about manufacturing the gas for chemical warfare. Later the SS would use the same firm and its deadly product to murder millions of Jews.

War in the Balkans and Persecution of Jews

Even before the SS and Wehrmacht had completed their plans for killing the Jews of Russia, the German armed forces took the initiative to slaughter Jews in Yugoslavia, particularly in Serbia. During the spring of 1941, Germany invaded Yugoslavia and Greece, principally for three reasons. First, Hitler moved to rescue his ally and friend, Mussolini, whose Italian armies continued to suffer serious defeats in Albania and, at the hands of the British, in North Africa along the Egyptian–Libyan border. The Germans realized that little popular support existed in Italy for the war and that only Mussolini's remaining in power in Rome assured Italy's loyalty to the Axis alliance.

Second, Hitler decided to invade the Balkans following a successful military coup against the pro-German government of Yugoslavia in late March 1941. Third, by invading the Balkans, Hitler aimed at securing the

Wehrmacht's southeastern flank for the war about to begin against the Soviet Union. On 6 April German and Italian troops attacked both Yugoslavia and Greece. The Axis forces triumphed in lightning fashion; Yugoslavia surrendered on 18 April, Greece three days later.

The victors divided Greece into various zones of occupation, but the country remained intact as a state. The Germans quickly plundered Greek and Jewish treasures. In Salonika, a significant center of Sephardic Judaism, the Einsatzstab Reichsleiter Rosenberg (ERR), assisted by units of the Wehrmacht, systematically seized five hundred-year-old Jewish literary and cultural riches as well as other valuable items, preserved in dozens of private and public libraries and synagogues. Also in Athens the ERR confiscated Jewish archives and libraries.

The ERR sent most pieces to Frankfurt/Main. Rosenberg had established there in 1939 the Institute for Research on the Jewish Question (*Institut zur Erforschung der Judenfrage*). The Institute contained a large library, which held a portion of the approximately three million books looted by the Nazis from Jews throughout wartime Europe. In addition to helping plunder the Jews, the institute provided the German Foreign Ministry and police with information on Jews in foreign countries that facilitated locating them for imprisonment or killing.

Moreover, the institute had a staff of pseudo-scholars—mostly historians, anthropologists, and geographers—that conducted "research on Jews" and aimed to provide "scientific" legitimacy for Nazi anti-Semitic propaganda. Altogether between 1935 and 1945, Rosenberg as well as the RSHA and Goebbels' Propaganda Ministry established thirteen such anti-Jewish institutes in Europe.

The Axis partners destroyed the Yugoslavian state, dividing its individual regions among them and implementing brutal occupation policies that enflamed the already bitter feuds there among the many different Slavic and other ethnic groups in the population. Primarily as a result of Axis policies, only two countries in Europe suffered more than Yugoslavia from the death and destruction of the world war: Poland and the western portions of the Soviet Union.

When German troops invaded Yugoslavia, approximately eighty thousand Jews lived in the country; some sixty-five thousand would fall victim to the Holocaust. In northern Yugoslavia the Germans annexed the supposed Germanic portions. Italy annexed areas in the north and along the Adriatic coast. The Axis divided the remainder of Yugoslavia into two parts. In Croatia the Germans and Italians established zones of occupation, but installed there a nominally independent satellite state under the leadership of extreme nationalist Croats, the Ustasha. The latter, a small and violent group of fanatics, soon plunged Croatia into bloody chaos by killing and expelling from the area local Serbs, Muslims, and Jews. The majority of Jews in Croatia were murdered in the numerous concentration camps of the Ustasha, such as those at Jasenovac and Stara Gradiska, and a small minority was deported to Auschwitz beginning in 1943. In addition, the Ustasha played off the Germans and Italians against one another.

In Serbia, the largest and most powerful province of the former Yugoslav state, the Germans occupied the territory and established a brutal military and police administration. While preparing for the war in the Balkans, the German Army High Command and Heydrich concluded an agreement originally reached for the attack on Soviet Russia. The agreement provided for Einsatzgruppen to accompany Wehrmacht units into the area, in order to "take executive measures" against local "civilian populations," which would include "emigrants, saboteurs, terrorists" and "Communists and Jews."[11]

At least initially, until the German invasion of Soviet Russia started and in deference to the existing pact between Hitler and Stalin, the Germans left Serbian communists relatively unmolested. Persecution of Serbian Jews, however, began immediately and on a widespread scale. Wehrmacht units and German police took the initiative. Only two days after Yugoslavia surrendered, a Wehrmacht execution squad, carrying out a reprisal for the killing of two German soldiers, shot or hanged thirty-six Jews and other Serbian civilians in Pancevo, a town twenty miles northeast of the capital, Belgrade.

On 19 April the Einsatzgruppe in Belgrade ordered the registration of all male Jews in the city; the Germans soon subjected the ten thousand registered to slave labor. Execution by firing squad awaited those discovered not identifying themselves. A few weeks later the German military commander ordered the Aryanization of Jewish property and the dismissal of Jews from all employment in civil service and private business. Simultaneously the Wehrmacht ordered Jewish businesses throughout Serbia marked and closed, the Star of David worn by Jews, reparations of one million Reichsmarks paid by Jews, and Jewish communities moved into ghettos.

It did not take the local population long to realize that, in a situation of indiscriminate slaughter, the resisters had a better chance of survival than did

those who cooperated. As a result, resistance to the occupiers steadily escalated. It began with former soldiers and officers of the Yugoslav army, who
formed the Cetniks. The latter especially tried to rally the Serbs to their side
and engaged in acts of sabotage and violence against the occupiers.

Moreover, the Cetniks waged a civil war against another local force
opposing the Italians and Germans, the Yugoslav Communists led by Josip
Tito. Following the German attack on the Soviet Union in June 1941, Soviet
Communists called on the Yugoslav Communist party to engage in partisan
warfare and mount a general uprising in Yugoslavia against the Axis to assist
the Russians.

While a struggle emerged between the Cetniks and Tito's partisans for
eventual control of postwar Yugoslavia, the partisans waged a guerrilla war
against the Germans. They attacked German military units, sabotaged
German communications and transportation lines, and killed German
troops. Initially, the Germans assigned the Einsatzgruppen and German
police units to fight the partisans. However, as the partisans' resistance spread
during the summer of 1941, Hitler ordered the Wehrmacht to put down the
insurrection. When the Wehrmacht had little success in doing so with military means, it turned to other methods. The most deadly were engaging in
reprisal killings and what would amount to genocide.

The Wehrmacht rounded up large numbers of Serbian Jews, Communists,
and some Gypsies as "hostages," and then for purposes of so-called atonement
(*Sühne*) shot or hanged them in public. Through the end of August 1941,
partisans killed thirty-two German soldiers in Serbia; during the same period,
the Wehrmacht and German police murdered more than one thousand Jews
and Communists, in both Belgrade and in towns in western and southern
Serbia such as Cacak and Krusevac.

Despite the determined repressive measures of the Germans, partisan and
other resistance spread throughout Serbia and soon controlled much of the
country except for the large cities. On 16 September Hitler appointed a new
German military commander in Serbia, an Austrian general Franz Böhme.
Böhme arrived with orders from Keitel to kill as many as one hundred
Serbian Jews and Communists as a reprisal for the death of one German soldier and fifty Communists for each German wounded.

On 10 October the ruthless Böhme and his staff issued their first directive regarding reprisals, in which they ordered the murder of *all* Serbian Jews.
The large-scale killings in Serbia, therefore, resulted primarily at the initia-

tive of local military commanders and not solely from orders issued by the OKW or other central authorities in Germany. The historian Christopher Browning has commented on Böhme's directive:

> This reprisal policy of Böhme . . . was not simply a minimal compliance with the Keitel guidelines. Not only did they adopt the maximum suggested ratio [of Keitel] of one hundred to one rather than the minimum of fifty to one, but they also explicitly included "all Jews," a group that Keitel had never mentioned. Why did they do this? The German military commanders in Serbia had long accepted the identification or at least the natural combination of Communist and Jew.[12]

Between October and December 1941 mass "reprisal" executions by the Wehrmacht became a common practice; Böhme and his staff constantly incited their troops to savage terror. In the last two weeks of October alone, German troops shot more than nine thousand Jews, Gypsies, and other civilians. Most of the victims were killed after deportation to concentration camps built by the Germans at Sabac and Nis and near Belgrade.

As the Wehrmacht withdrew from much of southern Serbia during October in the face of stiff partisan and Cetnik resistance, the German troops massacred in one day nearly two thousand "hostages" at the town of Kraljevo. Four days later, on 20–21 October, other Wehrmacht units further north in the town of Kragujevac shot 2,300 Jews, Communists, and other civilians, including men, boys, and school children. Many of the victims were buried in large mass graves.

The massacres at Kraljevo and Kragujevac had immediate repercussions. They provided significant instances in which the practical considerations of the German conduct of the war were subordinated to the needs perceived for the killing program. In Kraljevo the entire Serbian work force of an airplane factory producing for the German war effort was among the victims. The incident dismayed the OKW and contributed to a halt, at least temporarily, of the mass and arbitrary executions of Serbian civilians.

The decision, however, did nothing to help the Jews; pressure exerted by the Germans to find "hostages" elsewhere led the occupiers to focus even more intently on imprisoning and killing Jews. The same held true for Serbian Gypsies. The Germans executed a large number of Gypsies in reprisal operations, probably numbering in the thousands, primarily because military commanders considered them spies and supporting the enemy.

By the time Böhme was recalled from his post in Serbia on 6 December, after barely three months of duty, his troops had produced a murderous record that bore no relation to reprisals for partisan or other attacks on German forces. The German casualties of 160 dead and 278 wounded contrasted with 20,000 to 30,000 civilians who had been executed, including most adult male Jews, in Serbia. The fact that the overwhelming majority of the Wehrmacht forces in Serbia were Austrians, many of whom held a hatred for the Serbs that stemmed from World War I, added to the killers' enthusiasm for their task.

Meanwhile, the German police took most of the remaining Jewish women, children, and old men in Serbia, approximately eight thousand in number, to the Sajmiste-Semlin concentration camp near Belgrade. The Wehrmacht justified the Jews' imprisonment by accusing them of engaging in intelligence operations for the partisans. Between March and May 1942, however, the Germans gassed the prisoners at the camp in a van or truck equipped as a mobile gas chamber and sent from Berlin. In little more than one year, the Wehrmacht and German police had murdered nearly the entire population of seventeen thousand Jews in Serbia. The head of the German security police in Serbia, Emanuel Schäfer, would report in June: "Serbia is free of Jews."[13]

The Invasion of Russia: Mass Killings of Soviet POWs and Jews

The German attack on the Soviet Union, launched on 22 June 1941, caught the Russians by surprise and nearly led to the quick victory the Nazis expected. The Germans invaded with three massive army groups that made up the largest single invasion force in history, over three million troops, plus half a million from countries allied to or friendly with Germany; such countries included Rumania, Hungary, Italy, Spain, and the German puppet states of Croatia and Slovakia.

Army Group North struck into the Baltic States, overrunning Lithuania and much of Latvia in the first few days; Army Group Center seized the eastern portion of Poland annexed by the Soviets in 1939; and Army Group South plunged rapidly into the Ukraine. The Germans eliminated much of the large Russian air force, cut off and destroyed substantial parts of the Red Army, and penetrated deeply into Soviet territory. German leaders anticipated a Russian surrender soon.

The early dramatic victories not only produced crippling Soviet losses in dead and wounded as well as in equipment and transportation, but also the Germans captured hundreds of thousands of Soviet POWs. From the first days of the campaign, the invaders shot many POWs and also purposely killed vastly more by starving them to death or allowing them to die from disease and exposure. Hitler viewed members of the Red Army not as soldiers drafted to do military service, but as active agents of an allegedly criminal Jewish-Bolshevik ideology and decadent racial subhumanity. "For these reasons," an OKW directive observed on 8 September 1941, setting forth guidelines for the treatment of Soviet POWs, "the Bolshevist soldier has lost every right to treatment as an honorable soldier in accordance with the Geneva Convention."[14]

On the central front alone, between September and December 1941, over a quarter million Soviet POWS died in German captivity. Other parts of the Eastern Front had similar death rates of Russian POWs. Also Hitler, in anticipation that his armies would capture soon both Moscow and Leningrad, issued orders for his forces to burn or raze both cities to the ground and drive their inhabitants into the wastelands farther east or kill them.

Evidence indicates clearly that, despite the claims of postwar German apologists to the contrary, most Wehrmacht, German police, and civilian authorities participated in this atrocity both willingly and even enthusiastically. Only a small number of exceptional individuals objected. This purposeful slaughter of POWs fulfilled the crude Social Darwinian principle at the core of Nazi philosophy: opposing racial groups could never be assimilated, but only enslaved, expelled, or exterminated.

On the other side in the war in the East, the massacre spurred not only the Red Army, but also much of the Soviet civilian population to even greater resistance against the enemy. If local inhabitants did not see the large areas where the POWs died or the Germans had shot them, they either heard by word of mouth or saw the wounded or disabled soldiers deliberately left in the countryside to perish. About the German invader, Weinberg observed: "Here was an enemy who made even Stalin's labor camps look humane—a considerable accomplishment—and one with longterm political implications."[15]

Increasingly Soviet civilians, including some Jews, organized partisan groups, which operated from the forests, swamps, and fields and conducted a guerrilla war against the Germans behind the front lines. Already by 1942 the partisans played a significant role in organizing Soviet resistance to the enemy; almost from the start, German antipartisan operations generally failed.

The German policy of slaughtering huge numbers of POWs related closely to the policy of killing the Jews in the Soviet Union. Wehrmacht units, as shown later in this chapter, frequently shot Jewish civilians as well as Jewish POWs. Attached to the German armies as they moved forward were four Einsatzgruppen, which implemented the decision to murder the remaining Jews in the areas captured by the advancing armed forces.

Altogether the Einsatzgruppen, along with nine Order Police battalions, three Waffen-SS units, and a number of further special formations, totaled thirty-five thousand men. Almost a third of the killers wore the green uniform of the Order Police: 430 officers and 11,640 men. According to the postwar testimony of both Dr. Walter Blume, who headed a special detachment (*Sonderkommando*) in his Einsatzgruppe, and Otto Ohlendorf, the commander of another Einsatzgruppe, already during May and June 1941 the leaders of the killing units had received orally the secret directive to shoot *all* Jews in Russia.

In June Heydrich and other SS and RSHA officials held a series of lectures for leaders of the Einsatzgruppen about their duties and aims in Russia. Regarding the briefings, Blume, one of those present, recalled later: "At this time we were already being instructed about the tasks of exterminating the Jews. It was stated that eastern Jewry was the intellectual reservoir of bolshevism and, therefore, in the Fuehrer's opinion, must be exterminated."[16]

On 2 July Heydrich ordered the Higher SS and Police Leaders in Russia to murder, in addition to Communist functionaries and radical elements such as saboteurs, Jews in party and government positions. On 17 July he instructed the Einsatzgruppen and other mobile killing units, when sorting out elements among Soviet POWs, to eliminate Communist officials, Soviet intellectuals, and all Jews. Since the German leadership expected the war in Russia to last only a few months, the Einsatzgruppen received directions to slaughter the Jews as quickly as possible. This would give the appearance that the war had produced the killings, not that the killers had perpetrated such a policy purposely.

Initially the SS leadership worried that the earlier opposition of the Wehrmacht in Poland to the persecution and killing of Jews there might result in something similar in Russia. Himmler, Heydrich, and Daluege remained uncertain about how the generals would respond to the mass killing of Jewish women, children, and elderly men. Consequently, they urged the Einsatzgruppen chiefs and Higher SS and Police Leaders to collaborate with Wehrmacht commanders in their areas.

Also to remove such potential problems with the Wehrmacht, and to free the latter for other tasks, the Germans quickly established a civilian administration in the areas of the Soviet Union overrun by German forces. This added yet a new layer to the bureaucracies already there, Himmler's SS and police and the Wehrmacht, which competed often for control in occupation policy.

Hitler appointed Alfred Rosenberg Reich Minister for the Occupied Eastern Territories. Rosenberg, a Baltic German with some pseudo-knowledge of the East, had little influence in party and government circles mainly because of his ineffectiveness in various political offices. His only success had been plundering Jewish and other art in Europe. Also Hitler named Hinrich Lohse, a Gauleiter and state president of Schleswig-Holstein, Reich Commissioner for the East (*Ostland*), which included the Baltic States and Byelorussia, and Erich Koch, Reich Commissioner for the Ukraine.

Immediately clashes occurred between Himmler and Rosenberg over authority in the East, in which Rosenberg viewed the mass killings and planned SS Germanization operations as disruptive for economic and war production. However, at a high level meeting on 16 July Hitler ruled in favor of the Reichsführer. He outlined how he expected to exploit the newly won empire in the East solely for Germany's benefit and the settlement of large numbers of Germans in the conquered lands. During a discussion of the functions of the SS in the East, Hitler demanded that its forces "shoot anyone who even has a cross look."[17]

The following day he decreed that Himmler had the power to issue orders to civilian officials in the occupied territories regarding security matters. Because, with few exceptions, no one ever challenged Hitler's authority, even Göring agreed, showing himself willing to subordinate his economic and war production goals in the East to the widespread killings of alleged enemies.

The Einsatzgruppen and other mobile killing units had little doubt about their primary mission: they were to murder the Jews of German-occupied Russia, primarily on the pretext that Jews were the key enemy in the war in the East. The Jews, the Germans alleged, were Communists, saboteurs, partisans, agitators, marauders, and criminals. That all Jews were to be killed was reflected widely in the reports the units sent by telegram and radio to the

RSHA, copies of which the US Army discovered in Gestapo headquarters in Berlin after the war.

The units' initial 195 reports from June 1941 to April 1942 contained, variously, phrases such as "nearly the entire [Jewish] intelligentsia was trapped and liquidated," "Jews have been resettled," "the territory . . . was cleared of Jews," "the operations to clear the country of Jews," "as far as possible the localities are entirely purged of Jews," "the Jewish question is being solved," and "finishing off Jews and Communists."[18]

In reality, however, the Germans did not kill the Jews in Russia because they were partisans or saboteurs. According to the official reports of the Einsatzgruppen referred to above, the killing units slaughtered far greater numbers of Jews than partisans. Stalin's call on 3 July 1941 to Russians to engage in a partisan war behind the German lines provided Hitler and Nazi propagandists with a further opportunity to mix both groups—Jews and partisans—and use this to justify the mass murder of the Jews, particularly to the Wehrmacht. Also the Germans associated the Gypsies in Soviet Russia with the partisans and enemy spies. The Einsatzgruppen killed Gypsies without mercy, including women and children.

The Einsatzgruppen, each fully motorized and containing between six hundred and a thousand men recruited hurriedly from the Gestapo, Criminal Police, Order Police, and Waffen SS, entered Russia: Einsatzgruppe A operated in the Baltic States, assigned to Army Group North; Einsatzgruppe B in Byelorussia (White Russia), detailed to Army Group Center; Einsatzgruppe C in the north and central Ukraine, attached to Army Group South; and Einsatzgruppe D in the southern Ukraine, Crimea, and Caucasus, operating with the 11th Army.

In addition, some Order Police units, such as Battalions 307, 309, 316, and 322, joined the attack. They fell under the authority of the Higher SS and Police Leaders. The police battalions and Einsatzgruppen based much of their operational strategy on the fact that most of the five million Soviets Jews lived in the western portions of the country and were concentrated almost exclusively in cities. The mobile units moved closely behind the advancing Wehrmacht forces to reach as many Soviet cities as quickly as possible and trap the large Jewish populations there before the victims could learn their fate.

Several factors worked to blunt Jewish alertness to the danger. These included the lack of information in the Soviet press and on radio about the fate of Jews in Nazi Europe, including Poland; the traditional conviction of many older Jews, who remembered that in World War I the Germans had invaded Russia as semiliberators; and the difficulty in fleeing for the elderly, women, and children.

Moreover, few if any of the victims imagined or even contemplated in their wildest nightmares, until too late, that the Germans intended to kill them all. The killers were heavily armed, they standardized their murderous operations, and they worked quickly. The victims were unarmed and peaceful civilians, often gripped by confusion and fear, and despite outnumbering their murderers, unprepared to oppose the latter with acts of violence of their own.

Once the Wehrmacht and mobile killing units arrived in the cities, they frequently ordered local Jews to register with the Germans and wear a yellow Star of David. The Einsatzgruppen divided themselves into special detachments (Sonderkommando), some that accompanied the advance units of the German armed forces (*Vorkommandos*) and others that moved into remote areas off the main roads (*Teilkommandos*). Rarely did the Wehrmacht interfere with the killing operations and often, as discussed later, the soldiers participated in them.

Einsatzgruppe A, for example, moved quickly out of East Prussia through Lithuania, Latvia, and Estonia, and eventually entered the larger suburbs of Leningrad. Its first massacres were carried out in public. Already on the evening of 24–25 June, the killing unit, along with German police, executed 201 persons, mostly Jews, in the town of Garsden, just inside Lithuania.

Also at the end of June a Sonderkommando of Einsatzgruppe A had arrived in the Lithuanian capital, Kaunas, and encouraged the start of a local pogrom. Portions of the population there and in the rest of the Baltic States, which the Russians had forcibly occupied in 1940, viewed the Soviet regime as the greatest enemy and agreed with the Nazis' linking of Jews and communists closely together.

The pogrom in Kaunas, whose Jewish population numbered forty thousand, resulted in the burning of synagogues and the Jewish quarter and the killing of several thousand Jews. In the streets Lithuanian criminals and police who acted as security auxiliaries for the Germans clubbed Jews to death with crowbars. As they did so, crowds cheered, mothers held their children to see what happened, and German soldiers gathered round like spectators at a sporting event. Many soldiers snapped photographs.

In a nearby fort outside Kaunas, established by the Germans as a concentration camp, the same Sonderkommando, with the help of Lithuanian collaborators, tortured and executed eight thousand more Jews. During the roundup of the victims, an SS man seized an infant from its mother and ripped the body of the child in half as the mother looked on. A characteristic of the killers' behavior here and elsewhere in the Soviet Union during the war was that before they murdered many of their desperate victims they forced them to beg for their lives. The killers then buried the dead Jews, a number of them children and the elderly, and some still alive, in mass earthen graves. On 7 July the Germans ordered the remaining Jews in Kaunas moved into a ghetto.

The detachment repeated similar *Aktionen* (a word used by the Germans to describe and conceal terror operations that included mass shootings and deportations of Jews) in other towns. During the ensuing months the Sonderkommando moved back and forth in Lithuania, portions of Latvia, and near Minsk in Byelorussia, conducting extensive killing operations. Also during its sweeps the unit organized or assisted pogroms carried out by the local population. It did so in part because, administratively, every Jew killed in such local violent outbursts was one less burden for the Einsatzgruppe, and in part because, psychologically, the latter wanted the population to take part of the responsibility for the killings.

Regarding the last point, the Germans could use pogroms to defend themselves against accusers as well as to blackmail a local population that now had blood on its hands. Other districts near the Soviet border rapidly combed through by the Einsatzgruppen included Bialystok, Galicia, and Bessarabia. In the smaller Jewish communities the units eliminated nearly all of the inhabitants by organizing pogroms, carrying out mass executions of Jews, and deporting those who remained to labor camps. During the last few days of June 1941, mobs of Ukrainians, including some police, responding to rumors that the Germans had given them permission to carry out a "Jew hunt," murdered several thousand Jews in Lwów (Lemberg) and the surrounding area. In at least one instance, the Germans apparently had little or no hand in a local attack on Jews in Poland. On 10 July in Jedwabne, a village in the former Russian zone of Poland, Poles murdered some one thousand of their Jewish neighbors.

While the density of Jewish settlement and speed of the German advance in the lands along the Soviet frontier led to widespread killings of Jews, the Einsatzgruppen that moved farther to the east in Russia came upon fewer victims. East of the Ukraine and the White Russian areas, Jews were fewer in number and more widely distributed. Moreover, farther east the Moscow government had evacuated Jews along with others, and many Jews had fled on their own. On 12 September Einsatzgruppe C reported from the Ukraine: "Word seems to have passed among the Jews on the other side of the front, too, about the fate they can expect from us."[19]

At least a million Jews had fled before the advancing Germans arrived. However, the Einsatzgruppen, to draw or lure back large numbers of victims to their communities, where they were caught and murdered, practiced a number of ruses or deceptions. These included engaging in no killings for a time or promising to "resettle Jews for labor," a phrase used by the Germans to disguise their intention of killing Jews. Also Jews fleeing or hiding found doing so difficult: roads, villages, and fields offered little subsistence or protection; local populations refused to shelter strangers on the run; and some Jews fell into the hands of advancing German army units.

Within only a few months the Einsatzgruppen had killed several hundred thousand Soviet Jews. By mid-October Einsatzgruppe A reported it had killed 125,000 Jews; by mid-November Einsatzgruppe B had killed 45,000; by November Einsatzgruppe C had murdered 75,000; and by mid-December Einsatzgruppe D had killed 55,000.

Still, the hurried German advance into Russia had meant that the killing units had missed numerous Jewish communities. To strike at such areas, a second wave of killing units, comprised of a Gestapo force from East Prussia, police detachments from the Polish General Government, and more units of the Higher SS and Police Leaders swept into Lithuania and Byelorussia, killing tens of thousands more Jews.

Each Higher SS and Police Leader had a regiment of Order Police and some Waffen-SS units. These forces assisted the Einsatzgruppen, or participated themselves, in numerous large massacres. One of the worst occurred on 29–30 September, in the ravine of Babi Yar near Kiev; there, in little more than forty-eight hours, both an Order Police regiment and local Ukrainian militia assisted in the shooting of 33,771 Jews by a Sonderkommando of Einsatzgruppe C.

Between June 1941 and the spring of 1942, the Germans murdered at least seven hundred thousand Soviet Jews. In some instances, killing Jews took precedence over military considerations. For example, in early September 1941 in northern Russia, Himmler instructed the Higher SS and Police Leader, Prützmann, to use the Second SS Brigade for "cleansing" operations, which meant killing Jews, instead of employing the unit in the German army's attack on Leningrad.

Nearly everywhere the Einsatzgruppen and other mobile killing units followed the same procedure. Generally they chose a shooting site outside of town as a grave; sometimes deepened antitank ditches or shell craters served as graves, while other graves the killers dug specially. The killers herded victims in groups, men first, from the assembly or collecting point to the ditch. Although the SS leadership directed that the killing sites remain closed off to and concealed from outsiders, this was not always possible or enforced; numerous local inhabitants from nearby villages and the countryside, therefore, witnessed what was happening.

After the victims were forced to hand over their valuables and clothes to the leaders of the killing party, they were lined up in front of the ditch, shot in the back of the neck with submachine guns or other small arms, and toppled into the grave. Some commanders in the Einsatzgruppen, including Otto Ohlendorf, Paul Blobel, and Walter Haensch, wished to avoid personal responsibility for the killings and so used a different procedure, a firing squad shooting from a considerable distance. Still another method of the mass killings involved victims being stacked successively in layers from the bottom of the grave upward and killed by crossfire from above.

Some Order Police battalions, under the authority of the Higher SS and Police Leaders, contributed substantially to the slaughters. For example, already on 27 June, Battalion 309 had moved through Bialystok, a city in the former Soviet zone of east Poland and a center of Jewish settlement, and burned seven hundred Jews to death in a fire in the main synagogue. On 8 July Battalion 322 raided the city's Jewish quarter, executing twenty-two people.

That afternoon Himmler made an unexpected visit to Bialystok, inspected the booty from the raid, and urged the police to intervene more against the Jews. Both Himmler and Bach-Zelewski encouraged the practice of the policemen in automatically associating Jews with looting and consequently executing them. That evening, while Bach-Zelewski hosted a private dinner for Himmler, the police shot a thousand more Jews in the city. In Bialystok and the surrounding region, during the first three months of the German occupation, the invaders, often assisted by Ukrainians and Poles, murdered nearly fifty thousand Jews.

The war diary of Battalion 322 observed that the unit worked day and night. At the end of August the battalion participated in the killing of seven hundred Jews from the ghetto that the Germans had established in Minsk, the capital of Byelorussia. The ghetto had a Jewish population of eighty thousand, including some deported to it from surrounding towns.

For cities with such large numbers of Jews, the early pogroms and executions could not eliminate the inhabitants entirely; as a result, the Germans
began establishing ghettos and concentration camps in which to imprison
the remaining Jews. Also the ghettos often provided the Germans with slave
labor until the killers decided that they were ready to dispose of the Jews.

During August Himmler again visited western Russia to gain more
information on the progress of the killings. By 7 August Bach-Zelewski had
reported that the total number of executions of Jews in his sector had
exceeded thirty thousand. During the following two days the Germans killed
over ten thousand more Jews in Pinsk. A week later Himmler visited Minsk,
where he met Bach-Zelewski and Arthur Nebe, an SS general, Criminal
Police chief, and commander of Einsatzgruppe B. The Germans had started
executing the local ghetto inhabitants, but on a limited scale; moreover, the
ghetto would soon receive shipments of German Jews and serve as a killing
center for them.

While in Minsk Himmler watched a firing squad kill a hundred prisoners, many of them Jews, accused of partisan activity. The executioners, an
Einsatzkommando and Order Police Battalion 9, did their work poorly, at first
only wounding the women, which left the Reichsführer visibly uncomfort-
able. When Bach-Zelewski complained to Himmler about the psychological
repercussions of the killings on the killers, the latter received a speech from
Himmler. He demanded of them, he said, that they treat the Jews and Slavs
in only the most ruthless manner and obey orders unconditionally.

In the Ukraine, during August and September Order Police battalions
45, 303, 314, 320, and others engaged in widespread mass executions of Jews,
including killing nearly twenty-four thousand in several days at Kamenets-
Podolsk near the Dnestr River. Among the victims were sixteen thousand
Hungarian Jews whom the Hungarian government had expelled in June and
forced across the border into the Ukraine. One hundred miles north at
Berdichev, on 4 September Battalion 45 carried out mass killings of Jews in
the local ghetto. A few weeks later, the battalion participated in the Babi Yar
massacre by cordoning off the restricted areas.

While few German search operations in the Soviet Union specifically
targeted Gypsies for killing, the Einsatzgruppen and German police units
treated Gypsies as partisans or spies and shot those whom the killers encountered. Gypsy men, women, and children who happened to be around villages,
towns, or the countryside when the Germans moved through were murdered.

CHAPTER NINE

REPERCUSSIONS OF THE WAR AND DECISION FOR THE FINAL SOLUTION

PART OF THE SUCCESS of the mobile German killing units in Soviet Russia during the summer and fall of 1941 resulted not only from some in the local population, especially Ukrainians, Lithuanians, and Latvians, joining in the killings. The units also received widespread assistance from the German armed forces. To be sure, a few Wehrmacht officers and troops criticized or opposed the killings. But from the beginning of the invasion of Russia, many others in the armed forces, frequently without being instructed to do so, exceeded the actual letter of the orders to the Wehrmacht to kill certain categories of Soviet POWs and hostile civilians, including especially Jews.

The Wehrmacht and the Massacres of Jews

In some instances German military commanders even pushed the Einsatzgruppen into killing operations. Also German troops executed Soviet civilians, for the most part Jews and Communists, allegedly in reprisal for partisan actions such as ambushes, looting, and sabotage. The German 6th Army, during its advance into the Ukraine, participated in the massacres of Jews in Lutsk (2 July), Tarnopol (early July), Byelaya Tserkov (22 August), and Kharkov (October, December) and helped round up Jews for killing by

Einsatzgruppe C in Lubny (October). About the executions in Tarnopol, Einsatzgruppe B reported to Berlin: "The German Army demonstrates a gratifyingly good attitude towards Jews."[1]

Also in the Ukraine, at the end of July in Zhitomir a German infantry regiment commanded by Major Karl Rösler arrived at a mass shooting near a local railroad embankment, carried out by a German police battalion. Rösler and his staff discovered, as he reported to his superior later, that in "a wide circle around the pit stood scores of soldiers from the troop detachments stationed there, some of them in bathing trunks, watching the proceedings."[2] Although Rösler complained about the unpleasantness of the slaughter and how it violated German customs and rearing, not once did he mention Jews. A few days later in the same city, hundreds of 6th Army soldiers looked on from rooftops and platforms while the Einsatzgruppe hanged or shot more Jews.

Only since the mid-1990s has the army's widespread participation in the killings become public. Historians have explained such behavior in several ways. First, Wehrmacht troops had received extensive indoctrination both before and early in the war in anti-Semitic, anti-Bolshevik, and anti-Slavic ideology. Second, during the first months of the German attack on the Soviet Union, the heavy losses of the Wehrmacht in both manpower and equipment led to a brutalization and demodernization of its troops fighting in the East.

This process combined with other factors that led simultaneously to a dehumanization of the enemy and a worship of Hitler. During the war the German armed forces meted out massive punishment to their own troops to ensure submission to military discipline; the Wehrmacht executed some fifteen thousand of its own troops, mostly for desertion or other breaches of combat activity on the Eastern Front. In addition, once the invasion of Russia began, the army intensified Nazi propaganda even more among its soldiers, which encouraged their plunder and killing of Jews and Slavs.

On 10 October Field Marshal Walter von Reichenau, the Commander-in-Chief of the 6th Army, issued a directive that summarized the brutality his troops had been practicing. Hitler immediately praised the order as exemplary. Other officers, including Field Marshal Gerd von Rundstedt, head of Army Group South, and General Erich von Manstein, the 11th Army commander, either distributed copies of von Reichenau's order to their troops or elaborated on it by producing an even more radical version.

Contrary to some postwar military apologists, the order was not a spontaneous impulse on von Reichenau's part. Nor was it the result of widespread opposition in the Wehrmacht toward the mass murder of Jews. He directed his forces:

> The essential goal of the campaign against the Jewish-Bolshevik system is the complete destruction of its power instruments and the eradication of the Asiatic influence on the European cultural sphere.
>
> Thereby the [German] troops too have tasks, which go beyond the conventional unilateral soldierly tradition. In the East the soldier is not only a fighter according to the rules of warfare, but also a carrier of an inexorable racial conception and the avenger of all the bestialities which have been committed against the Germans and related races.
>
> Therefore the soldier must have *complete* understanding for the necessity of the harsh, but just atonement of Jewish subhumanity.[3]

Similarly in Byelorussia a commander in Army Group Center ordered his units "to make sure that the Jews are completely eliminated from the villages." He accused the Jews of being the sole supporters of the partisan movement and concluded: "Therefore, their annihilation is to be pursued ruthlessly."[4] During the last months of 1941, until the Red Army launched its first major offensive in the war and forced Army Group Center to employ nearly every one of its troops, the units of the Army Group carried out "cleansing" operations against Jews in villages and the countryside of White Russia.

When forces of Army Group Center reached Minsk, which German tank (*Panzer*) spearheads turned into a pile of ruins, they assisted in the killing of several thousand Jews and in establishing a ghetto for those who remained. Also elsewhere in the region the Wehrmacht helped the Einsatzgruppen and German police in the formation of ghettos at places such as Mogilev and Grodno.

Byelorussia had a special strategic importance for Army Group Center because the region contained key supply lines, crucial armament factories, and repair facilities. The Wehrmacht used the hundreds of thousands of Jews imprisoned in the ghettos of Byelorussia as slave laborers (*Arbeitsjuden*) in the army's rear area. Many of the enslaved died from malnutrition, overwork, and exhaustion; others were executed when the Germans no longer needed their labor. The massive German system of forced labor during the war is discussed in chapter ten.

Moreover, throughout Byelorussia between October and December 1941, the Einsatzgruppen, assisted by regiments of the Army Group and locally recruited auxiliary police forces, carried out largescale killings of ghetto inhabitants. Most of the victims were women and children. The Wehrmacht supplied trucks to transport Jews, troops to round up victims and cordon off areas, and units that served as execution squads. In addition, the Wehrmacht detailed engineers to cover mass graves by using explosive charges. During August and November the ghetto in Minsk, the largest in the occupied Soviet Union with one hundred thousand inhabitants, which included fifteen thousand Jews deported from Germany, suffered the worst massacres.

By January 1942 the Wehrmacht had murdered at least twenty thousand Jews in Byelorussia. In addition, the Rumanian armies that had accompanied the German forces into Russia and moved through portions of the southern Ukraine and Crimea, repeatedly invading Jewish quarters in cities and towns and murdering the inhabitants, often spontaneously and sometimes in collaboration with Einsatzgruppe D.

During October 1941 the 4th Rumanian Army executed as many as sixty thousand Jews in and near Odessa, the city with the largest Jewish population in the Soviet Union. This, however, left Heydrich dissatisfied with the Rumanians; both he and the head of Einsatzgruppe D, Ohlendorf, complained to the Rumanian government that the latter's forces had not done enough to eliminate Jews.

Effects of the Killings

Numerous issues regarding the mass shootings and other murders in the East concerned the leadership of both the Wehrmacht and killing units of the SS and RSHA. Einsatzgruppen commanders and their adjutants often visited the killing sites to observe the shootings and attempt to minimize their effects on the surrounding non-Jewish population and on those doing the killing. Above all, the officers sought to ensure that their units did everything to hide the massacres from local inhabitants.

However, the enormity of the killings and the sheer brutality with which they were carried out, meant that numerous local persons witnessed them, or at least heard about them. At first such onlookers seemed unworried and carefree about what happened, but soon this view faded away as increasingly they realized the harshness of German rule and feared for their own security and safety. According to Hilberg: "Gradually then, the local-non-Jewish witnesses of the destruction process perceived the true nature of the German racial ladder. The lowest rung was already afire, and they were but one step above it."[5]

Also the SS and RSHA sought to keep the officers and men in the killing units as silent about their work as possible. Himmler, Heydrich, and others issued orders forbidding members of the units from recording or discussing what they knew. However, word of the killings in the East, which became quickly and widely known in the occupied territories, soon filtered as well into Germany.

While the orders for secrecy were frequently repeated, they were also often disobeyed. Some of the men viewed the mass shootings as a duty, others as a curiosity, and still others as a sensation and popular entertainment. On numerous occasions the killers or other officers and men who witnessed what happened made a record of it, including taking photographs, writing letters back home to family and friends in Germany, and talking while home on leave about what they had seen.

One SS officer, Max Täubner, got into trouble for taking photographs of the torture and murder of Jews in the Ukraine, having them developed by a commercial chemist in Germany, and showing them to his relatives and friends. An SS court ruled that Täubner could not be punished for his actions because the Jews "have to be exterminated and none of the Jews that were killed is any great loss." The same court, however, condemned him for "the taking of tasteless and shameless pictures" and sentenced him to prison.[6] Himmler pardoned Täubner in January 1945.

Also some among the mobile killing units in the East exhibited psychological effects from the killing operations. At first they experienced anxiety: if Germany lost the war, it was said, there would surely be a heavy price to pay. But that feeling did not last long, especially as the German armies drove deeply into the Soviet Union, and it appeared Germany would soon win the war.

Individually, a few members of the killing units felt disgust or shame and suffered emotional problems. They had, it was claimed, terrible nightmares, they drank heavily, and some went mad and shot indiscriminately all around them. Nervous breakdowns and suicides also occurred. A handful of other men, for moral or other reasons, could not face the strain and refused to participate in the killings. The officers quickly weeded these out and sent them to other posts; although the men transferred might be called cowards, none suffered punishment for their refusal to involve themselves in the grisly work.

The excuse so often used by German war criminals and others after 1945 that "we would have been shot if we had refused," amounted to a myth. According to a 1988 study of over one hundred cases of Germans who refused to execute civilians during the war, "*none of them paid the ultimate penalty, death! Furthermore, very few suffered any other serious consequence!*"[7] Another important conclusion of the investigation was "the relative scarcity of documented instances of refusal by individuals or groups to carry out civilian or POW executions."[8] Neither the SS nor police needed to force or compel men to participate, because plenty of others volunteered to replace the miniscule number of defectors.

Most of the killers, for reasons that varied among them, accepted their orders obediently and soon settled into their work without conscience. They acted because, as Browning and other historians have emphasized, of pressure from peers for acceptance and conformity and the desire for promotions and rewards. Browning placed less emphasis on the role of anti-Semitism in motivating the killers, most likely because the postwar testimony of the policemen whom he studied made little or no reference to disliking Jews. Those testifying carefully avoided incriminating themselves with the courts.

Still other evidence suggests that anti-Semitism had a significant influence on the behavior of the killers. Police Battalion 310 acted because of its demographic makeup, brutalization in frontline combat, and—in the words of a recent study of the battalion—"commitment to the National Socialist *Weltanschauung*," which taught a savage hatred of Jews and Slavs.[9] A German historian, Konrad Kwiet, examined Police Battalion 322 and reached similar conclusions about the importance of ideology in explaining the battalion's actions. The battalion moved into Byelorussia and murdered six thousand Jews and others in the first weeks of the German invasion.

Daniel Goldhagen, with considerable justification, called the German police and other killing units involved in the Holocaust "willing executioners."[10] From the earliest moments of the war in the East, most members of the Einsatzgruppen and police units engaged agreeably in close-range shootings, rape, castration, dismemberment, and other forms of mutiliation of their victims.

By 1941, members of German police battalions and other killing units operating in the Soviet Union had lived for eight years in a Nazi society that had fed them a constant diet of rabid anti-Jewish propaganda. This had combined with propaganda emphasizing the rule over the East and its allegedly "inferior" peoples by the master race. Simultaneously, rigid Nazi censorship of the foreign media had screened out nearly all contrary views or voices.

One German policeman testified after the war, in defending his killing of Jews, that he was "at that time convinced that the Jewish people were not innocent but guilty. I believed all the propaganda that Jews were criminals and subhuman and that they were the cause of Germany's decline after the First World War. The thought that one should oppose or evade the order to take part in the extermination of the Jews never entered my head either."[11]

Commanders of the Einsatzgruppen and other killing units coped with the psychological effects of the massacres by attempting both to justify and repress their activities. Especially their choice of language used in written reports describing individual killing operations demonstrated their efforts at repression. They avoided the use of words such as "kill" or "murder," and instead substituted euphemisms, or terms designed to conceal or obscure the killings. Such words included "executed," "exterminated," "liquidated," "actions," "special treatment," "evacuation," "cleansing," "elimination," "resettlement," and "solution of the Jewish question."[12]

Wehrmacht soldiers who watched or participated in the killings reacted similarly to members of the mobile killing units. The soldiers too often wrote letters, talked, and sent photographs of mass shootings to their relatives at home; the soldiers, therefore, contributed also to information about the killings gradually reaching Germany. As an indication of what was happening, the Wehrmacht issued repeated instructions to the troops to stop sending pictures.

Yet in a classic case in Hitler's Germany of bureaucratic competition, Goebbels, the Reich Propaganda Minister and frequent rival of Himmler, published a book for propaganda purposes of letters sent home to Germany from the various war fronts. He included in the volume the letter of a German soldier to the latter's family that told of the mass murders. Moreover, Goebbels published an article in the German paper, *Das Reich*, which blamed the Jews for the war. He declared that Germany would deliver retribution by fulfilling Hitler's prophecy of 30 January 1939 that a war would result in the annihilation of European Jewry.

Also after the German conquest of Kiev in September 1941, the Wehrmacht invited foreign journalists to the Ukraine to view the destruction of the city, which the Germans blamed on the "Bolsheviks." The visitors, however, questioned their army hosts about mass shootings of civilians and refused to accept the army's denial of involvement in them. A Swiss army medical mission accompanying the German forces had similar information. One of its physicians, Rudolf Bucher, reported his experiences to superiors and discussed later what he had heard and seen among the Swiss public .

The World First Learns

Wholly unknown to the Germans, fairly precise knowledge of the killings in the East already had reached the British government. Since the beginning of the world war, Britain's military intelligence had broken the hand-based cipher of the German Order Police and intercepted and decoded on a regular basis the latter's radio messages regarding its activities.

The British, therefore, had picked up an array of information about the German occupation of Poland, in which the Order Police had participated. This included news about the transfers of Poles and Jews into the General Government and a requirement that the executions of such persons be reported to the commanding Higher SS and Police Leader. As a result, British intelligence analysts knew that German officials used euphemisms and a terminology of camouflage, such as "special duties" and "pacification," for describing extreme measures.

During the summer and fall of 1941, British decrypts of police messages included dozens of reports of mass killings in Russia directed by the Higher SS and Police Leaders and carried out by the Order Police and Waffen-SS. In one message on 7 August, Bach-Zelewski, the Higher SS and Police Leader for central Russia, boasted that the total number of killings in his region numbered more than thirty thousand. By the end of August, the British, including Prime Minister Winston Churchill, began to learn that Jews were the primary victims of the mass executions in Russia.

The following month, Britain's Secret Intelligence Service (SIS) concluded that the German "Police are killing all Jews that fall into their hands" in Russia, but decided not to report "these butcheries specially" to Churchill "unless so requested."[13] Some SIS analysts apparently worried that a previous Churchill speech, in which he mentioned the mass executions, might have tipped the Germans off to Britain's code-breaking success. Only Churchill and a few intelligence officials in the SIS knew of the top secret decrypt-analysis operation. Still, the analysts of the decrypts had sufficient information to conclude that Germany had a formal policy of destroying the Jews in the Soviet Union.

British intelligence, moreover, had other sources of early information about the killings. These included Russian radio broadcasts monitored in London that described in October 1941 what later came to be known as the Babi Yar massacre. A British Foreign Office official and chairman of his government's Joint Intelligence Committee, Victor Cavendish-Bentinck, treated such accounts with skepticism and claimed they represented primarily atrocity propaganda. However, as discussed later in this book, Britain sealed away as "top secret" the knowledge it had about the Nazi killings from the decrypted German police messages. Only decades after the war's end would researchers discover such "official secrets" in the British archives.[14]

Also the British received information from the Polish and Czech governments-in-exile in London and from accounts of the atrocities that reached neutral Switzerland and Sweden. As early as 4 January 1941, the Polish exile government requested that Britain's Royal Air Force (RAF) bomb the German concentration camp at Auschwitz. The exile government sent the RAF a report from sources in Poland that described the camp as "one of the worst organized and most inhuman concentration camps." The report continued: "It is a wonder how the prisoners manage to survive."[15]

The information reaching the government-in-exile, and subsequently the RAF, about Auschwitz was relatively accurate. In mid-January the RAF declined to bomb the camp because the effort would divert resources away from the Bomber Command's newly established primary objective, the destruction of German oil facilities. Moreover, the RAF attempted to preclude the exile government making a political appeal to Churchill or other members of the British government.

These events provide an additional context for evaluating the later failure of the Western Allies in 1944 to launch air attacks against the killing facilities located in the death camp at Auschwitz-Birkenau. The Allies, which by the end of 1941 would include both Britain and the United States, would only consider the issues of German war crimes, retribution, and the punishment of war criminals after pressured significantly to do so by the exile governments.

Still other pieces of information about the mass murder of Jews in Soviet Russia made their way to the West. During the fall of 1941 a variety of newspapers in Britain and neutral countries reported on particular massacres. The Jewish Telegraphic Agency newsman in Switzerland learned from a Ukrainian newspaper about the slaughter of Jews in Zhitomir; the *Jewish*

Chronicle in London reported that thousands of Jews had died in pogroms in the Ukraine. *The Times* of London reprinted a Swedish news account that claimed German Jews deported to Russia would die, one way or the other. Other British papers reported widely the deportations of Jews from Germany and Austria to the East.

In October Gerhart Riegner, a lawyer who had left Germany after the Nazis took power and ended up in Switzerland working for the World Jewish Congress (WJC), sent the organization's leaders a lengthy account of the killings of tens of thousands of Jews. Based on Riegner's information, the WJC provided the British Foreign Office with a lengthy report, filled with documentation, on the Nazi persecution of the Jews.

Almost simultaneously Richard Lichtheim of the Jewish Agency for Palestine, reported on the deportations of Jews from Germany, Austria, and the Czech Protectorate to the East, and possibly all the way to Russia. He made known his information to Chaim Weizmann, the prominent Zionist leader in London and President of the Jewish Agency. Lichtheim urged the agency to begin a campaign to publicize what was happening.

Despite receiving this news of the mass killings of Jews, most Jewish leaders in the West initially failed to perceive that a methodical campaign of extermination threatened their European brethren. They continued to think in terms of persecution and pogroms and did not realize the enormity of the killings. One can hardly blame the Jewish officials, however, because most everyone else in the West who read or heard reports of the mass killings not only expressed skepticism regarding them, but also misunderstood the unprecedented and horrifying reality of what the reports described.

In the United States, the reception of such news would be affected by attitudes held by most Americans regarding the war and refugees. The war produced among Americans a hysterical fear that a massive "fifth-column" existed in the United States, a spy network that many believed included Jewish refugees from Germany or Russia. Many Americans viewed Jewish refugees not only as potential German agents, but also as Communist informers for the Soviet Union. Although President Roosevelt had a hand in helping promote this illusionary threat by making uninformed remarks at a press conference, the State Department, the Federal Bureau of Investigation, and naval and military intelligence did the most to create it.

Anti-Jewish views existed in varying degrees at nearly all levels of the United States Army. In 1940, for example, the chief of the Army's War Plans

Division accepted the Nazis' wholly erroneous view of the distinguished scientist and German emigré, Einstein, who lived in the United States. The officer termed Einstein "an extreme radical" and Communist and recommended that he not be employed "on matters of a secret nature."[16] The Secretary of War, Henry Stimson, talked about an alleged Jewish problem in the United States and would at no time during the war express any strong feelings about the sufferings of Europe's Jews.[17]

Also in America, numerous powerful isolationists who wished to keep the United States out of the war held anti-Jewish views. On 11 September 1941, only a few months before the United States would enter the struggle, Charles Lindbergh, the aviator hero and admirer of Hitler, blamed the Jews for the war. In a notorious radio speech on behalf of the America First Committee, the most influential isolationist group, he alleged that American Jews pursued a "prowar policy" that would "lead our country to destruction." Moreover, Lindbergh claimed, American intervention in the war would be disastrous for the Jews themselves. They would be the first victims of the "war and devastation" that would quickly destroy the "tolerance" Jews enjoyed in times of "peace and strength."[18]

Despite the widespread anti-Semitism in America, information about the unfolding Holocaust in Europe continued to arrive in the United States from various sources. These included newsmen and diplomats in Germany and Europe. Yiddish newspapers in New York City reported about German killings of hundreds of Jews in western Russia. During October the *New York Times* published articles on the German slaughter of Jews and Serbs in Yugoslavia and of fifteen thousand Jews in Galicia; the paper based the latter report, titled "Slaying of Jews in Galicia Depicted," on eyewitness accounts from Hungarian soldiers.[19] Most of the articles in the *Times* and other papers relegated such reports to the back pages and generally treated them with skepticism.

During the fall the American embassy in Berlin reported that it expected all Jews in Germany would be deported soon to Russia for forced labor. An article in the *Times* on 21 October discussed something similar. None of the reports, however, indicated clear knowledge of the fate of the deportees. On 25 October President Roosevelt denounced publicly the German executions of innocent hostages in France, but made no mention of mass killings of Jews.

In a separate statement, Churchill condemned the Nazi killings in France and elsewhere, including countries in Europe and on the war front in

Russia. Although the prime minister said nothing of the slaughter of the Jews, he nevertheless suggested that punishment for such "crimes must henceforward take its place among the major purposes of the war."[20] Meanwhile, a few days later, the American military attaché in Berlin informed his government that SS units were killing Jews in many areas of Russia.

The First Armed Jewish Resistance

Unknown to the world were the first stirrings, by the fall of 1941, of organized and armed Jewish resistance in the German-occupied Soviet territories. Small resistance or underground groups appeared in some towns and ghettos, usually following largescale German massacres of their Jewish inhabitants. Most who joined the groups did so for reasons of revenge or because they realized that only death awaited them and their families and friends and they had nothing to lose by resisting the killers. Such groups included women and youth as well as men. Many were organized by prewar Jewish political parties and youth organizations, especially Zionists, Communists, and Bundists (socialists). In some ghettos the local Jewish leadership, the Judenräte, collaborated with the resistance.

In Byelorussia, small underground organizations arose, among other places, in Dyatlovo, Slonim, Starodub, Tatarsk, and Minsk. On 30 June 1941 units of the Wehrmacht had occupied Dyatlovo, where four thousand Jews lived, and quickly established a ghetto in the city. Periodic executions of Jews in July and the internment of four hundred in December in a nearby forced labor camp triggered the founding of a ghetto resistance group. Its leader, Alter Dworzecki, the deputy chairman and a principal official of the Judenrat, convinced sixty members of the underground to join the Jewish police in the ghetto. These Dworzecki transformed into a self-defense unit.

In the event the Germans carried out an Aktion, the resistance decided to organize an armed revolt that would enable the ghetto inhabitants to flee into the surrounding forests. Also Dworzecki's group attempted to spread anti-German feelings among the local non-Jewish population. Capitalizing on the resources of the Judenrat, Dworzeki acquired weapons that included two rifles as well as a pistol and munitions, which he smuggled into the ghetto in January 1942.

Although he favored fighting the Germans from inside the ghetto, in the spring Dworzecki escaped to the forests. But during a German Aktion that murdered twelve hundred Jews in the ghetto, the resistance made no attempt to attack the killers, primarily because local Soviet partisans viewed it as too risky. Later an ambush of the partisans killed Dworzecki, but his spirit lived on. Some of the remaining Jews in the Dyatlovo ghetto continued, with a measure of success under another resistance leader, Hirsch Kaplinski, to seek escape from the ghetto to the forests.

The Germans had overrun Slonim, a city with twenty-two thousand Jews, many of them refugees from Nazi-occupied western Poland, on 25 June 1941. Massacres of Jews in the city's ghetto on 14 July and 14 November killed 1,255 and 10,000, respectively, and led to the creation of a local Jewish resistance group. Calling itself an antifascist committee, the group consisted mostly of a handful of young Jews who worked for the Germans in munitions depots, from which they stole pistols, other guns, and grenades and smuggled them into the ghetto. The committee decided that, rather than organizing resistance inside the ghetto, it would contact partisans operating in the neighboring forests and distribute munitions and arms to them. With help from the Slonim Judenrat, the committee supported the partisans in other ways as well, but it could not stop the German murder during 1942 of nearly all the remaining Jews in the ghetto.

On 25 October 1941, local Jews in the towns of Starodub and Tatarsk, met with armed force the arriving Sonderkommando of Einsatzgruppe B. Because most of the Jews in both places perished, including 272 in Starodub, a German report of the battle remains the only account of what happened. In Tatarsk, the Germans shot all male Jews and three women, allegedly as punishment for not following German orders to return to the local ghetto.

Inside the much larger Minsk ghetto, a resistance movement developed amid the initial mass killings of the ghetto's inhabitants. The Germans had murdered five thousand in August 1941 and nineteen thousand in November. Each massacre intensified the activities of a ghetto underground organization, whose membership numbered about 450 persons, a third of them youth.

The group constructed a network of cells, distributed information from the military front, established a printing press, and made contact with Communist partisans in nearby woods and with other non-Jewish resistance groups in Minsk. Also the organization collected what few small-caliber weapons it could find. On one occasion, an emissary from the partisans secretly entered the ghetto and asked for money, which he received from the chairman of the Judenrat, Ilia Mushkin. The latter, a trade employee whose only qualification for his ghetto post was that he spoke German, in fact supported both the ghetto underground organization and the Communists with medicine, clothes, and the dispatch of Jews into the nearby forests to conduct partisan warfare. At the start of the massacre in August, the ghetto underground issued a despairing, but futile, appeal to the partisans outside the ghetto to assist more Jews in escaping into the woods.

Also in Lithuania, where massive killings of Jews began immediately with the German invasion of the Soviet Baltic States, small resistance movements appeared most notably in ghettos in Schaulen, Vilna, and Kaunas. Already by the end of 1941, after the Germans and Lithuanians had established a ghetto in Schaulen and murdered in the first months of occupation more than half of the 5,360 Jews, underground groups, comprised of Zionist and communist youth, had formed inside the ghetto. Although the groups managed to smuggle a few weapons into the ghetto, they were unable to produce a revolt among its population or stop later deportations.

In the large Vilna ghetto, Zionist youth also took the lead in creating a resistance organization. Sometime around New Year's day 1942, they met secretly, during which the manifesto of Abba Kovner, a ghetto resistance leader and writer, was read that declared, "Better to fall with honor in the ghetto than to be led like sheep to Ponar."[21] Since late June 1941 the SS and police killing units, assisted by Lithuanian auxiliaries, had shot thousands of Jews at Ponary, a nearby execution and mass burial site.

Kovner had learned of the massacres and appealed to the youth groups to organize an armed resistance against the Germans. Also participating in the meeting was Mordechai Tenenbaum, a founder and commander of Jewish resistance movements emerging not only in the Vilna ghetto, but also in the ghettos in Warsaw, Bialystok, and Grodno.

This meeting soon produced inside the Vilna ghetto an armed resistance group that would become one of the most important such organizations in the Holocaust. Created from the youth movements and different Jewish political parties represented in the ghetto, including the communists, the group called itself the United Partisan Organization (*Fareinikte Partisaner Organisatzije*, FPO). A Communist member, Yitzhak Witenberg, commanded the FPO, but significant differences existed between the Communist partisans outside the ghetto and the Jewish partisans inside.

The Jewish partisans prepared for a revolt in the ghetto when the Germans arrived to empty or destroy it; the Communists wanted the Jewish youth to fight the Germans in the woods outside the ghetto and city. Not content with engaging in only local anti-German operations, the FPO attempted to kindle resistance in various parts of Eastern Europe. Although the organization failed to incite a revolt inside the Vilna ghetto, it nevertheless eventually had several hundred ghetto fighters who joined the partisans in surrounding forests.

In addition, the FPO sent messengers to other ghettos, including Warsaw, to inform Jewish leaders about the murder of the Jews in Vilna and the rest of Lithuania. Although the FPO failed to establish contact with the Polish Underground Army (*Armya Krajowa*), it succeeded in establishing relations with a small non-Jewish Communist group. On at least one occasion the FPO attempted to send women as messengers through the battlelines on the Eastern Front, to report the mass murder of the Jews to the world and request help. As the messengers approached the frontlines, however, they were caught, but most managed to escape and return to Vilna.

Acquiring weapons represented the greatest problem for the FPO. Either it purchased small arms from the local population or FPO members who worked in a nearby German equipment depot smuggled a few weapons out and distributed them to the organization. Inside the ghetto, the FPO produced primitive grenades and Molotov cocktails. Mainly the FPO collected pistols and a small number of other guns, which it hid in the ghetto. Outside the ghetto, the organization worked to sabotage the German war effort; it destroyed rail sidings on which trains ran to the battlefront and damaged equipment and weapons in German factories where FPO members worked.

The chairman of the Vilna Judenrat, Jacob Gens, knew of the resistance movement inside the ghetto and retained good relations with its commanders until 1943. Gens, barely forty years old and a former Lithuanian officer, high school teacher, and businessman, was both a Lithuanian patriot and conscious Jew. He had also married a non-Jewish Lithuanian woman and insisted that she live outside the ghetto.

Gens's relations with the ghetto resistance would begin to dissolve in the spring of 1943, when the Gestapo discovered increased activities of the underground, which included arms smuggling and the escape of young people to the forests to join the partisans. The Germans warned Gens of terrible consequences for the ghetto inhabitants should this continue. When some of the escapees clashed with the Germans outside the city, in retaliation for the breakout the Gestapo seized the entire family of each Jew who had escaped. All were shot. Thereafter, if one person escaped a ghetto work party, the Germans ordered the entire group killed. A ghetto newspaper called escapees traitors "endangering the existence of our entire ghetto and the lives of their loved ones."[22] Gens agreed, demanding that the Jews remain behind the ghetto walls. Like most Judenrat leaders, he believed that the ghetto existed and survived because it served the Germans as a source of labor. He strove to turn the ghetto into a factory.

Then in mid-July 1943 the Gestapo discovered that Witenberg was also a member of the Lithuanian communist underground and demanded that Gens hand him over. Although the Jewish police arrested Witenberg, the latter escaped and the FPO refused to surrender him. The Germans insisted— either they receive Witenberg or the ghetto, along with its inhabitants, would be destroyed. The FPO, therefore, if it chose to defend Witenberg, faced a situation in which it would have to fight its fellow ghetto dwellers. Eventually, so as not to endanger the entire ghetto, Witenberg surrendered and later committed suicide in a German prison. A woman, Chaine Borowska, succeeded him as head of the communist underground. Shortly thereafter, when the Germans began massive deportations from the ghetto, relations between Gens and the FPO would collapse completely.

In the Kaunas ghetto, an antifascist organization emerged almost during the first months of the German invasion of Russia, which had produced immediate and massive killings of the city's Jews. The antifascists included mainly communists led by Chaim Yelin. The organization attempted to collect weapons and establish contact with local Soviet partisans. In addition to the communists, young people in the ghetto, most of whom belonged to Zionist youth groups, engaged in underground activities.

Also the ghetto's Jewish leadership cooperated with the resistance. The Judenrat, headed by a prominent physician and Jewish community leader, Elhanan Elkes, had close ties to the underground and assisted some of its members in escaping the ghetto to join the partisans. Elkes faced the Germans with great personal courage in other ways as well, including supervising clandestine efforts to rescue Jewish children from being killed by the Germans. The ghetto police, commanded by Moshe Levin, a right-wing Zionist, assisted the underground. Nevertheless, similar to most other Jewish resistance groups, the one in Kaunas had insufficient manpower and weapons to lead an armed uprising against the Germans.

The Transition to the Final Solution

The persecution and mass murder of the Jews particularly thrilled a German ally from the Middle East, Haj Amin al-Husayni, the extreme Arab nationalist and Grand Mufti of Jerusalem. He had fled to Berlin during 1941 from

Iraq, after Germany tried and failed to stop Britain's defeat of a revolt there led by a pro-German Iraqi prime minister. Both the Germans and Italians had hoped to use al-Husayni to incite Arab uprisings against the British in Palestine, Iraq, and elsewhere in the Middle East.

But although al-Husayni urged the defeat of Britain and approved of Germany's anti-Jewish policies, he had little influence in the Middle East and could do nothing to increase Axis power there. Hitler refused to support the Mufti's demand for Arab independence in the Middle East; the Nazi leader, obsessed with conquering Europe and Russia, feared alienating Italy, Vichy France, and Turkey and was guided by his ideology that viewed Arabs as racial inferiors.

German leaders, ecstatic about the massive initial victories of the Wehrmacht in Russia, turned to postwar planning in the summer of 1941 as quickly as they had during the previous year, when they believed the war had ended triumphantly for them in the West. Militarily they intended now to invade the Middle East, by moving German forces into the region from two directions: through southern Russia, the Caucasus, and Turkey and through North Africa and Egypt. The Germans envisioned that seizing the Middle East would destroy Great Britain's position there, help break up its global empire, and capture for Germany—and deny to the British and their allies—the vast oil reserves of the region to add to the supplies won by the Germans in the Caucasus.

Simultaneously, Hitler and his associates ordered in the first weeks of fighting in the East the implementation of what they termed "the Final Solution of the Jewish question." They apparently based this solution on the earlier plan Heydrich had submitted to Hitler in January for the extermination of the Jews. The Final Solution involved following up the mass murder of the Jews of occupied Russia with the murder of *all* of Europe's Jews that German military power could reach.

Triumph over the Soviet Union seemed assured. So did acquiring the extensive territory and resources there for Germany's future use during the remainder of the war and for long after. Hitler, Himmler, Heydrich, and Göring now believed they could do anything they wished—even murder a whole group of people, the Jews, whom they hated more than anyone else and for no other reason than such persons had been born.

During the first days of July 1941, Hitler apparently gave instructions for the Final Solution, most likely orally, to Himmler and Heydrich. It is doubtful that he issued a written order, perhaps in part because of his experience with the opposition of many Germans to the euthanasia program. Also his decision for the Final Solution resulted from the fact that he had received little objection from his subordinates to the mass slaughter of the Jews that had started in the Soviet Union. In fact, nearly everyone involved in the killing operations in Russia, including most of the Wehrmacht, agreed with, understood, and supported them.

During July and August his comments and actions and those of his top SS leaders indicate that he had issued the directive to murder every Jew in German-occupied Europe. He met on 21 or 22 July with Marshal Sladko Kvaternik, the commander of the Croatian armed forces, during which the German leader discussed removing the Jews from every European country and prophesied that Hungary would give up its Jews last. He mistrusted the Hungarians, primarily because they had refused to join him in his planned war in 1938 against Czechoslovakia.

Himmler, for his part, moved quickly to take the lead in this vast operation that Hitler had entrusted to him and the SS. He visited with key SS and police leaders in the East, repeatedly urging on them the destruction of the Jews, ordering them to prepare more effective places where, and techniques by which, the Jews could be eliminated, and proclaiming that this was the "Führer's order."

Sometime during the summer, most probably in mid-July, Himmler met in Berlin with Höss, the Reichsführer's longtime acquaintance and SS commandant at Auschwitz. During their private discussion, Himmler acted on his earlier idea of establishing an extermination center at the camp. According to Höss, Himmler informed him:

> The Führer has ordered the Final Solution of the Jewish question. We the SS have to carry out this order. The existing extermination sites in the East [likely a reference to the mobile killing units in the Soviet Union] are not in a position to carry out these intended operations on a large scale. I have, therefore, chosen Auschwitz for this purpose. First of all, because of the advantageous transport facilities, and secondly, because it allows this area to be easily isolated and disguised. . . .You now have to carry out this assignment. It is to remain between the two of us.[23]

Shortly thereafter, Eichmann visited Höss at Auschwitz. Eichmann explained to the commandant "the secret plans of the police roundups in the individual countries" and the intention to use poison gas to carry out the "mass annihilation" of the Jews.[24]

Then on 16–17 July Himmler received from Hitler extensive authority in the East over security matters and the resettlement of ethnic Germans there. Three days later Himmler visited Lublin, where the local SS and police leader, Odilo Globocnik, had built several concentration camps for Jews and Poles deported from western Poland. Globocnik, one of the numerous Austrians in the upper ranks of the SS, had demonstrated since his appointment in November 1939 an extraordinary ruthlessness in anti-Jewish policies. Himmler held his appointee in high regard and placed him in the Reichsführer's debt by naming him to the Lublin post after the latter's dismissal as Gauleiter of Vienna on charges of financial corruption. Also Globocnik had earned Himmler's notice by supporting the Reichsführer loyally in his repeated conflicts with Frank over the deportation of Polish Jews to the General Government.

During his visit to Lublin, Himmler, as a prelude to his plan to resettle after the war huge numbers of German peasants and security troops in the East, appointed Globocnik his deputy for the creation of SS and police residences and strongholds in the newly conquered territories. Himmler directed Globocnik to establish a permanent SS base in the Lublin area. It would be built from slave labor supplied by Jews and Poles imprisoned in local concentration camps, one a facility constructed in October that would become the future death camp, Maidanek. This project soon consumed large quantities of building materials and, to ship them, rail and trains, valuable resources that could have been used for the German war effort.

Himmler and Globocnik also discussed another important and looming matter. They reviewed what Eichmann had called in March 1941, in referring to Heydrich's proposal to Hitler for the extermination of the Jews, the final evacuation of the Jews to the General Government. This meant sending the Jews from the Polish and other ghettos as well as from Germany and the rest of Europe to die there in a system of concentration and extermination camps.

Deportations to Lublin and the surrounding area made necessary extensive arrangements and planning, including adding more manpower and developing more efficient killing techniques. Himmler, therefore, ordered Globocnik to organize the extermination of Jews in the General Government, an action which the Nazis later called *Aktion Reinhard*

("Operation Reinhard"), named after Heydrich, whom Czech partisans assassinated in May 1942.

Then the Reichsführer traveled to Kaunas, Lithuania, where the Germans had herded the remaining Jews into a ghetto and where he met Order Police chief Daluege. The latter informed Himmler about the resistance of the newly installed German civilian administration in the Baltic States (*Ostland*), headed by Lohse, a Rosenberg subordinate, to stop the executions of Jews and communists by Einsatzgruppen. Lohse favored instead the ghettoization of the Jews.

From Kaunas Himmler went to Riga, the capital of Latvia. Nazi officials there quickly introduced new anti-Jewish regulations and a few weeks later announced the formation of a ghetto in the city. Further, Himmler ordered the local Higher SS and Police Leader, Prützmann, to resettle the criminal elements in the area, which meant in this case primarily Jews, and to kill them. Subsequently, Prützmann forced Lohse to admit that the SS and RSHA had jurisdiction over the Jewish question in the Ostland, not Lohse and his subordinates.

Himmler also visited Baranowicze, the headquarters of Bach-Zelewski, the Higher SS and Police Leader for central Russia. The Reichsführer directed Bach-Zelewski to shoot all Russians suspected of supporting partisans, to burn the villages to the ground, to seize food and livestock, and to kill every Jew. Jewish women, added Himmler, should be driven into the swamps to die; he doubtless acted, in this regard, to spare local SS units shooting them.

Meanwhile, on 31 July in Berlin, Heydrich obtained from Göring, the latter acting in his role as head of the German war economy and placed by Hitler in 1938 in charge of the Jewish question, a written directive to plan, organize, and carry out the Final Solution in German-controlled Europe. Göring phrased the directive so that Heydrich could use it to gain assistance for the unprecedented killing campaign from official German agencies and offices not under his control. With the order Heydrich could demonstrate to them that the highest levels of the government had ordered and supported the campaign:

> To supplement the task that was assigned to you on 24 January 1939, which dealt with the solution of the Jewish problem by emigration and evacuation in the most suitable way, I hereby charge you with making all necessary preparations with regard to organizational, technical, and

material matters for bringing about a complete solution of the Jewish question within the German sphere of influence in Europe.

Wherever other governmental agencies are involved, these are to cooperate with you.

I request you further to send me, in the near future, an overall plan covering the organizational, technical, and material measures necessary for the accomplishment of the final solution of the Jewish question which we desire.[25]

Göring issued the directive either because he had received an order from Hitler to do so or because he knew of Hitler's wishes on the subject, if not in detail then in their broad outline. Moreover, during the following weeks Göring robbed from the German war economy to cater to Himmler. He transferred to the SS, adding to its extensive economic enterprises, several factories in Latvia that produced materials for the war. In addition, he stated that Jews under German rule had nothing more to live for, that they could only work in concentration camps when needed, and that they deserved to be hanged rather than given a more honorable death by shooting.

Eichmann, at his war crimes trial in 1960 in Israel, testified that Heydrich had told him that Hitler had commissioned Heydrich "with the physical extermination of the Jews."[26] Still further evidence of Hitler's knowledge of and intimate involvement in the killings emerged a day after Heydrich had received the new mandate. Heinrich Müller, the chief of the Gestapo, informed the Einsatzgruppen commanders that Hitler received regularly from the RSHA information on the activities of the mobile killing units. Astonishingly, given the repeated orders to the contrary in the SS and Wehrmacht, Müller asked the units to supplement their written reports to the RSHA with visual materials, including photographs.

Meanwhile, Himmler continued to search for new methods by which to slaughter Jews and to use the means already employed by the Nazis. In mid-August he received further evidence that the SS must develop new sites and techniques for the killings. While visiting the recently established ghetto in Minsk, he witnessed a mass shooting of partisans, many of them Jews. What he saw bothered him noticeably and prompted him to complain that one victim remained alive.

Before he left Minsk, he spoke briefly to the Sonderkommando that had done the killings and claimed, according later to the detachment's chief, Dr.

Otto Bradfisch, that orders for such murders had come from Hitler and that he and the Führer had sole responsibility for them. Also prior to leaving Minsk, Himmler concluded that shooting was not the most efficient method of killing those targeted for total destruction. The SS and police firing squads in Russia did not work with the speed, efficiency, and secrecy which Himmler and others preferred.

These factors, combined with the enormity of the Final Solution, that of killing additional millions of Jews from all over Europe, led the SS to look for new methods by which to slaughter the victims. The planned extermination of a whole people, which included huge numbers of men, women, and children, had never happened before, and thus the SS had no guidelines to follow.

In Lublin, Globocnik's troops experimented with using grenades to kill prisoners forced to lie down in large ditches. In Byelorussia, Nebe, the commander of Einsatzgruppe B, locked a group of mentally handicapped prisoners from Minsk in a bunker and blew it up. These sadistic methods proved as unsatisfactory to the Nazis as the traditional firing squads.

Then possibly at the end of August 1941 or even earlier in the summer, Hitler had given Himmler permission to borrow from the prior so-called euthanasia program both the killing techniques that used poison gas as well as the personnel that had experience in employing them. At the beginning of September, shortly after Hitler's order to reduce the euthanasia program in Germany, Himmler transferred gassing specialists from the euthanasia killing centers to Lublin to assist Globocnik.

One of those transferred was Christian Wirth, a technician at the Brandenburg euthanasia facility. Himmler also held discussions with officials of what would become early in 1942 the SS Economic-Administrative Main Office (*Wirtschaftsverwaltungshauptamt*). The office in Oranienburg and its chief, Oswald Pohl, drew up plans for the construction of new concentration camps at Maidanek and Belzec, both located in the easternmost part of the General Government, and at Auschwitz-Birkenau (Auschwitz II).

Globocnik constructed Maidanek on the outskirts of Lublin, initially to serve as a labor camp for Soviet POWs and, beginning in December 1941, Jews. Most of the earliest prisoners at Maidanek died from exhaustion and the terrible camp conditions or were shot shortly after arrival at the camp. SS men, also under Globocnik's control, started construction of Belzec in October 1941; within a few months it would become the first facility dedicated completely to extermination. From the murder of Jews and others at both camps and the confiscation of their belongings, Globocnik provided clothing and textiles for other concentration camps and the Waffen-SS.

Almost simultaneously the SS started murdering people in mobile gas vans or trucks, using carbon monoxide piped from the engine into trailer compartments on the vehicles to kill the victims. The vans derived their original technology and operational staff from the euthanasia campaign of 1940 and were used first by the SS in East Prussia and Poland. SS vans there had killed mentally handicapped patients, including some Jews.

The SS also deployed the gas vans to kill Soviet POWs at Sachsenhausen and POWs and Jews in the Ukraine. The vans, however, according to numerous eyewitness accounts of the gassings, produced a horrendous death for the victims. As the trucks moved, they manufactured only gradually lethal concentrations of carbon monoxide, leaving the passengers to scream and gasp in desperation for air during their final minutes.

Despite such problems the SS employed vans to carry out the first large gassings of Jews. This happened at Chelmno (Kulmhof), a new concentration camp built at the end of October or early November northwest of Lodz in the Warthegau. Possibly the Germans constructed the camp partly in response to pressure from Arthur Greiser, the Gauleiter of the Warthegau, to clear his district of Jews.

At Chelmno, on 7–8 December 1941, Jews from the surrounding area and about five thousand Gypsies imprisoned in a special section of the Lodz ghetto were taken to a local castle, herded into vans and gassed, and then buried in mass graves in a nearby forest. A special unit led by the SS captain, Herbert Lange, which had previous experience using euthanasia gas vans in 1940, carried out the killings. This made Chelmno the first operational death camp.

Although the Germans had introduced gas vans as one of the methods to make the murders more efficient and get around or avoid the need to involve SS men and German soldiers in direct acts of killing, the vans did not solve such problems. Numerous flaws existed in their mechanical operation, and during the rainy season they were impossible to use on muddy roads. "Nor," according to the Israeli historian, Leni Yahil, "was this method any easier from the psychological point of view. The sight of the contorted corpses was so terrible that SS troops usually preferred the previous method of killing."[27]

Meanwhile, at Auschwitz, where the SS had used the camp primarily for shooting Soviet POWs, officials had discovered a new poison gas to do the killing. It would prove to act somewhat faster than carbon monoxide, and the SS eventually used it more frequently. The SS did not do this to spare the suffering caused the victims, but rather to make easier the task of the killers, who waited outside the gassing facilities and had to listen to the victims' screams and banging on the walls.

The new gas was a pesticide, Zyklon B, a crystalline form of hydrogen cyanide manufactured by a German firm called Degesch and originally used to fumigate buildings infested with insects. Zyklon B turned gaseous when subjected to the air and killed all sorts of pests quickly. SS officers at Auschwitz had observed this characteristic of the gas, and during the first week of September 1941 they experimented with it on humans.

Wearing gas masks, they dropped blue chalk pellets of Zyklon B from canisters into a sealed basement torture cell, which created a haze of poisonous air; the gas killed those persons placed in the cell, which included six hundred Russians and another 250 sick inmates from the camp hospital. Death was not instantaneous as Höss, the commandant, would claim later. Even the next day apparently not everyone had died, and the SS men had to release more gas. Höss informed Eichmann of the experiments, and the two decided to use the pesticide for further killings. Soon Auschwitz ordered five hundred kilograms of Zyklon B, initially on the pretext of using it to delouse clothing and buildings, to begin largescale executions of prisoners.

Especially Höss saw the gassing as the method for the extermination of the Jews at the camp, which Himmler had ordered. In December the SS murdered another batch of Soviet prisoners with Zyklon B in the mortuary of the camp crematorium. Höss viewed the corpses and received assurances, completely erroneous, from camp physicians that the victims had not suffocated in agony.

Höss concluded, therefore, that death from the gas was bloodless and would spare his camp guards and other personnel the psychological burden of shooting the victims. The Germans established the first gas chamber in the mortuary, and during the early months of 1942 converted two farmhouses in nearby Birkenau (Auschwitz II) for gassings. At Birkenau, which Himmler had chosen several months before to be a large camp for murdering Jews from all across Europe, the SS construction company had begun work in October 1941.

Also the SS shipped quantities of Zyklon B elsewhere in the East, including to Minsk and Mogilev in Byelorussia. Another shipment of the lethal gas, this one to Riga, was cancelled for the lack of transport caused by military needs, which required most of the German trains sent eastward. SS personnel received training in the use of Zyklon B from the Hamburg pesticide company of Tesch and Stabenow.

For operation at Mogilev, moreover, where Bach-Zelewski had built a new forced-labor camp, the SS contracted with the Topf company of Erfurt to build and send there a huge crematorium, which arrived on 30 December. Already the SS preferred the gassing of the Jews and others whom it also wished to murder. Gassing the victims, the killers concluded, provided a greater technical efficiency as opposed to shooting them. Moreover, the procedure appeared to provide greater secrecy and practicality because it allowed the killers to gather the victims for annihilation in only a few locations.

The Beginning of Deportations

While the SS developed the poison-gas technology as a new means of exterminating the additional millions of Jews, it began also at Hitler's order, announced by Himmler on 18 September 1941, to deport to the East the first Jews who would be among some of the initial victims murdered in the Final Solution. These were the Jews remaining in Germany and Austria, who numbered approximately 230,662 in October 1941, and in the Protectorate of Bohemia-Moravia, which exceeded 118,000.

To emphasize the significance of the planned deportations, Hitler promoted Heydrich at the end of September to the additional powerful position of Reich Protector of Bohemia-Moravia, which made him directly subordinate to the Führer. Altogether during the war, 77,297 Jews from the Protectorate would die, most after the Germans had sent them to Theresienstadt, a ghetto Heydrich had constructed north of Prague. The Germans would use the ghetto in two ways. First, they imprisoned there some elderly German Jews as well as Czechs; and second, they claimed it a "model" ghetto and occasionally sought to use it to persuade the free world that Jews under German rule were not being mistreated. Most of the inhabitants of the ghetto, however, died from its brutal conditions or were deported to Auschwitz and killed.

Several reasons explain why Hitler ordered the deportations. First, he had intended for a long time to rid Germany of its Jews. By the fall of 1941 events in the war led him to conclude that he need or could not tolerate their continued presence in the country much longer. In this regard, he continued to believe fanatically in both an imminent German military victory over Russia and in the inferiority of the Slavs.

In northern Russia German armies had surrounded Leningrad, cutting off land communications to the city and beginning a long and bitter siege. The armored formations of Army Group South had captured Kiev, which had made possible the mass slaughter of local Jews nearby at Babi Yar. The Army Group had then headed south toward Kremenchug, located on the Dnepr River, destroying in its path massive Soviet forces and capturing over six hundred thousand POWs.

Similarly, during October on the central front two great armored breakthrough and envelopment operations enabled the Germans to tear up Soviet armies, seizing six hundred thousand more POWs, and move to within fifty miles of Moscow. Despite these overwhelming victories, neither Hitler nor most of his military leaders realized that the German forces had failed to achieve the primary military objective of Operation Barbarossa, that of forcing a quick Russian collapse with massive initial armored blows.

Second, Hitler ordered the deportations because he had received for some time pressure to remove the Jews from Germany and the areas of western Poland annexed to the Reich from the Gauleiters of the regions. Goebbels, acting in his role as Gauleiter of Berlin, had progressively intensified his demand to rid the capital of its remaining Jews. On 20 August Hitler agreed to a personal request from Goebbels that the Jews remaining in the Reich wear on their clothing a yellow badge with the Star of David on it.

When the Nazis decreed the wearing of the star on 19 September, they received a few unexpected adverse reactions from the German population, but otherwise no opposition to the measure. Hitler had decided by then to deport the German Jews, which Himmler had announced the day before. Clearly the Germans intended imposing the star to prepare the way for the deportations. The badge provided the Nazis with a quick means of identifying their victims. Moreover, forcing the Jews to wear the yellow star gave symbolic expression to the Nazi depiction of Jews as pariahs in the so-called Volksgemeinschaft.

During the following weeks and months, the German government enacted a stream of other laws and measures against the German Jews. These restricted their movement and travel, reduced their food rations, prohibited their use of public telephones, forbade them to leave their homes without police permission, and subjected them to lesser humiliations such as forbidding their owning of pets. Also if a "person of German blood" showed friendship toward a Jew in public, the police punished the offender by throwing him or her into a concentration camp.

For numerous Nazi officials, greed as much as ideology motivated them to demand and carry out such measures; they longed to seize for themselves dwellings vacated by the remaining Jews. Confiscation of the residences of the wealthiest Jews had already occurred in Munich and other large cities. Many ordinary Germans as well profited from the takeover of Jewish property. For example, the Gauleiter of Hamburg, Karl Kaufmann, cited a chronic housing shortage when he repeatedly urged Hitler to deport Jews from the city and surrounding area.

In Hamburg alone during the war the government confiscated or Aryanized more than three thousand pieces of land that had belonged to Jews. Also in the large northern seaport, the Germans after 1941 sold or auctioned off weekly gigantic quantities of household furniture and clothing of Jews initially from the city, then from all of Germany, and finally from Western Europe. Although some pieces had blood spattered on them and word traveled quickly among Hamburg residents about where the goods had come from, neither the wholesale buyers nor individual shoppers seemed deterred in their search for a bargain at the expense of the Jews.

Third, Hitler's decision to clear Germany, Austria, and Bohemia-Moravia of Jews probably resulted from his knowledge of the new technology for killing the deportees being developed by the SS. Himmler had likely instructed him on the course of developments and, according to Breitman, "it would have been like Hitler to conclude that he could now more quickly rid the Reich and the Protectorate of the people he considered vermin."[28]

But Hitler's ordering of the deportations before the war's end and before the SS could put the first death camps in operation produced a number of problems. For one thing, the deportations threatened to overwhelm the old-fashioned methods of the SS in the East for exterminating the Jews (i.e., shooting them or placing them temporarily in ghettos). Also German civilian authorities in the occupied territories of Poland opposed receiving more Jews.

Frank, for example, insisted on taking no more in the General Government and attempted during 1941 to rid the territory of most of its nearly two million Jews. In the Warthegau, the Lodz ghetto was overcrowded, and the Gauleiter, Greiser, pressed Hitler to remove the Jews from the ghetto and the territory. Auschwitz, which had only just begun a major expansion, could not handle the roughly 346,000 German, Austrian, and Czech Jews.

The deportations, moreover, provided the SS with legal and financial issues that required the support of various German government agencies. Shipping Jews by freight train from Germany or elsewhere in Europe to the East meant the SS had to receive the assistance of the Reich Transportation Ministry and of the Wehrmacht, which needed the trains for military shipments.

But the immense authority given by Hitler to Himmler and Heydrich enabled the SS leaders to have their way. The lack of trains would only slow down, not halt, the deportations, and eventually in most instances the SS received priority over the military in rail transports. Consequently, during the fall and winter months of 1941, the Germans used trains repeatedly to transport Jews east to be murdered instead of employing the rolling stock to ship winter clothing and supplies to German soldiers in Soviet Russia.

The SS sent the first German Jews to the Lodz ghetto. Some of the deportees were from Berlin, which caused unrest among certain groups of the population in the capital. While Himmler intended to deport sixty thousand Jews to Lodz, he promised Greiser that the deportees would later be shipped "farther to the east."[29] With this vague wording, Himmler meant the death camps at nearby Chelmno and Belzec and at Auschwitz, whose construction had begun at his order.

On 16 October 1941 the first trainload of German Jews arrived in Lodz, but protests from local German authorities against the shipments reduced the numbers sent there. Hitler hardly spoke by accident, therefore, when five days later he discussed privately with Himmler and Heydrich "exterminating" the Jews and how this would "do humanity a service."[30] On 25 October he told them: "It's good if the terror that we are exterminating Jewry goes before us . . . . I had to remain inactive for a long time against the Jews too."[31]

Meanwhile, the RSHA issued on 23 October an important edict that halted immediately the emigration of German Jews, closing off their last escape route. The same day, Eichmann announced at a meeting in Berlin the fate of the remaining German and Protectorate Jews. They would be deported to the German-occupied territories in the Soviet Union, and more specifically to the deadly Minsk and Riga ghettos.

Eichmann also ordered exemptions from the deportations for some Jews: Mischlinge (Jews of mixed ancestry), Jews in mixed marriages, and Jews over sixty years of age. Local Gestapo offices, however, disregarded such directives and placed many older Jews on the transports to the East. By 4 November, 19,837 Jews, primarily older women and men, had arrived in Lodz in twenty transports from Vienna, Prague, Berlin, Cologne, Frankfurt,

Hamburg, Düsseldorf, and occupied Luxembourg. In addition, five thousand Gypsies arrived, whom the SS imprisoned in a special section of the ghetto. Greiser demanded that the allegedly unproductive deportees be removed.

A few miles outside Riga, the SS had established a concentration camp. During November and December the SS and police deported some twenty-five thousand Jews from Germany and the Protectorate to Riga and approximately seven thousand to Minsk. In the deportations of Jews from Hamburg to Minsk, Riga, Lodz, and Kaunas, Reserve Police Battalion 101, which had returned to Hamburg, participated. The battalion did so despite the fact, as one of its members recalled after the war, it had learned that Jews in Minsk had been shot and "that our Hamburg Jews were to be shot there also."[32]

As this second wave of deportations began, the Germans implemented two more devastating measures against the German Jews. On 25 November 1941, a supplement to the Reich citizenship law permitted the German government to confiscate all remaining property of the deportees. The latter had lost their German nationality, the law proclaimed, because they had transferred their normal residence outside the Reich.

The Nazis, however, not only confiscated the Jews' property after their removal from Germany, they also forced the Jews to pay for their own deportation. Each deportee had to pay a substantial amount to the Reich Association of Jews in Germany, the sole political organization representing the German Jews, which in turn paid the Gestapo for future deportations.

With these initial deportations the Germans established the brutal procedures for the hundreds of other forced shipments of Jews from Germany and the rest of Europe to the East that soon would follow. A matter of much postwar controversy is whether or how much the Gestapo used the Reich Association of Jews in Germany and local Jewish cultural groups to assist in rounding up or "selecting" the deportees. In the view of some historians, most such organizations cooperated because they believed that would ease matters for their fellow Jews, but in reality they found themselves turned into tools of the Germans. Recently discovered documents of the association, however, cast substantial doubt on its participation in assisting the deportations.

Also the Gestapo established a ruse for persuading deportees that they were being resettled in the East for labor. This involved allowing the Jews to take with them personal belongings, including small tools and equipment, in suitcases or shoulder bags. The deportees, however, received a stamped

"Evacuated" in their passports and identity cards that, unbeknown to them, marked them for death when they arrived in the East.

Then the Gestapo loaded the Jews onto freight trains and sent an officer along with the transport. Approximately sixteen municipal policemen (*Schutzpolizei*) acted as guards for each one thousand Jews on the trains. Although German Jews exempted from the deportations included those over sixty years old, local Gestapo offices ignored the exception and continued to place many older Jews on the transports to the East.

While the transports left Germany and the Protectorate for Minsk and Riga, behind the scenes among the Nazi authorities bureaucratic quarreling continued over Jewish policy. The SS found its jurisdiction in security matters in the East challenged again by Rosenberg. As Minister for the Occupied Eastern Territories, he attempted once more to assert his control there over the SS and police.

The minister and his subordinates, Lohse and the Gauleiter and General Commissioner of Byelorussia, Wilhelm Kube, either complained about or openly resisted SS and police activities in the occupied Soviet territories, including opposing the murder of some Jews. The killings, Rosenberg argued, destroyed valuable laborers for the German war economy. But at a meeting of Himmler and Rosenberg on 15 November 1941, the minister backed down. Not only did he acknowledge SS authority, but Himmler also informed him of the details of the Final Solution, which Hitler had ordered.

Meanwhile, most of the German Jews who arrived at Minsk and Riga at the beginning of November held the illusion, encouraged at every opportunity by the German authorities, that they were being sent to the East for work. To prepare for the deportations to the Baltic States, Himmler replaced the Higher SS and Police Leader there, Hans-Adolf Prützmann, with Friedrich Jeckeln. Jeckeln's police and Einsatzgruppen in the Ukraine had executed far greater numbers of Jews there than German killing units had done elsewhere in Russia.

Although the ultimate fate of the Jews deported to the East was never in doubt, the timing and form of the extermination of the initial deportees varied, depending on where and when they arrived. At Minsk, Latvian auxiliary police, Gestapo, and SS units kicked and whipped the arriving German Jews off the train cars and herded them into a new ghetto.

Most of the victims, however, still did not realize what the Germans intended for them and believed they would be treated better than Russian

Jews they had seen as they passed the nearby main ghetto. While the Germans shot the Russian Jews first and buried them in large earthen pits, the winter conditions that hardened the ground and made digging further mass graves difficult helped most of the German Jews to remain alive until mid-1942.

At Riga the arrival on the night of 29–30 November of a thousand Jews from Berlin resulted in their immediate execution. Some had frozen to death in the unheated railway cars en route from the German capital. German police and Latvian collaborators shot and buried the others in large pits in a nearby forest called Rumbuli, along with fifteen thousand other Jews driven out of the ghetto with whips and clubs. A week later the police and Latvians murdered another eight thousand Jews in the same manner.

Although Jeckeln proudly reported the killings of the trainload of Berlin Jews to SS headquarters in the German capital, the murders produced complications. The executions had included elderly Jews as well as decorated Jewish war veterans, whom Himmler had not intended for immediate killing, but rather sent to the ghetto at Theresienstadt.

Obviously the deportation of elderly Jewish men and women discredited the public explanation that the transports took the Jews East to do heavy labor. Himmler had changed this by sending older Jews to the East via Theresienstadt. Apparently complaints reached Hitler that the Rumbuli forest killings were not secret enough and that they had negative consequences. Hitler, however, ignored the issue.

As the Final Solution began to unfold, Himmler and Heydrich also made preparations to move against Jews in all the countries of Europe conquered by or allied to Germany, or against Jewish citizens of countries within German territory. To assist them in acquiring agreement from those governments to seize their Jews, the SS leaders pursued the cooperation of the German Foreign Ministry and its head, von Ribbentrop. During the fall of 1941 Himmler resolved a number of previous disputes with von Ribbentrop and the ministry, primarily involving the Jewish question. The ministry cooperated with the RSHA and Wehrmacht regarding the fate of Jews in Serbia.

Soon von Ribbentrop and key figures in the ministry's Jewish section, Martin Luther and Franz Rademacher, learned about the Final Solution and what it meant. Already on 23 October, Rademacher had received a note from Paul Würm, an editor of *Der Stürmer*, which illustrated that talk of gassing Jews was even widespread among lower-echelon Nazi planners. According to Würm:

"On my return trip from Berlin I met an old party comrade, who works in the east on the settlement of the Jewish question. In the near future many of the Jewish vermin will be exterminated through special measures."[33] At the end of November, Heydrich invited Luther to attend a conference in eleven days at a villa on the Wannsee in Berlin, owned by the RSHA. Heydrich wished to use the conference, which was delayed to 20 January 1942, to gain the cooperation of German government ministries in the Final Solution. The Foreign Ministry made plans to pressure the governments of Rumania, Slovakia, Croatia, Bulgaria, and Hungary to deport to the East the Jews living in each country.

Also at the end of 1941 word of the Final Solution spread to other quarters. Legal problems for one of Frank's provincial governors in the General Government significantly weakened Frank politically with Hitler and others in the Nazi hierarchy. At the end of November Heydrich asked the General Government to send a representative to the Wannsee Conference.

Frank soon learned from Heydrich the subject of the meeting. The General Governor accepted the news, although he apparently knew nothing of the construction in his territory of the death camp at Belzec. Also the SS invited other government agencies to send officials to the Wannsee Conference, including the German Interior Ministry, whose state secretary, Wilhelm Stuckart, was informed that Hitler himself had ordered what topics the meeting would cover.

Information about the extermination of all Jews that German troops could reach in Europe also now extended outside the German government. On 16 November 1941, Goebbels wrote in a lead article in his weekly newspaper *Das Reich* that Hitler's prophecy on 30 January 1939 about the "annihilation of the Jewish race in Europe" was now coming true.[34]

Two days later Rosenberg, following his long meeting with Himmler three days before, briefed German journalists, declaring that the Jewish question could only be solved by the biological extermination of all Jews in Europe. It was necessary, he said, to push the European Jews beyond the Ural mountains in Russia or destroy them in some other way. He instructed the press, however, to give no details except for common phrases about "Bolshevism and its destruction."[35] A few weeks thereafter, when Rosenberg discussed with Hitler a speech the former intended to give, Hitler agreed with him that he should not mention the extermination of the Jews in public.

On 24 November, Himmler met with Stuckart and insisted that the "Jewish questions belong to me."[36] Also at the meeting Himmler surely initiated

Stuckart in much more than the Reichsführer's jurisdictional ambitions. When Stuckart's subordinate in the interior ministry, Bernhard Loesener, met with Stuckart a month later, the former relayed graphic reports of the recent mass killing of Berlin Jews in Riga. Stuckart replied: "Don't you know that these things happen on the highest orders?"[37]

A New Decision? The Intention to Extend the Killing of Jews outside Europe

At almost the same moment, Hitler appears to have made yet another major decision regarding the Jews. In this one, as in earlier decisions about the fate of the Jews, the war had a significant influence. Although the Soviet Union had not collapsed quickly, as Hitler and most of his associates had anticipated, from September to November 1941 German armies won victories at Kiev, in the Crimea and in central and eastern Ukraine, and in a renewed attack on Moscow. Suddenly the possibility emerged again for a complete German triumph in Russia and for an advance through the Caucasus into the Middle East.

On 28 November Hitler spoke with the Mufti of Jerusalem. During their conversation, Hitler referred to his earlier decision to remove the Jews from Europe and promised that Germany, at a suitable time in the future, would annihilate the Jews of Palestine and all others living in "non-European nations as well." He told the Mufti that Germany's sole interest in Palestine was killing the Jewish population there. Once German armies invaded the Middle East, he informed Haj Amin al-Husayni, they would ensure "the destruction of the Jewish element residing in the Arab sphere under the protection of British power."[38] At the time, this meant the Jews in Palestine, which numbered more than half a million, as well as the Jewish communities in Syria, Iraq, Iran, the Arabian Peninsula, Egypt, and French Northwest Africa.

Weinberg has concluded from this conversation that Hitler and those who operated the German war effort and killing program had now targeted for death the Jews living among peoples *outside* Europe. Since Hitler planned for Germany to conquer the Middle East, Africa, and other global areas, including eventually the United States, all Jews there would be killed. It is uncertain whether this decision to extend the Final Solution far beyond Europe represented something new in Hitler's thinking or he had intended it all along, if given the chance to do so. In this writer's view, the latter seems most likely.

Privately Hitler launched often during these weeks into tirades against the Jews. Repeatedly during his monologues before captive audiences at lunch or in the late evening at his military headquarters, he alluded to the destruction of the Jews as part of the war. Most such references, however, focused not on European Jewry, which Hitler had done previously, but discussed the "exterminating" of, getting "rid of," and seeing "the final ruin" of "the Jew" in general.[39]

The same theme of a wider global war against the Jews dominated his speech in Berlin on 12 December—the day after he had declared war on the United States—to the party's national leaders and Gauleiters. Goebbels summarized Hitler's comments in his diary: "With regard to the Jewish Question, the Führer is determined to make a clean sweep of it. . . . The world war is there. The annihilation of Jewry must be the necessary consequence."[40] Four days later, Frank told what he had heard from Hitler and Heydrich to officials in the administration of the General Government:

> But what should be done with the Jews? Can you believe that they will be accommodated in settlements in the *Ostland* [Baltic area and Byelorussia]? In Berlin we were told: why are you making all this trouble? We don't want them either, not in the *Ostland* nor in the *Reichskommissariat* [Ukraine]; liquidate them yourselves! Gentlemen, I must ask you to steel yourselves against all considerations of compassion. We must destroy the Jews wherever we find them, and wherever it is at all possible. . . .[41]

Although it did not mention the goal of murdering all Jews in Europe and elsewhere, the appointments diary of Himmler, discovered in 1999 in a Moscow archive, added further evidence showing Hitler was involved as the central decisionmaker in the Holocaust. The diary revealed that on 18 December 1941 the Reichsführer discussed the Jewish question with Hitler and that the result was "to exterminate [the Jews] as partisans."[42] The notation probably indicated the approval by Hitler of the propaganda line that had been pursued in the East toward the German soldiers and that could be used for Germans generally. It also confirmed the key role of Himmler in the Holocaust, who discussed the destruction of the Jews with Hitler and received his instructions.

Moreover, what is clear is that by the end of 1941 plans to destroy all Jews German arms could reach represented no idle threat. In Hitler's declaration of war on the United States on 11 December, four days after Japan's attack on Pearl Harbor, he proclaimed that Germany was now engaged in a "world war"—a term used until then almost solely to describe the war of 1914–1918.

Military decisions made already by the Germans demonstrated their commitment to a drive into the Middle East and to expanding the war even farther outside Europe. When a British offensive, begun on 18 November 1941 in North Africa, produced the first Allied defeat of a German army in the war, Germany shifted an entire air force fleet from the Eastern Front to the Mediterranean theater. Also the Germans dispatched numerous submarines to the Mediterranean. This latter move would have serious consequences for the Battle of the Atlantic, which would expand significantly following Hitler's declaration of war on the United States. The German navy, even though it had previously clamored for war in the Mediterranean and against America, now had to commit forces to the Mediterranean at a time it least wished to do so.

CHAPTER TEN

THE KILLING CENTERS AND DEPORTATIONS OF POLISH JEWRY, 1942

B Y THE TIME THE third year of the war opened, Germany had expanded the fighting enormously, with the immediate goals of conquering Soviet Russia and carrying out and protecting the systematic murder of the Jews. The decision for the Final Solution, however, had quickly made insufficient both the people and organizations initially believed necessary by the German leadership to accomplish the genocide.

Both Hitler and the SS leadership recognized that the killing program, now expanded to all of Europe and, if possible, outside it, needed the cooperation and involvement of numerous German government agencies. Seizing millions of Jews and deporting them to the killing centers under construction by the SS in the East required several major steps. These included approaching and persuading foreign governments to surrender their Jews, acquiring substantial numbers of rail lines and freight cars to transport them, and disposing of massive amounts of property and belongings plundered from them.

Also something else of significance resulted from the shift by the Germans from massacring Jews primarily by using mobile killing units, which had carried out the murder of the victims in a more or less unsystematic fashion, to stationary and carefully built killing facilities. No longer could the killers claim that their horrific work had connections to the demands of war, to removing alleged saboteurs or partisans. The new killing installations had the sole function of methodically slaughtering all Jews whom the Germans could reach and deliver to them.

The Wannsee Conference, Mischlinge, and Hitler's Public Statements

The SS intended at the Wannsee Conference on 20 January 1942 to draw significant portions of the German bureaucracy much more closely and directly into the planned genocide. Heydrich chaired the meeting. Attending were Eichmann, Gestapo chief Müller, and four other SS officers as well as functionaries from the party and Reich chancelleries. Present, above all, were senior civil servants, among them state secretaries, from Germany's most important government ministries. Represented were the Reich Ministry for the Occupied Eastern Territories, Interior Ministry, Office of the Four-Year Plan, Ministry of Justice, Office of the Governor General of Poland, and Foreign Ministry.

Heydrich opened the meeting by noting that both Göring and Hitler had entrusted him with preparations for the Final Solution, but that Himmler had charge of executing the policy. He then listed the numbers of Jews believed to be in each European country, which totaled eleven million and which the SS planned to deport for killing. He not only mentioned those in areas under German control, such as Poland and the Netherlands, and in Germany's allies and satellites, such as Italy, Croatia, and Finland. Also he included the Jews in England and even neutral countries, a clear indication of the plan of Hitler and Himmler to use the war to seize Jews throughout areas that had fallen, or might soon do so, under the control or influence of German forces.

Most of those present at the Wannsee Conference already knew of the mass killings of Jews. Their offices had received copies of the reports from the Einsatzgruppen in Russia. As Heydrich discussed with them the Final Solution, no one objected to what they heard and several reacted with enthusiasm toward it. After the conference Heydrich and Eichmann carefully altered the official written record of the meeting by inserting numerous euphemisms to conceal the real nature of the discussion.

Eichmann, however, later admitted to Israeli interrogators in 1961 that those present at the Wannsee meeting talked about the subject "quite bluntly" and "minced no words about it at all."[1] They understood that the

Final Solution involved the evacuation of the Jews to the East and then their extermination, one way or the other. "Europe," Heydrich told his listeners, "will be combed through from west to east" for Jews. Most of the fittest victims would be worked to death. Those that survived, Heydrich concluded, would have to be "dealt with accordingly" (i.e., exterminated) so that they would not "form a germ cell of new Jewish development. (See the lesson history teaches.)"[2]

After the meeting Heydrich and the other SS officers celebrated with cigars and cognac. According to some scholars, they rejoiced at the positive response and even enthusiasm of the government's leading bureaucrats toward the murderous policy Heydrich had outlined. More likely, however, Heydrich had expected little else from the bureaucrats, and he and his minions celebrated the official unveiling of the plan. The mass killing no longer involved solely the SS and police; now also the elite of the government administration had signed on.

Eichmann recalled later how the conference, in which the most prominent people, "the Popes of the Third Reich," had spoken about and planned the genocide, had dispelled his feelings of doubt about it. "At that moment," he said, "I sensed a kind of Pontius Pilate feeling, for I felt free of all guilt."[3] Heydrich, for his part, sought to bind the senior government officials to the policy by recording some of their comments later in the official minutes of the meeting. For the remainder of the war, the huge killing operation would become one of the major activities of numerous government ministries or agencies.

Most of the conference centered on what to do about the so-called Mischlinge, persons of mixed Jewish and non-Jewish ancestry, and the Jews married to Germans. No fewer than seventy-five thousand persons had been defined as Mischlinge first-degree (two Jewish grandparents) and some 130,000 as second-degree (one Jewish grandparent). Deciding on their fate confronted the Nazis with a thorny issue, which neither the Wannsee Conference nor later meetings in March and October 1942 resolved.

At the Wannsee meeting, the participants examined the possibility of murdering the Mischlinge; during the discussion, officials of the Reich Interior Ministry, the agency in charge of these matters, suggested the sterilization of such persons. The sterilization proposal resulted not from an effort by ministry officials to save Mischlinge from the Final Solution, as some bureaucrats claimed after the war in an attempt to exonerate themselves. Instead, it represented a step, as demonstrated recently by a German historian, on "the path leading to the second phase of the extermination policy—the 'final solution of the Mischling and mixed marriage question.'"[4]

As noted in chapter 13, while most of the Mischlinge and Jews in "mixed marriages" in Germany avoided deportation, from 1942 the Nazi government tightened the measures against them. For political and administrative reasons, the regime deferred a solution to the problem until after the anticipated final victory in the war. Both Hitler and Himmler regarded the combination of unwanted "Jewish blood" and valuable "German blood" as dangerous, but Hitler—whose personal views usually determined the status of Mischlinge—rarely supported deportation for such persons. Their deportation threatened to create political problems and incite possible protests from the Aryan relatives of those involved, exposing the existence of the extermination camps.

Likewise, in the German-occupied lands in Europe, while the Nazis developed no consistent policy toward Mischlinge and Jews married to Aryans, they nevertheless resolutely pursued the issue. In the Netherlands, persons with one Jewish grandparent were not resettled in the Amsterdam ghetto or deported. The 8,610 Jewish partners registered in mixed Dutch (i.e., Aryan) and Jewish marriages received a "choice" between deportation and sterilization. Elsewhere, such as in Slovakia and Croatia, most Mischlinge escaped the deportations.

In Poland, in contrast, the Germans imprisoned nearly all Mischlinge in ghettos and then deported them to the extermination camps. In Italy, following its surrender in the war in 1943, the SS deported 140–150 Jewish men and women in mixed marriages to Auschwitz. During 1942 in Lithuania, German police arrested twelve Jews, all in mixed marriages and all converts to Catholicism, as part of a campaign to pressure their wives to divorce them. For the occupied Eastern territories, Rosenberg's ministry urged at the beginning of 1942 that every person with a Jewish parent be defined as a Jew. All this suggested that the days of Mischlinge were numbered, especially if Germany won the war.

As discussed at the Wannsee meeting, the highest echelons of the SS originally intended to kill all Jews deported to the extermination camps within a short time after their arrival. The military situation on the Eastern Front, however, dictated otherwise. There German expectations of a quick victory had produced plans to acquire increased labor for war industries by dissolving fifty Wehrmacht divisions in the East and making slave laborers out of Soviet POWs.

But during 5–15 December 1941 and 1–10 January 1942, massive offensives of the Soviet armies all along the Eastern Front had surprised and badly battered the German forces. Moreover, the German policy of shooting Russian POWs, or leaving them to die from starvation and disease, had resulted in the deaths by February 1942 of 2.8 million of the 3.9 million prisoners captured to then by the Germans.

This military situation and enormous death toll of potential laborers for the Germans, combined with the shortage of workers inside the Reich stretching back before the war, forced Himmler to approve temporarily the use of some Jewish labor for war-related production. During February, various concentration camps involved in such production received one hundred thousand male and fifty thousand female Jews. Some of the Jews had been shipped to Poland from Germany and others from the occupied zone of France.

Despite his having to put some Jews to work instead of killing them, Himmler continued to make arrangements for the Final Solution. He issued written instructions to the Ministry for the Occupied Eastern Territories, ordering it to prepare measures for a solution to the Jewish question for all of Europe. Also the Reichsführer met on 5 March with Hans Frank, to ensure that the latter would not impede or block either the killings scheduled for the death camps in the General Government or the recovery by the SS of the belongings of the dead Jews. With the help of Lammers and Martin Bormann, Himmler forced Frank to agree that the SS and police should receive authority over all security and resettlement issues (i.e., all Jewish affairs) in the territory.

Both shortly before and after the Wannsee Conference, Hitler referred repeatedly in public and private to the extermination of the Jews. As he had done a year earlier, he recalled for Germans his speech of 30 January 1939, prophesying that war would result in the destruction of European Jewry. Also as previously, to emphasize his point he misdated the prediction to the day he had started the war—1 September 1939.

In his New Year's greeting to the German people on 1 January 1942, he spoke of the Reich's struggle against the alleged Jewish-capitalist-Bolshevist world conspiracy. A month later he declared in a speech at the Berlin Sportpalast:

We see our way clearly on the point that the war can end only in that either the Aryan peoples are annihilated or Jewry will disappear from Europe. On September 1, 1939 [sic], I declared in the German

Reichstag—and I guard myself against premature prophecies—that this war would not end as the Jews imagine, namely, that the European-Aryan peoples will be annihilated, but on the contrary that the consequence of this war will be the destruction of Jewry.[5]

He used almost the same phrasing in his "message" of 24 February to the "old fighters" of the Nazi party, read by one of the Gauleiters, celebrating the anniversary of the movement's founding in 1920: "Today the ideas of our National Socialist and fascist revolution have conquered great and mighty states, and my prophecy shall hold true that it is not the Aryan race that will be destroyed in this war, but rather it is the Jew who will be exterminated."[6] Then twice more during the year, on 30 September 1942 in another speech at the Sportpalast and on 8 November in an address to the party leadership in Munich, he recalled what he had said in 1939. In both instances, he claimed that the laughter of the Jews at his prophecy would soon subside everywhere.

During a private meeting with Goebbels on 14 February 1942, and then later with a group of military officers, Hitler angrily attacked the Jews and mentioned the close connection, in his mind, between the war and his plans for their annihilation. Goebbels recorded the diatribe in his diary:

> There must be no squeamish sentimentalism about it. The Jews have deserved the catastrophe that has now overtaken them. Their destruction will go hand in hand with the destruction of our enemies. We must hasten this process with cold ruthlessness. We shall thereby render an inestimable service to a humanity tormented for thousands of years by the Jews. . . .
>
> The Fuehrer realizes the full implications of the great opportunities offered by this war.[7]

A few weeks later Goebbels again discussed the Final Solution in his diary, this time in even more graphic terms. Also once more he identified Hitler as the driving force behind the use of the war to destroy the Jews:

> The Jews are now being pushed out of the General Government, beginning near Lublin, to the East. A pretty barbaric procedure is being applied here, and it is not to be described in any more detail, and not

much is left of the Jews themselves. In general one may conclude that 60% of them must be liquidated, while only 40% can be put to work . . . . The Jews are being punished barbarically, to be sure, but they have fully deserved it. The prophecy that the Führer issued to them on the way, for the eventuality that they started a new world war, is beginning to realize itself in the most terrible manner. One must not allow any sentimentalities to rule in these matters. If we did not defend ourselves against them, the Jews would annihilate us. It is a struggle for life and death between the Aryan race and the Jewish bacillus. No other government and no other regime could muster the strength for a general solution of the question. Here too, the Führer is the persistent pioneer and spokesman of a radical solution, which is demanded by the way things are and thus appears to be unavoidable. Thank God, during the war we now have a whole series of possibilities which were barred to us in peacetime. We must exploit them.[8]

German Military Success and the Killing Program

As Hitler indicated to Goebbels, the war's military situation made it possible for him to fulfill his prewar prophecy about the wartime extermination of the Jews. Although Germany and its Axis partners now faced a potentially formidable—and unlikely—alliance of Soviet Russia, the United States, and Great Britain, throughout most of 1942 Axis forces continued to hold the upper hand in the war.

For the Nazis, their armed forces both assisted and concealed the vast "shadow war" they had helped Hitler to launch, against the Jews. German forces occupied or controlled much of Europe during 1942 while others implemented the Final Solution in earnest in two principal ways: first, with the continued mass shootings of Jews in Russia by the mobile killing units and some Wehrmacht troops; and second, with the special large killing facilities or extermination camps, constructed by the SS in German-occupied Poland.

In this respect, Weinberg has concluded that "[a] major role of the German army fighting on the eastern front—and for most of the war this was most of the army—was to ensure continued German control of the killing centers in the East so that these could keep functioning."[9] Although the Soviets had checked the German advance on the Eastern Front during the winter of

1941–1942, the Wehrmacht went on the offensive in the East and elsewhere once more in the summer of 1942 in order to retake the initiative.

In North Africa, during May and June 1942 Axis troops seized Tobruk in a spectacular victory and stormed into Egypt. The Jewish community in Palestine appeared in immediate danger, a fact not lost on the Jewish Agency, the chief institution of the community. The agency seemed well informed about the fate of the Jews in Europe. One of its officials wrote the commander of the British 8th Army fighting the Axis: "There can be little doubt that if Palestine were overrun by the Nazis nothing less than complete annihilation would be the lot of the Jews of this country."[10] But during desperate fighting in July, the 8th Army held the German and Italian advance at El Alamein and in early September southeast of there at Alam el-Halfa. In the war at sea, the German navy, and most noticeably its submarines operating in the Atlantic Ocean, helped to keep the British and Americans from landing in Western Europe. This would prevent the Allies from disrupting the massive killings in Europe from the West.

Expansion of the Killings in the Soviet Union, Partisan Warfare, and Jewish Resistance

The mass shootings amid the war in the East represented a significant part of the Final Solution. Throughout 1942 and 1943, the Einsatzgruppen and police units continued in routine fashion to kill every Jew they could as well as destroy partisans in the Soviet Union and many Poles in the General Government. In western Russia between June 1941 and April 1942, during the so-called first sweep, discussed in chapter 8, the mobile killing units, with help from the Wehrmacht, murdered between 700,000 and 750,000 Soviet Jews.

In a second and more encompassing sweep during 1942 and 1943, these units murdered an additional 1,500,000 Jews. Similar to the first operation, the Einsatzgruppen functioned during the second at the forefront of the killings. Along with the Order Police and other security units, they continued the largescale ghetto murders that had started in Byelorussia and the Baltic States during the summer and fall of 1941.

In the end the German police, SS, and army units annihilated the Jews of the Ukraine, Byelorussia, and the Baltic States. Einsatzgruppen reports sent to Berlin during 1942 identified the Jews overwhelmingly as the primary targets. A report on 5 January declared: "Efforts are being made to purge the Eastern territory of Jews as completely as possible."[11]

The military crisis and heavy German casualties in the winter of 1941–1942, which would reach as high in the Wehrmacht as 150,000 per month during 1942, pressed many German rear area security troops, especially Order Police battalions, into frontline duty. How much this changed the nature and makeup of the units employed behind the lines in the racial war, as well as the course of the latter, is a subject of scholarly debate.

Browning concluded that Reserve Police Battalion 101 and other battalions declined in quality as security units, that they consisted of low categories of troops, and that they were commanded by elderly or incompetent officers. But other research suggests that no more than twenty of the approximately one hundred German police battalions established during the war consisted of over-aged reservists. Even among these reserve units, career policemen made up the majority of the officers and senior enlisted men.

What is clear is that the withdrawal of numerous security units from rear areas, together with the breaks opened through the German front by the Red Army, assisted the growing Soviet partisan movement. The partisans flourished most in the wooded and swampy areas of the northern Soviet Union, especially in the northern Ukraine, Byelorussia, and portions of the Baltic States and western Russia behind the fronts of the German Army Groups Center and North.

Not only did the partisans often control vast portions of rural areas, but they also attacked German military outposts and communications, especially cutting railway tracks, and collected intelligence for the Red Army. In addition, they punished suspected collaborators with the Germans and acted as an agent of the Soviet government in areas nominally under German control.

For the most part, the Germans had little success with antipartisan operations. SS, police, and Wehrmacht units swept through previously designated areas, slaughtered thousands of civilians, particularly Jews, burned as many villages and ghettos as possible, and occasionally killed a few partisans. Both the indiscriminate slaughter of civilians and the Germans' largescale program of recruiting forced labor in Soviet territories such as the Ukraine, persuaded an increasing number of the Soviet population to support the partisan effort. By the spring of 1942, the partisan movement had emerged as a substantial force, reaching almost a quarter million members and continuing to grow.

Some partisan units found assistance and cooperation from the increasing numbers of small Jewish resistance or underground organizations forming in the ghettos. Numerous tiny underground groups had already appeared in late 1941. The continuation by the Germans during 1942 of the massive ghetto Aktionen, or massacres of ghetto inhabitants, produced a steady growth, limited to be sure in size, of armed and other means of resistance among ghetto survivors.

Although severely limited in what they could and did achieve, and facing a determined and much better armed and trained enemy, some Jews fought back desperately. They sabotaged German military and police activities, smuggled weapons into the ghettos, planned revolts against their tormentors, published underground newspapers, and contacted and, where possible, fought alongside the partisans.

Not all Jews, however, were welcomed by the Soviet partisans. On the one hand, many encountered difficulties in being accepted, especially if they had few weapons of their own. Almost no Jews were trained soldiers, and many fled to the forests unarmed. On the other hand, anti-Semitic partisan groups turned away or even killed Jews. In Volhynia Ukrainian nationalist partisans slaughtered thousands of the survivors of ghetto Aktionen who had escaped to the nearby forests.

For Jewish families to survive, many had to turn to self-help. Some established family camps in the forests, the most famous of which was organized by Tuvia Bielski; he never turned away Jews who came to him and even made efforts to rescue them from surrounding ghettos. In the forests of eastern Poland, Byelorussia, and the northern Ukraine, some thirty thousand Jews fought against the Germans, always with inadequate weapons. Most died in the fighting; only recently opened Soviet archives have permitted historians to reconstruct some of their stories.

Small Jewish underground or resistance groups developed primarily in ghettos in the Baltic States (e.g., Riga, Schaulen, Vilna), the Ukraine (e.g., Brest, Lutzk, Kremenez, Rovno, Czortkow, Tutchin), and Byelorussia (e.g., Baranowicze, Bialystok, Dyatlovo, Grodno, Lachwa, Lida, Minsk, Mir, Nieswiez, Nowogrodek, Pinsk, Prushany, Slonim, and Volozhin). Eventually during the war, such groups would number nearly one hundred in ghettos in both the occupied Soviet territories and the former Poland.

In almost all of the Polish and Baltic ghettos the Jewish population at large did not side with the rebels; in many of the small Byelorussian ghettos they did, as they would do in the massive Warsaw rebellion in 1943. The main reason, according to Yehuda Bauer, the Israeli historian, seems to have been that in Poland and Lithuania working with the underground could not offer a real chance of survival, just a different type of death. [Byelorussia], on the other hand, had forests, which offered a slight chance of survival, as well as the real possibility of taking revenge, which probably explains the much greater support the rebels received from the Jews in the nearby ghettos.[12]

The activities and experiences of the resistance in Riga, Minsk, Grodno, and Nieswiez are instructive. An underground movement emerged in Riga in January 1942, shortly after the massacres of nearly twenty-eight thousand ghetto Jews in the nearby Rumbuli forest. Also the Germans had murdered Jews recently deported to the ghetto from Germany and the Protectorate.

A network of some twenty-five secret cells made up the resistance in Riga, which numbered three hundred members altogether and included twenty-eight of the Riga ghetto's forty Jewish policemen. The organization contacted underground elements outside the ghetto, in the hope of establishing ties to Soviet partisans. Moreover, resistance members procured a small number of weapons, chiefly through Jews who worked in German armaments depots, and smuggled them into the ghetto.

When ten members of the Jewish resistance left the Riga ghetto on 28 October for the Byelorussian border to join partisans, the Gestapo discovered and killed them. As a further reprisal, the Germans executed 108 Jews in the ghetto, uncovered and shot the Jewish ghetto policemen involved in the resistance, and in the ensuing days murdered many more Jews. After the destruction of the resistance, the surviving Jews attempted to stay alive by working at forced labor in the ghetto or nearby labor camps; however, further deportations during 1943 emptied the ghetto of most of the remaining Jews.

In Minsk both the Judenrat and the ghetto underground, comprised mainly of Communists, attempted unsuccessfully to sabotage the continuing massacres of the Jews. In February 1942 the Germans arrested and hanged the Judenrat's first chairman, Ilia Mushkin, for cooperating with the resistance and after he had been betrayed by a supposedly anti-Nazi German officer. Mushkin had helped to smuggle some 7,500 Jews out of the ghetto to nearby forests.

His successor, Moshe Jaffe, a refugee from Vilna, continued the collaboration with the resistance. A month later, when the Judenrat, urged to do so by the resistance, ignored orders by the SS to deliver five thousand more Jews for killing, the SS seized and murdered more than five thousand returning to the ghetto from their workplaces outside. When the Germans demanded that Jaffe hand over to them the underground leader, Hersh Smoliar, Jaffe pretended Smoliar had died by giving the Germans the corpse of a Jew whose face Jewish doctors had disfigured and in whose pocket they had placed Smoliar's false, blood-spattered passport.

Increasingly the SS carried out its Aktionen at night, murdering on 2 April alone over five hundred ghetto dwellers. Between 28–31 July the SS slaughtered approximately thirty thousand Jews in Minsk. Before the killings, the Germans forced Jaffe to comfort the unsuspecting victims. However, as the SS arrived at the place where the Jews had assembled, Jaffe suddenly screamed to the crowd. The Germans, he said, had deceived the people and they should run for their lives. In the subsequent confusion, the SS began massacring the people, which left only nine thousand Jews in Minsk out of the nearly one hundred thousand who had lived there the previous year.

As part of the slaughter the SS murdered Jaffe and a ghetto police commander, Blumenshtok. In place of the Judenrat, the Germans appointed a "ghetto directorate" comprised solely of Jewish collaborators. This group, whose members were criminals ready to do anything to save their own lives, soon handed over to the Germans Jewish resistance members who intended to escape into the forests.

Grodno, in part because of its location between Vilna and Bialystok, became a center of Jewish underground operations. The city, whose Jewish population numbered twenty-five thousand in 1939, contained one of the oldest and largest Lithuanian-Jewish communities and focal points of Zionism. Its ghetto was among the earliest Jewish communities to learn of the massacres of Jews at Ponary, outside Vilna.

At the beginning of 1942, numerous groups in the ghetto—non-Zionist and Zionist youth organizations, the Bund (Jewish socialist party), and Communists—founded an underground movement. Internal divisions, however, characterized the group; the Zionists urged fighting the Germans from inside the ghetto, while the Communists pushed for the resistance to join the partisans outside. Mordechai Tenenbaum, one of the founders and commanders of the resistance organizations in the Vilna, Warsaw, and Bialystok ghettos, arrived in Grodno and worked to unite the underground.

When the Germans began deportations of Grodno's Jews during November and December to the death camps at Auschwitz and Treblinka, the resistance attempted unsuccessfully to assassinate a German commander in the ghetto. The deportations continued during 1943, which drove some members of the resistance to flee into woods close by. Hunger as well as inhospitable non-Jewish partisans, however, forced them to return to the ghetto. Remaining there and fighting found increasing support among the survivors. Also numerous female resistance members, who possessed false travel papers, made secret visits to the Bialystok ghetto.

In yet another case of armed Jewish revolt, the Jews of Nieswiez rose against the Germans on 20 July 1942. The executions the previous October of almost 4,000 Jews of the town had left only 585 survivors, most of them imprisoned in a ghetto. In the wake of the killings, a small resistance organization had formed, headed by Shalom Cholawski, which included Jewish youth who worked in local German armaments plants and smuggled weapons into the ghetto.

The Nieswiez underground organization, which numbered forty-six men, had secret contacts with local partisans and planned for a revolt inside the ghetto should the Germans begin another Aktion to "evacuate" it. On 17 July Cholawski's group learned that the Germans had murdered all the Jews in a neighboring ghetto. The resistance mounted a machine gun on the roof of the Nieswiez ghetto synagogue and distributed a few small-caliber weapons to resistance members.

When the Germans and Byelorussian police entered the ghetto on 20 July to "select" all the inhabitants except thirty for execution, the members of the resistance opened fire on their attackers. Other Jews set their houses on fire and defended themselves with knives and similar weapons. Only a few Jews fled successfully into local forests; either the Germans shot many of those who tried to escape, or else the surrounding Byelorussian population captured and returned them to the Germans.

The SS and German police battalions operating in the occupied Soviet territories felt acutely the effects of the growing partisan and Jewish resistance and the crisis experienced by the German armies in the East during the winter of 1941–1942. Most SS and police units in the East now divided their time increasingly between fighting at the front alongside the Wehrmacht and combating the growing resistance in the rear lines.

For example, after Battalion 310 served on the frontlines near Leningrad between February and July 1942, the unit was assigned in August to Byelorussia. There it conducted several "pacification" and reprisal operations near Kobryn. Between 23 September and 9 October, it murdered in

surrounding villages 1,278 men, women, and children; battalion reports justified the "actions" by calling the victims "Eastern people" (*Ostmenschen*, or
Slavs).[13] Between 25 July and 1 August , a reserve police unit, Battalion 133,
executed near Lwów in Galicia 147 "partisan supporters," Gypsies, and other
enemies, including 69 Jews.

The killing by Battalion 133 and other police units of Gypsies in the
Soviet Union continued during 1942 much as it had previously. The battalion's execution of Gypsies apparently even exceeded the scope of the unit's
authority. Also in the Baltic States, the commander of the Order Police
attempted to dictate racial policy by persuading Reich Commissioner Lohse
in January 1942 that most Gypsies be "handled exactly as the Jews."[14]

Something else as well reflected the increasing German combat casualty
rates in the East among the security units and military forces in general. During
the first months of 1942, the police battalions assigned to the Leningrad front
lost on average 24 percent of their men. To make up for such losses, the SS and
police expanded the number of men recruited from local or native populations
into auxiliary units nearly tenfold, to three hundred thousand.

To assist in the killing operations and other police duties, the Germans
incorporated into their police structure local Byelorussian and Ukrainian auxiliaries termed by the Germans *Schutzmänner*. Initially such collaborators volunteered their services and were called *Hilfswillige*, or Hiwis, by the Germans.
The local police wore uniforms, received basic training at special schools in
their districts, and carried weapons. In addition, the collaborators took an oath
to obey German orders "in the struggle against murderous Bolshevism." A
Jewish survivor of the Holocaust in Russia observed about the Hiwis that they
were, "in my opinion, bandits and murderers." After the war an official in Mir
noted "that the local volunteers took pleasure in shooting Jews."[15]

The Germans recruited other collaborators primarily for police duty in
Poland. They included Ukrainians, Latvians, and Lithuanians found in
POW camps and then trained at the SS camp at Trawniki, a few miles
southeast of Lublin. There they received arms and black uniforms. The so-
called Trawnikis not only participated in shooting Jews, but they also
assisted in clearing ghettos. Further, approximately 90 to 120 would serve as
guards in each of the death camps.

Beyond helping the Germans meet increasing wartime demands on
manpower, the use of the Hiwis and Trawnikis helped shift the psychological
burden produced by the killings from the SS and German police to their col-

laborators. In this regard, Browning's conclusions about Reserve Police Battalion 101 are informative. While operating from June 1942 to November 1943 in the General Government, the five-hundred-man battalion participated in the direct shooting deaths of at least thirty-eight thousand Jews; it placed forty-five thousand more Jews on deportation trains to death camps. After the battalion's initial massacre of approximately fifteen hundred Jews at Józefów, fifty miles south of Lublin, the resulting demoralization and psychological problems among the men produced a major change in their work.

Thereafter, Trawnikis or Hiwis carried out most future operations directed by the battalion, including on-the-spot killings, clearing of ghettos, and deportations of Jews. This division of labor, Browning has observed, gave the German policemen the sense that others had done the killing and that the battalion really had not participated in or been responsible for the destruction of the Jews.

Clearing of the Polish Ghettos, Deportations, and the German National Railway

The major German focus in the Final Solution during 1942 was on deporting enormous numbers of Jews from German-controlled areas in Europe to the special killing centers, built in occupied Poland. The annihilation of Polish Jewry represented the single most important element in the Final Solution and an unprecedented massive operation: at the end of 1941, several hundred thousand Jews lived in the Polish territories annexed to Germany, including 380,000 in the Warthegau, and over 2 million lived in the General Government. Within a year, nearly 80 percent would be dead, murdered largely by gas in several extermination camps specially created for this purpose by the Germans.

The new facilities permitted the perpetrators less of a direct role in killing the victims and simultaneously expanded the numbers that could be and were murdered. Moreover, the camps would operate on assembly-line procedures with large gas chambers that required limited manpower and would kill in relative secrecy. The Germans established several such camps principally for killing the Polish Jews immediately on their arrival: Chelmno, built northwest of Lodz in the Warthegau; and Belzec, Sobibor, and Treblinka, located in the General Government.

Two more extermination camps were not designated solely for killing Polish Jews. These were Auschwitz-Birkenau in Upper Silesia, an area incorporated into the Reich, and Maidanek, just outside Lublin in the General Government. Both functioned not only as killing centers, but also as concentration camps and slave labor facilities for the SS and German industry.

SS and German police units as well as Trawnikis ruthlessly cleared the Polish ghettos and Jewish quarters, rounding up their weak and vulnerable inhabitants and forcing them onto the "special trains" (*Sonderzüge*), the death transports of endless freight cars, that took them to the killing centers. The clearing of the Polish ghettos followed a horrifying and similar procedure everywhere.

During the roundups of the deportees the Germans terrorized them by using surprise, speed, and violence, and exploiting the uncertainty of the victims about their fate. Ghetto inhabitants lived in constant fear and tension, caused by rumors of impending deportations to unknown destinations, the high death rates inside the ghettos, and the frequent beatings, shootings, and hangings of ghetto dwellers by the SS and police. The Germans purposely encouraged among the Jews the hope of a better life outside the ghetto by telling them that they were being sent to the East to work. Severe restrictions or bans on mail going in and out of most ghettos also helped to suppress among the inhabitants the truth about the deportations.

Often the Germans announced the deportations only a day or hours in advance and directed the Judenräte to assist in selecting and assembling their fellow Jews for deportation. A thick chain of heavily armed German police and East European or Russian collaborators would encircle the ghetto to prevent escape. In the larger ghettos the deportations took days or weeks and the Judenräte received orders to provide lists of many thousands of deportees, whom Jewish police would round up.

If the Judenräte and Jewish police failed to collect the number of deportees the Germans demanded, the latter would murder the Jewish leaders and their families and friends and search the ghettos, using further massive brutality, for more victims. Often during the round up of deportees, the Germans split family members, seizing some for deportation and leaving others in the ghetto; in other instances, the Germans attempted to force families to make the horrific choice of who among their members would board the deportation trains.

Also during the process the Germans beat or shot to death an undetermined number of victims in their dwellings or on the streets. This figure, which is one of the great uncertainties in the Holocaust, surely reached into the hundreds of thousands and especially included the elderly, frail, sick, or others who could not march to the trains. Tragically, the killing of such persons served to encourage the deception among the other Jews that they were being sent to work. So did the German order to the deportees to take with them only small tools and implements and enough clothes that could fit into a suitcase. Once the deportations began, not only did they often result in the separation of Jewish family members, most of whom never saw one another again, but also the Germans and their collaborators drove people onto the trains by beating them with leather whips and setting dogs on them.

For much of the first phase of the deportations of Polish Jews, from March to August 1942, the procedure went smoothly for the Germans. Through a combination of ruses, lies, secrecy, and mistreatment, they concealed from most of the Jews the real goal of the deportations. Not only had the Germans isolated the ghettos and cut them off from the rest of the world, but they also worked those inside so hard and fed them so little that most willingly boarded the trains to leave. The Nazi strategies of enslavement and genocide, therefore, merged conveniently for the killers.

Moreover, the Nazi effort to deceive the Jews into believing they were being deported for work fitted well into the typical policy of most Judenräte. The latter served neither as collaborators nor blind tools of the killers. Instead, most tried to extend the existence of the ghettos for as long as possible by providing the Germans with labor. If ghetto inhabitants could prove their productivity as workers, so the Judenräte assumed, they would continue to live, increase their chances of survival, and perhaps even see liberation. Most councils were convinced that the German war economy and local German authorities needed the Jews as a work force.

This view, although terribly erroneous, flourished especially at the end of 1941. By then it had become clear that Germany faced a continuing war. In the Warsaw ghetto, the chairman of the Judenrat, Adam Czerniakow, even as late as two days before the first large wave of deportations from the ghetto began on 22 July 1942, doubted the reliability of the rumors of the operation about to take place.

Czerniakow recorded in his diary, after talking with the last of several low-ranking members of the Warsaw Gestapo: "Finally, I asked whether I could tell the population that their fears were groundless. He replied that I could and that all the talk was Quatsch and Unsinn [utter nonsense]."[16] On 23 July, with the deportations underway, the Germans informed Czerniakow "that for the time being my wife was free, but if the deportation were impeded in any way, she would be the first one to be shot as a hostage."[17]

Czerniakow, however, refused to assist in the deportations and the next day swallowed cyanide. No one understood more clearly what the deportations meant than he did. As noted in chapter eleven, information had reached the ghetto about Chelmno and Belzec. At the time of Czerniakow's death, another ghetto dweller recorded in his diary: "The deportees are, to begin with, taken for killing."[18] After the war, a survivor of the ghetto and Holocaust would tell an interviewer regarding the beginning of the deportations from Warsaw that Czerniakow "came to the conviction that [the deportees] were being led away for extermination, and he poisoned himself. He could not stand it anymore."[19]

In this regard, contrary to the claims of numerous postwar writers, not all Judenräte, including those in most east Polish ghettos, had a part in the deportations; some were not asked for and did not deliver lists or groups of Jews to the Germans. The Germans themselves rounded up the victims. In some smaller ghettos, according to Bauer, the councils refused to cooperate at all in any way. The Minsk Judenrat, in fact, as noted above in this chapter, joined an organized underground resistance group in the Minsk ghetto.

Nevertheless, many Judenräte not only cooperated in the deportations during much of 1942, believing or deceiving themselves into thinking the deportees were heading to life-saving work elsewhere, but they also continued inside the ghettos their policy of "work for survival." This has made such Judenräte and their leaders the subject of much controversy. Czerniakow's friends, for example, viewed his suicide as an act of integrity, a testimony to his personal courage and sense of public responsibility. Resistance or underground commanders, however, saw his death as an act of weakness. They criticized the Judenrat chairman for not mustering the courage to warn the ghetto and call for resistance.

In addition to German police and their collaborators, other Germans involved themselves in the deportations of the Jews. Unclear is precisely how many of the German National Railway's (*Deutsche Reichsbahn*) half a million civil servants and 900,000 workers had anything to do with—scheduling, administering, or operating—or knew about the death transports. Some railroad employees assisted in driving the Jews into the freight cars. According to the principal study of the railway: "Without the provision of transport by the Reichsbahn, the Holocaust would not have been possible."[20]

Despite the top priority given the Wehrmacht in the use of the trains for shipping troops and equipment to the battlefronts, the SS nearly always had the death trains it demanded. At least twice the deportations were apparently halted temporarily because of the intervention of the army, which requested the trains for its use. The first time occurred in the summer of 1942, during the German offensive in Russia; and the second at the end of 1942, when train service to the Ukraine broke down because of poor weather and a shortage of rolling stock. In both instances, Himmler intervened successfully with the head of the Reich Transport Ministry to acquire the deportation trains.

Because of insufficient records that survived the war, precise numbers are lacking for how many trains the German railway used for the Holocaust. The most reliable evidence indicates that the railway, with the assistance of the Polish East Railway (*Ostbahn*), carried approximately three million Jews to their deaths, most of them transported to the extermination camps by at least two thousand trains. In addition, the railway carried the property seized at the killing facilities from the victims for use by the Germans.

Between the fall of 1941 and spring of 1945, more than 260 deportation trains hauled German, Austrian, and Protectorate Jews to the ghettos and extermination camps in Poland and Russia. Other trains took victims to Theresienstadt, the ghetto-transit camp near Prague for many elderly German Jews and decorated Jewish war veterans. Further, approximately 450 trains ran from Western and Southern Europe to the death camps: a minimum of 147 trains from Hungary, 87 from Holland, 76 from France, 63 from Slovakia, 27 from Belgium, 23 from Greece, 11 from Italy, 7 from Bulgaria, and 6 from Croatia.

Uncertain is how many deportation trains ran from the Polish cities and ghettos to the nearby killing centers, although the number surely reached into the many hundreds. Some 110 trains alone, for example, took approximately 138,325 Jews from Lodz to the death camps from January 1942 to November 1944.

Eichmann's Gestapo office organized and scheduled the deportation trains. At the beginning of the deportations, each transport carried a thousand people. Later in the war, the trains frequently held two thousand or even five thousand people, as the SS attempted to kill as many Jews as possible before the conflict ended. On every train the passengers were packed together in crowded, filthy, and terrifying conditions in freight cars, each containing between one hundred and two hundred persons. The SS and police nailed up and sealed the cars, which had neither food nor water and lacked adequate circulation and any toilet facilities.

Often those suffering inside the cars waited many hours and even days when their transports were delayed at railroad stations or on side-tracks. In the summer unbearable heat existed in the cars, and in the winter frigid temperatures. As many as 25 percent of the deported Jews died on the trains; they perished from thirst, hunger, suffocation, heat prostration, hypothermia, and exhaustion. The few police who guarded the transports routinely shot hundreds more. A report of 14 September 1942 by the head of the police detachment accompanying a trainload of Jews from Kolomea to Belzec noted: "The ever-increasing panic among the Jews, caused by the intense heat, the overcrowding in the wagons . . . the stink of the dead bodies—when the wagons were unloaded there were about 2,000 dead in the train—made the transport almost impossible."[21]

Amid such horrors, the German railway shipped millions of Jews to the extermination camps. Despite all delays and obstacles, hardly a single victim was spared because of a lack of transportation means. Although, according to Alfred Mierzejewski, "moving 3 million people to their deaths was well within the capabilities of the Reichsbahn even under wartime conditions," the Germans diverted from military and civilian use a "substantial" amount of rolling stock to the deportations.[22]

Many railway officials and employees realized that the railway was carrying thousands of people to their deaths. Such employees knew of the existence of the extermination camps near railroad lines; in postwar interrogations, some admitted having had knowledge of the destinations of the transports. Mierzejewski has revised the view that the German railway knew nothing about the Holocaust; regarding why the railway and many of its employees did their part to assist the killings, he concluded:

> There is no record of any member of the railway sections protesting the transports, let alone asking for a transfer. Again, fear for their jobs and the safety of their families, and the simple fact that most did not care because they were not personally involved and were caught up in their duties, explains their behavior. The Reichsbahn had a corporate consciousness based on its role as a common carrier that served the public and the government whatever demands were placed on it.[23]

Chelmno and the Lodz Ghetto

German preparations for gassing Jews began in the fall of 1941 at Auschwitz-Birkenau, Chelmno, and Belzec. Largescale gassing occurred at Chelmno in early December 1941 and continued until April 1943, when the Germans closed the camp; it reopened briefly in 1944 and early 1945. The camp functioned as the center for the murder of Jews in the Lodz ghetto and rest of the Warthegau. Estimates of the numbers of Jews killed from there vary widely, with the most realistic figure around 215,000.

In 1963 a German court issued a verdict in a trial of six members of the SS unit that operated the extermination camp, and the proceedings of the trial produced various details about the killings. Victims were taken to a "castle" at Chelmno, where gas vans marked "To the Baths" remained stationery while using carbon monoxide to murder them and then transport the dead to mass burial pits in a nearby forest. In this regard, Chelmno would represent a transition stage in the killings by gas, between the use of gas vans in some of the previous euthanasia killings carried out in the war's first months by the RSHA, and fixed gassing installations built at camps such as Belzec, Sobibor, and Treblinka.

An SS Sonderkommando, first led by Herbert Lange and then Hans Bothmann, each with previous experience in operating euthanasia vans, supervised the killings. Approximately ten to fifteen members of the Security Police and eighty Order Police ran the camp. A member of the gassing detachment recalled after the war the killing procedure at Chelmno. He observed that Bothmann had told him and other SS men "that in this camp the plague boils of humanity, the Jews, were exterminated."

> The extermination camp was made up of the so-called "castle" and the camp in the wood. The castle was a fairly large stone building at the edge of the village of Kulmhof [Chelmno]. It was here that the Jews who had been transported by lorry or railway were first brought. The Jews were addressed by a member of the Sonderkommando in the castle courtyard. . . .
> [He] explained to the Jews that they would first of all be given a bath and deloused in Kulmhof and then sent to Germany to work. The Jews then went inside the castle. There they had to get undressed. After this they were sent through a passageway on to a ramp to the castle yard

where the so-called "gas-van" was parked. The back door of the van would be open. The Jews were made to get inside the van. The job was done by three Poles, who I believe were sentenced to death. The Poles hit the Jews with whips if they did not get into the gas-van fast enough. When all Jews were inside the door was bolted. The driver then switched on the engine, crawled under the van and connected a pipe from the exhaust to the inside of the van. The exhaust fumes now poured into the inside of the truck so that the people inside were suffocated. After about ten minutes, when there were no further signs of life from the Jews, the van set off towards the camp in the wood where the bodies were then burnt.[24]

The first transports to Chelmno included Jews from nearby villages and communities as well as five thousand Gypsies, whom the Germans had imprisoned at the Lodz ghetto. Mass deportations of Jews from the large ghetto and their gassing at Chelmno began in mid-January 1942: 10,003 during 16–29 January; 34,073 during 22 February–2 April; 11,680 during 4–15 May; and 15,859 during 5–12 September. Included among the killed were approximately fifteen thousand Jews from the Greater German Reich and Bohemia-Moravia, whom the Germans had sent to Lodz.

Rumkowski, the chairman of the Lodz Judenrat, ruthlessly sought to preserve the ghetto, which he considered his personal dominion, by bargaining with the Germans to minimize the deportations. He fulfilled the unending series of deportation orders imposed on him by the Gestapo. The initial deportation quotas he filled with the unemployed, those on welfare, and politically outspoken resistance leaders—most of them Zionists, Bundists, and Communists—he thought had inspired widespread labor unrest inside the ghetto.

With these deportations, Rumkowski consolidated his power beyond any further challenge. His speeches and proclamations berated the people for their gossip and thinking they knew better than he about what the deportations meant. On 3 January 1942, while rumors circulated that deportations would soon begin, he told a crowd in the ghetto, "Nothing bad will happen to people of good will." Two weeks later, he declared to workers at a ghetto garment factory, "Only work can save us from the worst calamity."

But slowly, as the people had always rumored, the ghetto population began to disappear. Amid the end of the first wave of deportations, which had cost the lives of over seventy thousand, on 4 September Rumkowski informed those who remained: "A grievous blow has struck the ghetto. They are asking us to give up the best we possess—the children and the elderly." In the next breath, prompting terrified cries and wailing from among the assembled crowd, he demanded: "In my old age I must stretch out my hands and beg: Brothers and sisters, hand them over to me! Fathers and mothers, give me your children!"[25] Deporting the children and the elderly, he maintained, would save the lives of many other ghetto Jews, those who could work and would be strong enough to survive the persecution.

Substantial evidence exists, including from diaries of ghetto inhabitants, showing that Rumkowski and others in the ghetto, including the head of the Jewish police, Leon Rosenblatt, knew about the fate of the deportees. Rumors of the death camps kept circulating, including talk of a site at Chelmno, where the Lodz Jews were being exterminated. Rumkowski saw the rumors as a direct threat to his power, and he used all the force he could muster to suppress them.

On 16 May 1942 an official in the German administration of the ghetto, Friedrich Ribbe, sent Rumkowski a memorandum requesting that "you immediately investigate whether there is a bone grinder in the ghetto, either with a motor or hand-driven. The special commando in Kulmhof is interested in such a grinder."[26] Possibly Ribbe passed the memo procedurally on to Rumkowski in following up on a requisition from Chelmno. But it cannot be discounted that Ribbe left for history an almost undeniable piece of evidence, forced in front of Rumkowski, to end any question about the latter's complicity in his people's destruction.

Also the small, but diverse, underground organizations in the ghetto, which Rumkowski suppressed and which included members of youth movements, political parties, cultural groups, and a group that listened to foreign radio broadcasts, were powerless against the deportations. Although they too had little precise information about the death camps, they nevertheless recognized the danger that confronted the ghetto. The underground bitterly complained about Rumkowski and the Judenrat because, beginning in January 1942, they filled the deportation quotas given them by the Germans.

During his rule in Lodz, Rumkowski made the ghetto a self-sufficient and massively profitable enterprise for the Germans. It operated as a giant war industry, both arming its German enemy and demonstrating to it that the Jews were not, as Nazi ideology claimed, "parasites." Ghetto laborers produced tons of munitions, telecommunications equipment, uniforms, boots, lingerie, temporary housing, carpets, and all sorts of other goods.

From the production of ghetto workers and confiscation of their belongings, the SS Economic-Administrative Main Office in Berlin reaped a net profit of 46,211,485 Reichsmarks (about $21 million) during the ghetto's four years. Lodz would be the final ghetto in Eastern Europe the Germans would liquidate. On 20 August 1944 the Germans deported Rumkowski and his family to Auschwitz. Some of the Jews who survived the ghetto and war later considered him a hateful tyrant with no scruples and something of a war criminal; others believed he saved their lives.

Also during 1942 the Germans deported to Chelmno Jews from other parts of the Warthegau, a few hundred Poles, Soviet POWs, and eighty-eight children from the Czech village of Lidice. The SS distributed or sold much of the clothing and other property of the victims to the surrounding German population. By April 1943 the SS had suspended the transports to Chelmno and closed and destroyed the camp. At the time, almost the entire Jewish population of the Warthegau—except for the 86,000 who remained, most of them as slave laborers, in the Lodz ghetto—had been murdered.

Aktion Reinhard: Belzec, Sobibor, and Treblinka

Heydrich did not live to see the full implementation of the plan he helped formulate to kill Europe's Jews. On 27 May 1942 Czech assassins shot him. When he died a few days later, deportations of Jews had only begun from the General Government to Belzec and Sobibor. The bulk of Polish Jews lived in the five districts of the General Government—Warsaw, Lublin, Radom, Krakow, and Lwów; according to the estimates produced at the Wannsee Conference, the Jews in the territory numbered 2,284,000.

The Nazis termed the mass murder campaign against such Jews *Aktion Reinhard* after the slain Heydrich. Also as further brutal reprisals for Heydrich's death, Hitler ordered the execution of tens of thousands of Czechs and Jews and, in addition, the human and physical destruction of the Czech village of Lidice, a few miles northwest of Prague. The Germans chose Lidice for eradication because, they alleged, the village inhabitants had assisted Heydrich's assassins, which was erroneous, and were loyal to them.

Globocnik, the SS and Police Leader in Lublin, coordinated Aktion Reinhard with the assistance of another Austrian SS officer, Hermann Höfle. Because Himmler could not spare manpower for the massive project, Globocnik had to assemble his own staff and other personnel. He gathered around him numerous other Austrians. Some of them took charge of the extermination centers, while others handled transports of Jews arriving from the ghettos, other killing operations in the region, and collecting, sorting, and using the Jewish property seized at the extermination camps and in the emptied ghettos.

To carry out the huge ghetto clearing campaign, Globocnik created his own private forces, comprised primarily of three battalions of Order Police that totaled fifteen hundred men, small units of ethnic Germans, and numerous Trawnikis. For constructing and operating the gas chambers at Belzec and the other Aktion Reinhard death camps, Sobibor and Treblinka, Globocnik posted to each facility personnel from the euthanasia program in the Reich. This group numbered almost one hundred. It provided expertise on the design and construction of the killing centers.

Heading up the group was Christian Wirth, a police and SS officer who had gassed mentally handicapped Germans at Grafeneck and Brandenburg and shot victims at Hartheim. Wirth served as commandant at Belzec until August 1942. Globocnik appointed another former official from the euthanasia program as well as fellow Austrian, Franz Stangl, commandant of Sobibor in March 1942 and then of Treblinka in September 1942. Irmfried Eberl, the commandant of Treblinka during July and August 1942, had served as a senior physician-in-charge at the euthanasia centers.

Assembly-Line Murder

Essentially the three camps followed the same killing procedure. When the transports arrived, SS men and collaborators herded the Jews out of the train cars and camp prisoners cleared the dead from the transports. As the Jews arrived, especially those in the first phase of the deportations between March and August 1942, nearly all had no idea where they were. They believed SS officers, who told them they had reached a transit facility and would soon be sent to labor camps.

First, however, the officers moved the new arrivals to a transport yard amid chaos and turmoil produced by SS beatings of and screaming orders at the victims. Once at the yard, the Jews were ordered to undress, leave their clothing, money, and other valuables, and then proceed to the "bathing" and disinfecting area. The officials separated the men from the women and children and shaved the prisoners' heads. In keeping with their rule to plunder everything possible from the victims, the Germans used the hair for a variety of purposes; they processed it for industrial felt and spun it into thread for socks for German submarine crews and railway workers.

Then SS men and Ukrainian collaborators took the groups naked, women and children first, to the gas chambers, which the Nazis had disguised as showers. The guards hurried the Jews through a corridor or "tube" that connected the transport yard with the gas chambers, continually beating the people with whips and turning dogs on them. The killers intended to conceal the victims' fate from them to the end.

Most of the Jews had no idea of what was happening until the doors closed behind them and the gas began filtering into the chamber. Within twenty to thirty minutes, all had died. Initially with the deportations, from the moment the Jews arrived at the camps on the transports until the removal of their corpses from the gas chambers, the procedure took between three and four hours; later, as the killers built larger gassing facilities, it took barely two hours.

Each camp carried out the killings with hydrogen cyanide (prussic acid) pumped by fixed installations of diesel motors or tank engines through pipes into the hermetically sealed gas chambers. To dispose of the bodies, none of the camps had crematoria, but instead buried the victims in gigantic graves; only at the end of 1942 did the Germans begin burning the corpses on huge funeral piles to destroy the evidence of their crimes.

For removal of the bodies from the gas chambers, as well as stripping them of gold teeth and fillings and burying or burning the remains, the camps used hundreds of Jewish prisoners, who hoped to avoid in this way being gassed themselves. After a few days or weeks, however, the SS murdered such prisoners and replaced them with new arrivals off the transports. Other prisoner details collected and sorted the clothes and valuables of the dead. Still another Sonderkommando unloaded the deportees' luggage from the trains and cleaned the cars that had brought the victims to the camps; often they only completed their task as another transport arrived.

At Belzec, during the first four weeks, from mid-March to mid-April 1942, the Germans gassed approximately eighty thousand Jews: thirty thousand from the Lublin ghetto, fifteen thousand from Lwów, and thirty-five thousand from other ghettos in the Lublin district, the neighboring region of Galicia to the east, and the Reich. From mid-April through June, the killing operations at Belzec halted, while the killers, using Polish and Jewish labor, tore down the small wooden building that housed three gas chambers and replaced it with a large stone structure that had six larger chambers. The latter could hold and kill one thousand to twelve hundred people at a time, the equivalent of the number transported in twelve to fifteen train cars.

Repeatedly, however, the killing machinery experienced breakdowns and delays. Frequently the diesel engine that piped gas into the chambers malfunctioned. On one occasion the engine became inoperable for nearly three hours while Kurt Gerstein, the chief disinfection officer in the Waffen SS and police, visited the camp. All the while, seven hundred to eight hundred people stood naked in four of the chambers, and when the motor was finally activated, it took thirty-two minutes to kill the victims.

Once the killing operations resumed at Belzec during the second half of July, they continued until early December. From July to October, 130,000 Jews from the Krakow district, 225,000 from Lwów, and still more from the districts of Lublin and Radom died. A few transports, moreover, arrived with German, Austrian, and Czech Jews, whom the Germans had deported previously to Polish ghettos.

Estimates place the total number of persons killed at Belzec at six hundred thousand, almost all Jews, and a few thousand Gypsies and Poles. Belzec would end operations in December 1942, although on orders of the SS, which sought to erase the evidence of its unprecedented crimes at the camp, prisoner details there continued to unearth and burn the corpses and then rebury the ashes until late April 1943.

By the third week of July 1942, the two other extermination camps in Aktion Reinhard, Sobibor east of Lublin and Treblinka, about fifty miles northeast of Warsaw, had begun operation. For nearly two months Sobibor had received deportations of Jews from Lublin, Krakow, and Galicia. As the Germans emptied the Lublin district of its almost one hundred thousand Jews, trainloads of other Jews were moved into the district from Germany, Austria, the Protectorate, and the German puppet state of Slovakia. The Germans unloaded some in various Polish ghettos, with the foreign Jews temporarily taking the places of those who had recently been killed; the killers sent other victims directly to Sobibor.

At Sobibor, which the Germans built along a railroad line and in an isolated, thinly populated, and heavily forested and marshy region, the SS sent the substantial majority of the deportees immediately from the trains to the gas chambers. The camp consisted of four parts: the railroad platform, administrative buildings, and quarters for the SS and Trawnikis; a transport yard where arriving prisoners were taken to undress and have their hair shaven and valuables seized; a lodging area and workplaces for several hundred Jewish prisoners; and a killing complex, comprised of gas chambers, mass graves, and quarters for the prisoner detail that emptied the gas chambers of the dead and buried the remains.

From May to late July 1942, approximately one hundred thousand Jews died at Sobibor; most came from the vicinity of Lublin , roughly ten thousand from Germany and Austria, six thousand from Theresienstadt, and a thousand from Slovakia. During the summer, primarily to hide evidence of the killings, the SS at the camp ordered a prisoner detail to open the mass graves and burn the bodies, a procedure subsequently adopted for all transports.

About the burnings, the Israeli scholar, Yitzhak Arad, himself one of the resistance fighters of the Jewish underground in the war, wrote after the war:

> As a result of the hot weather in the summer of 1942, the buried corpses swelled, and the fully packed mass graves rose up above the surrounding surface. The entire area became infested with vermin, and a terrible stench pervaded the camp and its surrounding areas. The camp commanders feared that the drinking water, which came from dug wells, could be contaminated and poisoned. Therefore the decision was made to start burning the bodies in Sobibor.[27]

Also such mass cremations formed part of a much larger campaign begun by Himmler in June 1942 to conceal the mass murders. For that task, the Reichsführer appointed through Gestapo chief Müller an SS colonel, Paul Blobel, the former head of a Sonderkommando of Einsatzgruppe C. Blobel had participated in killings in Kiev and other places in the Ukraine. Müller named Blobel to head an SS unit that would cover up the traces of the vast executions carried out by the Einsatzgruppen and other German forces in the East.

Intended as top secret, Blobel's operation received the code name *Sonderaktion* (Special Operation) 1005. After experimenting with procedures for burning corpses at the Chelmno death camp, the special unit found a crudely efficient way to erase the German crimes. A large excavator and a detail of Jewish prisoners took the decomposed bodies out of the pits and arranged them on a large roaster built from old railway tracks laid over an empty hole. A special bone-crushing machine destroyed the bones that remained. Then the prisoners buried the ashes of the bodies and small fragments of bones in the pits from which the bodies had been removed.

At Sobibor the transports stopped temporarily during August and September, in part for repairs on the railroad leading into the camp, but mainly for construction of three more gas chambers. The killing facility could not keep pace with the transports arriving with Jewish victims. The expansion increased the killing capacity of Sobibor to twelve hundred persons at one time. At the beginning of October, deportations to the camp resumed, primarily of Jews from the Lublin region. Altogether, at least 250,000 Jews would perish at Sobibor.

The killing center at Treblinka, located in a thickly forested and concealed area, began gassing operations in July 1942. Initially the camp had a stone building that housed three gas chambers, each having a second door through which a Sonderkommando of prisoners removed the corpses and then buried them in mass graves two hundred yards away. For piping carbon monoxide into the gas chambers, the camp used engines from downed enemy planes. These often proved unreliable and malfunctioned, and German mechanics and engineers worked feverishly to keep them operating.

Between 22 July and 12 September, some 265,000 inhabitants of the Warsaw ghetto and 112,000 from other parts of the Warsaw district were deported to Treblinka and murdered. The SS first took at Warsaw the weakest in the ghetto, then those who lacked papers and permanent jobs, then relatives of those who had exemption papers, and finally even workers with proper papers.

Everyone was a potential victim. The ghetto's orphanage director, Janusz Korczak, accompanied his orphans, a tragic scene described in an account left behind by the ghetto's historian and archivist, Emanuel Ringelblum. The latter founded and administered a large secret ghetto archive and intelligence center, code-named *Oneg Shabbat* (Sabbath Delight), in which he and others recorded the horrors that befell the Jews of Warsaw and other ghettos.

Ringelblum and his colleagues successfully hid the documents in metal cases and milk cans in the ghetto during August 1942 and the spring of 1943. The archive survived the war and contained underground newspapers, diaries and papers of Ringelblum and other Jewish officials, and thousands of other original records. The collection remains the most important single source for the history of Polish Jewry during the world war.

Soon the gas chambers at Treblinka proved insufficient; between August and October, the SS constructed ten more. This expansion made possible the killing of twenty train carloads of victims at one time. Between 5–25 October, five transports from Theresienstadt deported eight thousand Jews to their deaths at Treblinka. Also killed there before the end of 1942 was a substantial portion of the 337,000 Polish Jews from the Radom region and 35,000 remaining in the Lublin district. In November the Germans expanded deportations to Treblinka of Jews in Bialystok, a city outside the General Government.

Moreover, during the summer and fall, SS personnel at Treblinka received and killed at least seven thousand Slovak Jews, whom the Germans had deported previously to ghettos in the General Government. The anti-Semitic Slovak state, Germany's most obedient satellite, had assisted the German invasions of both Poland and Russia. Not only did the Slovak government of the Catholic priest, Joseph Tiso, implement increasingly harsher measures against its Jewish citizens, but it was also the only government in Europe that asked the Germans to deport the Jews. The puppet regime in Bratislava could not fulfill its commitment to the Germans to supply them with a large number of Slovak laborers, so it suggested deporting Jews instead.

From March to October 1942 the Germans deported sixty thousand Slovak Jews, out of a community of some eighty-seven thousand, to Poland, where most died at Treblinka, Auschwitz, and Maidanek. Although Slovakia agreed to pay Germany five hundred Reichsmarks per deported Jew, including for those living in the Reich Protectorate, it soon changed its mind, believing the Germans were making too much money, and temporarily halted the deportations. The German Foreign Ministry urged the Berlin government to conclude a new property settlement with Slovakia, but the Ministry of Economics refused to give up the "blood money" that Germany had extracted from the puppet government.[28]

By the end of 1942 the killing centers of Sobibor and Treblinka had murdered over one and a half million Jews, most of them from occupied Poland. Of the nearly 1.2 million Jews who entered Treblinka in 1942 and 1943, only fifty-four are known to have survived; most of them escaped during an uprising of Jewish prisoners at the camp in August 1943. As 1942 drew to a close, already both Treblinka and Sobibor were near to shutting down. The killing capacity of Auschwitz would soon be expanded sufficiently for the murder of those Jews whom Germany could pry away or seize from its allies and satellites, such as Slovakia, and from the areas in Europe and elsewhere under German control.

Shortages of Transport and Forced Labor for the Wehrmacht and German Industry

When the newly opened Treblinka had begun gassing operations and run concurrently with Belzec and Sobibor, the deportations of Jews accelerated so quickly that they left a shortage of trains for use as transports. Also this scarcity arose because of the military situation in the East. The Wehrmacht needed urgently all trains for transporting more equipment and manpower to the Soviet Union, where the German summer offensive of 1942 had begun.

Germany also had pressured two of its satellites, Rumania and Hungary, into sending more troops to Soviet Russia to assist the German forces there. The Germans seized Voronezh and then moved southward toward Rostov and the lower Don River. In several battles, German armies had captured approximately two hundred thousand Soviet POWs. Hitler sent the German 6th Army toward Stalingrad and three other armies south in the direction of the Caucasus region.

His euphoria at what he viewed prematurely as a major victory led him to interfere even more than usual into military matters. In mid-July he moved his field headquarters from East Prussia to a new command post near Vinnitsa, in the eastern Ukraine. There the officers and secretaries could still smell the poorly buried corpses of the Jews murdered by the Germans after the Jews had completed work on the new headquarters.

The German military thrusts in the East made even greater the Wehrmacht's need of rolling stock for shipping supplies to the front. By August and September 1942, not only stiffening Soviet resistance, but also shortages of German supplies and reinforcements slowed down the German advance toward the Caucasus and at Stalingrad. Soviet offensives around Leningrad and on the central front spoiled planned German offensives and drained further German resources that the Wehrmacht replenished only with difficulty. Furthermore, as noted above in this chapter, the Germans had to contend with a rapidly growing partisan movement.

The increasing military demands, however, did not take precedence for long over the Final Solution. The killing program received priority over all else.

Large numbers of trains that could have hauled supplies and troops to the Soviet front instead continued to carry Jews to the death camps in Poland.

To witness the killing procedure, which he had previously envisioned and approved, Himmler visited the extermination centers. He went first to Auschwitz, which had started mass killings of Jews at the end of March 1942. There he watched SS officers use Zyklon B to gas a group of Jews from the Netherlands. Then he traveled to Lublin to see the gas chambers that employed carbon monoxide. Also he met Globocnik and witnessed a gassing at Sobibor.

While in Lublin on 19 July, the Reichsführer ordered the completion of Aktion Reinhard (i.e., the extermination of the entire Jewish population of the General Government) by the end of 1942. Almost immediately, deportations of Jews increased substantially. On 28 July Albert Ganzenmüller, the state secretary in the Reich Transportation Ministry responsible for the German railway, informed Himmler's SS adjutant, Karl Wolff: "Since 22 July a train carrying 5,000 Jews has been traveling daily from Warsaw to Treblinka via Malkinia. In addition there is a biweekly train carrying 5,000 Jews from Przemyl to Belzec."[29]

The same day, Himmler, after meeting with Hitler on 24 and 27 July, wrote Gottlob Berger, leader of the SS Central Office (SS-*Hauptamt*) and state secretary in Rosenberg's Eastern Ministry, protesting the ministry's concern to use Jews as labor. Himmler declared that "the occupied eastern territories will be cleared of Jews. The implementation of this very hard order has been placed on my shoulders by the Führer. No one can release me from this responsibility in any case. So I forbid interference."[30] On 13 August Wolff wrote Ganzenmüller that Himmler "was particularly gratified to learn . . . that for the past two weeks a train containing 5,000 members of the chosen people is traveling to Treblinka every day" and that "we are thus now in the position to carry out this population transfer at an accelerated pace."[31]

Although Himmler passed on his July directive from Hitler, it foresaw the deportation of nearly all the Jews from the Polish ghettos and therefore caused even greater supply problems for the Wehrmacht and the government's Ministry for War Production. The chief difficulty was that between May 1939 and May 1942, German civilian employment had fallen by 7.8 million people, mainly because of the increased conscription of Germans into the armed forces. As a result, the Germans met the demand for labor by relying primarily on "foreign workers" (*Fremdarbeiter*) and prisoners of war. Since 1941 the

Reichsführer-SS Heinrich Himmler begins his inspection of Mauthausen on April 27, 1941. (*Mauthausen Museum Archives*)

Due to his skill in writing propaganda, racial ideologue Alfred Rosenberg was made editor of the *Völkischer Beobachter*, the official Nazi newspaper, in 1921. He later headed a special unit, *Einsatzstab Reichsleiter Rosenberg*, which plundered objects of art and furniture belonging to Jews in occupied western Europe. (*William Gallagher*)

German Nazi and Luftwaffe leader Hermann Göring. In 1936 he was appointed Plenipotentiary of the Four Year Plan. Hitler placed him in charge of the "Jewish question" in 1938 and made him nominally responsible for the Final Solution. In 1940 he was appointed Reich Marshal, a special position reflecting Hitler's high regard for him. (*William O. McWorkman*)

Germans pass by a broken shop window of a Jewish-owned business destroyed during Kristallnacht in November 1938. (*National Archives*)

Austrian Nazis and local residents look on as Jews are forced on their hands and knees to scrub the pavement. This happened during the Anschluss in March 1938. (*Dokumentationsarchiv des Oesterreichischen Widerstandes*)

Reinhard Heydrich, at his Gestapo desk, was a crucial SS figure in planning and carrying out the Holocaust. (*KZ Gedenkstaette Dachau*)

A Nazi boycott of Jewish stores. This early measure of the Nazis in their persecution of German Jews began with a nationwide boycott on April 1, 1933. (*William Blye*)

Himmler and Hans Frank, the "Butcher of Poland," at a dinner held in Krakow in 1940. Frank was Governor General, the Nazi civilian administrator, of the region in Poland where much of the Holocaust happened. Himmler and Frank often clashed over control of Jewish and other Nazi racial-population policies. (*Muzeum Historii Fotografii*)

The hanging of two Jews, Moishe Kogan and Wolf Kieper, in Soviet Russia on August 7, 1941. All Jewish spectators were later killed by the *Gestapo*.

Passport photo of Raoul Wallenberg, a Swedish diplomat who saved thousands of Hungarian Jews in the summer of 1944. (*Hagstromer & Qviberg Fondkomission AB*)

Mordechai Chaim Rumkowski, the dictatorial leader of the Judenrat (Jewish Council) in Lodz. (*Jerzy Tomaszewski*)

Adam Czerniakow, the Judenrat leader in the Warsaw ghetto, meets with an officer of the Luftwaffe, circa November 1940.

Mordechai Tenenbaum, an important leader in the Jewish resistance in the Vilna, Warsaw, and Bialystok ghettos, here seen in 1943. (*Yad Vashem Photo Archives*)

Members of the Hashomer Hatzair Socialist Zionist youth movement, including Mordechai Anielewicz (top right), the leader of the Warsaw ghetto uprising in April 1943. (*Leah Hammerstein Silverstein*)

SS troops guard members of the Jewish resistance during the Nazi suppression of the Warsaw ghetto uprising. Note the presence of both male and female revolutionaries. (*National Archives*)

Jews, captured during the suppression of the Warsaw ghetto revolt, are marched to the *Umschlagplatz* (transfer point) for deportation. (*National Archives*)

Jan Karski, a Polish underground official, had witnessed Nazi atrocities in Poland and had escaped to the West. He provided the Allies, including Prime Minister Winston Churchill and President Franklin Delano Roosevelt, with a firsthand account of the Holocaust, but was often not believed.

Members of of Sonderkommando 4a of Einsatzgruppe C (mobile killing squad C) look through the clothing and other possessions of Jews massacred at Babi Yar, a ravine near Kiev, Ukraine. This photo was taken on September 30, 1941.

With the commandant of Auschwitz, Rudolf Höss, and with an official of the large German company IG-Farben, Himmler tours Monowitz, the slave labor camp at Auschwitz, in July 1942. The other men in civilian clothes are IG-Farben employees.

Arrival and selection of Hungarian Jews at Auschwitz in May 1944. (*Yad Vashem Photo Archives*)

The notorious Josef Mengele, SS doctor at Auschwitz. (*Panstwowe Muzeum w Oswiecim-Brzezinka*)

Adolf Eichmann, a major SS and Gestapo figure in the Holocaust, survived many years as a fugitive before Israel caught, tried, condemned, and executed him. Here Eichmann takes notes during his 1961 trial. (*Israel Government Press Office*)

The Sonderkommando burn bodies of gassed prisoners in the open at Auschwitz-Birkenau. (*Panstwowe Muzeum w Oswiecim-Brzezinka*)

Roza Robota was a key female member of Hashomer Hatzair in Ciechanow, Poland, and later in the Jewish underground movement in Auschwitz-Birkenau. She was among the first prisoners in the Birkenau women's camp. (*Yad Vashem Photo Archives*)

armaments industry had suffered from a huge shortage of workers that led the Reich government to recruit, and especially seize, foreign laborers.

Once the invasion of Russia had begun, the Germans impressed or kidnapped tens of thousands of Soviet citizens for slave labor in the economy, in part because the Wehrmacht's barbaric treatment of Soviet POWs, whom the Germans could have used as workers, had killed so many of the prisoners. Also the Germans conscripted large numbers of Poles for forced labor as well as workers from German-controlled Western Europe. By 1942 Nazi Europe had hundreds of labor camps that varied in size from a few workers to many thousands.

Slave labor, therefore, with its maltreatment and physical destruction of men and women compelled to work without pay and under appalling conditions, represented a crucial part of the war economy of Nazi Germany. While workers from Western Europe were treated better than those from the East, whom the Germans considered racially inferior, the Germans reserved the hardest lot for the Jews used as forced labor. Jews were tortured and even murdered in their places of work, whether in a ghetto, concentration camp, labor camp, or elsewhere. Beginning in 1942, as part of the Final Solution, the Germans implemented a deliberate policy of "destruction through work" (*Vernichtung durch Arbeit*).

In this massive system, most large German firms engaged in heavy industry and war production used forced labor. Counted among such firms were the state-owned corporations, such as Volkswagen and the Hermann Göring works, and the munitions and arms producers: Krupp, Rheinmetall-Borsig, Messerschmitt, Heinkel, and Junkers. The Volkswagen plant, for example, was only completed with the cooperation of the SS, which gave the company access to its enormous amount of cheap labor—civilian deportees, prisoners of war, concentration camp inmates, and finally Hungarian Jews deported in 1944 from Auschwitz. By the war's end, foreign labor would comprise over 85 percent of the workers at Volkwagen's main factory.

During the last two years of the war, nearly every major German firm— such as BMW (*Bayerische Motorenwerke*, Bavarian Motor Works), AEG-Telefunken, Siemens, Daimler-Benz, and IG Farben—had some function in the war economy and exploited the forced labor. These enterprises put Jewish prisoners to work in existing factories as well as in new ones built near the ghettos and concentration camps.

When Wehrmacht authorities and Albert Speer, the German Minister of War Production, learned in 1942 of Himmler's directive to complete Aktion

Reinhard by the end of the year, they protested vigorously. Himmler's order involved primarily forced labor in the General Government in the factories and workshops that produced or repaired goods for Germany's war effort and that used large numbers of ghetto workers. Among the approximately one million persons who worked for the armed forces in plants in the General Government, three hundred thousand were Jews, of which at least one-third were skilled craftsmen. A British historian observed as early as 1966 that "among the first Polish Jews who were gassed in the extermination camps were thousands of skilled metal workers from Polish armament factories."[32]

The first phase of the massive deportations from the Warsaw ghetto that ended in September 1942 cut the textile production of the ghetto in half. The military commander in the General Government, General Kurt Freiherr von Gienanth, complained that eliminating all Jews from the region would cripple war production. The desperate need for equipment indicated that every worker should be utilized.

Curiously, when the military officers responsible for war production suggested that Jewish laborers be replaced with Poles, they received little support from the OKW and Keitel. Yet senior SS officials in the General Government shared the concerns of the military. The SS not only employed substantial amounts of Jewish forced labor for its own large industrial enterprises, but it also sought to expand its armed units (Waffen-SS) within the military, which required even greater production and repair of war equipment.

At a meeting in late September 1942, during which quarrels broke out between Himmler and Speer over the organization of the armaments industry, Hitler declared his agreement with the demand of Fritz Sauckel, the Nazi plenipotentiary for labor procurement, that Jewish laborers in the General Government be used temporarily in war production. Although Himmler viewed all arguments for preserving Jewish labor as inconsequential, he nevertheless agreed to spare some Jewish workers if the SS could control every camp and ghetto that housed the laborers. He also insisted that the industrial plants requiring the prisoner labor be built in the camps themselves or that the camps be located near the plants.

As a result, the SS erected a number of new labor camps in which roughly forty-thousand Jews would eventually work: the main ones were located at Poniatowa and Trawniki in the Lublin district; and in the cities of Radom, Czestochowa, Plaszow near Krakow, and the Janowska camp outside Lwów. In addition, in the death camps of Auschwitz and Maidanek, the

Germans did not kill all Jews who arrived there immediately. A few whom the SS judged "capable of work," after they had survived a "selection" procedure at the train ramp that sent most deportees directly to the gas chambers, were assigned to work as forced laborers in the concentration camp portion of the two facilities.

Maidanek

Although Maidanek would function as one of the main German killing centers in the Holocaust, because of insufficient transport, building materials, and Soviet forced labor, it never reached more than half its planned size. Also the camp served as a slave labor facility for Poles and Soviet POWs, and at various times for Jews, who worked in SS plants in the Lublin area. The numbers of Jewish laborers at the camp varied from twenty-five thousand in the fall of 1942 to six thousand in late 1943.

Despite its construction on the edge of Lublin largely under the supervision of Globocnik, Maidanek never answered to him nor did it operate as part of Aktion Reinhard. Instead, the camp was supervised directly by the SS Economic-Administrative Main Office in Oranienburg. The camp drew most of its SS personnel, including its second commandant, the notorious Karl Otto Koch, not from the euthanasia program, but from the Buchenwald concentration camp in Germany.

Among the approximately three hundred thousand persons who died at Maidanek, nearly one-third were Jews. During the fall of 1942 the SS built three gas chambers at the camp, which used both carbon monoxide and Zyklon B. Of those who died at Maidanek during the war, the Germans gassed 25 percent; killed 60 percent from disease, lack of food, and overwork; and shot or beat to death the remainder.

While the agreement of Hitler in the fall of 1942 to spare some Jews for labor for the German war economy resulted in a temporary slowdown or delay in Aktion Reinhard, it did not change the basic German decision to kill all the Jews. Soon Hitler removed the uncooperative German general in Poland, von Gienanth, from his post. Himmler emphasized to the military and others that the agreement he and the Führer had made would last only for a limited time.

Meanwhile, the mass murder of Jews continued. The ideological fanaticism of Himmler and other SS leaders, always urged on and approved by

Hitler himself, demanded the killing of all Jews despite its impact on war production. On 16 December 1942, an SS corporal reported from Zamosc in Poland about the transport of 644 Poles to Auschwitz. The report recorded Hans Aumeier, the SS commandant of the Vaivara concentration camp in Estonia, as explaining that only Poles fit for labor should be delivered to Auschwitz and that, in order to relieve the camp, "limited people, idiots, cripples and sick people must be removed from the same by liquidation." The report continued, pointing to a policy at Auschwitz of exterminating the Jews, that "in contrast to the measures applied to the Jews, the Poles must die a natural death."[33]

CHAPTER ELEVEN

ATTEMPTED REVOLTS, AUSCHWITZ, AND THE BEGINNING DEPORTATIONS OF EUROPEAN JEWRY, 1942

DURING **1942** the massive deportations of Polish Jews had resulted in the murder of 2.2 million of them, which represented nearly 80 percent of Polish Jewry. As the large majority of the victims disappeared from ghetto after ghetto in Poland and from the surrounding countryside, and as reports circulated about what had happened to them, a growing number of those still alive began to grasp the awful truth.

Some even realized that they were doomed to total destruction, and the possibility of survival, even if in the most wretched conditions, was gone. A similar awareness had gripped some ghetto Jews in the occupied Soviet territories beginning in the winter of 1941–1942 and produced among them the first stirrings of armed Jewish resistance against the Germans. By the end of 1942, well over a million Soviet Jews had died at the hands of the Germans. Nevertheless, the substantial majority of the remaining Jews continued not to realize or understand that the Nazis intended to kill them all.

At the peak of the Germans' unprecedented mass murder operation, on 22 September 1942 Himmler had a lengthy meeting with Hitler. From what

Himmler wrote in his handwritten agenda notes, one subject may have been the extermination of the Jews. According to the notes, the two discussed the "Emigration of Jews" and "how [it] was to be further proceeded."[1] Also Himmler mentioned Globocnik, who had responsibility for carrying out the slaughter of Polish Jewry. Himmler's record suggested that either he updated Hitler on the mass murder of the Jews in the East or they decided on the next steps in the Final Solution.

The Polish Ghettos: Between Resistance and Revolt

During the fall of 1942, at least six months before the massive Warsaw ghetto revolt, small and isolated Jewish resistance or underground organizations had formed in a number of ghettos in occupied Poland. Some of these groups both planned and, on occasion, attempted to wage armed struggles to stop the deportations. Most of the underground cells developed, however, only as the deportations largely emptied many ghettos.

In contrast to the Russian Jews, whose murderers had hardly operated in secret by scattering themselves and carrying out killings throughout the occupied areas of Soviet Russia, Polish Jews, at least initially, had far fewer opportunities to learn about the German killing centers to which they were deported. In this regard, the German effort to murder more Jews and conceal the Final Solution by building the death camps (i.e., taking the victims to their killers) had enormously tragic results for the victims.

To be sure, some similarities existed between the situations of the Polish and Soviet Jews that influenced their fate significantly. Before the appearance of organized resistance in both occupied Russia and Poland, individual Jews had acted in various ways to resist, to escape, and as leaders—especially the Judenräte—to attempt to assure the survival of the Jewish community. But without hope of liberation or even the option of continued persecution and slavery, the small Jewish resistance groups nearly everywhere, according to Yitzhak Arad, "fought to choose the way they would die."[2] This stood in sharp contrast to the non-Jewish resistance, such as the Polish underground army (Armya Krajowa) and Soviet partisans, which fought for a way to live.

Also different from the non-Jewish resistance, which drew its strength from a surrounding and essentially intact population, the Jewish underground organizations had no Jewish masses, once the deportations began, from which they might have drawn substantial strength. Both Polish and Soviet Jews lived as a small minority isolated among most of the local non-Jewish populations and received little or no support (e.g., weapons) either from them or others in the outside world.

Indeed, in most places the local populations either barely reacted to the terrible fortune befalling the Jews or acted against them, usually for anti-Semitic reasons and fear of the Germans. Still another obstacle to the development of resistance was "collective punishment," the Nazi policy of killing large numbers of Jews as a reprisal for hostile Jewish acts.

Despite the enormous problems facing any Jewish effort at opposing the Germans, as the deportations of Jews in the General Government unfolded during 1942 those few who urged resistance found far more ready listeners among the Jews who had survived and who worked for German-owned factories or lived in hiding. Only gradually during 1942 had the truth about the deportations filtered into the Polish ghettos.

Already during the fall of 1941, reports from emissaries or messengers from Vilna and Kaunas had reached Warsaw about the mass killings of Jews in Lithuania. In January 1942 three gravediggers from the Chelmno death camp fled and made their way to Warsaw, where they arrived several weeks later. At the Warsaw ghetto, the small clandestine archival and intelligence center, the Oneg Shabbat, headed by the historian Ringelblum, interviewed the gravediggers about the camp and passed the information on to the Jewish underground press and also to the Polish underground.

Also during January, letters and postcards arrived in Warsaw from Jews living near Chelmno that informed their friends and families in the former Polish capital about the mass killings at the camp. During the spring, Ringelblum learned as well about Belzec and Sobibor and received reports about the extermination of the Jews in Lublin. Through a courier he transmitted the information to the Polish government-in-exile and through it to the British government.

When the BBC broadcast a report on 26 June 1942 about the death of 700,000 Polish Jews, Ringelbum and his colleagues in the Oneg Shabbat were ecstatic, believing they had "fulfilled a great historical mission. It has alarmed the world to our fate, and perhaps saved hundreds of thousands of Polish Jews from extermination. . . . We have struck the enemy a hard blow. We have revealed his Satanic plan to annihilate Polish Jewry, a plan he wished to complete in silence."[3] But a few days later, Ringelblum's mood had changed. He noted in his journal: "The more sober among us, however, warn against having any illusions. No compassion can be expected from the Germans. Whether we live or die depends on how much time they have. If they have enough time, we are lost. If salvation comes soon, we are saved."[4]

Elsewhere in Poland, at the end of March 1942 two Jewish women, Mina Astman and Malka Talenfeld, deported to Belzec from a town near the camp, escaped and returned to their home. There they secretly told friends what had happened. In April a Jewish underground newspaper, the Bundist *Nowe Tory* (*New Tracks*), wrote about the gassings at Belzec. Other information about Belzec came mainly from Poles who lived near the camp and from Polish railway workers, and it reached the Polish underground. From the latter's publication the Jewish resistance learned the news. Such knowledge, however, spread to only a limited number of Jews and did little to heighten the awareness of the Jewish masses about the dangers they faced.

Some distrusted what they heard from the Poles. One Jew, Yitzhak Lichtman, whom the Germans expelled in May from his town near Lublin to Sobibor, later explained: "On the train to Sobibor, we were told by some Poles that we were being taken to be burned. We didn't believe them. We thought that the Poles, who were anti-Semites, wanted to scare us."[5]

Other Jews refused to believe stories of annihilation, even after hearing the testimony of eyewitnesses; the listeners lived in a condition that psychologists and others term "suspended disbelief." This psychological state is similar to denial, in which people find what they hear too terrible to accept and therefore to comprehend and analyze. The disbelief of many Polish Jews at what they heard left them largely incapable of responding to the deadly threat facing them. Such disbelief also resulted for some Jews from their erroneous assumption that only people who had done something wrong could possibly be in danger. Who could believe someone would murder en masse millions of helpless and innocent people?

Gordon Craig has written that "[t]he problem of persuading people to believe reports of what was happening in the death camps was always difficult."[6] Nearly a year and a half after the Final Solution had begun, an inhabitant of the Lodz ghetto would write: "Persistent rumours circulate about the liquidation of the ghettos in various Polish cities. In my opinion, people are exaggerating as usual. Even if certain excesses have taken place in some cities, that still does not incline one to believe that Jews are being mass-murdered. At least, I consider that out of the question."[7]

Some Jews who lived near the death camps knew, or suspected, the worst of the Germans. A survivor of the Holocaust who had lived in Bedzin, a city not far from Auschwitz in eastern Upper Silesia, testified after the war to knowing about the camp. The survivor recalled that a leader of the Bedzin Judenrat, who cooperated with the Gestapo in rounding up local Jews for deportation, "knew that the Jews were going to Auschwitz, and he would assemble these Jews. He would send the old people to Auschwitz because he judged that an old person was already useless, he wouldn't bring anybody into this world, while young people could reproduce. But in time it became clear that he was simply a traitor to the Jewish people."[8]

During August and September 1942, rumors and information about Belzec and Treblinka and the actual fate of the deportees spread gradually among the remaining Jews in the ghettos and labor camps of the General Government. Regarding Treblinka, a Polish socialist railway worker helped a Bundist and "Aryan-looking Jew" from Warsaw, Zalman Friedrich, reach the railway branch line that led to the death camp. From people in the area Friedrich learned details about what went on at the place that consumed endless trainloads of people and left the smell of burned corpses hang over the surrounding neighborhood.

On 20 September a Bundist underground newspaper in Warsaw published accurate details about Treblinka. Also several prisoners had escaped from both the camp and deportation trains traveling there. Much greater secrecy continued to surround Sobibor, partly because of its location in a more remote and desolate area and partly because very few people escaped from the camp.

When the information about Belzec and Treblinka began reaching the Polish ghettos, the deportations ran much less smoothly than before. Jews hid inside the ghettos, and both the ghetto police and SS had greater difficulties taking them to collection areas and trains. In the more heavily wooded regions of northeastern Poland, groups of youth tried to escape and join partisan units. The local non-Jewish population betrayed some of the youth, such as those who had fled in December 1942 from the Solochew ghetto in eastern Galicia, to the Germans.

In other places small underground resistance groups formed, many of them by Zionist youth organizations that planned and sometimes attempted to incite Jewish revolts against the Germans and delay or sabotage the deportations. In Krakow during May and June 1942, the Judenrat, led by Artur

Rosenzweig, refused to cooperate with the Germans in helping the latter carry out the first massive deportations of the ghetto's Jews to Belzec. Consequently, the six thousand victims of the Aktion included the Judenrat.

In place of the Krakow council, the Germans appointed a new leadership body called the "Commissariat" and its head David Gutter. He had not lived in Krakow, but was ready to do everything the Germans demanded. During this Aktion the Jewish ghetto police assisted the German authorities by tracking down and arresting underground members.

By August Zionist youth had reacted by organizing two resistance groups, the *Hechaluz Halochem* (The Fighting Pioneers) and *Iskra* (The Spark). The groups soon established ties to the Warsaw-based Jewish Fighting Organization (*Zydowska Organizacja Bojowa*, ZOB). The young Zionist leaders included Zvi Bauminger, Aharon Liebeskind, Gola Mira, Shimshon Draenger, and Gusta Draenger-Dawidson. Influenced by the hostility of the Commissariat and Jewish police toward the underground, they prepared for an armed revolt against the Germans outside the ghetto, in the Aryan portion of Krakow.

From their base in the city, the young Zionists attempted numerous acts of resistance. Their greatest success occurred on 22 December 1942, when they bombed the Café Zyganeria, a favorite nightspot of German officers, in the city's center. The blast killed eleven Germans and wounded thirteen. Outside Krakow, several factors made the participation of the resistance in partisan operations difficult. These included the isolation of the Jews from the local Polish population and the hostile attitude toward the Jewish resistance of the Polish underground army.

Zionist youth also played the central role in the creation of a Jewish resistance organization in Sosnowiec, a city that had twenty-eight thousand Jewish inhabitants in 1939 and that was located a few miles west of Krakow. The Judenrat and its chairman, Moshe Merin, operated on the policy of "survival through work" and cooperated with the SS in recruiting forced labor from among the Jews and assisting in assembling Jews for deportations.

The Germans had given Merin broad powers over the Jewish communities in much of eastern Upper Silesia; his readiness to serve the Germans provided him numerous personal advantages. To acquire forced labor to satisfy German demands, he established a system of mandatory conscription, using all means possible to make it work, including extortion and issuing threats to the youth or their parents.

At least one historian has characterized Merin as a "pseudo-savior" suffering "from a messianic complex." Merin apparently dreamed of establishing his dominion over all the Jews of Europe under the auspices of the Nazi regime. "He was so blinded by pride," Leni Yahil concluded, "that in his mind's eye he saw the way was open before him alone, and he was determined to pursue it—only to find that it was merely a figment of his imagination."[9]

After deportations between May and August 1942 took 11,500 Jews to Auschwitz; the youth groups in the region and their leader, Zvi Dunski, called on the Jews to disobey the orders of the Judenrat and not report for the transports. The resistance tried unsuccessfully to contact the Polish underground. During the spring of 1943, when the Germans established ghettos at Sosnowiec and nearby towns, the youth organizations and a few other Jews procured a small caché of weapons. Also they built bunkers in which people could hide during deportations.

In Tarnów, a city east of Krakow that had a Jewish population of twenty-five thousand in 1939, the Germans carried out repeated deportations from the ghetto between June and mid-November 1942. These sent twenty-four thousand Jews to Belzec. In response, Zionist youth and other political groups established an underground movement. A few members of the Jewish ghetto police assisted the resistance by providing it with weapons. One underground group escaped to local forests where most of its members died fighting the SS. Others in the resistance continued their activities inside the ghetto and concentrated on organizing efforts to flee across the border to Hungary.

Auschwitz: A Concentration Camp and Killing Center

Germany's military situation during 1942 not only allowed the Germans to continuously operate the killing centers in the East that murdered, within eight months, the overwhelming majority of Polish Jewry. Also the occupation or control of much of Europe by German armies, despite problems on the Eastern and Mediterranean Fronts by the end of 1942, ensured as part of the Final Solution the beginning of the slaughter of Jews from Central, Western, and Southeast Europe. This portion of the Holocaust would extend into 1944.

Most of these victims would die in Auschwitz, the largest and most lethal of the German killing centers . There the killers followed a different procedure from the camps of Aktion Reinhard, which had murdered nearly all of their prisoners immediately on arrival. Auschwitz contained three camps in one: a killing facility, a concentration camp, and a group of slave labor camps.

Formation of Auschwitz I and II

The Germans had built the original or main camp, Auschwitz I, during 1940 on the site of a former Polish army barracks. It contained the head-quarters of the SS and living accommodations for SS officers and guards. Initially established as a concentration camp, Auschwitz I soon earned a reputation for savage treatment and murder of prisoners. Only the lucky few prisoners, or in fewer instances yet, the ones who helped one another, would ever survive.

In one building of the camp, the so-called Block 11, the SS constructed a bunker for meting out the severest tortures and physical abuses—including standing for a number of nights in a cell smaller than a square meter—to the prisoners, which almost always resulted in excruciatingly painful death. Next to the building stood the "black wall," where SS firing squads regularly executed inmates.

Initially the camp held Polish political prisoners and slave laborers; later it had primarily Soviet POWs and then Jews. By the end of 1941, the capacity of Auschwitz I reached eighteen thousand prisoners, and in 1943 the camp held as many as thirty thousand. This included a sector for women prisoners, established in March 1942, whose population rose to six thousand before the Germans moved it to Birkenau, the second and by far largest part of Auschwitz.

Also Auschwitz I killed prisoners by promoting the policy of "destruction through work," in which inmates died from backbreaking and exhausting labor, some of it intended as punishment. Meanwhile, above the front gate of the camp stood a large sign that declared, cynically, "Work makes one free" (*Arbeit macht frei*).

Following the decision to implement the Final Solution, in December 1941 the SS established a gas chamber in Auschwitz I, located in the mortuary of the camp's crematorium. Initially, the SS had used the mortuary to continue experimentation with the deadly prussic acid, Zyklon B, to gas Soviet POWs. Originally, the Germans had built the so-called old crematorium, later designated as crematorium I, for burning the bodies of prisoners who died a natural death or were killed or executed.

During 1941 Himmler ordered the establishment of the vastly larger and nearby Birkenau, known as Auschwitz II, for the projected mass annihilation of Europe's Jews. Construction began in October for a facility that would operate as both a killing center and concentration camp, the latter holding over one hundred thousand prisoners. At Birkenau in early 1942, the Germans converted two farm houses into gas chambers, called by the SS "bunkers 1 and 2." The first started operation in March and could hold eight hundred people at a time, and the second, which held twelve hundred, began functioning at the end of June. Woods surrounded the bunkers on all sides. Hedges screened from view large graves located nearby.

Following Himmler's visit to Auschwitz on 17 July, during which he witnessed the gassing of an entire transport of Jews in bunker 2, the SS began cremating the bodies instead of burying them. The SS unit headed by Blobel, commissioned with *Sonderaktion* 1005, arrived at Auschwitz to exhume the approximately one hundred thousand buried bodies, burn them, and scatter the ashes to prevent the possible reconstruction of the number of victims. Within a few months the unit had emptied all the mass graves.

The "Selections," Death, and Plunder

Between March 1942 and the end of the year, the two bunkers at Birkenau and the gas chamber at Auschwitz I carried out the systematic murder of most of the 175,000 Jews deported to Auschwitz from various German-occupied European countries. Unlike the Jews of Eastern Europe, some of whom had seen and heard of the massacres of Jews in Soviet Russia and Poland and rumors of gassings, most of those in Western Europe still remained unaware of what awaited them. Their German rulers continually told them they were being sent east for labor.

Trains carrying thousands of deportees, arranged by Eichmann's department in the Gestapo, traveled daily to Auschwitz. Once the transports pulled alongside a specially built spur of track near Birkenau, at the freight depot called the "Jewish ramp," SS guards forced the deportees with threats and beatings to leave the trains quickly and form two lines, men in one and women in the other.

SS doctors then carried out so-called selections; with a flick of the wrist they sent the large majority of the people, especially the elderly, children, and women, immediately to the bunkers to be gassed. The remainder they assigned to the camp for use in slave labor. The selections split up many families; most prisoners chosen for labor never saw their husbands, wives, children, or other loved ones sent elsewhere again.

SS guards who marched the victims, or loaded them on trucks to carry them to the bunkers, attempted numerous ruses to keep the people from learning what was happening. These included engaging the victims in innocent conversation and driving a car with a Red Cross emblem, which in fact often carried the canisters containing Zyklon B, alongside the processing column.

Once at the bunkers the SS men continued the deception. They told the prisoners that before taking up residence in the camp they had to go to the showers and undergo delousing. Also the prisoners were told to remember the spot where they left their effects. After they had followed orders to undress, either in one of the barracks or behind hedges, the SS chased them into the gas chamber, marked with a sign "To the Baths," under a rain of blows from whips and attacks by dogs.

Those packed inside the gassing facilities died a terrible death. One of the SS doctors who supervised the gassing procedure, Johann Kremer, testified after the war: "Shouting and screaming of the victims could be heard through that opening and it was clear that they were fighting for their lives. These shouts were heard for a very short while. I should say for some minutes, but I am unable to give the exact length of time."[10]

A special prisoner detail (Sonderkommando) then removed the corpses and plundered them further, extracting from them gold teeth, recovering jewelry, and cutting the women's hair. Another detail loaded the corpses onto trolleys on narrow-gauge tracks and transported them for burial, and beginning in the fall of 1942 for burning, to deep earthen pits.

Meanwhile, other Sonderkommando collected from the trains the mountains of luggage and other belongings, including money and valuables, left behind by the victims and seized by the Germans. The prisoners referred to the looted property as "Canada;" they associated the sheer amount of the plunder and its value with the riches they imagined existed in the far-away North American country. Under the closest supervision from the SS, the Sonderkommando carried the enormous loot to so-called Canada storage facilities, which eventually comprised dozens of barracks. There hundreds of other prisoners sorted and inventoried the stolen goods, viewed by the German government as state property, preparing them for shipment to Germany.

A decree by the SS Economic-Administrative Main Office in September 1942 required that the SS send much of the plunder to the government's Economics Ministry, SS offices in Berlin, and the special SS agency in charge of resettlement of ethnic Germans, the VoMi. The SS shipped money and valuables (diamonds, precious stones, pearls, and gold objects) seized at Auschwitz in armored cars and special railway transports to the SS Economic-Administrative Main Office, which sent the loot on to the Reichsbank in Berlin.

The bank, in turn, added some of the enormous booty to its own resources and deposited the remainder in special accounts for the SS, from which the latter could finance its extensive economic enterprises. According to the independent historian Milton Goldin, "what the SS took from persons it murdered and earned from Jewish slave labour financed the [SS as a] 'state within a state.'"[11]

The SS sent other items stolen from their victims, such as watches, fountain pens, pencils, shaving utensils, pen-knives, scissors, flashlights, and handbags to workshops of the SS Economic-Administrative Main Office for cleaning and repair before shipment to and sale at SS post exchanges. Moreover, the Germans sold some of the looted valuables in Switzerland. In other instances SS officials at Auschwitz illicitly appropriated large amounts of the property for themselves. German relief agencies acquired clothing, umbrellas, sunglasses, and briefcases plundered from the Jews and distributed them to the German population.

Few if any Jews at Auschwitz or the other Nazi killing centers were murdered until all their property and assets had been seized. The sole exception was gold teeth or fillings pulled from the mouths of the dead. Historians such as Goldin emphasize that Hitler was always concerned that Germany's home front should benefit sufficiently from the war not to revolt. Indeed, the Germans of the Third Reich never revolted against their regime. The 20 July 1944 attempt to kill Hitler involved only a tiny military and political group, whose members were subsequently condemned as traitors for their courageous action by many of their fellow countrymen.

Persecution

For the Jews who survived the initial selection on the railroad platform, the SS sent them to Auschwitz I or into the concentration camp portion of

Birkenau, which held various categories of prisoners. The SS registered nearly all such prisoners in camp files, in contrast to the Jews sent directly from the trains to the gas chambers, whom the Germans never kept records on.

Both men's and women's sectors of Birkenau held prisoners of many nationalities, most of them Jews and some Poles and Germans. Birkenau consisted of at least nine subcamps, surrounded and separated by electrified barbed-wire fences and equipped with gates and watchtowers. Heavily armed SS guards patrolled nearly everywhere. Long wooden barracks or huts, crudely built and constructed originally as horse stables, served as living quarters for most of the prisoners.

The women's sector at Birkenau eventually had nearly thirty thousand inmates, who suffered from a lack of the most basic sanitary and hygienic conditions and whom the SS subjected to frequent "selections" for gassing. Female SS guards or supervisors (*Aufseherinnen*) delighted in torturing the prisoners. Also Birkenau had a separate family camp for Gypsies as well as for Jews from the Theresienstadt ghetto.

Conditions for prisoners in the Auschwitz camps defy anything even remotely resembling accurate description. No words or pictures can portray the horrors endured there by the prisoners; nearly all died agonizing and painful deaths, usually after suffering one form or another of physical and psychological torture, humiliation, and degradation. SS guards meted out the most sadistic of beatings and other tortures to the prisoners. Persecution was perpetual. Severe punishments for minor infractions were routine. Inmates were whipped and beaten repeatedly; still others were placed several at a time into the small dark rooms known as standing cells (*Stehzellen*) with no space to sit down, or were shot or hanged.

The number of prisoners in the camps, mostly Jews, would rise steadily during the war, eventually totaling one hundred thousand. The camps marked a radical and irrevocable departure from the previous existence and lives of the prisoners. The latter found themselves in a wholly unreal world. When the prisoner entered either Auschwitz I or Birkenau, the Germans stripped him or her not only of all remaining personal possessions, but also of his or her identity and human dignity. All body hair of the prisoner was shaven off and a camp serial number tattooed on the prisoner's left arm, a practice unique to Auschwitz. Number replaced name, cold dark blocks or barracks replaced home, and a three-tiered, lice-infested wooden bunk with a thin layer of straw for a mattress replaced room and bed.

In the barracks or huts, which were not even fit for animals, massive overcrowding existed; filthy communal latrines and other unsanitary conditions produced epidemics of disease and dysentery. Thousands of prisoners, weakened from a severe lack of food, which never amounted to more than a small piece of bread and watery soup, and from hunger and starvation and a total absence of medical care, died from typhus.

The prisoners wore old wooden shoes and striped camp fatigues, with pieces of cloth sewn on them showing the person's serial number and prisoner category: a red triangle for political prisoners; green triangle for ordinary criminals; and black triangle for asocials. Other similar colored marks identified homosexuals and Jehovah's Witnesses. All Jewish prisoners wore a Star of David made of red and yellow triangles.

Those unable to adapt to the horrible existence soon sank into apathy and dejection and were called by others "Muslims" (*Muselmänner*), from the alleged resemblance of such prisoners, not able to stand on their feet, to Muslims in prayer in a bowed position. Such tragic figures hovered between life and death, their hunger-ravaged bodies little more than skeletons with yellowish skin and lifeless, sunken eyes. Most had given up any hope of survival.

Hunger and thirst so tormented prisoners before and after meals that stealing or hoarding (i.e., "organizing") of food was rampant. Many prisoners stole from others. In this regard, as in so many other instances in the camp, the Germans purposely forced the victims to participate in their own destruction. Primo Levi, an Italian anti-Fascist deported to Auschwitz in 1944, distinguished after the war between those in the camp whom he termed "the drowned and the saved." The former he identified as the Muselmänner, whose "life is short, but their number is endless."[12]

Also the prisoners endured daily early morning roll calls (*Appell*), in which they stood at attention in straight rows, often for hours in terrible cold or heat, so the SS, on the pretext of counting the prisoners, could torment them. Then prisoner work details or Sonderkommando left the camps for backbreaking forced labor that lasted twelve hours per day.

As the work groups moved out of Auschwitz I, a camp orchestra performed near the front gate; one musician would later call such work "playing for time" or survival. [13] Some Sonderkommando remained inside the camps, including those involved in the killing procedure or those laboring in various workshops and the camp kitchen and laundry. The prisoners worked under the supervision of an armed SS escort and the so-called *Kapos*, brutal prisoner foremen who pushed the slave laborers to exhaustion and often death.

At night, after returning to camp, the prisoners reported again for roll call, which—like the morning one—could last for hours if the SS could not account for all the prisoners. During and after roll call, the SS meted out individual or collective punishments to the prisoners; these included savage beatings and the most inhuman of other abuses. Nearly always the SS punished the prisoners arbitrarily. The most insignificant mistake made during the day by a prisoner or group of prisoners could mean death for any one of or the whole group.

The SS deliberately promoted inside Auschwitz I and Birkenau tensions and conflicts, including divisions between different nationalities and categories of prisoners. The Germans created a small though powerful layer of prisoners in positions of authority; such prisoners received favors from the SS and remained alive as long as the Germans deemed them useful in perpetuating the savage camp regimen. Prisoner Kapos had charge of labor squads, camp elders (*Lagerälteste*) of the entire prisoners' camp population, and prisoner elders of the blocks or barracks (*Blockälteste, Stubendienst*). Also some inmates held positions in the central administration of the camps.

German prisoners, despite their small numbers at Auschwitz, generally received positions of authority among the inmates. In Auschwitz I the SS assigned most official posts held by prisoners to Poles. At Birkenau, Jewish prisoners held such positions. Most inmates in positions of authority, especially Kapos and block elders, brutalized and mistreated their fellow prisoners.

Adding to this tense, emotional, and dangerous prisoner society, the inmates endured at Auschwitz the horrors of periodic "selections" by SS doctors of persons for killing in the gas chambers. The doctors, which numbered twenty-three, performed selections in the prisoner barracks and so-called medical or hospital blocks. In some instances the doctors picked their victims arbitrarily; in other cases they singled out for death the sick or persons alleged "unfit for work." Doctors also supervised the killings in the gas chambers.

Moreover, the doctors conducted a series of inhuman and criminal medical experiments on the prisoners. Such experiments at Auschwitz, as well as at other Nazi concentration camps, fell into two main categories and violated not only the ethic of patient consent, but also the oath that physicians had sworn since the time of ancient Greece to heal and do no harm.

According to Robert Lifton, a crucial factor in explaining the systematic genocide in Auschwitz and other mass German killing sites was the Nazis' "medicalization of killing—the imagery of killing in the name of healing." The way in which Nazi doctors justified their role in the mass murder of the Jews represented an extension of Hitler's fanatical ideology: the belief in the existence of "a deadly racial disease, the sickness of the Aryan race; the cure, the killing of all Jews."[14]

The German government or SS sponsored some experiments at Auschwitz, usually for a specific ideological or military purpose; other experiments reflected the sadistic scientific interest of a particular doctor. For example, Carl Clauberg and Horst Schumann conducted extensive sterilization and castration experiments using X-rays, primarily on Jewish inmates, both men and women. Most likely Hitler and Himmler intended to use mass sterilization after the war, which they expected Germany to win, to destroy the supposedly inferior Russians, Poles, other Slavs, and Gypsies. The experiments, carried out under the most primitive of medical conditions, often killed the prisoners or caused them painful burns, infections, and permanent mutilations and usually led to the doctors killing them or ordering them killed. Other doctors at Auschwitz experimented with their own interests, such as killing with phenol injections and operating on precancerous growths of the cervix.

The most notorious Auschwitz doctor, Josef Mengele, called by prisoners the "Angel of Death," selected tens of thousands of Jews for the gas chambers. Among those not selected were prisoners whom he subjected to X-rays, mutilations, virulent diseases, and toxic injections. His special interest was identical twins and dwarfs—some five and six years of age—whom he used in his so-called research. The latter, he believed, would allegedly further the Nazi mission of creating a genetically superior race. Also Mengele identified totally with Hitler and the Nazi party. Frequently he took gifts of candy and clothes to the children, joking with and even hugging and kissing them, but then a few hours or a day later he would torture them with barbaric experiments or murder them with injections and dissect their corpses. Some of the unsuspecting children even grew to like Mengele, substituting him for their father whom the Nazis had killed, and called him, innocently, "Uncle Mengele."[15]

Also in the name of alleged "medical" research, Nazi doctors killed eighty Auschwitz prisoners at the Natzweiler-Struthof concentration camp in 1943 near Strasbourg. The bodies were preserved in the Anatomy Institute of the

University of Strasbourg for eventual inclusion in a collection of human skeletons.

Nazi medical behavior in Auschwitz and at other concentration camps represented the ghastly end point of a gradual but steady process of attempts at supposed racial "purification" through medicine. The "medically" induced deaths and disfigurements of camp prisoners had their earliest origins in the eugenics movement in Germany before World War I. Gradually the Nazis had expanded this movement with the German sterilization law of 1933 and the later deadly wartime euthanasia program.

Slave Labor

Located over a wide area around Auschwitz I and Birkenau were approximately forty satellite camps, either directly affiliated with the main camps or serving as their branches. The satellites operated as slave labor facilities. They varied in size, some containing several dozen prisoner-slaves and others several thousand. The Germans established the satellites near mines, foundries, and other industrial enterprises; twenty-eight of the forty camps operated for the German armaments industry.

Of the nearly one and a half million people taken to Auschwitz during the war, four hundred thousand received prisoner status and many worked in the satellite camps. More than half of the slave laborers were Jews, most of the others Poles. In 1942 Auschwitz had twenty-four thousand prisoners, a figure that would increase almost fourfold two years later. Nearly all the mines and other industrial concerns in Upper Silesia, which belonged to some of Germany's largest companies, including the Herman Göring Works, Siemens-Schuckert, Krupp, and IG Farben, used the forced laborers.

The largest labor camp at Auschwitz was at Monowitz, called Auschwitz III, located a few miles from Auschwitz I and Birkenau. At Monowitz IG Farben built an enormous plant that covered roughly twenty square kilometers and had units for the production of methanol, iso-octane, carbide, and other chemicals. But its main factory, for producing synthetic rubber (buna), remained unfinished. By the spring of 1944, camp inmates, most of them Jews, composed nearly 30 percent of the approximately twenty-nine thousand workers at Farben's Auschwitz complex; they were treated much worse than the other workers, most of whom were Poles and some ethnic Germans.

The construction of the Farben plant at Monowitz did not go smoothly. A multitude of problems emerged that delayed the assembling and opening of Farben's factories; the methanol plant began operation in mid-1943 and all other units, except rubber, by the spring of 1944. Construction of the complex suffered from an insufficient supply of building materials as well as numbers of laborers, including skilled mechanics and machinists. But the most serious problem was the savage treatment of the workers by SS and other guards, which demoralized even the free laborers and undermined productivity.

During the last half of 1942, the SS decided to transfer many of the Polish workers to camps in Germany and replace them with more slave labor comprised of Jews arriving at Birkenau on the deportation trains from all over Europe. Hayes described "the rolling of a grisly human conveyor belt between the SS's rail sidings and Monowitz:"

> Able-bodied Jews were brought from Auschwitz, billeted three to a bed in stifling and verminous barracks, provided minimal food and clothing supplements to the standard camp issue, subjected to lengthy predawn roll calls in all sorts of weather, and put to work on eleven-hour shifts hauling or carrying heavy loads at a trot. Within three to four months of their arrival, such treatment literally consumed the inmates, reducing them to walking skeletons. Those who did not drop dead were sooner or later reclaimed by the SS and gassed. Either way, they were replaced, and the cycle resumed. In this manner, some 35,000 people passed through Monowitz during 1943–4; the toll of confirmed deaths came to about 23,000, or an average of 32 per day. At IG's mines in the neighborhood, the Fürstengrube, Janinagrube, and Gunthergrube, where the concern employed another 6,000 inmates during 1942–4, the mortality was even more frightful.[16]

While the SS collected an estimated twenty million marks in "wages" from Farben at the Monowitz camp, Farben's production and therefore profit from the plant never reached the firm's original goals. Although individual Farben officials occasionally sought to alleviate the plight of the prisoners, such officials were much more interested in the drive to finish the factories and begin production. Farben managers excused themselves from responsibility for the prisoners' fate by blaming it on the SS and the general shortage of supplies.

Moreover, for most Farben leaders, according to Hayes, "knowledge of the systematic annihilation of the Jews in gas chambers came later, more halt-ingly, and with less clarity." [17] Although senior executives visited Auschwitz, they never toured Birkenau; nor did they apparently realize that Degesch, a firm in which Farben had a financial interest, controlled the manufacture and distribution of Zyklon B, the poison gas used by the SS to murder the Jews at Auschwitz.

Yet, from the top of Farben on down, undoubtedly most officials heard the widespread rumors of what was happening at Auschwitz and did their utmost to remain ignorant about it. At Monowitz the horrible smell from the crematoria of Birkenau and Auschwitz I overwhelmed the official claim that the camps' battle with typhus made necessary the burning of dead bodies. By 1943 the inmates at Monowitz realized what awaited them, in part because some of Farben's supervisors not only spoke openly of the gassings, but also used them as an incentive to force the prisoners to work harder.

The War and Deportations in Central, Western, and Southeastern Europe

During 1942 the Nazis would have killed far greater numbers of Jews at Auschwitz, but three factors kept them from doing so. First, the camp's gas chambers had insufficient capacity to murder considerably more victims. Long before the gas chamber at Auschwitz I closed down in December 1942, the SS had contracted the German firm, Topf and Sons of Erfurt, and a con-struction company in Kattowitz, to build four large new crematoria at Birkenau that would contain gas chambers.

As early as October 1941, when the SS had placed the original order for a new crematorium from Topf and Sons, it stressed the urgency of the under-taking and demanded rapid delivery. But despite the hectic pace of the con-struction work, which went on day and night, the building firms failed to meet the approved deadlines for completing and installing the several cre-matoria. The latter would begin operation in the spring and summer of 1943, long after the SS had originally envisioned.

Second, the decision of Hitler and Himmler in the fall of 1942 to spare some Jewish workers in the East for labor for German war production resulted in fewer deportations of Polish Jews to Auschwitz. Third, the flow of depor-tees from Northern, Western, and Southern Europe to Auschwitz and other

German killing facilities in Poland was restricted because the RSHA and German Foreign Ministry had to negotiate with, and frequently place pressure on, foreign governments to hand over their Jews.

To press the governments to release their Jews for deportation, the Nazi regime conducted a two-pronged political attack. Eichmann's department in the RSHA set up a Jewish Office (*Judenreferat*) in countries such as France, Belgium, and the Netherlands or attached its officials to German embassies and missions abroad. In addition, the Foreign Ministry had a special section for Jewish affairs, led first by Luther, a hardline Nazi and protégé of von Ribbentrop, and his deputy, Rademacher. Altough a few of Germany's allies, satellites, and collaborator regimes either refused to give up their Jews or did so only reluctantly, most such governments accommodated the Germans in their murderous policy.

Slovakia

The discussion that follows of the deportations primarily to Auschwitz during 1942 is organized chronologically. The first victims of mass gassings at Birkenau included thirty thousand Jews from the nearby eastern portion of Upper Silesia. At the end of March the initial transports of Jews arrived from Slovakia and France; altogether in 1942 most of the nineteen thousand Slovak Jews and forty-two thousand Jews from France sent to Birkenau died in the gas chambers. Also the violently anti-Semitic Slovak government deported during 1942 much larger numbers of its Jews to their deaths at Treblinka and Maidanek.

Amid the deportations, some Slovak Jewish leaders saved fellow Jews. A secret Jewish organization in Slovakia, the so-called Working Group, headed by Gisi Fleischmann, a Jewess and representative of the Joint Distribution Committee in the Slovak capital, Bratislava, and Rabbi Michael Ber Weismandl, smuggled groups of young people and children from Poland into Slovakia. Between the fall of 1942 and summer of 1943, the Working Group, although apparently not aware until very late of the totality of the Final Solution, negotiated with and bribed Wisliceny, who was working for Eichmann, to stop the deportations. Eventually, the group even attempted to reach Himmler to bribe him to stop the trains to the death camps from all over Europe.

However, while the deportations of Slovak Jews in fact halted, it was not the bribing of the Germans that accomplished the action but rather the bribing of local Slovak officials and a decision by the SS that pressure no longer existed to kill the last Jews alive in Slovakia. When the Slovaks rebelled against the Germans in the fall of 1944, seeking to rehabilitate Slovakia with the Allies, the SS took renewed action against the local Jews. On orders of one of Eichmann's officials, Alois Brunner, Fleischmann was sent to Auschwitz and never seen again.

France

French policy toward the Jews, which would eventually become a blot on one of Europe's traditional and leading sources of civilization, had turned even more sharply against the victims during the spring and summer of 1942. In the German-occupied zone of France, the first deportation train left for Auschwitz on 27 March 1942, loaded with 1,112 persons. The transport departed from Drancy, a concentration and transit camp located in a dreary working class suburb northeast of Paris, which a Jewish survivor of the Holocaust later termed a "waiting room for Auschwitz."[18]

A major factor in the beginning of the Final Solution in France involved the German military command in Paris. During the fall of 1941, the command sought to end reprisal shootings of French hostages for assassinations of German officers by the French resistance. The assassinations, carried out mainly by French Communists, had started with the German invasion of Soviet Russia. Both Hitler and Keitel demanded draconian reprisal measures, including—as the Germans had implemented in Serbia—killing one hundred hostages for every German killed. The German military commander in France, General Otto von Stülpnagel, mainly for practical reasons, opposed the reprisal policy demanded at Hitler's headquarters. Mass shootings, Stülpnagel protested, risked losing for Germany the loyalty of the French population, making more difficult future cooperation between Germany and France, and compromising the French government.

Conflict among the Germans over the shooting of French hostages continued to escalate, until in mid-January 1942 Stülpnagel proposed to Hitler and Keitel a substitute for the killings that he knew his superiors would support wholeheartedly. The general suggested that Germany begin mass deportations of Jews and Communists in France "to Germany or the East."[19] He reasoned that apart from the Communists, especially the Jews, thanks to the widely held anti-Semitism in France, especially against foreign Jews who had immigrated into France from Eastern Europe after World War I, would receive little sympathy from the French population as long as there were no public shootings. Also because the assassins had included Jewish resistance fighters whom the Germans and French had arrested, the Germans could tie together repressive measures based on both political and ideological motives.

Although Stülpnagel resigned his command over the issue, his proposal soon became common practice. On 10 April it was formalized in a decree from Hitler which directed "that for each future assassination, apart from the execution by firing squad of a number of appropriate persons, 500 Communists and Jews are to be turned over to the RFSS [Reichsführer SS] and the German Chief of Police for deportation to the East."[20] From that moment on, shooting hostages and issuing deportation orders became automatic and, as noted above, the first mass deportation of Jews in France to the extermination camps in the East left from near Paris at the end of March 1942.

Almost simultaneously, Pierre Laval, who favored expanding collaboration with Germany, including by deporting Jews from France, reentered the Vichy government, at Hitler's insistence, this time as premier. Also Louis Darquier de Pellepoix, a notorious anti-Semite and pro-German who had no scruples in supporting the Germans in their murderous anti-Jewish policy, took over Vichy's General Commissariat for Jewish Questions (*Commissariat Général aux Questions Juives*). The French police, furthermore, concluded an agreement with the SS that provided the police with a high degree of autonomy but obligated it to combat the "enemies" of Germany.

The French prepared for the deportations from both Vichy and the occupied zone by forcing all Jews to wear the yellow Star of David (7 June 1942), imprisoning many Jews, and placing others under surveillance. To assist the process, Himmler installed a new Higher SS and Police Leader for France, Karl Albrecht Oberg, whose office no longer answered to the German military commander in the occupied zone, but to the Reichsführer.

During the summer and fall, Jews were deported from all over France. In mid-July the deportations expanded with the roundup and internment in Paris of 12,884 Jews; the French police seized other Jews as well and sent most of them to Drancy, from where they were shipped the long distance—nearly a thousand miles—and over a period of four or five days to Auschwitz.

Pressed consistently by Nazi Jew-hunters for deportations, the Vichy regime cooperated eagerly in arresting and deporting foreign Jews. Getting rid of unwanted foreigners pleased the government; it also sought to retain control over the French police and hoped to gain concessions from the Germans in a variety of areas. But in a more cautious and hypocritical fashion, Vichy officials ignored the arrests and deportations of smaller but not insignificant numbers of French Jews, carried out mostly by the Germans. In some instances, to satisfy German demands the government revoked the citizenship of French Jews to pave the way for their deportation.

Moreover, Vichy leaders found themselves restrained on the issue by the refusal of the Italians in their zone of southeastern France to deport local Jews. The Italian *comando supremo* (High Command), a French official in the Italian zone reported to the SS, "forbade the French authorities to carry out the internment of personnel of the Jewish race."[21] Italy's attitude made its zone a refuge, albeit an uncertain and potentially dangerous one, for Jews, French or otherwise, who fled there.

For Mussolini, anti-Semitism had not played a central role in his Fascist program, and with few exceptions he had viewed the Jewish question with indifference. This issue had contributed to strained relations between the Axis allies, whose officials already had a dislike for one another that stretched back to World War I and Italy's participation in the war against Germany.

Italian military and political leaders, in addition to opposing German Jewish policy in France, had disagreed sharply with the Germans over how to handle the Jewish question in other areas of Southern Europe occupied by Italian troops. Weinberg has written that to Italian officials "the German mania for killing Jews seemed to be just one more sign that their Axis partner had hardly progressed from the level of the Germanic barbarians who had invaded the Roman Empire centuries before."[22]

Germany

During 1942 the SS and police deported the first German Jews to Auschwitz. At the beginning of the year 131,823 Jews still lived in the old Reich. Technically the first German Jews deported to Auschwitz included many who had fled before the war to the countries of Western Europe; they were deported between March 1942 and the end of the year along with Jews from France, the Netherlands, Belgium, and Luxembourg.

On 13 July 1942 the Nazis deported the first Jews from the Reich itself to Auschwitz; these were thirty-nine persons from Stuttgart. Other German Jews had been sent during 1942 to the death camps at Belzec and Sobibor and tens of thousands to labor camps in the General Government; still others had been killed after shipment at the end of 1941 to Riga and Minsk. During 1942 the SS deported still more German Jews to the occupied Eastern territories: over 3,000 to Riga in January, a further 2,757 during the fall, and 811 to Reval in October.

Among the deportees from Germany, the approximately eleven thousand elderly Jews deported during the summer and fall of 1942 to the Nazis' ghetto at Theresienstadt had the greatest chance for survival. Still, the overwhelming majority of prisoners there would perish or be deported to their deaths at Auschwitz and other death camps. Of the 18,639 persons who arrived at the ghetto in September, the Germans soon sent 13,004 on to the extermination camps and 3,941 died in the ghetto. Numerous other Jews in Germany were sent to concentration camps such as Buchenwald, where most of them perished from malnourishment and repeated torture.

Amid the deportations, the Jews in the Reich lived in daily fear of both Gestapo terror and the intense dislike they felt from much of German society. Victor Klemperer, a Jewish professor in Dresden, a converted Jew, and the husband of a non-Jewish wife, recorded in his diary in the spring of 1942:

> The concentration of hate has this time turned into utter madness. Not England or the USA or Russia—*only*, in everything nothing but *the Jew*.— Pay attention to the mixture of hide-and-seek and open threat. 11:59, but shall we live to see the end of the day? It has now become a firm rule: On the day after a house search there are suicides. We heard of the new case at the same time as the Hitler speech. A couple called Feuerstein, living in Altenzeller Strasse, had been pillaged, then summoned to the Gestapo and beaten and kicked there; during the night the people were found dead in their gas-filled kitchen.—From day to day I wait for the house search to take place here. The apprehension is always worst in the evening between seven and nine. No doubt wrongly, for the squads are said to appear at any time of day. They are said to steal everything: even food that has been bought on coupons, writing paper, postage stamps, leather briefcases.[23]

Most German Jews worked at hard labor in factories and had little money and food, which often reduced them to begging from friends. The Reich Association of Jews in Germany, the sole organization since 1939 that had represented the country's Jews, estimated the wealth of the German Jews at less than three hundred million Reichsmarks (about $125 million), only a fraction of Jewish wealth in Germany in April 1938. Not only had they lost their property to Aryanization, but also they had to wear the Jewish star as a mark of identification and humiliation. In many cities they lived in crude barracks or "Jew houses," wholly isolated from the rest of society. The regime had banned them from using radios, telephones, typewriters, laundries, bicy-cles, most public transportation, market halls, parks, tobacco products, restau-rants, libraries, and barbers and from attending theaters, cinemas, concerts, and museums. Violations of any of the government's thousands of anti-Jewish measures could result in beatings, arrest, and deportation.

As early as March 1942 Klemperer noted that he had heard of Auschwitz, "or something like it," mentioned "as the most dreadful concen-tration camp. Work in a mine, death within a few days."[24] For a long time he retained a quiet hope that there would be news from Jewish friends or acquaintances who were disappearing all around him. Some around him listened secretly to reports of mass murders on enemy radio, the British Broadcasting Corporation (BBC). By mid-1942 stories of large-scale killings circulated through the Jewish *Mundfunk*, "word-of-mouth news relayed by friends and acquaintances."[25]

Other sources of information confirmed the rumors. Klemperer's wife visited with an army corporal, an Aryan family friend, home on leave from the Eastern Front. The soldier told her about the massacre of Jews at Babi Yar: "Ghastly mass murders of Jews in Kiev. The heads of small children smashed against walls, thousands of men, women, adolescents shot down in a great heap, a hillock blown up, and the mass of bodies buried under the exploding earth."[26]

Then on 17 October Klemperer observed in his diary that Auschwitz "appears to be a swift-working slaughterhouse." A week later he wrote that all conversations among Jews about the war and the problems of the Germans militarily in Russia "lead to the same reflection: 'If they [the Germans] have time, they'll kill us first.'"[27] He seemed to believe, however, that such accounts described isolated atrocities; he gave no indication that he realized they reflected the wholesale, systematic genocide suffered by the victims of the Holocaust.

By the end of 1942 far-reaching rumors spread in Germany about the gassing of Jews, but similar to Klemperer most Jews did not or could not grasp what the talk meant. According to the historian Marion Kaplan, one of the most effective barriers to the comprehension by German Jews of what deportation meant "was the sheer inconceivability of the genocide. Even those who received information frequently reacted with disbelief or repressed it. Some despaired upon learning of their fate, while others denied its possibility. . . . They expected the worst, they did not expect the unthinkable."[28]

The Netherlands

From July 1942 to the end of the year, the German occupation authorities in the Netherlands sent over forty transports carrying approximately thirty-nine thousand Dutch Jews to Auschwitz. Many of the deportees came from the Amsterdam ghetto. They boarded the transports without incident, apparently believing they were being taken to a work camp in Germany. Most of the trains left the Westerbork transit camp near the Dutch–German border.

At least one Jew in Amsterdam, however, suspected that death awaited many of the Jews deported. Anne Frank, the teenage daughter of a German Jew, hidden in the city with her family by Dutch friends, recorded in her diary on 9 October 1942:

> I've got only dismal and depressing news for you today. Our many Jewish friends are being taken away by the dozen. These people are treated by the Gestapo without a shred of decency, being loaded into cattle trucks and sent to Westerbork, the big Jewish camp in Drente. Westerbork sounds terrible. . . .
> If it is as bad as this in Holland whatever will it be like in the distant and barbarous regions they are sent to? We assume that most of them are murdered. The English radio speaks of their being gassed.[29]

Between 80 and 90 percent of the Dutch deportees died in the gas chambers at Auschwitz. Despite the long record of the Dutch in treating the Jews well and in opposing the anti-Semitic measures of the German occupation regime, the SS, Order Police, and German commissioner in the Netherlands, Seyss-Inquart, held a tight grip on the country. Seyss-Inquart played an active role in the deportation of the Jews to the East. He viewed their removal from Europe as Hitler's most important mission and did not want to leave the Final Solution exclusively to the SS, but hoped himself to belong to the initiators of the campaign.

Belgium

Beginning in August 1942 transports arrived at Auschwitz carrying Belgian and Croatian Jews. Similar to what happened in France, Belgium opposed deporting its own Jews (i.e., those with Belgian citizenship), which formed less than 10 percent of the ninety thousand Jews in the country. However, the chief Belgian civil administrator, Eggert Reeder, under German pressure, had agreed to deport alien or non-Belgian Jews.

Moreover, Reeder raised no objections to the deportation of Jewish refugees living in the country, which made Belgium the first German-occupied place in the West to do so. Already in December 1941 and the spring of 1942, the Germans had deported numerous Polish Jews in Belgium to Lodz for slave labor in textile factories. Such Jews suffered the same fate, however, as the approximately seventeen thousand Jews from Belgium deported to Auschwitz and gassed between August 1942 and the year's end.

Also the latter deportations included Jews with non-Belgian citizenship, such as Polish, Czech, Russian, and stateless Jews, most of whom had fled previously to Belgium. Similar to France, the Germans constructed a concentration camp that served as a transit or collection point for the deportees. This was at Malines, a small village between Brussels and Antwerp; 90 percent of the Jews in Belgium lived in the two cities.

Croatia

During the last months of 1942, SS authorities at Auschwitz gassed nearly five thousand Croatian Jews. Croatian extremists, the Ustasha, who ran the allegedly independent state of Croatia, which the Germans and Italians divided into zones each controlled by their respective armies, implemented draconian measures against the Jews. This included imprisoning them in numerous concentration camps, initially at Jadovno and Jasenovac and then at Djakovo and Loborgrad. Many hundreds of Croatian Jews died in the camps, particularly at Jasenovac.

Also the Ustasha regime of Ante Pavelic savagely hunted down and deported as many Croatian Jews as possible to Auschwitz. The Germans both encouraged and assisted the process. Local Italian military officers, however, protected the small numbers of Jews that either lived in the Italian zone of military activity or had escaped there from the German and Croatian murderers. The officers even successfully opposed Mussolini's decision, made as a result of German pressure on him in Rome, to hand over the Jews in the Italian zone to the Ustasha.

Norway

During October the deportation of Jews began in Norway, of which 532 arrived and died at Auschwitz. The Norwegian police and supporters of Quisling, the head of Norway's National Socialist party, assisted the Germans. Approximately half of Norway's eighteen hundred Jews fled to Sweden, and the Stockholm government expressed its willingness to grant asylum to them all. But the German government, and especially Ernst Freiherr von Weizsäcker, the state secretary in the Foreign Ministry, rejected the proposal. By the spring of 1943 the Germans had deported the other approximately 400 Norwegian Jews, 158 of them to Auschwitz.

Denmark

How much this experience would influence the Swedish government a year later to help rescue almost all of Denmark's Jews is unclear. In Denmark the Germans had chosen to work through the Danish government to control the country rather than annexing it to Germany or establishing an occupation regime there. This arrangement had helped force the Germans to act with restraint toward the Danish Jews, who had the sympathy of most of their fellow Danes.

But during the summer and fall of 1942, the RSHA had intensified its efforts to pressure the Danish government to give up its Jews. Von Ribbentrop, after discussing the issue with Hitler, pushed for the deportation of the Danish Jews. The Copenhagen government, however, held firm in resisting the German demands. Divisions regarding the issue characterized the Germans themselves. Especially the new German plenipotentiary in Denmark, the SS officer Werner Best, who had previously headed the SD in France, warned that any anti-Jewish action would lead to a solidification of widespread Danish resistance against Germany. Furthermore, Himmler remained unwilling to intervene in the question of the Danish Jews. Consequently, for the moment at least, the German efforts to seize and kill Denmark's Jews had failed.

Others

In November 1942, still other European Jews deported to their deaths at Auschwitz included thirteen thousand from Bialystok and several thousand others from Ciechanów in Poland. In addition, the Germans sent the first Greek Jews to Auschwitz. At least five thousand Jews of Greek ancestry, who had immigrated to Paris from Salonika during the early 1930s, fell into German hands and died after deportation to the killing center.

The War and Jews in the Middle East and North Africa

By November 1942 the German military experienced a number of reversals that would have significant implications for the Nazi war against the Jews. In North Africa, between 23 October and 4 November, the British 8th Army crushed the German and Italian forces at El Alamein in western Egypt. The British victory resulted from a variety of factors: a new commander of the 8th Army, General Bernard Montgomery; reinforcements and supplies rushed into the battle by the British and Americans, including the first batch of Sherman tanks from the United States; excellent intelligence information, some of it of the signals variety, acquired by the British; and Germany's inability to reinforce its troops because the fighting on the Eastern Front took enormous numbers of soldiers. The 8th Army, a significant portion of which was comprised of Muslim troops from India, began driving the Axis forces into retreat westward, quickly into and across Libya.

Almost simultaneously, on 8–9 November 1942, Anglo-American forces landed successfully in Northwest Africa. The landings caught the Germans completely by surprise; they believed that the shortage of Allied shipping caused by Germany's submarine attacks in the Atlantic Ocean made an invasion of North Africa impossible. Also the Allies had concluded an agreement with Admiral Jean Darlan, recently appointed by the Vichy government its representative in North Africa. Darlan directed French armed forces in Morocco and Algeria not to oppose the Allied invasion. Once the Allied troops had made it ashore, the Axis had practically no chance of driving them out, and the North African campaign soon turned into a race between the Allies and Axis to control Tunisia.

The halting of the Axis forces in North Africa ended the prospects for German armies to reach the Middle East, occupy the British mandate of

Palestine and the rest of the region from Egypt to the Arabian Peninsula, and murder the Jewish communities there. Hitler had previously assured the Grand Mufti of Jerusalem, Haj Amin al-Husayni, that Germany's primary interest in Palestine and the surrounding area was the killing of their Jewish populations.

The appointment of Montgomery and other new British commanders in North Africa in the fall of 1942 had ended elaborate British plans, drawn up earlier during the Axis advance into Egypt, to retreat along the Nile River and farther east into Palestine. Such a withdrawal would have left the Jews there for the Germans to massacre as well as allowed the oil fields of Arabia and Iraq to fall into Axis hands.

Also the Allied victories in North Africa saved the Jews of Libya, Tunisia, and Morocco. Hitler intended for Germany to gain control over important areas of Northwest Africa, mainly as a base for the future war he planned against the United States. Although nearly all Jews in North Africa had suffered persecution during the war, they survived in large part because of Allied, and to a degree, Italian policy.

In Tunisia the Vichy government had attempted the Aryanization of Jewish property, but because the measure would affect five thousand local Italian businesses, the Rome government protested vigorously. Only on the small island of Djerba off the southeast coast of Tunisia did the French succeed in plundering the Jewish community by looting its people's homes and seizing over a hundred pounds of gold. Consequently, the anti-Jewish program of the Vichy regime had less influence in Tunisia than in Morocco and Algeria.

Even after the arrival of German forces in Tunisia, the Germans could not realize their plans in the country to increase the Jewish persecution. Geographical considerations limited their freedom of action, and fears existed that soon the Allies would invade Tunisia from Morocco or Algeria. The SS and German police had sent a Sonderkommando to Tunisia, which soon arrested local Jewish community leaders.

Further, the supreme commander of German military affairs in Southern Europe and North Africa, Field Marshal Alfred Kesselring, ordered from his headquarters in Rome the use of Jews in Tunisia as forced labor for constructing military fortifications. The Germans exempted Italian Jews from such impressment because of protests from Rome. But in Tunisia the Germans achieved little with their program to enslave Jews and deported none of them. Also in Morocco and Algeria no deportations occurred, but the local French and other authorities interned numerous Jews in work camps in which severe conditions prevailed.

Approximately twenty-nine thousand Jews lived in the Italian colony of Libya. Only a relatively small number of Libyan Jews, among them several hundred with French and British citizenship, suffered deportation during 1942 to numerous internment and labor camps in Italy, including Fossoli, and then in 1944 to the Bergen-Belsen concentration camp in Germany. Nearly all the prisoners, however, survived their ordeal and returned to Libya at the war's end.

The Jews who remained in Libya during the war experienced a steady intensification of anti-Jewish measures implemented by the Fascist regime. On 7 February 1942 the Italians placed all Jews of Cyrenaica, in eastern Libya, in desert internment camps at Giado and Gasr Garian. During June the first anti-Jewish law for all of Libya limited the amount of property of Jews. That same month another law ordered all male Jews between eighteen and forty-five to do forced labor, which led to the construction of a new labor camp at Sidi Azaz, about a hundred miles from Tripoli. The camp housed four thousand Jewish prisoners.

Then during October 1942 the Italians implemented in Libya a 1938 Italian law regarding the so-called defense of the race. Italian newspapers, however, only published the decree on 17 December. This essentially rendered the law meaningless because the British 8th Army liberated Tripoli of Axis forces on 23 January 1943. One need not speculate too long to realize what would have happened to the Libyan Jews if Germany had occupied Libya following the Italian surrender in the war. As Weinberg has emphasized, few, if any, of the Indian Muslim forces or other members of the 8th Army realized that they were helping to rescue Jews in both North Africa and the Middle East from persecution.

Also on other military fronts by the end of 1942 the Germans began to run into difficulties. British air raids on German cities had steadily increased during the year, making the German air force defend its home and damaging German industry in the process. But most important, on the Eastern Front the Germans had lost the initiative. Between July and September 1942, the Red Army had slowed and then halted the German advance toward the Caucasus, and a bitter fight had begun for Stalingrad.

Near the city that bore Stalin's name, a vital communications and transportation center, the Soviets organized massive armies with orders to entrap and destroy the Germans. Moreover, Red Army offensives around Leningrad and along the central front spoiled planned German offensives and produced bitter fighting back and forth. Soviet partisan operations increased significantly, causing further troubles for the Germans and often attracting members of the Jewish resistance in the ghettos.

By the end of 1942, as the war continued in Russia, the German mobile killing units and Wehrmacht there had killed well over one million Soviet Jews. Nazi leaders, however, were by no means content with this result or the number of Jews murdered in occupied Poland. During 1943 they expected that further German victories in the war would extend German power both in and outside Europe and therefore also increase the number of Jews who could be killed.

CHAPTER TWELVE

GROWING JEWISH RESISTANCE AND CONTINUED DEPORTATIONS, 1943

D URING 1943 MASSIVE PRESSURES mounted on the German economy to replace the amount of military equipment and numbers of troops being consumed by the war. Already on 7 January, at a top-level military meeting in Berlin, Field Marshal Wilhelm Keitel, the commander of the OKW, reported that the German war in the East had a shortage of seven hundred thousand men. While "the monthly reinforcements sent to the Eastern Front comprise 60,000–65,000 men," Keitel continued, "by contrast the losses on the Eastern Front in terms of deaths, those missing, the wounded, sick etc. comprise 150,000 per month."[1]

No military or labor crisis, however, would halt the German deportations of Jews to the killing centers or the murder of Soviet POWs, even though the victims' use as laborers could have freed masses of Germans for service at the front. Instead, as far as the Nazi leadership was concerned, the problems in the war seemed only to make Germany's most critical wartime task, the extermination of the Jews, more urgent. About Hitler's determination in 1943, in this regard, one of his adjutants recalled after the war: "He spoke a great deal about his ideal of the European State in which it would be his objective to fight Jews and Communists and to destroy their influence in the world in every respect. He believed firmly that Providence had given him this task."[2]

Trains and Statistics: A Blueprint for More Killing

At just the moment Germany was about to lose the gigantic battle of Stalingrad, on 20 January 1943 Himmler sent an urgent letter to Ganzenmüller, the state secretary in the Reich Transportation Ministry. In the letter the Reichsführer discussed "the removal of Jews" from the General Government, the Eastern territories, and "the West." For this, he wrote Ganzenmüller, "I need your help and support. If I am to wind things up quickly, I must have more trains for transports." Himmler added: "I know very well how taxing the situation is for the railways and what demands are constantly made of you. Just the same, I must make this request of you: help me get more trains."[3] Almost immediately the SS and police chief received what he had requested.

At nearly the same moment, Himmler, whom the British writer, Gerald Reitlinger, once termed "a remote-control killer,"[4] sought to discover just how much "progress" his killers in the Final Solution had made. He commissioned a professional statistician on his staff, Richard Korherr, to compile a report that would measure the course and extent of the killings. Korherr, using the term "evacuation" frequently to camouflage his discussion of the killings, reported that between 1933 and 1942, the numbers of Jews in the Reich, including its incorporated regions, and General Government had dropped by 3.1 million. Based on Korherr's numbers the RSHA could calculate the expenditures from the murder of the Jews in a locale or country, establish the amount of railway cars needed for deportations, and determine the destination of them. A technocrat whose work meant everything to him, Korherr's statistical analyses offered a bureaucratic blueprint for the annihilation of the European Jews.

Another of Himmler's ideas that also surfaced as the New Year dawned involved his suggestion to Hitler that Germany establish a special camp for Jews from France, Hungary, and Rumania who had influential relatives in the United States. According to Himmler, the approximately ten thousand such Jews could be held as valuable hostages to maintain some leverage with the Allies. The camp Himmler envisioned was eventually built at Bergen-Belsen in northwest Germany.

Hitler grudgingly approved Himmler's proposal, but only if it brought Germany large amounts of foreign exchange. "Military and economic realities," the historian Breitman has concluded about this scheme, "were beginning to intrude on the Führer's dream of complete extermination."[5] Regarding all these issues—pressing for more deportation trains, assessing the progress of the Final Solution, and acquiring ransom money for Jews—one can only agree with Browning. He has concluded "that if one wants to know what Hitler was thinking about racial policy during this period, one should look first of all at what the reliable and perceptive Himmler was doing."[6]

A Turn in the Military Conflict

During 1943 steady, yet often dramatic, changes appeared in both the armed struggle raging in Europe and North Africa and the Holocaust. Germany's military situation deteriorated significantly on all fronts, which would have major consequences for the Nazis' war against the Jews. In January, at the Casablanca Conference of Prime Minister Churchill and President Roosevelt, the Western Allied leaders gave the highest priority to victory at sea that would eventually make possible an Allied invasion of Western Europe. Also at Casablanca the Allies announced publicly that they would remain in the war until the enemy surrendered unconditionally.

While Germany's European allies would eventually capitulate in such fashion or attempt to do so, the Germans would not. Instead they would choose to fight until the bitter end. According to Weinberg, "Certainly an important element in that [German] determination to continue the war was the recognition of having committed enormous crimes combined with a grim insistence on continuing the program of killing all Jews within German reach. . . ."[7]

In North Africa, where the Western leaders met, the Anglo-American victories and landings there and the victory of the British 8th Army at El Alamein at the end of 1942 laid the basis for the defeat of the Axis forces in Tunisia in May 1943. The Allies then took Sicily and, in September, landed on the Italian mainland. Elements of Mussolini's own Fascist party ousted him from power, and the Italians showed themselves unwilling to defend their homeland against the invading Allies.

Not only did these events force Hitler to send more German troops to Italy to defend and occupy large portions of the country, but also Germany established Mussolini in northern Italy as a puppet ruler. In addition, the

Germans occupied the Italian zones of control in France, Yugoslavia, Albania, and Greece as well as the Italian islands in the Aegean Sea. Moreover, because of Germany's continuing severe shortage of workers, it seized vast numbers of Italian soldiers and sent them for slave labor in camps in the Reich and elsewhere.

On the Eastern Front the crushing Soviet victory over the German 6th Army at Stalingrad by 2 February 1943 had severely undermined German morale, struck fear into the German home front, and delivered a major blow to Hitler's prestige among his people. The battle symbolized at the time, as well as thereafter, what to most observers was the great turn of the tide in the war in the Soviet Union.

The Germans only now began to mobilize their industrial and military output for the massive world war in which they found themselves a part. On 18 February, in the wake of Stalingrad, Goebbels demanded in a speech in the Berlin Sportpalast, which German radio broadcast, that Germany wage "total war" to rescue the Reich and the West from not only Bolshevism, but also from its evil originator, the Jews. The Propaganda Minister, to urge his listeners on to the utmost exertions in the war, connected the huge military struggle with the Holocaust.

Amid his lengthy vilification of international Jewry, Goebbels made a telling slip of the tongue about what was happening to the Jews. Germany, he declared, had no intention of "bowing" to the Jewish "threat, but means to counter it in time and if necessary with the most complete and radical exterm—[correcting himself]—elimination [*Ausrott—Auschaltung*] of Jewry. All these considerations have determined the military strain which the Reich has to bear in the East."[8] The large crowd received Goebbels' words with applause, shouts of "out with the Jews," and laughter.

Despite the subsequent shift of Germany toward a total war basis, the huge offensives in the East of both the German and Soviet armies continued to grind down the German forces. Especially the failure in July of the German tank attack to destroy the Kursk salient on the central Russian front eliminated any real possibility Germany had of returning to the offensive.

Thereafter the Red Army took the military initiative in the Donets Basin and along the Dnepr River, so that by the end of 1943 the Russians had cleared much of the Ukraine and the entire Caucasus region of German troops. Secret negotiations for a separate peace had even started in Sweden between the Germans and Soviets, which Hitler would prove unwilling to pursue. Stalin had apparently been the principal force behind the peace feelers. Not only did he realize that Russia was still in for a long and difficult war, but he was angry with his Anglo-American allies. They had not established a "second front" in Western Europe, something the Soviet leader desperately wanted to help relieve the German military pressure on the Soviet Union.

During 1943, however, the Western Allies began winning the war at sea and in the air against Germany, which would help lay the foundation for what Stalin demanded: the Allied invasion of Nazi-held France that would begin eventually on 6 June 1944. At the Casablanca Conference in January 1943, Churchill and Roosevelt had assigned top priority to the war against Germany's submarines.

Two months before, in November 1942, the Western Allies had suffered their greatest losses of the war at sea, when German submarines sank 720,000 of the total 860,000 tons lost. But by February 1943, for the first time in the war, Allied construction of new ships exceeded sinkings by submarines. A series of great battles in the Atlantic, in which the British and Americans used effectively the breaking of secret German submarine codes, resulted in the sinking of one submarine per day and turned the war at sea in favor of the Allies.

During the summer, the British and Americans initiated massive air raids on Germany that would force major diversions of the German military effort and resources. American bombers concentrated on attacking military and industrial targets, while the British struck German cities. The "combined bomber offensive" disrupted the German economy, helping to delay, for example, production of Germany's new weapon, the V-2 rocket.

The air war, moreover, forced the Germans to shift planes and pilots from the Eastern and Mediterranean war fronts to defend the skies over Germany. Beginning in the fall the Germans concentrated their air power on the home front. There the increase of aircraft production, and especially of pilots and fuel, could not keep pace with the losses in the sky. Furthermore, the expanded production and use of antiaircraft guns consumed more ammunition, but in contrast to traditional belief, such factors appear not to have reduced significantly the production of field artillery and tank guns available to the Wehrmacht.

Although between 1941 and 1944, the proportion of weapons and ammunition produced by Germany rose from 16 to 40 percent of overall industrial output, the war fronts needed every armaments worker and other type of laborer and every transport train. After the German defeat at

Stalingrad the demand for manpower in the armed forces rose so sharply that it produced a shortage in Germany of 1.5 million workers. No longer could the Reich rely on Soviet peoples for forced labor, nor could it meet its demands with labor conscripted from western and other parts of German-controlled Europe.

Nevertheless, from early 1943 to the end of the war, the Germans relied for such labor on the impressment of 2.5 million additional prisoners of war (which included six hundred thousand Italian soldiers) and foreign workers. This figure fell substantially short of the four million workers the Nazi head of labor procurement, Sauckel, planned to bring to Germany in 1944 alone. Although Sauckel recruited 391,000 French workers during the first half of 1943, the figure dropped to a mere 26,000 between August and December. According to Martin Kitchen, the Canadian military historian: "In large part this was due to the reluctance of the French authorities and workers to cooperate when the Germans no longer seemed quite so invincible."[9]

Revolt amid the Darkness[10]

One of the most violent acts of Jewish resistance against the Nazis occurred in January 1943 at Czestochowa, a city some 150 miles southwest of Warsaw, whose ghetto had originally held forty-eight thousand Jews. Although nearly ten thousand of the ghetto Jews worked as forced laborers in nearby German weapons and munitions factories, between May and October 1942 the SS deported some thirty-nine thousand Jews to Treblinka.

In December 1942 a branch of the Jewish Fighting Organization (ZOB) in Warsaw established an underground unit in Czestochowa that had approximately three hundred members. During January 1943, when the SS began another Aktion, the ZOB, led by Mendl Fiszlewicz, put up armed resistance. During the fighting in the ghetto, 251 Jews died and others were captured and deported to Treblinka. German reprisals followed immediately; the SS killed 127 Jewish intellectuals and 250 children and the elderly. Other members of the resistance operating outside the ghetto died in armed clashes with right-wing Polish partisans.

Also, on 10 January 1943, some four hundred Jews in Minsk Mazowiecka, forty miles east of Warsaw, rose in armed resistance against deportations of the inhabitants of the local ghetto. The Germans intended with the deportations to empty and close—termed by the Germans "liquidating"—the ghetto. German forces overpowered the ghetto fighters and forced them into a local school building and set it on fire, burning those inside alive.

Elsewhere, during the deportations from Bialystok in early February 1943 tens of thousands of Jews went into hiding. The Germans burned and dynamited houses to force the people to leave the hiding places. Fighting by Jewish resistance groups in the ghetto caused the Germans numerous casualties. In reprisal the SS shot two thousand Jews on the spot and deported ten thousand more to Treblinka.

Numerous underground groups in the Bialystok ghetto, comprised mainly of communist, Bundist, and Zionist youth, had collected a few weapons and organized the armed struggle. Although the resistance suffered heavy losses in the fighting, it continued to exist. Command of the oft-divided resistance soon fell to Mordechai Tenenbaum, a leader of one of the prominent Zionist youth organizations and a key figure in the attempted revolt.

Tenenbaum had started keeping a diary on 12 January 1943, and referred a week later in it to nearby Treblinka as a death camp. During February Tenenbaum drafted a manifesto, for "the moment when we proclaim the counteraction," stating that three million Jews had gone to their deaths in Chelmno, Belzec, Auschwitz, Treblinka, and Sobibor, and warning the Jews that all deportees were going to be killed. "We have nothing to lose anymore!" he declared. "Jews you are being led to Treblinka! They will poison us with gas like dogs with rabies and then they will burn us in ovens. We do not want to go like sheep to slaughter!"[11]

Also Tenenbaum concerned himself with educating the world and future generations in the catastrophe that had engulfed his people. At his initiative the underground established a secret ghetto archive, based on the model of the one in the Warsaw ghetto, the Oneg Shabbat. The chief archivist, Zvi Mersik, collected eyewitness testimonies and written accounts of the horrors of ghetto life as well as documents of the Judenrat and reports of its meetings. The archive, hidden somehow in the Polish portion of the city of Bialystok, survived the war and today provides an extraordinary primary source of the Holocaust.

The Judenrat chairman, the engineer and Zionist Ephraim Barash, supplied Tenenbaum with considerable sums of money, primarily to purchase weapons from the Polish underground army. Barash believed, however, as many Judenrat chairmen did, that the thousands of Jews already deported from the ghetto would guarantee the survival of the remaining Jews and the ghetto's continued existence.

Barash was strengthened in his conviction by the fact that the ghetto had numerous factories and served as a major industrial center for German war production. But his hope and desperation blinded him to the knowledge by then of growing numbers of Jews that only death awaited them all and not survival. As noted later in this chapter, the Germans would soon destroy the Bialystok ghetto.

These few examples of armed Jewish resistance illustrate an important point. For at least eight months before the Warsaw ghetto revolt in April and May 1943, other Polish ghettos had produced underground movements and even revolt, albeit on a much less substantial scale, against those who intended to kill every Jew they could seize. However, if the Warsaw uprising did not begin the armed Jewish resistance to the Germans, the revolt nevertheless had a far-reaching influence both on the relatively few remaining Jews in Eastern Europe and the Germans.

The Warsaw Ghetto Revolt

The ghetto revolt in Warsaw, except for the publicity it received and its success in encouraging Jews to fight the Germans, had numerous parallels with the previous Jewish attempts at armed resistance and the situation in which they happened. Both the non-Jewish population of Warsaw and the Polish underground army reacted with indifference to the terrible events of July–September 1942—the deportations of some 265,000 Warsaw ghetto inhabitants to Treblinka.

Amid the deportations, unarmed underground organizations in the ghetto that had operated since 1940 a secret press and communicated with political elements outside the ghetto formed the Jewish Fighting Organization (ZOB). The ZOB's leaders, most of them members of Zionist youth groups, included Mordechai Anielewicz, Yitzhak Zuckerman, Zivia Lubetkin, Josef Kaplan, and Israel Geller. Efforts by the ZOB to contact the Armya Krajowa, the Polish underground army, principally to acquire weapons, came to nothing. Some Poles eagerly assisted the Germans; only a handful attempted to help Jews. One organization, *Zegota*, the cover name for the Council for Aid to Jews, established by elements of the Polish underground and financed by the Polish government-in-exile in London, assisted in hiding hundreds of Jews and helping them survive.

The largescale deportations of Warsaw Jews changed dramatically the ghetto and the attitudes of the approximately sixty thousand remaining

Jews. For one thing, the deportations left the survivors feeling isolated, embittered, and demoralized. Many were young people who now reproached their families for not having opposed the deportations with armed resistance. They knew from various underground sources about the death factory at Treblinka and believed that the ghetto had nothing to lose by fighting back against the Germans.

Consequently, the ZOB found far more ready listeners and supporters among the thousands of ghetto survivors. Despair and fear gripped those still alive. One, Abraham Lewin, wrote in his diary on Yom Kippur, 21 September 1942:

> Those who are far away cannot imagine our bitter situation. They will not understand and will not believe that day after day thousands of men, women, and children, innocent of any crime, were taken to their death. And the handful of those remaining after nine weeks is in mortal danger and, it seems, can expect the same fate. Almighty God! Why did this happen? And why is the whole world deaf to our screams?
>
> Earth, earth, do not cover our blood, and let no place be free from our cries!
>
> A Jew has returned to our workshop who was taken away from here three weeks ago and worked as a gravedigger in Treblinka for nine or eleven days before escaping in a train-wagon in which the martyrs' belongings were being taken away. He tells horrific and shattering things. In any case we have another eyewitness to the fate of those who are deported. According to what he said, not only Jews from Warsaw and of the *gubernia* are being exterminated in Treblinka, but Jews from all over Europe—from France, Belgium, Holland, among others. Such a calamity has never before befallen us in all the bitter experiences of our history. In our courtyard Jews are praying, pouring out their cares to the Creator.[12]

Since the suicide in July 1942 of the Judenrat chairman, Czerniakow, and the subsequent deportations, the Judenrat had nearly ceased to exist. Although the Jewish police, which played a major role as helpers of the Germans in the deportations, and the Jewish managers of the ghetto workshops, wielded some authority, the leading place in the ghetto now fell increasingly to the ZOB and the few other underground elements. The latter included most political parties in the ghetto; they contributed small battle groups to the resistance, although one party, the Communists, refused to collaborate with the most conservative Zionists. The total ghetto fighting force may have numbered 750.

Slowly emissaries of the ZOB succeeded in contacting the Armya Krajowa and acquiring from it official recognition and a small supply of weapons, mainly revolvers, grenades, and explosives. Most of the ZOB's weapons, however, were purchased from middlemen who had bought or stolen them from the Germans. Even these modest successes provided the Jewish resistance with an important boost in morale.

Command of the ZOB fell increasingly to Anielewicz, a dynamic member of the youth group, *Hashomer Hatzaîr* (Young Zionists). He had been away from Warsaw during the deportations, involved in underground work in eastern Silesia; consequently, when he returned to Warsaw he had no hesitations or feelings of powerlessness that had eroded the fighting spirit of some of his ZOB colleagues. Anielewicz began immediate preparations for armed resistance against future deportations and arranged the assassination or attempts at assassination of Jewish ghetto officials who collaborated with the Germans. Only with such activities was the underground able to consolidate its control over the ghetto's inhabitants.

However, before the ZOB could complete its plans, Himmler visited the ghetto on 9 January 1943. He ordered its remaining industrial plants transferred to SS factories near Lublin and the deportation of eight thousand Jews who the SS alleged had improper papers. When the Germans began an Aktion on 18 January, they found the ghetto streets deserted and most of the Jews in hiding.

As the German columns moved farther into the ghetto, they were infiltrated by a group of ghetto fighters led by Anielewicz and armed with pistols. When the signal was given, the fighters stepped out and engaged the Germans in bloody street fighting. For the first time, Jews shot numerous German soldiers. Anielewicz's forces caught the Germans unprepared for any resistance, leaving them hesitant, cautious, and unwilling to search the ghetto for persons in hiding. Within four days the Germans withdrew and the Aktion ended.

The triumph electrified the remaining Jews and earned for the ghetto resistance even greater prestige and support from the people. Some erroneously believed that the Germans had intended in January to kill all the remaining Jews in Warsaw, which made the action of the resistance appear even greater. Further, the Jews in the ghetto viewed the events of January as proof that by using resistance one would be able to force the Germans to give up their plans. They held the misperception that the Germans would carry out the deportations only as long as the Jews remained passive and that because of the resistance and armed clashes they would delay further Aktionen.

Meanwhile, Anielewicz and the fighting organization worked even harder to prepare a strategic defense plan for the ghetto. They encouraged the people who had no weapons to build hideouts and bunkers below the ground and divided the ghetto into battle sectors to which they assigned armed fighting units. Also they persuaded the Armya Krajowa to provide the resistance with further modest amounts of weapons.

On 19 April, the eve of Passover, approximately two thousand SS, regular German soldiers, armed police, and Trawnikis entered the ghetto for what they believed would be a quick, three-day operation to round up and deport its remaining population to Treblinka. Instead, the fighting in what became known as the Warsaw ghetto revolt continued for more than a month.

Although the ghetto fighters had small arms such as revolvers, a few automatic weapons, and crude Molotov cocktails, the resistance proved much stronger than the Germans expected, and they had to withdraw. During the following weeks the German forces moved with tanks and heavy artillery into the ghetto street by street, purposely setting fire to and destroying the buildings, capturing and killing the people, dropping poison gas into the bunkers and sewers, and eventually crushing the resistance. The skies darkened with heavy smoke from the burning buildings.

Zuckerman recalled after the war the ghetto fighters' strategy in fighting the Germans. He noted that

> since the Germans couldn't conquer the whole ghetto, they had to devote a lot of forces to conquering every individual building. And when they did conquer a building, they had to leave a German force in it. In such a case, you could attack them in the courtyard, which is just what our fighters did, even though the Germans kept units and patrols at concentration points. When we switched to guerilla warfare, they didn't know who they were fighting against or where to look for the enemy; and then the Germans began setting fire to the ghetto.[13]

On 8 May the Germans overran the bunker to which Anielewicz and the ZOB staff had retreated and killed everyone inside. In the final analysis, a lack of automatic weapons and machine guns represented one of the worst problems for the Jewish resistance; its small caliber revolvers were unsuitable for fighting the massively armed Nazis. Also the rebels received almost no help from Polish civilians and little assistance from the Armya Krajowa. Despite their tenacity and courage, the ghetto fighters had lost.

However, the four-week revolt and bunker war deeply embarrassed the Germans, who had to combat the first armed uprising, including by Jews, in any major city in Europe. Repeatedly during the fighting, Jürgen Stroop, the SS officer in command for most of the struggle, would report prematurely to his superiors that his forces had broken the resistance and overpowered the revolt. The next day he would have to retract the claim and admit that the attacks had not ceased and that his forces continued to suffer casualties. Although reports at the time placed the number of Germans killed in the fighting at fourteen, later research would show that at least two hundred died.

Then on 16 May, with the ghetto reduced to enormous piles of smoldering rubble and dust, Stroop announced an end to the fighting, issuing a public report that boasted, "The Jewish Quarter of Warsaw is no more."[14] The Germans deported most of the Jews captured in the fighting to their deaths at Treblinka and Maidanek. Others they sent to labor camps near Lublin, principally those at Trawniki and Poniatowa.

But to a degree, reality differed from Stroop's report. Some of the ghetto Jews survived and lived below the rubble in underground sewers and caves; neither German dogs nor special search instruments discovered them. Hungry and resembling living shadows, they would emerge at night to seek food and water and to remain in contact with one another. Many eventually fled to the Aryan side of Warsaw, where Zegota and a few other courageous Poles sheltered them. Altogether approximately fifteen thousand Jews still remained in the city.

Many other Poles, however, including some in the Polish underground, betrayed the Jews to the enemy; this happened, for example, to most of the seventy survivors who managed to flee to the forests east of Warsaw. One, Zuckerman, remembered after the war that while the Armya Krajowa "fought the Germans," it "didn't accept Jews in its ranks and was composed of all sorts of elements, including antisemites . . . it also included a large bloc of Sanacja [a right-wing Polish political party], most of them antisemites, and we had to be careful of them; and there practically wasn't a single village that was sympathetic to the Jews."[15]

Also during the summer of 1943 the Germans sought to capture those in hiding in Warsaw by offering to allow them to travel outside German-occupied territory. This ruse led possibly as many as six thousand Jews to come out of hiding, whereupon the Germans shot them immediately or deported them to Auschwitz. Thereafter, the Germans continued to discover and kill Jews in the city. Moreover, during the revolt in August 1944 of the Armya Krajowa against the Germans, the latter as well as the Polish underground killed still more local Jews.

After the war a few of the Warsaw Jews who had managed to survive, including Lubetkin and Zuckerman, would emigrate to Palestine and help to found in 1949 in northern Israel Lohamei Haghetaot, the Ghetto Fighters' kibbutz. To perpetuate the memory of the ghetto fighters and Jewish resistance, the kibbutz created a museum and educational institute. According to the Israeli historian, Yisrael Gutman, himself a participant in the Warsaw ghetto revolt, "The Uprising was literally a revolution in Jewish history. Its importance was understood all too well by those who fought." In a similar thought, Anielewicz wrote on 23 April in his last letter to a fellow ghetto fighter: "We are aware of one thing only: what has happened has exceeded our dreams. The Germans ran twice from the ghetto . . . I have the feeling that great things are happening, that we have dared is of great importance."[16]

Uprisings in the Death Camps and Further Ghetto Revolts

News and rumors of the Jewish revolt in Warsaw soon reached some Jewish prisoners who still survived in other Polish ghettos, in labor camps, and in concentration camps in the German-occupied areas. Also information about what had happened spread to the war fronts in Europe, the Jews in Palestine, and the rest of the world. Some Jews living under what they realized was a death sentence from the Nazis identified with the battle in Warsaw; it moved them to take action because they too had little choice except to defend their lives and honor by fighting back. Still other Jews acted independently of the Warsaw uprising, having heard nothing about it and concluding on their own that they must resist their killers.

Two revolts exploded in the killing centers, first at Treblinka on 2 August 1943 and then at Sobibor on 14 October. These especially reinforced the concern of the Germans, raised by the events in Warsaw, that they must complete quickly and with adequate armed force the destruction of the remaining ghettos and labor camps in the East. To what degree such considerations influenced Hitler's directive to Nazi party leaders on 11 July 1943 is unclear. Through his party deputy, Bormann, he ordered: "Where the Jewish Question is brought up in public, there may be no discussion of a future overall solution. It may, however, be mentioned that the Jews are taken in groups for appropriate labor purposes."[17]

At Treblinka, Jewish resistance activity began initially during February and March 1943. The members of the Jewish Sonderkommando involved in the horrors of handling the deportees and their belongings realized that the SS was about to execute them and the other remaining prisoners as part of plans to close the facility. By then Treblinka had fulfilled the mission Himmler had set for it—the camp had killed most of the nine hundred thousand Polish Jews deported to it, except for a few transports from Bialystok.

During March and April the camp received several transports from outside Poland: 4,221 Jews from Greece, whom the Germans had sent from Thrace through Bulgaria; 7,122 from the portion of Macedonia annexed by Bulgaria from Yugoslavia; and almost 3,000 from Salonika. Additionally, two thousand Gypsies died at Treblinka. Although Bulgaria, a German ally in the war, refused to turn over its own Jewish population to the Germans for slaughter, it helped to arrange for the deportations of other Jews to their deaths.

After March the SS moved toward closing Treblinka. It scaled back the transports sent there and, at Himmler's order, began opening the mass graves, burning the bodies, and reburying the ashes. The prisoner Sonderkommando at the camp recognized the meaning of these efforts and suspected that without transports and work for them, the camp would be closed and they would be killed.

Several prisoner groups began to discuss both possible ways of rescuing themselves and the need to bring Treblinka and its horrors to the world's attention before it was too late. These talks soon led to the formation of a small underground organization that set forth to acquire weapons, prepare a revolt, and escape from the camp.

On 2 August members of the underground entered a weapons storeroom of the SS, but while doing so, another member at a barracks shot an SS officer, Kurt Küttner, who was about to learn of the rebellion from an informer.

The shots, however, alerted the camp guards before the prisoners had removed all the weapons from the storeroom. The prisoners then began shooting at the SS men and set a camp building afire.

Amid the ensuing battle, the SS shot numerous prisoners who attempted to storm the fence that circled the camp. Although German security forces searched the surrounding area, of the approximately one thousand prisoners, two hundred broke out and sixty survived. The SS executed on the spot some of the prisoners that remained in the camp and forced the others to help close the facility by tearing down the buildings and fences and removing all traces of the camp. The Germans then planted over some of the land with trees, turned a portion of it into a farm, and murdered the prisoners still there.

Two months later similar circumstances led to an uprising of prisoners at Sobibor. At the end of February 1943, Himmler had visited the camp and witnessed the gassing of a transport of Jewish women from the Lublin district. During March four thousand victims from France, most of them refugee or stateless Jews deported by the Vichy government, arrived and were murdered. Between March and July, thirty-five thousand Jews deported from the Netherlands died at the camp.

The SS employed extensive deception to hide from Jews of Western Europe both their destination and their fate. Many Dutch Jews arrived in normal passenger trains, were given tickets to reclaim their baggage, and ordered to send letters to relatives still in Holland asking them to write back. Such letters, which the SS termed "Operation Mail" (*Briefaktion*) and sent from Auschwitz-Birkenau at least as early as August 1942, had a dual purpose: first, to make the recipients believe that the deportations meant essentially nothing; and second, to reveal the addresses of more victims (i.e., the families of the deported) so that the SS could round up and deport them too.

By the summer of 1943 Sobibor had completed an eight-month-long slaughter of nearly eighty thousand Jews from the Lublin district and eastern Galicia. Altogether since its beginning, the camp had killed nearly 250,000 Jews from the General Government. On 5 July Himmler ordered the death camp closed and converted into a concentration camp for refinishing captured Soviet ammunition.

Thereafter the transports to Sobibor dropped sharply; in late September the last trains brought fourteen thousand Jews from the Vilna, Minsk, and Lida ghettos. This situation worried the camp prisoners; many feared they would soon be killed. Attempts by prisoners to escape, a few of them suc-

cessful, increased. The SS placed mines outside the camp fence to help prevent escapes and protect the camp from attacks by Polish partisans.

Leon Feldhendler, a prisoner and former Judenrat chairman from eastern
Galicia, had organized among the Jewish inmates an underground group that
planned a revolt and mass escape from the camp. After Soviet-Jewish POWs
arrived at Sobibor in late September, one of them, Lieutenant Alexander
Petschersky, took over command of the underground and Feldhendler
became his deputy. The prisoners planned to kill the SS guards, capture the
weapons storeroom, and fight their way out of the camp to freedom.

The insurrection began on 14 October. The prisoners killed eleven SS
men and numerous Trawnikis; the local SS unit had to call for help from various other SS bodies and the highest army and civil officials in the General
Government. Almost three hundred prisoners escaped from the camp, but
most fell victim to the SS, which pursued them into the countryside and shot
them. Moreover, the SS killed the remaining prisoners who had not participated in the revolt and stayed in the camp. Approximately fifty of the
escapees survived the end of the war. Shortly after the uprising the Germans
closed the camp in much the same way they did Treblinka.

The insurrections at Treblinka and Sobibor neither forced the ending of
operations of the two death camps nor stopped the killings in them. On the one
hand, as noted above, Himmler had made the decision to close them before the
revolts. By the time he visited the two camps in late February 1943, they had
already killed nearly all of the 1,700,000 Jews who eventually died there, most
of them from the General Government and victims of Aktion Reinhard.

On the other hand, the uprising in Treblinka hastened the closing of the
camp and therefore also the ending of the killings there. In Sobibor, the uprising produced a change in the plans for the camp. Originally the Germans had
intended to turn the killing facility into a concentration camp. But now the
SS destroyed and dismantled the camp.

Both revolts, from the viewpoint of most of the insurgents, represented
a success. They had achieved their principal aim of a mass escape and rescue
of at least some camp prisoners, all of whom were doomed to certain death
before the insurrections. As many as one hundred prisoners earned their freedom as a result of the two uprisings. One only has to contrast this with Belzec,
where no uprising occurred; there only two known prisoners survived, Rudolf
Reder and Chaim Hirszman, both of whom provided after the war eyewitness
accounts of the systematic mass murder at the camp.

As for the Germans, the revolts at Treblinka and Sobibor left them with worries about a further embarrassing loss of invincibility—the first being the Warsaw ghetto revolt—in the eyes not only of the Jews, but also of the non-Jewish peoples in the German-controlled lands of Europe. SS officers at both Treblinka and Sobibor feared punishment if investigations revealed that the rebels had organized underground activity in the camps. During the uprising in Warsaw, the SS had held the SS and Police Leader of the district, Ferdinand von Sammern-Frankenegg, responsible for the Jewish resistance and replaced him with Stroop.

The commander of Treblinka, Stangl, and his superiors in Lublin, Wirth and Globocnik, minimized the importance of the revolt and escape of the Jewish prisoners to the RSHA and attempted to keep the insurrection secret. They succeeded in doing so for a time, primarily because no German died in the uprising and only one suffered a wound. Deaths of SS men required reporting to the SS authorities in Berlin. The events at Sobibor, however, could not be concealed. Eleven SS men had died, the camp's security forces had called on other armed units in the General Government for help, and the SS men killed received a funeral in Berlin attended by high-ranking officials of the Führer chancellery.

The Germans, moreover, suffered other embarrassments at the hands of Jewish resisters. Prompted mainly by the growing Jewish resistance to them, they began the last deportations with the goal of liquidating the remaining ghettos. When they did so, they encountered continued insurrections of Jewish prisoners and an increasing coordination of action among the resistance.

On 25 June 1943 the SS began the sudden final destruction of the ghetto in Czestochowa, which caught the ghetto inhabitants by surprise. Nevertheless, inside the ghetto, a new branch of the ZOB, which included at least one member of the fighting organization that had survived the Warsaw ghetto revolt and managed to reach Czestochowa, tried to resist and stop the Germans. The SS, however, proved much too strong for the ghetto fighters; it stormed the underground bunkers of the resistance, killing its members, and then murdered nearly all of the remaining Jews in the ghetto.

On 1 August, when the SS neared completion of the destruction of the ghetto in Sosnowiec in southwest Poland, a small Zionist resistance group attempted an armed uprising to free its members from the ghetto. The group eventually gave up, however, after the SS killed its leader, Józek Kozuch, at the start of the Aktion. Still, a few members of the youth organizations and a small number of children tried hopelessly to resist with the few small arms they possessed. Although most of the rebels perished, the deportation the SS planned to complete in two days took two weeks.

The most serious such ghetto revolt occurred in Bialystok. When the Germans began on the night of 15–16 August to deport from the ghetto the thirty thousand Jews who remained in it, the armed ghetto underground, commanded by Mordechai Tenenbaum and Daniel Moszkowicz, led a revolt that lasted five days. Nearly every day three hundred ghetto fighters died in bitter street battles with the SS.

At the peak of the fighting the Germans entered the ghetto with tanks, artillery, and other heavy armor, and soon crushed the rebels. As the Germans increased their firepower against the Bialystok insurgents, nervous and frightened Jews in the ghetto, most of whom remained passive during the fighting, opposed the revolt. Tenenbaum and Moszkowicz likely committed suicide in a bunker before the Germans overran it. The SS soon deported most of the remaining Jews to their deaths at Treblinka and Maidanek and closed the ghetto.

Farther north, in the Vilna ghetto, bitter divisions by the fall of 1943 between the Judenrat and the principal resistance organization, the United Partisan Organization (FPO), assisted the Germans in their "liquidation" of the ghetto. During Aktionen on 4 and 24 August and 2 and 4 September, the SS rounded up over seven thousand Vilna Jews and deported them to a concentration camp in Estonia. During the September Aktionen, the FPO called on the ghetto inhabitants to ignore the orders to report for deportation and to rise in revolt. But the call found little response, because the inhabitants apparently—and incredibly—disbelieved the FPO's assertion that they would be deported to Ponary and murdered.

In the late afternoon of 1 September, the SS units that had encircled the ghetto exchanged gunfire with the underground, which killed the commander of one of the resistance groups, Yechiel Scheinbaum. To prevent further bloodletting between the resistance and the Germans, Jacob Gens, the chairman of the Judenrat, who feared the destruction of the ghetto and death of virtually all its people, offered a deal to the Germans. He would collect the Jews to fill the deportation quota demanded by the Germans if the SS would withdraw its forces from the ghetto. The Germans agreed and the fighting in the ghetto subsided; the deportations continued to Estonia.

On 14 September the Gestapo, suspicious of Gens, summoned and shot him on the spot. One can only imagine the desperation and despair that deluded him at this late date into believing he could still bargain with the Germans to save the ghetto and its people. The SS had murdered the substantial majority of the original one hundred thousand Jews in the ghetto.

Furthermore, many of the remaining Jews, including undoubtedly Gens, knew that death awaited them and that the possibility of survival no longer existed. The Germans emptied the ghetto on 23 and 27 September. They deported approximately 3,700 men and women to concentration camps in Estonia and Latvia. Over four thousand children, women, and old men were deported to Sobibor and gassed. In addition, the Germans took hundreds of old people and children to nearby Ponary and shot them. In the end, barely three thousand Vilna Jews survived the Holocaust.

Other ghettos in which Jews rose in revolt in 1943 included Bedzin (August) and Tarnow (September) and farther east at Kuldichvo (March), Brody (May), Lwów (June), and Kletsk (July). In Lwów, the SS officer who led the Aktion to liquidate the ghetto, Friedrich Katzmann, mentioned in his report that the Jews had purchased weapons from Italian soldiers. During the final hours of the ghetto's destruction, the Germans found the bodies of three thousand of its inhabitants, victims, the SS claimed, of suicide.

The Military Situation and *Aktion Erntefest*

By the fall of 1943 both Hitler and Himmler realized two things. First, to complete the most important part of the Final Solution, they would have to kill the only Jews who remained in Poland. Already the SS had begun liquidating the ghettos in Poland and farther east; soon it would also exterminate the tens of thousands of Jews who worked in slave labor camps in the Lublin district of the General Government.

Hitler and the SS leader had intended to destroy the work camps since their agreement a year earlier with the Wehrmacht to allow some Jews to work instead of being killed. As will be shown later, however, the decision to murder the remaining Jews ignored the ever-growing labor needs of the desperately embattled German armed forces in the war.

Second, the continuing Jewish resistance during 1943 in both ghettos and death camps had especially influenced Himmler. He feared further Jewish revolts and so ordered the rapid destruction by the SS and police of both the ghettos and labor camps, using surprise and more substantial armed force, which meant that neither the SS nor the police could be employed at the military fronts.

The Reichsführer's long speech on 4 October 1943 in Posen to senior SS officers illustrated his concern about the Jewish resistance. There he urged the SS onward to complete the Final Solution and justified the genocide. During the speech he violated his own rule of not speaking publicly about, as he called it, "the evacuation of the Jews, the extermination of the Jewish people." Although he had arranged for someone to tape the speech, he told the officers that he would mention the subject once because the German people, of which "each one has his decent Jew," had no sense of what it was like to carry out such a project. Nor did the people, unlike the SS, "know what it means when one hundred corpses are lying side by side, or five hundred, or one thousand."

Himmler praised the SS for implementing the killings and still, with "exceptions caused by human weakness," remaining "decent fellows." He termed the subject "a page of glory in our history which has never to be written and is never to be written." Recalling the alleged stab in the back in World War I, he noted that if Germany "still had Jews today in every town as secret saboteurs, agitators, and trouble mongers," the country "would now probably have reached the 1916–1917 stage when the Jews were still in the German national body."[18]

The severe labor shortages that confronted Germany, caused by its military setbacks and losses of manpower and other resources, seemed of little consequence to both Himmler and Hitler. They chose during the fall of 1943 to complete as quickly as possible the killing of most of the Jews remaining in the Polish and other ghettos in the East as well as those who worked in the Lublin district and other parts of Poland in labor camps, defense plants, and military repair shops. By the end of the year, except for Theresienstadt, only the ghetto in Lodz would remain.

During 3–4 November 1943, approximately two to three thousand Waffen-SS and police troops from the General Government and Reich as well as a special detachment from the Auschwitz death camp killed forty-two thousand Jews, primarily in three labor camps in the Lublin area—at Maidanek, Trawniki, and Poniatowa. The Germans code-named the massacres "Harvest Festival" (*Erntefest*), apparently a reference to what the killers viewed as eliminating the final remnants of Jewish communities in Poland. The killings over two days and carried out in a single campaign surpassed other similar executions, even the notorious Babi Yar murder of more than thirty-three thousand Jews outside Kiev. Only the slaughter by the Rumanian army of sixty thousand Odessa Jews in an operation in October 1941 exceeded the numbers killed in Aktion Erntefest.

To reduce the possibility of resistance from the victims, the killers acted simultaneously in all three places and with a maximum of surprise and armed force. In each instance, the Germans returned to the procedure of mass shootings of victims in large earthen pits that had characterized the early stages of the killing procedures in Soviet Russia in 1941.

The shootings began at Trawniki and Maidanek on the morning of 3 November and at Poniatowa the next day. At Poniatowa, where the Germans had sent thousands of Jews captured in the Warsaw ghetto revolt, the few former members among them of the Warsaw ZOB attempted to persuade the prisoners to rebel, in the event the Germans "evacuated" the camp. But the quickness of the German attack caught the resistance unprepared, and its members perished with most of the rest of the camp. In each camp, the Germans kept hundreds of Jews alive to burn the corpses of the victims, but then in turn murdered them.

The "Harvest Festival" slaughter ended Aktion Reinhard. Each of the death camps involved in the Aktion—Belzec, Sobibor, and Treblinka—had been shut down. By the close of 1943, little more than two hundred thousand Jews remained alive in German-occupied Poland, mostly in hiding, in partisan units, in the Lodz ghetto, and in numerous labor camps. In some of the camps, the Germans would continue to encounter resistance. During the night of 19–20 November, several groups of Jewish prisoners at the Janowska street camp in Lwów overpowered guards and escaped; the same day a prisoner cremation commando at the camp revolted.

The huge Aktion Reinhard had produced for the Germans an enormous amount of wealth plundered from the nearly two and a half million Jews who had died in the camps. In the ghettos from which they were deported, the Jews had left behind in their houses and businesses massive quantities of property, which the German authorities confiscated or which fell into the hands of the local non-Jewish populations.

The deported had taken with them to the killing facilities clothing and whatever other belongings they could pack in a piece of luggage, which included money, mostly cash, and valuables such as jewelry. A special camp in Lublin, which the SS attached to the nearby Maidanek death camp and which used primarily female Jewish prisoners, served as a collection and sorting place for all the valuables seized at Belzec, Sobibor, and Treblinka. Most of the money and valuables were then shipped to Berlin.

On 15 December 1943 Globocnik's Aktion Reinhard headquarters in Lublin submitted to Pohl, the head of the SS Economic-Administrative Main Office, a balance sheet that showed just how profitable killing the Polish Jews had been. The enterprise had produced total revenues of 178,045,961 Reichsmarks (about $85 million) in cash, plus gold coins and sixteen thousand carats in diamonds. At least two thousand freight cars of the German railway were used to carry the plundered materials to Germany. Globocnik did not indicate how much of the stolen property he and his staff, which included numerous Ukrainian camp guards, had appropriated for themselves.

Although the Aktion Reinhard death camps had closed, the SS made major efforts in each to unearth and burn the hundreds of thousands of corpses buried in mass graves. Himmler's visit to Treblinka at the end of February 1943, and the beginning of cremation at the camp immediately after he left, makes it likely that he personally ordered the burning of the corpses there. The Reichsführer, according to the Israeli historian, Arad, "was very sensitive about the erasure of the crimes committed by Nazi Germany."[19] Some SS officials, however, including Globocnik, at first refused to enforce the cremation, but then did so grudgingly. Globocnik had ideological objections. Germans, he complained, should be proud of having exterminated the Jews and should not hide the fact from future generations.

CHAPTER THIRTEEN

EXPANSION OF AUSCHWITZ, ALLIED VICTORIES, AND MORE DEPORTATIONS, 1943–1944

BEFORE THE RED ARMY overran it in January 1945, the huge killing facility at Auschwitz would become, as someone wrote once, the largest cemetery in human history. The most reliable estimates of the numbers of persons murdered and buried or cremated there range from one to one and a half million, which included at least 400,000 from Hungary in 1944, 300,000 from different parts of Europe, and 300,000 from former Polish regions. Between one-fifth and one-fourth of all the Jews slaughtered by the Germans during the world war were killed at Auschwitz.

Birkenau

Not until the spring and summer of 1943 did the largest part of the Auschwitz complex, Birkenau or Auschwitz II, take delivery and begin operation of the four huge crematoria and gas chambers of the type the SS had ordered built in the fall of 1942. Crematorium II and IV began functioning in March, crematorium V in April, and crematorium III in June. The SS officer, Dr. Hans

Kammler, head of construction for the SS Economic-Administrative Main Office and the builder of camps, supervised the expansion. Once the new killing facilities started operating, the SS closed down the two bunkers.

In the largest killing installations at Birkenau, crematoria II and III, each gas chamber could kill as many as two thousand victims at a time in approximately twenty minutes. Each crematorium contained five massive ovens that could incinerate twenty-five hundred corpses per day. The SS, in its efforts to increase the burning capacity of all four crematoria, reduced the incineration time and increased the number of bodies, which nearly doubled the number of corpses burned to eight thousand per day.

So excessive was the overloading of the furnaces that frequently it caused fires in and breakdowns of chimneys. Eventually the number of victims that arrived at the camp and were gassed far outstripped the capacity of the crematoria. When this machinery, whose efficiency SS engineers took great pride in, malfunctioned or delayed the killing procedure, the SS would begin burning the bodies in the open air and burying the remains in huge earthen pits.

The Germans attempted, where possible, to hide the four new crematoria from the view of the prisoners of Birkenau, enclosing the killing facilities with barbed-wire fences as well as with trees, bushes, and tall hedges. Each crematorium consisted of three basic components: a large dressing room, a gas chamber, and a furnace room. In crematoria II and III, the dressing room and gas chamber existed underground, connected by a narrow passage. SS men dropped Zyklon B pellets into vents above the gas chamber, which ran down induction shafts into the room.

The underground part of the buildings contained two other rooms, one to store hair, spectacles, and other effects taken from the murdered victims, and the second to hold canisters of Zyklon B. An elevator transported the corpses to the ground floor of the crematoria, both of which had three so-called retorts used to push the bodies into the furnaces. Near the entrance to crematorium II existed a dissecting room, and in crematorium III a room housed a melting pot to smelt gold teeth.

It took about four hours for the prisoner Sonderkommando, operating under SS supervision, to empty the gas chamber and deliver the corpses on the elevator to small trolleys that ran on rails to the furnaces. Before incineration of the women killed at Birkenau, the Sonderkommando cut the hair of the victims, removed jewelry from them, and extracted teeth with metal or gold fillings, crowns, and bridges from the mouths of all victims. If on inspection the prisoner detail failed to remove all gold teeth, the SS punished the prisoner accused of neglect by throwing him alive into the furnace.

While the killing facilities at Auschwitz expanded to accommodate many hundreds of thousands more Jews deported there to be murdered, so also the concentration and slave labor sections of the camp grew in size. In 1942 Auschwitz had twenty-four thousand prisoners. During 1943, the prisoner population expanded enormously, from 42,742 in February to 87,827 in November. By August 1944 the camp had 105,000 prisoners, almost one-fifth of the prisoner population of the massive Nazi concentration and labor camp system that extended throughout Central and Eastern Europe. Auschwitz's satellite camps held an additional fifty thousand Jewish prisoners.

A Further Turn of the Tide in the Fighting: Implications for the War against the Jews

By the time the Germans had expanded the killing center at Auschwitz in the spring of 1943, major changes had occurred on the military side of the world war. Eventually these would have significant results for the German war against the Jews and for the victims themselves.

Especially the war on the Eastern Front had begun to influence Germany's satellite states in Europe. Both Rumania and Hungary had increased their troops in 1942 fighting alongside the Germans in the Soviet Union. But in the great defeat of German forces during the winter of 1942–1943 at Stalingrad, the Red Army also had crushed both the Rumanian and Hungarian armies. Consequently, the government of each German satellite began searching for ways out of the war and even approached Great Britain and the United States about peace. Similarly, the Russians destroyed the Italian 8th Army, which increased Mussolini's efforts to urge Germany to conclude peace with the Soviet Union. The other Axis ally, Japan, had been an advocate of such a peace for a long time.

Also as the tide of the war appeared to turn against the Germans, both Rumania and Hungary showed a growing unwillingness to give up their Jewish populations to Germany for killing. Hitler himself continued to push the leaders of each satellite to hand over its Jews. On 13 April 1943 he told the Rumanian dictator, Ion Antonescu, that the Jews had been natural allies of Bolshevism and that he, Hitler, in contrast to Antonescu, believed that the more radically one proceeded against the Jews the better.

Three days later, during a visit to Germany of the regent of Hungary, Admiral Miklós Horthy, both Hitler and von Ribbentrop personally intervened with the regent to demand that Hungary surrender its Jews. According to minutes taken at their second meeting, von Ribbentrop, in Hitler's presence, replied to a point made by Horthy:

> On Horthy's retort, what should he do with the Jews then, after he had pretty well taken all means of living from them—he surely couldn't beat them to death—the Reich Foreign Minister replied that the Jews must either be annihilated or taken to concentration camps. There was no other way.[1]

Hitler almost immediately confirmed Ribbentrop's explicitly murderous statement at some length:

> Where the Jews were left to themselves, as for example in Poland, gruesome poverty and degeneracy had ruled. They were just pure parasites. One had fundamentally cleared up this state of affairs in Poland. If the Jews there didn't want to work, they were shot. If they couldn't work, they had to perish. They had to be treated like tuberculosis bacilli, from which a healthy body could be infected. That was not cruel, if one remembered that even innocent natural creatures like hares and deer had to be killed so that no harm was caused. Why should one spare the beasts who wanted to bring us Bolshevism more? Nations who did not rid themselves of Jews perished.[2]

For Rumania, its reluctance to cooperate with Germany on the Jewish question contrasted with its previous behavior. The Antonescu government earlier had turned over some of its Jewish citizens to German authorities for deportation and killing. In addition, during 1941–1942 the Rumanians had deported 150,000 of their Jewish inhabitants to Transnistria, a region in the southern Ukraine conquered by German and Rumanian troops and given by Hitler to Rumania as a reward for its participation in the war against Soviet Russia. Transnistria turned into a mass grave for Rumanian Jews.

Also the Rumanian armies invading the Soviet Union had assisted the Germans in murdering tens of thousands of Jews in Bessarabia and the Bukovina, lands recovered by Rumania from the Russians, and had carried out the largest single massacre of Soviet Jews at Odessa in the fall of 1941.

Increasingly the Antonescu regime had found it profitable to murder and plun-der Rumanian Jews and now refused to turn many of them over to the Germans.

In 1941 Rumania had 441,293 Jews; some 211,214 died during the war, most murdered by their own government. Moreover, the Rumanian government discussed schemes for the shipment of Rumanian Jews, especially children, to Palestine; during the summer of 1943 Antonescu proposed a plan to the Western Allies to ransom Rumanian Jews for money, which the Allies rejected.

The fighting in North Africa and later in Sicily and in Italy, Weinberg has observed, had "an ironically contradictory impact" on Hitler's hopes of expanding the killing of the Jews outside Europe.[3] On the one hand, as dis-cussed in the previous chapter, the Allied victory in North Africa in May 1943 precluded the planned German invasion of the Middle East and mur-der of the Jews of Palestine and Africa.

On the other hand, the German occupation of much of Italy, its islands in the Aegean Sea, and its zones in France, Yugoslavia, Albania, and Greece opened up those areas to the German program of killing Jews. Previously, Italian military and political officials had disagreed sharply with the Germans over how to handle the Jewish question, which had contributed to tense rela-tions between the two allies.

During February 1943 the German Foreign Minister, von Ribbentrop, even traveled to Rome to attempt to convince the Italian government to cooperate on the matter. Although Mussolini wavered, in nearly every instance, despite German pressure on them to do so, the Italians had refused to give up the Jews living under Italian rule.

Despite Germany's problems on the Eastern Front and in the Mediterranean, which forced the Wehrmacht by the summer of 1943 on the defensive in the East, the Germans still limited the Soviet Army to slow advances westward along the key central portion of the front. Only toward the end of 1943 and during early 1944 did the German forces, often against Hitler's orders, relinquish significant areas of the Ukraine to the Red Army, which began advancing west more rapidly.

The stiff German military resistance, always demanded to the utmost by Hitler, ensured the continued German control of the death camps in occu-pied Poland so that these could keep operating. This meant that the Germans could complete much of their second major goal of the Final Solution. That objective was to deport to the camps as many Jews as the Germans could pos-sibly seize or otherwise pry away from German-occupied countries and European satellites of the Reich.

Deportations from Europe

Most of the victims of the vast numbers of deportations from outside Poland during 1943–1944 died in the gas chambers at Auschwitz and Maidanek. From nearly every corner of Europe the deportation trains, moving their passengers in inhuman conditions like cattle, continued to roll to the two killing centers. To Auschwitz alone between January 1943 and November 1944, the Germans deported and killed at least 850,000 Jews.

The substantial majority of the victims earmarked by the RSHA for so-called special treatment had little or no knowledge of their destination or fate. Part of the reason was that most of the victims, in contrast to the Polish Jews who had perished in Aktion Reinhard, lived far from the killing factories in the East. A Rumanian Jewess deported from France to Auschwitz in the summer of 1943 told an interviewer after the war that even upon arriving at the camp and mistakenly moving into the wrong "selection" line, she "did not know that that was death."[4]

Only after the Germans began deporting large numbers of people did bits of information circulate in the West, primarily among Jewish and Communist resistance groups, about the meaning of the deportations. In the fall of 1942, a Communist underground cell in Paris, Solidarity, received information from a resistance member who had infiltrated the Wehrmacht transport division, noting that toxic gases were being used on Jewish deportees. On 20 October a French underground newspaper, *J'accuse*, confirmed the worst. "The news reaching us," the paper wrote, "despite the silence of the mercenary press, reports that tens of thousands of Jewish men, women, and children deported from France were either burned alive in the lead-shielded railcars or else asphyxiated to test a new toxic gas."[5]

Beginning that day, the search by the Jewish and other underground press in France intensified for information about the Final Solution, although this term was still unknown to the underground. In January 1943, *En avant!*, a newspaper for Jewish youth, confirmed the extent of the massacre of Polish Jewry with stunning accuracy: "Two million Jews killed in Poland. . . . Everything favors the Nazis in their attempts to achieve their goals: toxic gases, asphyxia in the sulfur chambers, executions, hangings." In May, another paper spoke of the gas chambers for the first time.[6] At almost the same moment, Solidarity listening posts in Paris and Lyons learned from the BBC that the last Jews in Warsaw were fighting the German troops that had invaded the ghetto.

How much the underground literature in France was read and believed by Jewish and other readers is impossible to know with any accuracy. What is certain is that both the German and French police closely monitored the press. After the war, researchers would find in the archives of the Gestapo in France numerous copies of the newspapers and other records from units of the police in various French cities.

France

The year 1943 opened in France with two indiscriminate police roundups of Jews. In Rouen, French police seized 222 Jews, of whom 170 were French citizens. Then in Marseilles, German and French police captured some eight hundred Jews, of whom a majority were French; all were soon deported to Auschwitz. In Paris on 10–11 February, a raid by French police, without an order from the Germans, resulted in the arrest of enough foreign Jews, numbering 1,549, to replace Jewish citizens of France about to be deported from Drancy to Auschwitz. But SS Colonel Helmut Knochen, the chief of the RSHA office in France, reported cynically, "Obviously both categories of Jews will be deported in this case."[7] A week later, French police searched Vichy to seize and deport on German orders two thousand male Jews, most of them foreigners, in reprisal for the killing by the resistance of two German officers in Paris.

During the spring and summer, arrests of Jews continued throughout France. Pressure from the Germans, who always sought to increase the number of their Jewish victims, escalated to force the French to hand over their Jewish citizens. Both German and French officials pressed the Italians, unsuccessfully, to release the approximately thirty thousand foreign Jews in the Italian zone in France. In addition, the Germans demanded that Vichy denaturalize some sixteen thousand Jews who had received citizenship after 1927; although both Laval and Pétain agreed, they soon hesitated and declined.

From September 1943 until the end of the war, German Jew-hunting units combed France, searching for Jewish deportees and making no distinction between French citizens and foreigners. In December Laval permitted French police to participate in the "Jew hunts" and made no more distinctions between citizens and foreigners. Consequently, more Jews were arrested in France during the first several months of 1944 than in any comparable period in 1943. Altogether during 1943–1944, a total of 33,788 Jews were deported from France, most to Auschwitz; for the entire war, 76,134 were killed—some 25 percent of all Jews in the country.

Several reasons explain why nearly three-fourths of the Jews in France managed to survive the Final Solution, despite the many pressures under which they lived. First, France was a relatively large country geographically, with extensive stretches of remote, sparsely populated, and often mountainous terrain in which people could hide. Second, some Jews escaped across France's borders into neighboring Switzerland and Spain, neutral countries in the war that received, often reluctantly, nearly fifty thousand Jewish refugees from France alone.

Third, the Germans allocated to France far fewer SS and police than they did to other Western countries, such as Belgium and the Netherlands. Instead, the Germans depended on the French police to minimize local political dissent, maintain order, and assist the Germans in largescale roundups of Jews. To preserve that relationship, the SS and German police had to avoid antagonizing the French officials and population unnecessarily.

German police, therefore, generally respected the concern of the Vichy regime and French population, to the extent that it existed, for Jews who were French. Yet one must not exaggerate or inflate the commitment of the Vichy government to protect its Jewish citizens. It was unenthusiastic at best and often nonexistent; throughout the German rule in France, tens of thousands of Jewish citizens were arrested and deported, and Vichy leaders did nothing. Moreover, from the end of 1943, Laval made no more distinctions, officially or otherwise, between Jewish citizens and foreigners. Widespread collaboration of the French public with the Germans, whether through support or indifference, helped make this tragedy possible; despite the resistance of a small minority of Frenchmen, their country was not the victim of Nazism that numerous post–World War II French writers would maintain.

Germany, the Mischlinge, and the Reich Association of Jews in Germany

Included among those deported to Auschwitz were almost 80 percent of the 51,257 Jews that remained in prewar Germany at the beginning of 1943. Large numbers of German Jews sent to Auschwitz in 1943 were those who had previously been spared because they worked as forced laborers in armaments industries. Many worked in factories in Berlin.

However, the Reich government, as it did with the Jews of other European states, had a greater interest in killing them than in using them for labor. On 27–28 February 1943, police raided the Berlin plants, arrested the

Jewish workers, and took them to collection points for deportation. Those seized included numerous Jewish men, perhaps as many as fifteen hundred, who had previously been exempted from deportation because they had married Aryan women. Such men were segregated and placed in a separate building on the Rosenstrasse, where their fate hung in the balance. Their wives—termed by the Nazis *Jüdischversippte* (Germans married to Jews or Mischlinge before 1935)—staged a major protest in the open street beginning on 28 February.

Consequently, after several days the police released the first of the prisoners. This episode illustrated the sensitivity of the Nazi government to German morale and public opinion. Similar to what the regime did in the face of widespread German opposition to the euthanasia program, it retreated from the obviously unpopular policy it had started of deporting the Jewish spouses of Germans.

Had there been no opposition to the arrests, the Nazis would have deported not only the Jewish spouses, but also the so-called Mischlinge, persons of "mixed ancestry" who had descended from marriages between Jews and non-Jews. The Nazi leadership had discussed and debated endlessly the issue of what to do with such persons since 1933. The subject had received extensive attention from Hitler himself and at the Wannsee Conference, and when the deportations began during 1942 pressures mounted to resolve the question. Nazi policies toward Mischlinge varied in the countries occupied by the Germans.

Quietly during and after 1942, the German government tightened the measures taken against the Mischlinge and prepared for a Final Solution of the Mischling and mixed marriage question after the expected victory in the war. But in at least one instance during the war, German bureaucrats and physicians attempted to destroy Mischling children.

During April and May 1943 the euthanasia killing center at Hadamar, on an order of the Reich Interior Ministry, established a special ward for Jewish children of mixed-ancestry (*Mischlingskinder*). Most of the children were healthy and sent to Hadamar because they were partly Jewish; there during 1943–1944 the staff killed with injections thirty-nine Mischling children of the first degree, i.e., persons with two or more Jewish grandparents. According to a leading authority on the Nazi euthanasia program, "Because the deportation guidelines exempted these children, the bureaucracy of the RmdI [Reich Ministry of Interior], not the RSHA, decided to destroy at least those Jewish hybrids in its control as wards of the state."[8]

Such killings likely illustrate what the German government intended for all Mischlinge once Germany had won the war and the regime no longer felt the need to concern itself with public opinion. On 20 February 1944 Hitler ordered the involvement of the party chancellery in all matters concerning Mischlinge. By the war's end the government condemned the Mischlinge of the first degree and Jüdischversippte to removal from the Wehrmacht and civil service (insofar as any such persons remained) to forced labor, and some even to deportation.

Following the unsuccessful 20 July 1944 attempt by a small group of German military and political officials to assassinate Hitler, all Mischlinge, including the so-called privileged ones of the second degree, persons with one Jewish grandparent, remaining in the bureaucracy were removed. In February 1945 the SS deported Jewish partners in mixed marriages to the Theresienstadt ghetto. Only the Allied victory over Germany in the war saved the Mischlinge from the Final Solution. The Nazi regime did not spare them, as some historians have suggested, because they viewed them as more German than Jewish.

Despite the uprising in Berlin that halted the deportations of the Jewish men married to Aryan spouses, between 12 January and 19 April 1943, twelve trains carried 13,934 Berlin Jews to Auschwitz; between June and December nine transports took 800 more. Most Berlin Jews remained ignorant of the trains' destination. A survivor of Auschwitz deported there from Berlin in 1943 testified immediately after the war that he had

> the impression that even the [Berlin] Jewish Council did not know [the destination of the deportations] because, even later when I was arrested, they supplied us with soap and pieces of clothing. . . . I think that if they had known where we were going, they wouldn't have done that for us. In Berlin nearly all Jews were arrested at once. . . . We just didn't know what was happening to us. All at once we were surrounded by [the SS]. We were trampled, kicked, and loaded into trucks.[9]

By the summer only 6,800 Jews remained in the German capital (from 160,564 in 1933). The police closed the offices of the city's once huge Jewish Gemeinde and all other Jewish organizations in Berlin and deported their remaining employees. Approximately 4,700 Berlin Jews survived the war. Some had married Aryans, others had joined the city's anti-Nazi underground, and still others had been hidden by Germans sympathetic to them.

When Goebbels told Hitler about the mass deportations of the city's Jews, Hitler praised him. "The Fuehrer," Goebbels recorded in his diary, "is happy over my report that the Jews have for the most part been evacuated from Berlin. He is right in saying that the war has made possible for us the solution of a whole series of problems that could never have been solved in normal times. The Jews will certainly be the losers in this war, come what may."[10]

Among those deported from Berlin in January 1943 were the last leaders of the Reich Association of Jews in Germany, the sole organization in Germany since 1939 that had represented the country's Jews and worked for their survival. Following the establishment of the association by the German government, the Reich Interior Ministry, and more specifically the RSHA, had formally subjected the organization to their control and appointed its leaders.

But the Reich Association of Jews in Germany was not, as some historians and others once claimed, merely a Nazi instrument for using Jews to promote the German government's anti-Jewish policies. During 1940 the association opposed the so-called Madagascar Plan. When Eichmann had discussed with leaders of the association the plan for resettling German Jews on the far-off island, they replied that only Palestine could come into question as a possible locale for Jewish resettlement. Following the deportation of Jews in October 1940 from Baden and the Pfalz to France, the association promoted numerous acts of protest. In response the National Socialists arrested and murdered Julius Seligsohn, one of the main representatives of the organization.

From then on the leadership of the Reich Association of Jews in Germany received increasing pressure from the German police; the latter deported many association leaders to concentration camps. One of the first victims was Otto Hirsch, who died in June 1941 at Mauthausen. Moreover, in June 1942 the Gestapo arrested and murdered several of the association's members as part of a reprisal for the anti-Nazi activities of the Baum Group (*Baum-Gruppe*), a Jewish underground organization in Berlin that had ties to the Communists. Many hundreds of other Jews in Berlin and surrounding locales died also as part of the Nazi vendetta.

Until October 1941, when the German government had officially forbidden the emigration of Jews, the Reich Association of Jews in Germany had promoted such emigration and cooperated with Jewish organizations in neutral countries to assist as many Jews as possible in leaving Germany. From then until the summer of 1942, when the deportations began to reach their peak, the association had established and assisted Jewish schools; the Gestapo, however, ordered the schools closed. But by the time of the deportation of the association's principal leaders, Leo Baeck and Paul Eppstein, to Theresienstadt in January 1943, the widespread suffering of the remaining Jews in Germany made welfare the group's most important work.

The Germans officially dissolved the association in July and suspended its publication, the *Jüdische Nachrichtenblatt*. Contrary to the claims of some postwar survivors of the Holocaust and studies by historians, the association did not participate directly or collaborate with the Gestapo in the deportations. This important point is supported by documents of the association scattered in archives in Germany, Israel, and the United States.

Still other German Jews deported to Auschwitz during 1943–1944 included many of those who had fled to Western Europe before the war. Most were sent to the extermination center from the Drancy transit camp near Paris, German-occupied Vichy France, and the Westerbork transit camp in Holland. Beginning in March 1943, transports with Jews deported in 1940 from southwest Germany to southern France left camps at Gurs, Les Milles, and elsewhere for Auschwitz. Transports also carried to the extermination camp and their death many German Jews who had managed to survive at Theresienstadt and at slave labor camps in Silesia and the General Government.

The shipment of some German Jews to the Minsk ghetto produced one of the strangest episodes in the history of the Nazi regime. During July 1943, Wilhelm Kube, the Nazi General Commissar for White Russia, despite his pronounced anti-Semitism, criticized the mass shootings by German Security Police and SD of Jews in Minsk and the brutal German policy toward the non-Jewish population. Kube demanded the halt of the transport of Jews from the Reich to Minsk. Concern for Jews or others, however, had nothing to do with his complaints; instead, he believed that the local SS and police carried out Aktionen over his head and weakened his authority. Kube died mysteriously on 22 September, apparently a murder victim of either "Bolshevist agents," according to the German press, or of a woman employed in his household.[11]

Finland

Only in the case of Finland, which fought alongside Germany against the Soviet Union, did the Germans not press the government to give up its small number of Jews. Approximately two thousand Jews lived in Finland, which included three hundred refugees from Germany, Austria, and Czechoslovakia.

The Finnish government made clear its unwillingness to hand any of them over. Traditionally, hardly any anti-Semitism had existed in Finland, and in the recent winter war against Soviet Russia the few Jews had contributed significantly to the Finnish war effort. The Germans decided not to press the issue, because they feared annoying the Finns, whose military presence on the Eastern Front Germany urgently needed.

Greece

But in most of the rest of Europe, beginning during the first half of 1943 German threats of armed action and other pressures against foreign governments yielded a huge number of victims for deportation. Some of the first came from Greece. After Germany's defeat and occupation of Greece in April 1941, the Germans had established a collaborationist Greek government and divided the country into three zones of occupation. During the next two years the Germans would deport 59,185 Greek Jews; only 8,500 would manage to avoid the deportations. In 1945 at the war's end, barely two thousand who had survived the deportations returned to their homeland.

The Italians held the Ionian peninsula, central and southern Greece, the strategically located Athens, and numerous Greek islands. The Germans occupied a portion of Macedonia in northeastern Greece, a strip along the eastern edge of Greek Thrace, a small area near Athens, and parts of Crete. Bulgaria occupied Thrace.

Although the Italians held most of Greece, tragically for the majority of the country's seventy thousand Jews, they lived in the German and Bulgarian zones in the north. In dividing up Greece, the Germans had insured this would be the case. The Bulgarians, wholly unconcerned for foreign Jews under their rule, sent the first Greek Jews to the death camps in Poland. In mid-February 1943 the Bulgarian government agreed to German demands that it deport the Jews from Thrace. Beginning on 4 March Bulgarian forces seized large numbers of Thracian Jews; these included 4,221 Jews shipped through Vienna and on to Treblinka, where they were gassed.

Also the Germans attempted in Greece to persuade Italy to cooperate with them to deport the Jews from both the German and Italian zones. When the Italians refused, the Germans decided to deport separately and at once the numerous Jews from their zone in northern Greece. This included primarily the Jewish community in Salonika, which had more than fifty thousand persons, many of them descended from Jews expelled centuries earlier from Spain and Portugal.

Already in October 1941 Hitler had authorized Himmler to include the Jews of Salonika in the Final Solution. During March and April 1943, Dieter Wisliceny and Alois Brunner from Eichmann's Gestapo office, with the assistance of the threatened and terrified Judenrat in Salonika, headed by the chief rabbi Zvi Koretz, organized the deportation by train to Auschwitz of many thousands of Jews. Most of them were gassed forthwith. On 9 May the Germans sent persons from the smaller Jewish communities in German-occupied Greece to Auschwitz, where most were gassed with victims of the seventeenth transport from Salonika. By then the Germans had deported over forty-two thousand Jews from Germany's zone of Greece.

The deportations resulted in mass protests from many Greeks and their officials who attempted to stop them. These included lawyers from Salonika, Jewish refugees from Salonika in Athens, prominent Greek intellectuals, Orthodox religious leaders, and even the head of the Greek puppet government, Konstantin Logothetopoulos. Such efforts had little success. Nevertheless, some Jews escaped by joining partisans or hiding with the help of non-Jewish Greeks.

Further, the Italian consulate in Salonika assisted Jews, several hundred of them, in fleeing to Italian-occupied Greece. More than three hundred Jews received false Italian papers from the consulate. In addition, diplomatic officials in Salonika from neutral Spain, Argentina, and Turkey saved Jews who asserted that they held citizenship in other countries. Such officials, who did not approve of the German slaughter of citizens of neutrals and complained to the Germans about their fate, encouraged Jews to claim citizenship in neutral countries.

This campaign worked only to a limited degree. In August 1943 the Germans sent the last transport from Salonika, which contained the seventy-four-person Judenrat, to a newly established camp for prisoners at Bergen-Belsen in Germany rather than to Auschwitz. The Germans constructed Bergen-Belsen originally as a transit or holding facility for persons who might be used as hostages in bargaining with the Allies, but then transformed it later in the war into a concentration camp. As discussed subsequently in this chapter, the collapse of Italy in September 1943 suddenly made many of the Jews in the Italian zone of Greece victims of the Germans.

The Netherlands

In the Netherlands during 1943 the Germans carried out periodic massive "Jew hunts." They had deported thousands of Jews from the Netherlands in 1942 and now collected tens of thousands more at the

Westerbork camp and other transit camps at Vught and Apeldoorn. From there, between March and July 1943, they sent 34,313 Dutch Jews to Sobibor, before the camp closed; only 19 survived. During 1943 and 1944, over twenty thousand Jews from Holland were transported to Auschwitz; barely fifteen hundred survived. During the same period the Germans sent 4,870 Jews, mostly German emigrants in Holland, to Theresienstadt, and 3,751 to Bergen-Belsen.

While only a handful of the Jews lived through the deportations, some Dutch families concealed other Jews and helped them hide or escape death. For example, Dutch associates and employees remained loyal friends to a German Jew living in Amsterdam, Otto Frank, and helped hide him and his family from July 1942 to August 1944.

Frank's teenage daughter, Anne, wrote with a youthful sense of hope in her diary about her family's Dutch friends that "it is amazing how much noble, unselfish work these people are doing, risking their own lives to help and save others. Our helpers are a very good example. They have pulled us through up till now and we hope they will bring us safely to dry land."[12] Six months later, the Gestapo discovered the Franks' hiding place and deported the family to Auschwitz. Anne died eventually at Bergen-Belsen. Only Otto Frank, among the family, lived through the ordeal; he was one of the approximately 20 percent of Jews in the Netherlands who survived the Holocaust.

Belgium

In Belgium, too, the Germans had deported during 1942 a large number of Jews from the country. Most of the victims did not hold Belgian citizenship. Many of the Jews who remained in Belgium by 1943 worked primarily in factories engaged in war production. The Germans, however, were more interested in killing Jews in Belgium than in using them for labor. During 1943–1944 ten transports with 8,285 Jews from Belgium arrived at Auschwitz, where the overwhelming majority died in the gas chambers.

One of the most significant examples of Jewish resistance to the Nazis occurred in Belgium during the night of 19–20 April 1943. A Belgian Jewish underground organization cooperated with a local Belgian resistance group in an armed attack on a deportation train carrying fourteen hundred Jews. Although only a few on the transport escaped, this is the only recorded instance of an armed assault in Europe on a train carrying Jews to their death.

Jews in Belgium had taken an active part in underground operations since 1940–1941, particularly in collaboration with local communists. Beginning in September 1943 Jews with Belgian citizenship lost their protection and were deported along with the foreign Jews.

Denmark

One of the singularly remarkable events of the Holocaust happened in 1943 in Denmark. A number of factors combined to save most of the approximately ten thousand Danish Jews from deportation. German policy toward Denmark changed completely in August 1943. Allegedly the shift resulted from anti-German disturbances caused by the Danes that produced German concerns for effects on the local armaments industry. On 29 August Germany proclaimed martial law in Denmark and replaced the Danish government with a military occupation regime.

The Germans, in a move that would increase—not lessen—anti-German sentiment and actions among the Danes, at once attempted to deport the Danish Jews. The RSHA scheduled the deportations to Auschwitz to begin on 1 October. Different German sources told Danish circles of the German plans; Ferdinand Georg Duckwitz, a member of the staff of the German plenipotentiary in Denmark, Werner Best, also informed the Swedish government.

The threatened Danish Jews, with the help of Danish fishermen and their boats, fled to Sweden. The operation began as a disorganized and spontaneous affair, but after the Swedish government declared its willingness to accept all the refugees from Denmark, the Danish resistance soon joined the effort and assisted the escape. In Denmark nearly every important group and individual participated in some way in the rescue—the king Christian X, the churches, the universities, and the Danish police. The rescue lasted three weeks during late September and the first days of October, when nearly all of Denmark's Jews arrived safely in Sweden.

Almost as unusual was the fate of the few remaining Danish Jews, 384 persons, roughly two-thirds of them from an old people's home in Copenhagen. During October the Germans seized and deported them to Theresienstadt, along with twenty more Danish Jews whom the German police sent to Germany, the women to the Ravensbruck camp and the men to Sachsenhausen. Most of the Danish Jews in Theresienstadt survived the war; in April 1945, negotiations between the Swedish Red Cross official, Count Folke Bernadotte, and Himmler freed them.

Italy and the Vatican

The surrender of Italy to the Allies on 8 September 1943 produced a tragically different outcome. Italy's collapse in the war doomed to German capture and killing large numbers of Jews in the country and in other areas formerly under Italian rule. Under Fascism, Italy's approximately thirty-four thousand Jews had lived with numerous restrictions, but they had remained alive.

The country's surrender represented a dramatic turning point for its Jews. The new Italian government of Pietro Badoglio fled to southern Italy where the British and Americans sponsored the reestablishment of the regime. The central and northern portions of the country fell under German control. Most calamitous for the bulk of the Italian Jews, they lived in Rome and the cities in the north, in the German-occupied region.

On 16 October 1943 several hundred German police and SS plundered the Jewish quarter in Rome, a former ghetto on the banks of the Tiber River, and arrested 1,259 Jewish men, women, and children. Two days later most were deported to Auschwitz; only 196 were not gassed right away, and of those 15 lived to see the war's end. Orders for the Aktion had come from the top of the Nazi hierarchy, first from Himmler's office in Berlin and then, when local German diplomatic and military officials in Rome had tried to block the deportation, from Hitler.

On 9 October, the German consul then in charge of the Reich's embassy in Rome, had received a telegram from the German Foreign Ministry, noting Hitler's involvement:

> The Reich Foreign Minister [Ribbentrop] requests that consuls [Rudolf] Rahn and [Eitel] Moellhausen be informed that, on the basis of a Führer instruction, the 8,000 Jews resident in Rome should be taken to Mauthausen (Upper Danube) as hostages. The Reich Foreign Minister requests that Rahn and Moellhausen be told under no circumstances to interfere in this affair, but rather to leave it to the SS.[13]

The words "Mauthausen" and "hostages" were likely verbal camouflage. As for Mauthausen, if Hitler meant what he said when he directed that the

Roman Jews be sent there, he was aware that it was possibly the deadliest of all concentration camps. The mortality rate there, especially for Jews, was terrible. Hitler surely knew, in the words of one historian, "that for the Jews to be deported from Italy 'as hostages' was their death warrant, whether it was to Mauthausen or whether this was simply a euphemistic deception on his part" that meant Auschwitz.[14]

In the north the Germans rounded up Jews in Trieste, Genoa, Florence, Milan, Venice, Ferrara, Verona, and elsewhere. After a brief stay in local prisons, the victims were interned in concentration camps at Fossoli and Bozen-Gries. The Fascist satellite state under Mussolini, established by the Germans in the north, ordered all Jews imprisoned in concentration camps and their property confiscated.

Because of the favorable attitude of most of the Italian population toward the Jews, the Germans carefully avoided issuing anti-Jewish decrees that forced Jews to wear the Star of David or to form ghettos and Judenräte. Instead, they concentrated on the less visible practices of seizing the victims, interning them in prisons or concentration camps, and deporting them from Italy.

Between September 1943 and the end of the war in April 1945, the Germans carried out further widespread manhunts in northern Italy, searching for Jews as well as for communist and partisan members of the anti-Nazi resistance. In January 1944 Eichmann dispatched to Italy one of his associates, Friedrich Bosshamer, to act as his "Jewish adviser" in the country. Often assisted by Italian collaborators and the Fascist police of Mussolini's satellite state, Bosshamer's police cadres imprisoned more than 20 percent of the Italian Jews for weeks and months, before sending them to Auschwitz.

Between November 1943 and late 1944, at least 3,198 Jews passed through the Fossoli camp, more than a third of the Italian Jews deported to Poland. Farther north the largest camp at Bozen-Gries held three thousand prisoners, of which approximately 20 percent were Jewish. During August 1944, as the Allies and war front approached Fossoli, the Germans sent its prisoners to Bozen-Gries. More transports of Jews left Bozen-Gries for Auschwitz, the last on 24 October, and later several went to concentration camps in Germany. Only a few Jews escaped the Italian camps, partly because of the hostility toward them and other Italians of the German minority in the surrounding South Tyrol.

The Germans established the most murderous camp at Trieste, a port on the Istrian Peninsula, which Italy had annexed in 1919. They took over direct control of the region and transformed an old rice factory just inside Trieste into a concentration and extermination camp called the Risiera di San Sabba. During the fall of 1943, two experienced German killers and SS officers, Globocnik, the leader of the recently concluded Aktion Reinhard in Poland, and Franz Stangl, the former commandant at Sobibor and Treblinka, worked in the area. Both had also participated in the euthanasia program in Germany, as had the SS officers who served as commandants of San Sabba, Christian Wirth and Dietrich Allers.

More than twenty thousand prisoners were interned in the camp; the SS murdered many of them, mostly by striking them in the head with a heavy club, and burned their bodies in the camp's crematorium. Also prisoners at San Sabba were killed by gas. The killers counted among their victims many dozens of Jews as well as partisans and communists. The SS deported about 650 Jews from San Sabba to Auschwitz or, at the end of 1944, to concentration camps in Germany. The last transport left Trieste on 11 January 1945.

Altogether the Germans deported 6,416 Jews in mainland Italy, including both Italian and foreign Jews, of which 820 returned to the country at the war's end. A variety of factors enabled the greater part of the Italian Jews to survive. Although some Italians, to be sure, had collaborated with the Germans in rounding up Jews, the population generally provided as much or more assistance to the Jews during the Holocaust as most other peoples.

Catholic clergy as well as other Italians supported and helped Jews, hiding them in the houses of Aryan friends, in remote villages, and in monasteries. Italian partisans gave other Jews refuge. Still more Jews lived to see the end of the war because they fled across the border to Switzerland or south to the portions of Italy liberated by the Allies.

At least at present, little evidence exists that Catholic churchmen received much direction or assistance from the Vatican. It is not surprising that Pope Pius XII remained silent about the roundup of the Roman Jews, inasmuch as he had said nothing publicly in the winter of 1939–1940 against the widespread murder of Catholic priests in Poland. Nor had he protested the killing of German Catholics in euthanasia hospitals or abortions performed by force on female foreign workers, many of whom lived in Catholic areas of Germany.

Neither had he said anything publicly during the war to condemn the mass slaughter of the European Jews, despite receiving countless dispatches describing the genocide. Requests that he speak out against the Nazi atrocities reached him from Catholic bishops in Europe, diplomats at the Vatican representing Britain, America, and other countries, and a personal envoy of President Roosevelt, Myron Taylor. Pius, furthermore, had witnessed along with the world the German crushing of the Warsaw ghetto revolt.

Only in his Christmas message of 1942 did the Pope mention in public in a single and vaguely worded sentence that "hundreds of thousands of people, through no fault of their own and solely because of their nation or race, have been condemned to death or progressive extinction."[15] On 6 March 1943, Konrad von Preysing, the bishop of Berlin, wrote the Pope and mentioned the Christmas message:

> Even more bitterly, the new wave of deportations of the Jews which just began in the days before 1 March particularly affects us here in Berlin. Several thousands are involved: Your Holiness has alluded to their probable fate in your Christmas Radio Broadcast. Among the deportees are also many [Jewish] Catholics. Is it not possible that Your Holiness tries once again to intervene for the many unfortunate innocents? It is the last hope for many and the profound wish of all right-thinking people.[16]

Even in his private reply to von Preysing, the Pope never responded directly to the bishop's appeal to intervene on behalf of the Jews.

About the seizure of the Roman Jews in October 1943, apparently Pius XII had been told about the roundup before it happened by the German ambassador to the Vatican. Consequently, the Holy See had opened some monasteries and convents to persons who requested asylum. How many found protection in such places or inside the Vatican itself is still disputed by historians. A number of the German trucks loaded with Jewish men, women, and children passed by Vatican walls.

In explaining why Pius XII did not protest the deportation of the Roman Jews, the historian Michael Phayer has cited three reasons—danger from the Germans to the remaining Jews in hiding as well as a similar danger to himself and to the city of Rome. "For lack of documentary evidence," Phayer has concluded, "we do not know which of these weighed most heavily on his mind. We know only that he remained voiceless."[17]

Also on this and the broader issue of the Pope's failure to speak out publicly against the Holocaust, long-buried Vatican files opened recently to a British scholar, John Cornwell, suggest that Pius had a poor sense of social Christianity and little respect for other cultures and faiths. He had a longstanding and secret antipathy toward the Jews, believing that they had brought misfortune on themselves and that the church's intervention on their behalf could draw the church into alliances with forces—mainly Communist Russia—that he feared and believed to be a greater danger to Christianity than Nazism.

Pius, according to Cornwell, believed that the Jews formed the driving element behind a Bolshevik plot to destroy Christendom. This was the same Pope who would inform the Western Allies in January 1944 that he hoped no black Allied troops would be allowed into Rome, once the Allies had liberated the city. A year later, Himmler would make a similar plea to the Allies to keep black forces from occupying Germany after the war.

The Pope, furthermore, acted toward the Jews in part from his desire to exercise absolute power over the church. For these reasons, Cornwell has concluded that Pius XII "was the ideal Pope for Hitler's unspeakable plan. He was Hitler's pawn. He was Hitler's Pope."[18] At the war's end, moreover, the Vatican would assist a number of SS and other Nazi war criminals in escaping Europe and punishment for their crimes.

It is nearly certain that during the war a public statement from the Pope against the German slaughter of the Jews would not have persuaded the German leadership to stop the killing. But almost as certain, a public utterance from the Vicar of Christ would have provided a much stronger moral justification for many Catholic clergy and their church members in Europe to help Jews. It may even have convinced some Catholics who participated in the Jewish persecution not to do so. The papal silence bordered on, if it did not indeed reflect, the immoral.

Also Pius, his advisers, and his assistants at the Vatican secretariat of state, contrary to the claims of Vatican defenders, rarely acted behind the scenes to help Jews. Outside Italy the Vatican intervened on only two occasions to oppose the deportations. First, in March and June 1942, without success it asked the German puppet regime in Slovakia, headed by the Catholic priest, Tiso, not to deport Slovak Jews. Then on 25 June 1944, the Pope would write to the Hungarian regent, Horthy, urging him to "stop the suffering" of the Jews of Hungary.[19] Pius's request, however, as shown in the next chapter, was much too late to prevent the killing of the several hundred thousand Jews from the Hungarian provinces.

In Italy the Holy See limited its protests against local anti-Jewish laws to measures affecting primarily converts to Catholicism and Jews in mixed marriages with Catholics; it acted similarly in helping Jews with emigration. The visits of Vatican officials to foreign Jews in Italian internment camps differed little from those to non-Jews and in no way eased their physical discomfort. Vatican diplomats rarely intervened for Jews threatened with deportation. No evidence exists that Pius himself issued a directive to church institutions to shelter Jews; instead the Pope remained uninvolved in such matters, even when they happened, in the words of one historian, "under his very windows."[20]

Something else is worth noting about the deportation of the Jews from Rome in October 1943. During the Aktion, the German ambassador to the Vatican, von Weizsäcker, played a double game. His diplomatic charge from Berlin, while the war entered its critical phase in Italy, was to encourage the Pope to retain his "impartiality"—i.e., silence—regarding the Final Solution.

Yet von Weizsäcker informed the Vatican ahead of time about the attack on Rome's Jews, and during the morning it happened he pleaded with the Holy See to issue a public protest against it. He and other officials representing Germany to the Vatican did not oppose the deportation on principle, but rather feared that it would produce a violent reaction from the Italian people, thereby damaging the German war effort in the country and elsewhere. The ambassador hoped that an immediate and strong papal denunciation might halt the SS, prevent further arrests, and pacify the population.

Former Italian-Occupied Areas in Europe

Also for many other Jews in Europe the removal of Italy from the war had fateful consequences. This held true for those in the former Italian zones in France, Greece, Yugoslavia, and Albania as well as for those on the Italian islands in the Aegean Sea. Immediately the Germans occupied the former Italian zone in southeastern France that had become a refuge for Jews. The SS captain, Brunner, one of Eichmann's henchmen, and a specially trained unit of German police, refusing to wait for the slow-moving French authorities and unwilling to distinguish between Jewish citizens and foreigners, launched their roundup of Jews in Nice. The Germans, however, had no way to determine who was Jewish; they lacked lists of Jews, searched for victims who wore no stars and had no identifying stamps on their documents, and had little native cooperation.

Consequently, the police seized and searched all suspects in a terrifying, brutal, and relatively ineffective way, "in a manner," according to one historian, "much more common in Eastern and Central Europe than in France."[21]

Altogether, approximately 1,800 French and foreign Jews in Nice and the surrounding area, from the local Jewish population of 25,000–30,000, were caught and deported. Most did not return. But the others survived, hidden by French non-Jews offended by the German savagery.

In the former Italian-occupied areas of Greece and in the Dodecanese islands, which Italy had seized in its war with Turkey in 1912, the Germans rounded up still more Jews for deportation. Led by Wisliceny and the butcher of the Warsaw ghetto, Stroop, the Higher SS and Police Leader for Greece, the Germans seized eight hundred Jews in Athens and deported them to Auschwitz on 24–25 March 1944, along with Jews arrested in small cities on the Greek mainland. Most were killed immediately. None of the 260 Jews seized on 21 May in Canea, the capital of Crete, and deported on a ship that sank, survived. On 6 June the Germans rounded up more victims on Corfu; almost eighteen hundred of the island's two thousand Jews deported to Auschwitz died there.

On 20 July 1944 the Germans captured and deported Jews that technically did not live in Europe, but in Asia. This would seem further clear evidence of the seriousness of Hitler in carrying out his promise to the Mufti of Jerusalem in November 1941 that Germany would get rid of not just European Jews but also of all others outside Europe. The Germans arrested 1,820 Jews on Rhodes, the largest of the Italian-held Greek islands in the Dodecanese, off the southwestern coast of Turkey. An associate of Eichmann's, Anton Burger, and the German army commander for the island, Lieutenant General Ulrich Kleemann, and for the Balkans, the Austrian Lieutenant General Alexander Löhr, organized the mass arrests and subsequent deportation.

Sent by ships to Piraeus, a port in southeastern Greece, and by train from Athens on a fourteen day journey to Auschwitz, during which 23 prisoners died, only 179 Rhodes Jews survived the death camp. On Rhodes the intervention of the Turkish consul, Saheddin Ulkumen, saved from deportation thirty-nine Jews with Turkish citizenship or Turkish spouses.

In Yugoslavia, under pressure from the Germans, Bulgaria deported 7,122 Jews at the end of March 1943 from its zone of control in Macedonia to the gas chambers at Treblinka. In Croatia, where the Italians also had a sphere of military activity and protected local Jews, many of whom had fled to the area from their prospective German and Croatian Ustasha killers, Italy's abandonment of its zone placed such persons in an ill-fated position. Although previously the Germans had sent some seven thousand Jews from the German-controlled zone of Croatia to Auschwitz, almost immediately upon taking over the Italian zone the Germans deported hundreds more Jews. Also during the war concentration camps in Croatia interned approximately twenty-six thousand Jews, most of whom were killed.

Germany's extremist Arab ally, the Mufti of Jerusalem, Haj Amin al-Husayni, contributed to the destruction of the Croatian and other Yugoslav Jews. He visited Croatia during March and April 1943. In collaboration with Himmler, whose need for Waffen-SS troops had reduced the SS's racial requirements and led to the creation of non-Aryan units, the Mufti supervised the formation of Muslim SS units in Croatian-dominated Bosnia and Herzegovina. These units skirmished for a time with Marshal Tito's Communist partisans, composed primarily of Christian Serbs; the Muslim forces distinguished themselves largely by committing a number of atrocities against local Jews and others.

Only in Albania, which the Germans took over from Italy after the latter's surrender, did the Germans act, at least initially, with relative caution in arresting and deporting the few hundred Jews in the country, which the Italians had generally protected. Under Italian occupation, Albania had become a haven for numerous Yugoslav and some Bulgarian Jews, especially following the German conquest of Yugoslavia. Once the Germans took over Albania, the issue of deportations of Jews stood in the way of the German effort to establish a collaborationist Albanian government.

But by the spring of 1944, the Germans gave up on building such a regime and dropped their reluctance to proceed against Albania's Jewish population. In April 1944 the SS deported a group of approximately three hundred Jews from the city of Pristina in neighboring Serbia; more than half of them died in Bergen-Belsen. Other Jews were interned in Albanian camps, some of which a Waffen-SS division used as hostages in reprisal measures against Albanian partisans. Estimates place the total number of Jews deported from Albania at 591, of which a considerable portion constituted refugees from other countries, including from Germany.

Bulgaria

Among the states of Eastern Europe allied to Germany, Bulgaria represented an unusual case regarding its role in the Holocaust. Despite Bulgaria's entry into the Tripartite Pact on 1 March 1941, its military involvement in the war remained limited to its troops following German forces into the Balkans and receiving a zone of occupation in the Macedonian portion of Yugoslavia and in Thrace in Greece. The Sofia regime resisted successfully German demands that it participate in the Russian campaign. Until the Red Army entered Bulgaria in September 1944, the latter retained diplomatic relations with the Soviet Union and both the Germans and Soviets viewed Bulgaria as a "window" to each other's enemy.

As noted in chapter eleven, under intense German pressure the Bulgarians surrendered to the Germans for deportation and killing 11,343 Jews in the areas of Yugoslavia and Greece occupied by Bulgarian forces. Yet Bulgaria was the only country in the Axis sphere of influence whose own Jewish minority survived the war. The Sofia government, despite anti-Semitic and pro-German officials heading it, was eventually forced during 1943 by its country's public opinion to refuse to turn over to Germany the approximately fifty-one thousand Jews from prewar Bulgaria. Anti-Semitism, although present in Bulgaria, had fewer roots there than elsewhere in Eastern Europe. The Bulgarians had traditionally directed more of their national and racial animosities toward the country's Greek, Turkish, and Muslim minorities than the Jews.

Nevertheless, even before Bulgaria joined the Tripartite Pact, its government implemented a series of anti-Jewish measures, including ordering the expulsion of approximately four thousand "foreign Jews," most of which were Turkish, Greek, and German or Austrian. As the Bulgarian government established closer relations with National Socialist Germany, Zionist organizations attempted to evacuate many Jews by ship to Palestine. This effort, however, met with tragedy in December 1940. That month, a vessel named *Salvator*, greatly overloaded with refugees, sank in the Sea of Marmora, the body of water between the Bosporous and Dardanelles in Turkey, killing about two hundred people.

The accident occurred almost simultaneously with the Bulgarian government's first anti-Semitic legislation, all of which caused an international scandal and ended other attempts to transport Jews to Palestine. Consequently, many Jews remained in the country. During 1942, under increasing pressure from the German Foreign Ministry and RSHA to surrender Jews in Bulgaria for deportation, the Sofia regime established a Commissariat for Jewish Questions that concluded an agreement with Germany. It provided for the deportation by May 1943 of twenty thousand Jews from Bulgaria and the regions it occupied in Yugoslavia and Greece.

The plans of the commissariat, however, did not remain secret. Strong opposition to the deportations emerged from Orthodox church leaders, the Bulgarian parliament, and widespread sectors of the population. The vice president of the parliament, Dimitur Pesev, helped to stop the police roundup of the Jews and delay the deportations. The fate of the Jews in Bulgaria attracted worldwide attention and produced appeals to King Boris and others in the government from the Swiss minister in Bulgaria, who represented the Swiss-based International Committee of the Red Cross, not to deport the Jews.

The situation also produced discussions among the British and American governments about the possibility of Britain's willingness to settle Bulgarian Jews in Palestine. During the last months of 1943 and much of 1944, the Western Powers made half-hearted attempts through both neutral Switzerland and Turkey to rescue Bulgarian Jews and Rumanian and Polish Jewish children.

As for the Germans, they steadfastly refused any discussion of such rescue efforts. Repeatedly the Mufti of Jerusalem urged von Ribbentrop not to permit the emigration of Jews from the Balkans to Palestine. Instead, the Mufti insisted, the Jews should be sent to Poland, where he knew that certain death awaited most of them.

Meanwhile, other factors contributed to the survival of the Bulgarian Jews, including the weakening of Germany's military situation and the actions of the Jews themselves. The defeat of German forces at Stalingrad, the anticipation of an Allied invasion of the Balkans, and the increasing partisan activities in Bulgaria gave some in the Sofia government pause about cooperating with the Germans on the Jewish question. Between February and May 1943 Jewish members of partisan groups, including the Jewess Violeta Jakova, assassinated numerous government and police officials.

Under continued pressure from the highest Orthodox leaders and other influential persons, the government finally changed course. At the end of May it ordered the Jews of Sofia, who numbered approximately twenty-eight thousand, to leave the capital for the countryside and provincial cities. Although the Germans believed this would be the first stage of the deportations, the Bulgarian government refused during the rest of the war to surrender the Jews to Germany. As the German military situation continued to deteriorate during the remainder of 1943 and 1944, the effectiveness of the German pressure on Bulgaria regarding the issue decreased proportionally.

Other Victims of Nazi Persecution

Much debate recently among students of the Holocaust has centered on the question of who were its victims. Does the word "Holocaust" refer solely to what the National Socialists termed the "Final Solution of the Jewish question," the systematic, government-directed effort to exterminate *all* Jews the Germans could seize? Or does the word mean, in addition to the Jews, the whole range of other Nazi victims: Soviet POWs, Gypsies, the handicapped, civilian Poles and Soviet peoples, homosexuals, Jehovah's Witnesses, political dissidents, and outspoken clergy? Some have termed such groups "the neglected Holocaust victims" and asserted that the emphasis on a uniquely Jewish tragedy has focused attention on certain groups of victims to the exclusion of others.[22]

Clearly, while the Nazis made the Jews their most numerous victims and singled them out as the only group for total physical elimination from the face of the earth, the perpetrators also persecuted a diversity of other groups of people and made them victims as well. Further, the Nazis developed divergent policies aimed at the various groups. They imprisoned and killed a number of political opponents and religious leaders, but in such cases the Nazis did not attempt to destroy all such persons. Instead they based their actions on the anti-Nazi views and behavior of the victims.

For instance, the National Socialists persecuted, deported, and even murdered many Jehovah's Witnesses because the latter incarnated much that the Nazis despised: internationalism, pacifism, Jewish influences from use of the Old Testament, and ironclad adherence to a religion that awaited the millennium of Jehovah on earth. The vast majority of the leadership and members of the Witnesses steadfastly refused to obey the state, behavior that stood in contrast to most Catholic and Protestant churchmen in Germany. The Witnesses refused to give the Nazi salute, to take part in Hitler's war or work at jobs supporting the military, to allow themselves to be intimidated into renouncing their faith, and even to escape from concentration camps, an action they equated with disobeying their beliefs. Nearly one-fourth of the twenty thousand Witnesses in Germany died during the Nazi regime, most killed in the camps.

Also the National Socialists developed no concerted campaign of mass murder of homosexuals equivalent to the Holocaust against the Jews. Since 1871 the German penal code had declared homosexuality a criminal offense.

Although at first certain Nazi circles, which included Hitler, tolerated or ignored homosexuality in their midst, such as in the SA, homophobia was widespread in the party as well as German society. It had numerous sources, including prejudices from previous generations and fears that existed of the sexual freedoms of the former Weimar regime. Nazi ideology, moreover, identified significantly with "manliness," which derived from the militaristic character of the party and state.

Himmler, for his part, argued that ties of homosexuals to one another would be stronger than their loyalty to the state. The Reichsführer maintained as well that most homosexuality existed not in the genes, but as the result of young boys seduced by older men; a sojourn in a concentration camp, he thought, would soon cure most homosexuals of their aberrations. Finally, since World War I widespread belief existed among Germans that they must increase their population, enough to fight the next war.

Principally for these reasons, a "homosexual panic" steadily gripped Nazi Germany. After 1933 the German police, which had evidence that two million men were members of homosexual organizations and clubs, raided numerous such groups and places. Often the police acted on denunciations and tip-offs from the public. Following the Röhm purge in 1934, Hitler declared that homosexuality would "result in the immediate dismissal of those guilty from the SA and Party."[23]

During the world war, the Nazi regime radicalized its policy toward homosexuals. At the end of 1941, Hitler, at Himmler's urging, proclaimed the death sentence for homosexuals in the SS and police. However, while the regime applied the ultimate penalty in some cases, it was not used consistently. Between 1939 and 1943 the German army brought 5,806 cases of homosexuality to trial. Altogether during the Third Reich, the courts convicted approximately fifty thousand men on the charge of homosexuality; the Nazi regime castrated some and interned between five thousand and fifteen thousand in concentration camps. While in the camps, many died from hard labor and torture. It seems likely that, had Germany won the war, both Himmler and Heydrich's successor as head of the RSHA, Ernst Kaltenbrunner, one of the most homophobic Nazi leaders, would have pushed for a Final Solution to the homosexual question.

Also neither African Germans nor other blacks in Nazi Germany and the occupied territories were singled out for extermination. Although the Nuremberg Laws identified blacks as having supposedly foreign or alien blood, the Nazis did not view their small population as a serious threat. Nevertheless, the Gestapo rounded up and persecuted the several hundred foreign mulattoes in the Rhineland, the offspring in 1924 of German women and black soldiers of the French occupation of the region. The Nazis sterilized many such African Germans, which Hitler and his followers undoubtedly intended for all blacks had the war ended in a German victory. During the war numerous black POWs as well as black concentration camp inmates and nonmilitary prisoners suffered torture and murder.

But most significant for after the war, the Nazi leadership planned to complete an enormous project of racial reorganization and purification, aimed primarily at the vast Slavic populations in Eastern Europe and the Soviet Union. This foresaw the enslavement, expulsion, or extermination of the Slavs and the German seizure of their lands, all of which the Germans began with their invasions of Poland, Southeastern Europe, and Soviet Russia. During the war, the Germans killed several million Poles and twenty-five million Russians and other Soviet peoples.

Of the latter figure, at most one-third were military deaths, which included over 3.3 million of the 5.7 million Soviet POWs—many of them Jews—captured by the Germans. German regular troops as well as police and SS formations either shot or purposely let starve or die from neglect approximately 57.5 percent of the Soviet POWs. In contrast, the Germans killed during the war 8,347 of approximately 235,000 Anglo-American POWs they captured, or 3.6 percent.

In both the Soviet Union and Yugoslavia, the German armed forces murdered hundreds of thousands of civilians in allegedly antipartisan and reprisal operations. Between 1.5 and 2 million of the peoples of Yugoslavia died in the war. Still other Slavs died in slave labor facilities and the death camps. Also most likely the Germans conducted the mass sterilization experiments in concentration camps for postwar use against the Slavs.

Substantial disagreement among scholars has arisen recently over whether the Nazis placed the Gypsies, or Sinti and Roma, in the same category as the Jews, targeting them for total extermination. The foremost representative of one side of the issue, Sybil Milton, concluded: "The Nazi regime applied a consistent and inclusive policy of extermination—based on heredity—only against three groups of human beings: the handicapped, Jews, and Gypsies."[24]

According to Milton, after the Nuremberg Laws of 1935 the National Socialist regime semiofficially classified Gypsies along with Jews and blacks as racially distinctive minorities with "alien blood." The German govern-ment subjected many Gypsies to internment in camps, where they experi-enced conditions that amounted to the "antechamber to Auschwitz."[25]

By 1938 anti-Gypsy agitation had spread widely in Germany. In December Himmler issued a decree for "Combating the Gypsy Plague," which distinguished between "racially pure" Gypsies, Gypsies of mixed ancestry (*Zigeunermischlinge*), and Gypsy-like itinerants (*Jenische*). While the law extended the various measures of control and discrimination to each category, it prescribed imprisonment for so-called asocial conduct, or for itinerant Gypsies of mixed ancestry and Gypsy-like itinerants who roamed about trav-eling and camping in groups similar to Gypsies. Also the decree placed Gypsy affairs under Himmler's detective force, the Criminal Police (Kriminalpolizei), and created a massive database on Germany's Gypsy population.

When the war began against the Soviet Union, the German police moved to imprison most of the approximately thirty-five thousand Gypsies in the Reich (which included eleven thousand in Austria). In the fall of 1941 the Germans added Gypsies to the transports deporting Jews from the Reich. The Reich Criminal Police Office (*Reichskriminalpolizeiamt*, RKPA) sent five thousand Gypsies to the Lodz ghetto in the Polish Warthegau, along with twenty thousand Jews. In Lodz nearly all the Gypsies died immediately, from overcrowding, star-vation, and epidemics. A few months later the Germans deported the surviving Gypsies to the nearby Chelmno death camp and murdered them alongside Jews.

During 1942 some Gypsies from the East and Germany were sent to Polish ghettos and murdered in the Aktion Reinhard killing centers. Also anti-Gypsy measures increased in Germany and Austria, which included pro-hibiting marriages not only among Gypsies and Germans, but also among the Gypsies themselves. German laws in 1942 discriminated in labor and social measures equally against both Jews and Gypsies; and the OKW excluded Gypsies from active military service.

Meanwhile, in the Soviet Union and Yugoslavia, the SS Einsatzgruppen shot Gypsies as well as Jews. In Croatia, a German ally, and in Serbia, local ethnic rivalries and the brutality of the German occupiers resulted in the murder of nearly all Gypsies and Jews. In the Czech Protectorate the Germans interned Gypsies in camps in which many died from disease, star-vation, and slave labor; those who remained died in the gas chambers at Auschwitz. Also the German occupation authorities in the Netherlands and Belgium deported nearly all local Gypsies to the East.

At Himmler's order, during February and March 1943 the Germans deported more than thirteen thousand German Gypsies to a special Gypsy camp at Auschwitz-Birkenau. Eventually, the camp would house nearly twenty-three thousand Gypsies, including some from other countries in occupied Europe, such as Poland and the Protectorate. Himmler's so-called Auschwitz decree that sent the Gypsies to Birkenau exempted some "racially pure" Gypsies from deportation, because the Reichsführer intended to keep a few Gypsies for exhibition or display after the Germans had won the war and destroyed the Gypsies.

However, according to Milton, local offices of the RKPA ignored the exemptions in Himmler's decree. Consequently, "pure Gypsies" were deported to Auschwitz along with Gypsies of mixed ancestry and Gypsy-like itinerants. At Birkenau, the Gypsy camp was a family one that allowed Gypsy men to live with the women and children, a privilege granted by the Germans only one other time, to Jews deported to Auschwitz from Theresienstadt. But the Gypsies suffered the same final destiny as that of the Theresienstadt Jews. On 2 August 1944 the SS gassed the Gypsies that had survived at Birkenau. There, altogether approximately twenty thousand Gypsies died.

On the other side of the scholarly debate about Nazi policy toward the Gypsies, substantially more writers have maintained that the Nazis developed no general program of extermination of the Gypsies analogous to the Final Solution for the Jews. The principal points of their argument follow. They note that despite the semiofficial classification by the Nazi regime after 1935 of Gypsies—along with Jews and blacks—as racially distinctive minorities with "alien blood," the government did not prevent marriages between Germans and Gypsies with a quarter or less of such blood.

Guenter Lewy, the American political scientist, has emphasized that Himmler's decree of December 1938 against the so-called Gypsy plague was "based on racial criteria, though it did not imitate the application of racialist principles to the Jews. 'Pure Jews' were the incarnation of evil and the arch-enemy of mankind but Mischlinge, being only partly Jewish, were treated somewhat less severely. In regard to the Gypsies, it was the other way around. Mischlinge were considered the bad element and pure Gypsies considered less of a threat."[26]

As the world war unfolded the radical measures implemented in Germany and Austria against the Gypsies resulted less from racial fanaticism than from pressure from below on the German government. Many local communities regarded Gypsies as asocial and criminal elements that had no place in a society that put excessive emphasis on law and order. It is likely that the Germans singled out and deported the primarily Austrian Gypsies in late 1941 to the Lodz ghetto in response to urging from the Nazi party and political officials, who for a long time had demanded freeing Austria of Gypsy influence.

It appears to Lewy improbable that the Germans deported the Gypsies with the idea of killing them. Many of those not deported from the Reich suffered sterilization, a procedure used since 1933 by the Nazi regime against numerous persons it judged as racial and social outcasts. These included "pure Gypsies" and settled and "socially adjusted" Gypsies of mixed ancestry, meaning they had jobs and a permanent residence.

The Germans marked the Gypsies for death for the first time during the German invasions of Yugoslavia and Soviet Russia. But the Einsatzgruppen did not massacre Gypsies in both countries in large numbers, often alongside Jews, for mainly racial reasons. Instead, Lewy concludes, the killers destroyed what they termed the foreign Gypsies because the Germans suspected them of spying for the enemy and of belonging to partisan units.

Here Lewy appears to have forgotten that the Germans gave the same euphemistic basis for killing many Jews. Nevertheless, he notes that while the Germans may have murdered nearly sixty thousand Gypsies in the Soviet Union, in many cases the killers left the so-called socially adjusted Gypsies alone. In both the Soviet Union and Yugoslavia, no overall German plan existed to exterminate every Gypsy, as there did to murder all Soviet, and later all European and other, Jews.

Lewy and other historians argue that the Germans deported to Birkenau in 1943 primarily only Gypsies of mixed ancestry. Himmler exempted "pure Gypsies" from deportation because he had a particular fascination with them. Evidently he believed the pseudo-scientific claim that the Aryans had originated with the Gypsies and therefore wanted those considered "racially pure" preserved as a potentially valuable addition to the stock of Aryan blood.

Unlike the Jews and other victims at Auschwitz, the SS did not subject the arriving Gypsies to "selections," but placed them in the newly built Gypsy family camp. Because of inadequate food and poor sanitary conditions, disease—especially typhus—in the camp spread rapidly. Moreover, the Gypsies suffered from deliberate cruelty at the hands of Kapos and SS guards. Also at Auschwitz, SS doctors, including Mengele, carried out unscientific and criminal medical experiments on Gypsy children, including twins, in which the doctors either left the victims badly maimed or killed them in order to harvest their organs and other body parts.

During the first months of 1944, the shortage of labor in Germany had increased, and between April and July the SS transferred approximately thirty-five hundred Gypsies from the camp at Auschwitz to concentration camps in Germany. There they worked as slave laborers in factories producing weapons and other equipment for the war effort. During the following months the Germans returned hundreds more Gypsies to the Reich for forced labor, which helped to reduce the number of younger Gypsies at Auschwitz. In March and early May, the SS gassed a number of Gypsies at Auschwitz who had typhus.

Unclear is who made the decision to destroy the Gypsy camp at Auschwitz and why. According to Lewy, strong circumstantial evidence points to the commandant of Auschwitz, Höss. On 8 May 1944, after an absence of several months from the camp, he had resumed command. Himmler had given him the special mission of preparing facilities for the murder of the hundreds of thousands of Hungarian Jews. When the first transports of Jews from Hungary arrived at Birkenau later in May, the capacity of the gas chambers and crematoria soon proved insufficient to kill the victims.

Consequently Höss had to find temporary housing for those who could not be murdered at once. He decided to make room for such Hungarian Jews by killing the Gypsies. As early as 16 May, the SS attempted to liquidate the Gypsy camp, but the effort ended in failure when the Gypsies revolted and refused to leave. Ten weeks later, the SS surrounded the camp barracks, rounded up the remaining Gypsies, most of them elderly and sick, and herded them to the gas chambers.

The Germans placed Hungarian Jews in the Gypsy camp at Auschwitz without much thought beforehand about the Gypsies' ultimate fate. Lewy concluded:

> Although conditions in the camp were atrocious, causing an extremely high rate of mortality, incarceration was not tantamount to a sentence of death [for Gypsies] nor was it meant to be such a sentence. The purpose of sending the Gypsies to Auschwitz was to get rid of them, not to kill them. . . . Deportation to Auschwitz was not part of a plan to anni-

hilate all Gypsies; instead it probably represented the lowest common denominator among various Nazi officials concerned with policy toward the Gypsies.[27]

This appears confirmed by Himmler's appointments diary, discovered two years ago. On 20 April 1942, after a meeting with Hitler, the Reichsführer made the notation: "No extermination of the Gypsies."[28] If the Nazis did not intend to murder all Gypsies, then how many of them did they kill? Lewy has provided estimates that range from ninety thousand to one-half million; Milton placed the figure at between one-quarter and one-half million. Although, according to Lewy, "no exact count will ever be attainable," whatever estimate is accepted "the losses in life experienced by the Gypsy community at the hands of the Nazis are clearly horrendous."[29]

CHAPTER FOURTEEN

THE FINAL SOLUTION AMID GERMAN DEFEAT, 1944–1945

DURING THE FINAL YEAR and a half of the war, as Hitler led Germany to military defeat and nationwide ruin, in his mind, as well as in the thinking of many in the SS and German armed forces, they were fighting more than ever to achieve what had been Hitler's top priority in the war since 1941. This was the continuation of the killing operations against the Jews and completion of the Final Solution. While Germany suffered one defeat after another on nearly every military front, Hitler, his associates, and the executioners pressed forward with the killings with ever greater speed and urgency.

By the first months of 1944, the position of the German armed forces had collapsed all along the Eastern Front. In January a Red Army offensive in the north completely freed Leningrad from German bombardment. At the southern end of the front, during April and May the Soviets inflicted on the Axis forces in the Crimea one of their most thorough defeats in the war. A large Soviet offensive drove the Germans out of most of the Ukraine and left the Red Army at the border of Rumania and Hungary.

Hitler's military strategy focused on holding the line on the Eastern Front and in Italy and on defeating the anticipated Anglo-American invasion of Western Europe. He assured a group of military officers on 26 May that Germany could not be beaten in the war. His listeners applauded when he claimed that the slaughter of the Jews and removal of all opposition to the Nazi regime at home made a stab in the back, which he believed had cost Germany victory in 1918, impossible. The generals' response indicated further how much the Wehrmacht served as a willing and active instrument in the Holocaust.

But the real chances of a German victory existed far less than Hitler thought. The Allies had built a formidable military coalition against Germany and, by the spring of 1944, they had established extensive deception operations in both the East and West that would help to mislead Hitler and his military leaders. On 6 June the Anglo-Americans began the D-Day invasion of France, landing successfully on the beaches of Normandy. Almost simultaneously the Soviets launched a huge offensive that drove into the forward most German position in the central portion of the Eastern Front. These final, massive assaults would lay the foundations for the subsequent Allied invasions of Germany in early 1945 and its surrender in May.

The war's last phase would point to yet other connections between the military side of the struggle and the Holocaust. In late July 1944, the rapid advance of the Soviet Army into Poland enabled the Russians to overrun and liberate the Maidanek death and concentration camp before the Germans could destroy its machinery of mass murder. At almost the same moment, however, when the Soviet Army crossed the Vistula River and moved to within fifty miles southeast of Warsaw, the Russian forces stopped to fortify their lines of supply and communications. From early August on, the Russians continued to wait outside Warsaw purposely allowing the Germans in the city to destroy the remnants of the Armya Krajowa, the Polish underground army. Once the Soviets resumed their advance in January 1945, it took them three days to reach Lodz, sixty miles west of Warsaw.

Had the Russians stopped their advance in the previous July three or more days later than they did, they might possibly have liberated most of the Jews, some sixty-seven thousand of them, remaining in the Lodz ghetto. Indeed those in the ghetto knew of the approach of the Soviet troops, which raised hopes among the ghetto dwellers that they would survive; they did not anticipate, however, that the revolt in Warsaw would delay the further advance of the Russians.

During August 1944, the Germans, determined not to allow the tens of thousands of Jews in Lodz to live, quickly liquidated the ghetto, sending its inhabitants to Auschwitz. Also, as the chapter that follows will show, had the war in Europe ended some months or even a week or two earlier than it did in the spring of 1945, thousands of Jewish and other innocent lives would have been saved.

The Deportations of Hungarian Jews

Since the formation of the Allied coalition at the end of 1941, its members had done little to lessen or deter Hitler's determination to kill as many Jews as possible. Except for continuing to fight the war against Germany, the Allies had managed only to issue several public declarations, which stated that after the war they intended to bring to trial and punish the perpetrators of war crimes. This issue is examined in chapter 15.

The Allied statements had little effect on the actions of the Germans. By 1944 the largest single remaining Jewish community that Germany could still possibly seize was that of Hungary, one of Germany's Axis satellites; it had approximately 725,000 Jews. For at least two years Hitler had had the idea of gaining hold of and killing the Hungarian Jews; in July 1941 he had predicted that Hungary would be the last country to hand over its Jews to Germany. As the Germans began to retreat on the Eastern Front and faced the possibility of defeat, Hitler and his subordinates pushed to capture and destroy the remaining Jews in their sphere of power.

During September 1943 they started to prepare to occupy Hungary to stop the country from leaving the war as Italy had done. Moreover, the Berlin government considered invading Rumania, the Axis satellite that had the second largest surviving Jewish community still within Germany's grasp. But before the Germans could seize control of Rumania, it succeeded in August 1944 in leaving the Axis side.

On 18 March 1944 Hitler summoned the Hungarian regent, Horthy, to a meeting. Hitler complained to him that "Hungary did nothing in the matter of the Jewish problem, and was not prepared to settle accounts with the large Jewish population in Hungary."[1] The following day Germany occupied Hungary and changed its government. The Germans did so when confronted with the disastrous defeat of their forces by the Red Army in the Ukraine, with the rapid speed with which Soviet troops were moving west, and with news that the Hungarians had made a serious attempt to conclude peace with the Western Allies.

Hitler forced Horthy to install a new regime in Budapest, headed by Döme Sztójay, the pro-German former Hungarian minister to Berlin. This course of events destroyed the delusion of Jewish leaders in Hungary that their country would preserve its sovereignty as a member of the Axis. Accompanying German troops that occupied Hungary were two members of Eichmann's staff, the SS officers Wisliceny and Hermann Krumey.

Hastily they established a Jewish council, an eight-member Central Committee of Hungarian Jews (*Zentralrat der Ungarischen Juden*), through which they issued orders to the country's Jewish community. Also the Sztójay government, under the supervision of Edmund Veesenmayer, Germany's plenipotentiary to Hungary, issued a flood of anti-Jewish measures that resulted in the isolation, identification, plundering, ghettoization, concentration, and finally, deportation of the Jews. Even before the German occupation, the strongly anti-Semitic Hungarian government had subjected the Jews to massive legal discrimination and forced many of them to do heavy labor for the army.

Because of the rapidly worsening military situation of the Axis, with the Red Army poised to invade Rumania, and because of difficulties in acquiring deportation trains, Eichmann himself soon arrived in Budapest. There, with swiftness even unparalleled in the Final Solution, he and others prepared and organized the deportations. This showed clearly the supreme importance the destruction of Hungary's Jews had for Hitler.

During the war the Hungarian Jewish community lost approximately 550,000 persons in the Holocaust. Between 15 May and 8 July 1944, approximately 437,402 Hungarian Jews were shipped in 147 trains to Auschwitz, most of whom were gassed immediately. The victims came from the provinces of Hungary or from regions Hungary had acquired from several of its neighboring countries between 1938 and 1941.

On 6 July 1944, Horthy halted the deportations "temporarily," but by then Hungary had become nearly "free of Jews," except for those of Budapest. He acted only after receiving considerable—but belated—international pressure to do so from Allied and neutral nations, including the papal nuncio in Hungary, Angelo Rotta, and the Pope, and after anticipating an eventual German defeat in the war. Also he was likely influenced by copies of documents he had received from two Slovak Jews who had escaped Auschwitz, from which he must have learned details of what he had already known in general—that he was complicit in the mass murder of his own citizens.

The rapidity with which the Final Solution was implemented in Hungary resulted from the indifference, with very few exceptions, of the

Hungarian people to what was happening. When not apathetic, they were hostile. The local Catholic Church, through its head, Cardinal Jusztinian Seredi, expressed extreme anti-Semitic views and during the deportations concerned itself only with the fate of Jewish converts to Catholicism.

At Auschwitz, since March 1944 the SS had prepared feverishly for the deportation of the Jews from Hungary, which would be as many or more people as had arrived at the camp in the preceding two years. The Germans laid railway tracks to the crematoria and reopened the second of Birkenau's gas chambers from 1942. The subsequent massacre of most of the victims occurred in crematoria II, III, and V. During the summer of 1944 the SS forced prisoners to dig large pits near the camp for rapid, open-air burning of the masses of corpses. When supplies of Zyklon B ran short the killers flung numerous victims still alive, which included children, headlong into the earthen infernos.

To carry out the murder of the Hungarian Jews quickly, Himmler had returned Höss to Auschwitz as its commandant. Höss, in his memoirs written in 1946–1947 while awaiting his war crimes trial in Poland, noted that "the huge fires could be seen from great distances at night," which produced complaints from the defense services of the German air force. "Nevertheless," Höss claimed, once again demonstrating how the Final Solution took precedence over the German military effort, "burnings had to go on, even at night, unless further transports were to be refused."[2]

Among the Hungarian Jews more information circulated about the meaning of deportation than had been the case previously with Jews in other countries. Allied radio had broadcast to Hungary information about Nazi killings; also Hungarian soldiers who had served in the East while on leave at home discussed what they had seen. Hungarian and Slovak Jews had also passed along what they knew. But even with such information, the Germans and their political allies in Budapest had caught the Jews in a trap, from which only a small percentage would escape.

To be sure, some Hungarian Jews living in remote areas knew little or nothing. The Jews of Sighet, a city in Transylvania, had heard rumors that Germany's defeat on the Russian front was imminent. Hitler, they believed, would be unable to do them harm. Anyway, they assured themselves, stories that the Germans intended to murder all of them could not possibly be true. They ignored warnings from one of their own religious leaders in the town who had escaped German captivity where he had witnessed mass shootings of Jews by Germans, including the killers' throwing babies in the air for rifle practice.

But suddenly one day the Gestapo arrived in Sighet, forced the Jews into a ghetto, and then deported them. When the train carrying them, including a young Elie Wiesel, reached a station with the name "Auschwitz," Wiesel recalled later, "No one had ever heard that name."[3] As the train stopped, however, the people saw to their horror "that flames were gushing out of a tall chimney into the black sky. . . . There was an abominable odor floating in the air."

A few moments later, after camp prisoners had emptied the Jews from the train and an SS officer with a truncheon in hand began the selection, Wiesel "did not know that in that place, at that moment, I was parting from my mother and [sister] Tzipora forever."[4] What the Jews of his community had believed could never happen had done so.

Jews from Poland also arrived at Auschwitz, most of whom were killed: approximately sixty-seven thousand from the remnant ghetto at Lodz, which the Germans liquidated, and twenty-three thousand cleared from the labor camps in the General Government. Rumkowski, the Judenrat leader in Lodz, had always claimed that he was saving the young and strong Jews of the ghetto by handing its children over to the Germans for deportation and turning the ghetto into a slave labor camp. Ghetto laborers produced valuable goods for the Germans and a large income for the local Nazi district leader, Greiser.

But during the spring of 1944, as the Soviet Army was about to advance into Poland, Himmler ordered the liquidation of the Lodz ghetto, the last of the large ghettos in Eastern Europe, except for Theresienstadt. Regarding the latter, the Germans deported still other Jews from it as well as from Slovakia and areas of Southern and Western Europe. Because of the Reich's acute labor shortage the SS kept a small portion of the victims alive and transferred them to labor camps for war work.

Nazi Ransom Schemes, the West's Negative Response, and Wallenberg

Historians and others have speculated widely about the motivations of the Nazis involved in German plans and offers toward the war's end to ransom some Jews. As the deportations of Hungarian Jews to Auschwitz began, a few transports with about twenty-one thousand Jews from southern Hungary remained stopped near Vienna, while officials awaited the results of negotiations between Zionists and some elements in the SS to rescue the Jews. The discussions in part involved an attempt by the SS to acquire massive wealth from the Jews in Hungary by employing some of them as hostages to extort money from the Allies. Even in the throes of military defeat the SS schemed to enrich itself from its victims.

Also the negotiations possibly represented Himmler's growing interest in concluding a separate peace with the West, seeking thereby to extract Germany from a two-front war, by using a small number of Jews as a pawn with which to bargain. Moreover, Himmler had learned previously from Hitler, during a meeting of the two in December 1942, that the Reichsführer could approve releasing small numbers of Jews in return for substantial amounts of foreign exchange. During the spring of 1944, a Himmler associate and Waffen-SS officer, Kurt Becher, as well as Eichmann and Wisliceny, discussed the ransoming of what remained of the Hungarian Jews with two members of the Jewish Rescue Committee (JRC) in Budapest, Rudolf Kasztner and Joel Brand.

But before these discussions proceeded very far, Becher arranged for the SS to take over the Manfred Weiss company, owned by Hungary's wealthiest Jewish family. He did this by bargaining with the family for the release of some of its members and to avoid violating the façade of Hungarian sovereignty. The Weiss Works, a mammoth corporation in Cespel, owned for the most part by the Aryan members of the Weiss family, had thirty thousand workers who produced trucks, bicycles, aircraft, and ammunition for the Wehrmacht. SS control of the company would permit Himmler first choice of military equipment for the Waffen-SS, both for the duration of the war and after it's end. Also Himmler could deny the company to Göring, who attempted to acquire it for purposes of aircraft production.

Himmler, therefore, intended with the transaction, which was completed on 17 May 1944, to continue building his SS empire, both militarily and financially. In return for its Aryanization of the company, the SS agreed that forty-eight members of the Weiss family could leave Hungary, while nine had to remain in Vienna as hostages to assure the "good behavior" of those who left. At least one group of the family made its way safely to Portugal.

Meanwhile, in mid-May, Brand, the JRC negotiator, carried a ransom demand from Eichmann to the Anglo-American governments. The Germans would release the approximately one million European Jews still in their hands in return for foodstuffs and ten thousand trucks for use on the Eastern Front. Both London and Washington turned down the offer on 19 July, a day before a small group of German military and political leaders attempted unsuccessfully to assassinate Hitler. The conspirators planted a bomb at his military headquarters, whose explosion left several of Hitler's aides dead but the dictator alive with only minor injuries. Subsequently the British arrested Brand on suspicion that he was a Nazi agent. Neither Allied government explored the "trucks for blood" offer, judging it a Gestapo plot, nor did they attempt to use it to play for time to possibly rescue Jews.

Becher continued to negotiate with Kasztner and suggested further that Himmler ransom a trainload of Jewish "notables" and allow them to travel from Hungary through Rumania to Palestine. Eichmann denounced the idea, claiming that it would harm Germany's close relationship to the Mufti of Jerusalem. Apparently Eichmann tried to frustrate most deals to free Jews; his greed then led him to insist on a much larger ransom price that finally reached one thousand dollars per Jew.

A train loaded with the so-called notables, 1,654 Jews, including Kasztner's family and friends, left Budapest on 1 July and traveled to a site near the Bergen-Belsen camp in Germany. There the Jews awaited further negotiations on the Austrian–Swiss border among Becher, Kasztner, and Saly Mayer, a retired Swiss manufacturer and official of the American Jewish Joint Distribution Committee. Mayer participated in the discussions at the request of the American War Refugee Board.

Although apparently Himmler hoped to use the Jewish negotiators to arrange peace talks between himself and the Western Allies, he nevertheless remained determined to complete the Final Solution. Hitler was even more committed to the goal. He warned Horthy that despite a few "exceptions" allowed Hungary by Germany regarding the Hungarian Jews, "[n]o delay of any kind in the execution of the overall measures against Jews [i.e., deportations] must take place."[5] Moreover, when Himmler's deputy and SS police chief, Kaltenbrunner, informed Hitler about Himmler's negotiating efforts through Becher, Hitler threatened death for anyone freeing Jews.

The nearly successful attempt to assassinate Hitler on 20 July only heightened his fanaticism for destroying the Hungarian Jews. Both he and Himmler had no intention of exchanging large numbers of Jews for goods or money from either the Allies or Jewish groups. At most they sought merely to bargain a few Jewish lives in return for large material benefits to Germany, while simultaneously pushing for the deportations to Auschwitz of their remaining hostages.

Becher and Eichmann continued the negotiations with Mayer and raised again the demand of Jews-for-trucks and other offers to ransom Jews. The American government, including the War Refugee Board, permitted Mayer to offer five million Swiss francs to the Germans and this time, unlike several months before, directed him to drag out the talks. By the beginning of September Becher had settled on a price of twenty-five million dollars to free the Jewish "notables" still imprisoned near Bergen-Belsen and the remainder of the Hungarian Jews. Haggling continued among Becher, Mayer, and Himmler, which eventually protected the notables, but produced freedom for no more Jews. During August and December, the notables were taken from Bergen-Belsen to Switzerland.

In the meantime the sudden collapse of Germany's military position in Southeastern Europe influenced Himmler even more toward separate peace negotiations with the West. In Rumania, by the end of August the Soviet army had encircled eighteen German divisions, and the King of Rumania announced that his country would switch sides in the war and join the Allies.

These disastrous setbacks made it crucial for Germany to retain Hungary's cooperation. Consequently Himmler deferred to the Horthy government regarding Hungary's Jewish question, apparently by ordering a halt to the deportations of Hungarian Jews. The Reichsführer, moreover, supposedly even approved an end to the killings at Auschwitz.

Also Germany's rapidly deteriorating military position led Himmler on 12 September 1944 to propose to Hitler the idea of separate peace talks, either with the Soviet Union or the Western Allies. Initially Hitler approved the proposal. To reach Washington and London, Himmler believed in the myth of Jewish influence in both capitals; he could ransom or exchange Jews in the West, he thought, for large amounts of either goods or money.

All this, in his mind, would satisfy Hitler while also improving the SS leader's image and negotiations with the Allies, the latter discussions that still continued at the Swiss border. But by October Himmler's policies had failed. The Western Allies refused to negotiate with the Germans and rejected the offer to exchange Jewish blood for ransom payments.

Meanwhile, during the fall of 1944 the killings at Auschwitz continued. In this regard, unclear is whether Hitler had rejected Himmler's ideas or, what is more probable, the latter had realized that Hitler disapproved of stopping the Final Solution. These decisions quickly had profound effects on Hungary's remaining Jews, most of whom lived in Budapest.

By mid-October the period of relative security for the Budapest Jews ended. Since June the Hungarian authorities had forced them to live in certain houses identified with a yellow Star of David. On 15 October Horthy attempted to remove Hungary from the war but failed. Consequently, a profascist and fanatically anti-Semitic movement in Hungary, the Arrow Cross, led by Ferenc Szálasi and aided by the Germans, took over the Budapest government.

Immediately the new regime began the deportations, which included marches on foot of thousands of Jews, many of them women, from Budapest toward Germany. Approximately 85,500 Jews from the city were deported to their deaths at Auschwitz. Also armed bands of Arrow Cross thugs roamed the streets of the Hungarian capital, beating, looting, and murdering other Jews.

At the beginning of December, with the Soviet armies about to encircle Budapest, nearly seventy thousand Jews in the city were placed in a ghetto in the Jewish quarter near the Dohóny Street synagogue. SS and Arrow Cross seized Jewish children from the ghetto and tortured and killed them. The killers gained additional time to keep on massacring their victims when the German armies defending the city fought bitterly against the approaching Soviets.

Many Jewish orphans were marched barefooted in the snow to the frozen Danube River and shot. "By that time," a survivor of the killings recalled long after the war, "the Danube was not the blue or brown Danube, it was a red Danube because of the Jewish blood."[6] Thousands of other ghetto inhabitants died of disease, starvation, and cold. The Soviets liberated Budapest during late January and early February 1945.

Amid the terrible suffering of the city's Jews, some courageous individuals attempted to help them. Zionist youth groups rescued a number of Jews by distributing false identification papers and providing the Jewish quarters with foodstuffs. Other Budapest Jews, above all children, owed their lives to persons associated with diverse Christian organizations and to members of the International Red Cross. Diplomatic representatives of neutral countries rescued still more Jews. The diplomat-heroes included especially Raoul Wallenberg, a thirty-one year old attaché at the local Swedish embassy, and Carl Lutz, a consul at the Swiss embassy.

Wallenberg, who apparently also worked for American intelligence and the War Refugee Board, arrived in Budapest on 9 July. Three weeks later he sent a dispatch to the Stockholm government that discussed the magnitude of

374 HITLER'S SHADOW WAR

the deportations and efforts of both German and Hungarian authorities in "defending the persecution of the Jews and denying what is happening at Auschwitz." He denounced official claims that mail delivery from the deported Jews was fully intact and reflected accurately the number of deportees:

> I checked on this immediately and found that only 14,000 postcards had been received from deported Jews from May 15 to July 12, i.e., representing at most 3 percent of the deportees. If you agree with the official German claim that most of the Jews are still alive, the statement that mail delivery is uninterrupted is patently absurd. . . .
>
> The figure representing the number of boxcars dispatched, as of my previous report (July 19) [sic], and left blank, is not available. The number of deportees as of July 1, however was approximately 333,000.[7]

For three months, Wallenberg, acting on behalf of a supportive Swedish Foreign Office, issued "protective papers" or passports bearing the emblem of the Swedish crown to thousands of Jews. Wallenberg talked Hungarian officials into accepting his contention that a Hungarian Jew with such a passport was a quasi-citizen of Sweden waiting to emigrate as soon as transportation became available.

To assist him Wallenberg assembled a staff at the Swedish Embassy that eventually numbered 350 and included many Jews who had received the passports. Also the Zionist youth movements in Budapest helped the diplomat significantly. To rescue Jews from deportation to Auschwitz, he drove to train stations, brickyards, ghettos, and other collection points, ordering officers in charge to release the people whose names he had on his list as holding Swedish documents. In some instances he even took people off the trains leaving for the death camp.

When Eichmann organized the forced marches of tens of thousands of Jews toward the German border, Wallenberg accompanied the convoy. Racing after the Jews, he acquired the release of hundreds of them who had the Swedish papers and returned them, in trucks that he had procured, to Budapest. On 12 December, in his first dispatch to the Swedish government since late October, and the last one he would send, Wallenberg described what had happened:

> Since the last report the situation of the Hungarian Jews has further deteriorated.

Probably in the vicinity of 40,000 Jews, of whom 15,000 men from the Labor Service and 25,000 of both sexes seized in their homes or in the street, have been forced to march on foot to Germany. It is a distance of 240 kilometers. The weather has been cold and rainy ever since these death marches began. They have had to sleep under rain shelters and in the open. Most have only been given something to eat and drink three or four times. Many have died. I learned in Mosonmagyarovar that 7 persons had died that day, and 7 persons the day before. The Portuguese secretary to the legation had observed 42 dead persons along the route, and [Hungarian] Deputy Prime Minister Szálasi admitted to me that he had seen 2 dead. Those who were too tired to walk were shot. On the border, they were received with kicks and blows by the Eichmann Special SS Command and were taken away to hard labor on the border fortifications. . . .

For a short time the columns marching toward the border were given food and medicine until the procedure was forbidden.

The sick have been picked up in rescue cars from the deportation staging points, about 200 persons in all.

By intervening in some way when the Jews were boarding the trains or being taken away, about 2,000 persons have been returned, of whom 500 [are] from Hegyeshalom. This practice has unfortunately had to cease after the Germans in the Eichmann Command threatened violent action.

The Jewish holders of Swedish protective passports have managed better, relatively speaking, than those under the protection of other countries.[8]

Wallenberg's heroic work represented possibly the first time during the war that an official from a foreign government confronted the Nazis and other killers of Jews with a personal request to save Jews. In this instance many thousands of Jews were saved, which made the failure of most governments during the war to use official methods to rescue Jews even more distressing. On orders from Eichmann the SS attempted unsuccessfully to assassinate Wallenberg by blowing up his car.

In a tragic turn of fate, however, the Red Army forces that soon occupied Budapest apparently suspected the Swedish diplomat of spying for the Germans and Americans. On 17 January 1945 friends last saw Wallenberg in Budapest, when he drove off to meet Soviet authorities to discuss protection for

Jews once the Red Army expelled the Germans. Wallenberg, termed by many in the West and Israel since the war "the righteous Gentile,"[9] disappeared mysteriously, most likely into imprisonment in the Soviet Union. During the first years after the war, German POWs in Soviet Russia who returned home reported sighting him in Soviet prisons and camps. The Soviets denied any knowledge of his whereabouts until 1957, when they announced that he had died of a heart attack a decade earlier in a Moscow prison.

Also following the war published reports discussed how Wallenberg, working together with the Judenrat in the Budapest ghetto, had thwarted a plan of the SS and Arrow Cross to blow up the ghetto. This effort alone possibly rescued as many as one hundred thousand Jews. Only many decades later, in November 2000, a statement from the chairman of a Russian commission on rehabilitation of victims of Soviet political repression indicated that the Soviets had shot Wallenberg, probably sometime before Stalin's death in 1953. In the West Wallenberg became a legend; in 1981 the American government declared him an honorary citizen, a distinction accorded previously only to Winston Churchill and a French officer who fought in America's War of Independence, the marquis de Lafayette.

Resistance and Revolt at Auschwitz

Amid the daily horror of Auschwitz, some prisoners made significant attempts at organized and other resistance, a subject often overlooked in studies of the camp. Resistance took different forms, most of it mutual help among the desperate inmates. A number of prisoners engaged in physical resistance and sabotage. On 23 October 1943 an unidentified Jewish woman who had arrived on a transport at Auschwitz from Bergen-Belsen grabbed a revolver from an SS man and shot two others.

Escape represented another form of resistance; during the camp's history, at least eight hundred prisoners succeeded in fleeing, many of whom were caught near the camp and executed. As discussed in chapter fifteen, the most successful escapees were two young Slovak Jews, Alfred Wetzler and Rudolf Vrba; they fled on 7 April 1944 to Pressburg in neighboring Slovakia. There they met local Jewish underground leaders and wrote a detailed report about Auschwitz that the underground smuggled to the West.

In June 1944 a Polish Jewess, Mala Zimetbaum, escaped from Auschwitz in a stolen SS uniform together with another inmate, Edek Galinski. The Germans recaptured both two weeks later and put them to death on 13 September. Zimetbaum's defiant opposition to her execution meant a great deal to all who saw it in the women's camp at Birkenau. One eyewitness who survived Auschwitz observed after the war that the SS had intended to hang Zimetbaum:

> [But] Mala had a razor [hidden] in her hand and at that moment cut several of her arteries. When the leader of the work service saw that she was cutting her arteries because she wanted to die her own death, he ran over to her, grabbed her and twisted her hands so that the blood should not run out. She stood up and slapped him twice, and she said, "I take on you the last vengeance for my sisters and brothers and children who have innocently perished." We heard it and we saw it. . . . She was taken to the crematorium in a little cart [where] she was shot to death by a prisoner who worked in the crematorium. Because he said, "Mala does not deserve to burn alive." When we heard that Mala was shot by one of our people, we were very happy.[10]

During 1943 a multinational resistance organization had formed that operated in both Auschwitz I and Birkenau. The nearby labor camp at Monowitz had its own resistance group, which made contact with the other one. Both groups helped supply inmates with food and medication; organized escapes, sabotage, and political protests; attempted to place political prisoners in important positions in the camp; and prepared a revolt of the prisoners.

The revolt occurred on 7 October 1944. A special prisoner detail that operated the crematoria organized and led the uprising, during which the prisoners blew up a portion of crematorium IV at Birkenau. This courageous action stood in contrast to the fact that none of the Allied Powers had attacked or bombed the killing facilities at Auschwitz, which numerous Jewish leaders in the West had repeatedly called for in the hope of ending the genocide at the camp.

All the participants in the insurrection, some 450, died in the subsequent fighting with the SS. Following the uprising the SS discovered that a group of young Jewish women from the Monowitz camp, led by a Polish and Zionist underground activist Roza Robota, had provided the explosives and smuggled them to the Sonderkommando. During the resulting investigation the SS tortured four of the women, including Robota, who refused to betray others in the camp resistance, and then executed them.

Before the revolt the members of the Sonderkommando carried out still another act of resistance; a few had managed to keep diaries, in which they detailed the horrors of life and death at Auschwitz. The prisoners buried the diaries, but following the war they were unearthed and became invaluable original sources describing Nazi atrocities at Auschwitz. Similarly the Sonderkommando of crematoria I constructed and left behind a written record.

A doctor and fellow prisoner who served as a physician to the Kommando, Miklos Nyiszli, managed to survive Auschwitz. He recalled after the war what motivated the members of the Kommando to write down their account and attempt to smuggle it outside the camp: "Eleven Sonderkommando squads had already perished and taken with them the terrible secret of the crematoriums and their butchers. Even though we did not survive, it was our bounded duty to make certain that the world learned of the unimaginable cruelty and sordidness of a people who pretended to be superior."[11]

Immediately after the uprising in Birkenau, the SS repeated what it had done before when prisoner revolts had occurred at other camps. Hurriedly Himmler suspended the gassings at Auschwitz and ordered the destruction of the crematoria. Also he wanted to avoid what had happened three months before at the Maidanek camp, near Lublin. There the Red Army had liberated the killing facility before the Germans could destroy the crematoria, gas chambers, barracks, and other traces of the crimes they had committed.

The "Death Marches"

In mid-January 1945 the Red Army resumed its offensive inside Poland, now in the direction of Krakow and Auschwitz, and the Germans ordered a hurried retreat. On 18 January the SS evacuated the approximately sixty-six thousand prisoners who remained at Auschwitz and its satellite camps, almost all of them Jews. They were sent on forced marches on foot, primarily to the west, to other concentration camps still relatively safe from enemy troops.

The Germans had begun dismantling the remaining crematoria at Auschwitz for shipment to the Gross Rosen concentration camp in Lower Silesia, where the Germans intended to continue killing Jews. But the SS had insufficient time to complete such plans. Instead, it dynamited the crematoria, destroying the last one on 22 January 1945, barely five days before Soviet troops arrived. The ruins are still visible today.

Prisoner details, before "evacuating" the camp, cleaned up around the crematoria, spread human ashes near the area, then covered it with earth and plants. Prisoners guarded closely by the SS emptied a few of the camp barracks that held property stolen from the Jews. Between 1 December 1944 and 15 January 1945 the Germans sent 514,843 pieces of looted clothing on trains to the Reich.

During the afternoon of 27 January, Soviet troops entered Auschwitz. In Birkenau they found the bodies of six hundred prisoners, murdered only hours before the liberation of the camp. The Soviets, however, rescued some 7,650 sick and exhausted prisoners from the three major parts of the camp. The Germans, in their hasty withdrawal from Auschwitz, had failed to empty numerous barracks that contained the plundered property of the victims.

Found by Soviet troops were mountains of clothing, ten thousand pairs of shoes, and almost seven tons of human hair. Surviving Nazi records do not contain data that make possible a rough or even partial estimate of the value of the property that the Nazis looted from the million or more victims of Auschwitz. It appears, however, that the cash value reached at least several hundred million Reichsmarks (more than $200 million). As early as 6 February 1943, Pohl, the chief of the SS Economic-Administrative Main Office, informed Himmler that 825 freight cars with clothing, bed feathers, and rags had been shipped to Germany from Auschwitz and Lublin; one entire car was filled with women's hair.

Evacuations such as the one at Auschwitz resulted from the hurried closing and destruction by the Germans of many concentration and labor camps during the final months of the war. The SS, assisted by some ethnic German guards, began forced marches of feeble and starving prisoners that increased quickly in number because enemy armies approached and threatened to overrun the camps that still held hundreds of thousands of both Jewish and non-Jewish prisoners. Included among the latter were many Russian, Polish, and other alleged racial inferiors. The evacuations marked yet another effort by the Nazis to conceal from the world what they had done in the camps.

Also the marches and evacuations continued to consume huge amounts of manpower and other resources that the Germans could have used against the onrushing enemy armies. Regarding the motives of the Germans who guarded the long columns of desperate prisoners, an American scholar has observed: "Guards did not have to be hardcore antisemites or even Nazis to realize that they were much safer moving with their charges into territories still in German hands rather than facing the alternative: a trip in the opposite direction where the enemies—partisans, Red Army or American soldiers— were armed and on the offensive."[12]

Also many Jews and other prisoners were taken back to Germany by train. The railroad historian, Mierzejewski, concluded:

> Seemingly irrational train movements were undertaken right up to the end of the war in an effort to keep Jewish prisoners in German hands. Whether this was to use them as a bargaining counter or simply to find an opportune place to kill them, or because the commanders involved had not received orders to do anything else, remains unclear. Yet, even in the last desperate days of the Third Reich, the Reichsbahn helped the Nazi regime pursue its racist goals through the provision of transportation.[13]

Even average Germans realized the extent to which the Nazi leadership persisted in subordinating the military side of the war to eliminating the Jews and other racial and political enemies. A member of an underground anti-Nazi group in Berlin recorded in her diary on 19 January 1945 about the deportations to Theresienstadt of local Jews married to Germans: "The trucks were ready; gasoline was available. Gasoline is always available when Jewish matters are involved."[14] Although the Germans called off such deportations from the capital, the Gestapo had begun in the fall of 1944 deporting some Jewish spouses from other cities in the Reich, the last group on 18 February 1945.

The lengthy and winding convoys of prisoners that trudged slowly away from the camps at gunpoint and under the worst of conditions were in fact "death marches" (*Todesmärsche*)—they represented another form of the German attempt to exterminate so-called racial inferiors. During the marches the SS and other guards deliberately tortured and murdered prisoners much as they had always done. Many prisoners were shot or beaten to death because they were not strong enough to keep up. Thousands, too, collapsed and perished from exhaustion and, during the winter of 1944–1945, the snow and freezing cold.

Still others died in the camps to which they had been moved mainly because of the complete breakdown of the German supply system. The latter could not provide even the minimum food and medical supplies the camp inmates were supposed to receive. Also the chaos of the final phase of the camps, which left the fate of prisoners even more than previously to chance and the whim and cruelty of local SS and other officials, contributed to the continued high death rate of the prisoners.

The death marches and closing of the concentration and labor camps began in the summer of 1944, when the Red Army initiated its gigantic offensive in the East and the Anglo-Americans landed in Normandy. Before the Germans evacuated its prisoners in July 1944, one labor camp in Poland, Skarzysko-Kamienna, some eighty miles south of Warsaw, had operated its own killing facility. Using exhaust gas, camp guards had murdered thirty-five thousand Jews "selected" as no longer capable of slave labor for the Hasag armaments works. Following still other selections, the guards had shot ten thousand more Jews. When they closed the camp, the Germans sent the seven thousand Jews remaining there to Hasag factories in Leipzig and further west in Poland.

Similarly, the SS sent westward to camps in Germany and Austria thousands of prisoners held in the Baltic States and elsewhere in the East: 3,360 from Warsaw on 28 July for Dachau; 4,000 from Yugoslavia for Hungary and then Sachsenhausen; 76,000 from Budapest on 8 November for the Hungarian-German border and then different concentration camps, especially Dachau and Mauthausen; 66,000 from Auschwitz on 18 January 1945 for Gross Rosen, Buchenwald, Dachau, and Mauthausen; 47,000 from Stutthof and its satellite camps in Pomerania for the west, but returned by the Red Army to Stutthof; and 40,000 from Gross Rosen and its satellites at the beginning of February for Dora-Mittelbau, Flossenbürg, Buchenwald, Mauthausen, Dachau, Bergen-Belsen, and Sachsenhausen.

As Soviet troops approached it during the night of 17–18 January 1945, in one camp, Chelmno, which the Germans had reopened in June 1944, the last forty-seven Jewish prisoners fought a bitter battle to save themselves. Certain of being shot as the Germans started to demolish the camp, the prisoners attempted to flee. Only two, however, managed to escape and survive the war.

By February 1945 Soviet armies had driven through the Baltic States, Poland, and Hungary and stood within a hundred miles of Berlin. Also in February British and American forces had fought their way into the Rhineland. On 7 March American soldiers seized a bridge on the Rhine River at Remagen which the Germans had failed to destroy, and crossed into the interior of Germany. By April Soviet, British, and American troops had advanced deeply into Germany from east and west. Soviet armies would soon lay siege to Berlin.

By this time, in Germany itself the SS evacuated one concentration camp after another and marched or transported the prisoners to fewer and fewer regions in the country that remained under German control. As of mid-March the besieged and war-torn Reich still imprisoned seven hundred thousand persons, which included two hundred thousand women. The regime employed approximately forty thousand SS men and women as well as some ethnic Germans to maintain the camps, guard the prisoners, and accompany the death marches.

During the final two months of what Nazi propaganda had always boasted would be the "thousand-year Reich," some 250,000 prisoners were evacuated from camps in Germany. Despite the regime's desperate military situation, the SS continued to divert military personnel and railway cars to the killing of its racial and political enemies, including Jews. On 1 April the Germans closed the Dora-Mittelbau camp in central Germany, where mostly non-Jewish prisoners had been worked to exhaustion and death building the V-1 and V-2 rockets. The SS sent the camp's remaining prisoners on a two-week death march to Bergen-Belsen. The guards led one of the columns into a barn, setting it afire with the victims inside; when American troops reached the scene the next day, they found hundreds of charred bodies.

Between 7–10 April, nearly forty thousand prisoners left Buchenwald and its satellite camps walking in long lines, often for destinations many hundreds of kilometers away. On 11 April the SS gave up the idea of evacuating the camp and fled; shortly thereafter, the remaining twenty thousand prisoners were liberated by American troops, and some pillaged the nearby town of Weimar. This enraged Hitler who, on or about 15 April, ordered that no concentration camp be surrendered before it was evacuated or all prisoners had been killed. A resulting directive from Himmler told the remaining camps: "Surrender is out of the question. The camp must be evacuated immediately. No prisoner may fall into enemy hands alive."[15] In addition, prisoners liberated at Buchenwald lynched nearly eighty SS guards and other camp officials, sometimes with encouragement from the American soldiers.

By this time, marches had begun from Flossenbürg, Sachsenhausen, Neuengamme, Magdeburg, Mauthausen, Ravensbrück, and different satellite camps of Dachau. Some prisoners, such as the clergyman Bonhoeffer and other members of the political resistance against the Nazi regime, were executed. Only a few weeks remained until Germany's surrender.

The closing of camps, evacuations of prisoners, and killings lasted until the final day and hours of the Third Reich. Between the summer of 1944 and Germany's capitulation, at least 250,000 prisoners were murdered or died while on the death marches and in the last chaotic days of the camps. On 1 May 1945, as the American army neared Mauthausen, the last death marches began from there to nearby subcamps; hundreds of prisoners collapsed as they walked, dying in the mud from exhaustion. Many, although not all, of the victims were Jews.

At Mauthausen, few local citizens showed the marchers sympathy; some bystanders clearly shared the view that the prisoners should not be freed. "In fact," one historian has noted recently, "on marches to or from Mauthausen, not just the SS guards got involved in killing stragglers, but so did soldiers, members of the Nazi Party, and ordinary citizens as well. Some locals took part in the massacres of Jews, and others shot Jews who happened to survive when they were left behind."[16]

Estimates of the numbers of German Jews killed and committing suicide during the war in the Germany of pre-1938 borders range from 160,000 to 195,000. At the war's end, less than 10 percent of the Jews present in Germany when the deportations began in late 1941, approximately fifteen thousand, had survived. Elsewhere in Europe, as summarized at the beginning of chapter eighteen, the Germans had carried out an even greater destruction of Jewish communities.

Goebbels referred to the Final Solution in his diary. He remarked about a report "in the American press that under no circumstances should Germany be given lenient treatment" at the war's end: "The Jews are reemerging. . . . Anyone in a position to do so should kill these Jews off like rats. In Germany, thank God, we have already done a fairly complete job. I trust that the world will take its cue from this."[17]

As for Himmler, the principal architect of the genocide that continued, he made final desperate gestures toward concluding peace with the West by offering to spare a handful of Jews and other prisoners. Like most Nazi leaders, Himmler now wanted to save his own skin. He realized the war was irredeemably lost and that Hitler would take Germany down into the abyss of Götterdämmerung rather than capitulate. He hoped to show himself in as good a light as possible to the Allies and perhaps even play a role in a postwar Germany.

During the spring of 1945 he met four times with Count Folke Bernadotte, the vice president of the Swedish Red Cross and a close relative of the King of Sweden, and offered to arrange a German surrender to the West. The Allies turned down the offer, an outcome, in the words of Kershaw, "as good as certain to all beyond the perimeters of the detached mental world of Nazi leaders."[18]

The War's End in Europe

Hitler learned on 28 April the sensational news about Himmler's proposal to the enemy. By then Soviet Army units were battering their way into Berlin from all sides. Holed up in an underground bunker near his Chancellery in the capital, physically exhausted and emotionally unstable, he frantically tried to have the city relieved with German army units that never had or no longer existed. These forces, he fantasized, would produce new German victories.

When he heard of Himmler's willingness to surrender, he flew into a rage at his "loyal" Reichsführer SS. This, along with Göring's last minute request that he be allowed to succeed Hitler, represented for the latter the utmost personal betrayal and stab in the back. He stripped both "traitors" of their offices and had Göring expelled from the Nazi party and arrested.

But such mindless intrigue hardly mattered anymore. The German capital, as well as most other cities of the Reich, lay under mountains of smoldering brick and concrete rubble from massive enemy bombing. Edward Westermann has shown recently that Allied air campaigns had dropped well over a million tons of bombs on Germany, killing nearly 300,000 civilians, wounding another 780,000, and destroying more than 3,500,000 industrial and residential structures. Hitler's racial and political hatred had led his nation to horrendous destruction, suffering, and defeat.

Yet his people, with a few courageous exceptions, had followed him loyally to the end. But unlike in 1918, when Germany had received little physical damage from World War I, in 1945 the Allies had carried the war deep inside the Reich and demonstrated clearly that they had defeated the country militarily. This would preclude a new stab-in-the-back debate in Germany of the kind that had so undermined the nation's politics after 1918.

On 29 April Hitler dictated a last will and testament, copies of which were sent out of the bunker. The will appointed a new German government. In the testament Hitler singled out the Jews one more time as his archenemy, using the same hateful and self-exculpatory rhetoric reminiscent of *Mein*

Kampf and his many speeches. He indicated one final time that he connected the war and the Jews and blamed the latter for it:

> It is untrue that I, or anyone else in Germany wanted the war in 1939. It was desired and instigated exclusively by those international states-men who were either of Jewish descent or who worked for Jewish inter-ests. . . . Centuries will pass away, but out of the ruins of our towns and cultural monuments the hatred will ever renew itself against those ulti-mately responsible whom we have to thank for everything: interna-tional Jewry and its helpers.[19]

He then mentioned once more, in a passing reference to the Final Solution, the fulfillment of the "prophecy" he had made in January 1939:

> I also left no doubt that, if the nations of Europe are again to be regarded as mere blocks of shares of these international money and finance conspirators, then that race, too, which is really guilty of this murderous struggle, will be called to account: Jewry! I further left no one in doubt that this time millions of children of Europe's aryan peoples would not die of hunger, millions of grown men would not suffer death, and hundreds of thousands of women and children not be burnt and bombed to death in the towns, without the real culprit having to atone for his guilt, even if by my more humane means.[20]

On 30 April 1945, with Red Army forces advancing to within a few blocks of his bunker, Hitler and his wife of a few hours, Eva Braun, took their own lives. He informed several of his servants that "he did not want to fall into the hands of the Russians either alive or dead and then be put on display in a freak show, meaning in Moscow. The bodies were to be burnt."[21]

Goebbels, too, committed suicide in the bunker with his wife, after arranging the murder of their six children. Bormann, Hitler's party secretary and also in the underground headquarters until the Führer's death, died on 2 May in a Berlin street by swallowing poison, rather than fall into Soviet hands. Himmler, following his arrest by the British, killed himself on 23 May. The Allies as well captured Göring, von Ribbentrop, Streicher, and a number of other ranking German leaders and would try them as war criminals. The German government appointed by Hitler to succeed him ended the war in

Europe by surrendering to the Allies in two phases, to the Anglo-Americans in France on 7 May and to the Soviets in Berlin two days later.

Unrecognized by the world until after the war, the Allies' hard-fought victory had denied Hitler and his closest Nazi associates triumph in the portion of the war they had most desperately wanted to win. This was their war for the extermination of *all* Jews which, in their view, would enable Germany to conquer much of Eurasia and acquire global domination. Nevertheless, the Nazis had achieved a substantial portion of their program to destroy those whom they hated the most. They had murdered Jews and other "racial" enemies until literally the final moments of the war.

Throughout the last years of the war, the Allies had shown what seemed to many Jews and others a callous indifference to the millions suffering and the approximately six million dying in the Holocaust. In response, Anglo-American leaders maintained that an Allied military triumph in the war represented the only certain way of stopping the horror and saving the rest of the world's Jews and other potential victims from Nazi racial hatred and the genocide it spawned.

CHAPTER FIFTEEN

BYSTANDERS: THE WORLD AND THE HOLOCAUST, 1942–1944

URING THE WAR, what had the world known about the Holocaust, and when did it know it? Also, as some postwar observers have asked, how could the world have stood by and allowed the Holocaust to happen? After mid-1941, first the Western Allies and then the neutral countries in Europe had learned—often in graphic detail—about the Nazi genocide against the Jews. But for various reasons, few had thought the information true and most had not acted to help the victims.

With only a couple of exceptions, outside intervention, including attempts to rescue Jews, remained almost nonexistent. The Allies and governments-in-exile, whose Western and Central European countries were under German occupation, issued several official declarations promising the killers retribution. Also a few brave persons in the territories occupied by or allied to Germany made efforts to hide or otherwise aid the victims. However, often the Anglo-Americans and neutral states as well as other world observers suppressed, both wittingly and unwittingly, the truth about what a British scholar has termed "the terrible secret."[1]

As early as the summer and fall of 1941, British intelligence had received reports from different sources, including decrypts of German police radio messages, about the mass slaughter of Soviet Jews. The decrypts, some of them sent during 1942 from Auschwitz, would end on 1 September, when the

Germans stopped reporting deaths by radio and recorded them only in writing. Furthermore, the decrypts from Auschwitz were decipherments of radio reports sent of the additions and subtractions to the regular, registered camp population; these reports omitted all unregistered Jews selected for gassing immediately on arrival. Although this information told nowhere near what was happening at the camp, it nevertheless indicated that numerous longterm prisoners were dying from executions and disease. The British, however, did little more than decode the messages.

In the United States, some newspapers had received information pointing to the massacres, but they usually reported it on the back pages. Almost none of the papers mentioned Hitler's repeated public boasts during the war about the extermination of the Jews. Neither Jewish nor other world leaders perceived in the initial news and other accounts of the killings anything much beyond what they believed amounted to persecution and pogroms.

1942: Numerous Reports and Allied Doubts

At the conference of British and American leaders in Washington during December 1941 and January 1942, the Allies prepared and issued the United Nations Declaration. It was signed by Britain, the United States, the Soviet Union, and China (and later by other nations also named joint declarers) and stated that the signatories intended as a principal war aim to fight to final victory against the Axis.

Simultaneously representatives from nine governments-in-exile met in London. They discussed reports from both occupied Poland and the Soviet territories about rampant killings of Jews and Slavs in the East. Officials from the new Allied coalition, Britain, the United States, and Soviet Union, attended the meeting, but only as observers unwilling to take any action regarding what some of their leaders considered claims of atrocities that remained unproven.

The Allies' view contrasted dramatically with that of the governments-in-exile. On 13 January 1942 the latter issued a joint statement, the St. James Declaration, which condemned the Nazi killings. Also the signatories declared their principal war aims, which included "the punishment, through the channel of organized justice, of those guilty and responsible for these crimes, whether they have ordered them, or in any way participated in them."[2]

How much the declaration influenced the start in January of discussions among Britain, the United States, Russia and other Allied nations about the subject of war criminals is unclear. Nevertheless, following the declaration, nearly a year passed before London and Washington would publicly acknowledge the reality of the Holocaust. During much of 1942, Britain's Secret Intelligence Service (SIS) analysts continued to decode German police and SS radio messages, which included daily reports about the prisoner population of Auschwitz and other Nazi camps.

Also the SIS read messages of the German railway and SS Economic-Administrative Main Office. These referred to shipments of categories of Jews to Auschwitz. According to Breitman, "The railway decodes must have contained even more detailed information, so British intelligence analysts must have known about the scale of deportations."[3]

While this information remained top secret and known only to a few intelligence specialists in the British government and Churchill, who himself stopped receiving SIS reports of executions of Jews in September 1941, other information filtered into Britain about Auschwitz and other German extermination camps. On 29 June 1942 the World Jewish Congress (WJC) held a press conference in London, during which it presented information from a report received through the Jewish Socialist party in Poland, the Bund.

The report discussed German actions against Polish Jews, placed the number already dead at seven hundred thousand, and warned that Hitler intended to murder all Jews of Europe. The WJC estimated that the Germans had murdered more than a million Jews, mostly in Eastern Europe and Russia. The British Broadcasting Corporation (BBC) carried much of the Bund's account, as did an article in London's *Daily Telegraph*, which even mentioned the German use of mobile gas chambers for killings.

Shortly thereafter, another secret account, substantiating the one from the Bund, came from a British soldier who had escaped from the Warsaw ghetto, where he and other British troops had been trapped and hidden. Interviewed by British officials and an American newsman in Lisbon, the soldier discussed the German murders of Jews by starvation and shootings.

Moreover, in the fall of 1942 a Polish agent based in London, Tadeusz Chciuk-Celt, who had parachuted twice into Poland, sent to London an account of the killings at Auschwitz and its expansion in size to slaughter more victims. In November the Polish underground reported that tens of thousands of people, mostly Jews and Soviet POWs, had arrived at Auschwitz and were killed immediately.

The American press and intelligence sources received some of these reports. In March 1942 the *New York Times* published an article that discussed the deportation and murder by the Gestapo of 240,000 Jews from Germany and other parts of Central and Eastern Europe. The paper based the account, which it published under the headline "Terror of Nazism in Balkans Told," on information from S. Bertrand Jacobsen, an official of the American Jewish Joint Distribution Committee.[4] He had talked to Hungarian soldiers who had served in the conquered Soviet territories; they had told of railroad cattle cars packed with Jews and of Jewish corpses floating in rivers.

Also American newsmen returning from their brief internment in Germany following Hitler's declaration of war on the United States published accounts of mass executions of Jews by the SS in the Baltic States and Soviet Union. These placed the death toll of Jews at two hundred thousand. During the summer of 1942 American diplomats and officials of international welfare organizations sent detailed descriptions of the brutal roundups and deportations of Jews from the unoccupied zone of France, controlled by the Vichy regime.

On 21 July 1942 a large rally in Madison Square Garden in New York City, held to protest German atrocities and sponsored by the American Jewish Congress (AJC), B'nai Brith, and Jewish Labor Committee, drew a crowd of twenty thousand. Both President Roosevelt and Prime Minister Churchill sent messages to the gathering that mentioned the need for holding the perpetrators of the Nazi crimes accountable. Each message, however, seemed restrained; Roosevelt's said nothing about the Nazis making Jews a special target or about any interest in rescuing the victims.

A few weeks later, news that offered a clearer picture of the general Nazi campaign against the Jews arrived in the West. First, on 30 July, a German industrialist, Eduard Schulte, whose company had mines not far from Auschwitz, had met with a Swiss business associate in Zurich. Schulte revealed to him that Hitler's headquarters had a plan to concentrate all the Jews of Europe in the East and murder them through the use of prussic acid. Altogether, Schulte said, four million Jews would die, and a giant crematorium would dispose of the bodies.

Schulte, while he uncovered a good portion of the Final Solution, apparently described the plan by the SS in 1942 to speed up the killing of Jews by constructing additional gas chambers and crematoria at Auschwitz. In 1943

Schulte would barely escape arrest for what he had done by fleeing to Switzerland on a tip from an official in German military intelligence. But in the late summer of 1942, his stunning account of Auschwitz reached Gerhart Riegner, the representative of the WJC in Geneva. Riegner had sent previ- ously to Britain and the United States reports of Nazi atrocities and killings of Jews in the East, and passed along Schulte's information in a telegram to American and British diplomats in Switzerland.

In America, State Department officials received the telegram with skep- ticism; the department described it for the American intelligence organiza- tion, the Office of Strategic Services (OSS), as "a wild rumor inspired by Jewish fears."[5] In Britain the information received through Riegner both con- firmed and extended the previous accounts of Nazi executions of Jews broad- cast during the summer of 1942 on the BBC.

A few months later the BBC launched a massive broadcast campaign on the extermination of the Jews. Information about the killings, including from Riegner, reached Rabbi Stephen S. Wise, the president of the AJC head- quartered in New York City, who passed it along to several top-level figures in the government. These included the Undersecretary of State Sumner Welles, Supreme Court Justice Felix Frankfurter, Secretary of the Treasury Henry Morgenthau Jr., and an official in the Justice Department, Oscar Cox.

Welles urged Wise not to publicize the information until the American government could investigate and confirm or deny it; Welles' inquiry into the question of Nazi policy toward the Jews, mainly done through Switzerland, took two months. Wise's agreement not to publicize the matter would later, following the war, produce accusations, many of them unjust, that he did not do enough in response to what he had learned from Riegner or what else he knew about the fate of the Jews in Europe.

Welles and the US State Department acquired some of their information from the humanitarian relief organization, the International Committee of the Red Cross (ICRC), headquartered in Geneva. Carl Burckhardt, the vice president of the ICRC, informed the US consul in Geneva, Paul Squire, that according to two well-placed German sources, Hitler had in 1941, they believed, ordered Germany to be made judenfrei, or "cleared of Jews."

The ICRC, however, had considerably more information on the perse- cution of the Jews than it shared with the Allies or announced publicly. Since the fall of 1939 it had received reports from numerous sources, often based on eyewitness accounts, about the persecution of German and other European

Jews and the mass executions of Jews by SS units. The sources included the ICRC's own representatives in Germany and other European countries, national Red Cross societies, and various charitable organizations. The ICRC focused much of its relief work on the groups traditionally the concern of the organization, POWs and civilian hostages.

Although a majority of members in the ICRC pushed in mid-1942 for it to make a public appeal against the worsening of conditions for civilians caught in the war, the appeal neither mentioned the Jews nor was it issued outside the ICRC. Some in the organization believed that the latter's competence did not extend to the victims of civil wars or political repression such as Jews.

The ICRC made no distinction between Jews and Aryans, and placed the former on the same footing as war victims of other peoples. Also the ICRC bowed to pressure from the Swiss government not to do anything the latter believed would antagonize the Germans and place Switzerland's neutrality at risk. The ICRC, too, put forth the specious claim that it had to maintain strict political neutrality to remain an effective humanitarian organization.

Consequently, after 1942 the ICRC confined its activities to sending relief supplies to the deportees in concentration camps, visiting the ghetto at Theresienstadt in June 1944 and March 1945, and appealing directly to governments of Germany's allies and satellites to resist German pressure to adopt anti-Semitic measures. The Germans generally duped the Red Cross representatives who visited Theresienstadt into believing the ghetto was a model one that treated prisoners well.

After the war the ICRC received considerable criticism, particularly regarding how much it knew of the Final Solution and what it tried, or rather failed, to do on behalf of victims of the Nazi persecution. In September 1988 the ICRC finally admitted to Swiss radio and the *Jerusalem Post* that the organization "did not do enough to save the Romanian and Hungarian Jews . . . but could not do more in favor of the Polish and Russian Jews under Nazi occupation."[6] A recently published book on the ICRC in the war concluded that the organization had "no choice but to recognise" that it "really should have spoken out."[7]

At the end of November 1942, when the State Department had completed its investigation and Welles informed Wise that each man's deepest fears were confirmed, Wise held press conferences in New York City and Washington that received extensive news coverage. He discussed how the

State Department had confirmed Riegner's previous information that the Germans planned to exterminate all the Jews.

But despite the publicity given Wise's statement, the *New York Times* only published it on page ten. The *Times* had printed articles about the massacres of Jews in Eastern Europe continuously during the summer and fall; one in July 1942 included brief mention about the gassings of victims at the Chelmno death camp. The account, which appeared under the seemingly unrelated headline "Allies Are Urged to Execute Nazis," observed that "ninety persons at a time were put in the gas chambers."[8]

The *Times* and much of the rest of the American press, while they told the American people about the development of the Final Solution, did so in such a way that elicited little notice or belief that it was happening. Instead, the press coverage produced doubts about the reports of the massacres and discouraged any public demand for retaliatory action. The press did this by publishing small headlines and placing the stories of the killings of Jews, most of them brief in length, on the back pages. The historian Deborah Lipstadt has shown that, in part, this resulted because the press reflected and played to a public mood of skepticism that was rooted in vague memories of World War I atrocity stories later claimed to have been invented.

Also skepticism among the American public was heightened by a belief that accounts of Jewish genocide represented propaganda designed to buttress America's entry into a war that was not really its concern. Furthermore, the press contributed to the disbelief of news about the Holocaust because journalists and editors rarely accepted information from sources they did not trust. They discounted reports from Europe of Germans, communists, and Jews, even when other persuasive evidence supported the information. According to Lipstadt, the *New York Times* went out of its way to avoid appearing to be too Jewish, by downplaying stories of the mass killings or burying them deep in the paper.

At almost the same moment Rabbi Wise met with the press, a Polish underground courier code-named Jan Karski arrived in London from Poland. He had traveled through occupied France to Spain with information, some of it contained in microfilm concealed in a key, that reinforced and confirmed the account in Riegner's telegram. The Germans, Karski discussed in some detail, planned to massacre all the Jews of Poland. He correctly identified the extermination camps of Operation Reinhard, where he had witnessed killings at Belzec, and emphasized that the Germans were not using the Jews for forced labor.

The WJC in London, which received a brief summary of Karski's information from the Polish exile government, realized quickly the significance of the account. The WJC urged the British Foreign Office to persuade the Allied governments to issue a statement about the Nazi extermination plan. The Foreign Office, however, whose officials had no access to the top-secret decrypts by the SIS of German police and SS messages, received Karski's report with distrust and questioned its reliability.

Nevertheless, the information about the Final Solution had begun to reach both the public and higher political levels in both Britain and the United States. No one could any longer live, in the words of a postwar British historian, in a "fool's paradise. Publication of the terrible facts had become an almost daily event."[9] Also during the fall of 1942, the British and Russians clashed sharply when Stalin accused Britain of treating Rudolf Hess too leniently and demanded that London try Hess immediately as a war criminal. The former deputy leader of the Nazi party, captured and imprisoned by the British after he had parachuted into Scotland in 1941, had apparently sought on his own to arrange a peace settlement between Britain and Germany.

On 8 December a small group of American Jewish leaders met with President Roosevelt and urged him to publicize the German killing of the Jews to the world and to attempt to stop it. Although the reports from Europe concerned the President and rekindled his prewar interest in finding havens outside Europe for Jewish refugees, his remarks on the subject to Jewish leaders, including Morgenthau, never seemed very realistic or reassuring.

In London the British Foreign Secretary Anthony Eden received increasing pressure to issue a joint Allied declaration denouncing the Nazi killings. This came from the WJC, the Polish exile government, the press, and certain British public figures, most notably the archbishop of Canterbury, William Temple. Consequently, Eden and the Soviet and American ambassadors to Britain, Ivan Maisky and John Winant, discussed and generally approved such a declaration.

Eden then informed the British ambassador in Washington, Lord Halifax, that German authorities doubtless aimed at the gradual extermination of all Jews, except for highly skilled workers. The Foreign Secretary asked Halifax to press Washington to accept a British proposal and wording for a joint Allied statement. The British War Cabinet and Churchill had accepted the proposal, and soon Roosevelt did also.

On behalf of the United Nations, then comprised of eleven Allied governments, including the United States and Soviet Union, Eden issued a statement on 17 December that said the German authorities "are now carrying into effect Hitler's oft-repeated intention to exterminate the Jewish people in Europe." The statement continued, "The number of victims of these bloody cruelties is reckoned in many hundreds of thousands of entirely innocent men, women, and children." It ended with a promise of justice for the victims: "Those responsible for these crimes shall not escape retribution and . . . [the United Nations will] press on with the necessary practical measures to this end."[10]

For the moment, however, the Allies took no further action, direct or otherwise, despite continued published reports about the Holocaust, such as that by Varian Fry in the *New Republic*, entitled "The Massacre of the Jews." Fry, an American journalist, had worked until late 1941 with the Emergency Rescue Committee, a private organization operating in Vichy France that assisted Jewish refugees to escape to neutral or Allied countries. Fry aided the rescue, for example, of the painters Marc Chagall and Max Ernst, the sculptor Jacques Lipchitz, and the philosopher Hannah Arendt. Despite his expulsion from France, Fry's work provided him with direct knowledge of German actions and plans and convinced him of the truth of the many reports that had reached the West.

Although the Western Allies had officially condemned the Nazi killings, they carried out their major military decisions and operations at the end of 1942 with little or no regard to their implications for the Jews. Neither Britain nor the United States had in mind the Jewish communities in the Middle East and North Africa when the British 8th Army defeated the Axis troops in Egypt and the Allies landed forces in Northwest Africa. Ironically, however, with the Allied triumphs in North Africa, which would lead to the surrender of the Axis forces there in May 1943, the Jews from Morocco to Palestine and in other areas of the Middle East, whom Hitler had targeted for annihilation, were saved.

1943–1944: Continued Allied Inaction and Growing Commitment to War Crimes Trials

The Allied statement of 17 December 1942 caused great excitement in the English Parliament and received wide publicity in both Britain and the United States. The knowledge that the Germans were involved in the most horrendous persecutions and atrocities undoubtedly affected one of the key decisions of Churchill and Roosevelt at the Casablanca Conference, held between 14 and 23 January 1943. There the two Western leaders announced the Allied policy of "unconditional surrender;" this declared that the Allies would conclude no separate peace with such a criminal regime as the one ruling in Berlin.

The announcement, however, produced little immediate effect on either German or Allied policy regarding the Jews. The Germans decided subsequently not to surrender but to fight to the bitter end. They did so in part because of the recognition by their government that it had committed atrocious crimes. Furthermore, Hitler and his associates insisted on continuing the program to kill as many Jews as possible.

As for the Allies, both their statement of December 1942 and the announcement at the Casablanca Conference produced no other actions on their part to assist the Jews. Information kept arriving in the West about the fate of the victims, including a rare wartime firsthand account published in the American magazine, *Collier's*, which contained photographs, of life in the Warsaw ghetto. Still, many officials in America and Britain continued to doubt the truthfulness of what they read and heard.

On 23 March 1943 the Polish underground reported that a new crematorium at Auschwitz-Birkenau disposed of about three thousand persons per day, most of them Jews. Although no one among the Allies knew it at the time, the information was remarkably accurate about the killing capacity of the two new crematoria, IV and V, that had begun operation that month.

Also the day before the revolt in the Warsaw ghetto exploded, a Polish underground courier surfaced in London and published a long report about his stay in Poland and Europe. He had lived in Auschwitz for a number of weeks, learned detailed information about the camp from Polish prisoners whom it had freed, and described minutely the gassing at Birkenau of large numbers of Jews. From May to August 1943 the Polish exile government provided other firsthand and largely accurate accounts of the German death camps, including Treblinka.

Similar evidence had reached several neutral governments. An anti-Nazi SS officer, Kurt Gerstein, who headed a department in the SS Institute of Hygiene and delivered Zyklon B to the death camps, had witnessed gassings at Treblinka and in August 1942 at Belzec. Gerstein told what he had seen to Swedish, Swiss, and papal diplomats in Berlin as well as to the German Protestant bishop, Dibelius. None of the recipients of the information, however, acted on it.

Despite the overwhelming evidence of what was happening, during 1943 intervention by the Allied or neutral governments to assist the Jews remained insignificant. Little resulted from the occasional requests by Rumania, Bulgaria, France, Switzerland, Sweden, and Ireland that Berlin release selected groups of Jews for transport to Palestine or neutral countries.

Amid the few efforts at rescuing Jews, Himmler, von Ribbentrop, and their associates had no intention of bargaining seriously with anyone for Jewish lives. The Germans consistently established conditions, and as shown in chapters 14 and 16, would continue to do so until the war's end, that made attempts at rescue politically and diplomatically unacceptable to the Allies. In negotiating with would-be rescuers, the Nazi aims appeared to be to stall for time while continuing with the Final Solution, to acquire substantial ransom money for freeing as few Jews as possible, or to convince the world, especially the Arabs, that the Allies were fighting the war for the Jews.

An Anglo-American conference met at the end of April 1943 in Bermuda, amid the first days of the Warsaw ghetto revolt. Originally the Allies intended for the conference to review the possibilities of assisting Jewish victims of persecution, but nothing practical resulted. In fact, both Allied governments seemed predisposed to ignoring each other's problems regarding the refugee issue. Their delegations viewed the Jews as only one of many groups threatened by the war and rated prisoners of war higher than Jewish and other refugees in receiving Allied aid. The meeting frustrated many Jewish leaders as well as other persons horrified at the fate of the Jews in Europe.

While meetings and words alone could not save any of the victims, it is also unclear what the Allies could have done to help them. Until the end of 1942, the Axis defeated the Western Allies militarily in one battle after another in the Pacific as well as at sea and in North Africa. The war at sea only turned in favor of the Allies beginning in the spring of 1943 and in the air at the start of 1944. The Allies had as their first priority to hang on militarily and combine their resources effectively to defeat the Axis.

Although Jewish organizations and prominent persons attempted to arouse both public opinion and government officials, hoping to pressure the United States and Britain to act militarily to rescue the Jews, the effort had little effect. This prompted Weinberg to conclude: "The great influence that anti-Semites everywhere always attributed to Jews had proved to be as imaginary as the other constructs sick minds projected onto a group without help or power in its hour of supreme peril."[11]

Numerous other factors combined to leave the Western Allies unwilling to assist the Jews actively, even by discussing publicly and condemning the Nazi crimes against the Jews. The British government, in fact, repeatedly opposed aiding Jewish refugees in Europe. It resisted Zionism and played a significant role in sealing the escape routes of the refugees, many desperately seeking to reach the British mandate of Palestine.

Especially British Foreign Office officials sought to silence Zionist activity in the United States, wishing thereby to protect Britain's postwar control of Palestine as part of British global imperial interests. The British, moreover, worried that defending or assisting Jews, and permitting their settling in Palestine, would stir up Arab disorders there and elsewhere in the Middle East against Britain.

Also some Foreign Office and other government officials in Britain suspected that reports of Nazi crimes resembled supposedly false Allied propaganda during World War I about enemy atrocities. British leaders, too, had difficulty believing that what they knew was happening was made largely possible by the horrible war. They maintained that rescuing Jews would detract from or undermine the Allied war effort.

Further, some officials doubted information from Jewish sources, thinking that Jews allegedly had an interest in exaggerating the suffering of their fellow Jews. According to a postwar British writer, there was "no doubt that anti-Semitism was in the air in Britain during the war," and officials "were not immune from infection by the public mood."[12]

Although Churchill did not share much of his government officials' reluctance to involve Britain in Jewish issues and held pro-Zionist sympathies, he nevertheless said nothing publicly about the Nazis targeting Jews for destruction. Nor did he raise the issue in War Cabinet meetings. Yet privately the Prime Minister could write to Eden, suggesting a grasp of the reality of the catastrophe overtaking the Jews in Europe. He told the Foreign Secretary: "This is probably the greatest and most horrible crime ever committed in the whole history of the world, and it has been done by scientific machinery by nominally civilised men in the name of a great State and one of the leading races of Europe."[13]

In addition, Britain's limited military options affected its response to the Holocaust. Bombing Germany in retaliation for atrocities had little support, and sending food and other supplies to Jews in the East probably had at best a slight chance of reaching the victims. Perhaps, as some observers suggested at the time and later, Britain could have broadcast more radio programs into enemy and neutral countries that informed Jews and others about what deportation meant.

Some in both the British and American governments, moreover, maintained that assisting Jews would provide support for the claim of Nazi propagandists—and Hitler—that the Jews had started the war and that the Allies fought it on behalf of and at the encouragement of the Jews. Such propaganda would appeal to the substantial anti-Semitic sentiments in both the British and American populations. While Anglo-Americans had no desire for the Jews to be killed, they could nevertheless oppose strongly what they viewed were efforts by their governments to help or favor Jews.

This view held true in the United States Army. During the Anglo-American invasion of French North Africa in 1942–1943, the Allied commander, General Dwight Eisenhower, refused to stop the persecution of local Jews so as not to risk antagonizing the Arab population. Eisenhower's subordinate, General George C. Patton, whom a historian recently termed "the crudest sort of racist anti-Semite," heightened the Allied commander's fear of an Arab–Jewish explosion.[14]

Eisenhower's wish to avoid favoritism toward Jews shaped significantly the policy on North Africa of the Army General Staff in Washington. The latter interpreted Eisenhower's position, "to give the comparatively few Jewish Semites a preferred status over the vastly more numerous Semites of Islam would almost certainly provoke an unfortunate and dangerous reaction on the part of the Moslems."[15] The Americans, therefore, did little to change the discriminatory policies of the French toward the Jews in North Africa.

For similar reasons the rabidly anti-Semitic chief of the Army's intelligence division, General George V. Strong, sought during the spring and summer of 1943 to persuade the United States government to join with Britain to oppose Jewish immigration to Palestine and a postwar Jewish state there. Strong not only emphasized the necessity of friendly relations to the Arabs to protect Allied wartime security in the Middle East, but also to ensure the postwar use by the United States of "the huge oil reserves in the Middle East."[16] Strong, however, failed to convince Stimson of the need for an official joint Anglo-American statement on Palestine, and the Secretary of War withdrew his support for it.

As Zionist organizations in America increased their activities, which included lobbying efforts aimed at the Jewish community as well as at

Congress and the American public at large, Army intelligence reacted accordingly. Already ever vigilant against alleged "unpatriotic and dangerous minorities" in America such as Germans, Italians, and Japanese, the army now intensified its surveillance of Jewish groups. In part this resulted from a heightened fear in the army of subversion from Communism, which focused negative attention on those persons many anti-Semitic minds associated with it, Jews.

Given this atmosphere in official military circles, when five hundred Jewish rabbis traveled to Washington to petition President Roosevelt and Congress to urge the rescuing of the Jews of Europe, army agents followed their every move, even filming part of the events. Agents also suspected B'nai B'rith and the Anti-Defamation League of subversion. An Army report, citing Communism as "absolutely the last stronghold for the international Jew," linked these groups to Jewish business, financial, and political interests supposedly reaching to close Roosevelt advisers.[17]

In addition to the xenophobia and anti-Semitism in substantial portions of the United States military and government, still other factors in America worked in varying degrees to prevent officials and the public from believing the truthfulness of the reports about the Holocaust and acting on them. Nazi brutality seemed a long distance away. The killing of millions of Jews for no reason except that they were Jews seemed incredible; such a prospect many Americans found extremely difficult to comprehend.

At first Washington only published "atrocity" reports if the latter could mobilize the public for greater efforts to win the war. But most Americans hardly saw Jews from other parts of the world—unlike far-away islands in the Pacific overrun by Japanese forces—as something for which to fight the war. Many officials in the U.S. State Department believed similarly with their colleagues in the British Foreign Office that any effort to rescue Jews would obstruct the war effort. Some officials, as noted previously, harbored anti-Jewish feelings that discouraged any impulse to intervene to help the victims. Such prejudices played a role in shaping the behavior of the State Department's Assistant Secretary of State, Breckenridge Long Jr., who had responsibility for refugees during the Roosevelt administration. Long was a paranoid anti-Semite, believing *Mein Kampf* "eloquent in opposition to Jewry and to Jews as exponents of Communism and Chaos."[18]

As for the Soviet government, it had almost complete disinterest in the Jewish persecution. Russia had its own long tradition of anti-Semitism, and the Communists never acknowledged Nazi racial ideology as the crucial factor in both the German invasion of the Soviet Union and in Germany's fanatical anti-Semitism. Stalin instead held suspicions toward the "capitalist" West and feared that the lack of an effort by his Anglo-American allies to establish a "second front" in the war in Western Europe signified their disloyalty to the Soviet Union.

Only at the end of 1942 did the Soviets broadcast, in German, from their radio station at Kuibychev, information about the extermination of the Jews. During late 1943 and the start of 1944, Soviet broadcasts discussed the gassings at Auschwitz. But even long after the war, the Soviet government refused to acknowledge that the Holocaust had happened and focused almost exclusively on the suffering caused the non-Jewish Soviet peoples from the German invasion.

However, Stalin's regime had in fact contributed to the early successes of the Germans in massacring Soviet Jews during and after 1941. The conclusion of the Soviet treaty with Germany in 1939 and the failure of Stalin to recognize the fanatical racial and anti-Semitic policies and actions of the German government, helped to leave the Soviet Union and its peoples—including most Soviet Jews—wholly unprepared for the German invasion.

For all these (as well as other lesser) reasons, well into 1943 the Allies did little to assist the Jews. Their sole effort, in this regard, was to send radio broadcasts to Germany, beginning with BBC and Soviet transmissions in December 1942 that provided highly accurate information on the fate of the Jews. Broadcasts during 1943 discussed the deportation of French Jews to Poland as well as the uprising of the Warsaw ghetto. Not everyone, however, believed the broadcasts; many Jews and other listeners dismissed the reports as war propaganda.

Efforts by Jewish and humanitarian groups in London to force the British government to act to save Jews in Europe had generally failed. But by October 1943 months-long public pressure and demonstrations of Jewish and liberal forces in the United States began to change the climate of opinion in that country toward favoring assisting the Jews. The switch in opinion occurred despite continued far-reaching anti-Jewish and anti-immigration sentiment in America.

Jan Karski, who had arrived in the United States, especially influenced President Roosevelt at their meeting on 28 July 1943. Karski steered the discussion to the concentration camps and eventually to the German persecution of the Jews which, Karski emphasized, differed from the German treatment of other peoples. Nazi policy, he told the President, aimed at the physical destruction of the Jews. The Allies, he insisted, had to intervene soon.

Shortly after this discussion, Roosevelt directed the United States Treasury Department to support the efforts of Rabbi Wise and the WJC to help relieve and rescue Jews in Rumania and France. While the Treasury Department agreed to the WJC's proposal, the State Department did much to obstruct it. High officials in the Treasury Department soon persuaded Secretary Morgenthau, a confidant of the President, the only Jew in the cabinet, and one of the most prominent Jewish Americans, to raise the WJC proposal and other problematic issues with Secretary of State Cordell Hull. Also Morgenthau was likely influenced to act because of his father's firsthand experience with the Ottoman genocide of the Armenians in World War I, while serving as American ambassador to Turkey.

This seemed to have an effect. During the fall the Allies took two actions that would prepare for the later trials of German war criminals at Nuremberg. First, on 20 October, they established a United Nations War Crimes Commission (UNWCC) in London, which did not include the Soviet Union as a member. Second, eleven days later, the British, American, and Soviet foreign ministers issued from their meeting in Moscow, on behalf of their governments, an official declaration on Nazi war crimes.

The latter, a document titled the "Declaration on German Atrocities in Occupied Europe," called for trials and punishment of German and other war criminals in Europe. But the proclamation, while it discussed "the monstrous crimes of the Hitlerites" against "all peoples or territories" under German rule, made no mention of the Jews or their extraordinary suffering.[19] Leaving out the Jews may have convinced Stalin to agree to the statement as much as or more than his satisfaction at the Western Allies' fighting in Italy and in the skies over Germany, and their increased shipments of military equipment to the Soviet Union.

By the time Roosevelt, Stalin, and Churchill met at Teheran from 28 November to 1 December 1943, the tide of the war had turned in favor of the Allies, and they had consolidated their alliance. Although unknown at the time, these factors would make a German victory in the war impossible, resulting in the saving of the majority of the world's Jews. But also unknown, yet suspected by a few horrified observers in the West, by the end of 1943 the Nazis had murdered nearly five million Jews, over one-quarter of world Jewry.

During 1944 the stream of information into the West about the geno-cide, and especially about Auschwitz, continued. At the end of January the report from a Polish underground agent, code-named "Wanda," reached London. Because the British knew of her reliability as a source, they distrib-uted the report to numerous American officials and the OSS office in London. It described the procedures at Birkenau of selection, killing, and cre-mation and estimated that through early June 1943 the Germans had gassed 645,000 Jews at the camp. Also the report noted that a large number of Gypsies had been murdered.

Moreover, several prisoners escaped from Auschwitz in the spring of 1944 and provided further details about the killing operations there. In April two Slovak Jews, Rudolf Vrba and Alfred Wetzler, fled the camp with the help of its prisoner underground and made their way to Slovakia. There they provided personal testimony for a thirty-page report, transcribed by a Judenrat leader from Bratislava.

The Jewish leadership in the Slovak capital had attempted since 1942 to prevent the deportations of local Jews by bribing Slovak and German offi-cials. An underground "Jewish Center," which existed apart from the so-called Working Group of Slovak Jews discussed above in chapter 11, had established intelligence networks, smuggled and aided some eight thousand Jews in reaching the then relative safety of Hungary, and passed information about deportations on to the West. The underground would do the same with the information provided by Vrba and Wetzler.

Their report described the organization of the Auschwitz complex and estimated that almost 1.75 million Jews had already been murdered there. They noted further that preparations had begun for the slaughter of nearly 800,000 Hungarian and 3,000 Czech Jews, the latter whom the Germans had deported months before from Theresienstadt. The Vrba-Wetzler document ended up in the possession of the Jewish underground in Bratislava, which also soon acquired information from two other Auschwitz prisoners who had fled the camp, Czeslaw Mordowicz and Arnost Rosin. Mordowicz and Rosin reported about the murder of Greek Jews and the beginning slaughter of the Jews of Hungary. Smuggling the Vrba-Wetzler and Mordowic-Rosin reports, which combined would be called the "Auschwitz Protocols," to the rest of the world proved difficult.

In mid-May a Swiss Jew received a copy of a shortened version of the pro-tocols and a letter from the Slovak underground that appealed to the Allies to bomb Auschwitz and the railroad lines leading to it. Moreover, the letter proposed warning Hungary, publishing facts about the mass murder of the Jews, sending the ICRC to Auschwitz, and providing money for rescuing the Hungarian Jews.

Also the underground in Bratislava got copies of the Auschwitz Protocols into the hands of Reszo Kasztner, a Zionist member of the underground in Hungary. Kasztner did not distribute the material, however, because he feared it would destroy negotiations then underway between Hungarian Jewish representatives and the SS for the release and rescue of Hungarian Jews. Other copies sent to Budapest, however, reached the local Judenrat as well as Rotta, the papal nuncio, and Horthy, Hungary's ruler. Furthermore, the papal representative in Bratislava received a copy of the protocols and sent them to the Vatican. Since much of the latter's archives still remain closed for the Nazi period, unclear is whether the information in the protocols influenced the Pope's intervention with Horthy at the end of June, urging him to prevent the further suffering of the Hungarian Jews.

Still another copy reached an official of the Czech exile government in Switzerland, who passed it to Riegner, the WJC's representative in Geneva. Riegner in turn dispatched a telegram summary of the protocols to the British embassy in Bern, which shared the materials with Allen Dulles, the head of the OSS in Switzerland. On 16 June 1944 the State Department in Washington received the protocols, as did the BBC and Swedish government a few days later.

Allied radio beamed to Germany increasing information, much of it highly accurate, on Auschwitz and gassing methods used in killings. During the fall, articles in the Western press appeared about Maidanek, recently overrun by the Russians and shown to Allied newsmen. Also the Polish underground agent, Karski, who had earlier met with and influenced Roosevelt with his information about the death camps, published his eyewitness testimony of killings at Belzec.

Misunderstanding the Purpose of Hitler's War

For most of the war, therefore, the Allies, who fought a total war militarily against the Germans, did not do so against the "shadow war" of Hitler and his Nazi associates, the Final Solution. Clearly only a few persons in the United States and Britain, which included neither Roosevelt nor Churchill, despite their periodic expressions of sympathy for the Jews, understood about the war what the National Socialists did: that Germany had initiated the military conflict in 1939 as a cover for a huge war for global domination against the Jews and other so-called inferior peoples long planned and then waged by Hitler. In this regard, both the bystanders and most of the victims did not realize the ultimate wartime goal of the Nazis.

Also other countries, such as the neutrals Sweden, Switzerland, Spain, Portugal, and the Vatican, failed or did not want to comprehend the true nature of the war Hitler had unleashed. At the Wannsee Conference held by the SS in January 1942, the list of countries in Europe whose Jews the Nazis planned to murder included each of the European neutrals.

While these states retained formal neutrality in the war, their attitudes and actions toward the Holocaust varied dramatically. On the one hand, the Swedish government helped save some Norwegian Jews in November 1942, most of the Danish Jews in October 1943, and unprecedented numbers of Jews with Wallenberg's mission in Budapest after July 1944.

On the other hand, throughout the war the Vatican and Pope Pius XII retained a silence toward the persecution of the Jews as well as other Nazi victims. At the war's end, both the Vatican and Spain assisted German war criminals to hide or escape. Also most neutral nations had received during the war substantial property deposited in their banks by German nationals and the Nazi government. Most of the property included assets looted from the German occupied territories and victims of the Holocaust.

In 1995 longstanding suspicions that Swiss banks held money plundered from Jews during the Holocaust burst forth. Since the war's end the Allied governments, but more especially the descendants and heirs of victims of the Nazis, had pursued with Switzerland a usually unsuccessful quest to acquire from the banks the assets to which such persons were entitled. The Swiss government and bankers intentionally dragged their feet. Repeatedly they fended off demands for compensation for victims' and their heirs with lies and claims that the banks held no assets or could not locate them. Also most Swiss claimed for their nation a neutral and heroic role in the war, allegedly in assisting Jewish and other refugees.

By the 1990s, however, several factors combined to increase the pressure for restitution on countries as well as on businesses and corporations that had profited immensely from the Holocaust. Such factors included a steadily growing international movement for human rights, the collapse of the Soviet Union and the Cold War, and the discovery of new information in Russian, East European, and Western archives.

Numerous victims of World War II demanded restitution for their suffering; the Koreans and Chinese sought compensation from Japan and the Japanese Americans from the United States. The governments of Bill Clinton in the United States and Tony Blair in Britain not only supported restitution to such victims, but they also declassified large numbers of records held by Washington and London on this and other important wartime issues.

During 1995 both the United States and Britain released official documents relevant to victims' assets in Switzerland. The WJC accused Swiss banks of hoarding such properties worth billions of dollars. Banking committee hearings in the United States Congress as well as a national commission appointed in Switzerland, investigated dormant Jewish bank accounts and so-called victim gold laundered by the Nazis in the country.

Moreover, class-action lawsuits filed in the United States against Swiss banks and discussion of an American boycott directed at the banks threatened to undermine their massive volume of business in America. Finally, after extensive negotiation, during which the Swiss offered grudgingly compensation that ranged from $32 million to $600 million, in mid-August 1998 they agreed to pay $1.25 billion to claimants to dormant Swiss accounts, refugees denied Swiss asylum, and victims of slave labor who had benefited the Swiss.

Amid the episode, numerous studies of Switzerland's wartime policies made a myth of the popular belief that the country had remained neutral in the war. The key examination, a book published by a Swiss historian in 1997, concluded that Switzerland "escaped World War II by virtue of shrewd, active, organized complicity with the Third Reich. From 1940 to 1945 the Swiss economy was largely integrated into the Greater German economic area."[20]

Swiss banks had provided Nazi Germany with the foreign exchange essential to its war effort. The banks had not only laundered gold looted from the banks of occupied Europe and from the bodies of Holocaust victims, but they had also granted Germany sizable loans. Even long before the war, a number of Swiss companies had rid themselves of Jewish directors or stockholders in exchange for more business opportunities in Germany. In addition, during the war the Swiss had supplied the German military with weapons, ammunition, and precision instruments. Furthermore, dozens of artworks, some stolen from Jews in Germany and elsewhere and others sold by German refugees desperate to raise cash to flee Nazi persecution, flowed through Swiss art galleries. Also repeatedly Jews seeking entry into Switzerland—perhaps as many as thirty thousand—found the country's borders closed to them, despite the fact that Swiss authorities knew it meant likely death for the refugees.

The reasons for the Swiss behavior varied. Greed motivated most of the bankers, art dealers, and others who exploited the persecuted; during the war and after they considered looting a legal enterprise and sought, while abandoning all morality, to make as much money as possible. A latent anti-Semitism afflicted the Swiss as much or more as most other Western peoples. Also the threat that Nazi Germany posed to Switzerland's independence guided the country's policies toward the Jews. Nearly everyone in the German government took for granted that the Reich would occupy and control Switzerland after winning the war. As a result, only when the war turned against Germany during 1943 and 1944 did the Swiss yield to Allied pressure to change their pro-German policies.

Among the motivations and actions of neutral nations regarding the war and Holocaust, Turkey had a mixed record. When the National Socialists seized power in Germany in 1933, nearly 10 percent of the thousands of German academics who had lost their jobs, including liberals, communists, and some Jews, found haven and employment in Turkey. During the war Turkey pursued its neutrality with determination and sought to remain out of the struggle, yet it cooperated with the Allies. The Turks rescued and assisted Allied soldiers and airmen as well as some Greek resistance fighters and Greek Jews.

Yet the Turks had a hand in the tragedy in the Black Sea in 1942. Responding in part to British pressure, Turkish authorities had refused to allow the *Struma*, a ship loaded with 769 Jewish refugees from Rumania headed for Palestine, to dock at Istanbul. The ship was sent into the sea, where it was mistakenly sunk by a Soviet submarine, killing nearly everyone on board. At least some Turkish and British officials who dealt with the affair realized the probable result of their action before forcing the ship back into the sea.

CHAPTER SIXTEEN

RESCUE, RELIEF, AND WAR CRIMES TRIALS

DURING 1944 the turn of the war clearly in favor of the Allies increased the possibility of saving Jews who still remained targets of the Nazi genocide and of interfering with or delaying the killings. Well known is the indifference, if not callousness, of much of the world, especially the West, during the 1930s toward accepting refugees from Nazi Germany. With a few minor exceptions, during the war this general unwillingness to care about the issue continued.

Rescue and Other Attempts to Aid the Victims

Neither the United States nor Britain made rescuing Jews even a secondary objective among their war aims. The official record of the major Allied conferences held during the war at Casablanca, Teheran, and Yalta, contains no mention of the murder of the Jews. The failure of the Bermuda conference in April 1943, held to address the refugee question and Jewish persecution in Europe, was almost predetermined by Washington and London. The two allies had an implicit understanding that America's delegates would not raise the thorny issue of immigration to Palestine, while the British representatives would avoid the controversial subject of American immigration laws.

Carefully documented studies have shown that the British government adamantly refused to admit significant numbers of Jewish refugees to Britain, Palestine, or the Empire. In some instances the British sealed off the escape routes from Europe of refugees fleeing for their lives. Despite Churchill's ardent pro-Zionist sentiments, he did almost nothing to rescue Jews. Moreover, his foreign secretary, Eden, who "preferred Arabs to Jews" and was an unshakable anti-Zionist, remained unsympathetic to rescue.[1] As for the role of Anglo-Jewish rescue groups, frequently their actions followed or reflected the restrictive immigration policy of the British government. Nevertheless, because of these refugee organizations, Britain admitted a larger number of foreign Jews than might have been the case without such groups.

Britain's opposition to Jewish immigration to Palestine both at the war's end and afterward would reflect a general policy of its government, described by the lawyer and historian Louise London, to avoid any longterm responsibility for large numbers of homeless Jews or other refugees. In March 1945 the War Cabinet specifically identified Jews among foreigners to be kept from settling in Britain and receiving citizenship. The "increase in our Jewish population," said the Home Secretary, "might increase the dangers of civil disturbances" because of "a strong undercurrent of anti-Semitism in some parts" of the country.[2]

The record of the United States in rescuing Jews generally resembled the unimpressive one of its Western ally. Late in the war the initiative in the United States for rescuing Jews came from Morgenthau and the Department of Treasury. Officials in the department had uncovered evidence that the Department of State had attempted to suppress information regarding the Nazi genocide against the Jews and to sabotage rescue efforts.

On 16 January 1944 Morgenthau presented a secret report to Roosevelt that opened with a scathing attack on the State Department. "One of the greatest crimes in history, the slaughter of the Jewish people in Europe," the report declared, "is continuing unabated."[3] Morgenthau then proposed the establishment of an intergovernmental agency that would focus on the refugee problem in Europe.

Immediately the President established the War Refugee Board (WRB), headed by John Pehle, a Treasury Department official, and aided by the American Jewish Joint Distribution Committee. As part of his order creating the WRB, the President obligated the War, Treasury, and State Departments to assist the new agency. Although the WRB had little success in rescuing Jews, it nevertheless made attempts to do so.

The WRB pressed the Hungarian government not to deport its Jews; in this regard, the board also appealed to all countries that had diplomatic relations with Hungary to apply pressure on the latter. Underground Zionist youth groups in Hungary received financial support from the WRB, which assisted some of their members to escape through Yugoslavia, Slovakia, and Rumania. The WRB, in addition to establishing a temporary camp for refugees near Oswego, New York, urged neutral countries in Latin America to accept refugees. The board, furthermore, pressed Switzerland to assist the Hungarian Jews.

Such activities, long overdue by 1944, saved only a tiny fraction of the victims. One problem involved the refusal of the War Department to cooperate with the WRB. Efforts to enlist the department and the Army in rescue and relief operations met with indifference, evasion, and inaction at nearly all levels. At the end of 1943 the Army had refused to rescue approximately four thousand Yugoslavian Jews evacuated by partisans to Rab, an island in the Adriatic Sea. The American commander in North Africa "determined that the military situation" did not permit "any direct assistance to these refugees."[4] Shortly thereafter the Germans reoccupied the island and deported the Jews.

Further, the Assistant Secretary of War, John J. McCloy, rejected a proposal from Morgenthau that the Army direct its theater commanders to assist the WRB. McCloy informed the army staff that he was "very chary of getting the Army involved in this while the war is on." Stimson, for his part, objected to most of the WRB's work. Special American laws, he insisted, had been introduced after World War I to prevent the "unrestricted immigration of Jews."[5]

Recently a Welsh historian, in discussing why the democracies did not save more Jews from the Germans, maintained

> that no Jew who perished during the Nazi Holocaust could have been saved by any action which the Allies could have taken at the time, given what was actually known about the Holocaust, what was *actually proposed* at the time and what was realistically possible. If there are any exceptions at all to this statement, their numbers may be measured in the dozens or hundreds rather than in some higher figure.[6]

The most significant barrier to rescuing Jews remained the Germans.

Interference with the Killings?

What possibilities existed of the Allies obstructing the killing process? During the fall of 1943 British cryptanalysts deciphered radio messages of the

German police and SS that provided in small but significant ways locations and activities of the Nazi killing operations in Europe. If the Allies had planned to interfere with such operations, the decodes would have provided valuable information. In mid-October, the British learned of the prisoners' escape from the Sobibor camp and that the SS had taken countermeasures against it. A radio message gave the location of the camp. Such messages could have been used by the Allies to plan attempts to interfere with the killing program, but none of the Allies made a move to do so.

Both during and especially after the war, a storm of controversy erupted over the question of whether the Allies could have obstructed or lessened the killings by bombing Auschwitz and the railroad lines leading to the camp. As noted in chapter nine, in January 1941 the Polish government-in-exile had urged the RAF to bomb the camp, which then held mostly Polish prisoners. The RAF had declined, citing operational considerations and technical limitations, and did its best to preclude a political appeal by the exile government directly to Churchill or other members of the British government.

During the spring of 1944 numerous Jewish and other groups made the same request (i.e., that the Allies bomb Auschwitz and its rail lines), especially as word spread in the West that the Germans had begun the deportation to the camp of the large Hungarian Jewish community. Those pleading for help argued that the world had indisputable proof of the mass killings at Auschwitz, that the Allies had captured control of the air space over Europe, that Allied planes had the ability to reach the target, and that such attacks had the possibility of rescuing the Hungarian Jews.

Despite the appeals, none of the Allies bombed Auschwitz I, Birkenau, or their rail lines, for reasons that ranged, according to critics, from deceit to indifference. In Britain both Churchill and Eden supported a proposal of the Jewish Agency for Palestine that the RAF bomb the camp and its rail lines. But high-ranking officials in the British Air Ministry and Foreign Office advised against such action, and apparently did so without even examining the practicability of the project. The London government, in its official answer to the Jewish Agency, claimed—much as the RAF had done to the Polish exile government in 1941—that technical difficulties made the operation impossible.

Similarly, the United States refused requests that its planes attack Auschwitz. At the end of June 1944 the War Department insisted that American air forces could not spare the planes tied up in the war's military campaigns. After the war, however, critics charged that the department never analyzed the feasibility of air operations against Auschwitz. It had not asked the opinion of the air command and bases in central Italy, from which Allied planes could reach much of Europe still controlled by Germany.

Officials in the department feared apparently that relief and rescue efforts would divert air power from military purposes. Subsequent requests to bomb Auschwitz, the last in November 1944, received such arguments from the American government for refusing to do so. According to Washington, only a quick end to the war would stop the killings at Auschwitz and elsewhere.

But clearly by the early summer of 1944, as the Jewish and other groups pleading for help noted, the Allies had achieved a sufficient military position to make such intervention possible. By then the Western Powers had supremacy over the German air force, established a firm position in Normandy, and seized the crucial airfields of Italy. Moreover, Auschwitz itself was a military objective; the camp lay in the midst of a region valuable for German industrial and war production. At Auschwitz-Monowitz German industry operated a synthetic oil refinery. Seven other refineries existed within fifty miles of Auschwitz, supported by the large coal resources of Upper Silesia.

In February 1979 the American Central Intelligence Agency released long-held aerial photographs of Auschwitz-Birkenau taken by Allied planes between April 1944 and January 1945. These showed with clarity the camp's gas chambers, crematoria, and prisoners at various stages of processing. The photos were almost an accidental byproduct of pictures taken of the IG Farben plant at nearby Auschwitz-Monowitz, which produced synthetic fuel.

From July to November 1944 some twenty-eight hundred American planes bombed the refineries and other industrial installations at or near Auschwitz. En route to their targets, nearly all flew over the important rail lines along which the deportation transports carried the last of the Hungarian Jews and other victims who would die in the huge killing facilities. At least twice, on 20 August and 13 September, the planes attacked an industrial plant only a few miles from the large gas chambers.

What the practical effect of bombing Auschwitz and the rail lines leading to it would have been is problematic. On one side of the issue, the Germans had not only shown their determination to murder Jews at all costs, but the perpetrators had become highly experienced and ingenious at devising the means of doing so. Furthermore, since 1943 the killers had searched for new categories of victims, including Jews still protected by Germany's allies as well as groups such as Mischlinge and Gypsies.

It is unlikely, therefore, that such dedicated murderers would have been deterred from their work by the bombing of a few rail lines and a gas chamber. At the most, the bombings may have slowed the frenzied pace of the killings and led the Germans to switch locations, and even perhaps the methods, of the murders.

But despite such considerations, even a few air raids on the killing facilities at or on rail lines leading to Auschwitz might have served several important purposes. First, they would have demonstrated to the desperate victims where the Allies stood on their behalf, which likely would have raised the victims' morale. Second, the bombings probably would have encouraged a few more persons to assist and comfort the persecuted. Third, military attacks on the camp may have helped a number of prisoners—how many is unclear—to survive the certain death the Germans intended for them. The failure to carry out even a symbolic armed strike on the killing facilities at Auschwitz would leave an undeniable blot on the Allies' war record.

However, in apportioning or analyzing responsibility for the Holocaust, one must again not lose sight of where the overwhelming bulk of the blame lay: with the perpetrators or killers. "Any general distribution of blame, the 'we are guilty' syndrome," Weinberg has observed, "only serves to exculpate the truly guilty. And they were not to be found among the Allies."[7]

The Shocking Reality

During the final days of the war in Europe, the United States and Britain, despite their many disagreements with the Soviet Union over issues that would affect the postwar world dramatically, agreed increasingly with the Russians on at least one subject. The three allies completed arrangements to implement the nearly unprecedented policy of placing on trial war criminals after the fighting had ended.

Since 1941 the Russians had experienced firsthand the horrors perpetrated by the Nazi regime. In America and Britain the steady flow of information from various sources in Europe about German atrocities had led by November 1943 to the Allies' Moscow declaration that those responsible would be tried and punished.

But in the fall of 1944, the American and British public had hardly reacted to pictures and news articles about Maidanek, the first of the major killing centers in Poland liberated by the Red Army. The Russians had given thirty Western newsmen a tour of the former camp, whose gas chambers had not been destroyed. Widespread disbelief greeted the resulting news accounts. The latter indicated that possibly as many as one and a half million persons from all over Europe had been "asphyxiated in gas chambers and their bodies cremated in huge furnaces." Maidanek, and later Auschwitz, also liberated by the Russians, seemed far away to Westerners. Moreover, at least one American magazine disapproved of the Soviet Army's overrunning of Poland and declared about Maidanek that "the parallel between this story and . . . atrocity tales of the First World War is too striking to be overlooked."[8]

Also news of such reports seemed insignificant in contrast to the war news from both the European and Pacific fronts. There the tide of battle had turned in favor of the Allies, but fighting remained intense, especially in the Pacific. The unreality of the numbers of Jews killed contained in reports arriving from Europe contributed as well to the public in America and Britain underestimating vastly the extent of Nazi murders. A Gallup poll in November 1944 showed that many Americans thought the figure numbered less than one hundred thousand.

But the disbelief of Americans began to end during April and May 1945. Mass circulation magazines such as *Newsweek* and *Life* and newsreel films confronted the public with images showing Anglo-American troops uncovering the horrors at concentration and labor camps in western and central Germany. On 12 April, the same day that President Roosevelt died, several of America's highest-ranking military leaders toured the Ohrdruf camp in the central German state of Thuringia, where they viewed, and photographers took pictures of, the dead and dying prisoners.

The officers included General Dwight Eisenhower, commander of Allied forces in Western Europe, and generals Omar Bradley, commander of the U.S. 12th Army Group, and George Patton, commander of the U.S. 3rd Army, whose troops were advancing toward Bavaria and Czechoslovakia. About their experience at Ohrdruf, Bradley would write after the war: "The smell of death overwhelmed us even before we passed through the stockade. . . . Eisenhower's face whitened into a mask. Patton walked over to a corner and sickened. I was too revolted to speak. For here death had been so fouled by degradation that it both stunned and numbed us."[9]

Almost simultaneously, when American troops liberated Buchenwald, they found piles of dead bodies, thousands of human skeletons who had survived the camp, and disease-ridden barracks. The Allies saw for the first time crematoria, execution rooms, and "hospital" facilities used for so-called medical experiments. British forces that entered Bergen-Belsen near Hanover on 15 April encountered a raging typhus epidemic that had killed thousands of prisoners each day; to help stop the disease the British had to use bulldozers to dig mass graves and push bodies into them.

A British army review reported the shock of British troops at what they found: "There had been no food nor water for five days preceding the British entry. Evidence of cannibalism was found. The inmates had lost all self respect, were degraded morally to the level of beasts. Their clothes were in rags, teeming with lice, and both inside and outside the huts was an almost continuous carpet of dead bodies, human excreta, rags and filth."[10] The victims included primarily Jews, Gypsies, and Slavs. Survivors resembled the half-dead, many of whom died after liberation.

On 29 April American troops reached Dachau, and on 8 May they discovered Mauthausen in Austria. The Soviet Army liberated Sachsenhausen on 22 April and Ravensbrück on 30 April, both north of Berlin, and Theresienstadt on 8 May. The eyewitness testimony, photographs, and news accounts describing the camps liberated by the British and Americans, provided by Allied journalists, photographers, and prominent public figures invited to see for themselves what the Germans had done, shocked the American and British peoples.

Edward R. Murrow, the American correspondent, delivered an emotional report from Buchenwald on the CBS radio network. After describing the liberated camp, with its thousands of bodies of dead prisoners piled like cordwood, and recounting the stories of unimaginable hell at the camp of two former prisoners, a Czech physician and a French professor, Murrow said, "I pray you to believe what I have said about Buchenwald. I reported what I saw and heard, but only part of it. For most of it, I have no words."[11]

The public in the West could no longer doubt or ignore the truth of what had happened. Allied soldiers—including the Soviets—would subsequently liberate many hundreds more smaller Nazi camps. These events, which represented something much different from the war's combat deaths and massacres, substantiated what had previously been reported extensively in the West, but rarely believed. According to Gordon Craig, Americans and other Westerners "reacted with almost as much surprise as horror when they learned what" Allied troops had found in the camps.[12]

Eisenhower, after visiting Ohrdruf, wrote General George C. Marshall, the American Army Chief of Staff, and observed that "[t]he things I saw beggar description. I made the visit deliberately, in order to be in a position to give *first hand* evidence of these things if ever, in the future, there develops a tendency to charge these allegations merely to 'propaganda.'"[13] What the Western Allies witnessed in such camps, ghastly as it was, would eventually pale in comparison to the truth about the enormous numbers of victims, mostly Jews, murdered at the killing centers in Poland, that would surface soon.

Trial of the Major War Criminals: The International Military Tribunal (IMT) at Nuremberg

The revelations of such horrors helped to prepare public opinion in the West for the Allies carrying out their policy, outlined at the Moscow Conference in 1943, of placing war criminals on trial after the war. The trials, when the Allies held them at the war's end, made crimes against the Jews a part of their proceedings, but such crimes never assumed a prominent place.

This in part reflected the fact that during the war Allied leaders had generally refused or failed to recognize that the Germans had made the Jews their special target in the mass killings. Moreover, except for the Nuremberg trial of the major German war criminals in 1945–1946, most of the subsequent Allied trials did not draw wide attention, nor did they recount the full history of the mass murder of the Jews. Nevertheless, the postwar trials would provide overwhelming evidence of the Holocaust and other criminality of the Nazi regime.

During the final months of the war the United States took the lead in developing Allied war crimes policy. Washington urged that criminals involved in atrocities committed in a single region or country be returned there for trial. For persons whose crimes covered a broader geographical area, the Americans pushed to have them tried before an international tribunal. This policy of the American government stood in contrast to much of its country's public opinion, which demanded the summary execution of captured German leaders.

Both the British government and public favored declaring the leading Nazis criminals and summarily executing them. This, Churchill and Whitehall argued, was what the Germans had done to millions of victims during the war. The Americans countered that such a policy would lead to charges equating the Allies with the Nazis. The Soviet Union agreed on bringing the major war criminals to trial, but Stalin also urged arbitrarily shooting thousands of lower level German military leaders or at least imprisoning them for many years.

As for the neutral states, they wished not to involve themselves in war crimes policy. Until mid-1944 most neutrals feared retaliation from Germany if they joined the Allies in the issue. But press reports of major Nazi figures seeking asylum in neutral countries prompted the Allies to request assurances from the neutral regimes that they would not offer such protection. Only reluctantly had the neutrals given their agreement.

Several, in fact, including Argentina and Spain, refused to cooperate with the Allies and, after the war, granted asylum to SS and other German war criminals. The Vatican, moreover, assisted SS and other Nazis in escaping during 1945 and after to the Middle East and Latin America. The most grievous example was Eichmann, who fled to Argentina. According to one historian of the subject, the Holy See both provided "money and credentials" to the fleeing Nazis and pressured "South American states to accept them."[14]

President Roosevelt summarized the American position on war crimes at the Yalta Conference in February 1945. On 2 May the new American president, Harry Truman, appointed Supreme Court Justice Robert H. Jackson to represent the United States in the preparations for international trials. Jackson met with the UNWCC and traveled to Europe. At the San Francisco conference founding the postwar United Nations organization, discussion of war crimes policy among the Allies focused on the American view that an international court should try the major war criminals.

On 26 June Jackson headed an American delegation that met with British, Soviet, and French representatives in London to decide the guiding principles for trying war criminals and plan the war crimes trials. The London Conference dragged on for nearly six weeks, as the delegations argued over issues that stemmed, in part, from the differences between Anglo-American common law and the European legal systems.

Finally, on 8 August, with the war about to end in the Pacific in an Allied victory, the Allies signed an agreement "for the prosecution and punishment of the major war criminals of European Axis" by an International Military Tribunal (IMT), comprised of judges from the four Allied powers. The agreement also provided a charter for the tribunal that defined the latter's jurisdiction, the procedures for it to follow, and the crimes it could prosecute. Such crimes included crimes against peace, war crimes, crimes against humanity, and participation in "a common plan or conspiracy to commit any of the foregoing crimes."[15]

Also the charter indicted six former German organizations: the leadership corps of the Nazi party; the SS, along with the SD as an integral part; the Gestapo; the SA; the general staff and high command of the armed forces; and the Reich

Cabinet. The tribunal would convict the first three organizations and declare them criminal. It rejected the prosecution's effort to declare the general staff and high command a criminal group, although the Soviet judge opposed the decision.

The Potsdam Conference of Allied leaders, which concluded on 2 August, only shortly before the war in the Pacific would end, scheduled the tribunal to start in November. The Allies originally planned to hold the IMT in Berlin, but instead it met in the southern German city of Nuremberg. For one thing, no room for the trial existed in the former German capital, most of which lay in ruin; approximately half of Nuremberg had been destroyed. For another, there was symbolic value in the victors holding the trial in a former stronghold of the Nazi party and place where Hitler had proclaimed the infamous Nuremberg laws in 1935.

Between 18 October 1945 and 1 October 1946, the IMT tried twenty-two "major" German and Austrian political, military, and economic leaders. It convicted eleven on most or all of the charges and condemned them to death, including Göring, von Ribbentrop, Keitel, Rosenberg, Frank, Streicher, and Seyss-Inquart. Tried in *absentia* and also sentenced to death was Martin Bormann, who had escaped capture. Göring committed suicide, but the others, except for Bormann, were hanged. The court sentenced three others to life terms in prison and four to lesser imprisonment. Three Nazis, including Schacht and von Papen, were acquitted.

All of the defendants, as well as their key witnesses, denied any direct involvement in or responsibility for the persecution and killing of the Jews. Some, including Rosenberg and von Ribbentrop, even denied knowledge of the policy of extermination. Frank blamed Hitler and Himmler for the Holocaust and complained that "[t]he orders were forced upon us against our will."[16] Keitel told a prison psychologist that he was only guilty of following directives from his superior, Hitler. "For a soldier, orders are orders!" he insisted. Streicher, whose own defense counsel at Nuremberg wondered whether his vulgar anti-Semitism did not spring from a diseased mind, asserted, "This trial is a triumph of World Jewry."[17]

But once prosecutors probed beneath the surface, making use of captured German records and interrogations of witnesses, they soon discovered that most of the defendants were not just poorly informed observers of the Final Solution, but were deeply involved in it. Prosecution witnesses, especially junior German officials and security officers who had both direct experience in and knowledge of the killing program, supplied details regarding it.

Most such witnesses, in addition, were taken to Nuremberg as war criminals destined for future trials; they included Wisliceny, an SS officer in Eichmann's Gestapo office, Otto Ohlendorff, commander of Einsatzgruppe D, and Höss, the commandant at Auschwitz. Interrogations of them revealed clearly that Hitler had a hand in authorizing the Holocaust, and that he first ordered the systematic murder of some categories of Jews in the East in the summer or early autumn of 1941.

Also Wisliceny testified that Eichmann had shown him an original copy of a written directive, signed by Himmler but based on "a Fuehrer Order," dated from April 1942, to undertake the "final disposition of the Jewish question," by which was meant, Wisliceny said, "the biological extermination of the Jews."[18] Fifteen years later, Eichmann, at his trial in Israel, would confirm Wisliceny's account, but corrected it, noting that the order for the Final Solution had been issued in the fall of 1941.

Further, the prosecution at Nuremberg filled in the details of operation of the death camps and began to verify the horrific figures on the numbers of Jews killed in the Holocaust. In this regard, Wisliceny recalled a chilling conversation with Eichmann in February 1945 about what would happen to them when the war had ended: "I laugh when I jump into the grave because of the feeling that I have killed 5,000,000 Jews. That gives me great satisfaction."[19]

What had caused the mass slaughter of the Jews? Interrogation transcripts from the IMT reveal that Allied interrogators generally assumed that anti-Semitic sentiment provided a sufficient explanation for the genocide against the Jews. Ironically, even today one of the debates about the causes of the Holocaust focuses on the validity of this assumption. The evidence from the interrogations of the IMT, as Richard Overy has demonstrated, suggested two things:

First, the role of anti-semitic propaganda and language was significant in creating a mindset in Germany in the 1930s that predisposed acceptance of racial policy even in its most radical forms. The constant repetition of anti-semitic sentiment, whether fanatical Party propaganda or the casual racial aside, lodged in the collective psyche in ways that reduced the ability of a great many Germans to question race policy and encouraged them to endorse it. . . .

Second, the pre-trial material shows the extent to which those who worked within the confines of the security apparatus and the camps, with their culture of secrecy and strict obedience, and their habits of physical and verbal violence, became inured to the harsh consequences of policy, however uncongenial. Such institutions display an inherent tendency to moral degeneration wherever they are established. In such an atmosphere the journey from physical abuse to murder was brief and unremarkable.[20]

Critics of the IMT, who included Pope Pius XII and the American senator, Robert Taft, opposed trying the war criminals. Some argued that the court had no basis in history or international law and that it represented victors' justice. Other opponents of the court denounced the presence of Soviet judges on the tribunal. However, the court was solidly anchored in international law, which had previously established the criminality of aggressive war. Numerous treaties and conventions existed on the rules of warfare; these stretched back to the nineteenth century and had prescribed certain protections for POWs and civilians.

Also at the end of World War I, in the Versailles treaty the victors had declared, the German emperor and many hundreds of German officers war criminals, but had mistakenly left the Germans with the task of trying them. Only twelve of the alleged war criminals were brought to judgment by a German court, of whom a majority was acquitted. A treaty signed in 1928 by fifteen of the world's nations and later ratified by forty-six others, including the Axis powers, renounced war as an instrument of national policy.

The IMT, whose proceedings were wholly open to the world press and covered extensively by it, hardly represented victors' justice. The court provided the defendants with due process, based on procedures from Anglo-American common law. The accused received legal counsel that had access to prosecution documents and could cross examine hostile witnesses. In addition, defense lawyers called friendly witnesses and presented documentary evidence on behalf of their clients.

Allied prosecutors had for their use at the trial hundreds of thousands of documents from the defendants' own and other German files, captured at the war's end by Allied soldiers. In addition, the Allies had seized films and still photographs made by the Germans of their persecution of Jews and others. Prosecutors submitted only a small fraction of these records to the court as evidence against the accused. As noted above, the prosecution as well called to testify against those on trial numerous subordinate German officials. In addition, the court heard testimony from many survivors of the

Holocaust and countless other victims of Nazi persecution. When evidence proved weak or insufficient, the defendants received lesser prison sentences or acquittals.

In its work the IMT established an important precedent regarding the responsibility of individual political and military leaders for their actions toward others. The court tried the war criminals as individuals and refused to allow them to protect themselves by claiming they had only followed the orders of the state they served. By doing so, the IMT—and Tokyo tribunal of 1946–1948 which tried Japanese war criminals—would lay the basis for the postwar international movement for the protection of human rights against the brutal actions of nation-states and their leaders. Not only would individual governments reinforce or extend the precedents at Nuremberg and Tokyo by bringing war criminals to trial, but also in 1993–1994 the United Nations established international tribunals to hear cases arising from atrocities committed in Rwanda and the former Yugoslavia.

Other War Crimes Trials

For subsequent trials of Nazi war criminals, the Allies produced still greater masses of captured enemy records and more witnesses against the defendants. However, altogether the Allies and other countries seized, tried, and punished only a fraction of all the German and other war criminals. The UNWCC named 36,529 suspected war criminals, with most of the names collected after the war. However, as noted in chapter 17, the number of persons involved directly in the Holocaust reached at least several hundred thousand.

Trials of lesser war criminals were subsequently held by the four Allied powers occupying Germany, by other countries of the new United Nations, and by the new governments in countries that were formerly enemies of the Allies. The military tribunals established by the United States and Britain pronounced a total of more than eight hundred death sentences, of which they carried out nearly five hundred. The United States placed 1,857 persons on trial before two separate sets of courts in the American zone; between December 1946 and April 1949, twelve military tribunals sat in Nuremberg and various military courts and commissions met mainly in Dachau.

The so-called subsequent proceedings of the twelve American tribunals tried 185 criminals from various branches of the SS, the OKW, officials of Germany's Foreign and Justice Ministries, doctors, and industrial and financial leaders. The military courts and commissions tried 1,672 accused, of whom 1,416 were convicted. Altogether in the trials conducted by the Americans, the latter sentenced 450 of the guilty defendants to death and 219 to life imprisonment. Also the U.S. Army conducted war criminals trials in Italy and Austria.

In the portion of Germany occupied by Britain, the latter's military courts charged 1,085 persons; the courts acquitted 348, sentenced 240 to death, gave life imprisonment to 24, and meted out various prison terms to 473. Also the British conducted trials in Italy and Austria. The most notorious British proceedings occurred at the end of 1945; over forty SS guards, among them twenty-one women, were tried for crimes committed against prisoners at Bergen-Belsen and Auschwitz. The court convicted and hanged eleven of the accused. Altogether after the war, no more than 789 of the roughly 8,000 SS men and women who served at one time or another at Auschwitz were ever tried.

Elsewhere in the West, the French charged 2,107 persons with war crimes; they acquitted 404, sentenced 104 to death, gave 44 life imprisonment, and meted out various prison terms to 1,475. In trials in Belgium, Denmark, Luxembourg, the Netherlands, and Norway, total convictions numbered 507, of which 54 resulted in death sentences.

Already by 1947, however, as Cold War tensions escalated between the West and Soviet Union, the United States and Britain sought to curry the favor of West Germany as a counterweight against the Russians. For this and other reasons, public opinion in the West soon lost interest in the war crimes trials; when American prosecutors at the trials returned home afterward, they were dismayed to find that few of their countrymen cared even to discuss the trials. Most Americans seemed unconcerned about the punishment of the Nazi leaders for their crimes. Both during and after the IMT, the American press had downplayed the court's role in meting out justice to the war criminals. Instead, the press had focused on the importance of the tribunal for discouraging the reoccurrence of such crimes—i.e., for establishing "the criminality of aggressive war in order to prevent future conflict."[21]

The West Germans, for their part, pressed increasingly for a general amnesty for war criminals. They criticized the trials, claiming that persons tried and imprisoned by the Western Powers were not war criminals but people who had followed orders. Also Pope Pius XII actively urged clemency for convicted war criminals.

As a result, the American tribunals began passing lighter sentences and established a board of clemency. At the end of 1949 the United States paroled sixty convicted German war criminals; a few months later, it reduced the punishment of seventy-eight other Germans. By the fall of 1951, half of the war criminals convicted and imprisoned in Germany by the Americans had already been discharged. During the first half of 1952 the United States released over one hundred more. By May 1955 only forty-five war criminals remained in the American prison at Landsberg, in Bavaria.

The British conducted a clemency policy along similar lines. By the end of 1957 both Britain and France had released all war criminals held in their zones of Germany; some had been former concentration camp guards. On 9 May 1957 the Americans freed the last four prisoners in Landsberg. Only major war criminals found guilty by the IMT remained behind bars at the Spandau prison in West Berlin, primarily as a result of Soviet insistence.

The Russians, who had experienced the horror of German atrocities first-hand in the war, held the first war crimes trials as early as 1943, long before the war had ended. Shortly after Germany's surrender, the Russians placed on trial in Smolensk, Leningrad, and other cities, a number of German military officers for wholesale atrocities against Soviet civilians and war prisoners.

By January 1947, according to Soviet sources, the Russians had charged 14,420 persons with war crimes; they sentenced 138 to death and 13,060 to various other penalties. The remaining142 were acquitted. In May 1950 the Soviets indicated that 9,717 German POWs were serving sentences for war crimes, while 3,815 were imprisoned awaiting further investigations. A different source estimated that immediately after the war Russian military tribunals brought to trial in the Soviet occupation zone of Germany nearly eighteen thousand persons.

Also the countries that fell under postwar Soviet rule—Poland, Rumania, Hungary, and Bulgaria—and Yugoslavia conducted war crimes trials. In Poland, most of the war criminals had fled with the retreating German armies; consequently, only 5,450 criminals were tried there after the war. Among those tried and hanged by the Poles were several key perpetrators of the Holocaust whom the Allies had extradited to Poland, including Arthur Greiser, Höss, and Stroop.

Beginning in 1950, shortly after the creation of the Federal Republic of Germany, the Allies authorized German courts to try all Nazi crimes, even those perpetrated against Allied nationals. In most instances German judges gave the minimum punishment to the guilty. As a rule the courts refused or failed to recognize that the crimes had occurred as part of the world war. Most appalling, they did not consider incriminating the fact that a defendant had belonged to a murder squad or an extermination camp staff.

From the end of the world war to 1992, German prosecutors initiated a total of 103,823 proceedings against persons suspected of having taken part in or having committed war crimes. Of this number only 6,487 were convicted. The Germans sentenced 13 persons to death, 163 to life imprisonment, and 6,197 to temporary imprisonment. Relatively speaking, the German record in trying war criminals after World War II seemed equally unimpressive as their record in 1919–1920.

In analyzing the results of Allied war crimes policies, a leading authority on the subject has concluded:

> In many respects the punishments meted out against German criminals by Allied and German courts alike bore no relation to the horrible crimes that had been perpetrated. . . . The pardon granted to German war criminals, among them some of the most notorious, seriously diminished the significance of the program to define and punish war crimes and effectively curtailed war criminals trials as a deterrent in the future.[22]

Doubtless more war criminals would have been seized and indicted had the Allies begun preparations and put in place sooner a mechanism for capturing the criminals.

However, both the American and British governments had dragged their feet in this regard. For reasons cited in chapter 15, the Western Allies acted as though their declaration of 17 December 1942, which promised retribution for Germans involved in war crimes, meant little. From 1943 on, both the American Department of State and British Foreign Office rejected or delayed efforts to rescue Jews as well as other war refugees and did almost nothing, even at the war's end, to prepare judicial proceedings for war criminals.

Also the British provided no relevant evidence from the police and SS decodes of radio messages, which British intelligence had gathered during the war, for war crimes trials involving offenses against Jews. This not only reflected both Britain's lukewarm commitment to postwar trials and its obsession with secrecy, but it also allowed some German and Austrian police and

SS officials to escape postwar de-Nazification procedures as well as war crimes trials. Especially the decodes of German police messages had contained numerous names of and information about SS and police officials working at Auschwitz and other concentration camps.

The failure of both Britain and the United States to act on the evidence they possessed made it difficult to correctly identify targets for prosecution. Even long after the war the Allies kept much evidence secret, which damaged later investigations of war criminals and bringing them to justice. The best known example of a war criminal to escape was Eichmann. But in 1960 Israeli agents captured him in Argentina, spirited him away to Jerusalem, and there tried and executed him. Other notorious examples of criminals who evaded the Allies were Josef Mengele, the SS doctor and so-called Angel of Death at Auschwitz, and Klaus Barbie, the Gestapo chief in Lyons, France beginning in November 1942.

In June 1945 the Americans took Mengele into custody and interned him in a POW camp, but his captors failed to identify him, which resulted in his release several months later. He remained in hiding in Bavaria until mid-1949, when he fled to Argentina, then in 1959 to Paraguay, and a year later to Brazil. In 1985 forensic experts identified as Mengele the body of a man who had died six years earlier in a drowning accident in Brazil.

Barbie had worked for a time after the war in Germany as an agent for American intelligence and in 1951 emigrated to Bolivia. The Nazi hunter, Beate Klarsfeld, discovered him in La Paz in 1971, and during the following decade both German and French authorities demanded his extradition to France for trial on war crimes charges. In 1983, after a change of government in Bolivia, the new regime expelled Barbie, and he was taken to France and tried and convicted of war crimes.

Also the Western Powers provided a number of war criminals, estimated in the thousands, with a haven or home in the Allies' own countries, enabling the criminals not only to escape justice but also to build new lives and benefit from the Allied victory. These included large numbers of auxiliaries or collaborators of the Germans in the Holocaust, the so-called Hiwis, mostly East Europeans such as Lithuanians and Ukrainians who had volunteered for and participated in the killings of the Jews.

At the war's end they fled Soviet rule and exploited the chaotic conditions in Europe to emigrate to the United States, Britain, Canada, and Australia. The Western Allies, all of them opposed to Communism, had much less information about the important role such collaborators had played in the Final Solution, which meant the emigrants could pose as innocent refugees from the Soviet Union.

Most of those entering the United States brazenly lied about their pasts and, with relative ease, fooled American immigration authorities. The latter, according to a leading Nazi hunter, "were either unable or unwilling to properly carry out the necessary investigations which would have exposed the false information submitted by the criminals."[23]

Only many years later did the American government act to remove the suspected war criminals from the United States. In 1979 it established an Office of Special Investigations (OSI), which identified suspected former war criminals living in America and examined whether they had entered the country illegally. The OSI estimated that at least ten thousand criminals had immigrated to America after the war; by 1991 the agency had investigated six hundred cases and deported sixteen persons for immigration and/or naturalization violations.

Among the best-known examples was Ivan Demjanjuk, a retired autoworker of Ukrainian descent living in the United States. He had entered America illegally after the war. The OSI discovered Demjanjuk, and the United States extradited him to Israel. There a court placed him on trial in 1986 and convicted him on charges that he had killed Jews while serving as a guard at Treblinka and acting as someone known to camp prisoners as "Ivan the Terrible." In 1993, however, evidence that included testimony found in archives in the former Soviet Union persuaded the court that while Demjanjuk had been a camp guard somewhere, he was not at Treblinka. The court reversed the conviction and freed him. In 1999 the United States reopened the case against him after learning that he had worked for the SS in Sobibor.

Between 1986 and 1994 the Simon Wiesenthal Center in Los Angeles submitted the names of over seventeen hundred suspected war criminals to twelve different countries where the accused lived. Until then, hardly anyone realized that thousands of the Nazis' local collaborators in Eastern Europe in carrying out the Final Solution were living in Western and other democracies.

The Wiesenthal center helped to influence several nations to pass long overdue special legislation to provide for the prosecution of war criminals living in them: Canada (in 1987), Australia (in 1989), and Britain (in 1991).

In addition, Sweden, New Zealand, and Iceland launched special investigations of war criminals living in their countries.

But nearly everywhere such efforts resulted in few prosecutions. The work of Nazi-hunters has suffered from legal obstacles, the death of some of the suspects, a lack of documents or witnesses, and the absence or loss of political will on the part of governments to hunt and prosecute the guilty. Governments and popular opinion, except for local Jewish communities and a few others, have complained about the high cost of funding investigations and trials. Also undermining the process is the anti-Semitism of local ethnic groups, right-wing extremists, and various politicians and public figures.

The determined attempts of the few to bring the war criminals to justice contrast with the worldwide indifference of so many others. Yet despite the frustrations and disappointment of the Nazi-hunters, crucial reasons still exist for uncovering Nazis more than a half century after they committed their crimes. One Nazi-hunter, calling his work "a unique privilege," has concluded:

Although the task is getting increasingly harder, it should not be considered impossible, nor should these crimes be relegated to the history books as long as their perpetrators are still living in our midst. On the contrary, we owe it first and foremost to the victims, but to ourselves and our children as well. . . . Beyond that, we, those who have undertaken to participate in this mission, can at least find consolation in knowing that, like Mr. Wiesenthal, we will one day be able to face the victims of the Holocaust and say proudly and with a clear conscience that, 'We did not forget you.'"[24]

CHAPTER SEVENTEEN

THE PERPETRATORS: TYPES, MOTIVES, AND THE POSTWAR ERA

THE HOLOCAUST IS the best documented of all genocides. At the war's end in 1945 the Allies captured a mountain of records from the Germans' own hands and made them available to the war crimes tribunals and later scholarly researchers. These included German security service, police, Einsatzgruppen, state, party, and administrative reports and military records. The Allies seized as well a large number of photographs and even films taken of the killings by SS officials, Wehrmacht troops, and other eyewitnesses.

Today a vast array of other records exists, including diaries, memoirs, letters, court testimony, and other records of Jews and non-Jews, as well as diplomatic and Allied intelligence materials and reports of the German Socialist party in exile. All the documentation has allowed the world to study the Holocaust in a depth and detail not possible in other genocides. Consequently, one can come closer to answering questions about the persons involved in the Holocaust—whether perpetrators or victims—than in the other examples of mass human destruction.

The perpetrators included, to a greater or lesser degree, most Germans: party, government, military, business, and professional leaders involved in decision making and policymaking; many "ordinary men" who served as executioners; and everyday Germans in the population, most of whom knew of or suspected the Holocaust but supported their government to its end. Also large numbers of Austrians as well as local collaborators in Eastern Europe and the Soviet Union assisted in the killings; and as shown elsewhere in this book, the Nazis received widespread collaboration or acquiescence in their murderous policy from much of the rest of Europe.

The Germans

After the war's end, most Germans claimed they had known nothing of the Holocaust. They blamed Hitler and his closest associates in the SS and government for what had happened. The former German officials in the dock at Nuremberg and other war crimes trials either denied knowledge of the Final Solution or defended themselves with rationalizations, self-justification, and recriminations.

The Elite and Executioners

With only a few exceptions, the members of Germany's political, military, business, and professional elite collaborated closely with Hitler from the start of his regime until its horrendous end. Many such persons not only had extensive knowledge of the extermination of the Jews, but they also had a high level of understanding for and agreement with it. Traditional conservative and nationalist political figures played a significant role in putting Hitler into power and keeping him there until 1945.

Top level officials in government ministries had read since 1941 reports from Soviet Russia of the Einsatzgruppen, which recorded the units' killings of many tens, hundreds, or thousands of Soviet Jews. Even in the Foreign Ministry's remote legations abroad, such as Uruguay, some diplomats knew about the killings. Much information passed orally inside the ministry and apparently even more often outside, through friends or family members.

One longtime professional diplomat, Curt Prüfer, while in Brazil serving as German ambassador, had heard "rumors" from German and enemy sources about the "mass deportation of Jews" to the East. When he returned to Germany in the fall of 1942, following the outbreak of war between Brazil and the Reich, Prüfer learned the truth about the deportations. He responded to the news with a combination of apathy and opportunism, recording in his diary:

> This morning they told me horrible stories concerning the treatment of the Persians [an expression for Jews on Berlin's Kurfürstendamm]. Men, women, and children have been slaughtered in large numbers by poison-gas or by machine guns. The hatred which inevitably must arise from that will never be appeased. Today every child knows this in the smallest detail.[1]

As evidence that he had little conscience about the atrocities, Prüfer knowingly purchased land confiscated at the order of the German government from Jews. His behavior was not atypical of many of his fellow civil servants. Their response to the Holocaust, which ranged from indifference toward the fate of the Jews to exploiting their misfortune for one's own financial benefit, resulted primarily from the officials' old-fashioned anti-Semitism and hatred of Bolshevism.

Others among the German elite participated more directly in the Holocaust. Germany's military leaders conquered much of Europe for Hitler. Only a tiny handful of courageous officers and political leaders, led by Colonel Claus Schenk von Stauffenberg, participated in the unsuccessful plot of 20 July 1944 to assassinate the German leader. How much of the conspirators' effort resulted from their disapproval of the German government's "horrible murder of Jews," which the wife of one of the would-be assassins has asserted, is a subject of considerable scholarly debate.[2]

On the Eastern Front, numerous Wehrmacht units assisted the Einsatzgruppen and German police battalions in mass shootings of Soviet Jews. Also the Wehrmacht engaged in the vast slaughter of Soviet POWs. Directives from field marshals and the OKW to soldiers defended the killings of "Jewish-Bolsheviks." Their orders, furthermore, betrayed a widespread leak in information about the massacres and attempts to keep them secret. Many of the reasons why the German armed forces behaved in this shameful fashion are discussed in chapter nine.

Still other elite groups contributed substantially to the Holocaust. Commanders of two of the four Einsatzgruppen held doctorate degrees; a third was commanded by Ohlendorf, an economist and lawyer. German engineers designed and constructed the huge gas chambers and crematoria at Auschwitz and the other killing centers. Similarly, they built the so-called euthanasia centers, in which numerous highly educated and trained German physicians, nurses, and technicians participated in the mass murder of tens of thousands of handicapped Germans. At Auschwitz and other camps, German doctors carried out criminal and unscientific "medical" experiments on Jewish and other concentration camp prisoners and selected hundreds of thousands of Jews to die. Mengele had two professional degrees, an M.D. and a Ph.D.

Finally, executives and managers of large German industries exploited the slave labor of masses of Jews and other Europeans imprisoned by the Germans and rented to the firms by the SS. Many of the enslaved died from the heavy and exhausting work. Numerous German corporations became caught up in war production and the plunder of Nazi victims, but not solely from pressure from the Nazi leadership. Instead, most firms made a rational choice to profit from the regime and the anticipated German victory in the war. As the corporations lost their workers to military service, they decided to use forced labor, much of it Jewish prisoners who died from the work, and thus made themselves accomplices to the Holocaust.

If the elite led the way in carrying out the orders for the Holocaust, recruiting ordinary murderers from lesser ranks of society became easy. At least several hundred thousand Germans were involved in varying degrees in the procedures used in the killings of the Jews. These included the "executioners," the members of the Einsatzgruppen, police battalions, Waffen-SS, and Wehrmacht units that massacred Jews in Soviet Russia and Poland; and SS guards and other officials at the concentration and death camps. Also railroad officials responsible for transporting the Jews to the killing centers, as well as administrators, clerks, and functionaries in the SS, police, and numerous government offices helped facilitate the killings.

Many of the actual Holocaust killers were both "ordinary men"[3] and enthusiastic and "willing executioners."[4] Often they were selected at random for their murderous tasks; some were not members of the SS, had joined the Nazi party late, or had never been party members. They would kill day and night, day after day, and month after month, stopping only for lunches, sleep, and leaves to return home to their families.

Why did they do so? The old excuse that they were forced to no longer has credibility; their superiors allowed them not to participate in the killings of the Jews or to opt out once the killings began without suffering serious consequences. No one who was reluctant or hesitant received a job of such importance to the Nazi regime. Chapter 9 has shown that the killers had many motives, ranging from anti-Semitic and racial prejudices to practical reasons that included avoiding the more dangerous alternative of service at the battlefront.

Numerous Nazis, in postwar trials for war crimes, offered a defense of themselves that suggested they were normal citizens and decent people, who had acted from professional ambition or the belief they must satisfy the demands placed on them by superiors . But Eric Johnson's recent study of the Gestapo emphasizes that low-ranking police functionaries entrusted with arresting and deporting Jews were not always solely carrying out orders from above. Such "local Eichmanns," according to Johnson, had considerable freedom to charge the victims and recommend punishments, and most embraced their role in persecution and murder "cruelly, efficiently, and willfully."[5]

Browning and others studying German police units that carried out the mass killings have issued a warning to modern civilization. If such "ordinary men" could become killers under such circumstances, what group of men cannot? Most societies have traditions, some stronger than others, of racism and other forms of bigotry, the fear of war or threat of it, respect for authority, bureaucratization, striving for wealth and career advancement, and pressures from peers to conform and obey.

Yet one must exercise caution in defining what "ordinary men" mean. Langer has observed that

> the universalizing tendencies implicit in Browning's final inquiry dilute the charge of German evil by deflecting our attention from the crimes that some men committed to ones that others might have committed but did not. . . . The fact is that when ordinary men agree to mass murder, for *whatever* reasons, they cease to be ordinary men like the rest of us and assume the role of killers . . . . It may be true, as Browning argues, that "everywhere people seek career advancement"; but the corollary does not necessarily follow that they do so by killing Jews. Once they have crossed that divide, they give us graver matters to consider than whether we would have done the 'same' thing in their circumstances.[6]

The People

Among the German public, a substantial majority had at least *some* knowledge of the extermination of the Jews. The historian, David Bankier, concluded in 1992 that "large sections of the German population, both Jews and non-Jews, either knew or suspected what was happening in Poland and Russia."[7] From the very beginning of the war, people heard of the slaughter of civilian Poles and Jews. German soldiers on leave discussed how Jews were pushed into ditches and killed with hand grenades or by shooting; some Jews, the soldiers said, committed suicide to escape the agony of dying at the hands of the SS.

At the start of the German invasion of Soviet Russia, more detailed and frightening accounts circulated in Germany. Soldiers on leave often told of the murder of Russian POWs and of the fate awaiting the Jews deported to the East. By the summer and fall of 1942, widespread discussion existed regarding the work of the Einsatzgruppen, including even that of the top-secret unit, Sonderkommando 1005.

Also Hitler and other German leaders such as Goebbels repeatedly mentioned the killings in public. Their continuous demands for the destruction of "Jewish-Bolshevism" helped to condition many Germans to view the war against the Soviet Union as a world-historical struggle, in which they accepted as part of the defeat of the enemy the killings carried out by the Einsatzgruppen. Moreover, numerous soldiers and civilians had no need to imagine what was happening because they had themselves witnessed the atrocities.

Yet another source for Germans about the extermination was the foreign slave workers in various German camps and other facilities in the East. When sent to work in Germany, such workers, most of whom had seen the murders themselves or heard about them, confided their experiences to Germans they trusted or who wished to know about what was happening. If the forced laborers managed to escape, their accounts occasionally even reached the Allies.

By the end of 1941 talk had begun among some Germans about the gassing of enemies of the country. Much of the discussion occurred in relation to information about the euthanasia program. In February 1942 Victor Klemperer recounted in his diary a discussion with other Dresden Jews about the Gestapo's recent brutal search of their house, during which the intruders asked: "Why do you all get so old?—Go on and string yourselves up, turn on the gas."[8] On 2 December 1942 the leader of a small anti-Nazi group in Berlin, which helped to hide Jews, observed in her diary: "The Jews are disappearing in throngs. Ghastly rumors are current about the fate of the evacuees—mass shootings and death by starvation, tortures, and gassings."[9]

By 1943 the use of gas as a killing method was fairly widely discussed, although inaccuracies and distortions led to rumors and misconceptions about the method of the killings. A popular rumor, which reached even foreigners such as a Spanish diplomat in Berlin and a Bolivian student in Frankfurt, stated that the victims had died in a gassing tunnel or in trains into which gas was injected.

Also SS guards and others working at the extermination centers spread news of the killings, despite the fact that the SS leadership attempted to keep the Final Solution secret. Some involved in the killings openly boasted about their work. Persons living close to Auschwitz knew that the camp served as a killing center. The camp and its satellite labor camps were situated near the German border in close proximity to several German population centers.

According to the postwar testimony of Pery Broad, an SS functionary in the political section at Auschwitz, railway workers "used to tell the civilian population how thousands were being brought to Auschwitz every day, and yet the camp was not growing larger at a corresponding rate. The same information was supplied by the police escorts of the transports." Still others living near the camp knew about it, said Broad, because "the great pyres [of burning corpses] were spreading such a stench that the whole countryside for miles around had been infected. At night, the red sky above Auschwitz was visible from far away."[10] The Auschwitz railway station was nearly always filled with civilians and soldiers on leave who could not fail to notice the clouds of smoke and smell.

Moreover, thousands of German civilians found employment in and around the death and concentration camps, where firms from nearly every branch of German industry set up factories and other installations to exploit the slave labor. The British historian, Walter Laqueur, has argued that many of these civilians came to know intimate details about the mass murder taking place daily in the camps, and presumably they communicated what they knew to German friends and family members on the outside.

Allied radio broadcasts, especially BBC transmissions, which numerous Germans listened to and discussed secretly, provided still another source of information on the exterminations. The Allies, including the Russians, broadcast extremely accurate information about the fate of the Jews, including details of the gassing methods. Furthermore, during 1943 Allied planes dropped leaflets over Germany that included data on the exterminations and warned Germans about the future consequences of the atrocities.

Also German newsmen had learned about the Holocaust. In June 1943, one reporter wrote after an official weeklong trip into the occupied Ukraine and noted the death toll of Jews for only a portion of the region:

We heard entirely clear and explicit announcements about the Jewish question. Among the 16 million inhabitants of the area controlled by the civilian administration in the Ukraine, there used to be 1.1 million Jews. They have all been liquidated. . . . One of the higher officials of the administration explained the executions with the words, 'the Jews are exterminated like roaches.'[11]

Moreover, once the deportations of German Jews began in October 1941, many Germans saw most of the Jews in the Reich gradually disappear and their abandoned property or belongings taken over by Nazi party and government officials or private individuals. The Gestapo, SS, and other police did nothing to conceal the deportations. Instead, they openly marched Jews under guard through the streets, gathered them in train stations, and shipped them on public streetcars en route to the terminals from where the transports would leave.

Albert Speer, appointed by Hitler Minister of Armaments in February 1942, observed in his postwar memoirs, in which he denied knowledge of the Holocaust much as he had done at his trial at Nuremberg, that during the daily drive to his Berlin office, "I could see . . . crowds of people on the platform of nearby Nikolascee [sic] Railroad Station. I knew that these must be Berlin Jews who were being evacuated."[12]

Although Speer claimed that "an oppressive feeling struck me as I drove past,"[13] his office journal captured by the Allies betrayed that he knew of and profited from the deportations. One of his biographers noted that party members often "asked Speer to get them large apartments" of deported Jews, and he obliged.[14] At the IMT, despite Speer's protests, Höss and others identified him as one who constantly pressed the Gestapo for more concentration camp labor for the German armaments industry. Unclear is whether or not in 1978 Speer finally admitted to what he had known during the war. He purportedly told the South African Jewish Board of Deputies: "My main guilt . . . I still see today in my tacit acceptance of the persecution and the murder of millions of Jews."[15]

To counter the ever-growing information about the killings in the East, Bormann, the head of Hitler's party chancellery, felt it necessary in the fall of 1942 to issue new propaganda directives to party officials. He ordered them to combat the information by arguing that cleansing the Reich of Jews through emigration was no longer feasible because Germany's territory had expanded and the number of Jews increased. "Therefore," Bormann insisted, "the complete displacement, that is the elimination, of millions of Jews living in the European economic area is an imperative rule in the struggle to secure the existence of the German people."[16]

How did Germans respond to what they heard, read, or witnessed about the extermination of the Jews? Many who understood the policy of their government and were in a position to attempt some form of opposition or organized rescue operation did nothing. The Christian churches especially fell into this category. The Protestants, including most of the Confessing Church, asked converted Jews wearing the yellow star not to attend worship services or, failing that, to make themselves inconspicuous.

When the mass deportations of German Jews began in October 1941, Germany's Catholic hierarchy limited its intervention with the government to Catholic non-Aryans. Four months later, Wilhelm Berning, the bishop of Osnabrück, noted privately that "the plan for a total elimination of the Jews clearly exists," but he never acted on his thought of protesting from the pulpit.[17] In July 1944, a key member of the conservative resistance and plot to kill Hitler, Helmuth von Moltke, who realized that only a small portion of the deported Jews survived the killings in the East, discussed the subject with the Catholic bishop of Berlin, von Preysing. The latter, however, similar to most of the rest of the Catholic leadership, remained silent.

The vast majority of the population chose not to respond and tried not to know; they closed their eyes and ears. Some reacted with apathy and did not care sufficiently about Jews to oppose their persecution. Others feared for their own lives if they spoke up. However, Johnson's study of Gestapo terror does much to challenge the view that such intimidation discouraged ordinary people from opposing Nazism. Also Robert Gellately has concluded that the Gestapo's success was due not to the passivity of ordinary German citizens, but rather in large part to their cooperation with the police in singling out suspected "enemies" in their midst: "People cooperated when it came to enforcing anti-Semitism and the racial measures aimed at foreign workers, and they were certainly not reluctant about informing when it came to ordinary crimes."[18]

Prior to 1942 open hostility toward the Jews characterized the majority of Germans. Bankier concluded, "The Nazi policy succeeded because it was anchored in deeply rooted anti-Jewish sentiments which permeated all classes" and in German victories in the war.[19] Although numerous Germans reacted negatively to the government's introduction in September 1941 of the yellow star to be worn by Jews, they did so because when confronted with what they did not wish to see they felt obligated to change their everyday behavior. Most Germans disliked actions, even against outcast Jews, that violated their sense of order and decency. As long as the government segregated and isolated the Jews from public visibility, people could claim ignorance and deny the reality created by the anti-Semitic policy. Eventually, however, most Germans accepted the yellow badges.

Many knew, or at least suspected, that the deportations of Jews meant death for the deportees. Some Germans, who profited from the deportations, advocated and endorsed them. Others protested the deportations or simply responded with indifference. For the most part, those who objected did so not because they opposed the principle of deporting Jews, but because they disliked a particular aspect of the measure. These Germans put forth the well-known objection that "some of my best friends are Jewish" (i.e., defending the local Jews they knew but remaining silent about the deportation of others).

Only a few brave individuals criticized the deportations for humanitarian or moral reasons; these included the Catholic clergy, Cardinal Faulhaber of Munich, and the Berlin priest Lichtenberg. Some Germans, deeply affected by the persecution of the Jews and often at great risk to themselves, helped Jews to hide and survive or flee Germany. A handful of people actively and courageously opposed Hitler and joined the resistance that attempted to bring down his government.

Among these was a small circle of students belonging to the White Rose group centered at Munich University; the students denounced anti-Semitism and exposed the extermination of the Jews in anti-Nazi pamphlets they distributed. But by April 1943 the Gestapo had arrested and executed its leaders. The persecution of the Jews also appalled others in the resistance whom the Nazis executed after the 20 July 1944, such as Julius Leber, a socialist and labor leader; Bonhoeffer, the Protestant pastor; and von Stauffenberg, the officer who planted the bomb at Hitler's headquarters on 20 July.

But most Germans who disapproved of the deportations did so from self-interest. Many feared Jewish vengeance and especially Allied retribution, the latter primarily in the form of heavy air raids. Self-interest motivated numerous Berlin residents after an Allied air raid on the capital in March 1943. Thousands of homeless Berliners sat on street curbs with what few belongings they had saved; they waited for transportation and complained indignantly when trucks, which they demanded for their own use, carrying Jews to deportation trains passed by. Most German industrialists associated with armaments production also saw the Jewish question in terms of their own self-interest. They objected to deportation because of the scarcity of workers and the desire to retain Jews for forced labor.

Despite such factors and the enormous wartime propaganda of the German government blaming the Jews for the war and German suffering, beginning during 1942 most Germans responded even more with indifference and passivity to the fate of the Jews. The countless suicides of German Jews, who wished to avoid deportation, had little impact on the non-Jewish masses.

Although basic anti-Jewish sentiments pervaded the German population, Nazi propaganda failed to intensify the people's anti-Semitism. Historians have offered several reasons for this paradox. For one thing, progressive military defeats in the East and in North Africa beginning in 1942 dimmed hopes for victory and fueled progressively greater fears of enemy retribution. This increased people's awareness of being accomplices who shared the guilt and shame for what was happening to the Jews sent East, which led to greater apathy and passivity toward the victims. People hoped with such indifference to evade moral responsibility for their government's criminality.

Also thoughts of being made answerable for the atrocities by Germany's enemies existed among the Nazi leaders. This was especially true following the proclamation in January 1943 by the Western Allies of their policy of "unconditional surrender." Concern about enemy reprisals, including fears of retribution against the Reich from a Jewry allegedly determined to rule the world, pushed the Nazi officials to further killings. They had gone too far and could not turn back. Speer recalled after the war hearing Hitler tell a small group in the spring of 1943: "Gentlemen, the bridges behind us are broken."[20] Speer added that he had suspected the remark referred to the Jews.

On 2 March Goebbels explained the situation in his diary. "On the Jewish question, especially," he recounted the words he had told Göring earlier in the day, "we have taken a position from which there is no escape. That is a good thing. Experience teaches that a movement and a people who have burned their bridges fight with much greater determination than those who are still able to retreat."[21]

Hardly surprising, Goebbels made this theme a dominant one in German propaganda. Designed to push the people to the utmost wartime sacrifices, it emphasized that an enemy victory would mean a frightful enemy vengeance.

But such propaganda had limited success because it could not overcome the people's declining hopes of victory and concern about a bitter end to the war. Clearly fearful about the future, Germans responded increasingly with apathy toward both the propaganda and the Jewish issue.

Still another reason why, as the war dragged on, Germans were increasingly indifferent to the Jewish fate was that other concerns seemed more important to them. These included, according to Kershaw, "the growing pressures of war, the worries about relatives at the Front, fears about bombing raids, and the intensified strain of daily existence." Moreover, the National Socialists had successfully used policy and propaganda to "isolate" Jews from and "depersonalize" them among Germans.[22]

The Swiss historian Marlis Steinert, in a pioneering study of popular opinion in Nazi Germany, explained the apathy in yet another way. Steinert noted that "rumors, talk, and hints about mass executions were, for many individuals, ideas beyond rational comprehension."[23] On 4 February 1944 a Berlin resident recorded in her diary about the killings of Jews: "'They make them dig their own graves,' people are whispering. 'They take their clothes away—shoes, shirt. They send them to their death naked. They go naked to eternity.' This horror is so inconceivable that imagination rebels at grasping it as a reality. Some sort of contact is broken here."[24]

Despite such findings, Bernd Weisbrod, a German historian, has concluded that at the war's end a widespread sense of guilt existed among Germans. When American troops moved initially into western Germany near Aachen during the fall of 1944, they heard Germans mention frequently that the people deserved punishment because of "wrongs" done to peoples "in the East."[25]

In a similar fashion, Johnson asserted that "millions of German citizens did come to know about the mass murder of the Jews before the war was over. . . . [B]y early 1943 at the latest, the sources of information about the mass murder were so plentiful, so detailed, and so credible that it became difficult for millions of Germans not to know and not to know a lot."[26]

The Postwar Era

Whatever the responses of most Germans during the war to their government's genocide of the Jews, whether it was indifference or hostility toward the victims or participation in the killings, they had complied willingly, some more than others, with Nazi ideology and policy. An equally sad and dark legacy of the Holocaust resulted from the longtime postwar response of Germans to the war crimes perpetrated by many of their officials and others. In the words of a prize-winning book in 1997, the Nazi past produced a "divided memory" in the two postwar Germanys and one that was influenced significantly by Cold War politics.[27]

In the Soviet-dominated East German regime, the German Democratic Republic, the Stalinist dictatorship deliberately kept the people from any real engagement or confrontation with the Nazi past. Stalinist ideology explained National Socialism as a tool of Western capitalism and not as an independent set of ideas that had its own goals, chief of which was the destruction of enemy "races" such as the Jews. Consequently, most East Germans did little after 1945 to confront or address the Holocaust and their role in it.

West Germans referred often in the postwar era to 1945 as *Stunde Null*, a historical *tabula rasa* created by the war's end and establishment four years later of the democratic Federal Republic. But some German as well as foreign critics have questioned the validity of this claim. The critics pointed to continuities between the Nazi regime and Bonn Republic and to the failure, as well as the refusal, of many Germans "to come to terms with" or "work through" the past. After 1945, for example, most of the so-called German Christians, the small but influential Protestant movement in Hitler's Germany that had tried to unite its depraved racial version of Christianity with National Socialism, returned to the German Protestant Church with few, if any, questions asked.

Still other critics emphasized that postwar West Germany built its democratic values and economic successes not on reconciliation with the Jewish and other victims of Nazism, but "on a swampy mire of national guilt and confusion over the events of the Holocaust."[28] In at least one instance regarding the non-Jewish victims of Nazism, the Bonn regime did not alter views from the Third Reich. Registration files for Gypsies created during the Nazi era were transferred to postwar successor agencies, and police surveillance of Gypsies continued in German states such as Bavaria. Such practices, Sybil Milton concluded, "only proves that stereotyping, scapegoating, and persecution had not ceased with the collapse of the Nazi regime and were still endemic in the German political landscape."[29]

The International Military Tribunal at Nuremberg, which tried the major Nazi war criminals, had little effect on the attitudes of most Germans toward both the Holocaust and Nazism. They generally viewed the IMT and subsequent war crimes tribunals as victors' justice and refused to believe the mass of evidence presented by Allied prosecutors showing German war crimes. Few such attitudes changed when the Allies forced some Germans at the war's end to view the masses of dead in the former concentration camps. Thirty years later a noted German historian would write: "The IMT was not an international court of justice but a victor's tribunal."[30]

Indeed, for several decades after the war, West Germans responded to the Holocaust by seeking to deny, repress, or simply forget what had happened rather than confront it. It is worth recalling, in this regard, that the Germans had not been the ones to end the Holocaust, nor had they returned themselves after 1945 to democracy; the responsibility for these events rested with the victorious Allies. Unlike fascism in Italy and later Spain and Bolshevism in the former Soviet Union and Eastern Europe, National Socialism was not defeated indigenously.

In West Germany anti-Semitism persisted long after the war, and indeed even after the reunification of 1989. A 1987 survey found 33 percent of the population potentially anti-Semitic, 12 percent strongly so, and 7 percent vehemently so. The images of Jews held by Germans had changed little since the two decades after the world war; a substantial number of Germans, approximately 30 percent, viewed Jews negatively as "calculating," "shrewd," and an "oversensitive group that sticks together."[31]

Although by the end of the 1980s young and better-educated West Germans increasingly accepted Jews, relatively few of those polled (12 percent) claimed to know Jews personally. Also connections still existed in the Federal Republic between its anti-Semitism and the people's rejection of guilt for the Holocaust and wishes to end discussion of the past. Following reunification, studies on anti-Semitism conducted during 1990–1991 concluded "that East Germans were less anti-Semitic in all areas of prejudice than West Germans."[32]

Ernestine Schlant, an American scholar of modern German literature, concluded "that despite increasingly available knowledge about the Holocaust, Germans individually and collectively have been unable to work through and to mourn the crimes perpetrated, if working through demands 'the possibility of judgment' that is 'argumentative, self-questioning, and related in mediated ways to action.'"[33] Most West German novelists from 1949 to 1990 employed various strategies to circumvent, repress, or deny knowledge of the Holocaust. Such writers, according to Schlant, including even Günter Grass and Heinrich Böll, produced a consistent "literature of absence and silence contoured by language."[34]

With rare exceptions, similar sentiments and efforts have characterized the German public's attitudes toward the Holocaust. Between 1946 and 1948 widespread avoidance or repression by Germans of the Holocaust helped, among other factors, to undermine the Allied de-Nazification campaign. There was hardly a former Nazi who, to avoid punishment by de-Nazification, could not count on friends and contacts to provide letters of support and character references.

Although the postwar de-Nazification procedures generally failed to uncover and punish local former Nazis, the four postwar powers occupying Germany banned the Nazi party and successor organizations. This would help free the new West German regime after 1949—as well as today's reunified state—of the threat of extreme rightist parties of the type that had destroyed the Weimar Republic.

Nevertheless, while the small neo-Nazi parties that emerged beginning in the 1950s had only limited success, barely 11 percent of West Germans approved of their government's concluding of an agreement in September 1952 with Israel to pay 3.5 billion marks to the Jewish state as "compensation" for the Holocaust. The United States pressed the Chancellor of the Federal Republic, Konrad Adenauer, to complete the agreement by indicating that doing so would assist the admission of West Germany to the North Atlantic Treaty Organization.

Adenauer, in contrast to Germany's leaders after World War I, who had gone to great lengths to avoid paying reparations, a policy that had produced disastrous results for the Reich and other European states, realized that Germany would benefit if it paid reparations to the victims of Nazi barbarism. He extended compensation as well to individual families; by 2000 Germany had awarded nearly 105 billion marks to Jewish victims .

German corporations that had profited enormously from the Holocaust, however, would only agree much later to compensate Jews and others whom the companies had exploited for slave labor or other purposes. They would do so in December 1999, when forced by political and economic pressures similar to those exerted shortly before on Swiss banks by the United States government and Jewish organizations. Nearly seventy German corporations agreed to pay ten billion marks (approximately $5.2 billion) to hundreds of thousands of persons used by the Nazis for forced labor, many of them Jews, or plundered in other ways by the companies.

Moreover, as the corporations came under greater scrutiny regarding their possible links to the Nazis and Holocaust, at least six—Allianz, Degussa

A.G., Bertelsmann, the Deutsche Bank, Ford, and Adam Opel (the German subsidiary of General Motors)—hired prominent historians and other researchers to investigate their business dealings during the Third Reich. A senior official at the National Archives in Washington, Greg Bradsher, commented on the race by the firms to find incriminating or other embarrassing material before others did: "If I was general counsel for one of these companies, I would be looking to find everything I could."[35]

During the early 1960s a significant majority of West Germans, in addition to their disapproval of reparations payments, opposed the so-called Auschwitz trials in Frankfurt/Main, held to prosecute SS members who had operated the death camps. However, the visit in December 1970 of the West German Chancellor and Social Democrat, Willy Brandt, to the memorial in Warsaw for victims of the Nazi destruction of the ghetto during 1942–1943 represented a genuine expression of mourning for those who died in the Holocaust. Brandt received worldwide recognition when he dropped to his knees at the memorial and bowed his head. The first high official of the Federal Republic to travel to Poland, he had done so ostensibly to sign the Polish–West German treaty as part of his new Eastern policy (*Ostpolitik*) of rapprochement with the Soviet bloc nations and Russia.

Meanwhile, between 1965 and 1979, the West German parliament, the Bundestag, debated the extension of the statute of limitations for bringing to trial Nazi war criminals. But the parliament only finally abolished the statute altogether after the airing in the Federal Republic of the American television series *Holocaust*. The film reenacted the experience in Nazi Germany of both a German and a Jewish family, the members of the latter dying in a death camp. The film captured West Germans' attention, moved the conscience of many, and stirred a public debate on an unprecedented scale.

Nevertheless, the 1980s witnessed an upsurge of neo-Nazi revivalism. In 1983 the magazine *Der Stern* caused a national sensation by publishing the "diaries" of Adolf Hitler, which the German Federal Archives soon pronounced a forgery. The news that Mengele, who had killed or selected for death hundreds of thousands of Jews at Auschwitz, had died in Brazil produced a mass of apologias from Germans who denied Nazi crimes and who portrayed the German people as victims of Nazism.

Also when Rudolf Hess, Hitler's deputy Führer until 1941 and the last of the major Nazi war criminals imprisoned at Spandau in West Berlin, died from suicide, rightist groups in West Germany accused the Allied powers of murdering him. During the spring of 1985 the Bundestag passed the so-called

Auschwitz lie law, which made it criminal to claim that Auschwitz never existed. Since the 1970s an increasingly vocal group of anti-Semites, neo-Nazis, and other xenophobes in West Germany—and elsewhere in the West—had denied that the Holocaust had happened.

The German parliament, however, severely diluted the "Auschwitz lie" law by linking its passage to the issuing of another law that made it equally criminal to deny that Germans were expelled at the end of World War II from Germany's former eastern territories. The law as it still stands today thus equates the denial of Auschwitz with denial of the expulsions of Germans from Eastern Europe.

At nearly the same moment, the Bundestag voted 398 to 24 favoring the controversial visit of the American President, Ronald Reagan, to the German military cemetery at Bitburg. Included among those buried at the cemetery were forty-nine members of the Waffen-SS. The conservative German Chancellor, Helmut Kohl, incensed by the Allies' refusal to invite him to ceremonies at Normandy commemorating the fortieth anniversary of the D-Day landings, insisted that Reagan go to Bitburg.

In the United States, when the scheduled visit became public, the news prompted massive demonstrations of Jewish groups, veterans' organizations, and outraged citizens as well as opposition from a large majority of American congressmen and senators. They urged Reagan to cancel the trip. But in Germany a number of newspapers and magazines, reminiscent of forty years before, alleged that the American Jewish community had immense powers and sought to change Reagan's plans. Also the press accused the Jews of persisting in a vendetta against the peace-loving Germans. Such great influence usually attributed to Jews by anti-Semites and others proved imaginary once again. Reagan visited Bitburg on 5 May 1985.

Three days later Richard von Weizsäcker, the President of the Federal Republic and son of the former secretary of state in Hitler's Foreign Ministry, delivered a speech commemorating the fortieth anniversary of the end of World War II in Europe. "All of us," said Weizsäcker, "whether guilty or not, whether old or young, must accept the past. We are all affected by its consequences and liable for it. . . . We must understand that there can be no reconciliation without remembrance."[36] A large majority of the West German people, however, did not share his view. One year later public opinion polls revealed that barely 12 percent of them agreed with their President about the importance of remembering "the past."

Perhaps reflecting the growing importance of this issue, between 1985 and 1988 a war of words exploded among prominent West German historians, resulting in an affair known as the "historians' controversy" (*Historikerstreit*). The matter revolved around the publications of two well-known scholars, Andreas Hillgruber, a Cologne historian, and Ernst Nolte, a Berlin political scientist who had written previously on the rise of fascism. Hillgruber equated the Nazi genocide of the Jews with the defeat of the Wehrmacht by the Soviet army in 1944–1945. The Holocaust and Germany's disappearance from the East, he suggested, had weakened Western civilization by destroying its key Central European element, by which he meant both German and Jewish.

Nolte went even further. Not only did he attempt to "normalize" the Holocaust within the framework of twentieth-century history, but he also argued that the Holocaust was neither unique nor a German national crime. He alleged that the Final Solution had originated in the mass killings of Soviet citizens perpetrated by the Bolsheviks and Stalin. Hitler, Nolte maintained, was driven to murder the Jews by his own fear of what the Russians might do to Germany if they were victorious.

Furthermore, Nolte asserted, world Jewry had declared war on Nazi Germany in 1939. His remark that "Chaim Weizmann's statement in the first days of September 1939, that in this war the Jews of all the world would fight on England's side" cannot and should not be interpreted in any other way. Nolte then alleged that Weizmann's words provided "a foundation for the thesis that Hitler would have been justified in treating the German Jews as prisoners of war and thus interning them."[37]

Both Nolte and Hillgruber contended that Auschwitz was no different from the Allied bombing in February 1945 of the German city of Dresden or of Hiroshima six months later. The Jewish victims of Hitler's Germany, Nolte insisted, were similar to the Armenians massacred by the Turks in 1915–1916 and the peasant landowners and Ukrainians killed by Stalin during 1929–1933.

Such illogical and misinformed views held by establishment historians produced a storm of controversy in West Germany. The Frankfurt social philosopher, Jürgen Habermas, as well as several West German historians such as Hans and Wolfgang Mommsen and Hans-Ulrich Wehler, refuted the claims. They noted that Nolte and Hillgruber robbed the Holocaust of all particular meaning by equating it with other so-called similar events. The intention, the critics showed, was to revise history by relativizing or normalizing the Holocaust.

The "historians' controversy," however, indicated that the place of the Holocaust in the Federal Republic's history and political life had changed; the issue had now become one of national public debate. In 1988 public pressure forced Philipp Jenninger, the president of the Bundestag, to resign following a speech he presented on the fiftieth anniversary of the Kristallnacht. During his address, it appeared to many that he used Nazi language in an effort to promote understanding and justification for the savage pogrom.

A year later the Holocaust dominated numerous debates among Germans about the reunification of their country, which soon followed the collapse of the Berlin Wall. Günter Grass opposed unification. He argued against "a new version of a unified nation that in the course of barely 75 years, though under several managements, filled the history books, ours and theirs, with suffering, rubble, defeat, millions of refugees, millions of dead, and the burden of crimes that can never be undone."[38] In contrast, Martin Walser, another popular West German writer, favored reunification. Walser insisted that his country's stable democracy and membership in the Western alliance illustrated that Germans had learned the main lessons of their history.

For other Germans reunification marked what they hailed as a new beginning in German–Jewish relations. A number of Soviet Jews arrived in Berlin and Frankfurt in the late 1980s and early 1990s, joining immigrant Jews already there from Eastern Europe. Today possibly as many as one hundred thousand Jews live in Germany, of which approximately half are unaffiliated or not registered as Jews.

Still, during the 1990s the complex relationship of Germans to their Nazi past and to Jews remained ambiguous. On the one hand, the award-winning movie Schindler's List, Hollywood's version of the story of the Moravian-German manufacturer of enamelware who, during the war, managed to save about one thousand Jewish workers in his Polish factory from Auschwitz, played to huge audiences in Germany. The reception in the country of Goldhagen's book, Hitler's Willing Executioners, whose German translation appeared in August 1996, was unparalleled for books on the Holocaust and largely mirrored that in the United States. While the German public received the book and its author with enthusiasm, most German historians criticized the volume for the same reasons that most American scholars had attacked it.

Also Jewish culture has attracted the interest of increasing numbers of Germans. Some young German Jews and Jews writing in German discuss living in post-Holocaust Germany and how they want to be viewed and accepted there—"not," in Schlant's words, "as objects but as subjects of their own history with voices of their own." Even a few German writers, among them W. G. Sebald in his book, *The Emigrants*, which reconstructs the lives of several German Jews in exile, have begun to mourn the destruction of Jews in Germany—"a unique achievement in German literature," according to Schlant.[39]

On the other hand, one finds disturbing and worrisome the endless debates and recriminations among Germans about locating a Holocaust memorial and Jewish Museum in Berlin, reunified Germany's new capital. These and similar controversies about remembrance and memorialization, which are discussed in chapter eighteen, not only illustrate the general knowledge of Germans about the Holocaust, but also their problematic attitudes—avoidance, circumvention, repression, or insensitivity—in confronting it.

Similarly, the opening in Hamburg in March 1995 of an extensive photographic exhibition titled "The German Army and Genocide" unleashed a storm of public criticism. Since the war the Wehrmacht's role in the Holocaust had received little attention. For various reasons, including the popular place of the armed forces in German history, such forces had represented to Germans the millions of good people among them as opposed to the bad hundreds of thousands in the SS that had committed the war crimes. But both the exhibit and the meticulous archival work of historians at the German Military History Research Office in Freiburg exploded this fantasy about the armed forces. These carefully documented the systematic nature of the violation of the laws of war on the part of the Wehrmacht and many ordinary soldiers.

Also revelations and denials continued regarding the Nazi past of prominent figures in the German professions. During 1993 doctors from Germany, the United States, Canada, and Israel campaigned against the election of Dr. Hans Joachim Sewering, a leader in German medicine for many years, as president of the World Medical Association. Critics charged that Sewering, while a young physician in the Third Reich and early member of the SS, had sent in 1943 a teenage girl to death at Eglfing-Haar, "a well-known euthanasia center of the Nazis."[40] Sewering denied the accusation.

Postwar silence about the complicity of German academics in the Nazi regime produced a different controversy. In 1998 a group of young historians attacked the previous generation of leading university professors, which included Wehler, Jürgen Kocka, and the Mommsen brothers, for not having questioned the Nazi past of their mentors. The latter, namely Theodor Schieder, Werner Conze, and Karl Dietrich Erdmann, were accused of having provided, while young historians in Hitler's Germany, justification for Nazi expansionism in the East and possibly even genocide. After 1945 the three had remained silent about their collaboration with National Socialism, and each became a leading figure in West Germany's historical profession.

Of greater concern since the 1990s, however, have been the steadily mounting incidents of racial violence and hatred in Germany. Neo-Nazis and skinheads, some of them young East Germans still disoriented and uneducated about Nazism, have killed foreigners living and working in the country, attacked and beaten them in their homes, and behaved reminiscent of Nazi gangs during the Weimar and Nazi years. The attackers, furthermore, targeted Jews with their violence, setting synagogues afire, desecrating Jewish cemeteries, and sending death and bomb threats to Jews.

Ordinary German citizens have reacted to the hate crimes in a mixed fashion. Although occasionally in the past large numbers of the population protested the violence, recently a similar response from the people has resulted only after earnest pleas for it by some civic leaders. Moreover, while the German government has moved toward banning the neo-Nazi National Democratic party, conservative politicians have whipped up a national debate on immigration and insisted that minorities must adopt German culture. That amounts to "verbally playing with fire," Paul Spiegel, a Jewish leader in Germany, has warned.[41]

Peter Gay, the distinguished American historian whose family fled Nazi Germany after the Kristallnacht, mentioned in an address in Munich in January 2000 an example of what he termed a continued naiveté among many Germans about the history of the 1930s. Gay discussed

a conversation I had in Berlin several years ago with an influential and intelligent German public servant who had a good knowledge of history, and whom I had come to know fairly well. One evening he asked me, evidently ill at ease, why German Jews had gone like lambs to the slaughter. This made it plain to me that even among well-informed Germans there must be many who had not an inkling how Jews had lived in Nazi Germany, how little such Germans knew about their former fellow citizens, and how the world outside the German dictatorship looked to the German Jews; it was for them a world that was reluctant to accept as immigrants lawyers and businessmen who, for the most part, knew only German.[42]

Six months after Gay's appearance in Munich, an incident in Germany seemed to lend greater credence to his view. A prominent German cultural foundation awarded the historian Nolte one of Germany's most prestigious literary prizes named for West Germany's first chancellor, Adenauer.

Although many Germans have attempted to come to terms with the Holocaust, and some contemporary writers and others mourn the destruction and loss of the victims and acknowledge the Jewish presence in Germany, today the issue still divides the people. Most who admit the truth about what happened in the death camps do so with a feeling of shame and sorrow, but substantially less of those who still believe that reports of the camps were exaggerated feel similarly.

The continuing interest of both Germans and others in the heritage of Germany's past is not surprising. But unlike the country's first experiment at democracy in the 1920s, the present Federal Republic has individuals and groups who recognize the dangers posed by extremists for a civilized society. Moreover, Germans have important incentives to avoid another world war: the crushing defeat of their nation in 1945 that left no doubt—unlike in 1918—it had lost the war; the prosperity and freedom most of them enjoy; and the subsequent reintegration of their country into a new European-wide political and economic system. Shortly after the reunification, Weinberg wrote about "a new Germany in a new world" and concluded: "The legacy of the past cannot and will not and should not disappear; the appropriate prescription after half a century is amnesty, not amnesia."[43]

The Austrians

In their Moscow Declaration of 1 November 1943, the Allies described Austria as "the first free country to fall victim to Hitlerite aggression" and promised to reestablish "a free and independent Austria" after the war.[44] For

many years following the war the Austrians portrayed themselves as the "first victims" of Nazi aggression, when Hitler completed the Anschluss in March 1938.

In reality, however, Austria actively courted the German annexation,
and when it happened in 1938 enormous crowds of Austrians welcomed it.
A majority of Austrians supported the Anschluss arrangement and the
German effort in the war to the end. Between 1938 and 1943 the Nazi party
enrolled proportionately far more members in Austria than in the Germany
of pre-1938 borders. Although Austria's population of nearly seven million
made up only 8 percent of the population of the Greater German Reich,
approximately seven hundred thousand Austrians joined the party; by 1945
they comprised 14 percent of the SS.

Far-reaching and deeply rooted anti-Semitism played a major role in
Austrians' broad support of Hitler. Many of them hoped that he meant what he
said when he promised that he would settle accounts with the Jews. The overwhelming majority of Austria's Jews lived in Vienna. During 1938 the extent of
the anti-Semitic violence in the city that accompanied the Anschluss, in which
large mobs joined Nazi gangs in the savagery, shocked even the Germans.

During the Kristallnacht in Vienna, much more than in any other city
of the Reich the crowds attacked, beat, robbed, and humiliated Jews. Faced
with perpetual terror and wholesale expropriation of their wealth, Austrian
Jews had little doubt that they must get out of the country as quickly as possible. Well over half managed to flee the country between 1938 and 1941.

Once the deportations of Austrian Jews began in the fall of 1941, crowds
of Austrians often lined the streets of Vienna shouting their approval as
trucks loaded with Jewish men, women, and children passed in broad daylight
on their way to the railroad stations. How much the onlookers knew about
the fate of the deported Jews is unclear. According to Evan Bukey, who has
written about popular sentiment in Austria in the Nazi era:

> Although ordinary Viennese had no knowledge of these dreadful plans,
> there is little reason to suppose that a large number would have disap-
> proved. This is not to suggest that the silent majority would have coun-
> tenanced mass murder; most Viennese simply wanted the Jews to
> disappear. Nevertheless, it would be foolish to presume that many of
> them imagined the Jews would escape harsh treatment. Given the mag-
> nitude and intensity of popular anti-Semitism, massive expulsion was
> simply the next logical step.[45]

Moreover, Austrians comprised some 40 percent of those involved in killing operations, both in the T4 euthanasia program and at the death camps. For the Austrian Jews the Anschluss and war were catastrophic. The Nazis forced almost 130,000 Austrian Jews to leave their home and country; 65,459 remaining Jews died in the Final Solution.

After the war, despite the establishment of a parliamentary democracy in Austria, extensive anti-Semitism persisted in the country. The approximately 4,500 Jewish concentration camp survivors who returned to Austria beginning in the summer of 1945 received little sympathy. Part of the reason for this was that, at the time, some six hundred thousand former Austrian members of the Nazi party, SS, and SA lived in the country and with their immediate families made up one-quarter of the population.

Most Austrians blamed the Germans for their suffering and the Holocaust and never reexamined their own strong prejudices or collaboration with the Germans in what had happened. The postwar Austrian government confronted the problem of deeply rooted anti-Semitism in the country either by denying it or promising to curtail it. Both during and after the Allied occupation of Austria, which ended in 1955 with the reestablishment of Austrian sovereignty, the country's federal and state governments had an extremely weak record for de-Nazification and trying Nazi war criminals. By 1948 the government had amnestied 90 percent of former Nazi party members and by 1957 nearly all the others, including Gestapo and SS officials.

Also the government only slowly after 1955 agreed to pay reparations to victims of political persecution in the war, but compensated persons who were nonresidents with barely a fraction of the value of their property. Even before the victims were compensated, the government had restored in 1952 the property of former Austrian Nazis. The Austrians accepted only a moral, not a legal, responsibility for making compensations, a position they continued to hold to in the 1990s.

Although a Jew and socialist, Bruno Kreisky, served as Austrian chancellor from 1970 to 1983, he repudiated many specifically Jewish concerns and even appointed in his first government several former members of the Nazi party. In 1986 the Austrians elected as President Kurt Waldheim, the former Secretary-General of the United Nations. They did so even though it had been discovered that Waldheim had neglected to mention the more embarrassing aspects and "missing years" of his wartime activities.[46] He had concealed his wartime service in the Balkans as a German officer, first as part of a unit that had massacred Yugoslavian partisans and then in Greece, when Greek Jews were being deported to Auschwitz.

The Waldheim affair produced an international outcry, placed in question Austria's memory of the Anschluss and war years, and focused worldwide attention on the issue of Austrian complicity with Nazi Germany. In 1990 the Vienna government allocated almost two hundred million dollars in financial restitution to Jewish victims of Nazi persecution. But many Jews and others viewed the settlement as inadequate. Some Holocaust victims continued to demand a greater amount from the government and Austrian companies that had seized the property and assets of the victims during Nazi rule.

Furthermore, public opinion polls during the 1990s revealed several disturbing things. Anti-Semitism had increased among Austrians, as had their disapproval of the continued prosecution of Nazi war criminals and desire for an end to further discussion of the Holocaust. The polls showed as well that a third of the people still viewed Austria as Nazi Germany's "first victim." At the beginning of 2000 the European Union and United States condemned the inclusion in a coalition government in Vienna of the extreme rightist and xenophobic Freedom party. Jorg Haider, the party's leader and governor of the southern province of Carinthia, had once expressed admiration for the SS and Hitler's labor policies and consistently opposed immigration in Austria.

Collaborators in the Holocaust

During the war, in the German-occupied Eastern territories local peoples frequently joined the Germans in the mass killings of Jews. The enormity of the killings and the sheer brutality with which the killers carried them out meant that numerous local persons witnessed or at least heard about them, and some collaborated in the slaughter. In Lithuania , the Ukraine, and Byelorussia, many local men, called by the Germans "Hiwis," at first volunteered to join the Germans as armed police auxiliaries or accomplices to assist the Germans in the persecution and murder of Jews. Eventually the SS recruited several hundred thousand such collaborators. These included the "Trawnikis," some of whom worked as guards at the killing centers and labor camps in the General Government and at Auschwitz.

Eastern Galicia, for example, was a region comprised mainly of Poles and Ukrainians. The local population often spontaneously murdered Jews, contrary to assertions that no pogroms ever started without German influence.

By May 1942 transports of Jews from eastern Galicia began to arrive at Belzec; there more than a quarter of the region's Jews died. But what distinguished Galicia in the Holocaust was that the primary means of killing Jews remained mass shootings, even long after the killing centers existed. One in eleven Jews who died in the Holocaust lived in eastern Galicia; of 540,000, only 2 to 3 percent survived.

What motivated some of the Poles, Ukrainians, Byelorussians, and Baltic peoples to join in the killings? While few identified wholeheartedly with the Germans, they showed even less sympathy for the conditions of the Jews. Both the Poles and Ukrainians had long traditions of anti-Semitism, and both associated the Jews with the Bolsheviks. The Ukrainian anti-German underground provided little support for Jewish partisan groups, and Ukrainian citizens frequently reported on Jews they found in hiding. Just as often, Ukrainian partisans slaughtered Jews who had managed to escape the German destruction of the ghettos. Some Poles, too, murdered Jews, as for example at Jedwabne, or assisted the Germans in the killings. Partly for these reasons, the German architects of the Holocaust chose Poland and Russia as the principal sites for it.

Most of the local collaborators in the East acted for one or more reasons: fear of the Germans if they did not cooperate, anti-Semitism, sadism, and a desire to profit personally from the killings. Once the collaborators had cast their lot with the Germans and participated in the mass horrors of genocide, they discovered, much as the Germans did, that there was no turning back or quitting. Polish participation in the Jewish persecution would undermine post–World War II claims of many Poles that Poland had been an innocent victim of Nazi aggression.

Similar to the SS and other Germans involved in the mass killings, the local police and other collaborators believed that their only hope of survival depended on their continued killing of Jews and a victory in the war. After the war most of the collaborators escaped punishment. With the rapid onset of the Cold War, many escaped to the West and settled there by disguising their identities, falsifying immigration papers, and masquerading for the Western Allies as informers against the Soviet regime.

CHAPTER EIGHTEEN

THE VICTIMS: DESTRUCTION, RESISTANCE, AND MEMORY

NEARLY ONE-THIRD of the world's nineteen million Jews perished in the Holocaust. World War II, which Hitler started, made possible his massive "shadow war" against the Jews. According to the most reliable estimates, a minimum of 5,290,000 and maximum of slightly over 6 million Jews died. Numerous European countries lost 70 percent or more of their Jewish population: Poland (2,700,000, 90 percent); Yugoslavia (65,000, 90 percent); Greece (59,185, 83 percent); Slovakia (70,000, 79 percent); Hungary (550,000, 76 percent); the Netherlands (102,000, 73 percent); Germany (165,000, 70 percent); the Protectorate (77,297, 65 percent); Rumania (211,214, 48 percent); the Soviet Union (2,100,000, 45 percent); Norway (758, 42 percent); Austria (65,459, 35 percent); Belgium (28,518, 32 percent); France (76,134, 25 percent); Italy (6,513, 19 percent); and Denmark (116, 0.019 percent). Additionally Luxembourg lost 1200 Jews and Albania lost 591.

Destruction of Those Who Survived

After the war few of the Jewish survivors of the Holocaust returned to their former homelands. Poland provided an example of the fate of the survivors from Eastern Europe. Warring German and Soviet armies had left enormous physical destruction in Poland and primarily the Germans the death of nearly three million Polish Jews and several million more Poles.

At the war's end barely three hundred thousand Polish Jews had survived and lived in desperation in the country, with its new borders pushed farther west. But the liberation of Poland by Red Army troops had not ended the country's anti-Semitism. Many Poles had profited materially from the Jewish persecution and concerned themselves with securing control over stolen Jewish property.

When the Polish Jews attempted to resettle in their homeland, pogroms prevented them from doing so, such as the one in Krakow in August 1945 and the most violent one in Kielce on 4 July 1946, which killed forty-one Jews. The Poles expelled other Jews, many of whom eventually emigrated to Palestine, the United States, and Australia. Only five thousand Jews, mostly the ill and elderly, remained in postwar Poland.

Many other Jewish survivors had a similar experience. By the end of 1946 more than 150,000 Jews had moved into "Displaced Persons" (DP) camps in Germany and Austria operated by the Allies. Some Jewish DPs had fled Poland after the Kielce pogrom while others had migrated westward from the Soviet Union and Soviet-held territories. A portion of the DPs had survived the death camps, usually in a condition more dead than alive. But once in the DP camps, they often encountered poor conditions, including low rations. The editors of a recent publication on the Holocaust described the refugees' situation: "The history of the Holocaust did not end in 1945 with the liberation. It is an unfolding story that continues in the efforts of survivors to rebuild their lives, renew their spirits and document their experiences."[1]

In Austria, clandestine Palestine-based Zionist organizations, assisted by funds from the American Jewish Joint Distribution Committee, soon ran the DP camps informally and established a well-functioning underground organization that took the Jewish refugees to the Mediterranean coast. From there Haganah, the main Jewish underground army in Palestine, controlled by the Jewish Agency, transported them illegally to the British-held land. While American authorities in Austria and elsewhere did not interfere in the operation, the British, who continued to restrict substantially Jewish immigration to Palestine, attempted to sabotage it. Britain's blockade of Palestine led to the capture of fifty thousand Jewish refugees, who were detained in camps in Cyprus.

Nevertheless, both Austria and Italy served as critical transit points for the mass exodus of Polish and other Eastern European Jews to Palestine and elsewhere. Between 1945 and 1948, thousands of Jewish DPs entered Palestine illegally. Still, by January 1948, some 250,000 Jews lived in DP camps in Germany alone. Once the state of Israel was formed in 1948, during its first three years nearly 374,000 Holocaust survivors entered the new country. Between 1946 and 1953 almost 140,000 known survivors arrived in the United States. Altogether, one-third of Jewish DPs settled in America and nearly all the others in Palestine (later Israel).

The Holocaust not only left postwar European Jewry almost wholly destroyed. For its survivors the Holocaust had left them with a lifelong void created by the loss, in nearly every instance, of entire families and other loved ones. Yet, remarkably, somehow many survivors adapted to their new countries, rebuilt their lives, and established new families. They did so with great difficulty and in most places, including both America and Israel, in the face of initial widespread insensitivity and indifference to their plight among both local Jews and Gentiles. The title of one survivor's memoir, *Triumph of Hope: From Theresienstadt and Auschwitz to Israel*, reflected the kind of journey made by many survivors.[2]

Despite outward appearances, "living with the Holocaust," in the words of an important book on the subject, meant that survivors suffered both psychologically and physically from the horrors and trauma they had experienced.[3] According to Bartov, "When memory of Holocaust survivors comes, it is a memory of loss and separation, absence and uprooted identity, repressed, fragmented, traumatic."[4] Nightmares, depression, and feelings of guilt tormented most of them. Many survivors were haunted by their utter powerlessness in the Final Solution and by the fact that they had managed somehow to live through the genocide while others dear to them had not. Jewish tradition and history, which had placed on each Jew an obligation not only for his or her own life, but also for the survival of the community, heightened the sense of loss and guilt.

In diaries, testimonies, and memoirs left behind by some who died in the Holocaust as well as by a number who survived, the authors reproached themselves for not having done enough to save a beloved family member or friend. Primo Levi, a survivor of Auschwitz and author of important books on the camp, committed suicide in 1987, which demolished the view of many observers that he had recovered from the awful pain and humiliation he and others had suffered.

Langer has written extensively about the struggle of survivors in rejoining the human community healed and whole :

One of the most perplexing dilemmas of taking or watching Holocaust testimonies, which I have been doing for nearly ten years, is understanding the difficulty so many witnesses have believing that they are without fault for the doom that consumed them and members of their families. Whether we speak of annihilation by gas, disease, starvation, or exhaustion, Nazi Germany frequently conspired to force its victims to participate in their own destruction. With utter contempt for those victims, the murderers knew that the instinct to stay alive would too often take precedence over the moral will to resist, especially when one was faced with the uncommon threats to life of gassing, starvation, or physical exhaustion.[5]

Langer concludes that in the misplaced shame and remorse of many Holocaust witnesses, "blame is deflected from the real culprits," the killers, "to the victims themselves." Readers of such testimonies, he warns, must not "be beguiled into endorsing them as valid images of the truth."[6]

The Holocaust had not only shattered the lives of many survivors, but also their belief in mankind—and some even in God. Some, such as Levi, never recovered. Their experience took them, in the words of one survivor who also committed suicide, to "the mind's limits." Jean Améry explained how the Nazis had dispossessed him and other Jewish prisoners of their dignity as humans and Jews, "tortured because [the Nazis] were torturers," and left him with the pains of exile and alienation:

> Every morning when I get up I can read the Auschwitz number on my forearm, something that touches the deepest and most closely intertwined roots of my existence; indeed I am not even sure if this is not my entire existence. Then I feel approximately as I did back then when I got a taste of the first blow from a policeman's fist. Every day anew I lose my trust in the world. The Jew without positive determinants, the Catastrophic Jew, as we will unhesitatingly call him, must get along without trust in the world.[7]

For some survivors, especially those who had engaged in active or violent resistance against the Nazis, such issues presented fewer problems. Aaron Hass has concluded from studying the psychological effects of the Holocaust on survivors and their children "that those who actively fought back as partisans emerged from the Holocaust with a greater part of their self-worth intact. They were not paralyzed by feelings of powerlessness. Their wartime activities also allowed for the discharge of a rage which has gone unexpressed for most survivors."[8]

How much influence fear and trauma played in the postwar testimony of the few Holocaust survivors who assisted former Nazis to escape punishment for war crimes is unclear. In the 1950s Israeli society was rocked by two trials involving Rudolf Kasztner, one of the leaders of the Jewish community in Budapest during the war who had organized various rescue operations.

Kasztner had immigrated to Israel after the war, but charges surfaced that he had testified on behalf of a major Nazi war criminal, the SS officer Kurt Becher. The latter had played a key role in the deportation and death of the Hungarian Jews. Although the Israeli Supreme Court cleared Kasztner of most of the accusations against him, it could neither understand nor forgive him for assisting Becher. Why Kasztner did so may never be determined. Many continue to suspect that it had something to do with a deal he had worked out with Becher that enabled a trainload of six hundred of Kasztner's friends and family members to escape to Switzerland.

Was There No Resistance?

Most agonizing for nearly all Holocaust survivors, the postwar era produced a devastating accusation against both them and those who had died in the genocide. Charged with emotion, moral judgment, and controversy, and first leveled in the 1950s and 1960s by several Jewish scholars—most notably Hilberg and the survivors Bruno Bettelheim and Arendt—it alleged Jewish complicity in the Holocaust.

Jews, said the allegation, had gone to their deaths with little or no resistance, as "lambs to the slaughter." Even worse, the critics asserted, Jewish ghetto leaders, officials of the Judenräte, had cooperated with the Germans in helping organize deportations and become themselves instruments of murder. According to Hilberg, who based his view almost entirely on German sources and continued to hold to it in a later edition of his book, *The Destruction of the European Jews*, the councils "responded to German demands with automatic compliance."[9] This response, he maintained, had characterized the behavior of Jews for two thousand years in surviving persecution. Many more Jews may have survived the Holocaust, Hilberg implied, if they and their leaders had resisted their killers openly.

Arendt made an even stronger attack on the compliance or accommodation of Jews in the Holocaust when she wrote: "To a Jew this role of the

Jewish leaders in the destruction of their own people is undoubtedly the darkest chapter of the whole dark story."[10] A leaderless and chaotic Jewry, she maintained, would have had much greater chances for survival. Even today some Jewish writers from both the secular liberal and ultra-orthodox sides, albeit for different reasons, accuse the Jewish leaders of the 1930s and 1940s, both inside and outside Europe, of betraying their people.

However, during the past three decades, with the discovery of vastly more Jewish and other records from the Holocaust, scholars as well as survivors have refuted such assertions. For one thing, little non-Jewish resistance occurred to Nazi rule in Europe, and when it did, with the exception of the partisans in the Soviet Union and Yugoslavia, it experienced extreme difficulties and nearly always costly failure. In 1972 Isaiah Trunk showed in his standard book on the subject, *Judenrat*, that the Jewish councils responded in a variety of ways to the Holocaust—not solely with compliance—and that the Nazis forced council members to serve on such bodies and provide services to the Germans. The survivor Améry concluded about Arendt that in her view of Eichmann and what Jews had encountered in Nazism, "there is no 'banality of evil.'" She "knew the enemy of mankind," Améry continued, "only from hearsay, saw him only through the glass cage" in which Eichmann had sat during his trial.[11]

Also about the critics—contemporary or otherwise—of the Jewish leadership, Yehuda Bauer has emphasized that such persons are "incapable of accepting the sad fact that the Jews during the Holocaust were absolutely powerless."[12] Of Jewish resistance in the Holocaust, he notes:

> Contrary to a widely held belief in the immediate postwar period and the 1950s, there was a great deal of armed Jewish resistance throughout Europe. Contrary to a widely held belief later on, it was not—it could not be—massive; quantitatively speaking, it was marginal. And contrary to widely held beliefs today, it was qualitatively an important series of events and is an important component of collective Jewish memory— quite rightly so.[13]

Assertions that if only more Jews had openly fought their killers many more would have survived the Final Solution seem dubious at best. The victims were up against the most determined and heavily armed of killers. Hitler and his government refused to permit any considerations—rational, military, or otherwise—to interfere with the carrying out of their killing program. A few more Jewish revolts, similar to a few more Allied cuts of railway lines or the bombing of a gas chamber, would hardly have halted the large number of Germans dedicated to the mass killing, and who saw their own careers and even well-being tied to its continuation.

Moreover, the victims, in their varied and numerous attempts to resist, always faced enormous obstacles: an almost total lack of weapons, little or no military training, poor communications and frequent political and other differences with one another, largely hostile or apathetic non-Jewish populations living nearby, physical weakness from hunger and disease, and the Allied armies far away from the ghettos and concentration camps. In either the ghetto or camp, only the lucky few among the prisoners, who also had a fanatical will to live, survived.

Indeed, given the overwhelming odds against survival, a recent study of the Holocaust has concluded, "[T]he fact that there was any Jewish armed resistance at all in Eastern Europe is more impressive than its modest dimensions."[14] Small Jewish underground or resistance organizations, most of them dominated by members of Zionist youth groups, arose in approximately one hundred ghettos in Poland, Lithuania, Byelorussia, and the Ukraine. Each planned and/or attempted to incite a revolt inside its ghetto or to escape and join partisan groups in nearby forests.

The majority of ghetto fighters and others in the underground resistance, who included numerous women, saw little possibility of armed opposition rescuing Jews from death. Instead most of them fought primarily because they knew and acknowledged, once they learned by the fall of 1942, after vast numbers of Jews had been murdered, the truth about the deportations—that death awaited them and that the possibility of survival was gone. Also they revolted to avenge the murder of other Jews and to justify their behavior to and inspire later generations.

Even after information filtered into the ghettos that deportation meant death, the underground groups in the Polish and Lithuanian ghettos encountered serious problems in rallying the masses of inhabitants to resist the killers. In most of Poland and Lithuania, working with the resistance did not offer a real chance of survival, just a different type of death; unlike Byelorussia, few forests existed that offered even a slight chance that one might escape.

Nearly everywhere most ghetto Jews responded to the information about the mass killings with disbelief and shock, which limited their acceptance of what they heard. Nothing could have prepared the victims for comprehending the systematic and wholesale murder of *all* of them. Nor could the awful news be verified easily in the isolated ghettos or concentration camps. Experience and rationality, furthermore, made the reports inconceivable. Who could believe the deliberate destruction of a whole people innocent of any wrongdoing and who provided the German war industry with valuable labor in wartime? For many Jews the sheer horrors they faced increased their inability to perceive the truth. Physically devastated by malnourishment and mistreatment, they lapsed into despair and masses died.

Nevertheless, for some Jewish prisoners in ghettos and several of the killing centers, including Sobibor, Treblinka, and Auschwitz-Birkenau, such feelings of hopelessness, coupled with the recognition that they too would soon be killed, motivated them to revolt. Furthermore, in numerous European countries, including Belgium, the Netherlands, France, Hungary, and Germany, small Jewish underground organizations formed and concentrated on rescuing Jews from deportation. Occasionally the groups succeeded in sabotaging German military operations and organized other armed opposition.

Resistance included as well countless actions of Jews in the ghettos and concentration camps of a material or spiritual kind—sometimes called "evasion" of German policies— designed to help keep the people alive and retain their human dignity. In his pioneering study of survivors, Terrence Des Pres concluded that the life of most prisoners in the death camps, despite the Nazis' efforts to make it such, was not a war of all against all in which the prisoners cooperated in their own destruction. Instead, the relationship of the prisoners to one another was intensely social and depended on basic components of humanness—on the prisoners' sense of conscience and dignity, on innumerable small acts of help and sharing, and on collective forms of resistance. To stay alive was to remain human and to enable the survivor to one-day bear witness to what had happened: "the survivor task," as one wrote to Des Pres.[15]

Some have criticized Des Pres's conclusions because they rested mainly on the testimony of few of the prisoners who managed to survive the camps. Moreover, his findings challenge the view of some survivors and others that camp life so destroyed the human spirit that most prisoners were wholly depersonalized and dehumanized.

How does one judge the actions of the controversial Jewish ghetto leaders, the Judenrat members? Of 720 such officials studied by Trunk, nearly 80 percent died in the Holocaust; in many cases they were murdered or removed by the Germans because they refused to obey German orders. Also Bauer notes that in many Polish and Lithuanian ghettos the Judenräte were not asked for and did not deliver lists of Jews to the Germans. In numerous smaller ghettos the councils refused to cooperate at all in any way.

Aharon Weiss's study of Judenrat chairmen in the General Government reveals that most of the first chairmen, many of them longtime pre-war leaders of local Jewish communities, represented the interests of the communities and did not bend to German pressure. But a different situation arose when primarily the Germans appointed the successors of the original chairmen, who had been removed or murdered. With the new or second wave of chairmen, a substantial increase occurred in their number who showed obedience to German demands to provide Jews for deportation and slave labor.

The unrestrained Nazi terror and commitment to killing Jews and total lack of opportunities and resources for Jews to thwart German plans left Judenrat chairmen with only ineffectual and futile strategies for saving their people. Employing tactics such as bribery, bargaining, compliance, or "rescue through work" nearly always failed. So did attempts by Judenräte, which took place in some cases, at outright opposition to the Nazis and collaboration with ghetto resistance groups. Disobeying the Germans usually meant death, not only for oneself, but also for one's family and many others in the ghetto.

Someone wrote once that most Judenrat leaders not only sought the preservation of Jews, but they also worked to preserve the Jewish people. One suspects that such leaders would have agreed with the postwar comment of a Jewish partisan in Lithuania who lived through the Holocaust: "Without Jewish survival, victory over Nazism was not a victory to me."[16]

Bauer wrote recently, "In the moral dilemma that the Judenräte faced, no simple answers could be given."[17] In judging the Jewish leadership, Dawidowicz observed, correctly in this writer's opinion:

> For all their weaknesses, failings, and wrongdoings, these men—Rumkowski, Merin, Gens—were not traitors. . . . The accusation that some Jewish leaders "cooperated" or "collaborated" with the Germans arises out of distortions of the historical record. Cooperation and collaboration with the Germans were policies voluntarily undertaken by leaders of nations that retained all or part of their independence and autonomy. In the ghettos of Poland, where German rule was total . . . Germany did not ask for or get either cooperation or collaboration. SS

force and terror extracted compliance from the Jews and aimed to bring them to a state of unresisting submissiveness. Unlike Quisling, Laval, and [Andrei] Vlasov [a Soviet general captured by the Germans in the war and who made a futile effort to form an army of Soviet POWs to fight alongside the Germans], no Jew—not even an underworld black-guard who sold information to the Gestapo—ever awaited German victory. . . . To say that they "cooperated" or "collaborated" with the Germans is semantic confusion and historical misrepresentation.[18]

Elie Wiesel, himself a survivor of the Holocaust and an eloquent spokesman for its victims, has deplored the very question "Why so little resistance?" as if somehow it is the victims who have been placed on trial:

> The world kept silent while the Jews were being massacred, while they were being reduced to the state of objects good for the fire; let the world at least have the decency to keep silent now as well. Its questions come a bit late; they should have been addressed to the executioner. . . . Do not wait for the dead to come to our rescue. Their silence will survive them.[19]

A final aspect of Jewish resistance that students of the Holocaust frequently ignore or overlook is connected directly to the world war. Jews played a significant role in the military defeat of the Germans and their allies. Even before the war Jews had joined the struggle against Nazism and Italian Fascism. During the civil war in Spain (1936–1939), many had fought in the international brigades, armed groups comprised of volunteers from numerous countries that supported the Spanish republicans against the Nazi and Fascist-backed military rebels. Jews, in fact, constituted almost 20 percent of the approximately forty thousand brigadists.

During World War II, 1,400,000 Jewish men (and women) fought in the armed forces of the Allied alliance, including approximately 400,000 in the Red Army and 700,000 in the British and American armies. In Palestine thirty-five thousand Jews volunteered for the British Army; ten thousand of them later formed a so-called Jewish Brigade. In addition, numerous other Jews belonged to the partisan or guerrilla units of the European countries. Possibly as much as 10 percent of the world's entire Jewish population fought in the war, in one military fashion or another, against Hitler's Germany.

The numbers of medals and citations earned by Jewish soldiers in the various Allied armies reflected the soldiers' motivation in participating in the huge struggle. Some 160,772 Jewish soldiers received decorations in the Soviet Army, 36,352 in the American Army, and many thousands more in other Allied forces.

Numerous memoirs and testimonies of Jewish soldiers make clear that not only did they view their participation in the war as a means by which they could defend their homeland from the enemy, but they also had an ideological motivation. They were conscious of fighting against the destroyer of their fellow Jews and felt an intense desire to take revenge against the murderers. The postwar Nazi hunter, Simon Wiesenthal, recalled after the war that following his liberation from the Mauthausen camp in 1945, his "first American friend" was a Jewish soldier who "took it upon himself to look after the liberated Jewish inmates."[20]

Another Jew liberated in Buchenwald by American troops remembered similarly. He noted immediately after the war: "We got out and went to meet them. To our great joy, in one of the first three tanks that came in was a Jew, an American soldier. Right away he gave us cakes to eat. We simply couldn't imagine, a Jew, an American soldier! We were liberated! The joy, I can't picture it in words."[21] Almost all Jews in the Allied countries able to bear arms had done so.

Consciousness and Memorialization

How must the Holocaust and its victims be remembered? How should one study or attempt to reimagine as accurately as possible what happened in an event so horrific and unprecedented as the Final Solution? As Langer reminds his readers, there exists an "incessant anxious dialogue about how our civilization may absorb into its reasonable hopes for the future the disabling outburst of unreason we name the Holocaust, as it continues to assault memory and imagination with immeasurable sorrow and undiminished force."[22]

Today, the Holocaust has become in the West, in the words of a recent writer, the single "most talked about and oft-represented event of the twentieth century."[23] A series of public opinion surveys in the early 1990s in the United States concluded that approximately 95 percent of Americans had heard of the term *Holocaust*, and almost as many believed they knew what it meant. *Holocaust* is a word familiar to an overwhelming majority of both

Jewish and non-Jewish Americans and an event that has entered into the nation's consciousness.

Commemoration of the victims of the Holocaust has become institutionalized, in both physical structures and other ways, in America and elsewhere in the West. Numerous and different "shapes of memory" characterize "Holocaust remembrance."[24] Recently architecture has emerged alongside literature as a primary avenue for discussion and memorialization.

Although architecture is a relatively new field for discourse about the Holocaust, James Young, an American scholar of English and Judaic studies, speaks of a "veritable explosion of Holocaust monuments in recent years."[25] Young served as the sole foreigner and Jew on the panel to find an appropriate national memorial in Berlin to Holocaust victims. His research has also explored the works of numerous artists in the West—such as Art Spiegelman, Shimon Attie, David Levinthal, and Rachel Whiteread— which help the world remember the Holocaust in the "after-images" of its history.[26]

In April 1993 the United States Holocaust Memorial Museum opened on the mall in Washington, D.C. Built on public land with private funds and originating in a unique combination of initiatives of President Jimmy Carter and the White House staff, the museum was the culmination of a fifteen-year effort to create a national memorial in America to victims of the Holocaust. Countless other Holocaust memorials have appeared across America as well. These range from museums and monuments to the establishment of university professorships and courses in Holocaust studies. Also legislatures in several states have mandated that elementary and high schools teach about the Holocaust.

The extraordinary surge of Holocaust consciousness in America is exhibited in still other ways. Popular films such as *Sophie's Choice* received widespread public attention. Steven Spielberg's 1993 movie, *Schindler's List*, won seven Academy Awards and made over $221 million at foreign theaters. Also Spielberg established a one hundred million-dollar project to collect videotaped testimonies of Holocaust survivors. Educational companies and universities have produced hundreds of other films, based on original footage or still pictures shot by the Germans themselves and captured by the Allies, of the persecution of the Jews.

Even Goldhagen's lengthy doctoral dissertation on the Holocaust, published in 1996, drew enormous popular interest in both America and Europe. In the United States alone the book sold hundreds of thousands of copies. On still another level of Holocaust institutionalization, the United States Justice Department operates the OSI, an office that hunts down former Nazi war criminals living in America and has them expelled from the country.

The Eichmann trial in Israel in 1961 first attracted widespread popular attention to the Holocaust. The massive publicity surrounding the trial led many Americans to make Eichmann a universal symbol of evils, such as blind obedience to authority and a lack of individual conscience that lay hidden, they alleged, within all people. A few years later many American and other Jews feared that Israel's Six-Day War in 1967 and Yom Kippur War in 1973 threatened the Jewish state with a new Holocaust.

Nearly 120 million Americans viewed the NBC mini-television series *Holocaust*, which ran four consecutive evenings in April 1978 and further transformed the Holocaust into an event that evoked strong emotions and a discussion of basic societal values. The show's soap-opera style of portraying the Holocaust through the experiences of the Weiss family, captured the attention of the American public and made the term *Holocaust* a household name. The film also had a huge impact in Europe, especially in West Germany.

This "Americanization of the Holocaust"[27] has led, furthermore, to Hollywood-like representations of the Holocaust in sensational books and movies, picture postcards, and toys and games. In the United States and elsewhere, Holocaust tourism is gigantic. Each year millions of visitors pass through the Holocaust museums in Washington and other American cities; more than twelve million visited the Washington museum alone in its first six years, with four out of five visitors being non-Jews. Still other Americans, as well as many foreigners, visit the State Museum at Auschwitz, the Anne Frank House in Amsterdam, and the Holocaust national memorial in Jerusalem, Yad Vashem (the Holocaust Martyrs' and Heroes' Remembrance Authority).

In Germany a lengthy and bitter controversy has only ended recently over the proposed location in Berlin of a large national memorial to the victims of the Holocaust. Other Holocaust memorials in the city include the exhibit in the Schoeneberg district's Bayerisches Viertel, the Wannsee house exhibition, and a monument near the Grunewald train station, where the deportation trains had left for Auschwitz.

During the past two decades still other architectural disputes regarding who and what to memorialize have embroiled Germans. In 1982 the city of Berlin initiated plans for a public park or playground at the site of the ruined and former Gestapo headquarters, to commemorate those who had died or been killed there by the police. But establishing a recreation area at a former place of torture and killing indicated a disturbing lack of understanding of what the site had signified.

During 1993 protest erupted when the German chancellor Helmut Kohl made the *Neue Wache*, the historic guards barracks built in 1818 in Berlin, a memorial for the victims of both world wars, tyranny, racial persecution, resistance, expulsion, and terrorism. Kohl, similar to the German historian, Nolte, sought to "normalize" or "relativize" German history by commemorating the victims of the Nazi regime and Holocaust along with the German perpetrators and the perpetrator generation.

Elsewhere, in Israel, the United States, Poland, and the Netherlands, each of the memorials presents the Holocaust differently and reflects its own view of the event and world war. Yad Vashem emphasizes the "martyrs and heroes"—the resistance to Nazism in general, the Warsaw ghetto revolt in particular, and the "righteous" who rescued Jews. The memorial has a gigantic archive of documents, testimonies, photographs, and films and a library containing more than eighty thousand titles, mainly studies of the Holocaust, World War II, fascism, Nazism, and anti-Semitism.

Its new Museum of Holocaust Art advances the idea of art as a form of resistance and survival. In the words of the museum's curator, "For some of the artists [caught in the Holocaust], art was a way to describe what they and those around them saw and experienced . . . . For others, art was a device that made psychological survival possible."[28] Also an underlying assumption of the memorial, built as directed by a law passed in 1953 by the Israeli parliament, the Knesset, is the helplessness of Jews in the Holocaust and Diaspora and their rebirth in the postwar state of Israel.

In Washington the Holocaust museum tells the story of the Holocaust with an exhibition of artifacts, photographs, films, and documents. It serves, moreover, as both the central archive in North America for documents and artifacts and an education center, the latter used primarily to teach youthful visitors about the Holocaust. The museum demonstrates, historian Michal Berenbaum has observed, "that the Holocaust has a place in the American national memory and the American future."[29]

The Auschwitz museum, established soon after the world war, provided until recently several inaccurate descriptions of the death camp. Initially, during the Cold War, with Poland in the Soviet bloc, Communist propaganda proclaimed that the former camp represented fascist aggression and its defeat by the Soviet Union. But once the Soviet Union and Iron Curtain collapsed in 1990–1991, Auschwitz was made to symbolize the German persecution of the Poles. Then, faced with demands from historians and others in the West that it reflect what in fact the Nazis had used the camp for, the museum began to focus more attention on the role of Auschwitz in the murder of European Jewry. Franciszek Piper, the head of the museum's historical research department, and the latter's staff have contributed important details about the camp's history. During the past several years, the name Auschwitz has become even more than previously a synonym for the "Holocaust."

Long before the explosion of Holocaust consciousness, some who lived through the Holocaust, including Elie Wiesel, who would play a key role later in founding the museum in Washington, decried what they termed the trivialization of it by writers, filmmakers, and others who, the critics believed, had little or no right to represent it. Wiesel, a winner of the Nobel Prize for Peace in 1986, has viewed the Holocaust as something that cannot possibly be reimagined by anyone who had not lived through it.

Soon after World War II, the issue had surfaced of whether or not literature was an appropriate vehicle through which to express and remember the Holocaust. In 1949 Theodor Adorno, the eminent social philosopher and exile who had returned to Germany, declared emphatically "no" and insisted that "to write poetry after Auschwitz is barbaric." But later Adorno apparently changed his mind. "The enduring suffering," he wrote in 1966, "has as much right to expression as does the tortured man to scream."[30]

The world's authorities on Holocaust literature, which include Langer and Ernestine Schlant, have generally taken issue with Adorno's original view. According to Schlant, "To succumb to a moral or aesthetic imperative that demands the silence of the Holocaust would be tantamount to not acknowledging the very barbarism of which Auschwitz stands as the horrifying exemplar. It would extend the inhumanity of the action to the inhumanity of nonarticulation."[31] Still, Langer has issued a pointed warning to those who write about the Holocaust:

> There is simply no connection between our ordinary suffering and [the victims'] unprecedented agony, nor do our trivial inclinations toward sin resemble in any way the minds that devised such terminal torture. Literalist discourse about the Holocaust—and I must stress that I am speaking only about the Holocaust—leads nowhere but back into the

pit of destruction. At least it has the grace to acknowledge that we learn nothing from the misery it finds there.[32]

Other artists, including the filmmaker Spielberg, attempt to reconstruct elements of the Holocaust for the public in a movie set or in some other pop-ular and creative fashion. While Spielberg has sought to educate the masses, critics of his and other efforts to acquaint the public with the Holocaust return to the concerns voiced by Adorno and Wiesel. Films and other con-temporary art forms that depict the Holocaust, they maintain, gloss over or cannot begin to represent the horror and tragedy of the event.

The "Big Lie" and "Holocaust Industry"

The massive public awareness of the Holocaust has produced several recent reactions. First, it has led neo-Nazis to make Holocaust denial the focus of their propaganda. The deniers borrow from Hitler's technique of telling the "Big Lie" by denying that the gas chambers existed and the Holocaust hap-pened. According to the British scholar, Richard Evans, "a good deal of them [the deniers] seemed to be linked to racial hatred and antisemitic animosity in the most direct possible way."[33] Especially since the 1980s, in the words of American historian Deborah Lipstadt, the deniers have organized a "growing assault on truth and memory."[34]

Such denials of the factual record not only threaten Jews, but they as well undermine the very principles of objective scholarship that support the world's faith in historical knowledge. They also—in a perverse inversion of victim and perpetrator—call the Holocaust a hoax created by an interna-tional Jewish conspiracy to defame Germany and cost it millions in repara-tions. Furthermore, the denials are surely deeply offensive to the many thousands of Nazi victims who survived the concentration and death camps and now hear people telling them that virtually nothing of what they had suf-fered had ever happened.

But any effort to deny the Holocaust loses all plausibility in the face of the mountains of documents, photographs, and testimony since 1945 show-ing the mass murder by the firing squads and in the gas chambers of the exter-mination camps. The fraud of denial was confirmed most recently in April 2000 in a London court. The court overwhelmingly rejected the libel suit of the British writer, David Irving, against Lipstadt and the publisher of her book, *Denying the Holocaust*, for calling Irving "one of the most dangerous spokespersons for Holocaust denial."[35]

Further, the Americans Michael Shermer and Alex Grobman published recently the first extensive analysis and refutation of Holocaust denial. They use the issue, according to the authors, "as a classic case study in how the past may be revised for present political and ideological purposes."[36] In the process Shermer and Grobman refute the deniers' claims and arguments, present an in-depth analysis of the deniers' personalities and motives, and show precisely, with detailed evidence, how historians and others know the Holocaust happened.

Only a step away from denial is the attempt of some persons to white-wash Hitler and National Socialism with an insidious "yes but" kind of claim, designed to blur the boundaries between fact and fiction and between perse-cuted and persecutor. The ultimate objective is not unlike that of the deniers: to revise, in this case by marginalizing or relativizing, the history of Nazism to make it look less criminal.

Yes, such persons say, there was a Holocaust, but everyone in the world war committed similar war crimes, such as America's internment of Japanese Americans and the Allied bombing of civilians in German and Japanese cities. With such assertions, Lucy Dawidowicz concluded, one can "blur the distinctiveness of Jewish fate and consequently one can disclaim the presence of anti-Semitism, whether it smolders in the dark recesses of one's own mind or whether it operates in the pitiless light of history."[37]

There has been a second principal reaction to the explosion of Holocaust consciousness. Some writers, especially Peter Novick of the University of Chicago, criticized the phenomenon as the creation of an American media controlled and manipulated by Jewish organizations for their own purposes. Novick argued that during the last quarter century, American Jewish leaders purposely chose "to center the Holocaust—to combat what they saw as a 'new anti-Semitism'; in support of an embattled Israel; as the basis of revived ethnic consciousness."[38]

For Novick and others who share his opinions, this has produced crass, kitschy, and seemingly ever-present commercial and political exploitation of the Holocaust. Novick questioned whether the Holocaust teaches useful lessons, such as sensitizing people to atrocities; and he asked why there is no museum of American slavery. Also, he has warned, "The life expectancy of memories in today's society appears greatly diminished." He predicted that in future years Holocaust consciousness will weaken because "[m]uch of the original impetus behind the Jewish drive for centering the Holocaust is, if not spent, at least declining in power."[39] This includes the deaths of the increasingly few remaining Holocaust survivors.

While such criticisms may hold some truth, they are surely overdone. The assertion that Jews have conspired to manufacture "the Holocaust industry"[40] for political and financial gain is wholly erroneous and a dangerous invitation to anti-Semitism. Any base exploitation of the Holocaust or the ubiquitous presence of the subject in society should not result in silence and less learning and teaching about the subject. Instead these should inspire the world to learn more about it, teach it better, and produce quality works of scholarship. At present the role in the Holocaust of several European countries and their collaboration with the Germans still remains substantially unexamined—or not admitted by their leaders and populations.

Moreover, the fascination of the Holocaust for millions today is not the result of Jewish manipulation of the subject, the media, or anything similar. It is instead the consequence in large measure of the Holocaust itself and what is known about it. A huge documentation from the Holocaust survived it and has enabled historians and others to study and write about it in a depth and detail not possible in other genocides. Scholars continue today to uncover new and original evidence about the Holocaust, some of it in recently opened archives such as those in Russia.

Despite the multitude of Holocaust memorials, however serious or exploitative, the great task of representing the meaning of the Holocaust to the world is best done—not flawlessly, to be sure—by scholars researching and writing about it. "Good historical writing," a historian reminded readers in her recent book on the Holocaust, is where "the reader is brought into a constructed, controlled, directed engagement with the texts, and is invited to join the writer's search for their meanings."[41] As the number of Holocaust survivors continues to dwindle, an increasingly greater share of the responsibility for understanding and remembering the Holocaust will shift from its eyewitnesses to researchers and writers.

Victims' Assets and Compensation

A final testimony to the victims of the Holocaust is the widespread attention given since the mid-1990s to recovering their enormous assets looted by the Nazis and various governments of wartime Europe. In recovering victims' assets paid to Jewish survivors, Jewish organizations in the United States and the latter's government have led the way. In 1998 banks in Switzerland were forced to pay restitution to Jewish and other victims, and a year later similar pressures led large German corporations to agree to compensate former slave laborers.

Currently, pressure from Jewish organizations and American officials mounts on former Soviet-bloc countries in Eastern Europe to return prewar Jewish properties or provide financial compensation to survivors. Investigators have discovered as well looted artworks in museums in the United States that were never returned to Holocaust victims or their heirs.

For example, a midwestern art institute claims ownership of a painting by the Frenchman, Edgar Degas, which once belonged to Fritz Gutmann, a son of the founder of the Deutsche Bank. Henri Matisse's *Odalesque*, a work seized from Paul Rosenberg in France in 1940, is in an art museum on the west coast. To examine and investigate this troubling issue further, the United States established a Presidential Commission on Holocaust Assets, one of eighteen such commissions operating in Western nations that deal with victims' assets and seek return of the property. In 1999 the National Archives in Washington published a one thousand page finding guide to its records on "Holocaust-era assets."[42]

By January 2001 the presidential commission reported that it had found over two thousand books in the Library of Congress and other objects at universities and museums brought to the United States at the war's end by American troops and, largely through inattention, never returned. The commission promised that, where possible, it would seek the return of the items to rightful owners.

Recent public revelations have implicated America's vast global conglomerate, International Business Machines (IBM), in helping facilitate the Holocaust. The company acknowledged that its German subsidiary, Dehomag, had supplied machines to the Nazis to assist them in compiling, sorting, and classifying information on their Jewish and other victims. But in February 2001, the lawyer for Holocaust survivors seeking legal judgments against IBM declared: "It is time for IBM to answer for its culpability."[43] The continuing discovery and opening in Europe, Russia, and America of private and government records on the Holocaust should contribute further to long-awaited justice for many Holocaust and other wartime victims and their families.

CHAPTER NINETEEN

LEARNING FROM
THE PAST

"THE PAST," the author of a college textbook wrote once, "is not a meaningless tale."[1] Without knowledge of our history, we cannot fully know ourselves, because people, institutions, and values from the past shape us all. Yet unfortunately people seldom learn from history. The Holocaust has much to teach us about mankind in general and the Western world in particular. With the dawn of a new century, with all its promise as well as perils, it is more urgent than ever for people to heed the lessons of the Holocaust, for reasons that may involve the very safety and survival of humanity.

To begin with, while the genocide we call the Holocaust was a product of human action similar to all other genocides, it was nevertheless very different from the others in at least one major respect: it represented a radicalization of genocide, with the most radical of implications for the world. In addition to what happened to the Jews at Nazi hands, other genocides that belong to the same species of human behavior have marked modern history: the slaughter of Native Americans by Europeans and their descendants, the Turkish massacre of Armenians in World War I, the mass killings of Soviet peoples in the 1930s by Stalin's government, the bloodbath perpetrated by the Pol Pot regime in Cambodia, the Hutu slaughter of the Tutsis in Rwanda, and the Serbian murder of masses of Albanians and Bosnian Muslims in the former Yugoslavia.

But unlike these other terrible massacres, in which the killers targeted and murdered a portion of a national, ethnic, or racial group, the Holocaust involved a planned attempt to annihilate physically every single member of such a group. In this regard, the Holocaust speaks loudly to both present and future generations. "The warning contained in the Holocaust," one scholar has written, "is surely that the acts of the perpetrators might be repeated, under certain conditions, by anyone."[2]

If so, what could happen to others should the Holocaust of the Jewish people become a precedent for similar actions? For one thing, we are all possible victims, members of peoples who could be targeted for complete destruction; and we are also possible perpetrators and bystanders. But a second, and even greater, danger exists. With the continuation today of many of the hatreds that produced the Holocaust and with the world acquiring evermore destructive military and biological weapons, humanity is confronted with the ultimate question: could a future war and genocide threaten *all* of humankind, as the Jews were in World War II, with total physical extinction?

What also makes the Holocaust worthy of careful study is that it had deep roots in the history of the West. At a recent lecture, Browning reminded his audience: "The Holocaust occurred within and was a product of our civilization, and we cannot simply dismiss it as something other cultures and peoples do but which has little to say about ourselves."[3] How, then, is the Holocaust a product of Western civilization? How is it imbedded in our history? And what might we learn by examining it in that context?

Perhaps most important to realize is that numerous prejudices from Western history combined together by the twentieth century to make the Jews, in the view of many Westerners, the most hated and dangerous enemy of not only the world, but of all mankind. The Holocaust was inconceivable without the presence of such deep-seated intolerance. A persistence of similar hatred today among some Westerners, and its intensification elsewhere in the world, as, for example, in the Middle East and portions of Asia, is both highly problematic and ominous.

The Holocaust could not have happened without the widespread religious anti-Semitism in Europe and elsewhere in the West, which resulted from the two-thousand-year-long antagonism of Christianity toward the Jewish minority and Judaism. Today a major question is whether, following World War II, the Holocaust influenced the Christian churches to admit to and eliminate their long history of anti-Jewish sentiment. Historian Michael Phayer has observed that while the death of Pope Pius XII in 1958 "closed the door on a dismal period of church history, at least insofar as the Holocaust is concerned," the Catholic church soon "began to rethink its relationship to Judaism during the Second Vatican Council, a process that led to the church's renunciation of anti-Semitism in 1965."[4]

How much the Church's attitude toward Jews has changed, however, is questionable. A Vatican commission's report on the Church's responsibility, if any, for the Holocaust, issued in March 1998, concluded that the Church had none. The report distinguished between "anti-Judaism," of which some unnamed and uninformed Christians were unfortunately guilty in the past, and "anti-Semitism," which led to the Holocaust and which "was essentially more sociological and political than religious."[5] A recent study of the report has concluded: "This argument, sadly, is not the product of a Church that wants to confront its history."[6] Nor have Protestant churches made significant efforts to grapple with their failed response to the Holocaust and resulting implications for Protestant theology regarding Judaism and Jews.

Second, during its commercial and industrial revolutions of the fifteenth through nineteenth centuries, the West spawned a new brand of anti-Jewish sentiment, one charged with xenophobia. The revolutions produced in many rich and poor Westerners alike a virulent economic anti-Semitism. It fostered a suspicion and dislike of Jews, most of whom had been forced off the land and into business occupations during the Middle Ages, as financial competitors and manipulators, forces of an insidious "modernism," and undeserving "outsiders." Widespread myths about the "rule" of Jewish "finance capital" would add later to the hatreds that made the Holocaust possible.

Third, the genocide of the Jews in World War II resulted from the fusing of extreme nationalism and racism, begun in Europe and America during the last half of the nineteenth century. This racial nationalism intensified the destructive forces of intolerance, including the hatred of Jews. Germany, one of the West's newest nations, formed only in 1871, would subsequently produce the most fanatical and widespread racial anti-Semitism.

Today similar extremist elements still lurk near the surface of Western society and politics, and occasionally break forth in violence against so-called foreigners, including Jews, blacks, and immigrants—whether Hispanics, Asians, Arabs, or whomever. Incidents of terrorist violence in the West, especially those exported from the Middle East or other non-Western areas, threaten to intensify xenophobia.

Only an important and fragile layer of political culture based on human rights and democracy protects most Western societies from the forces of hatred not unlike those that unleashed the Holocaust. In the United States, white supremacist groups such as the Aryan Nations, Ku Klux Klan, the militias, and skinheads spew forth racial, political, and cultural hatreds that copy many of Hitler's. Moreover, America still discriminates officially and in other ways against homosexuals. In countries of the European Union, rightist political movements and neo-Nazi organizations exist, and in some places thrive.

Fourth, the Holocaust was the consequence of both the powerful and modern nation-state as well as advanced technology, each having originated in the West and developed significantly in Germany. In this regard, perhaps the most important and frightening lesson of the Holocaust is that the great accomplishments of the Western intellect, especially in science and technology, can be turned on the world, including our own civilization, with vast destructive power. The West, throughout its history, has repeatedly harnessed science and technology to serve both peaceful and violent ends. However, the application of scientific and technological achievements to war accelerated dramatically in World War I.

World War II produced even more calamitous results from the wedding of technology and killing. But what defined the war of 1939–1945 most, in this regard, was not solely the use by its competing armed forces of weapons that caused unprecedented death and other destruction, the greatest single example being the discovery and use by the United States of the atomic bomb to end the war against Japan.

Instead, the war was characterized equally or more by the new type of *institution* it produced, one designed and constructed by highly trained engineers and technocrats solely to destroy a portion of the human race "as a punishment for having been born."[7] The death camps of "the Holocaust kingdom," in the words of a survivor of the Warsaw Ghetto uprising and forced labor at Maidanek and in Germany,[8] were original with Nazi Germany and represented, in the use for which they were intended, a gigantic leap of civilization toward self-destruction.

For all these reasons, as well as others, the systematic mass murder of the Jews in World War II represented the most radical and extreme example of genocide that has happened. The long history, intensity, and zealousness of the hatreds and other forces that drove it forward and sustained it to the utmost ends, and the determination of the killers to complete it, had important roots in the West and even exceeded the ideological fanaticism of Stalinism.

No other genocide, moreover, can match the vast geographical scope of the Holocaust. Millions of persons were murdered from all parts of Europe and Russia. Only Germany's defeat in the war kept the killers from expanding the Holocaust farther. In addition, there is no parallel with the systematic manner, or the speed, efficiency, and thoroughness with which the National Socialists implemented the genocide.

Also the Holocaust helps to explain why, after World War II, important areas of the world developed as they have. At the war's end, the Allies did not rearrange the regions and peoples in Europe most affected by the fighting and German racial policies by applying the post–World War I peace settlement. The Allies had based that settlement on the principle of national self-determination. Their effort in 1919 to make geographic boundaries fit peoples so as to provide such persons with their own nation had left the Germans most unhappy, although this solution had benefited Germany significantly.

Consequently, at the end of World War II the Allies applied to the Germans the policy that the latter had implemented during the war against their conquered peoples, which had been, in Weinberg's words, "to draw the boundaries first and then push the people around to fit the boundaries."[9] In 1945–1946 the Allies moved approximately twelve million Germans from Czechoslovakia, East Prussia, Danzig, and other former eastern German territories turned over to Poland. Also millions of Poles, to accommodate the Soviet Union's new western border, had to move from the eastern portions of their pre-1939 country westward to lands taken over from Germany.

In the Middle East the war and Holocaust significantly influenced the postwar creation of Israel as a state. The war had weakened further Britain's hold both on its former mandate in Palestine and imperial position in India, Iraq, and Egypt. British plans before World War II had called for a partition of Palestine into Jewish and Arab sectors. Shortly after the war's end the British gave up their rule over India and therefore also over Palestine. They had used the latter previously to protect the northern approach to their vital link to India, the Suez Canal.

Owing to the Allies' success during the war in keeping the Germans out of Palestine, a small but substantial Jewish community remained there. After 1945 it supplied a basis for the subsequent establishment in Palestine of a Jewish state. The new state would also become home for many Jews who had survived the Holocaust, especially Polish Jews, but who could not return to their former lands because of violent opposition from local populations.

The full revelations of the horrors suffered by the Jews in the Holocaust, coupled with the desperate postwar situation of Jewish survivors, made at least some portions of world opinion sympathetic to the Jews' plight. So did the wartime alliance of extreme Arab nationalists, including the Mufti of Jerusalem, with the Germans. These factors helped by 1948 to persuade the United Nations to approve the newly proclaimed state of Israel, and in a form considerably larger than that previously planned by Britain.

Finally, the Holocaust raises important and complex issues, some of them very personal, for everyone. How must one incorporate the Holocaust into his or her moral and historical view of both the past and future? What would I have done under similar circumstances? What makes some people resist and others obey authority? What is the role and responsibility of the individual in society? Where does one draw the line between obeying the law and obeying one's conscience? Should people follow one all-powerful leader or political group? For what purposes should the new and unprecedented powers of science and technology be used—the protection and sustenance of human life or its destruction?

And ultimately, how might such events as the Holocaust and world war, the most deadly yet of horrors perpetrated by man against man, be prevented in the future? The preceding study has suggested a crucial answer. One must foster far more successfully in the West and other parts of the world three of the West's most significant and peaceful traditions: human rights protected by the rule of law; democratic government; and a liberal education and philosophy that places supreme value on all humanity.

Without these, as Germany's history during 1939–1945 illustrated, one of the world's traditionally most literate and cultured nations unleashed on the earth unprecedented war and death. In doing so, Hitler and his followers threatened to pull "the whole world," as Winston Churchill told Parliament in June 1940, "into the abyss of a new Dark Age, made more sinister, and perhaps more protracted, by the lights of perverted science."[10]

But almost no one at the time, including the British prime minister, could have known or even imagined the extent of the sheer evil the war would soon bring, of which the Holocaust represented an unparalleled part. Today, barely a half-century later, remembering the war and Holocaust and the close relationship between them is more important than ever. Both events continue to warn the world of the potentially horrific dangers of singling out for hatred foreigners or social outsiders whose nationality, race, religion, or lifestyle is perceived as alien.

ENDNOTES

Notes for Introduction

1. Louis P. Lochner, ed., *The Goebbels Diaries, 1942–43*, trans. Louis P. Lochner (Garden City, N.Y.: Doubleday, 1948), 86.
2. Ronald Smelser, *Robert Ley: Hitler's Labor Front Leader* (Oxford: Berg, 1988), 295.
3. Gerhard L. Weinberg, "The Holocaust and World War II: A Dilemma in Teaching," in Donald G. Schilling, ed., *Lessons and Legacies: Teaching the Holocaust in a Changing World* (Evanston, Ill.: Northwestern University Press, 1998), 26–40.
4. Lucy S. Dawidowicz, *The War against the Jews, 1933–1945* (New York: Holt, Rinehart and Winston, 1975).
5. *Hitler's Table Talk, 1941–1944: His Private Conversations*, trans. Norman Cameron and R. H. Stevens (London: Phoenix Press, 2000; first pub. 1953), 332.
6. Gerhard L. Weinberg, *A World at Arms: A Global History of World War II* (Cambridge: University of Cambridge Press, 1994), 898–99.
7. Gordon A. Craig, *Politics and Culture in Modern Germany: Essays from* The New York Review of Books (Palo Alto, Calif.: Society for the Promotion of Science and Scholarship, 1999), 268–69.
8. Gerald Fleming, *Hitler and the Final Solution* (Berkeley: University of California Press, 1987).
9. Wolfgang Benz, *The Holocaust: A German Historian Examines the Genocide*, trans. Jane Sydenham-Kwiet (New York: Columbia University Press, 1999), 12.
10. Robert S. Wistrich, *Hitler and the Holocaust* (New York: Modern Library, 2001), 41. The italics are those of Wistrich.
11. Michael R. Marrus, *The Holocaust in History* (New York: Meridian, 1987).

12. Karl A. Schleunes, *The Twisted Road to Auschwitz: Nazi Policy toward German Jews, 1933–1939*, Illini Books ed. (Urbana-Champaign: Illinois University Press, 1990).

13. Yehuda Bauer, *Rethinking the Holocaust* (New Haven, Conn.: Yale University Press, 2001), 25–26.

14. Omer Bartov, *Mirrors of Destruction: War, Genocide, and Modern Identity* (Oxford: Oxford University Press, 2000), 125.

15. Christopher R. Browning, *The Path to Genocide: Essays on Launching the Final Solution* (Cambridge: Cambridge University Press, 1992), 169.

16. Daniel Jonah Goldhagen, *Hitler's Willing Executioners: Ordinary Germans and the Holocaust* (New York: Vintage, 1997), 77.

17. Geoff Eley, ed., *The "Goldhagen Effect": History, Memory, Nazism—Facing the German Past* (Ann Arbor: University of Michigan Press, 2000), 5.

18. Goldhagen, *Hitler's Willing Executioners*, 442.

19. Richard Breitman, *The Architect of Genocide: Himmler and the Final Solution* (New York: Knopf, 1991).

20. Götz Aly, *"Final Solution": Nazi Population Policy and the Murder of the European Jews*, trans. Belinda Cooper and Allison Brown (London: Arnold, 1999).

21. Ian Kershaw, *Hitler, 1936–45: Nemesis* (New York: Norton, 2000), 479, 481.

22. Eric A. Johnson, *Nazi Terror: The Gestapo, Jews and Ordinary Germans* (New York: Basic Books, 2000), 381.

23. Lawrence L. Langer, *Preempting the Holocaust* (New Haven, Conn.: Yale University Press, 1998), xii.

24. Edward B. Westermann, "'Ordinary Men' or 'Ideological Soldiers'? Police Battalion 310 in Russia, 1942," *German Studies Review* 21 (1998): 41–68.

Notes for Chapter One

1. Robert S. Wistrich, *Anti-Semitism: The Longest Hatred* (London: Thames Mandarin, 1995), 3–54.

2. Joel Carmichael, *The Satanizing of the Jews: Origin and Development of Mystical Anti-Semitism* (New York: Fromm, 1992), chaps. 1–4.

3. Keith H. Pickus, *Constructing Modern Identities: Jewish University Students in Germany, 1815–1914* (Detroit: Wayne State University Press, 1999), 69.

4. Wistrich, *Anti-Semitism*, xv–xvi.

5. Jacob Katz, *From Prejudice to Destruction: Anti-Semitism, 1700–1933* (Cambridge, Mass.: Harvard University Press, 1980).

6. Richard L. Rubenstein, *The Cunning of History: The Holocaust and the American Future* (New York: Harper Torchbooks, 1987), 8.

7. H. R. Trevor-Roper, ed., *Hitler's Table Talk, 1941–1944: His Private Conversations*, trans. Norman Cameron and R. H. Stevens (London: Phoenix Press, 2000; first pub. 1953), xxxix.

8. Yitzhak Arad, Yisrael Gutman, Abraham Margaliot, eds., *Documents on the Holocaust: Selected Sources on the Destruction of the Jews of Germany and Austria, Poland, and the Soviet Union*, 5th ed. (Jerusalem: Yad Vashem, 1993), 15–18.

9. Nicholas Goodrick-Clarke, *The Occult Roots of Nazism: Secret Aryan Cults and Their Influence on Nazi Ideology, The Ariosophists of Austria and Germany, 1899–1935* (New York: New York University Press, 1992), 2.

10. Gerald Fleming, *Hitler and the Final Solution* (Berkeley: University of California Press, 1987), 15.

11. Adolf Hitler, *Mein Kampf*, trans. Ralph Manheim (Boston: Houghton Mifflin, 1943), 2:679–80.

12. Raul Hilberg, ed., *Documents of Destruction: Germany and Jewry, 1933–1945* (Chicago: Quadrangle, 1971), 11.

13. Norman Isenberg, *Between Redemption and Doom: The Strains of German-Jewish Modernism* (Lincoln: University of Nebraska Press, 1999), 3.

14. Karl A. Schleunes, *The Twisted Road to Auschwitz: Nazi Policy toward German Jews, 1933–1939*, Illini Books ed. (Urbana-Champaign: Illinois University Press, 1990), 44.

15. Hitler, *Mein Kampf*, 2:653.

16. Quoted in Gerhard L. Weinberg, *Germany, Hitler & World War II: Essays in Modern German and World History* (Cambridge: University of Cambridge, 1995), 51.

17. Ingo Müller, *Hitler's Justice: The Courts of the Third Reich*, trans. Deborah Lucas Schneider (Cambridge, Mass.: Harvard University Press, 1991), 91.

18. Carole Fink, "Prelude to the Holocaust? The Murder of Walther Rathenau," in Rochelle L. Millen et al., eds., *New Perspectives on the Holocaust: A Guide for Teachers and Scholars* (New York: New York University Press, 1996), 39–56.

19. Christopher R. Browning, *Fateful Months: Essays on the Emergence of the Final Solution*, rev. ed. (New York: Holmes & Meier, 1991), x.

20. Geoffrey J. Giles, *Students and National Socialism in Germany* (Princeton, N.J.: Princeton University Press, 1985), 71.

21. Donald Niewyk, "Solving the 'Jewish Problem'—Continuity and Change in German Antisemitism, 1871–1945," *Leo Baeck Yearbook* 35 (1990):369.

Notes for Chapter Two

1. J. Noakes and G. Pridham, eds., *Nazism, 1919–1945: A Documentary Reader*, 3 vols. (Exeter, UK: University of Exeter Press, 1982–1988), 3:628–29.

2. Noakes and Pridham, *Nazism, 1919–1945*, 3:628–29.

3. Richard Breitman, *Official Secrets: What the Nazis Planned, What the British and Americans Knew* (New York: Hill and Wang, 1998), 20.

4. Michael Burleigh and Wolfgang Wippermann, *The Racial State: Germany, 1933–1945* (Cambridge: Cambridge University Press, 1991).

5. Karl A. Schleunes, *The Twisted Road to Auschwitz: Nazi Policy toward German Jews, 1933–1939*, Illini Books ed. (Urbana-Champaign: Illinois University Press, 1990), 70, quotes from the directive of 1932.

6. Richard Bessel, ed., *Life in the Third Reich* (Oxford: Oxford University Press, 1989), 8.

7. Marion A. Kaplan, *Between Dignity and Despair: Jewish Life in Nazi Germany* (New York: Oxford University Press, 1998), 20.

8. Martin Gilbert, *The Holocaust: A History of the Jews of Europe during the Second World War* (New York: Holt, Rinehart and Winston, 1985), 33–34.

9. Avraham Barkai, "Volksgemeinschaft, 'Aryanization' and the Holocaust," in David Cesarani, ed., *The Final Solution: Origins and Implementation* (London: Routledge, 1996), 38.

10. Yitzhak Arad, Yisrael Gutman, Abraham Margaliot, eds., *Documents on the Holocaust: Selected Sources on the Destruction of the Jews of Germany and Austria, Poland, and the Soviet Union*, 5th ed. (Jerusalem: Yad Vashem, 1993), 37.

11. Michael H. Kater, *Doctors Under Hitler* (Chapel Hill: University of North Carolina Press, 1989), 184, 190.

12. Jean Medawar and David Pyke, *Hitler's Gift: Scientists Who Fled Nazi Germany* (London: Richard Cohen Books, 2000).

13. Max Weinreich, *Hitler's Professors: The Part of Scholarship in Germany's Crimes against the Jewish People* (New Haven, Conn.: Yale University Press, 1999; first pub. 1946), 29.

14. Sybil Milton, "Sinti and Roma in Twentieth-Century Austria and Germany," *German Studies Review* 23 (May 2000):318.

15. Noakes and Pridham, eds., *Nazism, 1919–1945*, 2:454–55.

16. Alan E. Steinweis, *Art, Ideology, and Economics in Nazi Germany: The Reich Chambers of Music, Theater, and the Visual Arts* (Chapel Hill: University of North Carolina Press, 1993), 108.

17. Jay W. Baird, *To Die for Germany: Heroes in the Nazi Pantheon*, First Midland ed. (Bloomington: Indiana University Press, 1992), 101.

18. Robert P. Erickson and Susannah Heschel, eds., *Betrayal: German Churches and the Holocaust* (Minneapolis: Fortress Press, 1999).

19. Peter Matheson, ed., *The Third Reich and the Christian Churches: A Documentary Account of Christian Resistance and Complicity during the Nazi Era* (Grand Rapids, Mich.: Eerdmans, 1981), 12–16.

20. Doris L. Bergen, *Twisted Cross: The German Christian Movement in the Third Reich* (Chapel Hill: University of North Carolina Press, 1996), 32.

21. Dietrich Bonhoeffer, *Letters and Papers from Prison*, ed. Eberhard Bethge (New York: Touchstone, 1997), 360.
22. Dietrich Bonhoeffer, *The Cost of Discipleship*, revised and unabridged ed. (New York: Macmillan, 1959), 116, 117.

Notes for Chapter Three

1. Gordon A. Craig, *Germany 1866–1945* (New York: Oxford University Press, 1978), 587.
2. Holger H. Herwig, *Hammer or Anvil? Modern Germany 1648–Present* (Lexington, Mass.: Heath, 1994), 286.
3. Detlev J. K. Peukert, *Inside Nazi Germany: Conformity, Opposition, and Racism in Everyday Life*, trans. Richard Deveson (New Haven, Conn.: Yale University Press, 1987), 71–72.
4. Marion A. Kaplan, *Between Dignity and Despair: Jewish Life in Nazi Germany* (New York: Oxford University Press, 1998), 45.
5. Yitzhak Arad, Yisrael Gutman, Abraham Margaliot, eds., *Documents on the Holocaust: Selected Sources on the Destruction of the Jews of Germany and Austria, Poland, and the Soviet Union*, 5th ed. (Jerusalem: Yad Vashem, 1993), 65.
6. Arad et al., *Documents on the Holocaust*, 46.
7. Kaplan, *Between Dignity and Despair*, 53.
8. Robert Wistrich, *Who's Who in Nazi Germany* (New York: Macmillan, 1982), 10–11.
9. Quoted in Kaplan, *Between Dignity and Despair*, 53.
10. Lucy S. Dawidowicz, *The War against the Jews, 1933–1945* (New York: Holt, Rinehart and Winston, 1975), 190.
11. Kaplan, *Between Dignity and Despair*, 72.
12. Raul Hilberg, *The Destruction of the European Jews*, student ed. (New York: Holmes & Meier, 1985), 41.
13. Kaplan, *Between Dignity and Despair*, 5.
14. Max Domarus, ed., *Hitler: Speeches and Proclamations, 1932–1945*, trans. Chris Wilcox and Mary Fran Gilbert, 3 vols. (Wauconda, Ill.: Bolchazy-Carducci, 1992–1997), 2:686.
15. David Bankier, *The Germans and the Final Solution: Public Opinion under Nazism* (Oxford: Blackwell, 1992), 34.
16. J. Noakes and G. Pridham, eds., *Nazism, 1919–1945: A Documentary Reader*, 3 vols. (Exeter, UK: University of Exeter Press, 1982–1988), 3:531.
17. Albert Fischer, "The Minister of Economics and the Expulsion of the Jews from the German Economy," in David Bankier, ed., *Probing the Depths of*

German Anti-Semitism: German Society and the Persecution of the Jews, 1933–1941 (Jerusalem: Yad Vashem, 2000), 216.

18. Shelley Baranowski, "Conservative Elite Anti-Semitism from the Weimar Republic to the Third Reich," *German Studies Review* 19 (1996):530.

19. Noakes and Pridham, *Nazism, 1919–1945*, 3:538–39.

20. Karl Schleunes, ed., *Legislating the Holocaust: The Bernhard Loesener Memoirs and Supporting Documents*, trans. Carol Scherer (Boulder, Colo.: Westview, 2001), 16.

21. Alan E. Steinweis, *Art, Ideology, & Economics in Nazi Germany: The Reich Chambers of Music, Theater, and the Visual Arts* (Chapel Hill: University of North Carolina Press, 1993), 111.

22. Domarus, *Hitler*, 2:710–11.

23. Arnold Paucker, "Jewish Resistance in Germany: The Facts and the Problems," 6. The pamphlet was published by the German Resistance Memorial Center, Berlin, 1991.

24. Richard Mandell, *The Nazi Olympics*, reprint ed. (Urbana-Champaign: University of Illinois Press, 1987), 64.

Notes for Chapter Four

1. Karl A. Schleunes, *The Twisted Road to Auschwitz: Nazi Policy toward German Jews, 1933–1939*, Illini Books ed. (Urbana-Champaign: Illinois University Press, 1990), 135.

2. Ian Kershaw, *The 'Hitler Myth': Image and Reality in the Third Reich* (Oxford: Oxford University Press, 1989), 126.

3. Gerhard L. Weinberg, *The Foreign Policy of Hitler's Germany: Diplomatic Revolution in Europe, 1933–1936* (Chicago: University of Chicago Press, 1970), 245.

4. Peter Hayes, "State Policy and Corporate Involvement in the Holocaust," in Michael Berenbaum and Abraham J. Peck, eds., *The Holocaust and History: The Known, the Unknown, the Disputed, and the Reexamined* (Bloomington: Indiana University Press, 1998), 204. A significant portion of this section is based on Hayes's study.

5. J. Noakes and G. Pridham, eds., *Nazism, 1919–1945: A Documentary Reader*, 3 vols. (Exeter, UK: University of Exeter Press, 1982–1988), 2: 550.

6. Charles W. Sydnor Jr., *Soldiers of Destruction: The SS Death's Head Division, 1933–1945* (Princeton, N.J.: Princeton University Press, 1977), 20.

7. Noakes and Pridham, *Nazism, 1919–1945*, 2:547–48.

8. Max Domarus, ed., *Hitler: Speeches and Proclamations, 1932–1945*, trans. Chris Wilcox and Mary Fran Gilbert, 3 vols. (Wauconda, Ill.: Bolchazy-Carducci, 1992–1997), 2:938–42.

9. *Documents on German Foreign Policy, 1918–1945* (Washington, D.C.: Government Printing Office, 1949), Series D, Vol. 1, No. 19.

Notes for Chapter Five

1. Harold James, *The Deutsche Bank and the Nazi Economic War against the Jews: The Expropriation of Jewish-Owned Property* (Cambridge: Cambridge University Press, 2001), 43.
2. Evan Burr Bukey, *Hitler's Austria: Popular Sentiment in the Nazi Era, 1938–1945* (Chapel Hill: University of North Carolina Press, 2000), 134.
3. Gordon A. Craig, *Germany 1866–1945* (New York: Oxford University Press, 1978), 635.
4. Jonathan Petropoulos, *Art as Politics in the Third Reich* (Chapel Hill: University of North Carolina Press, 1996), 189.
5. James, *Deutsche Bank*, 214.
6. James, *Deutsche Bank*, 215.
7. James, *Deutsche Bank*, 38.
8. Petropoulos, *Art as Politics*, 57.
9. Craig, *Germany*, 635.
10. Richard Breitman, *The Architect of Genocide: Himmler and the Final Solution* (New York: Knopf, 1991), 50.
11. Anthony Read and David Fisher, *Kristallnacht: The Unleashing of the Holocaust* (New York: Bedrick Books, 1989), 68.
12. *Documents on German Foreign Policy, 1918–1945* (Washington, D.C.: Government Printing Office, 1949), Series D, Vol. 4, No. 501.
13. David I. Kertzer, *The Popes against the Jews: The Vatican's Role in the Rise of Modern Anti-Semitism* (New York: Knopf, 2001), 281–82.
14. Bukey, *Hitler's Austria*, 146.
15. Yitzhak Arad, Yisrael Gutman, Abraham Margaliot, eds., *Documents on the Holocaust: Selected Sources on the Destruction of the Jews of Germany and Austria, Poland, and the Soviet Union*, 5th ed. (Jerusalem: Yad Vashem, 1993), 108.
16. Arad et al., *Documents on the Holocaust*, 108.
17. Arad et al., *Documents on the Holocaust*, 112.
18. Breitman, *Architect*, 58.
19. Robet S. Wistrich, *Hitler and the Holocaust* (New York: Modern Library, 2001), 68.
20 Robert H. Abzug, ed., *America Views the Holocaust, 1933–1945: A Brief Documentary History* (Boston: Bedford St. Martin's, 1999), 76.

21. Joseph W. Bendersky, *The 'Jewish Threat'*: *Anti-Semitic Politics of the U.S. Army* (New York: Basic Books, 2000), 250.

22. Arad et al., *Documents on the Holocaust*, 125–26.

23. *Documents on German Foreign Policy*, D, 4, 158.

24. Fyodor Dostoyevsky, *The Brothers Karamazov*, trans. Constance Garnett (New York: Modern Library, 1948), 855.

25. Max Domarus, ed., *Hitler: Speeches and Proclamations, 1932–1945*, trans. Chris Wilcox and Mary Fran Gilbert, 3 vols. (Wauconda, Ill.: Bolchazy-Carducci, 1992–1997), 3:1449.

26. Robert E. Herzstein, *Roosevelt and Hitler: Prelude to War* (New York: Paragon House, 1989), 293.

27. Ian Kershaw, *Hitler, 1936–45: Nemesis* (New York: Norton, 2000), 151.

28. Arad et al., *Documents on the Holocaust*, 119–21.

29. J. Noakes and G. Pridham, eds., *Nazism, 1919–1945: A Documentary Reader*, 3 vols. (Exeter, UK: University of Exeter Press, 1982–1988), 3:739.

30. Office of United States Chief of Counsel for Prosecution of Axis Criminality, *Nazi Conspiracy and Aggression* (Washington, D.C.: Government Printing Office, 1946), 7:752–54.

Notes for Chapter Six

1. Lucy S. Dawidowicz, *The War against the Jews, 1933–1945* (New York: Holt, Rinehart and Winston, 1975), 110–11.

2. J. Noakes and G. Pridham, eds., *Nazism, 1919–1945: A Documentary Reader*, 3 vols. (Exeter, UK: University of Exeter Press, 1982–1988), 3:1051.

3. Hamburg Institute for Social Research, ed., *The German Army and Genocide: Crimes against War Prisoners, Jews, and Other Civilians in the East, 1939–1944*, trans. Scott Abbott (New York: New Press, 1999; hereafter *German Army and Genocide*), 24.

4. Noakes and Pridham, *Nazism, 1919–1945*, 3:1057.

5. Christopher R. Browning, *Ordinary Men: Reserve Police Battalion 101 and the Final Solution in Poland* (New York: Harper Perennial, 1998), 40.

6. Valids O. Lumans, *Himmler's Auxiliaries: The Volksdeutsche Mittelstelle and the German National Minorities of Europe, 1933–1945* (Chapel Hill: University of North Carolina Press, 1993).

7. Charles W. Sydnor Jr., "Executive Instinct: Reinhard Heydrich and the Planning for the Final Solution," in Michael Berenbaum and Abraham J. Peck, eds., *The Holocaust and History: The Known, the Unknown, the Disputed, and the Reexamined* (Bloomington: Indiana University Press, 1998), 165–66.

8. Max Domarus, ed., *Hitler: Speeches and Proclamations, 1932–1945*, trans. Chris Wilcox and Mary Fran Gilbert, 3 vols. (Wauconda, Ill.: Bolchazy-Carducci, 1992–1997), 3:1886.

9. Raul Hilberg, *The Destruction of the European Jews*, student ed. (New York: Holmes & Meier, 1985), 79.

10. Hilberg, *Destruction of the European Jews*, 85–86.

11. Hilberg, *Destruction of the European Jews*, 95.

12. Michael R. Marrus, *The Holocaust in History* (New York: Meridian, 1987), 115.

13. Noakes and Pridham, *Nazism, 1919–1945*, 3:1069.

14. Richard Overy, *Russia's War: A History of the Soviet War Effort, 1941–1945* (New York: Penguin, 1997), 136.

15. Overy, *Russia's War*, 135.

16. Henry Friedlander, *The Origins of Nazi Genocide: From Euthanasia to the Final Solution* (Chapel Hill: University of North Carolina Press, 1995), 64.

17. Friedlander, *Origins of Nazi Genocide*, 113.

18. Noakes and Pridham, *Nazism, 1919–1945*, 3:1035.

19. Friedlander, *Origins of Nazi Genocide*, 22.

Notes for Chapter Seven

1. Marlis G. Steinert, *Hitler's War and the Germans: Public Mood and Attitude during the Second World War*, ed. and trans. Thomas E. J. DeWitt (Athens: Ohio University Press, 1977), 56.

2. Leni Yahil, *The Holocaust: The Fate of European Jewry*, trans. Ina Friedman and Haya Galai (New York: Oxford University Press, 1990), 172.

3. Philippe Burrin, *France under the Germans: Collaboration and Compromise*, trans. by Janet Lloyd (New York: New Press, 1996).

4. *The Secret Conferences of Dr. Goebbels, October 1939–March 1943*, ed. and selected by Willi A. Boelcke, trans. Ewald Osters (London: Weidenfeld and Nicolson, 1967), 68.

5. J. Noakes and G. Pridham, eds., *Nazism, 1919–1945: A Documentary Reader*, 3 vols. (Exeter, UK: University of Exeter Press, 1982–1988), 3:1077.

6. Christopher R. Browning, *The Final Solution and the German Foreign Office: A Study of Referat D III of Abteilung Deutschland, 1940–1943* (New York: Holmes & Meier, 1978), 38.

7. Charles W. Sydnor Jr., "Executive Instinct: Reinhard Heydrich and the Planning for the Final Solution," in Michael Berenbaum and Abraham J. Peck, eds., *The Holocaust and History: The Known, the Unknown, the Disputed, and the Reexamined* (Bloomington: Indiana University Press, 1998), 171. The italics are Heydrich's.

8. Yehuda Bauer, *Rethinking the Holocaust* (New Haven, Conn.: Yale University Press, 2001), 90.
9. Sydnor, "Executive Instinct," 171. The italics are Heydrich's.
10. Robert Edwin Herzstein, *The War That Hitler Won: Goebbels and the Nazi Media Campaign* (New York: Paragon, 1987), 312, 314.

Notes for Chapter Eight

1. Gerhard L. Weinberg, "The 'Final Solution' and the War in 1943," *Fifty Years Ago: Revolt amid the Darkness* (Washington, D.C.: U.S. Holocaust Memorial Museum, 1993), 1.
2. Charles W. Sydnor Jr., "Executive Instinct: Reinhard Heydrich and the Planning for the Final Solution," in Michael Berenbaum and Abraham J. Peck, eds., *The Holocaust and History: The Known, the Unknown, the Disputed, and the Reexamined* (Bloomington: Indiana University Press, 1998), 175.
3. Eberhard Jäckel, *Hitler in History* (Hanover, N.H.: University Press of New England, 1984), 53.
4. Lucy S. Dawidowicz, *The War against the Jews, 1933–1945* (New York: Holt, Rinehart and Winston, 1975), 110.
5. Richard Breitman, *The Architect of Genocide: Himmler and the Final Solution* (New York: Knopf, 1991), 156.
6. Peter Hayes, *Industry and Ideology: IG Farben in the Nazi Era*, new ed. (Cambridge: Cambridge University Press, 2001), 351.
7. J. Noakes and G. Pridham, eds., *Nazism, 1919–1945: A Documentary Reader*, 3 vols. (Exeter, UK: University of Exeter Press, 1982–1988), 3:1087. The italics are Hitler's.
8. Noakes and Pridham, *Nazism, 1919–1945*, 3:1086–87.
9. *German Army and Genocide*, 30.
10. Jürgen Förster, "Jewish Policies of the German Military, 1939–1942," in Asher Cohen, Yehoyakim Cochavi, and Yoav Gelber, eds., *The Shoah and the War* (New York: Peter Lang, 1992), 58.
11. *German Army and Genocide*, 38.
12. Christopher R. Browning, *Fateful Months: Essays on the Emergence of the Final Solution*, rev. ed. (New York: Holmes & Meier, 1991), 49.
13. Walter Manoschek, "The Extermination of the Jews in Serbia," in Ulrich Herbert, ed., *National Socialist Extermination Policies: Contemporary German Perspectives and Controversies*, trans. from the German (New York: Berghahn, 2000), 164.

14. *German Army and Genocide*, 140.

15. Gerhard L. Weinberg, *A World at Arms: A Global History of World War II* (Cambridge: University of Cambridge Press, 1994), 300–301.

16. *Trials of War Criminals before the Nuernberg Military Tribunals under Control Council Law No. 10, Nuernberg, October 1946–April 1949*, 15 vols. (Washington, D.C.: Government Printing Office, 1952), 4:140.

17. Breitman, *Architect*, 183.

18. Yitzhak Arad, Shmuel Krakowski, and Shmuel Spector, eds., *The Einsatzgruppen Reports: Selections from the Dispatches of the Nazi Death Squads' Campaign against the Jews in Occupied Territories of the Soviet Union, July 1941–January 1943* (New York: Holocaust Library, 1989), 78, 91, 119, 128, 156, 161, 195.

19. Arad et al., *Einsatzgruppen Reports*, 131.

Notes for Chapter Nine

1. Yitzhak Arad, Shmuel Krakowski, and Shmuel Spector, eds., *The Einsatzgruppen Reports: Selections from the Dispatches of the Nazi Death Squads' Campaign against the Jews in Occupied Territories of the Soviet Union, July 1941–January 1943* (New York: Holocaust Library, 1989), 12.

2. Ernst Klee, Willi Dressen, and Volker Riess, eds., *"The Good Old Days": The Holocaust as Seen by Its Perpetrators and Bystanders*, trans. Deborah Burnstone (New York: Konecky & Konecky, 1988), 118.

3. Omer Bartov, *Hitler's Army: Soldiers, Nazis, and War in the Third Reich* (New York: Oxford University Press, 1991), 129–30. The italics are von Reichenau's.

4. *German Army and Genocide*, 128.

5. Raul Hilberg, *The Destruction of the European Jews*, student ed. (New York: Holmes & Meier, 1985), 128.

6. Klee et al., *"Good Old Days,"* 201, 203.

7. David H. Kitterman, "Those Who Said 'No!': Germans Who Refused to Execute Civilians during World War II," *German Studies Review* 11 (1988):241. The italics are Kitterman's.

8. Kitterman, "Those Who Said 'No!'" 252.

9. Edward B. Westermann, "'Ordinary Men' or 'Ideological Soldiers'? Police Battalion 310 in Russia, 1942," *German Studies Review* 21 (1998): 52–63.

10. Daniel Jonah Goldhagen, *Hitler's Willing Executioners: Ordinary Germans and the Holocaust* (New York: Vintage, 1997); and his article, "The Evil of Banality," *The New Republic*, July 13–20, 1992, 49–52.

11. Klee et al., *"Good Old Days,"* 220–21.

12. Hilberg, *Destruction of the European Jews*, 133–34.

13. Richard Breitman, *Official Secrets: What the Nazis Planned, What the British and Americans Knew* (New York: Hill and Wang, 1998), 96.

14. Breitman, *Official Secrets*, 96.

15. Edward B. Westermann, "The Royal Air Force and the Bombing of Auschwitz: First Deliberations, January 1941," *Holocaust and Genocide Studies* 15 (2001):70–85.

16. Joseph W. Bendersky, *The 'Jewish Threat': Anti-Semitic Politics of the U.S. Army* (New York: Basic Books, 2000), 307.

17. Bendersky, *'Jewish Threat'*, 314.

18. Bendersky, *'Jewish Threat'*, 285.

19. *New York Times*, 9, 26 October 1941, on pages 10 and 6, respectively.

20. Breitman, *Official Secrets*, 106.

21. Yitzhak Arad, "The Armed Jewish Resistance in Eastern Europe: Its Unique Conditions and Its Relations with the Jewish Councils (*Judenräte*) in the Ghettos," in Michael Berenbaum and Abraham J. Peck, eds., *The Holocaust and History: The Known, the Unknown, the Disputed, and the Reexamined* (Bloomington: Indiana University Press, 1998), 594.

22. Michael R. Marrus, *The Holocaust in History* (New York: Meridian, 1987),133.

23. Rudolph Höss, *Death Dealer: The Memoirs of the SS Kommandant at Auschwitz*, ed. Steven Paskuly, trans. Andrew Pollinger (New York: Da Capo, 1996), 27.

24. Höss, *Death Dealer*, 28.

25. J. Noakes and G. Pridham, eds., *Nazism, 1919–1945: A Documentary Reader*, 3 vols. (Exeter, UK: University of Exeter Press, 1982–1988), 3:1104.

26. Noakes and Pridham, *Nazism, 1919–1945*, 3:1105

27. Leni Yahil, *The Holocaust: The Fate of European Jewry*, trans. Ina Friedman and Haya Galai (New York: Oxford University Press, 1990), 259.

28. Richard Breitman, *The Architect of Genocide: Himmler and the Final Solution* (New York: Knopf, 1991), 205.

29. Breitman, *Architect*, 204.

30. *Hitler's Table Talk, 1941–1944: His Private Conversations*, trans. Norman Cameron and R. H. Stevens (London: Phoenix Press, 2000; first pub. 1953), 79.

31. See the careful translation in Richard J. Evans, *Lying About Hitler: History, Holocaust, and the David Irving Trial* (New York: Basic Books, 2001), 72–73.

32. Christopher R. Browning, *Ordinary Men: Reserve Police Battalion 101 and the Final Solution in Poland* (New York: Harper Perennial, 1998), 43.

33. Christopher R. Browning, *Nazi Policy, Jewish Workers, German Killers* (Cambridge: Cambridge University Press, 2000), 47.

34. Ian Kershaw, *Hitler, 1936–45: Nemesis* (New York: Norton, 2000), 482.

35. David Bankier, "The Use of Antisemitism in Nazi Wartime Propaganda," in Michael Berenbaum and Abraham J. Peck, eds., *The Holocaust and History: The Known, the Unknown, the Disputed, and the Reexamined* (Bloomington: Indiana University Press, 1998), 42.
36. Browning, *Nazi Policy*, 49.
37. Browning, *Nazi Policy*, 49.
38. *Documents on German Foreign Policy, 1918–1945* (Washington, D.C.: Government Printing Office, 1964), Series D, Vol. 13, No. 515.
39. *Hitler's Table Talk*, 68, 79, 87, 117.
40. Quoted in Kershaw, *Hitler, 1936–45*, 490.
41. Yitzhak Arad, Yisrael Gutman, Abraham Margaliot, eds., *Documents on the Holocaust: Selected Sources on the Destruction of the Jews of Germany and Austria, Poland, and the Soviet Union*, 5th ed. (Jerusalem: Yad Vashem, 1993), 248.
42. Yehuda Bauer, *Rethinking the Holocaust* (New Haven, Conn.: Yale University Press, 2001),5.

Notes for Chapter Ten

1. Raul Hilberg, ed., *Documents of Destruction: Germany and Jewry, 1933–1945* (Chicago: Quadrangle, 1971), 102–3.
2. Reinhard Rürup, ed., *Topography of Terror: Gestapo, SS and Reichssicher-heitshauptamt on the "Prinz-Albrecht-Terrain," A Documentation*, trans. Werner T. Angress, 2nd ed. (Berlin: Verlag Willmuth Arenhövel, 1991), 148–49.
3. Hannah Arendt, *Eichmann in Jerusalem: A Report on the Banality of Evil*, rev. and enlarged ed. (New York: Penguin, 1994), 114.
4. Annegret Ehmann, "From Colonial Racism to Nazi Population Policy: The Role of the So-called Mischlinge," in Michael Berenbaum and Abraham J. Peck, eds., *The Holocaust and History: The Known, the Unknown, the Disputed, and the Reexamined* (Bloomington: Indiana University Press, 1998), 128.
5. Lucy S. Dawidowicz, *The War against the Jews, 1933–1945* (New York: Holt, Rinehart and Winston, 1975), 110–11.
6. Götz Aly, *"Final Solution": Nazi Population Policy and the Murder of the European Jews*, trans. Belinda Cooper and Allison Brown (London: Arnold, 1999), 265.
7. Louis P. Lochner, ed., *The Goebbels Diaries, 1942–43*, trans. Louis P. Lochner (Garden City, N.Y.: Doubleday, 1948), 86.
8. See the translation in Richard J. Evans, *Lying About Hitler: History, Holocaust, and the David Irving Trial* (New York: Basic Books, 2001), 87–88.

9. Gerhard L. Weinberg, "The Holocaust and World War II: A Dilemma in Teaching," in Donald G. Schilling, ed., *Lessons and Legacies: Teaching the Holocaust in a Changing World* (Evanston, Ill.: Northwestern University Press, 1998), 34.

10. Walter Laqueur, *The Terrible Secret: An Investigation into the Suppression of Information about Hitler's 'Final Solution'* (London: Weidenfeld and Nicolson, 1980), 187.

11. Yitzhak Arad, Shmuel Krakowski, and Shmuel Spector, eds., *The Einsatzgruppen Reports: Selections from the Dispatches of the Nazi Death Squads' Campaign against the Jews in Occupied Territories of the Soviet Union, July 1941–January 1943* (New York: Holocaust Library, 1989), 276.

12. Yehuda Bauer, *Rethinking the Holocaust* (New Haven, Conn.: Yale University Press, 2001), 137.

13. Edward B. Westermann, "'Ordinary Men' or 'Ideological Soldiers'? Police Battalion 310 in Russia, 1942," *German Studies Review* 21 (1998): 56–58.

14. Westermann, "'Ordinary Men' or 'Ideological Soldiers'?", 62.

15. Martin Dean, *Collaboration in the Holocaust: Crimes of the Local Police in Belorussia and Ukraine, 1941–1944* (London: Macmillan, 2000), 68, 71.

16. Raul Hilberg, Stanislaw Staron, and Josef Kermisz, eds., *The Warsaw Diary of Adam Czerniakow: Prelude to Doom*, trans. Stanislaw Staron and Staff of Yad Vashem, Elephant paperback ed. (Chicago: Ivan R. Dee, 1999), 383.

17. Hilberg et al., *Warsaw Diary of Adam Czerniakow*, 385.

18. Chaim Kaplan, *Scroll of Agony: The Warsaw Diary of Chaim A. Kaplan*, ed. and trans. Abraham I. Katsh (Bloomington: Indiana University Press, 1999), 382.

19. Donald L. Niewyk, ed., *Fresh Wounds: Early Narratives of Holocaust Survival* (Chapel Hill: University of North Carolina Press, 1998), 140.

20. Alfred C. Mierzejewski, *The Most Valuable Asset of the Reich: A History of the German National Railway*, 2 vols. (Chapel Hill: University of North Carolina Press, 2000), 2:114.

21. Ernst Klee, Willi Dressen, and Volker Riess, eds., *"The Good Old Days": The Holocaust as Seen by Its Perpetrators and Bystanders*, trans. Deborah Burnstone (New York: Konecky & Konecky, 1988), 235.

22. Mierzejewski, *Most Valuable Asset*, 2:128.

23. Mierzejewski, *Most Valuable Asset*, 2:126.

24. Klee et al., *"Good Old Days,"* 217–18.

25. Alan Adelson and Robert Lapides, eds., *Lodz Ghetto: Inside a Community under Siege* (New York: Viking, 1989), 201, 207, 328.

26. Adelson and Lapides, *Lodz Ghetto*, 492.

27. Yitzhak Arad, *Belzec, Sobibor, Treblinka: The Operation Reinhard Death Camps* (Bloomington: Indiana University Press, 1987), 171.

28. Christopher R. Browning, *The Final Solution and the German Foreign Office: A Study of Referat D III of Abteilung Deutschland, 1940–1943* (New York: Holmes & Meier, 1978), 99.

29. Klee et al., *"Good Old Days,"* 233.

30. Christopher R. Browning, *Nazi Policy, Jewish Workers, German Killers* (Cambridge, Mass.: Cambridge University Press, 2000), 173.

31. Klee et al., *"Good Old Days,"* 233.

32. Tim Mason, "The Primacy of Politics—Politics and Economics in National Socialist Germany," in Henry A. Turner, ed., *Nazism and the Third Reich* (New York: Quadrangle, 1972), 195.

33. Quoted in *The Irving Judgment: David Irving v. Penguin Books and Professor Deborah Lipstadt* (London: Penguin, 2000), 147.

Notes for Chapter Eleven

1. Richard J. Evans, *Lying About Hitler: History, Holocaust, and the David Irving Trial* (New York: Basic Books, 2001), 89–90.

2. Yitzhak Arad, "The Armed Jewish Resistance in Eastern Europe: Its Unique Conditions and Its Relations with the Jewish Councils *(Judenräte)* in the Ghettos," in Michael Berenbaum and Abraham J. Peck, eds., *The Holocaust and History: The Known, the Unknown, the Disputed, and the Reexamined* (Bloomington: Indiana University Press, 1998), 594.

3. *Notes from the Warsaw Ghetto: The Journal of Emmanuel Ringelblum*, ed. and trans. Jacob Sloan (New York: Schocken, 1974), 295, 296.

4. *Notes from the Warsaw Ghetto*, 298.

5. Yitzhak Arad, *Belzec, Sobibor, Treblinka: The Operation Reinhard Death Camps* (Bloomington: Indiana University Press, 1987), 242.

6. Gordon A. Craig, *Politics and Culture in Modern Germany: Essays from* The New York Review of Books (Palo Alto, Calif.: Society for the Promotion of Science and Scholarship, 1999), 276.

7. Martin Gilbert, *The Holocaust: A History of the Jews of Europe during the Second World War* (New York: Holt, Rinehart and Winston, 1985), 608.

8. Donald L. Niewyk, ed., *Fresh Wounds: Early Narratives of Holocaust Survival* (Chapel Hill: University of North Carolina Press, 1998), 49.

9. Leni Yahil, *The Holocaust: The Fate of European Jewry*, trans. Ina Friedman and Haya Galai (New York: Oxford University Press, 1990), 206, 210.

10. *KL Auschwitz Seen by the SS: Rudolf Höss, Pery Broad, Johann Paul Kremer*, trans. Constantine Fitzgibbon and Krystyna Michalik (Warsaw, Poland: Interpress, 1991), 162n50.

11. Milton Goldin, "Financing the SS," *History Today* 48 (June 1998):34.
12. Primo Levi, *Survival in Auschwitz: The Nazi Assault on Humanity*, trans. Stuart Woolf (New York: Collier, 1993), 90.
13. Fania Fenelon, *Playing for Time* (New York: Atheneum, 1977).
14. Robert Jay Lifton, *The Nazi Doctors: Medical Killing and the Psychology of Genocide* (New York: Basic Books, 1986), 14, 16.
15. Lucette Matalon Lagnado and Sheila Cohn Dekel, *Children of the Flames: Dr. Josef Mengele and the Untold Story of the Twins of Auschwitz* (New York: Penguin, 1992), 9.
16. Peter Hayes, *Industry and Ideology: IG Farben in the Nazi Era*, new ed. (Cambridge, Mass.: Cambridge University Press, 2001), 359.
17. Hayes, *Industry and Ideology*, 361.
18. Leo Bretholz and Michael Olesker, *Leap into Darkness: Seven Years on the Run in Wartime Europe* (New York: Anchor, 1999), 149.
19. Ulrich Herbert, "The German Military Command in Paris and the Deportation of the French Jews," in Ulrich Herbert, ed., *National Socialist Extermination Policies: Contemporary German Perspectives and Controversies*, trans. from the German (New York: Berghahn Books, 2000), 142.
20. Herbert, "The German Military Command in Paris," 143.
21. Jonathan Steinberg, *All or Nothing: The Axis and the Holocaust* (London: Routledge, 1990), 108.
22. Gerhard L. Weinberg, "The 'Final Solution' and the War in 1943," *Fifty Years Ago: Revolt amid the Darkness* (Washington, D.C.: U.S. Holocaust Memorial Museum, 1993), 10.
23. Victor Klemperer, *I Will Bear Witness: A Diary of the Nazi Years*, trans. Martin Chalmers, 2 vols. (New York: Random House, 1999), 2:45.
24. Klemperer, *I Will Bear Witness*, 2:28.
25. Henry Ashby Turner Jr., "Victor Klemperer's Holocaust," *German Studies Review* 22 (1999):392.
26. Klemperer, *I Will Bear Witness*, 2:41.
27. Klemperer, *I Will Bear Witness*, 2:155, 156.
28. Marion A. Kaplan, *Between Dignity and Despair: Jewish Life in Nazi Germany* (New York: Oxford University Press, 1998), 194, 195.
29. *Anne Frank: The Diary of a Young Girl*, trans. B. M. Mooyaart-Doubleday (New York: Bantam, 1993), 38–39.

Notes for Chapter Twelve

1. Jeremy Noakes, ed., *Nazism, 1919–1945: A Documentary Reader*, vol. 4 (Exeter, UK: University of Exeter Press, 1998), 239.

2. Nicolaus von Below, *At Hitler's Side: The Memoirs of Hitler's Luftwaffe Adjutant, 1937–1945*, trans. Geoffrey Brooks (London: Greenhill, 2001), 200.

3. Martin Gilbert, *The Holocaust: A History of the Jews of Europe during the Second World War* (New York: Holt, Rinehart and Winston, 1985), 526.

4. Gerald Reitlinger, *The SS: Alibi of a Nation, 1922–1945* (New York: Viking, 1968), 287.

5. Richard Breitman, *The Architect of Genocide: Himmler and the Final Solution* (New York: Knopf, 1991), 241.

6. Christopher R. Browning, *Nazi Policy, Jewish Workers, German Killers* (Cambridge: Cambridge University Press, 2000), 172.

7. Gerhard L. Weinberg, "The 'Final Solution' and the War in 1943," *Fifty Years Ago: Revolt amid the Darkness* (Washington, D.C.: U.S. Holocaust Memorial Museum, 1993), 4.

8. Noakes, *Nazism, 1919–1945*, 4:491.

9. Martin Kitchen, *Nazi Germany at War* (London: Longman, 1995), 161.

10. Quoted from *Fifty Years Ago: Revolt amid the Darkness* (Washington, D.C.: U.S. Holocaust Memorial Museum, 1993).

11. Raul Hilberg, *Perpetrators, Victims, Bystanders: The Jewish Catastrophe, 1933–1945* (New York: HarperCollins, 1992), 181–82.

12. Abraham Lewin, *A Cup of Tears: A Diary of the Warsaw Ghetto*, ed. Antony Polonsky, trans. Christopher Hutton (Oxford, UK: Basil Blackwell, 1988), 183–84.

13. Yitzhak Zuckerman ("Antek"), *A Surplus of Memory: Chronicle of the Warsaw Ghetto Uprising*, ed. and trans. Barbara Harshav (Berkeley: University of California Press, 1993), 376.

14. Sybil Milton, ed., *The Stroop Report: The Jewish Quarter of Warsaw Is No More*, trans. Sybil Milton (New York: Pantheon, 1979).

15. Zuckerman, *Surplus of Memory*, 396–97.

16. Israel Gutman, *Resistance: The Warsaw Ghetto Uprising* (Boston: Houghton Mifflin, 1994), xx.

17. Yitzhak Arad, Yisrael Gutman, Abraham Margaliot, eds., *Documents on the Holocaust: Selected Sources on the Destruction of the Jews of Germany and Austria, Poland, and the Soviet Union*, 5th ed. (Jerusalem: Yad Vashem, 1993), 342.

18. Gilbert, *Holocaust*, 615.

19. Yitzhak Arad, *Belzec, Sobibor, Treblinka: The Operation Reinhard Death Camps* (Bloomington: Indiana University Press, 1987), 174.

Notes for Chapter Thirteen

1. Quoted in Richard J. Evans, *Lying About Hitler: History, Holocaust, and the David Irving Trial* (New York: Basic Books, 2001), 92.

2. Evans, *Lying About Hitler*, 93.
3. Gerhard L. Weinberg, "The 'Final Solution' and the War in 1943," *Fifty Years Ago: Revolt amid the Darkness* (Washington, D.C.: U.S. Holocaust Memorial Museum, 1993), 2.
4. Donald L. Niewyk, ed., *Fresh Wounds: Early Narratives of Holocaust Survival* (Chapel Hill: University of North Carolina Press, 1998), 314.
5. Adam Rayski, "The Jewish Underground Press in France and the Struggle to Expose the Nazi Secret of the Final Solution," in Michael Berenbaum and Abraham J. Peck, eds., *The Holocaust and History: The Known, the Unknown, the Disputed, and the Reexamined* (Bloomington: Indiana University Press, 1998), 622.
6. Rayski, "The Jewish Underground Press in France," 623.
7. Susan S. Zuccotti, "Surviving the Holocaust: The Situation in France," in Michael Berenbaum and Abraham J. Peck, eds., *The Holocaust and History: The Known, the Unknown, the Disputed, and the Reexamined* (Bloomington: Indiana University Press, 1998), 499.
8. Henry Friedlander, *The Origins of Nazi Genocide: From Euthanasia to the Final Solution* (Chapel Hill: University of North Carolina Press, 1995), 295.
9. Niewyk, *Fresh Wounds*, 260.
10. Louis P. Lochner, ed., *The Goebbels Diaries, 1942–43*, trans. Louis P. Lochner (Garden City, N.Y.: Doubleday, 1948), 314.
11. Raul Hilberg, *The Destruction of the European Jews*, student ed. (New York: Holmes & Meier, 1985), 151.
12. *Anne Frank: The Diary of a Young Girl*, trans. B. M. Mooyaart-Doubleday (New York: Bantam, 1993), 146.
13. Evans, *Lying About Hitler*, 99.
14. Evans, *Lying About Hitler*, 101.
15. Robet S. Wistrich, *Hitler and the Holocaust* (New York: Modern Library, 2001), 142–43.
16. Wistrich, *Hitler and the Holocaust*, 143.
17. Michael Phayer, *The Catholic Church and the Holocaust, 1930–1965* (Bloomington: Indiana University Press, 2000), xvii.
18. John Cornwell, *Hitler's Pope: The Secret History of Pius XII* (New York: Viking, 1999), 296–97.
19. Cornwell, *Hitler's Pope*, 325.
20. Susan Zuccotti, *Under His Very Windows: The Vatican and the Holocaust in Italy* (New Haven, Conn.: Yale University Press, 2000).
21. Zuccotti, "Surviving the Holocaust," 499.

22. John A. S. Grenville, "Neglected Holocaust Victims: The Mischlinge, the Jüdischversippte, and the Gypsies," in Michael Berenbaum and Abraham J. Peck, eds., *The Holocaust and History: The Known, the Unknown, the Disputed, and the Reexamined* (Bloomington: Indiana University Press, 1998), 315–26.

23. Geoffrey J. Giles, "The Institutionalization of Homosexual Panic in the Third Reich," in Robert Gellately and Nathan Stoltzfus, eds., *Social Outsiders in Nazi Germany* (Princeton, N.J.: Princeton University Press, 2001), 236.

24. Sybil Milton, "Correspondence," *History Teacher* 25 (1992):516.

25. Sybil Milton, "Antechamber to Birkenau: The Zigeunerlager after 1933," in Michael Berenbaum and Abraham J. Peck, eds., *The Holocaust and History: The Known, the Unknown, the Disputed, and the Reexamined* (Bloomington: Indiana University Press, 1998), 387–400.

26. Guenter Lewy, *The Nazi Persecution of the Gypsies* (New York: Oxford University Press, 2000), 55.

27. Lewy, *Nazi Persecution*, 165.

28. Yehuda Bauer, *Rethinking the Holocaust* (New Haven, Conn.: Yale University Press, 2001), 66.

29. Lewy, *Nazi Persecution*, 222.

Notes for Chapter Fourteen

1. Quoted from minutes of the meeting in Richard J. Evans, *Lying About Hitler: History, Holocaust, and the David Irving Trial* (New York: Basic Books, 2001), 95.

2. *KL Auschwitz Seen by the SS: Rudolf Höss, Pery Broad, Johann Paul Kremer*, trans. Constantine Fitzgibbon and Krystyna Michalik (Warsaw, Poland: Interpress, 1991), 89.

3. Elie Wiesel, *Night*, trans. Stella Rodway (New York: Bantam, 1982), 24.

4. Wiesel, *Night*, 25–27.

5. Richard Breitman and Shlomo Aronson, "The End of the 'Final Solution'? Nazi Plans to Ransom Jews in 1944," *Central European History* 25 (1992):189.

6. Nora Levin, ed., *The Holocaust Years: The Nazi Destruction of European Jewry, 1933–1945* (Malabar, Fla.: Krieger, 1990), 320.

7. Raoul Wallenberg, *Letters and Dispatches, 1924–1944*, trans. Kjersti Board (New York: Arcade, 1995), 241–42.

8. Wallenberg, *Letters and Dispatches*, 265, 267.

9. John Bierman, *Righteous Gentile: The Story of Raoul Wallenberg, Missing Hero of the Holocaust* (New York: Viking, 1981).

10. Donald L. Niewyk, ed., *Fresh Wounds: Early Narratives of Holocaust Survival* (Chapel Hill: University of North Carolina Press, 1998), 318.

11. Miklos Nyiszli, *Auschwitz: A Doctor's Eyewitness Account*, trans. Tibère Kremer and Richard Seaver (New York: Arcade, 1993), 123.

12. Doris L. Bergen, "Death Throes and Killing Frenzies: A Response to Hans Mommsen's 'The Dissolution of the Third Reich: Crisis Management and Collapse, 1943–1945,'" *Bulletin of the German Historical Institute* 27 (Fall 2000):28.

13. Alfred C. Mierzejewski, *The Most Valuable Asset of the Reich: A History of the German National Railway*, 2 vols. (Chapel Hill: University of North Carolina Press, 2000), 2:124.

14. Ruth Andreas-Friedrich, *Berlin Underground, 1938–1945*, trans. Barrows Mussey (New York: Paragon, 1989), 192.

15. Robert Gellately, *Backing Hitler: Consent and Coercion in Nazi Germany* (Oxford, UK: Oxford University Press, 2001), 250.

16. Gellately, *Backing Hitler*, 251.

17. *Final Entries 1945: The Diaries of Joseph Goebbels*, ed. Hugh Trevor-Roper, trans. Richard Barry (New York: Putnam's, 1978), 126.

18. Ian Kershaw, *Hitler, 1936–45: Nemesis* (New York: Norton, 2000), 819.

19. Kershaw, *Hitler, 1936–45*, 821–22.

20. Kershaw, *Hitler, 1936–45*, 822.

21. Anton Joachimsthaler, *The Last Days of Hitler: The Legends, the Evidence, the Truth*, trans. Helmut Bögler (London: Arms and Armour, 1996), 138, 144.

Notes for Chapter Fifteen

1. Walter Laqueur, *The Terrible Secret: An Investigation into the Suppression of Information about Hitler's 'Final Solution'* (London: Weidenfeld and Nicolson, 1980).

2. Arieh J. Kochavi, *Prelude to Nuremberg: Allied War Crimes Policy and the Question of Punishment* (Chapel Hill: University of North Carolina Press, 1998), 20.

3. Richard Breitman, *Official Secrets: What the Nazis Planned, What the British and Americans Knew* (New York: Hill and Wang, 1998), 116.

4. *New York Times*, 14 March 1942.

5. Breitman, *Official Secrets*, 139.

6. Nora Levin, ed., *The Holocaust Years: The Nazi Destruction of European Jewry, 1933–1945* (Malabar, Fla.: Krieger, 1990), 332–33.

7. Jean-Claude Favez, *The Red Cross and the Holocaust*, ed. and trans. John and Beryl Fletcher (Cambridge, UK: Cambridge University Press, 1999), 282.

8. *New York Times*, 2 July 1943.

9. Martin Gilbert, *Auschwitz and the Allies* (New York: Holt, Rinehart and Winston, 1981), 87.

10. Kochavi, *Prelude to Nuremberg*, 142.
11. Gerhard L. Weinberg, "The 'Final Solution' and the War in 1943," *Fifty Years Ago: Revolt amid the Darkness* (Washington, D.C.: U.S. Holocaust Memorial Museum, 1993), 14.
12. Bernard Wasserstein, *Britain and the Jews of Europe, 1939–1945* (London: Oxford University Press, 1979), 351.
13. Wasserstein, *Britain and the Jews of Europe*, 259.
14. Joseph W. Bendersky, *The 'Jewish Threat': Anti-Semitic Politics of the U.S. Army* (New York: Basic Books, 2000), 315.
15. Bendersky, *'Jewish Threat,'* 316.
16. Bendersky, *'Jewish Threat,'* 325.
17. Bendersky, *'Jewish Threat,'* 294.
18. Robert S. Wistrich, *Hitler and the Holocaust* (New York: Modern Library, 2001), 190.
19. Michael R. Marrus, ed., *The Nuremberg War Crimes Trial, 1945–46: A Documentary History* (Boston: Bedford, 1997), 20–21.
20. Jean Ziegler, *The Swiss, The Gold, and the Dead: How Swiss Bankers Helped Finance the Nazi War Machine*, trans. John Brownjohn (New York: Harcourt Brace, 1998), 18.

Notes for Chapter Sixteen

1. Robert S. Wistrich, *Hitler and the Holocaust* (New York: Modern Library, 2001), 207.
2. See W. M. (45) 37th Conclusions, 28 March 1945, Public Record Office, London, CAB 65/49, frame 164.
3. Nora Levin, ed., *The Holocaust Years: The Nazi Destruction of European Jewry, 1933–1945* (Malabar, Fla.: Krieger, 1990), 325.
4. Joseph W. Bendersky, *The 'Jewish Threat': Anti-Semitic Politics of the U.S. Army* (New York: Basic Books, 2000), 332.
5. Bendersky, *'Jewish Threat,'* 334, 336.
6. William D. Rubinstein, *The Myth of Rescue: Why the Democracies Could Not Have Saved More Jews from the Nazis* (London: Routledge, 2000), x. The italics are Rubinstein's.
7. Gerhard L. Weinberg, "The Allies and the Holocaust," in Michael Berenbaum and Abraham J. Peck, eds., *The Holocaust and History: The Known, the Unknown, the Disputed, and the Reexamined* (Bloomington: Indiana University Press, 1998), 490.
8. Quoted from the *Christian Century*, 13 Sept. 1944, in Robert H. Abzug, ed., *America Views the Holocaust, 1933–1945: A Brief Documentary History* (Boston: Bedford/St. Martin's, 1999), 182.

9. Omar N. Bradley, *A Soldier's Story* (New York: Modern Library, 1999; first pub. 1951), 539.

10. Martin Gilbert, *The Dent Atlas of the Holocaust: The Complete History*, 2nd ed. (London: J. M. Dent, 1993), 226.

11. David A. Hackett, ed., *The Buchenwald Report*, trans. David A. Hackett (Boulder, Colo.: Westview, 1995), 10.

12. Gordon A. Craig, *Politics and Culture in Modern Germany: Essays from* The New York Review of Books (Palo Alto, Calif.: Society for the Promotion of Science and Scholarship, 1999), 276.

13. Craig, *Politics and Culture*, 276. The italics are Eisenhower's.

14. Michael Phayer, *The Catholic Church and the Holocaust, 1930–1965* (Bloomington: Indiana University Press, 2000), 165–75.

15. Arieh J. Kochavi, *Prelude to Nuremberg: Allied War Crimes Policy and the Question of Punishment* (Chapel Hill: University of North Carolina Press, 1998), 224–25.

16. Richard Overy, *Interrogations: The Nazi Elite in Allied Hands, 1945* (New York: Viking, 2001), 179.

17. G. M. Gilbert, *Nuremberg Diary* (New York: Da Capo, 1995), 6, 7.

18. Overy, *Interrogations*, 359–60.

19. Overy, *Interrogations*, 192.

20. Overy, *Interrogations*, 197.

21. Brian Keith Feltman, "Window to Nuremberg: The American Press and the International Military Tribunal, 1945–46," M.A. thesis, Clemson University, 2002.

22. Kochavi, *Prelude to Nuremberg*, 247.

23. Efraim Zuroff, *Occupation: Nazi-Hunter: The Continuing Search for Perpetrators of the Holocaust* (Hoboken, N.J.: KTAV, 1994), 35.

24. Zuroff, *Occupation*, 366.

Notes for Chapter Seventeen

1. Donald M. McKale, ed., *Rewriting History: The Original and Revised World War II Diaries of Curt Prüfer, Nazi Diplomat*, trans. Judith M. Melton (Kent, Ohio: Kent State University Press, 1988), 11.

2. Marion Yorck von Wartenburg, *The Power of Solitude: My Life in the German Resistance*, with an introduction by Peter Hoffmann, ed. and trans. Julie M. Winter (Lincoln: University of Nebraska Press, 2000), 20.

3. Christopher R. Browning, *Ordinary Men: Reserve Police Battalion 101 and the Final Solution in Poland* (New York: Harper Perennial, 1998), 188.

4. Daniel Jonah Goldhagen, *Hitler's Willing Executioners: Ordinary Germans and the Holocaust* (New York: Vintage, 1997).

5. Eric A. Johnson, *Nazi Terror: The Gestapo, Jews and Ordinary Germans* (New York: Basic Books, 2000), 21.

6. Lawrence L. Langer, *Preempting the Holocaust* (New Haven, Conn.: Yale University Press, 1998), xiii–xiv. The italics are Langer's.

7. David Bankier, *The Germans and the Final Solution: Public Opinion under Nazism* (Oxford, UK: Blackwell, 1992), 103.

8. Victor Klemperer, *I Will Bear Witness: A Diary of the Nazi Years*, trans. Martin Chalmers, 2 vols. (New York: Random House, 1999), 2:12.

9. Ruth Andreas-Friedrich, *Berlin Underground, 1938–1945*, trans. Barrows Mussey (New York: Paragon, 1989), 83.

10. *KL Auschwitz Seen by the SS: Rudolf Höss, Pery Broad, Johann Paul Kremer*, trans. Constantine Fitzgibbon and Krystyna Michalik (Warsaw, Poland: Interpress, 1991), 134–35.

11. Quoted in Gerhard L. Weinberg, *A World at Arms: A Global History of World War II* (Cambridge: University of Cambridge Press, 1994), 474.

12. Albert Speer, *Infiltration*, trans. Joachim Neugroschel (New York: Macmillan, 1981), 255.

13. Speer, *Infiltration*, 255.

14. Matthias Schmidt, *Albert Speer: The End of a Myth*, trans. Joachim Neugroschel (New York: Collier, 1984), 188.

15. Gitta Sereny, *The German Trauma: Experiences and Reflections, 1938–2000* (London: Allen Lane/Penguin Press, 2000), 284–85.

16. Marlis G. Steinert, *Hitler's War and the Germans: Public Mood and Attitude during the Second World War*, ed. and trans. Thomas E. J. DeWitt (Athens: Ohio University Press, 1977), 141–42.

17. Robert S. Wistrich, *Hitler and the Holocaust* (New York: Modern Library, 2001), 131.

18. Robert Gellately, *Backing Hitler: Consent and Coercion in Nazi Germany* (Oxford, UK: Oxford University Press, 2001), 261.

19. Bankier, *Germans and the Final Solution*, 121.

20. Sereny, *German Trauma*, 281, 282.

21. Louis P. Lochner, ed., *The Goebbels Diaries, 1942–43*, trans. Louis P. Lochner (Garden City, N.Y.: Doubleday, 1948), 266.

22. Ian Kershaw, *Popular Opinion and Political Dissent in the Third Reich, Bavaria, 1933–1945* (Oxford, UK: Clarendon, 1984), 360.

23. Steinert, *Hitler's War and the Germans*, 145.

24. Andreas-Friedrich, *Berlin Underground*, 116–17.

25. Quoted in Doris L. Bergen, "Death Throes and Killing Frenzies: A Response to Hans Mommsen's 'The Dissolution of the Third Reich: Crisis Management

and Collapse, 1943–1945,'" *Bulletin of the German Historical Institute* 27 (Fall 2000):32.

26. Johnson, *Nazi Terror*, 437.

27. Jeffrey Herf, *Divided Memory: The Nazi Past in the Two Germanys* (Cambridge, Mass.: Harvard University Press, 1997).

28. Andrei S. Markovits and Beth Simone Noveck, "West Germany," in David S. Wyman, *The World Reacts to the Holocaust* (Baltimore: Johns Hopkins University Press, 1996), 401.

29. Sybil Milton, "Sinti and Roma in Twentieth-Century Austria and Germany," *German Studies Review* 23 (May 2000):317.

30. Werner Maser, *Nuremberg: A Nation on Trial*, trans. by Richard Barry (London: Allen Lane, 1979), 279.

31. Werner Bergmann and Rainer Erb, *Anti-Semitism in Germany: The Post-Nazi Epoch Since 1945*, trans. Belinda Cooper and Allison Brown (New Brunswick, N.J.: Transaction, 1997), 111, 116.

32. Hermann Kurthen, Werner Bergmann, and Rainer Erb, eds., *Anti-Semitism and Xenophobia in Germany after Unification* (New York: Oxford University Press, 1997), 23.

33. Ernestine Schlant, *The Language of Silence: West German Literature and the Holocaust* (New York: Routledge, 1999), 13.

34. Schlant, *Language of Silence*, 1.

35. "Chroniclers of Collaboration," *New York Times*, 18 Feb. 1999.

36. Markovits and Noveck, "West Germany," 434.

37. *Forever in the Shadow of Hitler? Original Documents of the Historikerstreit, the Controversy Concerning the Singularity of the Holocaust*, trans. James Knowlton and Truett Cates (Atlantic Highlands, N.J.: Humanities Press, 1993), 8.

38. Harold James and Marla Stone, eds., *When the Wall Came Down: Reactions to German Unification* (New York: Routledge, 1992), 57–58.

39. Schlant, *Language of Silence*, 19.

40. "Top German Doctor Admits SS Past," *New York Times*, 16 Jan. 1993.

41. "Berlin Recalls a Night in 1938 with a Solemn Rally," *New York Times*, 10 Nov. 2000.

42. Peter Gay, "'My German Question,'" *New York Review*, 10 Jan. 2000, 22.

43. Gerhard L. Weinberg, *Germany, Hitler, & World War II: Essays in Modern German and World History* (Cambridge: Cambridge University Press, 1995), 324.

44. Evan Burr Bukey, *Hitler's Austria: Popular Sentiment in the Nazi Era, 1938–1945* (Chapel Hill: University of North Carolina Press, 2000), 207.

45. Bukey, *Hitler's Austria*, 150.

46. Robert Edwin Herzstein, *Waldheim: The Missing Years* (London: Grafton, 1988).

Notes for Chapter Eighteen

1. Michael Berenbaum and Abraham J. Peck, eds., *The Holocaust and History: The Known, the Unknown, the Disputed, and the Reexamined* (Bloomington: Indiana University Press, 1998), 693.
2. Ruth Elias, *Triumph of Hope: From Theresienstadt and Auschwitz to Israel*, trans. Margot Bettauer Dembo (New York: Wiley, 1998).
3. Aaron Hass, *The Aftermath: Living with the Holocaust* (Cambridge: Cambridge University Press, 1995).
4. Omer Bartov, *Mirrors of Destruction: War, Genocide, and Modern Identity* (Oxford: Oxford University Press, 2000), 85.
5. Lawrence L. Langer, *Preempting the Holocaust* (New Haven, Conn.: Yale University Press, 1998), 135.
6. Langer, *Preempting the Holocaust*, 133.
7. Jean Améry, *At the Mind's Limits: Contemplations by a Survivor on Auschwitz and Its Realities*, trans. Sidney Rosenfeld and Stella P. Rosenfeld (Bloomington: Indiana University Press, 1980), 31, 94–95.
8. Hass, *Aftermath*, 10.
9. Raul Hilberg, *The Destruction of the European Jews*, student ed. (New York: Holmes & Meier, 1985), 76.
10. Hannah Arendt, *Eichmann in Jerusalem: A Report on the Banality of Evil*, rev. and enlarged ed. (New York: Penguin, 1994), 117.
11. Améry, *At the Mind's Limits*, 25.
12. Yehuda Bauer, "A Past That Will Not Go Away," in Michael Berenbaum and Abraham J. Peck, eds., *The Holocaust and History: The Known, the Unknown, the Disputed, and the Reexamined* (Bloomington: Indiana University Press, 1998), 18.
13. Yehuda Bauer, *Rethinking the Holocaust* (New Haven, Conn.: Yale University Press, 2001), 136.
14. Donald Niewyk and Francis Nicosia, *The Columbia Guide to the Holocaust* (New York: Columbia University Press, 2000), 100.
15. Terrence Des Pres, *The Survivor: An Anatomy of Life in the Death Camps* (New York: Oxford University Press, 1976), 40.
16. Yitzhak Arad, *The Partisan: From the Valley of Death to Mount Zion* (New York: Holocaust Library, 1979), 120.
17. Bauer, *Rethinking the Holocaust*, 82.
18. Lucy S. Dawidowicz, *The War against the Jews, 1933–1945* (New York: Holt, Rinehart and Winston, 1975), 348.
19. Roselle K. Chartock and Jack Spencer, eds., *Can It Happen Again? Chronicles of the Holocaust* (New York: Black Dog and Leventhal, 1995), 263.

20. Simon Wiesenthal, *Justice Not Vengeance*, trans. Ewald Osers (New York: Grove Weidenfeld, 1989), x.

21. Donald L. Niewyk, ed., *Fresh Wounds: Early Narratives of Holocaust Survival* (Chapel Hill: University of North Carolina Press, 1998), 181.

22. Langer, *Preempting the Holocaust*, xix.

23. Tim Cole, *Selling the Holocaust: From Auschwitz to Schindler, How History Is Bought, Packaged, and Sold* (New York: Routledge, 1999), 3.

24. Geoffrey H. Hartman, ed., *Holocaust Remembrance: The Shapes of Memory* (Oxford, UK: Berg, 1994).

25. Ernestine Schlant, *The Language of Silence: West German Literature and the Holocaust* (New York: Routledge, 1999), 239.

26. James E. Young, *At Memory's Edge: After-Images of the Holocaust in Contemporary Art and Architecture* (New Haven, Conn.: Yale University Press, 2000).

27. Hilene Flanzbaum, ed., *The Americanization of the Holocaust* (Baltimore: Johns Hopkins University Press, 1999).

28. Yehudit Inbar, "Art in the Face of Adversity: The New Museum of Holocaust Art," *Yad Vashem Quarterly Magazine* 20 (2000):10.

29. Michael Berenbaum, "United States Holocaust Memorial Museum," in Walter Laqueur, ed., *The Holocaust Encyclopedia* (New Haven, Conn.: Yale University Press, 2001), 661.

30. Schlant, *Language of Silence*, 8, 9.

31. Schlant, *Language of Silence*, 9–10.

32. Langer, *Preempting the Holocaust*, 22–23.

33. Richard J. Evans, *Lying About Hitler: History, Holocaust, and the David Irving Trial* (New York: Basic Books, 2001), 109.

34. Deborah E. Lipstadt, *Denying the Holocaust: The Growing Assault on Truth and Memory* (New York: Free Press, 1993).

35. *The Irving Judgment: David Irving v. Penguin Books and Professor Deborah Lipstadt* (London: Penguin, 2000), 9.

36. Michael Shermer and Alex Grobman, *Denying History: Who Says the Holocaust Never Happened and Why Do They Say It?* (Berkeley: University of California Press, 2000), 2.

37. Lucy Dawidowicz, *The Holocaust and the Historians* (Cambridge, Mass.: Harvard University Press, 1981), 16.

38. Peter Novick, *The Holocaust in American Life* (Boston: Houghton Mifflin, 1999), 280.

39. Novick, *The Holocaust in American Life*, 268.
40. Norman G. Finkelstein, *The Holocaust Industry: Reflections on the Exploitation of Jewish Suffering* (London: Verso, 2000).
41. Inga Clendinnen, *Reading the Holocaust* (Cambridge: Cambridge University Press, 1999), 180.
42. Greg Bradsher, comp., *Holocaust-Era Assets: A Finding Aid to Records at the National Archives at College Park, Maryland* (Washington, D.C.: National Archives and Records Administration, 1999).
43. "How IBM Helped Facilitate the Holocaust," *International Herald Tribune*, 23 Feb. 2001.

Notes for Chapter Nineteen

1. Marvin Perry et al., *Western Civilization: Ideas, Politics & Society*, 6th ed., 2 vols. (Boston: Houghton Mifflin, 2000), 2:xv.
2. Yehuda Bauer, *Rethinking the Holocaust* (New Haven, Conn.: Yale University Press, 2001), 19.
3. Christopher R. Browning, "Why Study the Holocaust?" 5–6, Frank Porter Graham Chair Inaugural Lecture, University of North Carolina-Chapel Hill, 30 March 2000.
4. Michael Phayer, *The Catholic Church and the Holocaust, 1930–1965* (Bloomington: Indiana University Press, 2000), xvii, and esp. chap. 12.
5. Quoted in David I. Kertzer, *The Popes against the Jews: The Vatican's Role in the Rise of Modern Anti-Semitism* (New York: Knopf, 2001), 6–7.
6. Kertzer, *Popes against the Jews*, 6.
7. Gerhard L. Weinberg, *A World at Arms: A Global History of World War II* (Cambridge: University of Cambridge Press, 1994), 899.
8. Alexander Donat, *The Holocaust Kingdom: A Memoir* (New York: Holocaust Library, 1978).
9. Gerhard L. Weinberg, "The Holocaust and World War II: A Dilemma in Teaching," in Donald G. Schilling, ed., *Lessons and Legacies: Teaching the Holocaust in a Changing World* (Evanston, Ill.: Northwestern University Press, 1998), 38.
10. Winston S. Churchill, *The Second World War*, 6 vols. (Boston: Houghton Mifflin, 1949), 2:226.

SUGGESTIONS FOR
FURTHER READING

OR THE GENERAL READER or nonspecialist wishing to examine the Holocaust and World War II in some detail, he or she can do so easily with sources in English. Many of the collections of relevant documents as well as a good portion of the best work done by foreign scholars have been translated. The exception to this used in the present study, primarily for the numbers and figures it provides, is Wolfgang Benz, ed., *Dimension des Völkermords. Die Zahl der jüdischen Opfer des Nationalsozialismus* (Munich: Deutscher Taschenbuch Verlag, 1996).

The reading list that follows does not include the sources in the endnotes, except for several books of essays that are cited according to the editors rather than authors of essays in the volumes. The list hardly begins to present the enormous literature on the Holocaust, even in English, but instead contains additional sources useful for researching this book and for a further examination of its subject. Readers will find a helpful annotated bibliography in Donald Niewyk and Francis Nicosia, *The Columbia Guide to the Holocaust* (New York: Columbia University Press, 2000), part 5.

Adelson, Alan, and Robert Lapides, eds. *Lodz Ghetto: Inside A Community under Siege*. New York: Viking, 1989.
Allen, William Sheridan. *The Nazi Seizure of Power: The Experience of a Single German Town, 1922–1945*. Rev. ed., 1965. New York: Franklin Watts, 1984.

Aly, Götz, Peter Chroust, and Christian Pross. *Cleansing the Fatherland: Nazi Medicine and Racial Hygiene*. Trans. Belinda Cooper. Baltimore: Johns Hopkins University Press, 1994.

Ascheim, Steven E. *Culture and Catastrophe: German and Jewish Confrontations with National Socialism and Other Crises*. New York: New York University Press, 1996.

Barkai, Avraham. *From Boycott to Annihilation: The Economic Struggle of German Jews, 1933–1943*. Trans. William Templer. Hanover, N.H.: University Press of New England, 1989.

Bartov, Omer, ed. *The Holocaust: Origins, Implementation, Aftermath*. New York: Routledge, 2000.

Bauer, Yehuda. *The Jewish Emergence from Powerlessness*. Toronto: University of Toronto Press, 1979.

———. *A History of the Holocaust*. New York: Franklin Watts, 1982.

———. *Jews For Sale? Nazi–Jewish Negotiations, 1933–1945*. New Haven, Conn.: Yale University Press, 1994.

Bauman, Zygmunt. *Modernity and the Holocaust*. Cambridge, Mass.: Polity Press, 1989.

Baumel, Judith. *Double Jeopardy: Gender and the Holocaust*. Portland, Ore.: Valentine Mitchell, 1998.

Berenbaum, Michael. *Witness to the Holocaust: An Illustrated Documentary History of the Holocaust in the Words of Its Victims, Perpetrators and Bystanders*. New York: HarperCollins, 1997.

Berenbaum, Michael, and Abraham J. Peck, eds. *The Holocaust and History: The Known, the Unknown, the Disputed, and the Reexamined*. Bloomington: Indiana University Press, 1998.

Berger, Alan L., and Naomi Berger, eds. *Second Generation Voices: Reflections by Children of Holocaust Survivors and Perpetrators*. Syracuse, N.Y.: Syracuse University Press, 2001.

Berkowitz, Michael. *The Jewish Self-Image in the West*. New York: New York University Press, 2000.

Black, Peter. *Ernst Kaltenbrunner: Ideological Soldier of the Third Reich*. Princeton, N.J.: Princeton University Press, 1984.

———. "Rehearsal for 'Reinhard'? Odilo Globocnik and the Lublin Selbstschutz." *Central European History* 25 (1992): 204–26.

Bloxham, Donald. *The Holocaust on Trial: The War Crimes Trials and the Formation of History and Memory*. Oxford: Oxford University Press, 2001.

Borowski, Tadeusz. *This Way for the Gas, Ladies and Gentlemen*. New York: Penguin, 1959.

Botwinick, Rita Steinhardt. *A History of the Holocaust: From Ideology to Annihilation*. 2nd ed. Upper Saddle River, N.J.: Prentice Hall, 2001.

Braham, Randolph, ed. *The Destruction of Hungarian Jewry: A Documentary Account*. 2 vols. New York: World Federation of Hungarian Jews, 1963.

———. *The Politics of Genocide: The Holocaust in Hungary*. Condensed ed., 1982. Detroit: Wayne State University, 2000.

———. *Studies on the Holocaust: Selected Writings*. Vol. 1. New York: Columbia University Press, 2000.

———, ed. *Vatican and the Holocaust: The Catholic Church and the Jews during the Nazi Era*. Boulder, Colo.: Social Science Monographs, 2000.

Browder, George C. *Foundations of the Nazi Police State: The Formation of Sipo and SD*. Lexington: University Press of Kentucky, 1990.

———. *Hitler's Enforcers: The Gestapo and SS Security Service in the Nazi Revolution*. New York: Oxford University Press, 1996.

Burleigh, Michael. *Death and Deliverance: "Euthanasia" in Germany, c.1900–1945*. Cambridge: Cambridge University Press, 1994.

———. *Ethics and Extermination: Reflections on Nazi Genocide*. Cambridge: Cambridge University Press, 1997.

———. *The Third Reich: A New History*. London: Macmillan, 2000.

Burrin, Philippe. *Hitler and the Jews: The Genesis of the Holocaust*. Trans. Patsy Southgate. London: Edward Arnold, 1994.

Campbell, Bruce. *The SA Generals and the Rise of Nazism*. Lexington: University Press of Kentucky, 1998.

Cargas, Harry James. *Voices from the Holocaust*. Lexington: University Press of Kentucky, 1993.

Cesarani, David, ed. *The Final Solution: Origins and Implementation*. New York: Routledge, 1996.

Chary, Frederick. *The Bulgarian Jews and the Final Solution, 1940–1944*. Pittsburgh: University of Pittsburgh Press, 1972.

Cholawsky, Shalom. *The Jews of Bielorussia during World War II*. Amsterdam: Harwood Academic, 1998.

Cohen, Asher. *The Halutz Resistance in Hungary, 1942–1944*. New York: Columbia University Press, 1986.

Cohen, Asher, Yehoyakim Cochavi, and Yoav Gelber, eds. *The Shoah and the War*. New York: Peter Lang, 1992.

Cohen, Richard. *The Burden of Conscience: French Jewish Leadership during the Holocaust.* Bloomington: Indiana University Press, 1987.

Conway, Martin. *Collaboration in Belgium: Léon Degrelle and the Rexist Movement.* New Haven, Conn.: Yale University Press, 1993.

Czech, Danuta. *Auschwitz Chronicle, 1939–1945.* New York: H. Holt, 1990.

Dallin, Alexander. *German Rule in Russia, 1941–1945. A Study of Occupation Policies.* London: Macmillan, 1957.

Davidson, Eugene. *The Trial of the Germans: An Account of the Twenty-two Defendants before the International Military Tribunal at Nuremberg.* New York: Collier, 1966.

Deschner, Günther. *Reinhard Heydrich: A Biography.* New York: Stein & Day, 1981.

Diner, Dan. *Beyond the Conceivable: Studies on Germany, Nazism, and the Holocaust.* Berkeley: University of California Press, 2000.

Dobroszycki, Lucjan, ed. *The Chronicle of the Lodz Ghetto, 1941–1944.* Trans. Richard Lourie, Joachim Neugroschel, and others. New Haven, Conn.: Yale University Press, 1984.

Donat, Alexander. *The Death Camp Treblinka: A Documentary.* New York: Holocaust Library, 1979.

Durlacher, Gerhard. *The Search: The Birkenau Boys.* Trans. Susan Massotty. London: Serpent's Tail, 1998.

Dwork, Debórah. *Children with a Star: Jewish Youth in Nazi Europe.* New Haven, Conn.: Yale University Press, 1993.

Dwork, Debórah, and Robert Jan van Pelt. *Auschwitz, 1270 to the Present.* New York: Norton, 1996.

Edelheit, Abraham J., and Hershel Edelheit, eds. *History of the Holocaust: A Handbook and Dictionary.* Boulder, Colo.: Westview, 1994.

Engelking, Barbara. *Holocaust and Memory: The Experience of the Holocaust and Its Consequences: An Investigation Based on Personal Narratives.* Ed. Gunnar S. Paulsson. Trans. Emma Harris. London: Leicester University Press, 2001.

Epstein, Helen. *Children of the Holocaust: Conversations with Sons and Daughters of Survivors.* New York: Penguin, 1988.

Ezergailis, Andrew. *The Holocaust in Latvia, 1941–1944: The Missing Center.* Riga: Historical Institute of Latvia; Washington, D.C.: United States Holocaust Memorial Museum, 1996.

Fenyo, Mario. *Hitler, Horthy and Hungary: German–Hungarian Relations, 1941–1944.* New Haven, Conn.: Yale University Press, 1972.

Ferencz, Benjamin B. *Less Than Slaves: Jewish Forced Labor and the Quest for Compensation.* Cambridge, Mass.: Harvard University Press, 1979.

Jürgen Förster. "Securing 'Living-Space.'" In Militärgeschichtliches Forschungsamt (Research Institute for Military History), Potsdam, Germany, *Germany and the Second World War,* trans. Dean S. McMurry, Ewald Osers, and Louise Willmot. Vol. 4. Oxford: Clarendon, 1998.

Fogelman, Eva. *Conscience and Courage: Rescuers of Jews during the Holocaust.* New York: Anchor, 1995.

Freeden, Herbert. *The Jewish Press in the Third Reich.* Trans. William Templer. Providence, R.I.: Berg, 1993.

Friedländer, Saul. *Nazi Germany and the Jews: The Years of Persecution, 1933–1939.* New York: HarperCollins, 1997.

Friedlander, Henry, and Sybil Milton, eds. *The Holocaust: Ideology, Bureaucracy, and Genocide: The San Jose Papers.* Millwood, N.Y.: Kraus, 1980.

———, eds. *Archives of the Holocaust: An International Collection of Selected Documents.* 25 vols. New York: Garland, 1989–95.

Friedlander, Saul. *Memory, History, and the Extermination of the Jews of Europe.* Bloomington: Indiana University Press, 1993.

Friedrich, Otto. *The Kingdom of Auschwitz.* New York: HarperPerennial, 1994.

Fulbrook, Mary. *German National Identity after the Holocaust.* Cambridge, UK: Polity Press, 1999.

Gay, Peter. *My German Question: Growing Up in Nazi Berlin.* New Haven, Conn.: Yale University Press, 1998.

Gellately, Robert. *The Gestapo and German Society: Enforcing Racial Policy, 1933.* Oxford, UK: Clarendon, 1991.

Gellately, Robert, and Nathan Stoltzfus, eds. *Social Outsiders in Nazi Germany.* Princeton, N.J.: Princeton University Press, 2001.

Gerlach, Wolfgang. *And the Witnesses Were Silent: The Confessing Church and the Persecution of the Jews.* Ed. and trans. Victoria J. Barnett. Lincoln: University of Nebraska Press, 2000.

Gitelman, Zvi, ed. *Bitter Legacy: Confronting the Holocaust in the USSR.* Bloomington: Indiana University Press, 1997.

Goldsmith, Martin. *The Inextinguishable Symphony: A True Story of Music and Love in Nazi Germany.* New York: Wiley, 2000.

Gordon, Sarah. *Hitler, Germans and the 'Jewish Question.'* Princeton, N.J.: Princeton University Press, 1984.

Greenspan, Henry. *On Listening to Holocaust Survivors: Recounting and Life History.* Westport, Conn.: Praeger, 1998.

Gregor, Neil. *Daimler Benz in the Third Reich*. New Haven, Conn.: Yale University Press, 1998.

———, ed. *Nazism*. New York: Oxford University Press, 2000.

Gutman, Israel, ed. *Encyclopedia of the Holocaust*. 4 vols. New York: Macmillan, 1990.

Gutman, Yisrael, and Chaim Schatzker. *The Holocaust and Its Significance*. Jerusalem: Zalman Shazar Center, 1984.

Gutman, Yisrael and Michael Berenbaum, eds. *Anatomy of the Auschwitz Death Camp*. Bloomington: Indiana University Press, 1994.

Harris, Mark Jonathan, and Deborah Oppenheimer. *Into the Arms of Strangers: Stories of the Kindertransport, The British Scheme That Saved 10,000 Children from the Nazi Regime*. London: Bloomsbury, 2000.

Hayes, Peter, ed. *Lessons and Legacies: The Meaning of the Holocaust in a Changing World*. Evanston, Ill.: Northwestern University Press, 1990.

Headland, Ronald. *Messages of Murder: A Study of the Einsatzgruppen of the Security Police and Security Service, 1941–1943*. Rutherford, N.J.: Farleigh Dickinson University Press, 1991.

Herbert, Ulrich. *Hitler's Foreign Workers: Enforced Foreign Labour in Germany under the Third Reich*. Trans. William Templer. Cambridge: Cambridge University Press, 1997.

———. *National Socialist Extermination Policies: Contemporary German Perspectives and Controversies*. Trans. from the German. New York: Berg, 2000.

Herf, Jeffrey. *Reactionary Modernism*. Cambridge: Cambridge University Press, 1984.

Herzstein, Robert Edwin. *When Nazi Dreams Come True: The Horrifying Story of the Nazi Blueprint for Europe*. London: Abacus, 1982.

Hilberg, Raul. *The Destruction of the European Jews*. Chicago: Quadrangle Paperbacks, 1967.

Hirschfeld, Gerhard. *Nazi Rule and Dutch Collaboration: The Netherlands under German Occupation, 1940–45*. Oxford, UK: Berg, 1988.

Hochhuth, Rolf. *The Deputy*. New York: Grove, 1964.

Hoffmann, Peter. *The History of the Germann Resistance, 1933–1945*. Trans. Richard Barry. Cambridge, Mass.: MIT Press, 1977.

———. *Stauffenberg: A Family History, 1905–1944*. Cambridge: Cambridge University Press, 1995.

Holliday, Laurel, ed. *Children in the Holocaust and World War II: Their Secret Diaries*. New York: Pocket Books, 1995.

The Holocaust Chronicle: A History in Words and Pictures. Lincolnwood, Ill.: Publications International, 2000.

Horowitz, Sara R. *Voicing the Void: Muteness and Memory in Holocaust Fiction.* Albany: State University of New York Press, 1997.

Ioanid, Radu. *The Holocaust in Romania: The Destruction of Jews and Gypsies under the Antonescu Regime, 1940–1944.* Chicago: Ivan R. Dee, 2000.

International Military Tribunal. *Trial of the Major War Criminals.* 42 vols. Nuremberg, 1947–1949.

Jaskot, Paul B. *The Architecture of Oppression: The SS, Forced Labor and the Nazi Monumental Building Economy.* New York: Routledge, 2000.

Jones, David H. *Moral Responsibility in the Holocaust: A Study in the Ethics of Character.* Lanham: Rowman & Littlefield, 1999.

Katz, Steven T. *The Holocaust in Historical Context.* New York: Oxford University Press, 1994.

Keegan, John. *The Second World War.* New York: Penguin, 1990.

Keneally, Thomas. *Schindler's List.* New York: Touchstone, 1993.

Kermish, Joseph, ed. *To Live with Honor and Die with Honor! Selected Documents from the Warsaw Ghetto Underground Archives "Oneg Shabbat."* Trans. M. Z. Prives et al. Jerusalem: Yad Vashem, 1986.

Kershaw, Ian. *Hitler 1889–1936: Hubris.* New York: Norton, 1998.

Koehl, Robert L. *The Black Corps: The Structure and Power Struggles of the Nazi SS.* Madison: University of Wisconsin Press, 1983.

Kogon, Eugen. *The Theory and Practice of Hell: The German Concentration Camps and the System behind Them.* New York: Berkeley, 1998.

Kogon, E., H. Langbein, and A. Rückerl, eds. *Nazi Mass Murder: A Documentary History of the Use of Poison Gas.* New Haven, Conn.: Yale University Press, 1993.

Korczak, Janusz. *Ghetto Diary.* New York: Holocaust Library, 1978.

Kozinski, Jerzy. *The Painted Bird.* Boston: Houghton Mifflin, 1965.

Krakowski, Shmuel. *The War of the Doomed: Jewish Armed Resistance in Poland, 1942–1944.* Trans. Orah Blaustein. New York: Holmes & Meier, 1984.

Krausnick, Helmut, and Martin Broszat. *Anatomy of the SS State.* Trans. Richard Barry, Marian Jackson, and Dorothy Long. New York: Walker, 1968.

Kremer, S. Lillian. *Women's Holocaust Writing: Memory and Imagination.* Lincoln: University of Nebraska Press, 1999.

LaCapra, Dominick. *History and Memory after Auschwitz.* Ithaca, N.Y.: Cornell University Press, 1998.

Lamberti, Marjorie. *Jewish Activism in Imperial Germany. The Struggle for Civil Equality*. New Haven, Conn.: Yale University Press, 1978.

Langer, Lawrence, ed. *Art from the Ashes: A Holocaust Anthology*. New York: Oxford University Press, 1995.

Landau, Ronnie S. *Studying the Holocaust: Issues, Readings, and Documents*. London: Routledge, 1998.

Lanzmann, Claude. *Shoah: An Oral History of the Holocaust. The Complete Text of the Film by Claude Lanzmann*. New York: Pantheon, 1985.

Laqueur, Walter, and Richard Breitman. *Breaking the Silence: The Secret Mission of Eduard Schulte, Who Brought the World News of the Final Solution*. London: Bodley Head, 1986.

Lazare, Lucien. *Rescue as Resistance: How Jewish Organizations Fought the Holocaust in France*. Trans. Jeffrey F. Green. New York: Columbia University Press, 1996.

Leiser, Erwin. *Nazi Cinema*. Trans. Gertrud Mander and David Wilson. New York: Macmillan, 1975.

Leitz, Christian. *Nazi Germany and Neutral Europe during the Second World War*. Manchester, UK: Manchester University Press, 2000.

Levi, Primo. *The Drowned and the Saved*. Trans. Raymond Rosenthal. New York: Summit, 1986.

Levin, Dov. *Fighting Back: Lithuanian Jewry's Armed Resistance to the Nazis, 1941–1945*. Trans. Moshe Kohn and Dina Cohen. New York: Holmes & Meier, 1985.

Levin, Itamar. *Survival in Auschwitz: The Nazi Assault on Humanity*. Trans. Stuart Woolf. New York: Collier, 1993.

———. *The Last Deposit: Swiss Banks and Holocaust Victims' Accounts*. Trans. Natasha Dornberg. Westport, Conn.: Praeger, 1999.

Levy, Richard S., ed. *Antisemitism in the Modern World: An Anthology of Texts*. Lexington, Mass.: Heath, 1991.

Lewis, Rand C. *The Neo-Nazis and German Unification*. Westport, Conn.: Praeger, 1996.

Lipstadt, Deborah. *Beyond Belief: The American Press and the Coming of the Holocaust, 1933–1945*. New York: Free Press, 1986.

London, Louise. *Whitehall and the Jews, 1933–1948: British Immigration Policy and the Holocaust*. Cambridge: Cambridge University Press, 2000.

Lukas, Richard C. *The Forgotten Holocaust: The Poles under German Occupation, 1939*. Lexington: University Press of Kentucky, 1985.

Lukacs, John. *The Hitler of History: Hitler's Biographers on Trial*. London: Wiedenfeld and Nicolson, 2000.

Maier, Charles S. *The Unmasterable Past: History, Holocaust, and German National Identity*. Cambridge, Mass.: Harvard University Press, 1997.

Marszalek, Józef. *Majdanek: The Concentration Camp in Lublin*. Warsaw, Poland: Interpress, 1986.

Mayer, Arno J. *Why Did the Heavens Not Darken? The "Final Solution" in History*. New York: Pantheon, 1990.

Mazower, Mark. *Inside Hitler's Greece: The Experience of Occupation, 1941–1944*. New Haven, Conn.: Yale University Press, 1993.

Michaelis, Meir. *Mussolini and the Jews: German–Italian Relations and the Jewish Question in Italy, 1922–1945*. Oxford, UK: Clarendon, 1978.

Michalczyk, John J., ed. *Medicine, Ethics, and the Third Reich: Historical and Contemporary Issues*. Kansas City, Mo.: Sheed and Ward, 1994.

Mendelsohn, John, and Donald Detweiler, eds. *The Holocaust: Selected Documents in Eighteen Volumes*. 18 vols. New York: Garland, 1982.

Mommsen, Hans. *From Weimar to Auschwitz*. Trans. Philip O'Connor. Princeton, N.J.: Princeton University Press, 1997.

Morgan, Michael L., ed. *A Holocaust Reader: Responses to the Nazi Extermination*. New York: Oxford University Press, 2000.

Morse, Arthur D. *While Six Million Died*. London: Secker and Warburg, 1968.

Mosse, George L. *Toward the Final Solution: A History of European Racism*. New York: Harper & Row, 1978.

———. *The Crisis of German Ideology: Intellectual Origins of the Third Reich*. New York: Schocken, 1981.

Müller, Filip. *Eyewitness Auschwitz: Three Years in the Gas Chambers*. 1979; Chicago: Ivan R. Dee, 1999.

Müller-Hill, Benno. *Murderous Science: Elimination by Scientific Selection of Jews, Gypsies, and Others, Germany, 1933–1945*. Trans. George R. Fraser. Oxford: Oxford University Press, 1988.

New, Mitya, ed. *Switzerland Unwrapped: Exposing the Myths*. London: I. B. Tauris, 1997.

Nicholls, A. J. *Weimar and the Rise of Hitler*. 3rd ed. New York: St. Martin's, 1991.

Nicosia, Francis. *The Third Reich and the Palestine Question*. Austin: University of Texas Press, 1985.

Niewyk, Donald L. *The Jews in Weimar Germany*. Baton Rouge: Louisiana State University Press, 1980.

————. *The Holocaust: Problems and Perspectives of Interpretation.* 2nd ed. Boston: Houghton Mifflin, 1997.

Nyiszli, Miklos. *Auschwitz: A Doctor's Eyewitness Account.* Trans. Tibère Kremer and Richard Seaver. New York: Arcade, 1993.

Ofer, Dalia, and Lenore J. Weitzman, eds. *Women in the Holocaust.* New Haven, Conn.: Yale University Press, 1998.

Office of United States Chief of Counsel for Prosecution of Axis Criminality. *Nazi Conspiracy and Aggression.* 9 vols. Washington, D.C.: Government Printing Office, 1946–1948.

Pauley, Bruce F. *Hitler and the Forgotten Nazis: A History of Austrian National Socialism.* Chapel Hill: University of North Carolina Press, 1981.

————. *From Prejudice to Persecution: A History of Austrian Antisemitism.* Chapel Hill: University of North Carolina Press, 1992.

Pawelczynska, Anna. *Values and Violence in Auschwitz: A Sociological Analysis.* Trans. Catherine S. Leach. Berkeley: University of California Press, 1979.

Paxton, Robert O., and Michael Marrus. *Vichy France and the Jews.* New York: Columbia University Press, 1981.

Perechodnik, Calel. *Am I a Murderer? Testament of a Jewish Ghetto Policeman.* Ed. and trans. Frank Fox. Boulder, Colo.: Westview, 1996.

Petropoulos, Jonathan. *The Faustian Bargain: The Art World in Nazi Germany.* New York: Allen Lane Penguin Press, 2000.

Poliakov, Leon. *Harvest of Hate: The Nazi Program for the Destruction of the Jews of Europe.* New York: Holocaust Library, 1979.

Porat, Dina. *The Blue and Yellow Stars of David: The Zionist Leadership in Palestine and the Holocaust, 1939–1945.* Cambridge, Mass.: Harvard University Press, 1990.

Proctor, Robert N. *Racial Hygiene: Medicine under the Nazis.* Cambridge, Mass.: Harvard University Press, 1988.

Pulzer, Peter G. J. *The Rise of Political Antisemitism in Germany and Austria.* Cambridge, Mass.: Harvard University Press, 1988.

Readings on Night. Ed. Wendy Mass. San Diego: Greenhaven, 2000.

Reynaud, Michel, and Sylvie Graffard. *The Jehovah's Witnesses and the Nazis: Persecution, Deportation, and Murder, 1933–1945.* Trans. James A. Moorhouse. New York: Cooper Square, 2001.

Rich, Norman. *Hitler's War Aims.* 2 vols. New York: Norton, 1973, 1974.

Roland, Charles G. *Courage Under Siege: Starvation, Disease, and Death in the Warsaw Ghetto.* New York: Oxford University Press, 1992.

Rosenbaum, Alan S. *Prosecuting Nazi War Criminals.* Boulder, Colo.: Westview, 1993.

———. ed. *Is the Holocaust Unique? Perspectives on Comparative Genocide.* Boulder, Colo.: Westview, 2000.

Rosenfeld, Alvin. *A Double Dying: Reflections on Holocaust Literature.* Bloomington: Indiana University Press, 1980.

Ross, Robert. *So It Was True: The American Protestant Press and the Nazi Persecution of the Jews.* Minneapolis: University of Minnesota Press, 1980.

Rothberg, Michael. *Traumatic Realism: The Demands of Holocaust Representation.* Minneapolis: University of Minnesota Press, 2000.

Schilling, Donald G., ed. *Lessons and Legacies: Teaching the Holocaust in a Changing World.* Evanston, Ill.: Northwestern University Press, 1998.

Schonfeld, Walter T. *Nazi Madness: Highlighted at Nuremberg.* London: Minerva, 2000.

Schumann, Willy. *Being Present: Growing Up in Hitler's Germany.* Kent, Ohio: Kent State University Press, 1991.

Sebald, W. G. *The Emigrants.* Trans. Michael Hulse. New York: New Directions, 1997.

Segel, Binjamin W. *A Lie and a Libel: The History of the Protocols of the Elders of Zion.* Ed. and trans. Richard S. Levy. Lincoln: University of Nebraska Press, 1995.

Shandler, Jeffrey. *While America Watches: Televising the Holocaust.* New York: Oxford University Press, 1999.

Sheftel, Yoram. *The Demjanjuk Affair: The Rise and Fall of a Show Trial.* Trans. Haim Watzman. London: Gollanz, 1994.

Smith, Bradley F. *Reaching Judgment at Nuremberg.* London: André Deutsch, 1977.

Smolar, Hersh. *The Minsk Ghetto: Soviet-Jewish Partisans against the Nazis.* Trans. Max Rosenfeld. New York: Holocaust Publications, 1989.

Spector, Shmuel. *The Holocaust of Volhynian Jews, 1941–44.* Jerusalem: Achva Press, 1990.

Spiegelman, Art. *Maus: A Survivor's Tale.* 2 vols. New York: Pantheon, 1997.

Spitzer, Leo. *Hotel Bolivia: The Culture of Memory in a Refuge from Nazism.* New York: Hill and Wang, 1999.

Steiner, Jean. *Treblinka.* New York: Simon & Schuster, 1967.

Steinhoff, Johannes, Peter Pechel, and Dennis Showalter, eds. *Voices from the Third Reich: An Oral History.* New York: Da Capo, 1993.

Styron, William. *Sophie's Choice.* New York: Bantam, 1980.

Tal, Uriel. *Christians and Jews in Germany: Religion, Politics, and Ideology in the Second Reich, 1870–1914.* Trans. Noah Jonathan Jacobs. Ithaca, N.Y.: Cornell University Press, 1975.

Taylor, James, and Warren Shaw, eds. *Dictionary of the Third Reich.* London: Penguin, 1997.

Taylor, Telford. *The Anatomy of the Nuremberg Trials: A Personal Memoir.* New York: Knopf, 1992.

Tec, Necama. *Defiance: The Bielski Partisans, The Story of the Largest Armed Resistance by Jews during World War II.* Oxford: Oxford University Press, 1993.

Tory, Avraham. *Surviving the Holocaust: The Kovno Ghetto Diary.* Ed. Martin Gilbert. Trans. Jerzy Michalowicz. Cambridge, Mass.: Harvard University Press, 1990.

Trachtenberg, Joshua. *The Devil and the Jews: The Medieval Conception of the Jew and Its Relation to Modern Antisemitism.* Philadelphia: Jewish Publication Society, 1983.

Trunk, Isaiah. *Judenrat: The Jewish Councils in Eastern Europe under Nazi Occupation.* Lincoln: University of Nebraska Press, 1996.

Waite, Robert G. L. *Vanguard of Nazism: The Free Corps Movement in Postwar Germany, 1918–1922.* New York: Norton, 1969.

Wank, Ulrich, ed. *The Resurgence of Right Wing Radicalism in Germany: New Forms of an Old Phenomenon?* Trans. James Knowlton. Atlantic Highlands, N.J.: Humanities Press, 1996.

Webster, Paul. *Pétain's Crime: The Complete Story of French Collaboration in the Holocaust.* Chicago: Ivan R. Dee, 1991.

Wegner, Bernd. *The Waffen-SS: Organization, Ideology, and Function.* Trans. Ronald Webster. Oxford, UK: Blackwell, 1990.

Weinberg, David. *A Community on Trial: The Jews of Paris during the 1930s.* Chicago: University of Chicago Press, 1977.

Weinberg, Gerhard L. *The Foreign Policy of Hitler's Germany: Starting World War II, 1937–1939.* Chicago: University of Chicago Press, 1980.

Weiss, Aharon. "Jewish Leadership in Occupied Poland—Postures and Attitudes," *Yad Vashem Studies,* 12 (1977):335–65.

Weiss, David W. *Reluctant Return: A Survivor's Journey to an Austrian Town.* Bloomington: Indiana University Press, 1999.

Weiss, John. *Ideology of Death: Why the Holocaust Happened in Germany.* Chicago: Ivan R. Dee, 1996.

Westermann, Edward B. *FLAK: German Anti-Aircraft Defenses*, 1914–1945. Lawrence: University Press of Kansas, 2001.

Wilt, Alan F. *Nazi Germany*. Arlington Heights, Ill.: Harlan Davidson, 1994.

Wyman, David S. *The Abandonment of the Jews: America and the Holocaust*, *1941–1945*. New York: Pantheon, 1984.

———, ed. *The World Reacts to the Holocaust*. Baltimore: Johns Hopkins University Press, 1996.

Young, James E. *The Texture of Memory: Holocaust Memorials and Meaning*. New Haven, Conn.: Yale University Press, 1994.

Zertal, Idith. *From Catastrophe to Power: Holocaust Survivors and the Emergence of Israel*. Berkeley: University of California Press, 1998.

Ziegler, Herbert. *Nazi Germany's New Aristocracy: The SS Leadership*, *1925–1939*. Princeton, N.J.: Princeton University Press, 1989.

INDEX

Abetz, Otto, 169
About the Jews and Their Lies (Luther), 12
Adenauer, Konrad, 442, 449
Adorno, Theodor, 468
Africa, 248, 304–7, 334
air force (Luftwaffe), 69, 118
air raids, 312
Aktion Erntefest. *See* Harvest Festival (Erntefest)
Aktion Reinhard, 224–25, 264–75, 328–29, 359, 393. *See also* camps, death
Aktionen, 202, 217, 252, 325
al-Husayni, Haj Amin, 221–22, 238, 305, 353
Allers, Dietrich, 348
Allies, 19, 366;
after World War II, 477; coalition of, 388; conferences of, 408; peace talks with, 372. *See also* Western Allies
Aly, Götz, 9
Amann, Max, 84
America First Committee, 216
American Central Intelligence Agency, 412
American Jewish Congress (AJC), 390
American Jewish Joint Distribution Committee, 409, 455
American War Refugee Board, 371

Améry, Jean, 457, 459
amnesty, for war criminals, 422
ancestry, 15–16. *See also* Mischlinge
Anielewicz, Mordechai, 315, 317–19, 320
Anschluss, 95, 98–99, 450, 451, 452
Anti-Comintern pact, 81
anti-Jewish: legislation, 39, 46–48; measures, 34; policy of SS, 88; political parties, 13; stereotypes, 113
anti-Nazi uprising. *See* Nazis; resistance
anti-Semitism, 2, 11, 441; eliminationist vs. exterminationist, 8; genocidal, 8; Jew-haters and, 14; organizations supporting, 32; Protestants, 12, 56–58, 440; religion and, 11–12, 56–58; in universities, 32–33, 48–49; Zionism, response to, 14, 67. *See also* Arrow Cross; *specific countries*; xenophobia
antifascist committee, 218, 221
Antonescu, Ion, 332–34
Arad, Yitzhaf, 268, 329
armed forces, 72; **Commander-in-Chief of, 94**. *See also* military; Wehrmacht
army, 29, 61
Army Group Center, 196, 208
Armya Krajowa, 315, 317, 318, 319, 365
Arrow Cross, 373

ABOUT THE AUTHOR

Donald M. McKale was born in 1943 in Clay Center, Kansas. Since 1988, he has been the Class of 1941 Memorial Professor of Humanities in the History Department at Clemson University. He is the author of numerous books and articles on modern German history, including *Hitler: The Survival Myth* (also available from Cooper Square Press); *The Nazi Party Courts*; and *War by Revolution: Germany and Great Britain in the Middle East in the Era of World War I*, winner of the Charles Smith Award from the European Section of the Southern Historical Association. He and his wife, Janna, live in Clemson, South Carolina.

Auschwitz I

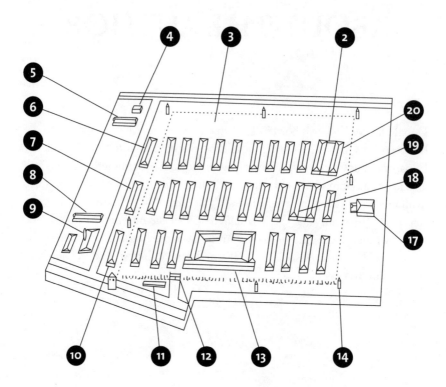

1. Gas Chambers and Crematoria
2. Black Wall
3. Living Barracks
4. Camp Commander's Quarters
5. Main Guard House
6. Command Post
7. Administration
8. Political Section
9. Crematorium
10. SS-Chief Medical Office
11. Block Commander's Room
12. Entry
13. Camp Kitchen
14. Watch Tower
15. Women's Camp
16. Watch Tower

From Yehuda Bauer, *A History of the Holocaust* (New York: Franklin Watts, 1982), 216–17.

Auschwitz II (Birkenau)

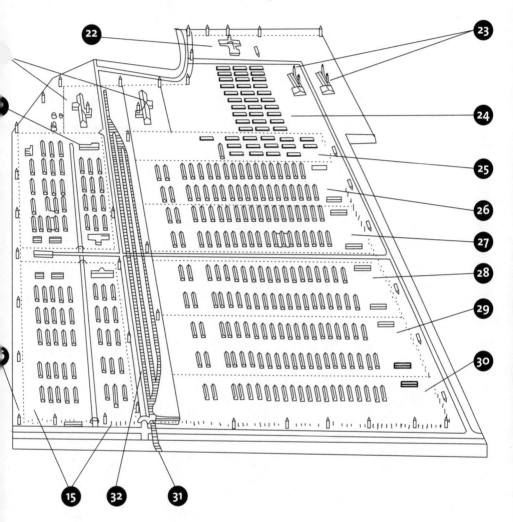

17. Storeroom of Victims' Property
18. Barrack 21—Prisoners' Hospital
19. Barrack 20—Infectious Diseases
20. Bunker (Jail) Barrack
21. Women's Camp
22. Bath
23. Gas Chambers and Crematoria
24. Storerooms of Victims' Property

25. Prisoners' Hospital
26. Gypsy Camp
27. Men's Camp
28. Hungarian Camp
29. Family Camp
30. Quarantine Camp
31. Entry
32. Auschwitz Rail Connection